J.D. Edwards OneWorld:
A Developer's Guide

J.D. Edwards OneWorld: A Developer's Guide

Steven L. Hester and Chris Enyeart

Osborne McGraw-Hill

Berkeley New York St. Louis San Francisco
Auckland Bogotá Hamburg London Madrid
Mexico City Milan Montreal New Delhi Panama City
Paris São Paulo Singapore Sydney Tokyo Toronto

Osborne **McGraw-Hill**
2600 Tenth Street
Berkeley, California 94710
U.S.A.

For information on translations or book distributors outside the U.S.A., or to arrange bulk purchase discounts for sales promotions, premiums, or fund-raisers, please contact **Osborne/McGraw-Hill** at the above address.

J.D. Edwards OneWorld: A Developer's Guide

1234567890 DOC DOC 019876543210

ISBN 0-07-212316-8

Publisher Brandon A. Nordin	Bonnie Bills Chrisa Hotchkiss
Associate Publisher & Editor In-Chief Scott Rogers	**Proofreaders** Linda Medoff Paul Medoff
Acqusition Editor Gareth Hancock	**Indexer** Rebecca Plunkett
Project Editor Emily Rader	**Computer Designer** Roberta Steele
Acquisitions Coordinator Tara Davis	Lucia Ericksen Lauren McCarthy
Tech Editors Reid Turnquist Linda Doherty	**Illustrator** Michael Mueller Robert Hansen Beth Young
Developmental Editor Catherine Robbins	**Series Design** Roberta Steele
Copy Editors Carol Henry Marilyn Smith Andy Carroll	**Cover Designer** Ted Holladay

This book was composed with Corel VENTURA™ Publisher.

To the ladies of my life, Kathy and Lauren.
Words can never say how much I love both of you.
Steven

For Angela.
C.E.

About the Authors

Steven L. Hester is a OneWorld application developer and consultant for marchFIRST in Cleveland, Ohio. In the past couple of years, he has focused on designing and implementing third-party applications from the ground up, and on implementing interoperability between OneWorld and other systems. Steven received an M.S.E.S. from the University of Toledo, where he studied reliability and performability modeling of client/server systems. He also holds a B.S.E.E. from the University of Mississippi, where he was one of the university's webmasters; during his tenure there, the university's web site was named by Yahoo! as one of the top 100 college web sites. Steven worked for other notable institutions as well, such as the Mississippi Center for Supercomputing Research, the Argonne National Laboratory, and the United States Navy. He enjoys spending his spare time with his lovely wife and darling daughter.

Chris Enyeart is a OneWorld technical consultant based in Denver, Colorado. In October 1994, he began working for J.D. Edwards as a developer of manufacturing, distribution, and logistics OneWorld applications. During his five years at J.D. Edwards, he worked on many parts of the OneWorld base product before leaving to cofound Mountain Business Solutions (www.mountainbusinesssolutions.com). He specializes in customizing and designing new enhancements for OneWorld software. Chris has a bachelor's degree from Benedictine College in Atchison, Kansas, where he studied Mathematics and Computer Science. Outside of work, Chris enjoys traveling with his wife and spending time in the mountains skiing and hiking.

About the Contributing Author

Steve Wilburn is a OneWorld senior technical consultant for marchFIRST, and is based in Atlanta, Georgia. He specializes in developing enhancements and modifications for OneWorld applications. Previously, he developed add-on tools for J.D. Edwards WorldVision applications. He also has extensive experience developing client/server applications using Visual Basic. Steve has a B.S. in Computer Information Systems from DeVry Institute of Technology in Atlanta, Georgia. Outside of work, Steve enjoys time with his wife, Kathie, and his sons, Ryan and Austin.

About the Technical Reviewers

Reid Turnquist joined J.D. Edwards after several years in industry, in various private and public accounting, as well as IS management roles. At J.D. Edwards, he served an initial tenure as a developer, and then graduated to Client Services, serving throughout Europe and the Middle East, and implementing various systems in 17 countries. After

Europe, he returned to Denver, joining Partners in Development, where he managed the development of several World and OneWorld modules. Reid conceived and helped form the "OneWorld Developer Immersion" training program, participated in one of the early classes, and was among the first to achieve OneWorld Developer certification.

Reid is now an independent management consultant working with select JDE business partners and clients, and assisting them with topics ranging from requirements analysis and design, to configuration, implementation, and training on various JDE World and OneWorld asset- and infrastructure-centric modules in both the public and private sector.

While not actively practicing as a CPA, Reid maintains his membership in the Colorado Society of CPAs, and is a member of the Project Management Institute (PMI).

Linda Doherty has worked with OneWorld for more than seven years. She has extensive experience with the software, ranging from installation programming, application development, and custom modifications, to CNC transfer and deployment. She is currently a technical consultant with The Implementation Partners, LLC, in Denver. She lives with her husband and two sons in Thornton, Colorado.

About the Developmental Editor

Cathy Robbins is a senior technical writer at J.D. Edwards. She has been a technical writer for eight years, four with J.D. Edwards, where she has written various types of documentation for OneWorld Development Tools. Cathy has an M.S. in Technical Communication and a B.A. in English.

Contents at a Glance

PART IV

Interfacing with OneWorld

PART V

Appendixes

Contents

PART I
OneWorld System Architecture for Developers

PART II
Client Modifications Using OneWorld

PART III
Advanced Application Development

PART IV
Interfacing with OneWorld

PART V
Appendixes

Foreword

J.D. Edwards OneWorld is making a surge in the e-business arena; and its stable foundation gives you, the user, some comfort in the ever-changing, unpredictable technology world. Many Quest members are coexisting between WorldSoftware and OneWorld, while others are taking the OneWorld plunge. Whether you are coexisting or moving straight into a OneWorld implementation, *J.D. Edwards OneWorld: A Developer's Guide* brings important and helpful technical information to the J.D. Edwards community.

J.D. Edwards recognizes that technology must be able to evolve in order to suit your changing business needs; and OneWorld was designed with this firmly in mind. It is the first network-centric solution that separates business rules from the underlying technology, allowing businesses to capitalize on new functionality without disrupting ongoing business. This comprehensive guide shows J.D. Edwards' commitment to providing practical information to both new and experienced OneWorld developers.

Similarly, Quest strives to help its members gain the most from their J.D. Edwards investments; and our support of this publishing project demonstrates our continued backing of J.D. Edwards' effort to communicate useful technical information to users. The partnership between J.D. Edwards and Osborne/McGraw-Hill that created J.D. Edwards Press is very much in tune with Quest's mission to provide information to its user community. Without this communication and support, those implementing OneWorld, or coexisting between WorldSoftware and OneWorld, would not have the information needed to implement it successfully nor gain the most from their software investment. *J.D. Edwards OneWorld: A Developer's Guide* delves deep into the technology of OneWorld, giving users the "Ins and outs" of the software while focusing on application development and customization.

As the e-business world changes at phenomenal speeds, technology must rapidly adapt to keep pace. Here is your chance, as a current or prospective OneWorld developer, to delve into information specifically aimed at helping your organization successfully develop and modify OneWorld applications to get the most out of its J.D. Edwards investment.

The technology world will keep changing. J.D. Edwards Press will help you keep up.

Robert A. Rosati
President, Quest J.D. Edwards User Group

Acknowledgments

My sincerest appreciation and gratitude goes to the following people who helped to make this book possible:

Gareth Hancock, who guided me through this whole process and gave me the opportunity to write this book.

Catherine Robbins, who endured hours of editing my material and probably wonders how I got the opportunity to write this book.

Reid Turnquist, who served as the wise elder who kept me honest and in line throughout this book.

Linda Doherty, who spent many hours paying attention to the technical details of each example and discussion in this book.

Last but not least, Kathy and Lauren, who sacrificed many long hours waiting for me to finish this book.

Sincerely,
Steven L. Hester

Writing this book was a great experience, and I would first like to thank Gareth and Steven for giving me the opportunity to take part.

I would also like to thank Catherine and Emily, whose contributions to my chapters were invaluable. Sorting through my writing, I know, was not easy.

Reid and Linda's technical advice and guidance played an integral part in producing correct, clear chapters. For this, they deserve much credit.

Tara should also be thanked for successfully controlling the flow of all figures; illustrations; and edits, and edits, and edits . . .

And finally, I need to thank my wife, who put up with me during the writing of this book.

Sincerely,
Chris Enyeart

Introduction

J.D. Edwards OneWorld is a comprehensive suite of business applications that extends the features and functionality of its legacy counterpart, WorldSoftware, that established J.D. Edwards as the leader in financial, human resources, distribution, manufacturing, and other systems for businesses. J.D. Edwards OneWorld comes with its own set of application development tools for modifying and building applications within it. The application development toolset provides application developers the state-of-the-art toolset that can build and modify any application a business requires.

The one feature that distinguishes J.D. Edwards OneWorld from its competitors is that it is built on the Configurable Network Computing (CNC) technology that J.D. Edwards created. CNC extends the client/server model to the next level of adaptability, configurability, extensibility, and stability. These features make J.D. Edwards OneWorld a truly revolutionary concept and system, because OneWorld actually embeds the characteristics of platform independence in network-centric-based computing, to provide a superior IT system for any company today.

J.D. Edwards OneWorld: A Developer's Guide is targeted at professional software development companies and individuals who develop third-party or customized software for J.D. Edwards OneWorld. It presents the theory and practice of application development in OneWorld, and is intended to be used as a reference by the professional software developer.

If you are a Visual Basic or Java application developer, you will find that working with OneWorld allows you to build applications with less coding. OneWorld applications are based on the core principles of the object based event-driven execution model. These principles are the same ones that your previous applications were based on, and you will find the transition to OneWorld relatively painless.

If you are a developer migrating from the WorldSoftware platform, you will find this book invaluable because it presents the examples and the background information you need to upgrade your programming skills for OneWorld.

If you are a current OneWorld application developer, this book will stay with you throughout your career. This book presents the basic and intermediate concepts you use every day when building applications. It also demonstrates the advanced techniques that you will need to know as you move to more difficult development projects for your clients or employers.

Ultimately, what this means to you, as a developer, is that this book delivers the knowledge and expertise that enable you to take advantage of the full capabilities of OneWorld. Each chapter starts with theory and technical background information, so you can proficiently operate and develop in OneWorld. Then, the focus moves to the actual OneWorld toolset and applications needed to perform the specific task for that chapter. Every topic's discussion is backed up with real-world examples to aid in rapid understanding of OneWorld application development.

Each chapter includes one or more special Developer's Corner section. The Developer's Corners discuss practical issues that arise during development of third-party and customized applications in OneWorld. All of the information in these sections is intended to supply you with helpful shortcuts in the development cycle; and it comes from the trenches of real software development taking place in industry today.

Part I, "OneWorld System Architecture for Developers," begins with high-level OneWorld concepts that inform the developer what OneWorld is and how it is implemented. The focus then changes to the single most important issue relating to OneWorld: the user perspective. Discussion of the user perspective provides the developer with essential information on how the user will operate and interact with applications. The rest of Part I covers system administration and configuration issues that impact third-party software development.

Part II, "Client Modifications Using OneWorld," opens with a big picture discussion of the OneWorld development cycle and its two major categories: third-party and custom application development. Part II then exposes the essential tools, Form Design Aid and Report Design Aid, for performing any type of software modification or creation in OneWorld. The primary language, Event Rules, used in all development tools, is analyzed in Part II, as are the basic environment tools needed to become proficient in testing and debugging applications. Part II provides the common foundation that all types of software programmers need in order to function competently in OneWorld application programming.

Part III, "Advanced Application Development," has no central theme, as its predecessors do, but it contains all of the advanced development topics related to OneWorld: processing options, currency, messaging, business functions, and workflow. All of these features can be added to interactive, batch, and web-based applications to enhance and enrich application operation.

Part IV, "Interfacing with OneWorld," shows you the many ways in which you can integrate your applications, as well as third-party applications, into OneWorld's modules. Part IV also shows you how to enable the built-in e-commerce capabilities of OneWorld to extend your business processes to your suppliers, customers, and employees.

Part V offers tips and technical summaries that allow you to quickly look up the information you will need while you are building applications and OneWorld interfaces to external systems. The Glossary continues the summary information by providing you with definitions for common terms and acronyms that are used in OneWorld.

PART I

OneWorld System Architecture for Developers

CHAPTER 1

Essential OneWorld Concepts for Developers

Enterprise Resource Planning (ERP) System Fundamentals

Configurable Network Computing (CNC) Architecture

CNC Fundamentals

CNC Deployment Strategies

Examining Computers in a OneWorld Environment

OneWorld Development Toolset

Putting It All Together

OneWorld is a unified environment that includes an integrated set of development tools. Each development tool is built from the ground up to work with the other tools, and most of them are graphical user interface (GUI) based to provide point-and-click application development. This unique combination provides a setting for rapid application construction, in which any object or application in OneWorld can be created and modified.

Because the OneWorld toolset generates the bulk of software code used for defining objects, developers spend less time and effort in programming as compared to text editor–based environments. In addition, the OneWorld tools support the application in the environment where it is executed. Therefore, most of the time and effort spent on application development is focused on creating business logic and functionality, rather than writing the supporting code.

Each OneWorld development tool has one or more built-in Business Activators to further increase your productivity as a developer. Business Activators are part of a broad product and technology suite called ActivEra that enables OneWorld to easily adapt itself to existing and future business requirements. The primary purpose of an Activator is to automate tasks that you regularly perform. For example, you can quickly generate a simple report for your company's financial department by using an Activator built into the report writing development tool—without writing one line of code.

DEFINITION

Business Activators *are part of OneWorld's ActivEra suite. ActivEra is a collection of applications that provide a flexible framework for fast customization and snap-in functionality with low application-development overhead.*

What the OneWorld development toolset means to you as a developer is that your time isn't wasted in trying to integrate development tools from different vendors. And your productivity is dramatically increased during application development because your efforts are focused on writing code that supports business operations.

This chapter provides an overview of OneWorld and its development toolset, including

- **Enterprise Resource Planning (ERP) System Fundamentals**   This section explains the fundamentals of Enterprise Resource Planning (ERP). ERP systems assist corporations in managing their data. Your ability to write effective software code depends on your knowledge of ERP systems. By understanding each application's position within a large and complex enterprise, you have the proper know-how to tackle big development projects in OneWorld.

- **Configurable Network Computing (CNC) Architecture**   Understanding the concepts of network-centric computing and how you can leverage them to build and modify sophisticated applications allows you to effectively develop OneWorld applications, because all OneWorld applications depend on CNC.

- **CNC Fundamentals**   The CNC architecture provides three essential components for your applications: seamless operation, scalability, and application partitioning. Your development projects are directly affected by the components, because they determine the infrastructure of how your applications are designed and built.

- **CNC Deployment Strategies**   This section provides you with a description of all configurations that OneWorld can have for an installation. It will assist you in understanding how OneWorld applications are impacted by the different configurations, and what you need to do to prepare your applications for each one.

- **OneWorld Development Toolset**   Knowing how each tool is used in a development project ensures that you will make the best use of your time while developing applications.

Enterprise Resource Planning (ERP) System Fundamentals

ERP systems are business management systems that contain many diverse sets of modules. These modules work together to manage information that supports a business's daily operations. A *module* is a set of applications that perform tasks on a specific set of data in the database, such as General Ledger (GL), Accounts Payable (AP), Accounts Receivable (AR), or Inventory.

Some modules are combined to provide advanced analysis and functionality that a business needs to manage itself. For example, the Sales and Procurement applications combine the financial modules GL, AP, and AR, with Inventory and Transportation Management to optimize the costs and revenues of materials required to meet customer and internal demands. Another example is the combination of the Human Resources and Customer Service modules to optimize costs and personnel required for management of projects that support the customer base.

Because so many modules are combined within applications, ERP systems are very large and complex. Therefore, most ERP systems reside on several servers that contain relational databases for storage and management of corporate information and applications. This infrastructure supports the configuration and deployment of ERP and all of the user applications.

This section describes the distributed computing environment that supports ERP, and the spectrum of users supported by the ERP-based applications.

Distributed Computing Environment

All modern ERP packages use the *distributed computing environment (DCE)* as the underlying system to support ERP operations. The DCE is a corporate network infrastructure comprising the network that connects many clients and servers. These clients and servers communicate through the network to gain access to shared applications and data.

N O T E

In a DCE, application execution and data storage generally are not centralized on one machine, but rather are shared across the various machines on the corporate network. For example, the Accounts Payable department server may store all data and execute all applications related to the Account Payables module.

Let's take a look at the four components in a DCE: clients, servers, the network, and user access security.

Clients

A client is a user-centric machine that provides the user interface for anyone using the DCE. A client generates requests to various servers for information needed by users. Typically in a DCE, there is a many-to-one relationship of clients to servers.

Client machines on the network can exist in many forms, and they are discussed in greater detail in the CNC sections of this chapter. A client could be a laptop computer that interacts with OneWorld through a web browser, or a tower desktop that developers use to build and modify applications. In the OneWorld environment, client machines are categorized as fat clients, thin clients, and zero clients.

Fat Client A *fat client* (also called a *workstation*) is usually a desktop system that contains substantial hard disk space, processing power, and memory. Advanced users and developers are users of fat clients, because they execute computationally intensive applications and typically manipulate large amounts of data, which they access and sometimes download from the servers.

Thin Client A *thin client* is one in which nearly all applications are viewed from a server over the network via a browser. A thin client executes applications that add, change, inspect, and delete information from a database on a server. Thin clients cost less than fat clients because they use dramatically less memory and processing power than their fat client counterparts.

Zero Client A *zero client* does not execute applications; it can only display information and capture user input. All of the application execution needed by a zero client occurs on a server. The advantage of a zero client is that an older computer can easily display the information and capture the input, even though it cannot execute a OneWorld client session.

One of the main issues of trying to support more than one client type in an ERP system is that each client type typically requires its own development tools for application development. OneWorld is one of the few ERP systems that provide application development for any client type within the same application. Therefore, you will not have to deal with the overhead of maintaining multiple versions of applications for each client.

Servers

The server in a DCE provides centralized services to clients, and management functions for system administrators. Servers furnish central storage for corporate information, support file and printer sharing among clients, enforce corporate security, monitor network activity, manage fax and e-mail communication, and provide network directory services. Typically, one server does not perform all these functions. Instead, multiple servers are used to ensure reliability and availability of services to clients.

In a distributed environment, many servers perform the same tasks, with each server strategically positioned to serve a certain group of clients. As a result, the applications executed by a client experience higher performance. Also, the ERP system is more reliable because more than one server is available on the network to serve client machines.

Networks

As a developer in a DCE, one of your main concerns is the network. A network is inherently slower by several orders of magnitude than any single computer. Your ability to provide distributed applications across a network while maintaining a high degree of performance on the user's computer will always be limited by the network.

The performance of several popular networks is summarized in Table 1-1. You'll notice that network speed varies drastically from network to network. Local area networks (LANs) provide the highest speed possible and are substantially faster than wide area networks (WANs). Network speed over WANs is slowed by the large distances, measured in miles, that connect the units of the network. In comparison, LANs typically measure their maximum distance in feet or meters.

Let's look at an example. Figure 1-1 is a hypothetical corporate network that connects offices in Chicago, Atlanta, and Denver through a WAN. Each office has its own LAN, and each city needs to access computer resources in the other cities. All of the data and applications are centrally located in Denver. As the Atlanta and Chicago offices use the applications, the WAN will experience major amounts of message traffic, and the users will experience conspicuous slowdown in application execution across the WAN. To improve performance across the corporate infrastructure and to lower message traffic on the WAN, the information and applications used most by a particular city must reside locally on that city's LAN. By optimizing the applications in this manner, users in a particular city will have all the resources locally on their LAN, and the end result will be better application performance.

Network	Type	Speed
LANs	Ethernet	10–1,000 Mbps
	Token Ring	4–16 Mbps
WANs	T3	45 Mbps
	T1	1.544 Mbps
	Frame Relay	32–768 Kbps
	Leased	9.6–56 Kbps
Dial-ups	Analog	9.6–56 Kbps
	Digital (ISDN)	> 128 Kbps

TABLE 1-1.   Speeds of Common Network Topologies

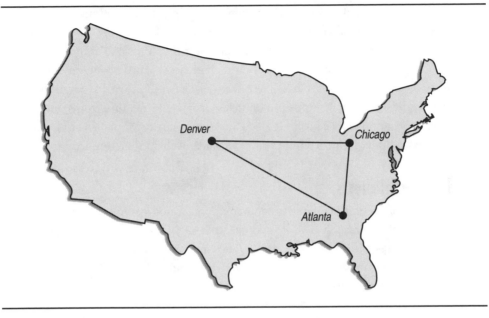

FIGURE 1-1.   Corporate network example

In the past, many developers embedded network infrastructure logic into business applications for them to operate in an ERP system. In these circumstances, however, applications quickly become obsolete whenever new technology is introduced into the network, because the application must be rewritten to incorporate the new technology. The cure is to build applications in an environment that isolates them from the underlying technology.

User Access Security

Once a DCE is operational, security is the next primary concern. The security system prevents competitors and unauthorized employees from gaining access to proprietary information and inflicting great damage on a company through global distribution or other subversive measures. User access security is required in most DCEs.

User access security ensures that individuals who need corporate information are allowed to view and interact with it. All other individuals are restricted from viewing it. Typically, users can only access information required by their job function. Basing security on the roles users perform in the company dramatically reduces the occurrence of security problems. For example, too little security assigned to an individual will increase the probability of compromising daily operations. Too much security assigned to an individual prevents that individual from doing his or her job.

Your development projects may quickly bog down if you have to enforce user access security in every application. OneWorld eliminates security concerns for developers by enforcing it in the CNC architecture. The end result of separating security from business applications is a dramatic decrease in the time you spend modifying applications for security. It also eliminates security loopholes caused by developers who forget to incorporate security mechanisms in their applications.

User Spectrum

Every employee in a company requires some computing resources to fulfill their duties within the organization. This is especially true for DCEs. For example, resource requirements are generally low for secretaries and clerks doing only viewing, preparation, and editing of data (such as working with data in the company financial or inventory systems). Managers and executives, on the other hand, need higher levels of resources for reporting, summarizing, and performing statistical analysis of information located in the corporate database.

Figure 1-2 shows how the *user spectrum* determines required computational resources and security for any individual in a company, based on the tasks he or she executes every day for the company.

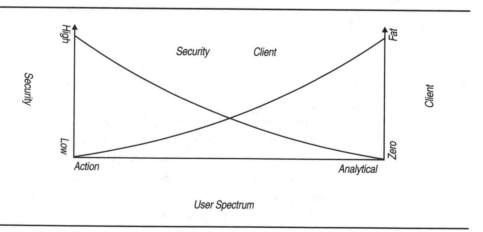

FIGURE 1-2. Security and client computing requires dependency on the user spectrum

As shown in Figure 1-2, all users in the corporation fit into a range defined by *action users* at one end, and *analytical users* at the other end.

Action Users

Action users view and update corporate information that is specific to the job they perform for the company. They are typically involved with the operational tasks of the business. Action users require a very limited set of corporate data to fulfill their jobs, and for this reason user access security is higher, as shown in Figure 1-2. Thin or zero client machines may be sufficient computation resources for action users, since the majority of the computations required are typically located on the server that contains the database.

Applications built for action users generally contain simple user interfaces and logic routines. The user interfaces can be simple because action users require only a means of viewing and editing information pulled from a database. Action user-based applications employ only simple logic routines because the database operations on the server execute the bulk of the logic.

Analytical Users

Analytical users accumulate, analyze, and distribute information for the organization. They are involved with tactical and strategic decision making for the company. In order to make sound decisions for the company, analytical users require access to very large segments of company data. User access security for analytical users is therefore low, as shown in Figure 1-2. Also, for optimum performance, analytical users require fat client machines to support their tasks of accumulating and analyzing substantial amounts of data at any given time.

Applications built for analytical users can be very complex. These user interfaces may need plentiful data so that users can view, summarize, edit, and transform information from a majority of tables in the database. Analytical user-based applications support forecasting, high-level summaries with drill-down capability, and data mining.

Configurable Network Computing (CNC) Architecture

CNC architecture is a new paradigm in corporate computing. It is totally focused on network-centric computing. The CNC architecture isolates business applications from the configuration and administration issues of the underlying technology of the corporate network infrastructure. By isolating technology from applications, businesses can focus on their operations, where they have expertise, rather than on technology, where they may have little or no expertise.

In comparison to the CNC architecture, client/server architecture is inefficient because it focuses on application-centric computing. The client/server paradigm centers on the application and how it can be supported by the clients and servers on the network. The result is applications that are highly dependent on the underlying technology and very sensitive to any changes in the technology. Expert knowledge of the business applications and the underlying technology is necessary to understand the functional operation of each application.

With the CNC architecture, applications are independent of the underlying technology that supports the network. Therefore, applications in the CNC architecture are easier to maintain because they do not contain technology-dependent logic existing on the network. The result is that applications are focused on business practices and are independent of the network that supports OneWorld.

The importance of thoroughly comprehending the CNC architecture is critical and cannot be overemphasized. Without an understanding of the CNC architecture's affects on your applications, you are likely to restrict yourself to basic applications that merely view and update data for users. Sophisticated applications for analytical users, such as interfacing data that exists outside of OneWorld, will be out of your development reach if you don't know how the CNC architecture is used.

In upcoming sections, you'll study some strategies for deploying the CNC architecture.

CNC Overview

The CNC architecture tracks the location of all information and applications on the corporate network for the OneWorld environment. As shown in Figure 1-3, all client/server communication on the network is directed through the CNC architecture for properly routing requests and enforcing security. Without the CNC architecture, all OneWorld operations cease to exist, because the CNC architecture manages all configuration issues of OneWorld.

From a developer's perspective, CNC is viewed as a logical server, because it directs all the communication between computers in the OneWorld environment. As shown in Figure 1-3, the CNC logical server sits in between all clients and servers in the OneWorld environment to manage all corporate information and network

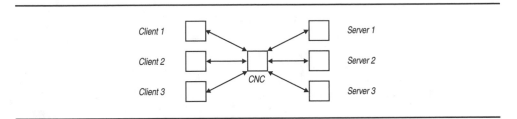

FIGURE 1-3. CNC directs all communication between clients and servers

resources. The CNC logical server is not physically implemented on one machine, but rather is located on every client and server that operates in the OneWorld environment.

NOTE

Although CNC is not really a logic server, the logic server analogy is a good approach for most developers trying to understand how it is used in their applications. The logic server analogy for the CNC architecture only applies to it during execution of an application.

For example, a client machine needs to execute an application that its user is requesting. The client consults the CNC logic server first, to determine if the user has the proper user-access security permissions to execute the application. If the user has the proper security, the client consults the CNC logic server again to determine the location of the database on the network, and then issues the request to the server that contains the database. These steps occur whether the data and application are stored on the client or the server.

The CNC logic server in Figure 1-3 is further illustrated in Figure 1-4, which shows the components that make up CNC. The CNC layer is responsible for three major functions: deployment of system components; administrative services; and system services.

Deployment

The deployment component, which is further explained in the "CNC Deployment Strategies" section, later in the chapter, involves configuration of all clients and servers on the corporate network. Processing modes determine the type of operations, whether

OneWorld System Architecture for Developers

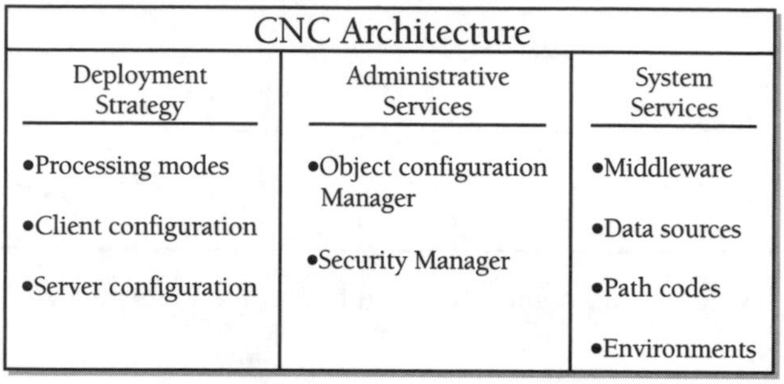

CNC Architecture		
Deployment Strategy	Administrative Services	System Services
•Processing modes	•Object configuration Manager	•Middleware
•Client configuration	•Security Manager	•Data sources
•Server configuration		•Path codes
		•Environments

FIGURE 1-4.   Major components of the CNC architecture

direct connection or offline, that occur between clients and servers. Every client and server in the OneWorld environment can be configured in various ways to enhance performance and reliability on a daily basis.

DEFINITION

*A **deployment strategy** explores all the available options for OneWorld deployment and implementation at a business. The deployment strategy represents all the clients and servers on the network and defines the role each will play in OneWorld configuration, design, development, and execution.*

Administrative Services

Administrative services are management applications that control configuration settings for OneWorld, and they are fully covered in Chapter 3. The Object Configuration Manager (OCM), for example, stores the location of all objects and data on the network. The Security Manager enforces object and data security for users at runtime to ensure no one has the ability to access information they are not allowed to see.

System Services

System services comprise the essential layers of the CNC architecture that support proper operation across the entire OneWorld environment. This component includes the definition of data sources, path codes, and environments (Chapter 2). The *middleware*, which is covered in Chapter 15, contains all the database communication routines. Runtime engines for all clients and servers on the network are also managed in system services.

CNC Fundamentals

Your development projects are directly affected by the CNC architecture. The CNC architecture provides you with the maximum amount of flexibility for your applications by enabling them to execute in any medium. For example, one application can easily be used for a Windows-based client on a LAN or for a Web-based client over a WAN.

The CNC architecture provides three essential components that enable maximum flexibility for your applications: seamless operation in a heterogeneous environment, scalability, and application partitioning.

Seamless Operation in a Heterogeneous Environment

The most powerful feature of the CNC architecture is its ability to integrate heterogeneous computing platforms and database systems into one homogeneous environment. Incompatible computer platforms such as Windows NT and UNIX workstations, and competing database systems such as Oracle and SQL Server, can be mixed and matched with ease. The CNC architecture integrates incompatible systems in OneWorld without any impact on business applications.

The biggest benefit of CNC's isolating the technology from business applications is that developers and technical support personnel can coexist without playing the blame game when an application does not perform to expectations. Developers can concentrate on the design and development of business applications without worrying about network environment instability. Technical support personnel can upgrade, modify, and reorganize the network architecture that supports OneWorld without impact to any business application.

Figure 1-5 is an example of a corporate network that has implemented a CNC architecture. All of the communication between any device on any LAN or WAN is performed through the CNC logical server, as shown in Figure 1-3. The clients and servers communicate without concern for each other's hardware and operating systems. In Figure 1-5, any communication between servers (in this case, a mix of Sun and AS/400 machines) and clients (a mix of Windows NT workstations, web browsers and Windows Terminals) is identical. The CNC architecture provides a

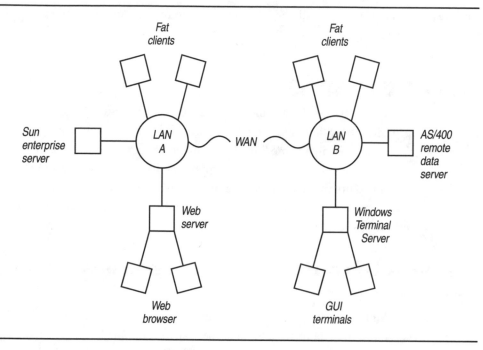

FIGURE 1-5. Example of a "homogenized" corporate network

heterogeneous network infrastructure, transformed in Figure 1-5 to a homogenous environment for OneWorld operations.

The CNC architecture isolates technology from business applications in three major areas: client/server platforms; server configurations; and database systems.

Client and Server Platforms

The CNC architecture integrates many computer platforms, such as AS/400, RS/600, HP 9000, Sun Enterprise Server, and Windows NT, for any client and server on the network. The ability to integrate incompatible computer platforms in a single architecture allows businesses to implement the user spectrum concept for optimal use of corporate computing resources. As shown in Figure 1-5, the CNC layer buries the technical details of operation of the remote AS/400 server with the Sun enterprise server.

As shown in Figure 1-6, the CNC architecture isolates the technical details of computer platform incompatibility from the business applications. CNC handles the

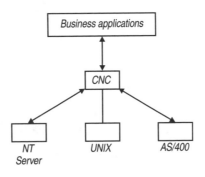

FIGURE 1-6. CNC handling of incompatible computer platforms

details of routing data and applications to particular servers, and determines how to execute the requests for a specific server. This architecture also simplifies integration of new computer-platform technology without disrupting business applications.

Server Configurations

CNC allows multiple configurations of servers for optimizing network resources, such as network bandwidth. As illustrated in Figure 1-7, CNC server configuration ranges from a simple, centralized server to a complex, hierarchical, multiple server configuration.

For example, the corporate network in Figure 1-5 shows the AS/400 being used to minimize message traffic across the WAN by using CNC. The AS/400 maintains a replicated database. The replicated database allows all of the client machines on LAN B to access data locally without overburdening the WAN with requests for data on LAN A.

Database Systems

The CNC architecture transforms database systems that are incompatible into a harmonious operating database system for OneWorld operations. CNC provides the medium through which the incompatible databases can easily interchange data. As illustrated in Figure 1-8, CNC handles the location, storage, and communication of applications and data.

A CNC architecture allows DB2, SQL Server, Oracle, and Access databases to store and retrieve data interchangeably, as if they were built by the same software company. The example in Figure 1-5 depicts data replication between an Oracle database, which

OneWorld System Architecture for Developers

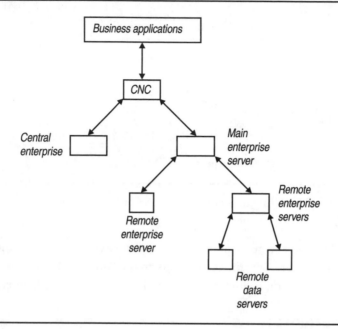

FIGURE 1-7.   CNC server configurations

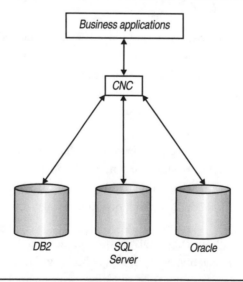

FIGURE 1-8.   CNC and incompatible database systems

resides on a Sun server, and a DB/2 database, which resides on an AS/400, without any knowledge or interaction required of the user or developer.

Scalability

One factor having impact on most ERP systems is the ability to scale the system as the company grows. ERP systems quickly become obsolete if they can't easily scale up or down as the company expands or retracts. A CNC architecture provides a solid framework that accommodates network evolution without affecting the supported applications. Developers have often been frustrated by state-of-the-art network technology that sometimes renders their applications useless. Applications developed in OneWorld, however, execute reliably as network technology changes, providing a stable environment for related application evolution.

For instance, the network in Figure 1-8 can be changed if the company acquires another business and needs to make a WAN connection to the new business's LAN. Providing another remote server to communicate to more clients on another LAN will involve minimal effort. Or, if the division that contains LAN B is sold, the network configuration could easily change over to a single-server system with little or no impact on the ERP system.

Application Partitioning

Even when user interaction with an application occurs on a single computer, several clients and servers behind the scenes may execute various portions of the application. Execution of an application across many computers exists because most applications are made up of one or more objects. Defining the execution location of each object for an application is called *application partitioning*.

Typical corporate applications have five layers: the presentation layer, presentation logic layer, application logic layer, data logic layer, and database management layer. Each layer contains one or more objects that support the features and functionality of the application.

For example, the presentation layer is a simple form that is displayed on the monitor for capturing user interactions. How the form behaves in the application is embedded in the presentation logic layer. The application logic layer contains business logic that is used to enforce business rules. The data logic layer performs data integrity validation of the data that flows in and out of the database. The database management layer performs administrative tasks, such as replication and exporting of data, on the database.

OneWorld System Architecture for Developers

With application partioning, each of the objects assigned to an application layer can exist on different machines across the network. The advantages to application partitioning are its ability to decrease the amount of network traffic generated by the application, and to improve the application's overall performance. OneWorld includes five modes of application partitioning, illustrated in Figure 1-9 and discussed in the sections that follow.

Remote Presentation

The remote presentation mode is typically a zero client that communicates with a mainframe. Most of the application execution is located on the mainframe, because the zero clients only present the information on the screen and capture user input. Zero clients are useful in environments in which high reliability is required, and during terminal failure when a quick turnaround time is critical. An example of a zero client is a dumb terminal that communicates to a mainframe computer on the network.

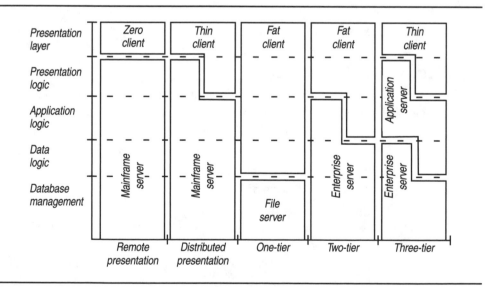

FIGURE 1-9. Application partitioning modes in the CNC environment

N O T E

Proper partitioning of an application across a network will reduce the message traffic occurring on the network, resulting in a decrease in application response time.

Distributed Presentation

The distributed presentation mode is normally implemented as a dumb terminal communicating to a mainframe computer. In distributed presentation mode, all of the objects are centrally located on the server, and the client is used only to display information on the screen and capture user inputs.

One-Tier System

The one-tier system is typically implemented with fat clients on the network, that access data located on a file server and perform the bulk of application execution and database management. One-tier systems are only used in the OneWorld environment for servers that provide remote storage of data to minimize message traffic across the network.

Two-Tier System

The two-tier system is typically implemented with a thin or fat client on the network, and is typically used by analytical users and developers in an organization. This type of client shares application execution with a server that handles database management.

Three-Tier System

The three-tier system is normally implemented as a thin client communicating to two servers. The objects are partitioned across the two servers—for example, a client executing web pages that contain Java applets. The thin clients for the three-tier system are used for WANs.

N O T E

Many non-OneWorld applications use a development toolset for each partitioning mode, dramatically increasing the amount of redundant code needed. OneWorld applications avoid this by partitioning objects across the network to implement each partitioning mode, thereby eliminating redundant code.

OneWorld System Architecture
for Developers

CNC's Impact on OneWorld Applications

You are probably swimming in a sea of confusion at this moment, due to the amount of condensed information in the preceding pages. In all likelihood, the topic causing you the most grief is how the CNC architecture impacts applications in OneWorld. To illustrate what we have been talking about in the previous pages, Figure 1-10 shows a simple application that embodies most of the principles we have discussed up to now.

The Guest and Client Search and Select application shown in the figure is part of a hotel reservation system. In particular, the application is used to search for guests or the clients they represent who have used the hotel services of the company in the past. For example, a reservation clerk uses the application to find a particular guest and their billing address by their name, the company they represent, or their address.

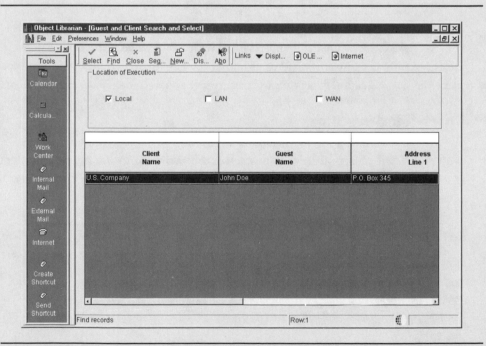

FIGURE 1-10. Guest and Client Search and Select application

The application provides you with the functionality to execute the same lines of code on different clients and servers on the network. By selecting one of the three check boxes (Local, LAN, or WAN) and clicking the Find button, the application will execute on your machine, on a server located on the same LAN, or on another server located across the WAN from your machine. In all three cases, the application manipulates a set of tables that reside on the same LAN where it is executing.

The following Event Rule (ER) code listing shows the lines of code built into the application. For local execution, you can see that the lines of code delete all the records in the F56SLH1 table and refresh it with data from the F560040, F0101, F0116, and F0101 tables. For LAN and WAN execution, identical code is written into two different business functions, and each one of the functions are mapped to a local server on the LAN and to another server across the WAN.

```
If FC Local is equal to "1"
   F58SLH1.Select All
   F58SLH1.FetchNext
   While SV File_IO_Status is equal to CO SUCCESS
         F58SLH1.Delete
         F58SLH1.FetchNext
   End While
   F560040.Select All
   F560040.FetchNext
   While SV File_IO_Status is equal to CO SUCCESS
         F0101.FetchSingle
         F0116.FetchSingle
         F0101.FetchSingle
         F58SLH1.Insert
         F560040.FetchNext
   End While
End If
If FC LAN is equal to "1"
   Refresh the F58SLH1 Table for LAN
End If
If FC WAN is equal to "1"
   Refresh the F58SLH1 Table for WAN
End If
```

Local　When you select the Local check box and click the Find button, the application executes very slowly. In fact, it takes over six minutes for the manipulation of the tables to occur, as shown in the output of the debug log (Jdedebug.log). This is due to the fact that each record from the database has to be transferred to the client, and the client has to then send the modified record back to the database.

```
       .
       .
       .
15:19:39 ** 296/62      SELECT  *  FROM TESTDTA/F58SLH1
       .
       .
       .
15:25:51 ** 296/62      RESET: INSERT INTO TESTDTA/F58SLH1 VALUES
(?,?,?,?,?,?,?,?,?)
```

LAN Things dramatically improve when you execute the same code on the server that contains the database by selecting the LAN check box and clicking the Find button. Just as with the Local option, during execution the application makes a remote procedure call to the server to execute the business function that manipulates the tables. As shown in the following code listing, it takes about one second for the entire process to execute. The reason for the massive improvement is that all of the calls to the database reside on the same machine, instead of over the network.

```
       .
       .
       .
15:14:21 ** 296/62      Calling Business function
RefreshTheF58SLHTable1 on S102RY3M for SHESTER.
       .
       .
       .
15:14:22 ** 296/62      RT: <<<Finished  ER: Write Grid Line-After
App: P58SLH      Form: W58SLHB
```

WAN When the machine is physically located across the WAN, the performance of application execution varies depending on the location of the database to the server. When the database is on the same LAN as the server, the application execution takes about 15 to 30 seconds. The performance is not as good for the WAN as for the LAN, because the WAN has a smaller bandwidth capacity that results in delaying the amount of time it takes to transmit the data.

When the database is on a different LAN than the server, the performance is even worse than in the first case. The calling machine issues a remote procedure call to the server across the WAN to execute the other business function, and the same server has to retrieve all the data from another database across the WAN. The same requests that are made by the client machine in the local execution are made by the server in this execution, but they are made over a network (WAN) that is substantially slower than a LAN. After all of the tables are manipulated over the network, the results are returned in about 30 minutes to the machine that made the original request.

From this example, we can learn some important points:

- *Spend the time to properly partition an application.* Even though the CNC architecture provides you with the tools to execute an application or business function anywhere on the network, it does not tell you the best technique for partitioning the execution of the application across the network. The best rule of thumb you can use to help you properly partition an application across the network is to execute the logic that directly manipulates database tables on the machine that contains the database.

- *Embed as much database manipulation logic as you can into a business function.* If you do this, you will be able to dynamically partition the execution location of the business function at any time, and that will allow you to test for the best execution location on the network. Dynamic application partitioning saves you time because you don't have to recompile the code for a different server; you just map the execution location of the business function to a different server.

- *Monitor the network traffic your application creates.* Do not sit idly by hoping your applications won't generate excessive messages to support their operations. It's important to monitor the network traffic your applications generate because it can solve a lot of performance and network bandwidth problems. That way, you will never be in a situation in which you have the application, the database, and the server all located on different points on the WAN, eating up a lot of network bandwidth.

CNC Deployment Strategies

The CNC deployment strategy, which is one component of the CNC paradigm, is the foundation for the OneWorld environment. Only when the underlying network infrastructure is properly designed and implemented will OneWorld operate properly with its CNC layer.

Understanding the possible ways in which OneWorld can be configured at a business can make or break your projects. You will save much time and effort on a project if you are thoroughly familiar with the various configurations in which servers and clients can be arranged. This section presents a high-level overview of the configurations available in the CNC architecture.

Processing Modes

OneWorld provides several processing modes for client/server interaction. Each processing mode provides different methods of communication between a client and server on the network to optimize network bandwidth. The more bandwidth that is available, the more responsive your applications will be. OneWorld's four processing modes are discussed next.

Direct Connect Mode

All interactive and batch applications initiated from the client machine in the direct connect processing mode are executed immediately by the server, as shown in Figure 1-11. Direct connect provides interaction with a single application to perform editing and creation of data through the application. Also, direct connect is ideally suited for employees who perform their tasks within work sites that are connected to the server through a LAN.

The direct connect processing mode is highly dependent on database resources and results in a high volume of network traffic. Such volume is intolerable for WANs and dial-up networks because it eats up network bandwidth and dramatically slows down application execution.

Store-and-Forward Mode

The store-and-forward processing mode is for users who need to enter transactions through OneWorld while disconnected from the server. Employees perform their tasks in OneWorld offline and then forward the new data to the server when a network connection becomes available. For example, a sales representative on the road can

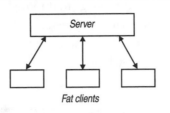

FIGURE 1-11.   Direct connect processing mode

enter orders on a laptop and then forward the orders later when the laptop can be connected to the server.

Figure 1-12 is a simple diagram of the store-and-forward processing mode. All of the data integrity checks are performed on the data while the user enters the information, and this ensures that the user doesn't have to modify the data later. The data is temporarily stored in OneWorld's Z files.

DEFINITION

Z files are standard OneWorld tables that are available for importing and exporting data to and from OneWorld. Z files store data that is waiting to be processed, or data that failed to be imported into OneWorld.

When OneWorld detects that the laptop is connected to the network by modem or network card, OneWorld then uploads the data from the Z files on the laptop to the same Z files on the server. The server then executes business logic to validate all entries that have been deposited into its Z files, to ensure data integrity. After

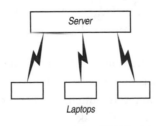

FIGURE 1-12.   Store-and-forward processing mode

validation, OneWorld sends a status message to the employee's Work Center mailbox providing the status and success or failure of the upload process. OneWorld is then notified to execute a batch process, which handles all transactions in the Z files and enters the data into the corporate database.

DEFINITION

The **Employee Work Center** is an application (P012501/ZJDE0002), and it is used to send and receive messages from the system or to another user.

Another advantage of store-and-forward mode is that it allows program execution on networks that have low reliability, such as dial-up networks. The data stored in the client's Z file is transferred to the server's Z file, and the data is retained in the client's Z file until it can verify that the data has been successfully transferred to the server. If the network connection becomes unreliable, the data stored in the Z file on the client machine remains in a hold status until the data can be reliably transferred. This lets individual users be sure that their data will get to its destination properly.

One drawback of the store-and-forward processing mode is that it requires more application interaction than the direct connect mode. Store-and-forward requires a GUI application for data entry, and another application to store information in the local Z files and reliably transfer the data to a corresponding Z file on the server. Another application on the server imports the Z-file data into the proper application modules.

Batch-of-One Mode

Batch-of-one processing mode combines the performance of the store-and-forward mode with the real-time transaction updating of direct connect mode. Instead of the client storing data locally in its own Z files, the data is stored in Z files on a server. Therefore, transactions that the client creates are automatically entered into the system. The processing of the transaction by the server is performed in one of two ways: subsystem and online.

When the server is set up to execute the batch-of-one processing mode as a subsystem job, the user's entry is processed behind the scenes without the user's knowledge. Once the subsystem job is launched, no other user input is required. In this way, users can progress to the next task without waiting for system notification of the results. Notification of the entry's status is sent to the user's Work Center mailbox.

In the online method, the user interacts with the batch by providing options during execution. The results then can be viewed instantaneously or delayed until a specified time.

Stand-Alone Mode

The stand-alone processing mode is a completely freestanding system that operates on a single computer (a client on which the entire OneWorld client and server software is installed). The client does not use OneWorld servers to operate, because those services are completely installed on the client.

There are only two uses for the stand-alone processing mode: for demonstration (demo) and for the OneWorld Software Development Kit (SDK). The OneWorld demo application allows salespeople to show the OneWorld environment on a single computer without transporting several servers around the country. The demo also allows potential customers to test-drive OneWorld and decide if they want to install the product for their businesses.

The SDK version of OneWorld is the demo version augmented with solutions to the tutorial exercises for developers. Its sole purpose is for developers to practice creating applications using the SDK tutorial.

Client-Side Configuration

Computing requirements vary across the user spectrum, based on users' roles within a business. Solutions are provided for the three types of CNC clients: fat, thin, and zero.

Fat Client

Fat clients are powerful workstations that are used by analytical users and developers. As shown earlier in Figure 1-9, fat clients are used in two-tier systems to share the workload with the server, and this increases the server's availability for other clients. Typical OneWorld fat clients use the direct connect processing mode with the enterprise server, as shown in Figure 1-13.

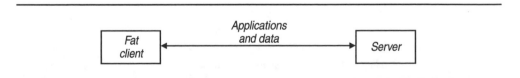

FIGURE 1-13.   Fat client configuration

OneWorld System Architecture for Developers

Because of the direct connect mode, message traffic is high, impacting network bandwidth and application execution. Fat clients must be located on the same LAN where the enterprise server is located to prevent overburdening the network, such as when used with a WAN or dial-up network. Application execution is fast on a fat client, but too many users with fat clients on a LAN will degrade performance because of all the message traffic generated.

N O T E

OneWorld applications that are configured for fat clients should use direct connect processing only, because of the substantial amount of message traffic occurring between the clients and servers.

Thin Client

Thin clients are stripped-down versions of fat clients that are used by action users. The bulk of application execution is off-loaded to a server, and the client only executes logic that is related to presentation of the application on screen. As shown earlier in Figure 1-9, there are two types of thin clients that are distinguished by the type of partition mode they implement (distributed presentation and three-tier). Configurations of the two thin-client solutions are shown in Figure 1-14.

The distributed presentation mode used on a thin client offloads all application execution onto the enterprise server. The difference between a OneWorld fat client and a OneWorld thin client with a distributed presentation partitioning mode is that with the latter, a smaller number of OneWorld applications are installed on the client. If the client needs to execute an application that it does not have installed, the client will perform a just-in-time installation (JITI) of the application at the moment of the request.

One example of a three-tier system with a thin client is a web-based solution that off-loads the bulk of application execution to a OneWorld web server, which is called a Java Application Server (JAS). JAS interprets information flowing to and from the enterprise server and sends Java applet–enabled web pages to the client.

N O T E

In Figure 1-14, the distributed presentation on a thin client is a stripped-down version of the fat client in Figure 1-13. In contrast, the combination of JAS and the thin client in Figure 1-14 make up a single fat client, as shown in Figure 1-13.

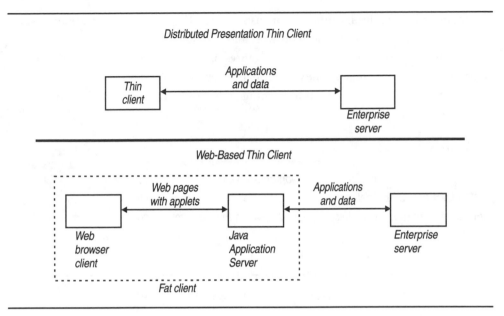

Distributed Presentation Thin Client

Thin client ←→ Applications and data ←→ Enterprise server

Web-Based Thin Client

Web browser client ←→ Web pages with applets ←→ Java Application Server ←→ Applications and data ←→ Enterprise server

Fat client

FIGURE 1-14. Thin-client configurations

For example, if a salesperson enters a sales order through the three-tier mode on a thin client, the request can be passed to the JAS. The JAS validates the client and any data integrity checks. The enterprise server then receives the request from JAS, and enters the sales order into the system. No special logic is required of the enterprise server for the web-based sales order, so that server processes the order as if it came from a fat client.

T I P

This three-tier implementation of a thin client requires developers to modify fat-client applications so that they operate properly with a web browser. The Form Design Aid (FDA) tool can build both Windows- and web-based applications.

Zero Client

Zero clients are the leanest type. All application execution is on the server and the display is exported to the zero clients, as shown in Figure 1-9. A zero client requires a monitor to display the information from any application, and a keyboard and mouse for the user to provide input. Zero clients receive interface control messages that tell the monitor how to display information, as shown in Figure 1-15. There are two types of OneWorld zero clients: the web browser and Windows Terminal Server.

The web browser–based zero client requires no installed OneWorld-specific code. This zero client's only functionality is through a web browser. This client communicates to the same web server that the thin client uses, but the zero client receives only web pages with HTML control codes.

N O T E

For web browser–based clients, application development is different from that in Windows-based applications. Application development is focused on the development of web pages that are passed between the web browser and a web server.

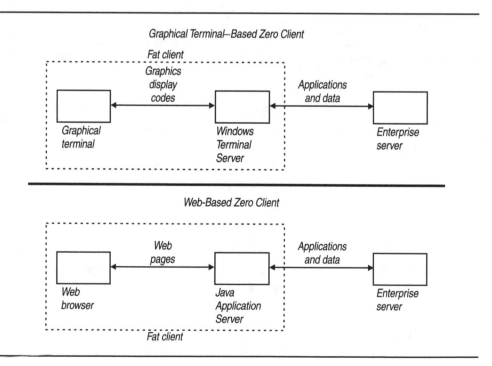

FIGURE 1-15. Zero-client configurations

The other type of zero client communicates with a Windows Terminal Server. All of the application execution is performed on the Windows Terminal Server, and the graphics are exported to the client through interface control codes.

N O T E

The web browser–based zero client in Figure 1-15 is the web-based thin client in Figure 1-14, except the zero client processes only web pages with HTML. The graphical terminal–based zero client in Figure 1-15 is the fat client in Figure 1-13, with all the processing on the Terminal Server, and the display exported to a graphics display.

Server-Side Configuration

Several server-side configuration options are available in OneWorld, but they are not as clearly defined as on the client side. Each server-side configuration option is not mutually exclusive of the others. They can be combined in many ways to provide a highly reliable and available corporate OneWorld system. The four server-side options are discussed next.

N O T E

There is no server-side application development in OneWorld. However, applications that are built in OneWorld can be mapped to execute on the server through the Object Configuration Manager (OCM) application.

Multitier Architecture

The two most common architectures for operation of OneWorld are two tier and three tier (see Figure 1-9), and both can exist simultaneously on the same network in OneWorld. The two-tier architecture is predominantly used by fat clients operating in the direct connect processing mode, and the three-tier architecture is used by thin and zero clients. For example, the network in Figure 1-5 contains two-tier architecture for fat clients, and three-tier architectures for thin and zero clients (web browsers and GUI terminals).

NOTE

Three-tier application partitioning and three-tier architecture have virtually the same definitions. Three-tier application partitioning is totally focused on applications and how they are distributed among machines, whereas three-tier architecture is mostly focused on the system that supports the applications.

The reasons for using two- and three-tier architectures will depend on the network infrastructure. As shown in Table 1-1, slower network connections such as dial-up networks and WANs require three-tier architecture. Faster networks such as LANs, on the other hand, are best suited for two-tier architecture.

Hierarchical Server Configuration

Strategic use of hierarchical configuration of servers localizes network traffic. Placing servers for each department and node on a WAN contains most of the network traffic to the LAN, instead of running it across the entire corporate network. The end results are applications with high responsiveness and reduced network traffic.

In Figure 1-5, the two LANs are connected by a WAN; each LAN contains a server. The hierarchical server configuration in Figure 1-5 contains a remote server on LAN B that synchronizes its content with the central server on LAN A. If the company that owns the network in Figure 1-5 added another LAN, the LAN would have its own server in order to limit message traffic across the WAN to necessary traffic only.

Data Replication

Data replication synchronizes content among servers on a corporate network and is nothing more than copying data from server to server. Data replication does, however, require significant network bandwidth to keep all the servers synchronized, due to the amount of data each server needs.

You can avoid saturating the WAN with network traffic required for data replication by performing data replication periodically at specific times. It's a good idea to select an off-peak time of WAN usage, such as midnight, to perform data replication. For example, the corporate network in Figure 1-5 synchronizes its servers on LAN A and B at night to leave network bandwidth available for users during the day.

TIP

Information that must be updated on all servers before the next synchronization event is not used for data replication. The data inconsistency between servers can disrupt business operations when servers do not have up-to-date data.

High-Availability Clustering

For mission-critical software and hardware operations, a single server will not do, because service is dependent on a single point of reliability. To ensure that single-point failures don't exist in corporate mission-critical systems, you should cluster the hardware and software. Clustering allows OneWorld servers to continue operating if one server fails.

Typically, you use the main enterprise server and JAS servers for clustering. You need the enterprise server for high availability and reliability—especially for all of the data and applications on the central enterprise server that supports the business's CNC architecture. Without the CNC architecture operating properly, all OneWorld operations will cease. You cluster the JAS servers to ensure that all electronic storefronts and commerce applications are always available for business. Unavailable JAS services for business on the Internet equate to lost revenues and opportunities.

Examining Computers in a OneWorld Environment

All clients and servers that operate in the OneWorld environment must be properly defined and identified for use in the OneWorld environment. The Machine Master and Detail tables (F9650 and F9651) are used to define all clients and servers on the network that are used for OneWorld operations.

The F9650 and F9651 tables provide detailed information for the CNC layer, about the unit's location and type of computer. Some of the information includes the machine platform, such as NT or HP9000; name; primary user; and the unit's installed OneWorld software packages. You use the Deployment Locations application (P9654A) to add and modify the information in the F9650 and F9651 tables.

Here are the steps to use the Machine Identification application (P9654A) to find all servers and clients that are available to the OneWorld environment:

1. At the OneWorld Explorer, type **GH9611** in the Fast Path edit box to access the Advanced Operations menu (GH9611).

2. Execute the Machine Identification application (P9654A).

3. The Work With Locations and Machines form (Figure 1-16) appears with nothing but the Location/Machine Information data item displayed in the window. To view all servers and client workstations that are in the OneWorld environment, click the Find button at the top of the application.

4. To view the details on each machine, highlight a machine and click the Select button. The relevant information is displayed in the Revisions screen that is linked to the Machine Identification Detail table, as shown in Figure 1-17.

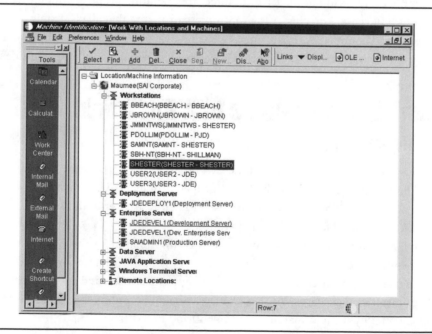

FIGURE 1-16.　Work With Locations and Machines form of Machine Identification application (P9654A)

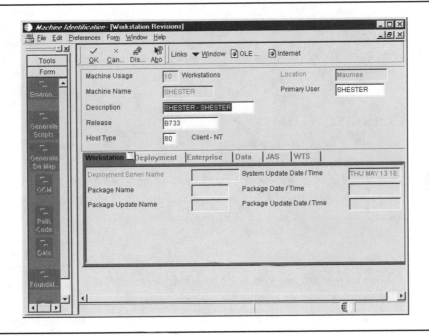

FIGURE 1-17.   Workstation Revisions form of Machine Identification application
(P9654A)

OneWorld Development Toolset

The OneWorld development toolset is a large set of utilities to perform any function required by a development project. The toolset ranges from common tools that you use to modify and build typical applications, to very specialized programs that perform a single function, such as importing data from outside OneWorld.

This section gives you a high-level overview of the entire development toolset in OneWorld. With this overview you will be able to understand how the tools are used for a particular project.

Base Application Development Tools

Any attempt to develop a OneWorld application must start with the base application development tools. Any OneWorld developer must know these tools well to develop or modify applications. The base application development tools are discussed next.

Data Dictionary (DD)

The Data Dictionary integrates applications and databases by maintaining a central repository for all data items used in OneWorld applications. The definition of a data item determines the item's appearance on any application; the type of data entry validation it provides; and the column and row descriptions it uses. Each definition also includes a glossary definition for field-sensitive help.

The Data Dictionary is an Activator for OneWorld, because of the dictionary's ability to react dynamically to changes in data item definitions. Any change made to a data item is immediately displayed across all clients. The Data Dictionary is covered in more detail in Chapter 11.

Table Design Aid (TDA) Tool

You use the Table Design Aid tool to create or modify tables for the applications you build. You add data items to the tables through TDA and then generate the table to a particular database. TDA also allows you to create new keys for a table as needed, for performance and increased search capability. TDA is explained in Chapter 11.

Business View Design Aid (BDA) Tool

The Business View Design Aid tool allows developers to create and modify views of
tables and table joins. Business views provide a consistent means to access tables from
anywhere in OneWorld, whether from interactive or batch applications. The BDA
provides four types of joins: simple, left, right, and outer. For any join, a maximum
of five tables can be combined. The BDA is fully explored in Chapter 11.

N O T E

*BDA is an Activator that generates the SQL statements based on the table and
columns defined for a particular business view. You use business views to
identify the required data items in application, which ensures that only
necessary data is transmitted across the network.*

Form Design Aid (FDA) Tool

You use the Form Design Aid tool to create and modify interactive OneWorld
applications. The FDA, too, is explained in Chapter 5. This tool directly interacts with
the database tables through business views assigned to forms within the application
you create. All of the elements on the form come from the Data Dictionary, by way of
the data items defined in the business view, to enforce consistency of Data Dictionary
items from the database to the interactive applications.

Some unique features of OneWorld-based forms are the query-by-example (QBE)
bar, and versions. Grid-based forms offer a powerful means of searching database
tables, using the query-by-example bar built at the top of each grid. Users who have
no knowledge of SQL can type criteria into the QBE bar, and a moment later the grid
contains the results of a search on those criteria.

Users can create many different looks for a form by customizing it and storing it
as a *version*. The user can change the values for the processing option of an application,
and the logic can be put in place to adjust the application's behavior based on those
values. To ensure that the user's changes will be available next time, and that any
previous changes won't be deleted, the newly modified form can be stored as a version
for all OneWorld users to execute.

OneWorld System Architecture
for Developers

Processing options are parameters input to an interactive or batch application. For example, the Address Book application (P01012/ZJDE0001) in the Address Book module provides a processing option to determine what types of addresses (employees, customers, or suppliers) are viewed in the application.

Report Design Aid (RDA) Tool

You use the Report Design Aid tool to build and maintain two types of report applications: *Reports*, which provide current information on the contents of a database, are designed to be flexible in aiding OneWorld users. The other type of report is called a *batch*—a process used to modify database tables. You can also use batches to administer and automate tasks within OneWorld.

RDA provides a graphical environment for report creation and modification that allows you to see the reports as you construct them. Like FDA, RDA lets you customize existing forms for your own needs without overwriting existing reports. RDA is discussed in Chapter 6.

RDA contains an Activator that helps you quickly build a report without writing any code. This is particularly useful when you are just interested in getting basic functionality embedded into a report.

Advanced Development Tools

For experienced OneWorld developers, advanced development tools provide features that allow the use of sophisticated techniques. With the advanced development tools you can gain access to the lower layers of OneWorld and modify the OneWorld environment to enhance application execution and performance. The advanced development tools are discussed next.

Menu Design Tool

The menu in OneWorld Explorer is the starting point for all OneWorld users and developers, because application execution starts at the menu. To access applications in OneWorld, the applications must be available to the users through a menu item in

OneWorld Explorer. A good, logical menu layout will enable users to quickly find the application they need to execute.

The Menu Design tool implements a menu layout for OneWorld, and is covered in Chapter 11. Developers design a menu layout for the applications they develop, and use the Menu Design tool to implement it in OneWorld. If modification to the menu is needed later, a system administrator or developer can do this by returning to the Menu Design tool.

T I P

The time you spend on designing a menu layout will go far toward ensuring that users can easily find the applications you build for them. If a user can't find an application, then your effort to build it is wasted.

Web Generation Facility

The primary benefit of the Web Generation Facility is that it gives you a single application for performing development and maintenance of applications for use on Windows- and web-based clients. The Web Generation Facility helps you build and maintain any application using the FDA tool, and then easily generate it to a web-based application based on one of two types of web pages: HTML with Java applets, or HTML.

- Web pages based on HTML with Java applets provide the thin-client solution, covered earlier in this chapter, for OneWorld. The thin-client solution is necessary when communication among clients and servers is on a slow network connection, or when the client machine's user requires full computation power at the workstation.

- Web pages based on HTML provide one of two zero-client solutions. The zero-client solution is needed in situations in which a kiosk for public access is required, or users need only to perform information entry and lookup for their jobs. A useful place for a kiosk in any company, for example, is in the human resources department, and in a situation in which employees need easy access to their information for viewing and editing purposes.

OneWorld System Architecture for Developers

Object Configuration Manager (OCM)

The Object Configuration Manager (OCM), discussed in Chapter 3, is the heart of the CNC architecture. OCM stores the network location for all objects that execute in OneWorld; it is the mechanism that gives the CNC architecture its dynamic ability to change object location at runtime.

NOTE

With the OCM, development of client-side and server-side–only applications is blurred. Developers spend time building and modifying applications, and the OCM maps the application's execution location, whether it's a server or client.

With OCM, you no longer have to spend time defining the locations for all objects in client/server architectures. OCM helps you define, at runtime, the location of all objects in any OneWorld environment. This flexibility lets you store or execute objects on any client or server machine that exists on the corporate network.

NOTE

The OCM is a Technology Activator that provides dynamic changes to the mapping of data and applications across the network. With the OCM, you get the ability to select a new deployment strategy without impacting the software code for an application.

Security Manager

The Security Manager provides user security to prevent users from accessing applications and data that they are not allowed to view or execute. The Security Manager (Chapter 3) controls user access by individuals and groups of users in OneWorld. Developers don't need to spend time on building discrete applications meant for a specific group of users, because the Security Manager provides an efficient way to control user access to applications and data. Security measures can be placed to limit users from executing an application, performing specific functions within it, accessing particular table columns or rows, and accessing database security.

Workflow Management

Paper-based business processes are very slow in reacting to business processes that are inefficient. Businesses that require paper as the medium for communication lose sales to their competitors due to the length of the paper-based business process. To automate paper-based processes, OneWorld provides the Workflow Management development tool.

Consider, for example, the typical business process used by most companies when a customer exceeds their credit limit. The business process defines all the steps required to either increase the customer's credit limit or reject the customer's order. You use Workflow Management to automate business processes like this one, to reduce the cycle time of the process.

You build workflow processes by sequencing applications from start to finish. Each step in the sequence is an application that executes a required step in the business process. Workflow processes require very little application coding, and you can easily change them at any time as your business changes its internal operations.

N O T E

One of the key tools in ActivEra's architecture is Workflow, which is an Activator itself. Many of the ActivEra applications, such as Composer, are built using workflow.

AutoPilot

AutoPilot, is a GUI scripting tool that automates quality assurance (QA) testing and automates applications that require repetitive data entry. A major benefit of AutoPilot is that the scripts it creates are small and compact, because all of the logic for data validation and program execution is embedded into the application being manipulated.

AutoPilot increases the productivity of the advanced developer. AutoPilot can take the mundane verification of proper program execution out of the hands of people, which results in better QA testing. Also, many of the development and administrative tasks that you perform to build and maintain OneWorld applications can easily be automated through AutoPilot to save development and data entry time.

OneWorld System Architecture for Developers

Interoperability and Integration Tools

Any business that requires interoperability and integration of OneWorld with any other ERP systems must use the tools discussed in the following sections, and fully covered in Part 4. These tools provide all the necessary applications and interfaces to import and export data to and from OneWorld

Interoperability Tables and Processes

Interoperability tables, which are called *Z tables*, and processes, which are called *Z processes*, are special tables and batch applications inside OneWorld that allow you to import data from outside OneWorld. Z tables are used for temporary storage of data to and from non-OneWorld systems. Z processes verify accuracy of the data in the Z tables, and then insert the valid data into the main OneWorld environment. When the Z process is finished, it provides a status for every record in the Z table it has processed.

For example, the first step in processing data for the General Ledger (GL) from a foreign data source is to import the data into the GL Z table (F0911Z1). When importing is complete, the GL Z process (R09110Z) creates a report that displays the status of each record in the GL Z table. The status indicates whether the GL Z process successfully processed each record. The GL Z process inserts all of the valid records it processes as an unposted journal entry into the account ledger table (F0911). The new journal entries get posted to the general ledger when their batch is executed.

N O T E

The OneWorld table-naming convention is FMMXXXX, where MM is the module number, and XXXX is the object number within the module. For example, the General Ledger module number is 09, and the Journal Entries table object name is F0911.

Table Conversion Tool

The Table Conversion tool, covered in Chapter 9, provides high-speed manipulation of data in OneWorld with minimal application development effort. The tool manipulates any OneWorld table, or any external table supported by OneWorld. Data conversion, table replication, and batch record deletion are some of the manipulations performed by this tool.

The Table Conversion tool is the primary development tool for importing and exporting data in OneWorld. In most cases, imported data will come from files that store ASCII data, and you use the Table Conversion tool to build a batch application that imports the data from the file into one of the Z tables (for instance, the GL Z table F0911Z1).

DEFINITION

*A **foreign data source** is any database that is not a part of the OneWorld environment. Examples of foreign data sources include a directory of plain ASCII text files, an Access database, and an Oracle database.*

Open Data Access (ODA)

Open Data Access is a read-only ODBC driver that you use to access OneWorld data stored in an Access database. ODA converts column names, data types, and security rules to present the data properly to the outside world. ODA offers a quick and reliable method of exporting data to non-OneWorld applications, with low programming overhead.

COM Generator

The COM Generator tool gives you access to OneWorld business functions through Microsoft's interprocess communication standard, the Component Object Model (COM). COM is used in OneWorld to provide a wrapper around a set of OneWorld objects, letting a non-OneWorld application execute the OneWorld objects in the COM wrapper.

The COM generator produces fully functional COM servers that can be exported to the outside world. The user executing the COM server code must have a OneWorld license located on the machine, and must log onto the OneWorld environment during execution of the COM server.

OneWorld System Architecture for Developers

Know Your Servers!

Probably the most difficult technical detail for new OneWorld developers to understand is the number of servers needed by a company for supporting OneWorld, and the function each server performs. The schematic diagram shown in Figure 1-18 is that of a hypothetical corporate OneWorld server configuration that contains every type of server supported by OneWorld.

Enterprise Server

The center of the OneWorld production environment is the *enterprise server* because it is the central storage area for corporate data and applications. All other servers in the Production environment interact with the enterprise server for data and applications.

The enterprise server's Production environment is the environment used by all employees, except for developers and programmers, for daily tasks. The Production

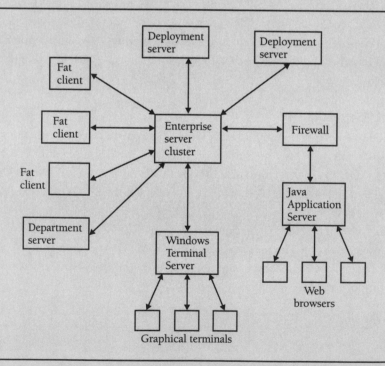

FIGURE 1-18. Example of a OneWorld installation at a company

environment is physically separated from the Development and Testing environments to ensure that any enhancements do not accidentally enter the Production environment until they are ready.

The enterprise server also enforces corporate-wide sign-on security. When an employee logs onto OneWorld, the enterprise server verifies the user's name and password. If the employee passes sign-on security, then the OneWorld Explorer is displayed. If the employee fails sign-on security, a dialog box appears and informs the user.

The enterprise server has minimum requirements for hard disk space, as shown in Table 1-2.

NOTE

The hard disk space required for the enterprise server with a database is on the conservative side for the Production environment. Experience has shown that doubling the minimum required disk space in this case is a good rule of thumb.

For reliability and availability of the corporate enterprise server, the enterprise server in Figure 1-18 is configured as a cluster. The cluster of servers or the *enterprise server farm* requires more financial overhead and initial investment for support, but it provides the mission-critical reliability and availability required by many corporations for their ERP systems.

Deployment Server

The *deployment server* is the one on which OneWorld is installed and configured. The configuration process includes setting up the Machine Identification tables (see the

Platform	Deployment Server	Enterprise Server	SQL Database	Oracle Database
NT	18GB	10GB	15GB	10GB
UNIX	18GB	10GB	NA	10GB
AS/400	18GB	20GB	12GB	10GB

TABLE 1-2.   Minimum Disk Space Requirements for OneWorld

section "CNC Overview," earlier in this chapter) to identify all computers on the network. Then the deployment server defines the CNC architecture for the particular OneWorld installation. At the end of the installation process, the deployment server builds full software packages for installation on all client workstations.

As business applications are built and modified, you need to perform periodic updates of software packages on all computers in the OneWorld environment. The deployment server's primary task after installation is to export partial-update software packages to all enterprise servers and full software packages to client workstations.

TIP

Ensure that the software packages for servers and clients in the OneWorld environment are updated at the same time. This will save you massive amounts of time debugging applications that do not work because they are not identical on the server and clients.

Since initial and update package builds occur sporadically, the deployment server has two other secondary roles to help support operations in the OneWorld environment. One of these tasks is to enforce license security for OneWorld. License security ensures that you will never exceed the number of seats or users that are allowed to sign onto it, and the number of seats are controlled by how many users are allowed to sign onto it at one time. As the enterprise server enforces user sign-on security, the deployment server verifies that sufficient licenses exist for an employee to obtain a OneWorld session.

The other supportive role for the deployment server in the OneWorld environment is to provide one storage location for all the business application source code. As developers modify and create objects for their applications, the source code for each object resides on the deployment server.

TIP

If you do not have access to any of the directories under the J.D. Edwards OneWorld directory for your enterprise and deployment servers, then license security and checking objects in and out will fail.

Due to the number of environments it must store, the deployment server requires more hard disk space than the enterprise server (see Table 1-2). The deployment server builds all the packages for all servers and clients on the network, and stores each package on its hard drive. For each OneWorld environment, there can be several packages built in that correspond only to that environment. The benefit of this approach is that you can maintain the applications for a single environment without worrying about affecting the other environments. The main drawback of this approach is that you can saturate all available disk space by keeping old packages on the deployment server.

Probably the most confusing thing about the deployment and enterprise servers is the various configurations that each one can have. They each can have their own hierarchical tier architecture because each one operates independently of the other. The enterprise server is strictly for production usage, and the deployment server is for version control, security, and packaging.

For example, a company may have ten enterprise servers configured in a very complex, hierarchical fashion, and only one deployment server. This ratio of enterprise to deployment servers is possible because the demand for the deployment server is only during package installation and upgrades—sporadic and transient operations during which performance is not essential.

Development Server

A *development server* is an enterprise server that has one environment installed on it and used for development purposes only. The advantage to a development server is that your application developers construct applications on a different server, which physically isolates the development and production environments to prevent any conflicts. The downside to this approach is that it requires more hardware and software to support the development server. Minimum requirements for the development server are comparable to the amounts presented in Table 1-2 for the deployment server.

Windows Terminal Server

As stated earlier, the Windows Terminal Server provides the functionality for graphical terminal–based zero clients, which interact with the enterprise server through the Terminal Server. The Terminal Server requires NT Server 4.0, 30MB of RAM per user, and 1.5GB of hard drive space per user. The GUI client can be a 486 CPU with minimal hardware, because all of the processing is performed on the server.

OneWorld Web Server

The minimum requirements for the *OneWorld web server* (Java Application Server, JAS) and the client are shown in Table 1-3. The web server can be arranged in a cluster, as shown in the earlier schematic, to create a typical web farm that provides high availability for e-commerce customers. The most important factor to keep in mind when installing a corporate web server or web farm is to place the servers on the opposite side of the firewall from the enterprise server. The last thing a OneWorld and systems administrator wants to deal with is an attack on the corporate enterprise server due to the loss of firewall protection from the web server.

Department Server

The *department server* is located across the WAN from the enterprise server and is used to localize unnecessary network traffic and keep it from consuming all the WAN bandwidth. The department server can be set up in a one- or two-tier architecture. The one-tier architecture for the department server is a simple file server, with a database that contains replicated tables from the enterprise server to provide read-only privileges for its client. The two-tier architecture is a full enterprise server that provides more functionality to its clients than just a file server. The two-tier

Machine	CPU	RAM	Hard Drive	Operating System	Required Software
Web server	Pentium 200 MHz	512MB	8GB	Windows NT Server 4.0	Internet Information Server, Microsoft Java Virtual Machine build 3167 or later, and JRunPro
Web client	Pentium 166 MHz	32MB	10MB	Any OS that supports JDK 1.1	Internet Explorer 4.01 or Netscape Navigator 4.0

TABLE 1-3.   Minimum Web Server and Client Requirements

architecture is more expensive, but it cuts down on network update traffic because the one-tier architecture department server can't write any data to its tables.

Fat Client

Although fat clients are not servers, they are machines that power user and developer interaction with OneWorld. We added fat clients to the list of OneWorld servers because the sizing requirements for fat clients are quite large. At most OneWorld installations, the number of fat clients are factored into the total cost of ownership because their cost can drive up the expense of installing and maintaining OneWorld.

Fat clients are Windows-based machines that are used as clients in OneWorld. The advantage of fat clients is that users have the full capabilities of the computer and all installed software applications that your company uses. However, the costs of providing all employees in your company a fat client is expensive, because the minimum requirements for it, shown in Table 1-4, are expensive.

N O T E

When the fat client is used by developers, we recommend that the minimums be at least doubled to accommodate installation of other software development packages, such as the Java Development Kit and Microsoft Visual C++, to build and test each object.

CPU	RAM	Hard Drive	Operating System	Required Software
Pentium 120 MHz	64MB	2GB	NT Workstation 4.0	Access 97, Internet Explorer 4.01, and ODBC drivers for enterprise server database

TABLE 1-4. Minimum Fat Client Required Configuration

Putting It All Together

OneWorld represents a paradigm shift from other modern ERP systems because of its CNC architecture. The CNC architecture allows the total integration and operation of the network and information infrastructures to optimize every bit of computing resources for a corporation. The CNC architecture leverages many technologies, such as state-of-the-art and legacy, by allowing them to mutually exist. The end result of the CNC paradigm is that you will have applications that are no longer dependent on the underlying technology.

Knowledge of the entire OneWorld development toolset is required for you to develop applications efficiently and with confidence. You may not use each tool on a daily basis, but forcing one development tool to build an application when another tool is better suited for the job is a waste of your time and resources. Spend the time and effort to get familiar with the entire OneWorld development toolset—in the long run, you will develop superior applications.

The rest of this book tells you how application development occurs in OneWorld, and how you can get the most from the development toolset. The parts of the book are based on the experience level of the developer. As you progress throughout your OneWorld application development career, you will find all the parts and chapters in this book to be of great value for the development projects to which you are assigned.

CHAPTER 2

OneWorld Configuration for Developers

Initial development projects for OneWorld developers usually focus on building and maintaining simple interactive and batch applications. As you become more experienced with OneWorld, your development projects will become more complex. For now, however, you need an understanding of OneWorld configuration and its impact on development. This chapter focuses on configuration issues and how they affect decisions you make at development time.

Two development areas deeply influenced by OneWorld's configuration are *foreign tables* and *application performance*. Tables that are not a part of the standard OneWorld system are called foreign tables, and they are typically used to import and export data for OneWorld. The configuration of the OneWorld environment becomes an issue when you use foreign tables, because the tables must be defined in order for OneWorld to communicate with and modify them.

Performance, too, is influenced by OneWorld configuration. If OneWorld is configured to have most applications communicating with a server on the other side of a WAN, the performance of these applications can suffer tremendously. However, if servers are configured strategically across the network, then applications will perform better.

At the lowest levels of the CNC architecture are definitions of the location of databases, applications, and servers on the network. These definitions are used to support OneWorld. The low-level definitions in the CNC layer are

- **Data Sources**   Data sources are building blocks in OneWorld that define all the databases and enterprise servers on the network. The data source definition provides applications with pointers to the location of databases and servers on the network and information about how to communicate to them.

- **Database Data Sources**   A database data source is used in OneWorld to store and manipulate data. Every database that the system uses must be defined as a database data source, so that OneWorld can easily communicate to it.

- **Logic Data Sources**   A logic data source is an enterprise server that is available for executing batch applications and business functions. The advantage of logic data sources is that you can distribute the execution of batch applications and business functions to increase their performance, especially when they manipulate a database.

- **Data Sources Required by OneWorld**   OneWorld requires several data sources in order for it to operate properly. These data sources are broken down into system and environment data sources.

- **Path Codes**   Path codes define the location where OneWorld batch and interactive applications are stored. There are usually many path codes for a OneWorld installation, and this allows various applications to exist in OneWorld without affecting one another.

- **Environments**   Environments define a specific set of applications, databases, and enterprise servers that are used for a particular OneWorld session. This definition is formed by combining a particular path code with a set of defined data sources for a user.

- **Windows Registry and Jde.ini**   The Windows registry and Jde.ini file are critical components for OneWorld on every client and server machine on the network. Both these components define initialization settings for OneWorld and how it behaves for users.

Data Sources

All applications in OneWorld require access to databases for information, and to enterprise servers to execute batch applications. Access is provided by the use of data sources, which are the essential building blocks for the system. Each data source defines the location of every database or enterprise server on the network, and the drivers required to communicate with them.

There are two major categories of data source in OneWorld: *database* and *logic*. Database data sources define all databases that are available for use in the system, and they provide the core functionality for using multiple databases to support a particular OneWorld system. The definition of the database data source includes the pointer to the location of the database, and the database driver for communicating with the database.

N O T E

Data sources point to a particular database or server on the network that stores information or executes applications, respectively. When a computer needs to find one of these resources on the network, the computer uses the data sources as pointers to the proper server or database.

Logic data sources define the network location where execution of batch application and business function logic occurs in OneWorld. Batch applications and business functions are the only OneWorld objects that can execute on a logic data source. A logic data source is typically a OneWorld enterprise server on the network.

All definitions of data sources for OneWorld exist in the Data Source Master table (F98611). There is one Data Source Master table for all clients on the network, and one for each server. The single table for all clients ensures easy and centralized administration of the table. Every enterprise server has its own Data Source Master table because the server's mappings will be different from the client mappings, and different from the mappings on other servers.

This section examines in detail the characteristics of database data sources and logic data sources, as well as the two groups of data sources required for proper operation of the unified OneWorld environment.

Database Data Sources

As discussed in Chapter 1, OneWorld allows you to store data across one or more databases to support system operations. In order for a database to be used in OneWorld, the database has to have a definition in the Data Source Master table (F98611) as a valid database data source. The database data sources define all the valid locations for database data, and which Open Database Connectivity (ODBC) or OLE Control Extension (OCI) driver the client will use to communicate with the database management system (DBMS).

A database data source is defined by its name, its table owner, the name of the server on which it's located, and the name of the dynamic link library (DLL) driver through which OneWorld communicates with the database.

Data Source Name

The data source name contains the location of the database on the network, and the database drivers required for communicating with it in OneWorld. A data source name is up to 30 characters long, and is case and space sensitive. The name in this field must be identical to the data source name (DSN) in the Tnsnames.sql file for Oracle, or the ODBC definition for all other databases. The DSN is the actual component used for communicating with the database.

Table Owner

All database tables have an owner, which determines who is allowed to manipulate and manage the table. The owner is not an actual person, but rather a database administrator (DBA) that maintains the database.

Server Name

The server name identifies the server on which the database is located. The name must exist on a valid computer that is defined in the Machine Identification table (F9650). Server names are discussed in the Developer's Corner titled "Know Your Servers!" in Chapter 1.

DLL Name

The dynamic link library (DLL) driver allows OneWorld to communicate with a particular database. A driver is built for each database type (such as Oracle or SQL Server) and for each platform (such as Intel or AS/400). Table 2-1 lists the DLLs that are used for a particular server platform and database type.

N O T E

On client workstations, use ODBC drivers for Microsoft-based database products, and use OCI drivers for Oracle databases.

Database Type	AS/400	HP9000	RS6000	Intel	Digital
DB2/400	Dbdr	Libjdbnet.sl	Libjdbnet.so	Jdbodbc.dll	Jdbnet.dll
Oracle	Jdbnet	Libora80.sl	Libora80.so	Jdboci80.dll	Jdboci80.dll
SQL Server	Jdbnet	l ihjdbnet.sl	Libjdbnet.so	Jdbodbc.dll	Jdbodbc.dll

TABLE 2-1.   DLLs for Various Databases and Hardware Platforms

OneWorld System Architecture for Developers

Viewing Database Data Sources in OneWorld

As a developer, you will need to view database data sources in order to find out where data for a particular environment is stored. Here are the steps for viewing a database data source:

1. From OneWorld Explorer, type **GH9011** in the Fast Path edit box and press ENTER. The System Administration Tools menu appears.

2. Double-click the Database Data Sources application (P986115/XJDE0001) menu item that is located halfway down the right-hand panel of OneWorld Explorer. The Database Data Source application appears. Shown in Figure 2-1 is the Machine Search and Select form of the Database Data Sources application; its purpose is to prompt the user to select a server.

3. Highlight the server that contains the database data source and click the Select button. The Work With Data Sources form for the Database Data Source application appears, as shown in Figure 2-2.

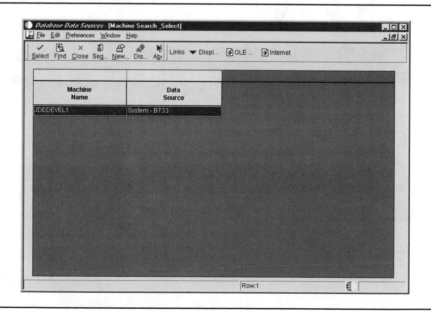

FIGURE 2-1.   Machine Search and Select form of the Database Data Source application (P986115/XJDE0001)

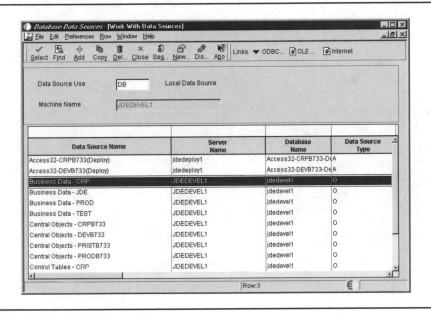

FIGURE 2-2. Work With Data Sources form of the Database Data Source application (P986115/XJDE0001)

4. To view all data source names in the application, click the Find button and scroll down the list displayed in the grid. All of the data sources displayed in the grid are the ones assigned to the server that you selected in step 3. To view the full definition of a database data source, highlight it and click the Select button. The Data Source Revisions form of the Database Data Source application appears, as shown in Figure 2-3.

Logic Data Sources

A logic server is a OneWorld enterprise server that executes business functions and batch applications for clients and servers on the network. This allows the clients and other servers to offload an application's computational workload to a logic server. When appropriate for the configuration, logic data sources can increase application performance and decrease network traffic.

For example, a network that contains several logic servers can reduce its message traffic if it is properly planned. By taking batch applications that generate substantial database requests and moving them to the server that contains the database, and by

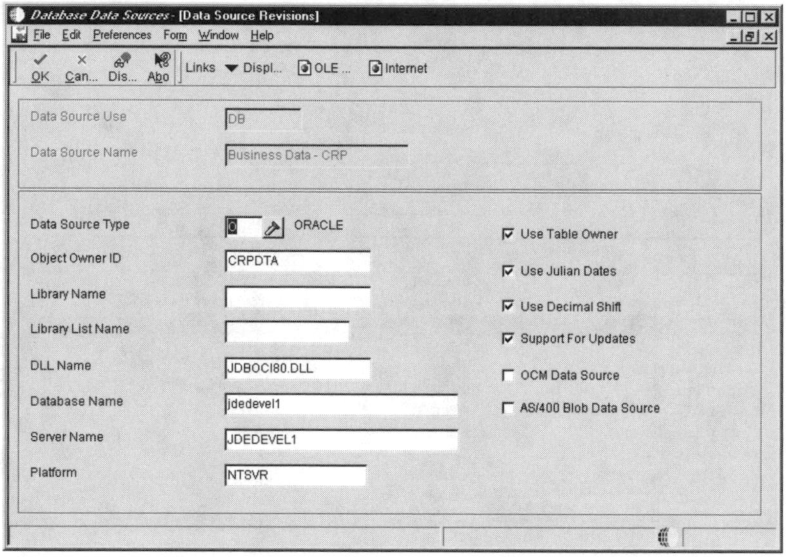

FIGURE 2-3. Data Source Revisions form of the Database Data Source application (P986115/XJDE0001)

assigning each server to a group of clients, thereby localizing network traffic generated by those clients, you can provide applications that perform better and a network with higher availability.

In OneWorld, logic servers are defined using logic data sources. The OneWorld application that defines and maintains logic data sources is identical to the one used for database data sources. All information related to any data source is stored in the Data Source Master table (F98611).

Logic data sources are nothing more than pointers to enterprise servers. These data sources are defined using the same fields as for database data sources. The Data Source Name field for logic data sources contains the name of the enterprise server. The Table Owner Name field contains the name of the enterprise server's server map.

Viewing Logic Data Sources in OneWorld

Here are the steps for viewing all logic servers on the network:

1. From OneWorld Explorer, type **GH9011** in the Fast Path edit box. The System Administration Tools menu appears.

2. Execute the Logic Data Source application (P986115/XJDE0002); the Machine Search and Select form appears. Notice that the form is identical to the one in Figure 2-1 that is used for database data sources.

NOTE

The Database Data Source (P986115/XJDE0001) and Logic Data Source (P986115/XJDE0002) applications are the same application with different versions due to modified input settings. The input settings are modified through the use of processing options, which are covered in Chapter 14.

3. Highlight the server that contains the logic data sources in which you are interested, and click the Select button. The Data Source Revisions form of the Logic Data Source application appears, as shown in Figure 2-4.

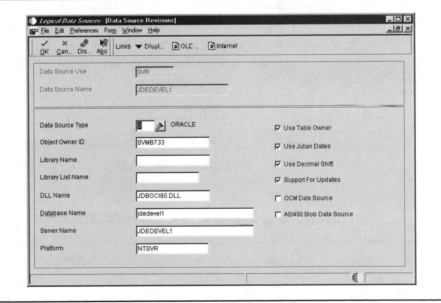

FIGURE 2-4.   Data Source Revisions form of the Logic Data Source application (P986115/XJDE0002)

OneWorld System Architecture for Developers

As shown in Figure 2-4, the only information defined for the logic data source is the location of the server mappings. We will discuss server mappings in the next section.

Data Sources Required by OneWorld

For OneWorld to operate properly, a set of required data sources must exist. The required data sources are categorized into two groups: environment data sources and system data sources.

Environment Data Sources

Environment data sources are defined on a per-environment basis. In other words, each OneWorld environment contains its own set of environment data sources, to prevent other environments from manipulating its data. JDE recommends that every OneWorld installation include at least four major OneWorld environments: Production (PRD733), Conference Room Pilot (CRP733), Development (DEV733), and Pristine (PRT733). Each of these environments will need its own set of defined data sources.

For DBMSs that support tablespaces, every environment data source exists in its own tablespace, as shown in Table 2-2. A *tablespace* is a logical storage area on a hard disk where a DBMS stores its data and indexes for tables. The tablespace is the owner of the tables. For example, a table that contains the business data for the Production environment (PRD733) is owned by table owner PRODDTA.

Environment	Business Data	Control Tables	Central Objects	Versions
PRD733	PRODDTA	PRODCTL	PROB733	PROB733
CRP733	CRPDTA	CRPCTL	CRPB733	CRPB733
DEV733	TESTDTA	TESTCTL	DEVB733	DEVB733
PRT733	PRISTDTA	PRISTB733	PRISTB733	PRISTB733

TABLE 2-2. Mapping of Environments and Data Sources to DBMS Tablespaces

N O T E

The tablespace name can be used as the short name for the data source, and typically it is the name used by most developers when referring to a data source.

For databases that do not support tablespaces, you use the database for client-side caching of data. The OneWorld environment uses these databases for local storage of information from the tables that reside on the servers, or for stand-alone operating modes. Owners are not assigned to tables that do not have tablespace support, such as the tables in an Access database.

Following are descriptions of the five data sources required for each environment:

Business Data Data Source

The business data contains all the business or testing data for the environment. All financial, inventory, manufacturing, sales, and forecasting applications store their data in the business data source. It is the largest data source for any environment.

Control Tables Data Source

The control tables data source stores user-defined codes, menus, and next numbers. The information in this data source is basically static when compared to the business data source, which is dynamic and usually cached to the database on each client.

Central Object Specifications Data Source

OneWorld objects are defined by a set of specification files. These specifications describe each OneWorld object by its main purpose, attributes, any input and output parameters, and source code. There are two types of specification files: *central objects* and *replicated objects*.

Central objects store the definitions of each object in the central object specification data source. Central object specifications contain the central master definition of every object, and no object can execute in OneWorld without one. If the object has any source code associated with it, the source code is stored on the deployment server.

OneWorld System Architecture for Developers

N O T E

Central object specifications are also called relational database (RDB) specifications. *RDB specs are the master specifications for all OneWorld objects.*

During development, you create and modify objects on your local machine. These modifications are then uploaded into the central objects specification data source (or RDB specs) when you check the object back into the environment. During package building for clients and servers, the central objects are used to generate the replicated objects.

T I P

If you need the specifications before the next OneWorld client update package, check out each object and the system will automatically download the modified specifications to your client. Otherwise, you will receive new specifications when your client installs a new update package.

Replicated object specifications exist on all machines on the corporate network and are used during runtime to execute the objects as they are requested. The OneWorld runtime engines use these specifications to execute the objects and their logic. The replicated object specifications are stored in a J.D. Edwards proprietary format called *Table Access Method (TAM)* and are the runtime copies of RDB specifications.

The central object specification data source comprises the database tables in the RDB Spec column of Table 2-3. This table maps the relationship of central objects/RDB specifications to replicated objects/TAM specifications, and the purpose of each specification. To view the RDB and TAM specs, as shown in Table 2-3, see the example located in the section "Windows Registry and Jde.ini," later in this chapter.

C A U T I O N

There are times when the TAM specs on your client are incorrect. The best way to fix this situation is to delete only TAM specs. The only TAM specs that you can delete on a client workstation are DDDICT, DDTEXT, and GLBLTBL.

Replicated Object (TAM Spec)	Central Object (RDB Spec)	Purpose
DDTABL	F98710	Table information.
DDCLMN	F98711	Information for each column in a table.
DDPKEYH	F98712	Information for each index in a table.
DDPKEYD	F98713	Information for each column in an index.
BOBSPEC	F98720	Information for the definition of business views.
GBRLINK	F98740	One record for each event that has event rules (ER) code for applications, reports, and tables.
GBRSPEC	F98741	One record for each line of event rules (ER) code.
DSTMPL	F98743	Information for the definition of data structures.
FDATEXT	F98750	Text information for interactive applications.
FDASPEC	F98751	Detail information, such as columns, grid lines, buttons, and edit boxes, for interactive applications.
ASVRHDR	F98752	Header information for Form Design Aid and Software Version Repository.
ASVRDTL	F98753	Detail information for Form Design Aid and Software Version Repository.
RDATEXT	F98760	Text information for batch reports.
RDASPEC	F98761	Detail information, such as section, column, sort, and constants, for batch reports.
JDEBLC	F98762	Information for the definition of business functions.
DDDICT	F9200	Header information for data dictionary items.
DDTEXT	F9200, F9202, F9203, F9207, F9210	Detail information for data dictionary items.
GLBLTBL	N/A	Cache of just-in-time installation (JITI) specifications for items from the data dictionary and table definitions.
SMRTTMPL	F98745	Information for smart field named mappings.
POTEXT	F98306	Text information for processing options that belong to interactive and batch applications.

TABLE 2-3. Replicated and Central Object Specification Mappings

OneWorld System Architecture for Developers

Versions Data Source

Versions contain the preselected processing options and additional settings that modify the behavior of an application without modifying the base application. The system stores version information in a set of specifications in the versions data source. This information is stored separately from the base application's specifications.

The versions data source contains two database tables: the Versions List (F983051) and the Processing Option Text (F98306). These tables store the version specifications and the processing option settings for a particular version.

Before other users can check out and use any version, you must check it into the Versions List table. The version specifications, which are similar to TAM and RDB specs, must be on the client in order for the client to execute the version properly.

CAUTION

The Versions List table is stored locally, and it is overwritten when the client machine accepts a full package. If you do not check in the version before installing the next full package on your client, that version is lost forever when the full package creates a new version data source.

Cache Tables Data Source

The cache tables data source points to the directory in which local data is stored, such as Microsoft Access data. The amount of data cached locally depends on the processing mode of the client. The direct connect mode requires very little cached data, and typically contains the user-defined codes and menus that are located in the control tables data source. The store-and-forward mode requires a lot of cached data in order to maintain OneWorld operations while disconnected from the enterprise server.

The directory of the cache tables is /B7/*path code*/data; for example, /B7/DEVB733/data.

TIP

Access databases can become very large over time, even if the amount of data within them does not increase. You should periodically compact your Access database to save space on hard drives.

System Data Sources

System data sources provide centralized storage and management of system-related tables that are required for OneWorld to operate. System data sources are different from their environment data source counterparts because there is only one set of system tables per release.

Following are descriptions of the tables defined by the system data sources for OneWorld.

Data Dictionary Data Source

The Data Dictionary data source is used to manage all data items defined in OneWorld. The Data Dictionary contains definitions of all fields used in a OneWorld environment. It defines the item type, edit rules, visual assist, glossary definition, and display rules. The Data Dictionary data source points to an appropriate tablespace on a named enterprise server, such as the DDB733 tablespace for a B733 environment.

Object Librarian Data Source

The Object Librarian is a repository of all applications in OneWorld and is located in the OBJB733 tablespace. Any object that you want to modify must be checked out through the Object Librarian application (P9860). The Object Librarian manages all objects for a development group to ensure that modifications are performed in a cohesive manner without conflict.

System Tables Data Source

The system tables data source, which is stored in the SYSB733 tablespace, contains all the technical tables that support the OneWorld environment. Sign-on security, environment definitions, user and group profiles, machine definitions, and object mapping data for clients are all stored in the system tables.

Server Map Data Source

The server map data source, located in the SVMB733 tablespace, contains information used only by a logic data source. Each logic data source owns a server map, and it contains the object mapping data for that logic data source. The logic servers use the server mapping to identify the location where execution of batch applications and business functions on the server will occur, and where to find data that is stored in tables on that server.

The object mappings for clients and for logic servers are different because the logic server requires special mappings beyond what clients use. The separation of object mappings for clients and logic servers helps to prevent confusion when developers modify or maintain those mappings.

AS/400 Data Sources

AS/400-based enterprise servers require additional data sources, because the AS/400 cannot translate binary large objects (BLOBS). The names of these added data sources are similar to the environment and system data sources discussed previously, except that the characters DNT (for Do Not Translate) are appended to the end of the tablespace name or data source name. For example, the AS/400 stores the binary data for the system table data source in the data source called the SYSB733DNT, and the other data in the SYSB733.

Setting Up a Foreign Table as a OneWorld Data Source

To demonstrate the importance of data sources, the following example defines a foreign table as a valid database data source.

DEFINITION

In OneWorld, a **foreign table** is any table that is not part of the standard installation. The foreign table has to exist in a valid OneWorld database, such as Oracle or SQL Server, or in a text file.

It is very common to use foreign tables for importing data to and exporting data from OneWorld. You can use this technique to import test data into tables that do not yet have applications for input; or you can use it to integrate OneWorld with an external ERP system.

To define the foreign table for use in OneWorld, you have to perform the following steps:

- Define an ODBC data source name for the foreign table.

- Define a OneWorld database data source.

Define an ODBC Data Source Name to the Foreign Table

Before you create a OneWorld data source, you must create an ODBC data source for any foreign table. Here are the steps to do this:

1. In the Windows Control Panel, double-click the ODBC 32 icon.

2. Select the System DSN tab, which contains all data source names for the computer.

3. In the System DSN tab, click the Add button.

4. Select the Microsoft Access driver.

5. In the Data Source Name field, type **Foreign Database** as the data source name. (Remember the exact name that you assign to a data source, because OneWorld uses it in the OneWorld database data source setup.) Type **Foreign Table for Chapter 2** as the Description.

6. Enter the location of the Access database. In this example, the foreign database is located in D:\OWBook\Chapter 2\Foreign Table.mdb.

7. Click the OK button. The finished DSN definition should resemble Figure 2-5.

OneWorld System Architecture for Developers

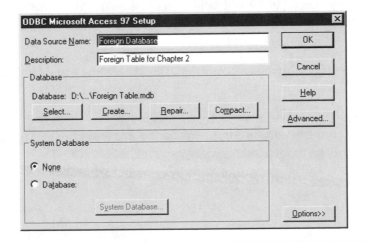

FIGURE 2-5.   ODBC System DSN dialog box for a foreign table

Define a OneWorld Database Data Source

NOW that the ODBC data source exists for the foreign table, you can create a database data source in OneWorld. Here are the steps:

1. From OneWorld Explorer, type **GH9011** in the Fast Path edit box, and press ENTER. The System Administration Tools menu appears.

2. Execute the Database Data Sources application (P986115/XJDE0001). The system displays the Machine Search and Select form of the Database Data Source application, shown earlier in Figure 2-1.

3. Highlight the server that will contain the data source definition and click the Select button. The system displays the Work With Data Sources form, shown earlier in Figure 2-2.

4. Click the Add button. The Data Source Revisions form (shown earlier in Figure 2-3) appears with blank fields.

5. Type **Foreign Database** as the descriptive name in the Data Source Name field

6. Type an **A** in the Data Source Type field, to identify this data source as an Access database.

7. Type **Jdbodbc.dll** in the DLL field. You use this DLL for Access databases and ASCII files. If you have another database that you want to use, consult Table 2-1 to determine which DLL to use.

8. In the Database Name field, enter the ODBC data source name defined in step 5.

N O T E

Ensure that the name entered in the Database Name field (step 8) exactly equals the name of the particular data source defined by ODBC or by OCI. The name in this field is what the system uses to identify a particular database on the network.

9. Type **Local** in the Server Name field. Most foreign tables reside on the local client machine.

10. Type **Local** in the Platform field to indicate the foreign data source is on the client machine.

11. Leave all of the check boxes blank on the form. You'll use them for databases that support tablespaces, such as Oracle or SQL Server.

12. Click the OK button. Your screen should resemble the one in Figure 2-6.

TIP

You can also use the foregoing procedure for ASCII text files. You use the text file ODBC driver for ASCII files, and the DSN points to a directory. ASCII text files have a data source type I instead of type A, as shown in step 6.

Data Sources by Release

The Data Dictionary, Object Librarian, and versions data sources are sensitive to each OneWorld release. Organization by release provides a mechanism to have separate data sources for each release. These three data sources are managed by release to prevent data migration to and from different releases.

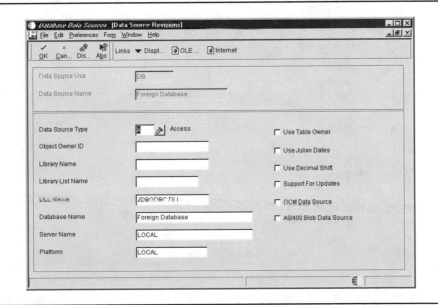

FIGURE 2-6. OneWorld database data source definition for a foreign table

For example, there are different Data Dictionary data sources for B73.1, B73.2, and B73.3. If you attempt to copy or transfer data from the Data Dictionary from B73.1 to B73.3, the operation will fail because the source and destination releases are not identical. Also, if you try to copy or transfer data from a Data Dictionary data source that is not assigned a release, the operation will fail.

You must assign data sources to a release so that objects can be properly copied and transferred. The Release/Data Source Map application (P00948), shown in Figure 2-7, manages this assignment for Data Dictionary, Object Librarian, and version data sources. The Release/Data Source Map application is located on the Environments menu (GH9053).

Path Codes

A path code is a pointer to a set of OneWorld objects and applications. Path codes manage a set of objects and their locations in OneWorld, and each environment has

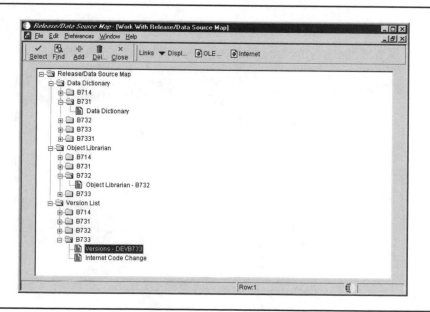

FIGURE 2-7.   Work With Release/Data Source Map form of the Release/Data Source Map application (P00948)

one path code. Each path code contains its own set of objects, which allows different versions of objects per path code. Having a path-code–specific set of objects prevents conflict with other objects in other path codes, and ensures that OneWorld knows what path code to use for a particular user session.

Every path code manages two sets of objects: the runtime objects and the data sources. The path code is maintained in the Object Path Code Master (F00942) table. The runtime objects are the executables and specifications needed for a computer to operate in the OneWorld environment. The data sources, discussed in the preceding section, manage data access for the path code.

The runtime objects managed by the path code are contained in a directory with the same name as the path code, as shown in Figure 2-8. Examples of standard path code names for OneWorld are PRTB733 for the PRT733 (Pristine) environment, DEVB733 for the DEV733 (Development) environment, PRDB733 for the PRD733 (Production) environment, and CRPB733 for the CRP733 (Prototype) environment.

Every path code contains the same directory structure, as shown in Figure 2-8:

- The Bin32, include, lib32, make, obj, and source directories contain all of the components necessary to build a complete OneWorld package (including DLLs, header files, source code, make files, and binary objects).

- The res directory contains all of the icon (.ico), sound (.wav), and movie (.avi) files for the OneWorld Explorer and applications.

- The spec directory contains the TAM specifications.

- The work directory contains the support files needed to build a OneWorld package, which is discussed in Chapter 3.

Path codes perform different functions depending on the purpose of execution. For example, the duties of the path code at installation time are different from those at runtime. Let's take a look at the three categories of execution in OneWorld: installation, runtime, and development.

Path Codes During Installation Time

Installation and update packages, which are discussed in Chapter 3, are applied to clients and servers across the network to update their OneWorld applications. The deployment server knows which data sources and runtime objects to install on clients and which ones to install on servers, because the data sources assigned to each path code provide the

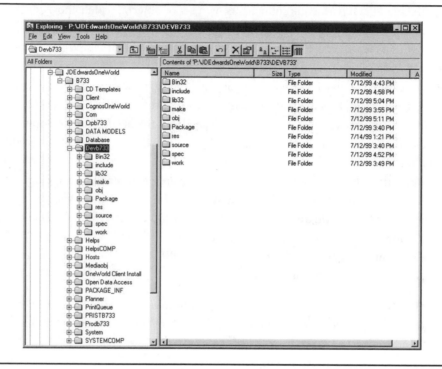

FIGURE 2-8.   Directory structure for the DEVB733 path code

information. The number of path codes that a deployment server can install on a server is almost unlimited, but client workstations can hold significantly fewer.

When a package is installed on a client, the client can have only one active OneWorld environment. This restricts the client to one path code in use at any time. Installing one path code on a client generally is not a problem. Most users perform their daily tasks in a single environment, such as the Production environment.

T I P

Developers usually need more than one environment and path code installed. To override the single-environment limitation, you can use SnapShot. This workaround is discussed further in the upcoming Developer's Corner, titled "SnapShot."

Path Codes During Runtime

During runtime, if the object does not exist in the path code of your client, OneWorld will force a just-in-time installation (JITI) of that path code's missing object. JITI selects the object missing from the path code and converts and installs it locally as TAM specifications on the client machine. JITI ensures that the client is never without a runtime object or specification that it is requesting.

TIP

If you modify an object but the changes you made never appear, delete the GLBLTBL, DDDICT, and DDTEXT TAM specs for the path code. The next time you sign onto OneWorld, the system will force a JITI of new TAM specs.

Path Codes During Development Time

During development time, you select a path code to check objects in and out. The check-in process takes the object that you modified or created and performs two steps: First, it takes your modified local TAM specs for the object and converts them to RDB specs for the environment that you selected. Second, any associated source code for the object is copied from your workstation to the corresponding source code for the objects that reside on the deployment server.

During the check-out process, the server updates your workstation. When you check out, the process converts RDB specs from the enterprise server to TAM specs on your workstation. If the object has any source code, the source code is copied from the deployment server to the appropriate directory on your workstation.

Viewing Path Code Definitions

To view the details for a particular path code, follow these steps:

1. From OneWorld Explorer, type **GH9053** in the Fast Path edit box and press ENTER. The Environments menu appears.

2. Open the Path Code Master application (P980042). The Work With Path Codes form appears, as shown in Figure 2-9.

3. To examine the definition of a path code, highlight any path code and click the Select button. The Path Code Revisions screen, as shown in Figure 2-10, then displays all the detail information for the selected path code.

SnapShot

As stated in the next section of this chapter, "Environments," a OneWorld client can have only one environment active at a time, which can sometimes be restrictive for developers. Sometimes you may need to create and modify a few applications in the Development environment, and then quickly switch to the Prototyping environment to test and verify other applications. To meet these needs, you can use SnapShot to manage multiple environments installed to a single client workstation.

SnapShot is an application that enables installation of multiple environments on a client. You execute SnapShot from Microsoft Windows. The executable (Snapshot.exe) can be found on any OneWorld client in the \B7\System\Bin32 directory.

TIP

The size of each OneWorld environment for a client is about 2GB, so storing many environments on one machine consumes substantial hard disk space. Therefore, you should periodically search through old environments that were stored using SnapShot, looking for any that can be deleted to recover disk space.

To accommodate the existence of multiple environments on the client, SnapShot renames the active OneWorld directory and stores its registry settings, the Jde.ini file, and its license security files into an inactive directory with a different name. Once SnapShot is finished renaming and storing the essentials of an environment, you can install a new OneWorld environment without causing a conflict with the previous one, and without having any OneWorld license security problems.

To rename an environment, follow these steps:

1. Move the Snapshot.exe program from the \B7\System\Bin32 directory to a directory outside the \B7 directory structure. Moving the application from the \B7 directory protects the application from possible corruption when the name of the \B7 directory is changed. We suggest you store the executable in your Windows directory.

2. Execute the Snapshot.exe program. The following dialog box appears:

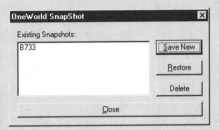

3. Click the Save New button to display the next dialog box:

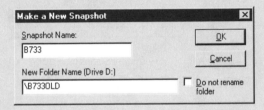

4. Type the new directory name in the New Folder Name field. Rename the directory to be stored, using a name other than B7, to prevent conflicts with the active environment. Assign a name that will help you remember which environment it represents.

5. Click OK, and SnapShot renames the \B7 directory and moves the registry settings, the Jde.ini file, and the license security files into the new, stored directory.

After you install a new environment, there will exist one active OneWorld environment and many other environments that were renamed by SnapShot. SnapShot allows you to switch among any environments that are already installed on your client. You do not have to perform any installation or administrative tasks.

To switch among environments, follow these steps:

1. If a \B7 directory exists, use SnapShot to rename the environment (as just described). This ensures that there is no corruption of existing environments.

2. Using the existing Snapshot box, select the environment you want to activate in the dialog box shown here:

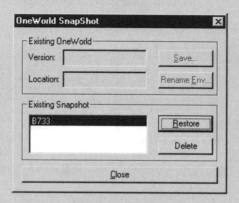

3. Click the Restore button, and SnapShot renames the environment to \B7 directory. The next time you sign onto OneWorld, the session will be in the new environment.

You can execute the SnapShot application at the command line to avoid the GUI-based version or to automate a few tasks. The command-line version of SnapShot includes the following options:

```
SnapShot /S [SnapShot name] /R [SnapShot name] /U /D /A /T [Target
directory]
/S [SnapShot name] saves the active environment to the new SnapShot
   name.
/R [SnapShot name] restores the existing SnapShot name to the active
   environment.
/U disables the warnings, errors and the user interface of SnapShot.
/D do not rename the OneWorld installation directory, for example
   \B7.
/A when restoring an existing SnapShot name, overwrite the active
   environment.
/T [Target directory] specifies the target directory where an
   existing SnapShot resides that needs to be restored to the
   active environment.
```

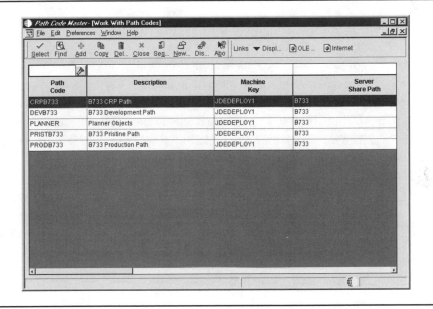

FIGURE 2-9.   Work With Path Codes form of the Path Code Master application
(P980042)

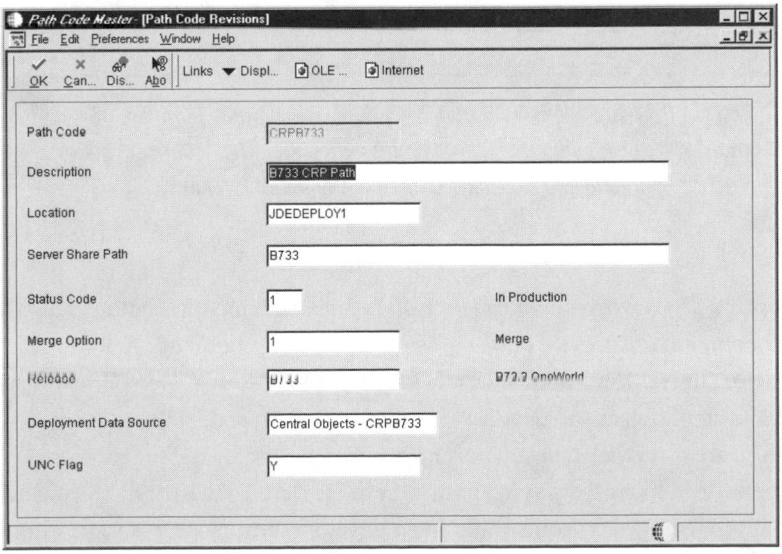

FIGURE 2-10.   Path Code Revisions form of the Path Code Master application
(P980042)

Environments

In OneWorld, environments are the center of all operations during a user's OneWorld session. You assign path codes and data sources to environments so that each one knows which objects to execute and which data to use. The CNC architecture configures OneWorld by mapping objects and data around the corporate network on a per-environment basis. Users are assigned only to the environments they need to do their jobs. You can install only one package at a time to a workstation, and you can have only one active environment on a workstation.

CAUTION

Never delete a path code to remove a OneWorld environment. The license security for the client workstation will not be properly uninstalled and will prevent you from installing another environment.

OneWorld can have as many environments as there are combinations of path codes and data sources. This flexibility allows applications to use many different sets of data, such as production and testing data, and allows data to use many different sets of executable objects.

TIP

If you need to use an existing path code with a different data source, create a new environment and assign the data source to the path code. This technique Is typically used for importing and exporting data into and out of foreign data sources.

Only one active environment can be installed on a client workstation. This single active environment ensures that no confusion exists during execution in the OneWorld environment. An environment points to a single path code, to avoid confusion at runtime about which set of objects needs to be executed. The path code, in turn, contains a single set of data sources that tells the environment where to find its data at runtime.

The benefit of having discrete environments is that it separates objects and data from other environments. You should keep development, testing, and production environments separate to prevent conflicts and ensure that progress can be made in each environment without influencing the others. Experience has shown that discrete environments help reduce the pain of migration and development for a business. Rushing modified objects directly to production before they are properly tested can halt business operations and dramatically reduce productivity.

NOTE

Production and development servers are nothing more than enterprise servers with a single installed environment. In our examples, the production server contains the PRD733 environment, and the development server contains the DEV733 environment.

This section examines the characteristics of environments required by OneWorld, and the tables that support them.

Environment Required by OneWorld

Six environments are recommended for optimum OneWorld operation. Four of the environments are for normal OneWorld operations:

- Production (PRD733)

- Conference Room Pilot/Prototyping (CRP733)

- Development (DEV733)

- Pristine (PRT733)

The other two environments are for special purposes:

- Test (TST733)

- Planner/Deployment (DEPB733)

NOTE

OneWorld developers typically refer to an environment by its short name. For example, developers generally mention "the DEV733 environment" when referring to the development environment for the B733 release.

OneWorld System Architecture for Developers

Production (PRD733)

The PRD733 Production environment is where all business processing and transactions take place. PRD733 is a stable environment that is isolated from development and testing. Objects and data that exist in this environment have been properly tested for software bugs and examined for proper operations with other OneWorld applications. The PRD733 environment ensures a stable setting in which users can work without worrying about conflict with developers modifying applications.

Conference Room Pilot/Prototyping (CRP733)

The CRP733 environment is practically a mirror of the PRD733 environment. You use this Conference Room environment to ensure that any object on its way to the production environment operates properly. The CRP733 environment is the staging and quality assurance environment for OneWorld. You use the data in the CRP733 environment to test the operation of an application with real-world data.

Development (DEV733)

The DEV733 environment is the development environment for OneWorld, used to modify and create objects that will eventually operate in the Production environment. The Development environment contains data that allows you to perform boundary testing of objects to ensure they meet expectations.

Pristine (PRT733)

The PRT733 environment contains all unmodified OneWorld objects. You should not make modifications or changes in the Pristine environment, because it is intended to contain the pure data and applications from J.D. Edwards. The protection offered objects and data in the PRT733 environment gives you a backup environment.

While difficult software issues and nagging defects plague your development projects, you can compare the defective environment with the Pristine environment to determine what lines of code may be causing the problem. By leaving the data and applications in the Pristine environment untouched, you maintain the ability to accurately compare the modified environment.

CAUTION

If you make any changes to objects in the PRT733 environment, any re-installation or upgrade will completely overwrite that environment with new objects, and all of your changes will be lost.

Test (TST733)

The TST733 Test environment uses the CRP733 path code with the DEV733 data. This environment allows you to test CRP733 objects with DEV733 data.

Planner (DEPB733)

Only installation teams use the DEPB733 environment, and it is used for installing OneWorld at a new business or upgrading OneWorld to a new release. The deployment server is the only computer on the corporate network that has access to the DEPB733 Planner environment, because it is a skeleton version of OneWorld for performing installations and upgrades.

Environment Tables

Three tables define and provide access security for OneWorld environments:

- Library List Control (F0093) table
- Library List Master (F0094) table
- Environment Detail (F00941) table

Library List Control Table (F0093)

The Library List Control table assigns environments to each user. Users are assigned at least one environment to give them access to OneWorld; they can only sign onto an environment that is explicitly assigned to them. The Library List Control table provides another layer of security and access control.

Library List Master Table (F0094)

The Library List Master table contains the name of the environment and its description. The table is only used for coexistence between OneWorld and its predecessor, World. Coexistence allows OneWorld and World to operate in unison, and it is used as a migration path for businesses that operate World.

Environment Detail Table (F00941)

The Environment Detail table is for OneWorld use only and contains the environment's name and its assigned path code. For example, the DEV733 environment has the DEVB733 path code assigned to it.

Creating a New OneWorld Environment

You might want to create a new environment if you often need to import or export data to or from a foreign data source. You must assign the foreign data source to an environment so that an application can locate the data, and indicate which path code to use for the foreign data source.

After you assign a data source to an environment, use the OCM application (discussed in Chapter 3) to override the path codes so you can use the foreign data source. The following example shows you how to assign the foreign data source you created previously in this chapter:

1. From OneWorld Explorer, type **GH9611** in the Fast Path edit box, and press ENTER. The Advanced Operations menu appears.

2. Execute the Environment Master application (P0094). The Work With Environments form appears, as shown in Figure 2-11.

3. On the Work With Environments form, click the Add button. The Environments Revisions form (Figure 2-12) appears.

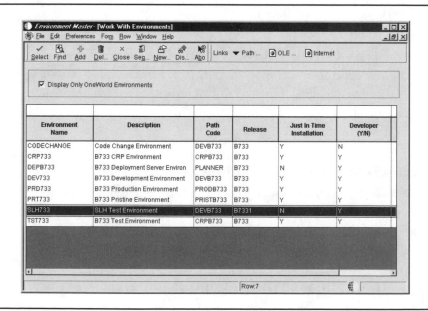

FIGURE 2-11. Work With Environments form of the Environment Master application (P0094)

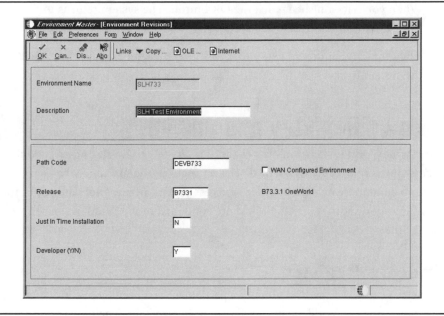

FIGURE 2-12.   Environments Revisions form of the Environment Master application (P0094)

4. In the Environment Name field, type the name of the new environment, which is **SLH733**. This name is unique and is used throughout the system to refer to the new environment.

5. Enter a qualitative description in the Description field.

6. Type the name of the environment's path code, which is **DEVB733**, in the Path Code field. The path code must be the path code that is assigned to the client. (You will assign the foreign table to the new environment in Chapter 3.)

7. In the Release field, enter the OneWorld release version number. This value must equal the current release of OneWorld.

8. Typer N (No) in the Just-in-Time Installation field. This field should only be set to Y (Yes) when you are working with one of the following environments: PRD733, CRP733, DEV733, or PRT733.

9. In the Developer field, type **Y** (Yes). This allows you to modify and build objects in the environment.

OneWorld System Architecture
for Developers

10. When you have finished, click the OK button. The system returns to the Work With Environments form.

11. Click the Find button to verify that the new environment has been added to the system.

Windows Registry and Jde.ini

For every OneWorld installation on a client or a server, certain settings are required to be configured to execute OneWorld. The settings tell the machine what servers and database to communicate with in order to access needed information and applications. The configuration settings for OneWorld are contained in the Windows registry and in the Jde.ini file.

Windows Registry

The registry settings are used to identify a particular version of OneWorld, and are only installed on OneWorld clients, as shown in Figure 2-13. The only registry settings of concern to you as the developer are located in the \Hkey_local_machine\Software\ Jdedwards\Oneworld\Install.ini registry key.

N O T E

The registry settings are only valid for a single OneWorld client package. Therefore, trying to use the same registry settings for another package or enterprise server will corrupt that machine's environment.

The Install.ini key contains the B733 registry key in which the version information for a particular OneWorld client software package resides. The BasePackage setting is the name of the particular OneWorld package built for clients, and its build date is the AppBuildDate setting. The CurrentPathcode setting defines what path code the package is based on; as shown in Figure 2-13, this is set to DEVB733. The InstallPath setting is the location of the root OneWorld directory. The location where user security is validated at sign-on is set in the SecurityPath registry setting.

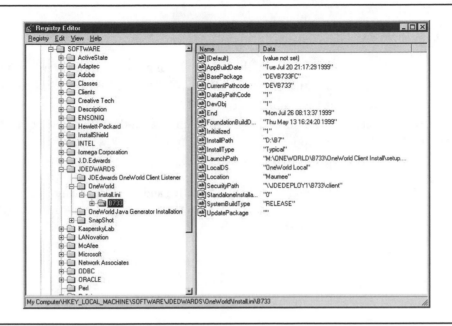

FIGURE 2-13.   Registry settings for OneWorld

Jde.ini File

The Jde.ini file provides the runtime and initialization settings for OneWorld. This file, which resides on every OneWorld client and server, provides the settings for each OneWorld package to identify the location of essential resources across the corporate network.

The Jde.ini file is formatted into the section-key format that is used in Microsoft Windows 3.*x* operating systems. Each section defines a group of related keys, and the keys define a particular setting available for the section. For example, all Jde.ini files have the section named DB SYSTEM SETTINGS, which defines the default environment, path code, and database used for a particular OneWorld package. Here is an example.

```
[DB SYSTEM SETTINGS]
Default Env=DEMOB7A
```

```
Default PathCode=DEMO
Base Datasource=System B733
Database=System B733
```

For ease of system administration, the Jde.ini file for each enterprise server resides on the deployment server in the \JDEdwardsOneWorld\Hosts\ directory. The client's Jde.ini file is stored in the C:\Winnt directory for Windows NT machines, and in the C:\Windows directory for Windows 95 and 98 machines. All the Jde.ini settings for clients are fully detailed in Appendix F.

Following are descriptions of some very useful settings in the Jde.ini file:

- To view debugging statements from interactive and batch applications in the C:\Jde.log and C:\Jdedebug.log files, set the following keys in the DEBUG and UBE sections:

```
[DEBUG]
Output=Both
   .
   .
   .
[UBE]
UBEDebugLevel=9
```

- To view a Data Dictionary item's alias for a field in an interactive application, set the value of ShowAlias key to 1 in the EVEREST section. The alias is located in the pop-up menu, as shown in the following illustration, when you right-click a field.

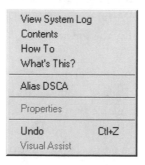

Viewing the RDB and TAM specs

The Universal Table Browser (UTB) is part of the OneWorld toolkit that allows you to view any valid OneWorld table on the network. The UTB is the only tool that you can use to read RDB and TAM specs on the client or server; however, the option for this capability is initially disabled in the Jde.ini file.

TIP

If you experience any strange problems with any OneWorld application, it's a good idea to check the RDB and TAM specs with the UTB. If these settings are not identical, you will encounter a lot of frustration and spend many hours needlessly troubleshooting phantom problems.

To view the RDB and TAM specs through the UTB, set the value of the following key in the Jde.ini file:

```
[INTERACTIVE RUNTIME]
TAMMenus=SHOW
```

With this setting, the next time you sign onto OneWorld and type **UTB** in the Fast Path edit box of OneWorld Explorer, the UTB application will have new menus and icons. These new menus and icons will let you view the local and remote TAM specs, as shown in Figure 2-14.

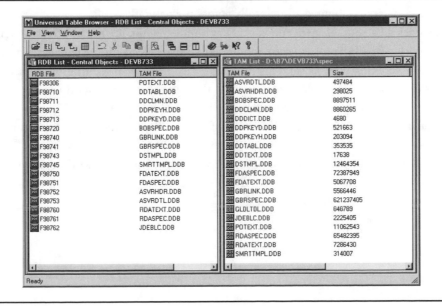

FIGURE 2-14. Modification of UTB application to view central and replicated objects

Putting It All Together

As a developer, your initial development projects are usually focused on building and maintaining interactive and batch applications. As you become a more experienced OneWorld developer, however, your projects become more complex. In most cases, their complexity is due to special low-level CNC definitions of data sources, path codes, and environments.

The CNC architecture uses data sources, path codes, and environments to define the location of data and applications on the network. These are the static components of the CNC layer. Without these definitions in OneWorld, the CNC layer would be unable to find anything on the network, and no OneWorld operations would function.

OneWorld configuration affects some aspects of your development projects, including the process of accessing foreign tables from OneWorld, and the performance of your applications. Specifically, your OneWorld applications will sometimes need data that exists in foreign tables. In order for the foreign table to be available to OneWorld, OneWorld must be configured so the system knows where the foreign table is and how to talk to it. In terms of application performance, you will see signficant negative effects if OneWorld is configured to have most of the applications talk to a server on the other side of a WAN. On the other hand, application performance will improve when servers are configured strategically across the network.

Besides data sources, path codes, and environments, the Jde.ini and registry settings contain all the information required for any machine on the corporate network to know where to access data and applications. Only a few Jde.ini settings were discussed in this chapter, but you'll encounter more of them in the material of other chapters. A more detailed discussion of the Jde.ini file is located in Appendix F.

The last and most important component of the CNC layer is the Object Configuration Manager (OCM), which is discussed in Chapter 3. OCM is the glue that brings together the data sources, path codes, and environments into a network to support OneWorld operations. OCM provides dynamic functionality to the CNC layer for its runtime configuration and operations.

System Administration for Developers

We have mentioned in previous chapters that OneWorld application development is focused on the construction and management of network-centric applications. This chapter discusses the major concepts of operating and supporting the network applications you build in OneWorld.

The essence of network-centric applications is that they are part of a large and robust system that spans a corporate network and resides on many computers. As a developer, you soon learn that the applications you are modifying or creating are microcosms in a larger environment. They are not isolated objects interacting only with users, like stand-alone applications. Rather, network-centric applications are integrated into a system that controls all objects and how they behave for the users.

Your knowledge of how network-centric applications operate and are managed in OneWorld is critical to your success as a OneWorld developer. You need to understand the impact system administration functions have on application execution and behavior, even if you do not necessarily know the workings of those functions in excruciating detail. This chapter focuses on the following tools for system administration:

- **User Profiles** OneWorld employs user profiles to manage settings for users that interact with applications. Profiles allow OneWorld to manage the various system settings required by many of the users in an organization. User profiles also provide the functionality to assign users with similar profiles to groups, for effective management of all the organization's profiles.

- **Object Configuration Manager (OCM)** The OCM stores the location for every network object, whether data or application related, and provides the location of objects when they are requested by an application at runtime. These two functions give the CNC architecture the flexibility it needs to accommodate all data and applications on the network. Also, OCM provides a little-known, powerful feature called *dynamic application partitioning,* which allows you to change application or data locations on the fly.

- **Security in OneWorld** The Security application restricts access to the organization's applications and data. Individuals have restrictions at the user or group level, and these limits are verified every time a user requests access to an application or object.

- **Package Management** The OneWorld system builds and distributes resource packages for clients and servers through the Package Management module. This module provides the tools to define, build, and deploy software applications to any computer on the network, regardless of that computer's role.

User Profiles

It's a tedious and laborious task to write applications that allow an organization's users to modify applications based on their preferences. In most cases, the additional software required by the applications will exceed the amount of code needed to support their base features and functionality. The application has to contain logic for retrieving the user's preferences, modifying the GUI application at runtime based on the preferences, and then storing any changes made to the preferences during a session.

OneWorld removes the burden of developing and maintaining user preferences by employing *user profiles*. Profiles allow OneWorld to manage the various system settings required by many users in an organization. In OneWorld, every user is identified by a profile. The user profile stores unique information and preferences for a user, such as which environments and menus they access. The primary advantage of user profiles is that users can move among the computers within the OneWorld environment, and their profile follows them.

DEFINITION

User profiles *provide the functionality in OneWorld to manage settings for users that interact with it. The primary advantage of using profiles is that they allow users to keep their settings as they roam from computer to computer on the network.*

Profile Hierarchy

Maintaining user profiles for every user in a company can be very difficult, requiring a full-time employee just to manage and build the profiles. To allow for better administration and organization of user profiles, OneWorld user profiles are organized hierarchically.

The hierarchical organization of profiles allows administrators to define user profile settings for the entire company, groups of common users, and specific users. Any OneWorld subsystem or application that requires the resources of user profiles searches for user preferences hierarchically, checking first in the user's profile, then the group profile, and then in the *PUBLIC profile.

User Profile

When an application begins execution, it checks the user's profile to see if any user preferences are set for that application. If the user has special settings for the application, it then retrieves the settings and modifies itself based on those settings. After it retrieves the information from the user profile, the application terminates its search for user preferences.

Group Profile

If it doesn't find any preference settings for a particular user, the application then searches for settings in the group profile. In the group profile, the settings represent common preferences for a group of users; most users within the same department will have similar settings because they share common roles. If an application finds group profile settings for itself, it retrieves them and terminates the search for preferences.

For example, users within the accounts receivable department of a company are assigned to the AR group. Typically, most of the preferences for the users in that department will be defined in the AR group profile rather than in individual employees' user profiles. When an account is needed for a new user in the AR group, very few preferences have to be set in the new profile because the bulk of the settings are the AR group profile.

*PUBLIC Profile

If it doesn't find any user *or* group profile settings, the application then searches the *PUBLIC profile. The *PUBLIC profile is not a user or group account, but a special user group in OneWorld that identifies all valid OneWorld users. Any settings that are assigned to the *PUBLIC profile are the default settings for all OneWorld users.

DEFINITION

PUBLIC is not a "real" user account or group profile, but rather a default setting built into OneWorld to represent all users. This allows definition of profile settings that are common for all users in an organization.

Building User and Group Profiles

You will often need to create special profiles for the users and groups who will access your applications. The most common applications requiring user profiles are the Object Configuration Manager (OCM) and Security Manager, both discussed later in this chapter. The OCM and Security Manager mappings in OneWorld provide or restrict access to objects and data throughout the corporate network.

The process to build both user profiles and group profiles is similar, and you build these profiles in the same application.

TIP

Build the group profiles before you build the user profiles. This way, you can assign users to groups as you define each user.

Here are the steps:

1. From OneWorld Explorer, type **GH9011** in the Fast Path box and press ENTER. The System Administration Tools menu appears.

2. Execute the User Profiles application (P0092). The Work With User Profiles form appears, as shown in Figure 3-1. To display a list of all users, click the Find button.

3. To add a new profile, click the Add button. The User Profile Revisions form appears (Figure 3-2).

4. Enter the username into the User ID field.

5. In the User Class/Group field, enter the name of the group with which the user is associated.

6. If you're creating a group profile, enter the name of the group in the User ID field. In the User Class/Group field, enter ***GROUP**. In this example, Steven is the name of the user profile; user Steven is assigned to the DEVEL group.

7. Set the Allow Fast Path field to Y (Yes) or N (No) to indicate whether the user or group can see the Fast Path box in OneWorld Explorer.

8. Enter the user's address book ID in the Address Number field.

CAUTION

The User Profiles application (P0092) does not validate the address number. Before you enter anything in the Address Number field, ensure that the user has an address book entry. This entry will affect the system operation—for example, any workflow-based application.

OneWorld System Architecture
for Developers

9. If you want to restrict the user/group to viewing a particular menu, enter the name of that menu (such as GH9011) in the Menu Identification field.

10. If you want to use your own icons, enter the location of the icons in the Default Icon File text box.

11. Developers typically do not use the rest of the fields in the User Profile Revisions form, so click the OK button when you've finished to submit the new entry. When you return to the Work With User Profiles form, click the Find button to verify that the user profile was added.

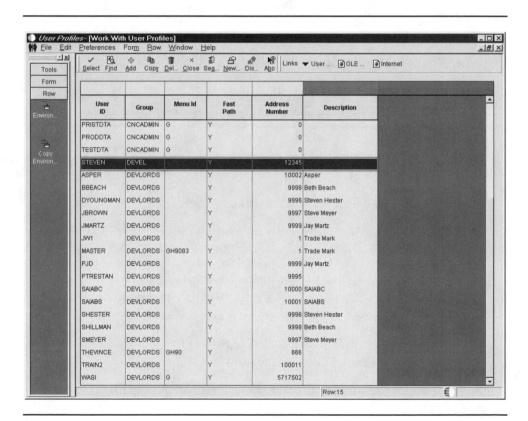

FIGURE 3-1. Work With User Profiles form from the User Profiles application (P0092)

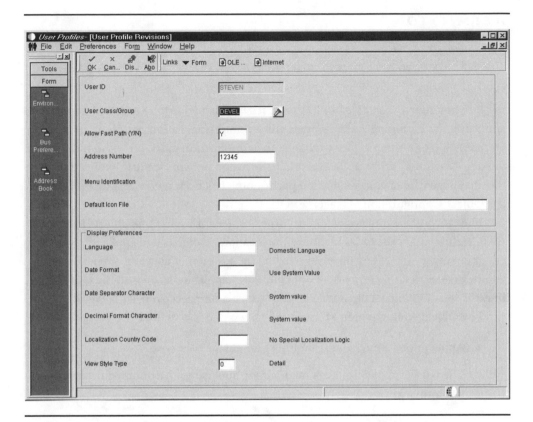

FIGURE 3-2. User Profile Revisions form from the User Profiles application

Object Configuration Manager (OCM)

As developers began to build network-centric applications, it became apparent that the main focus was on *application partitioning*. Up until now, application partitioning has been static. For example, you determine the partition between the server and client, and then build an application for each server and client on the corporate network. If you need to adjust the application partition at any time, you have to go back and modify the applications for the client and server as well.

DEFINITION

Application partitioning *means dividing up an application across the network. The application is typically partitioned among clients and servers.*

For true network-centric applications, it's unreasonable to expect to determine application partitioning at development time (static application partitioning). Organizations need the ability to change their application partition without the aid of a developer. With OneWorld and its focus on network-centric applications, the challenge of dynamic application partitioning has been met with a tool called the Object Configuration Manager, or OCM.

The OCM is the director of all the corporate network's data and objects for the CNC architecture. The OCM identifies the location of all data and applications on any client or server, and at any time can redefine the location of data and applications to another computer on the network. All OneWorld applications consult the OCM first to find the location of data or another application, before proceeding with execution.

The Object Configuration Manager offers two major benefits:

- Applications are no longer built just for clients or servers.

- The overhead of developers maintaining application partitioning in applications is eliminated.

By letting the OCM determine the application partition, your developed applications do not have to be aware of what type of computer they reside on, such as a server or client. The OCM blurs the lines between client- and server-side application development, letting you focus on application development. This results in a staff of developers who are an integrated group, ready to develop network-centric applications rather than assigned to client or server applications.

NOTE

The OCM blurs the lines between client-side and server-side application development, and creates a robust environment for network-centric applications.

Because of the OCM, you can eliminate the overhead of maintaining the application partition in your applications. Therefore, you can focus on implementing needed features and functionality in your applications instead of worrying about where the features and functionality will exist.

The applications that you build and modify are directly impacted by the operations that the OCM performs. To develop high-impact applications, you need to have expert knowledge of the OCM. This section examines the OCM method of object management and how the Manager determines object location at runtime.

OCM Object Management

The OCM mappings are stored in the Object Configuration Master table (F986101). There are at least two sets of OCM tables for a particular OneWorld installation: one centralized OCM table for all client machines, stored in the system data source (SYSB733); and one OCM table for each logic data source that is stored in the server map data source (SVMB733). As discussed in the "Data Sources" section of Chapter 2, clients and servers need their own set of OCM mappings because of their differing requirements.

Each OCM mapping is defined by the following parameters:

- Environment

- Object name

- Data source

- User class/group

- Object type

As discussed in Chapter 2, the environment parameter identifies a path code and the set of data sources that it uses. The path code points to a set of unique objects that an environment is allowed to execute. The data source points to the database and logic data sources used by an environment.

The object name and type allow you to make OCM mappings for a group of objects instead of for one object at a time. For example, you can set the object name to DEFAULT and the type to TABLE to create an OCM mapping for all table objects for a particular environment.

DEFINITION

DEFAULT is not a "real" object in OneWorld, but a value that represents all objects in OneWorld. **TABLE** has the same purpose as DEFAULT, except it applies to all tables.

OneWorld System Architecture
for Developers

Here are the valid object types:

- Business functions (BSFN)

- Tables (TBLE)

- Batch applications (UBE)

- Interactive applications (APPL)

- Media objects (GT)

- Business views (BSVW)

- Data structures (DSTR)

Each object in OneWorld must be assigned to a logic or database data source. UBEs and BSFNs are assigned to a logic data source identifying where the object is executed. Table objects are assigned to a database data source identifying where the object is stored.

NOTE

Business functions (BSFNs) and batch applications (UBEs) are the only objects that can be assigned to secondary data sources through the OCM. Secondary data sources only apply to logic servers, which execute BSFNs and UBEs.

Last, the OCM uses the User Profile tables to assign each mapping to a user, a group, or to all users (*Public). This last assignment provides an efficient means of managing OCM mappings for an entire company down to a specific user. OCM mappings that are common for everyone are assigned to *PUBLIC, whereas special mappings are created for a particular user or group as required.

OCM Determination of Object Location at Runtime

As an application executes and generates requests for data or another application, it consults the OCM, which determines where the resources are located on the network. The OCM then passes the request to the assigned computer for completion. The OCM knows where to send the request because each OCM mapping is assigned to a data source. When an application requests data from a *table*, that causes the OCM to send the request to the assigned *database* data source. A request for another *application* causes the OCM to send the request to the assigned *logic* data source.

The OCM needs the following information to determine the location of data and applications on the network: the requesting user, the user's environment, and the requested object.

OneWorld contains many OCM mappings because they are set for any combination of users, environments, and objects. Each OCM mapping is assigned to a single OneWorld environment. A user is any valid OneWorld user defined in the User Profile application. The object is the name of any OneWorld object, such as the Journal Entries table (F0911), or any generic object, which is called DEFAULT.

Once the OCM has the needed information, it begins the hierarchical search for the first active setting. OCM performs two types of hierarchical searches: for data and for applications.

DEFINITION

*An **active mapping** in the OCM table is any entry that has the value AV (Active) in its Object Status column. The value NA (Inactive) is always ignored.*

Search for Data

When OCM finds the first active mapping during its search, it terminates the search and sends the request to the database data source identified in the mapping. When the database data source has finished with the request, the results are sent back to the requesting application.

Table 3-1 shows how the OCM goes about its hierarchical search. In this example, the user is STEVEN, who belongs to the DEVEL group, and the object is table F0911 (the Journal Entries table).

Let's step through this search for data:

1. The OCM begins the search to find an active mapping for the F0911 table and the user STEVEN. If an active mapping is found, OCM executes step 7.

2. If no mappings are found in step 1, the OCM finds the group to which the user belongs. The OCM then searches for the requested data based on the table (F0911) and the group (DEVEL). If an active mapping is found, OCM executes step 7.

3. If no mappings are found yet, OCM searches for an active mapping for the F0911 table for all users (*PUBLIC). If an active mapping is found, OCM executes step 7.

4. If no mappings are found yet, OCM looks for DEFAULT mappings for any table. The OCM searches for an active mapping for the DEFAULT table and the user STEVEN. If an active mapping is found, OCM executes step 7.

5. The OCM then proceeds to search for a DEFAULT table mapping for the group DEVEL. If an active mapping is found, OCM executes step 7.

6. Last but not least, the OCM will use the active mapping for the DEFAULT table and all users (*PUBLIC).

7. The active mapping has a database data source assigned to it. The OCM sends the request to that database data source for processing.

CAUTION

*There will always be an active mapping for *PUBLIC and for any DEFAULT object in the OCM table for table objects. If there is no default OCM mapping for all users for step 7, then OneWorld displays a "Select/Failed" error message.*

Sequence	Object Name	User
1	F0911	STEVEN
2	F0911	DEVEL
3	F0911	*PUBLIC
4	DEFAULT	STEVEN
5	DEFAULT	DEVEL
6	DEFAULT	*PUBLIC

TABLE 3-1.   Sequence of OCM's Hierarchical Search for Data

When it issues the request to the database data source, the OCM sends the request through the middleware component called JDEBase, which is discussed in Chapter 25. JDEBase generates the SQL statement to the third-party database. After the SQL statement is executed, the results are returned to the OneWorld application that generated the request.

Search for Application

In a search for an application, the OCM searches for the first active mapping just as it does in the search for data. When it finds the OCM mapping, OCM terminates the search and sends the request to the logic data source assigned to that particular mapping. Once the logic data source has finished with the request, the results are sent back to the requesting application.

Table 3-2 shows the sequence of OCM's hierarchical search for applications. The user is STEVEN, who belongs to the DEVEL group; and the object is business function B0900049, which is for journal entry management of the General Ledger.

Let's step through this search for applications:

1. The OCM begins the search to find an active mapping for the B0900049 business function and the user, STEVEN. If an active mapping is found, OCM executes step 7.

2. If no mappings are found in step 1, the OCM finds the group to which STEVEN is assigned. The OCM then searches for the requested data based on the business function (B0900049) and the group (DEVEL). If an active mapping is found, OCM executes step 7.

3. If no mappings are found yet, OCM searches for an active mapping for the B0900049 business function for all users (*PUBLIC). If an active mapping is found, OCM executes step 7.

4. If no mappings are found yet, OCM looks for DEFAULT mappings for any table. The OCM searches for an active mapping for the DEFAULT business function and the user STEVEN. If an active mapping is found, OCM executes step 7.

OneWorld System Architecture for Developers

5. The OCM then proceeds to search for a DEFAULT business function mapping for the group DEVEL. If an active mapping is found, OCM executes step 7.

6. Last but not least, the OCM searches for an active mapping for the DEFAULT business function and all users (*PUBLIC).

7. If the OCM finds an active mapping, it issues a request to the logic data source that is assigned to the mapping. If no active mapping is found, OCM executes the request on the local machine that generated the request.

When it issues the request to the logic data source, OCM sends it through the middleware component called JDENet, which is discussed in Chapter 20. JDENet informs the logic data source, or enterprise server, to execute the application. When the application has finished executing, the results are returned to the OneWorld application that generated the request.

Assigning a Foreign Data Source to an Environment

When you are importing or exporting data to or from a foreign data source, a good technique to avoid table conflicts is to assign the foreign data source to its own environment. A common problem that occurs is that the same table exists in both

Sequence	Object	User
1	B0900049	STEVEN
2	B0900049	DEVEL
3	B0900049	*PUBLIC
4	DEFAULT	STEVEN
5	DEFAULT	DEVEL
6	DEFAULT	*PUBLIC

TABLE 3-2.   Sequence of OCM's Hierarchical Search for Applications

the foreign and OneWorld data sources. If you create another environment with the same table assigned to it, you'll be able to successfully import and export data between the two data sources.

In this next example, you will assign the foreign data source you created in Chapter 2 (in the section "Setting Up a Foreign Table as a OneWorld Data Source") to the environment you created in that same chapter (in the section "Creating a New OneWorld Environment"). Follow these steps with the OCM application (P986110) to assign and activate the foreign data source for use in the OneWorld environment.

1. From OneWorld Explorer, type **GH9011** into the Fast Path box and press ENTER. The System Administration Tools menu appears.

2. Execute the Object Configuration Manager application (P986110).

3. When the Machine Search and Select form appears (Figure 3-3), select the enterprise server to which the OCM settings are applicable. Select the enterprise server with the OCM table (F986101) in the system data source (SYSB733).

N O T E

If the foreign data source is to be used by an enterprise server, you must add an entry into that server's OCM mappings. Remember that each enterprise server owns an OCM table.

4. On the Work With Object Mappings form (Figure 3-4), click the Add button.

5. The Object Revisions form appears, as shown in Figure 3-5. Enter the following information into the fields of the Object Mappings Revisions form:

Environment Name:	**SLH Test Environment**
Object Name:	**DEFAULT**
Primary Data Source:	**Foreign Database**
User:	***Your OneWorld user name***
Object Type:	**TBLE**

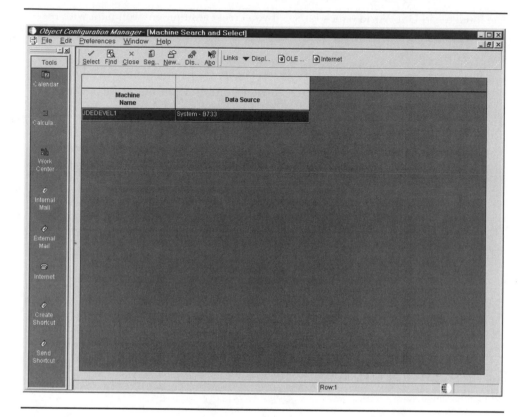

FIGURE 3-3. Machine Search and Select form of the OCM application (P986110)

6. When you have finished, click OK to return to the Work With Object Mappings form.

7. Click the Find button to search for the mapping you just created. To activate it, highlight the new mapping and choose Change Status from the Row menu. The status of the OCM mapping changes from NA (inactive) to AV (active).

N O T E

If you do not activate your OCM mapping, it will not take effect. You should also restart OneWorld so that the local cache will recognize the new OCM setting.

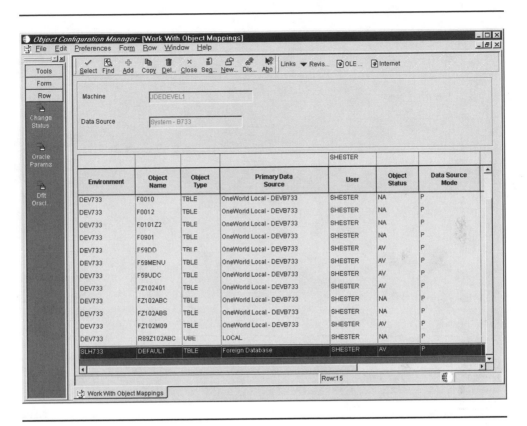

FIGURE 3-4. Work With Object Mappings form of the OCM application (P986110)

Application Partitioning

As stated earlier, you use the OCM to partition applications across the network in order to boost performance and reduce network traffic. It's important to be able to recognize where and when an application needs to be partitioned across the network. You also need to know how the application executes, the requests it makes across the network, and when to use the OCM to partition the application differently to increase performance.

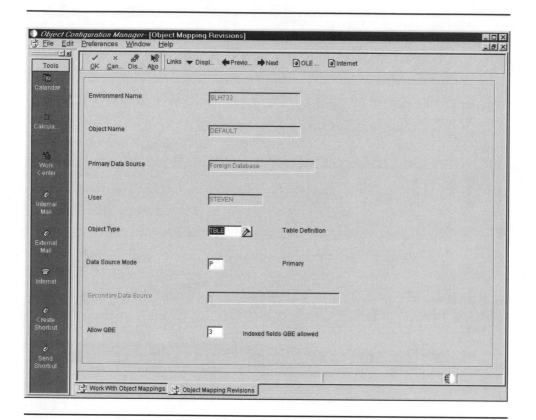

FIGURE 3-5. Object Mapping Revisions form of the OCM application (P986110) for the foreign data source example

---

N O T E

The primary focus of application partitioning is to increase the performance of an application that executes over a network.

Keep the following guidelines in mind when partitioning applications:

- Keep the business function (BSFN) that processes and validates data located physically near the database where the data is stored. Long distances between the BSFN and the data can be a factor in delay times.

- Build all the processing and validation logic required in an application into a BSFN or a set of BSFNs, which allows you to use the OCM to map the location of the BSFN to the server on which the data is stored.

- If the BSFN is part of a transaction processing application, map the Master Business Function (MBF) supporting the transaction processing near or on the server that stores the data needed by the MBF. (Master Business Functions are discussed in Chapter 21.)

An Example of Partitioning

Figure 3-6 illustrates how application partitioning helps in the overall performance of an application. This example shows a fat client with a server arranged in a two-tier system, and the message traffic that occurs between them. The fat client's GUI applications physically reside where the heavy message traffic occurs, and the fat client is requesting a record that contains a single detail record. The network connecting the fat client and server is a LAN—the only type of network that is used for this configuration.

The GUI application cannot proceed to the next step of execution until the request for data is fulfilled by the database. Since the application requires the record and its detail record, at least two network turns are required, and the application must wait for both requests to take place. If validation of both records fails, then more network turns are required and the application has to wait even longer.

Figure 3-6 is not realistic because it shows only a single record with a single detail record, while in reality most applications will have several records with many corresponding detail records. This amount of traffic dramatically increases the number of network turns during application execution.

N O T E

The performance of a network-centric application is directly affected by the physical location on the network of the objects that make up the application, and the amount of message traffic it generates.

To better the application's performance, you use the OCM to map the business functions that process the application's requests to the database, mapping those functions to reside on the server. By mapping the business functions on the server, all of the requests for fetching and validating data will occur on the same machine; thus the number of network turns is reduced.

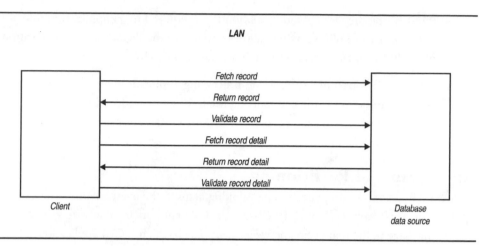

FIGURE 3-6.   Example of two-tier application partitioning mode

If performance is still below expectations, consider the configuration in Figure 3-7. This shows a thin client with two servers arranged in a three-tier mode, and the message traffic that occurs between them. The thin client's GUI applications are physically separated from the heavy message traffic, and the thin client is requesting a record that has a single detail record. A WAN connects the thin client to the servers.

The same number of network turns occur in Figure 3-7 as in Figure 3-6—but in Figure 3-7, they only occur between the logic data source and the database data source.

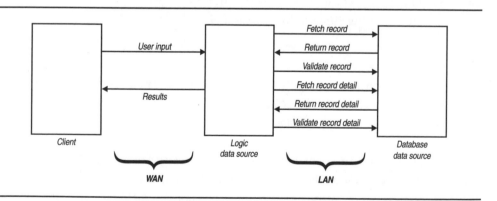

FIGURE 3-7.   Example of three-tier application partitioning mode

The GUI application can execute asynchronously until it requires the information from the logic data source. The logic data source relatively quickly performs all the processing and validation of data from the database data source, because the network connecting the two servers is a LAN. The amount of network traffic across the WAN is dramatically lower than on the LAN, achieving tolerable application performance.

Changing the Execution Location of a BSFN

An MBF contains a set of BSFNs and is used for transaction-based processing. MBFs generate a lot of message traffic on the network, because of all the processing and validation of database records. To prevent an MBF from dramatically reducing the performance of an application, we suggest mapping the MBF to the server that owns the database tables needed by that MBF, or mapping the MBF to a logic data source or enterprise server that is physically close to the database.

The steps that follow explain how to map the Journal Entries MBF (B0900049) for the General Ledger to a logic data source:

1. From OneWorld Explorer, type **GH9011** into the Fast Path box and press ENTER. The System Administration Tools menu appears.

2. Execute the OCM application (P986110).

3. When the Machine Search and Select form appears (shown earlier in Figure 3-3), select the enterprise server to which the OCM settings are applicable. Select the enterprise server with the OCM table (F986101) in the system data source (SYSB733).

4. On the Work With Object Mappings form, click the Add button.

5. Enter the following information into the fields of the Object Mapping Revisions form, as shown in Figure 3-8:

Environment Name:	**DEV733**
Object Name:	**B0900049**
Primary Data Source:	**JDEDEVEL1**
User:	***PUBLIC**
Object Type:	**BSFN**

6. When you have finished, click OK to return to the Work With Object Mappings form.

7. Click the Find button to search for the mapping you just created. To activate it, highlight the new mapping and choose Change Status from the Row menu. The status of the OCM mapping changes from NA (inactive) to AV (active).

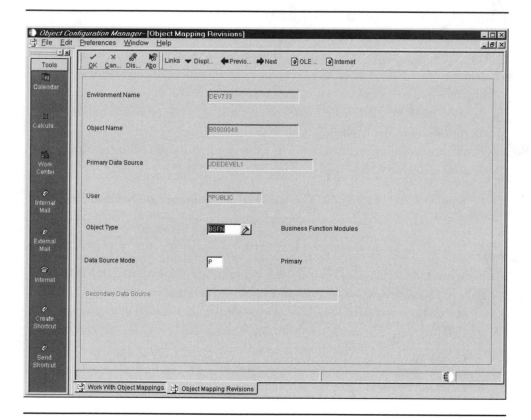

FIGURE 3-8.   Object Mapping Revisions form of the OCM application (P986110) for the Journal Entries MBF

Security in OneWorld

A developer with any experience at all in working with applications for an ERP system knows that security issues are a dark cloud constantly looming above all development projects. Restricting unauthorized users from viewing and editing data and applications is a tough job, and the finished arrangement typically requires substantial development overhead to maintain and enforce. Many development projects have been sidelined due to lack of support and resources for security.

In OneWorld, security is built into all applications and can be enabled and disabled at any time. No programming overhead is required to enforce the security setup, because every object in OneWorld already contains security features. You can concentrate on building and modifying applications without worrying about security and how it manages the applications you create.

Typically, system administrators enforce security in OneWorld. This section explains the enforcement principles you need to know in order to ensure that all of your applications are built properly for security. Administration of security in OneWorld is accomplished by a simple but powerful application that manages all user access to applications and data in the system. Applications, objects, and data in OneWorld are subject to security to ensure that only authorized users interact with them. You can set security restrictions for an entire application or for a single cell in a table, and you can make changes to the security level at runtime.

OneWorld's security is flexible because it is built to complement the OCM application. OCM mappings provide all the locations of data and applications on the network, while the security mechanism either grants or restricts access to the data and applications managed by the OCM. Security and OCM work together to provide the ability to map objects across the network and restrict access to them. The relationship between the two is examined in the following Developer's Corner, titled "Using the Scheduler."

Using the Scheduler

The Scheduler application in OneWorld is an invaluable system administrator's tool for developers. The Scheduler is useful when you want to run batch jobs that take up too many resources during normal working hours, or when you want to automatically perform mundane tasks without burdening development staff. Another useful role for the Scheduler is to execute a batch application on a server in another country during your local working hours, without bothering developers in the other country.

The Scheduler is actually a server-side process that resides on any OneWorld enterprise server, and launches all batch applications and monitors them for execution state. The Scheduler uses the Job Master (F91300) and the Job Schedule (F91320) tables to store all the information needed for its tasks.

NOTE

Before you can use the Scheduler process, it must be activated on your enterprise server.

All jobs for the Scheduler are initially defined in the Job Master table, which contains the information about the application to be executed. When a job in the Job Master table is assigned to execute at a particular time, an entry for each occurrence is placed in the Job Schedule table. The Job Schedule table contains information related to the status of the job (such as Active, Success, and Failed).

The Scheduler uses a modified version of Universal Time Coordinate (UTC) that counts the number of minutes instead of the number of seconds. At one-minute intervals, the Scheduler looks in its Job Schedule table to check the status of active batch applications, and launches a new job. By modifying UTC counting, the system resources on the server are not exhausted by the Scheduler's continual checking of job status and launching new jobs.

The following steps show you how to create a scheduled execution of a batch application through the Scheduler application.

1. From OneWorld Explorer, type **GH9015** into the Fast Path box and press
   ENTER. The Job Scheduler menu appears.

2. Execute the Scheduler application (P91300) to open the Work With
   Versions form:

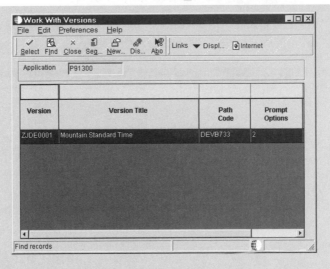

3. On the Work With Versions form, choose the time zone in which you want the application to execute. The Work With Scheduled Jobs form appears next:

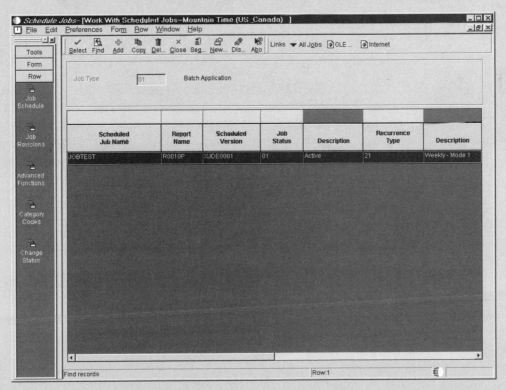

4. To create a new job, click the Add button. The Scheduling Information Add form appears next:

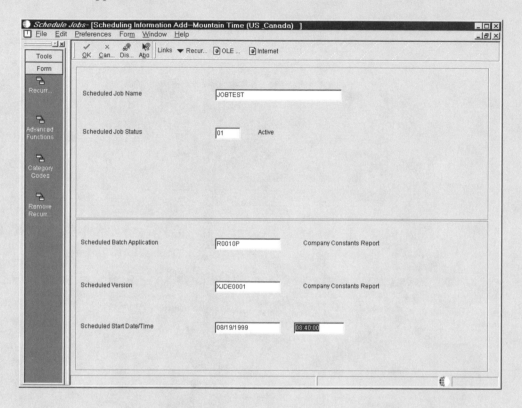

5. Enter the following information:

- Type **JOBTEST** into the Scheduled Job Name field.

- Type **R0010P** into the Scheduled Batch Application field. The R0010P application is the Company Constants report.

- Type **XJDE0001** into the Scheduled Version field.

- In the Scheduled Start Date/Time field, enter the time to execute the application, five minutes from now.

6. If this is a one-time execution of a batch application, jump to step 8; otherwise, proceed to step 7.

7. From the Row menu, choose Recurrence. In the Recurring Scheduling Information Revisions form that appears, fill in the data according to your needs.

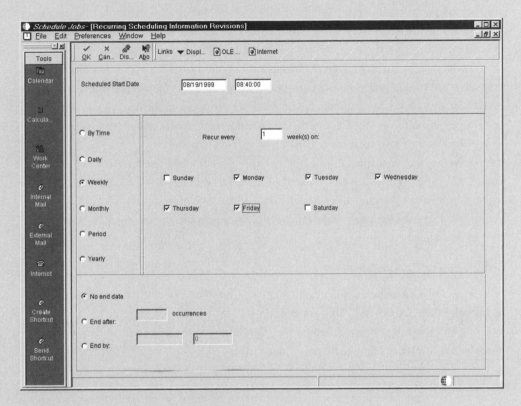

8. When you have finished, click OK twice to return to the Work With Scheduled Jobs form. To verify that your job has been entered into the Scheduler, click the Find button.

NOTE

The Scheduler process must be activated on your enterprise server in order for your job to execute. If Scheduler is not activated, a dialog box will inform you.

9. Wait five minutes for your job to be executed by the Scheduler.

Object-Level Security

All OneWorld security settings are stored in the Security Workbench table (F00950) in the system data source (SYSB733). This single table allows OneWorld to enforce security for the entire environment on any machine on the network. For example, if a user tries to get around a restriction by using another machine to access the restricted application, security ensures that the user doesn't inadvertently gain access to that application.

The focus of security in OneWorld is to either grant or restrict access to objects, and all OneWorld applications are composed of objects. This *object-level security* provides the lowest level of security possible in OneWorld, which gives you the flexibility to implement security in any way you choose. On the other hand, there are thousands of objects in OneWorld, and managing security can quickly become unwieldy.

To ensure that managing object-level security does not become an overwhelming task, OneWorld's security operates like the OCM. The end result is a security system with robust functionality, as well as adequate controls to meet all security requirements possible. It uses object identity and user profiles to accomplish security at the object level.

Object Identity

The Security Workbench application (P00950) gives you the ability to apply security to any object in OneWorld. This application lets you restrict or grant access to a single object or a group of objects, based on the objects' name, system code, and one or more menus that uniquely identify them in OneWorld.

NOTE

The Security Workbench application applies security to a single object or to a group of objects by system codes and menus.

Any OneWorld object may have special restrictions placed on it to ensure the finest level of security in OneWorld. However, this object-level control can become very cumbersome. For example, if you applied the security mechanism to each object for every OneWorld user, the job could take months to enforce and verify.

To overcome this problem, you can group objects by system code and by menu, allowing OneWorld security to enforce restrictions "in bulk." System codes and menus typically group objects by module. For example, all General Ledger objects are marked with the system code 09. All General Ledger applications are attached to menus that start with G09.

When objects are grouped by system code and menu, you can enforce security by module. The typical OneWorld user can only access certain modules and menus within OneWorld Explorer. Enforcing security by module allows you to manage object security efficiently without being overburdened.

User Profiles

Regardless of what application requests the services of an object, OneWorld security enforces restrictions on the user if that user is not permitted to access the object. For example, a particular object may be used by three different applications, but it can be restricted from all access except by privileged users.

Every security setting stored in the Security Workbench table (F00950) restricts access to an object by assigning a user profile to it. All security settings that are common for all employees or members of an organization are applied to the *PUBLIC user profile; likewise, security settings that are common for a department are applied to the group user profile of that department. Any unique security settings for a particular employee are applied to the employee's user profile.

N O T E

Object-level security ensures that applications cannot inadvertently execute objects that are restricted from certain users.

To access an object, any user must pass all his or her own security requirements, the requirements of the user's group, and the requirements for all users. By approaching security in this manner, security administrators can organize the system hierarchically to allow easy management and prevent security loopholes.

N O T E

*For a user to gain access to an object, security restrictions cannot exist on the object at the user, group, or *PUBLIC levels. Access is provided to a user only if that individual is allowed access at all three levels.*

Security Types

In real-world OneWorld implementations, many users need to execute a portion of an object's functionality as part of their daily tasks. For example, most users require searching and viewing capabilities for an application, but few users need to modify or add new information in an application. OneWorld's robust set of security types for objects, described in the following paragraphs, allow users to access parts of an object's functionality as needed.

Application Security   Application security restricts users from running or installing an application and all of its objects. This type of security ensures that all parts of an application are not accessible to a particular user.

Action Security   Action security prevents certain users from executing a particular action in an application. This type of security allows users to search and view data, but they cannot create, delete, modify, or copy data within an application.

Row Security   Row security restricts users from accessing certain grid rows within an application. This control is particularly useful when users are allowed to view only certain business units within a table. For example, a clerk may only be allowed to view and modify data for business unit 10 of company 1.

Column Security   Column security restricts users from viewing certain columns of data within a grid. This control is useful when a user needs to access data for a particular company, but is not allowed to see any totaling or cost associated with the item. For example, you can restrict payroll clerks from viewing the salaries of their coworkers within the payroll department.

Processing Option Security   Processing option security restricts a user from changing input values in an application. This type of security is useful when applications are customized with certain processing option values, and you want to prohibit users from modifying those values.

Tab Security   Tab security disables tabs within an interactive application, thus restricting users from accessing other forms within the application.

Exit Security   When you apply exit security, the exit bar located to the left of any OneWorld application is disabled. This control prevents users from accessing and modifying data in applications that are executable from the current application.

Exclusive Application Security   Exclusive application security allows a user to execute the application regardless of the security restrictions set for the group or *PUBLIC. This allows users to override any existing security that applies to their associated group. Exclusive application security only lifts restrictions for a particular *application*; it does not lift all restrictions imposed on the group or on *PUBLIC.

External Calls Security   External calls security prohibits stand-alone execution of applications that are external to OneWorld. For example, you can restrict access to the OneWorld development toolsets that are physically executed from outside the OneWorld environment.

Assigning Application Security to the Journal Entry Application (P0911)

Limiting access and usage of the application to a user or group of users is the most common function that you will perform with the Security Workbench application. When you turn on application security for a user, the menus that normally display a particular selection will no longer display that selection for the user. The following example shows you how to apply application security to the Journal Entry application.

1. From OneWorld Explorer, type **GH9052** into the Fast Path box and press ENTER. The Security Maintenance menu appears.

2. Double-click the Security Workbench application (P00950) to open the Work With User/Group Security form, as shown in Figure 3-9.

3. From the Form menu, choose Setup Security Application. The Application Security form appears (Figure 3-10).

4. Apply security to the Journal Entries application (P0911) for the user STEVEN. Type **STEVEN** in the User/Group field.

5. Type **P0911** into the Application field.

6. To restrict the user from executing and installing the application object, click to check the Run Security and Install Security check boxes.

7. From the Row menu, choose Secure To All.

8. Click the Find button, and expand the Secured item in the lower grid. The display will resemble Figure 3-10.

OneWorld System Architecture for Developers

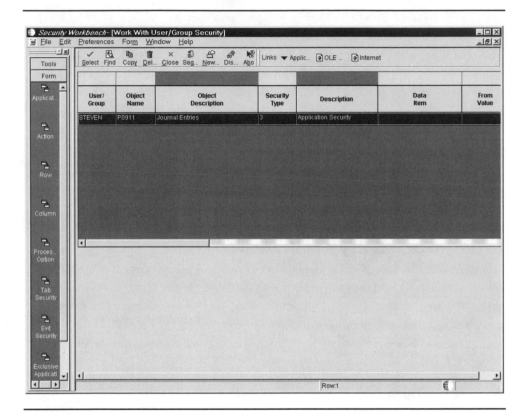

FIGURE 3-9.   Work With User/Group Security form of the Security Workbench
application (P00950)

TIP

*At this point, exit and restart OneWorld, because all security settings are cached
locally. The security information in the local cache is only updated when
OneWorld is started.*

9. To remove the application security restriction on the Journal Entries
   application (P0911), highlight the P0911 icon under the Secured item,
   and choose Remove All from the Row menu.

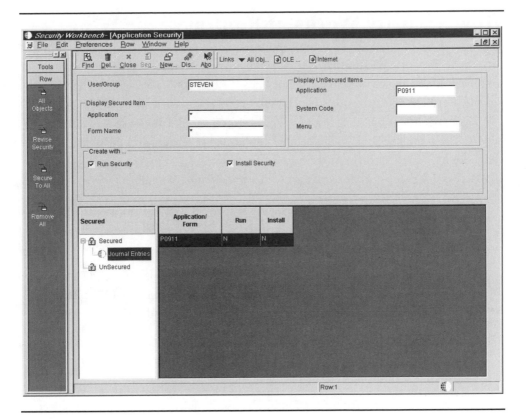

FIGURE 3-10.   Application Security form of the Security Workbench application (P00950)

NOTE

Users with access to the Object Librarian can execute applications from the Object Librarian. However, if the user does not have permission to execute the object, a dialog box notifies the user that execution of the application is denied.

10. Click OK when you have finished. The system returns to the Work With User/Group Security form. Click the Find button to verify that your entry has been made.

How Security Works at Runtime

All verification of object-level security in OneWorld is performed before execution of any application or object for the user. When OneWorld verifies user access security for an object, it terminates its search when it finds the first applicable security restriction for the user in the Security Workbench table (F00950).

Table 3-3 shows the sequence of a typical search to validate the security of an object. The user is STEVEN, who belongs to the DEVEL group; and the object is the table P0911, which is the Journal Entry application.

Here are the steps of the search for security validation of an object:

1. The search sequence starts by locating security restrictions for the P0911 application that are assigned to the user STEVEN. If a security restriction is found, the search is terminated and the user is notified.

2. The sequence continues to search for security restrictions for the P0911 application that are assigned to the user's group assignment, DEVEL. If a security restriction is found, the search is terminated and the user is notified.

3. Last, the sequence searches for security restrictions for the P0911 application that are assigned to all users, or *PUBLIC. If a security restriction is found, the search is terminated and the user is notified.

4. If no security restrictions are found, the user is allowed to execute the object.

Enforcing Application Security for the Journal Entry Batch Processor Application (R09110Z)

It is useful to know how security works in OneWorld. However, it is even more useful to know how security works when unauthorized users attempt to execute

Sequence	Object Name	User
1	P0911	STEVEN
2	P0911	DEVEL
3	P0911	*PUBLIC

TABLE 3-3. Sequence of Security Validation Search

applications. Testing OneWorld security on a variety of your applications will give you a comprehensive understanding of the system's inner workings. The following steps show you how to make sure that security for the Journal Entry Batch Processor application (R09110Z) is operating to specifications in OneWorld.

1. Verify that your Jde.ini file, located in the C:\Winnt directory, contains the following settings:

```
[DEBUG]
Output=Both

[UBE]
UBEDebugLevel=9
```

2. Perform steps 1 through 10 of the preceding example for the Journal Entry application, but this time set the application security for the Journal Entry Batch Processor application (R09110Z). Also, apply the application security to your own OneWorld username instead of to the username STEVEN.

TIP

At this point, exit and restart OneWorld Explorer, because all security settings are cached locally. The security information in the local cache is updated only when OneWorld Explorer is started.

3. From OneWorld Explorer, type **BV** into the Fast Path box and press ENTER. The Batch Versions application (P98305) appears, as shown in Figure 3-11.

4. Type **R09110Z** into the Batch Application field. This is the name of the Journal Entry Batch Processor application.

5. Open the C:\Jdedebug.log file in your text editor, and delete all contents in the file except one character. Make sure there's a single character left in the file before you save it.

CAUTION

If you do not leave at least one ASCII character in the Jdedebug.log file, the file will become unusable to OneWorld.

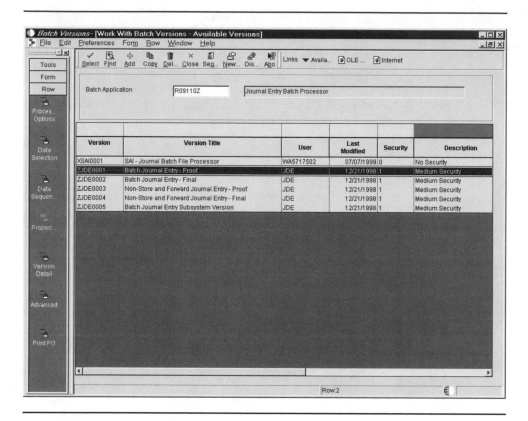

FIGURE 3-11.   Work With Batch Versions form of the Batch Version application
(P98305)

6. Click the Select button. A dialog box appears, notifying you that you are
   restricted from executing this application.

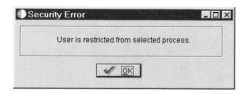

7. Reopen the C:\Jdedebug.log file in your text editor. Near the top of the
   file, you should see the following lines notifying you that your request to
   execute R09110Z failed. The OneWorld batch runtime engine executes the

CheckUBESecurityinF00950 BSFN (B983052), which verifies user security for the R09110Z object.

```
RT:   BSFN: Calling : CheckUBESecurityinF00950 App: P98305
Form: W98305A
Calling Business function CheckUBESecurityinF00950 for STEVEN.
(BSFNLevel = 1)
      Entering JDB_InitBhvr
      Entering JDB_FreeBhvr
      Return value is 2 for CheckUBESecurityinF00950.
(BSFNLevel = 1)
RT:  BSFN: Returned 2:CheckUBESecurityinF00950 App: P98305
Form: W98305A
RT:      BSFN DID NOT RETURN SUCCESS CheckUBESecurityinF00950
```

8. If your security setting failed, the R09110Z application will proceed with execution, and the following lines will appear in Jdedebug.log:

```
RT:      BSFN: Calling : CheckUBESecurityinF00950 App: P98305
Form: W98305A
Calling Business function CheckUBESecurityinF00950 for STEVEN.
(BSFNLevel = 1)
      Entering JDB_InitBhvr
      Entering JDB_FreeBhvr
      Return value is 0 for CheckUBESecurityinF00950.
(BSFNLevel = 1)
RT: BSFN: Returned 0: CheckUBESecurityinF00950 App: P98305
Form: W98305A
```

N O T E

It is a good idea to remove application security from the R09110Z object, to verify that the lines in step 8 exist in the Jdedebug.log file. This will ensure that application security is operating properly.

Package Management

Probably the most enigmatic aspect of any development project is how to build your newly created and modified objects into packages and distribute them to users and customers. Typically, this effort is performed well into the development cycle. The result is utter chaos and terror as you try to get the build process to build reliable, deliverable executable objects. OneWorld circumvents this turmoil by providing an effective set of package management and deployment tools. No longer do you have to create a separate development project that is used to define a reliable package-build process, because OneWorld already has that process defined and operational.

Your job may or may not include the duties of package management, but knowledge of the process will make your life easier. In this section, we'll examine the fundamentals of package management, followed by a close look at the importance of just-in-time installations. Finally, we'll walk through the procedure of creating an installation CD from an existing OneWorld package.

What Is Package Management?

The OneWorld package management system provides all the functionality you need to build and deploy a package to any client or server defined in the CNC architecture. This system reduces the headache for systems administrators and developers of keeping track of all objects for a particular platform and whether it belongs to a client or a server.

OneWorld provides full, partial, and update packages.

Full Package

A full package is a snapshot of the OneWorld central objects for a particular environment. The full package contains all the source code, applications, and development tools for the environment and is installed on any client or server.

The main advantage of the full package is that it installs every licensed OneWorld application onto the client. This reduces the time it takes to perform just-in-time installation of applications.

NOTE

Full packages are required only by client workstations that are used by developers and by power users. For normal production, a thin client or zero client package installation on a client is adequate.

The main disadvantage of a full package is that it requires a substantial workstation or server for OneWorld to operate properly. Typically, a full package needs a little less than 2GB of hard disk space and about 64MB of RAM for efficient execution.

The steps to build a full package are as follows:

1. Create the package directory.

2. Create the .inf file for the package.

3. Create the following directories:

   Res
   Source
   Include
   Work
   Make
   Bin32
   Lib32
   Obj

4. Copy all the source and header files from the current environment that the package is based on, into the Source and Include directories.

5. Build the TAM specification from the central objects.

6. Execute the BusBuild program to compile all BSFNs and DLLs. The BSFN objects are copied into the Object directory; the DLLs are copied into the Bin32 directory; and all libraries are copied into the Lib32 directory.

7. Create a compressed file for each directory.

TIP

OneWorld uses Microsoft's CAB file compression technique to compress files. To view .cab files, you can use any version of WinZip that is 7.0 or later.

Partial Package

A partial package is a minimum OneWorld configuration that requires a limited number of OneWorld applications. The partial package is only available for client machines, because it contains only the applications needed to execute the OneWorld Explorer.

There are a couple of advantages to using the partial package: it requires a minimum amount of hard disk space, and it only installs the applications that are executed by the user. The partial package initially requires about 200MB. As the user requests applications, just-in-time installation (JITI) installs them. The end result is that only the applications that interact with the user are installed on the client machine.

The main disadvantage of partial packages is the network traffic that is generated by just-in-time installation of applications. As requests are made to install applications that are missing on the client, the message traffic generated to fulfill the requests eats up a lot of the organization's network bandwidth. Therefore, it is best to install partial packages onto clients that reside on the same LAN as the deployment server that stores all packages.

Here are the steps to build a partial package:

1. Create the package directory.

2. Create the .inf file for the package.

3. Create the following directories:

    Res
    Work
    Make
    Bin32
    Lib32
    Object

4. Build an empty set of TAM specifications.

5. Execute the BusBuild program to compile all BSFNs and DLLs. The BSFN objects are copied into the Object directory; the DLLs are copied into the Bin32 directory; and all libraries are copied into the Lib32 directory.

6. Create a compressed file for each directory.

Update Package

An update package is the means of updating OneWorld clients and servers across the entire organization. Update packages are a point-in-time snapshot of the OneWorld central objects that are used to refresh the existing full or partial packages installed on clients or servers. Update packages contain only objects that have been modified or created and need to be deployed to clients and servers. Objects that are not included in the update package are left alone.

N O T E

As a developer, you should never install a partial package, because you will not have a true snapshot of the central objects for the development environment.

The steps to build an update package are as follows:

1. Create the package directory.

2. Create the .inf file for the package.

3. Create the following directories:

   Res
   Source
   Include
   Work
   Make
   Bin32
   Lib32
   Obj

4. Build the TAM specifications from the central objects for all the objects defined in the update package. The Software Package Detail table (F9631) contains a list of all objects in the update package.

5. Execute the BusBuild program to compile all BSFNs and DLLs. The BSFN objects are copied into the object directory; the DLLs are copied into the bin32 directory; and all libraries are copied into the lib32 directory.

6. Create a compressed file for each directory.

Just-in-Time Installation

A client with a partial package installed does not contain any applications. The applications are installed at runtime by a process called just-in-time installation (JITI), as the user requests them. The advantage of JITI is that it allows a minimal footprint—only OneWorld applications that are executed by the user—to be installed on the client.

A JITI event occurs when an application requested by the user is not installed on the client machine. When one of OneWorld's runtime engines does not find the requested application, OneWorld forces a JITI event to download the TAM specs for the application from the server and then proceeds with execution when the JITI process is complete. Therefore, the only applications that are installed with JITI are TAM spec–based applications.

N O T E

TAM spec–based applications are the only type of applications that use JITI for client-side installation.

TAM spec–based applications, such as interactive and batch applications, are the only applications that can be installed with JITI. TAM specs are composed of J.D. Edwards' own interpretive language, called Event Rules (ER). The GUI or batch runtime engines interpret all ER source code at runtime when a user executes an application or batch process. The following OneWorld objects exist in TAM specs:

- Interactive applications

- Batch applications or reports

- Processing options

- Data structures

- Business views

Modules and functions that are built using BSFNs cannot be installed using JITI. BSFNs are based on compiled languages, such as C and J.D. Edwards's own Named Event Rules (NER), and must be compiled into DLLs. These OneWorld objects are built into DLLs:

- BSFNs

- Data structures for BSFNs

- Data structures for generic text and media objects

- Table Event Rules (TER)

- Named Event Rules (NER)

- Icons

Creating an Installation CD for a Package

For companies with users and developers spread across a WAN, it is not recommended that they update their clients across the WAN with the newest OneWorld package. In particular, development teams spread across a WAN that requires installation of full packages on its clients cannot install the package in a reasonable amount of time.

The following procedure explains how to create an installation CD from an existing OneWorld package. This process is an easy means of creating a remote development site for a company, and cuts down on network traffic due to the installation process. (A typical full-package installation takes 30 minutes over a LAN, and approximately 350MB of data are transferred over it.)

1. Create a directory on your computer that will contain all the OneWorld files needed for installing a full development environment from a CD to a client machine. For this example, we created a directory called D:\Install CD\.

2. Create the following directories under the D:\Install CD\ directory:

   OneWorld Client Install
   HELPSCOMP
   SYSTEMCOMP
   DEVB733
   DEVB733\package
   DEVB733\package\Datacomp
   DEVB733\package\PCKDEVFF
   PACKAGE_INF

NOTE

PCKDEVFF is the name of the full package to install on the client.

3. Copy the files listed in Table 3-4 from the \JDEdwardsOneWorld\B733\ directory on your deployment server, to the same directories that you created in step 2 in your computer's D:\Install CD\ directory. There are about 350MB of files to transfer.

4. Adjust the following lines in the SrcDirs section of the PCKDEVFF.INF file, which is located in the D:\Install CD\PACKAGE_INF\:

```
SDEVB733=..\DEVB733\package\PCKDEVFF
SSYS=..\SYSTEMCOMP
SDEVB733DATA=..\DEVB733\package\Datacomp
SHELP=..\HelpsCOMP
```

5. Adjust the line in the FileLocations section of the INSTALL.INF file, which is located in the D:\Install CD\OneWorld Client Install\ directory, to read as follows:

```
PackageInfs=..\PACKAGE_INF
```

6. Burn the entire contents of the D:\Install CD\ directory to a CD, but not the directory itself.

7. When ready to use the CD to install the package to a client, execute the InstallManager.exe file in the OneWorld Client Install directory.

Directory	Files
OneWorld Client Install	All files and subdirectories
HelpCOMP	Help.cab, Helpcomp.inf, and the Disk1 subdirectory
SystemCOMP	System.cab, Syscomp.inf, and the Disk1 subdirectory
DEVB733\Package\Datacomp	Data.cab, Devpackagedatacomp.inf, and the Disk1 subdirectory
DEVB733\Package\PCKDEVFF	All *.cab files
PACKAGE_INF	PCKDEVFF.INF

TABLE 3-4.   Files to Copy Locally for Creating a OneWorld Installer on a CD

NOTE

The only network request generated by the installer on the CD will be for validating and installing license security on the client.

Putting It All Together

The focus of this chapter was to show you how to manage and operate the applications you build or modify in OneWorld. You cannot successfully develop applications in OneWorld without knowledge of user profiles, OCM, security, and package management.

User profiles provide the functionality in OneWorld to manage settings for OneWorld users. Profiles allow OneWorld to manage the various system settings required for users in an organization. Profiles also allow assignment of users with similar profiles to groups, enabling effective management of all profiles for an organization.

The OCM stores the location for every object, whether data- or application-related, on the network. OCM also provides the location of the object when it is requested by an application at runtime. These two functions give the CNC architecture the flexibility it requires to handle all data and applications on the network. And the dynamic application partitioning enabled through OCM lets you change the location of applications or data on the fly.

With OneWorld's Security application, you can impose restrictions on access to applications and data. You can limit access at the user or group level, and the limits are verified every time a user requests an application or object.

The system builds and distributes packages for clients and servers through the Package Management module. Package Management provides the tools to define, build, and deploy software applications to any computer on the network, regardless of its role as client, enterprise server, or Java application server.

OneWorld System Architecture for Developers

PART II

Client Modifications Using OneWorld

CHAPTER 4

Overview of OneWorld Development

Development in OneWorld

Application Types

The Object Librarian

Putting It All Together

Every developer's primary focus is to design and create a set of applications to meet or exceed the requirements of the business. As a developer, you have to be aware of many issues for application development and support. To support the project itself, however, you also need to perform many tasks that are not related to development. This chapter focuses on those tasks. The topics covered in this chapter give you essential information for achieving optimum productivity and efficiency as a OneWorld developer.

- **Development in OneWorld**   The first section, "Development in OneWorld," helps you see how to determine the scope and complexity of a project, so that you have the proper resources and administrative functions to efficiently support the project. Without a clear sense of the scope and complexity of development needed, individuals assigned to the project may be overburdened by unrealistic expectations.

- **Application Types**   It is essential to understand the application types used in OneWorld and where they are used. Too many projects have gone down the wrong path and failed because of inadequate knowledge of what an application can and cannot do.

- **The Object Librarian**   The last section of this chapter discusses the single most important application that supports development in OneWorld: the Object Librarian. You use the Object Librarian to create, delete, and launch objects that OneWorld applications comprise. It is the one tool that you will use the most.

Development in OneWorld

Development in OneWorld always includes both building and customizing, whether you are building a new application or modifying an existing one. A given project can be as simple as changing a few processing options on an application, or as complex as creating an entirely new module and integrating it with existing OneWorld modules.

The initial challenge for any development project is to understand the enhancements and changes that are required for the application. Knowing this helps you gauge the amount of time and effort required. All OneWorld development projects comprise one or more of the following enhancements and changes:

- Modification or creation of the specifications for an object; for example, adding or modifying a field on an application.

- Modification or creation of the source code, such as C or the named event rules (NER), for a business function.

- Modification or creation of data that impacts the functionality of an application; for example, the application's processing options.

- Modifications that affect the operation of the production environment.

- Modifications that require deployment of an update package to all OneWorld clients.

As enhancements and changes are proposed and implemented during a development project, its size and complexity will increase. Therefore, it is crucial that you know exactly where the modifications will impact the project so that you can effectively prepare for them. Being ready for the impact of enhancements and changes requires attention to two primary factors: the level of complexity of the changes, and the way you administer the progress of development. We'll begin by examining levels of complexity in OneWorld development projects.

Levels of Complexity

The types of changes needed are what determine the level of complexity for a development project. This level of complexity directly influences the amount of time and effort you'll need to finish the job. Let's take a look at the five levels of complexity, from lowest to highest.

Modifying or Creating Data

The lowest level of complexity in OneWorld development is modifying or creating data in certain tables that affect the functionality of OneWorld applications. The tables that affect application functionality are system setup values, menus, User-Defined Codes (UDCs), and processing option values. These changes require replication of data across the corporate network; they are the only changes that do not require deployment of update packages.

Modifying or Creating Versions

Modifying or creating versions of applications is the primary technique of customizing OneWorld applications for a company. When you modify versions, you change processing options, or certain sections inside a report. These types of changes typically do not require significant knowledge of application development.

Application Enhancement

Application enhancement involves modifying an existing application to meet the requirements of a company. You typically use the Form Design Aid (FDA) or Report Design Aid (RDA) to make these modifications, including changing the application's Event Rules (ER).

Customizing Existing OneWorld Modules

When you customize existing modules, you change the way in which the modules perform certain tasks. This level of complexity requires altering the majority of applications in a module to meet the company's requirements. A good example of module customization is changing the applications in the General Ledger module to reduce the number of journal entries created throughout a given period.

Creating a New Application Suite

You create a new application suite in OneWorld when you need highly specialized, third-party applications and modules for a specific industry. This level of complexity incorporates the tasks of all the other complexity levels, and requires a high degree of expertise in OneWorld application development. The complexity of building new modules in OneWorld increases along with the number of modules implemented.

Development Administration

Along with your knowledge of the impact that changes will have, careful administration is necessary for you to monitor and control the progress of development. The goal for administration of a development project is not to choke it with unnecessary bureaucracy, but to ensure that the design is heading down the right path to completion. Proper administration guarantees that modifications to the OneWorld project are performed in a timely manner with few application errors. Development administration includes the responsibilities described in the following sections.

Resource Planning

Resource planning ensures that you realistically estimate and monitor the size and complexity of the development project. In the initial stages, resource planning includes analyzing the project in terms of the types of changes and level of complexity required, as well as determining the proper staff and equipment needed. During development itself, resource planning helps you monitor progress, helping to keep the project within initial estimates and thereby avoid delays and cost overruns.

Change Management

Change management helps you control and monitor enhancements that are introduced to OneWorld as development progresses. Proper control of changes ensures that interdependent enhancements are performed in the correct sequence, to prevent project delays. In addition, you can more easily measure the real progress made during the project, and you can use this data for resource planning as well.

Deployment Management

Deployment management helps you control the introduction of software enhancements into the production environment. This process is critical; adequate management of deployment means you don't introduce problems into the daily operations of the business.

Upgrades

Managing upgrades is important during any development project. There are two major types of upgrades: the upgrade of the OneWorld environment and the upgrade of previously enhanced applications. When the OneWorld environment is upgraded, you must verify that previous versions of applications are not damaged or rendered ineffective by the upgrade. As you add new enhancements, you incorporate them into the development environment first for testing of application features and functionality. The advantage of this approach is that it will help you identify problems early before the applications are introduced into the production environment for OneWorld.

Quality Assurance

Quality assurance, ensures that modifications and enhancements of applications are thoroughly tested and have a minimum of errors. Nothing is more frustrating for an organization than to roll out a new application to the production environment only to find it not yet ready for daily operations.

Training and Documentation

Training and documentation help affected individuals in an organization to be educated and ready to use the applications you create. Training includes walking users through all the features and functions of the new application, or using a computer-based training (CBT) program. Documentation ranges from technical information for developers (discussed in the following Developer's Corner, titled "Critical Design Documents for a OneWorld Development Project") to online help and manuals for end users.

Critical Design Documents for a OneWorld Development Project

For any development project, you need to write certain critical design documents that explain the requirements of the project. We are not saying these critical documents are the *only* ones needed for a successful development project, but rather that neglecting to prepare them will jeopardize the projects's success.

Although many types of design documents are available for use in your development projects, in most cases, you'll be able to make good use of only a few. For OneWorld development projects, the following three design documents are critical to the project's success:

Entity Relationship Diagram

The entity relationship diagram (ERD) captures the essence of a business's operational model and requirements, and you use the ERD to define the required database schema to support business operations. The entities in the ERD design document directly translate to tables in the database. The relationships between entities in the diagram become foreign keys in the tables that represent the entities.

The likelihood of your project's success is dramatically increased by an ERD, and you'll find many books available to instruct you in building this document. The ERD's basic elements are summarized in Figure 4-1.

Window Navigation Diagram

The window navigation diagram (WND) defines the menu layout within the OneWorld environment, and shows how users navigate through OneWorld Explorer to find the applications they need to perform their tasks. The WND document starts at the top level of the menu and identifies all the decisions required by users to execute an application. You need to ensure that the menu layout is logical and makes sense to those who interact with.

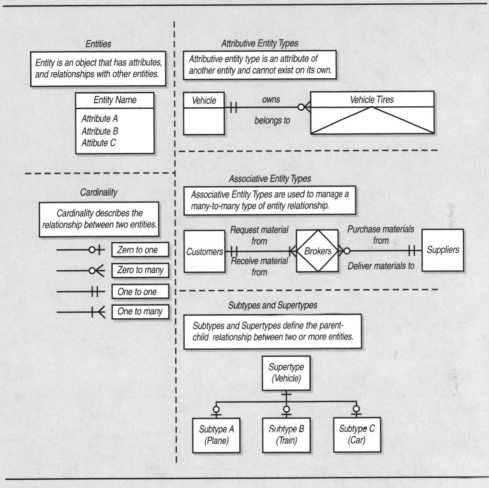

Entities

Entity is an object that has attributes, and relationships with other entities.

Entity Name
Attribute A
Attribute B
Attibute C

Attributive Entity Types

Attributive entity type is an attribute of another entity and cannot exist on its own.

Vehicle — owns / belongs to — Vehicle Tires

Cardinality

Cardinality describes the relationship between two entities.

	Zero to one
	Zero to many
	One to one
	One to many

Associative Entity Types

Associative Entity Types are used to manage a many-to-many type of entity relationship.

Customers — Request material from / Receive material from — Brokers — Purchase materials from / Deliver materials to — Suppliers

Subtypes and Supertypes

Subtypes and Supertypes define the parent-child relationship between two or more entities.

Supertype (Vehicle)

Subtype A (Plane)   Subtype B (Train)   Subtype C (Car)

FIGURE 4-1. Summary of schematic elements used in entity relationship diagrams

Figure 4-2 shows the WND document for the Address Book module. It starts at the main menu in OneWorld Explorer and shows the selections that a user makes to get to the Address Book Revisions (P01012) application.

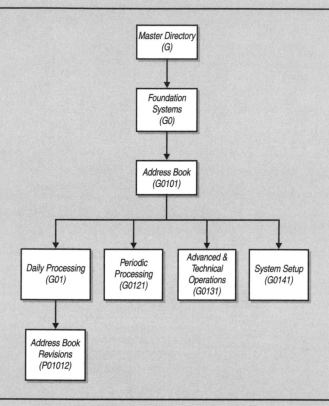

FIGURE 4-2.   Window navigation diagram for the Address Book module

Application Navigation Diagram

The application navigation diagram (AND) defines the layout of an application by providing all possible actions generated by the users. The AND document starts at the menu item that launches the application, and then describes actions that occur as the user selects buttons and row exits in the application. The graphical view of the AND ensures that your application contains all the functions needed by its users.

146

Figure 4-3 shows the AND document for the Address Book Revision and Phones applications. It starts at the menu item that launches the Address Book Revision application, and then shows actions that will occur as users select buttons, row exits, and form exits in the applications.

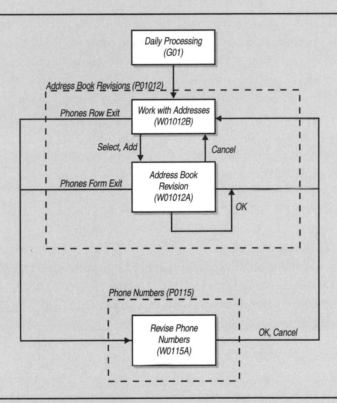

FIGURE 4-3. Application navigation diagram for the Address Book Revisions application (P01012)

Development Cycle

After you have completed the analysis and design documentation for your OneWorld development project, you will follow a development cycle as shown in Figure 4-4. This straightforward development sequence begins with the Data Dictionary and ends with menu design, and each step in the cycle is dependent on the preceding step. For example, you cannot build business views until you create the data items and tables to be used by your application.

The actual starting point for an application in the OneWorld development cycle is determined by the changes and enhancements being made for the application. The cycle begins where the changes and enhancements are *not* dependent on the preceding steps. For example, if a column name needs to be changed in a report already being used in production, then the Report Design step in Figure 4-4 is the only step that you need to perform. However, if you need to create a new application, then the development cycle starts at the Data Dictionary step.

Each step of the development cycle in Figure 4-4 is accomplished with a separate design tool, as explained next.

Data Dictionary

The Data Dictionary (DD) application (P92001) manages all data items in OneWorld and is located in the Data Dictionary menu (GH951). Data items appear as fields on all reports and forms, and in all columns in a table. The primary advantage of the Data Dictionary is that any changes made to a data item in OneWorld are automatically incorporated in all applications in which those data items are used. The DD application also performs the following functions:

- Validating data entry for all forms

- Assigning row and column descriptions

- Providing text for field-level help

Table Design Aid

You use the Table Design Aid (TDA) to modify and create tables and indexes in OneWorld. TDA uses data items to build all the columns in a table. However, a single data item can only be defined once in a table. If you want a table to contain more than one instance of a data item, you must add that data item as many times as there are instances of it in the table.

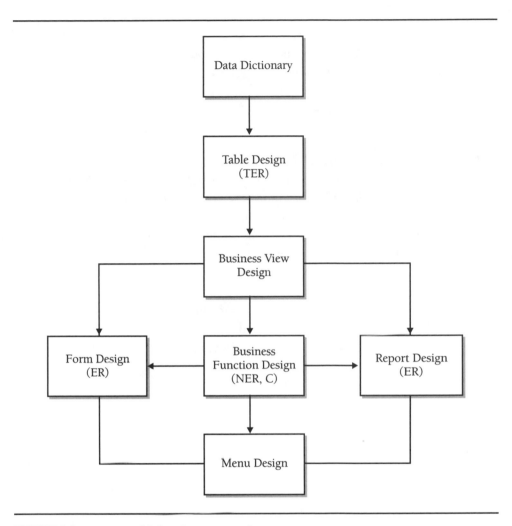

FIGURE 4-4. OneWorld development cycle

Use the following naming convention for all tables that you create in OneWorld: *fmmmmxxx*. The letter *f* uniquely identifies the object as a table; *mmmm* is the system code associated with the table; and *xxx* is a unique identifier for the table in the module. For example, the object name for the main table in the Address Book module (01) is called the F0101 table.

Business View Design Aid

The Business View Design Aid (BDA) tool allows you to modify and create *business views,* which provide the links between database tables and applications developed in OneWorld. A business view defines the data items in the tables that are used in an application. The naming convention for business views is similar to that for naming tables, except that business views start with a *V* instead of an *F* (for example, V550001).

Form Design Aid

The Form Design Aid (FDA) tool allows you to modify and create GUI applications that consist of a set of forms. Forms provide the visual link between the user and the information stored in the database tables. The naming convention for forms is similar to that for tables and business views, except that application names begin with the letter *P* (for example, P0101).

Report Design Aid

The Report Design Aid (RDA) allows you to modify and create batch applications and reports. Reports provide the application users with the current state of data stored in various tables. Batch applications modify the data stored in tables, such as table purge programs and posting of journal entries. Names for reports and batch applications begin with the letter *R* (for example, R5501).

Business Function Design Tools

You use *business function design tools* to modify and create business functions (BSFNs). BSFNs encapsulate specialized logic and are available for execution by any application or other business function through Event Rules. You can write BSFNs in either C/C++ or with Named Event Rules (NER). Each language has its own development tool to build BSFNs.

N O T E

NER-based BSFNs are useful for business logic only, whereas C/C++-based BSFNs are good for embedding low-level logic. For example, NER business functions are used for field- and record-level validation, and C-based business functions are used in transaction processing.

Menu Design Tool

The Menu Design Tool application (P0082), located in the System Administration Tools menu (GH9011), manages all menus and menu items that are displayed in OneWorld Explorer. Menu items are the launching point for applications that are executed by users. Menu names begin with the letter *G* (for example, GH9011).

Application Types

To build effective applications in OneWorld, you need a solid understanding of the different types of application you can create. There are four major application types in OneWorld, each used to perform a specific type of task.

Interactive Applications

An interactive application is a graphical interface with which a user interacts in the OneWorld environment. The interactive application provides an intuitive, easy-to-use interface containing images and graphical elements as clues and assistance to users on how to properly manipulate the application.

Interactive applications comprise one or more forms that are nothing more than individual screens or dialog boxes representing the sequence of the application. Forms allow users to provide input, select data, and view information that is stored in the OneWorld database tables. Data is viewed and modified in a form through the controls that are assigned to it by the developer. For example, a form can contain check boxes, pull-down lists, buttons, text fields, and grids.

The two important attributes of a OneWorld form are its form type and its runtime data structures.

Form Types

OneWorld includes seven types of forms, each with special characteristics to accommodate different user interactions and tasks.

Find/Browse   The find/browse form (Figure 4-5) is the normal starting point for most applications. This form allows users to search, view, select, and delete records in one or more tables. It also contains a Query-by-Example (QBE) line located at the top of the grid to provide powerful but simple database search capability.

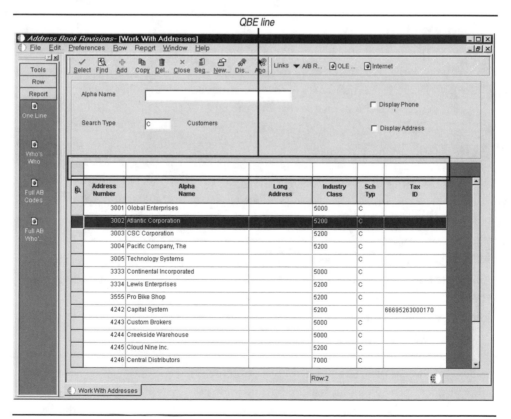

FIGURE 4-5.   The find/browse form enables searching for and working with Address Book entries

Fix/Inspect   The fix/inspect form (as shown in Figure 4-6) allows users to add, view, and update records for one or more tables. You can only view or edit one record at a time.

Header Detail   The header detail form (Figure 4-7) enables users to work with data from two tables having a one-to-many relationship. One table contains header records that own one or more detail records stored in another table. This unique feature presents an input-capable grid allowing users to add, update, and delete detail records.

Headerless Detail   Similar to the header detail form, the headerless detail form (Figure 4-8) provides a view to a single table that is not normalized. This form also contains an input-capable grid in which users can add, update, and delete records residing in a table.

Client Modifications Using OneWorld

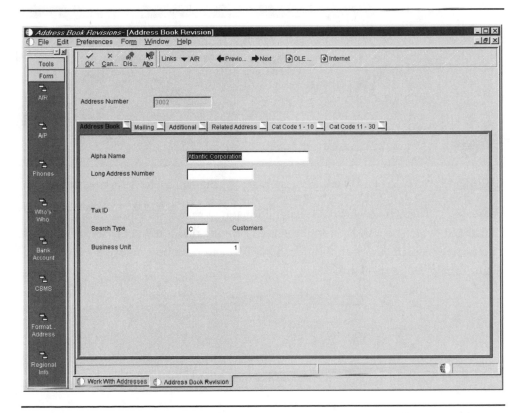

FIGURE 4-6.   The fix/inspect form enables adding and updating Address Book entries

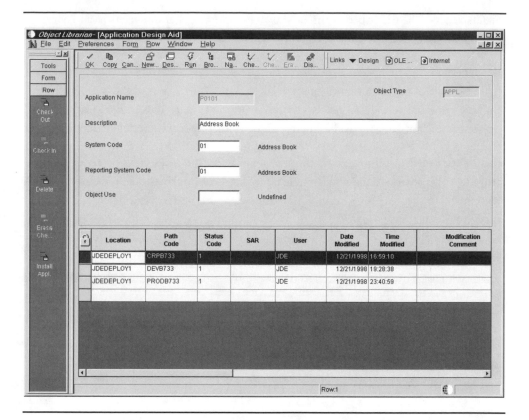

FIGURE 4-7.   The header detail form enables working with objects for applications

Message   The message form displays information or requests action from users, as illustrated next. The message form is modal, meaning that it restricts users from interacting with any other application. Static text and push buttons are the only controls allowed in this form.

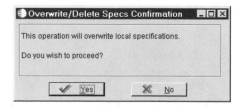

Parent/Child   Parent/child forms (see Figure 4-9) present information from tables that have a parent-child relationship. These forms contain a parent/child control, which offers the information as a tree relationship. The parent/child control can show all the details of the table, or only data at one level in the tree.

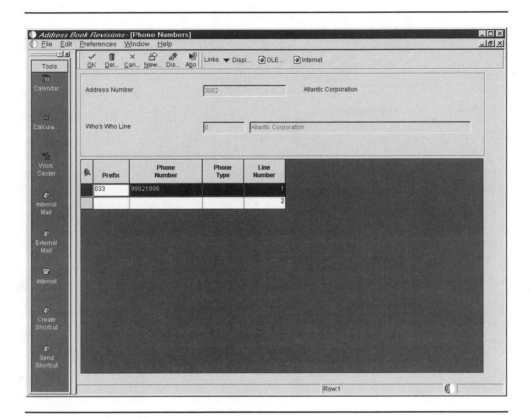

FIGURE 4-8.   The headerless detail form enables working with phone numbers for an address book entry

Search/Select   Search/select forms (Figure 4-10) allow users to search for one or more values in one or more tables, and then to return the selected values to the form that called the search/select form. Users execute a search/select form by clicking the visual assist button, which resembles a flashlight, beside a field. The grid in a search/select form is not input capable and only allows users to select items located in a table.

Runtime Data Structures for Interactive Applications

Runtime data structures are blocks of computer memory that contain data processed by a form during execution of the application. Each runtime data structure corresponds to a unique component located in the form, and is used to store temporary data for the form. For example, any information that is contained in the grid is stored in the Grid Column runtime data structure. A two-character code identifies the runtime data structures within the form.

The data can easily be passed among the runtime data structures through the use of ER.

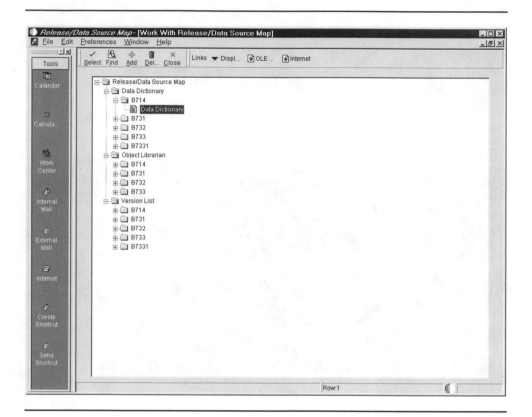

FIGURE 4-9.   The parent/child form enables working with data sources for different releases of OneWorld

The eight important runtime data structures for all forms in OneWorld are described in the following paragraphs.

Business View Columns (BC)   The BC runtime data structure stores data for each column in a business view for the form and grid. The columns are populated with the values from the database when a fetch or save is performed.

Grid Column (GC)   The GC runtime data structure stores data for each column in a grid. The data located in the GC data structure is from the highlighted row in the grid, because the data structure can only store one row of data at a time.

Grid Buffer (GB)   The GB runtime data structure is a temporary storage buffer for data in the grid. The data in the GB data structure is independent of the current data in the grid, and you use it when you want to manipulate records in the grid. The GB data structure can only store one row of data at a time.

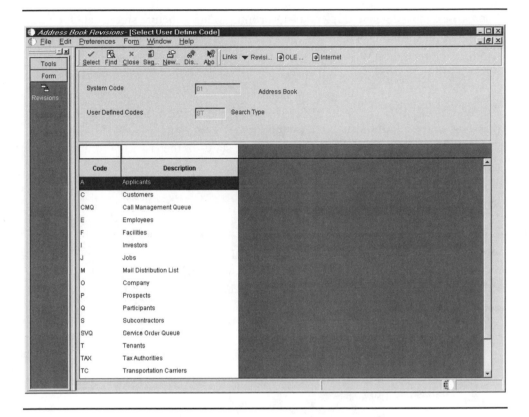

FIGURE 4-10. The search/select form enables selecting an address book entry type

Form Control (FC)   Every control on a form has an assigned FC runtime data structure. The FC data structure contains either the data from the corresponding BC data structure, or data that is typed in by the user.

Form Interconnection (FI)   Any values that are passed from form to form are passed through the FI runtime data structure. This data structure is used to read or write data between two or more forms. An example use of the FI data structure is when data is passed between forms that are related through a row exit.

Processing Options (PO)   Values that are assigned to the processing options of an application are passed through the PO runtime data structure. The processing options are assigned when the application is started, and any form within it can access the PO data structure. Processing options are particularly useful for versions of interactive applications.

Client Modifications Using OneWorld

Query-by-Example Column (QC)   The QC runtime data structure stores data for each column in the QBE line. Wildcards can be stored in the QC data structure, but not comparison operators. When the data in the grid is updated to a table, the data in the GC and BC data structures is not affected.

System Variables (SV)   The SV runtime data structure stores systemwide variables that exist in the environment. One example of a system variable is the FILE_IO_STATUS flag that provides the success or failure status of the last fetch or update to a table.

Batch Applications

A batch application processes without user interaction, except for processing options attached to it. When a user launches the batch application, no user control is available during execution. User control is prohibited because the Universal Batch Engine (UBE), which executes batch applications, does not stop execution until the application ends. The four types of batch applications are

- Reports
- Table conversion
- Database output
- Subsystem jobs

Report batch applications in OneWorld allow users to view data in an online format or printed document. Reports contain information on financial status, number of items in inventory, and employee information. The main focus of a report is to extract and present information stored in OneWorld's databases.

Table conversion batch applications manipulate data from table to table, or within a table in OneWorld. Table conversion is particularly useful for importing and exporting data to and from foreign tables, or for making changes to a new database schema for OneWorld. Table conversion applications can also purge data within a table or copy data to another environment.

Database output is a hybrid of the report and table conversion batch applications. Database output generates a report that presents the information stored in the database, but this batch application also adds or updates information in one or more tables during report execution. Database output applications are particularly useful when you need summarization and extraction of data from one or more tables.

Subsystem jobs constantly run batch applications that occur in the background on an enterprise server. The background processes periodically examine the state of the system to determine if any action or work needs to be performed. One example of a subsystem job is the Workflow Management's Check for Escalated Activities batch application (R98810). This batch application periodically checks the message queue to determine if a message needs to be forwarded to another user when no action has taken place within a specified time.

Two important attributes of a OneWorld batch application are its section types and its runtime data structures.

Section Types

Every batch application contains at least one of the following types of sections: header, footer, and body. These sections are modules that build the batch application. For example, there are sections for initialization, shutdown, and processing every record. The three major section types for most batch applications are described next.

DEFINITION

Header sections and *footer sections* are dependent on other sections in a report. Such dependent *sections are called* level-two sections. *Body sections are independent of other sections in a report. These* independent *sections are called* level-one sections.

Header Section   The header section at the beginning of a report contains information that identifies the report. This information includes the report title, version, object name, date, and user.

Footer Section   The footer section at the end of a report contains information that summarizes the data in the report. This summary information includes the page number, report status, and any grand totals for the report.

Body Section   The body section contains all the main processing that a batch application performs. As processing occurs in the body section, certain events occur. You can embed business logic (ER) into these events to create the required functionality for the report. There are three types of body sections for OneWorld batch applications. The difference between the three is in how they present the data in the report:

- **Columnar**   A columnar section presents data in a column format just like a spreadsheet. Each row in the report is a single record, and every column contains related information for every row in the report, as shown here:

Address Number	Alpha Name	Area Code	Phone Number	Mailing Name	Address Lane 1
281	Almacen Compania 28-ESTE			Almacen Compania 28-ESTE	
283	Almacen Compania 28-OESTE			Almacen Compania 28-OESTE	
77	Canadian Company			Canadian Company	35021 Queen Street
80	Colombian Company			Colombian Company	
505	Consignment Agent		303-555-1111	Consignment Agent	1212 Main Street

- **Group**   The group section combines common records that are spread across many tables into a single report. As shown in the following illustration, the group section presents the data by grouping the information in row and column format. Here the name of the company is grouped with its address and phone contact information.

Address #	Mailing Name	Phone Number		Type	P/C
1	Financial Distribution Company 8055 East Tufts Avenue, Suite 1331 Denver CO 80237	303	555-0100	FAX	

- **Tabular**   A tabular section presents detailed and summarized financial information in a single section. The following illustration shows the detailed records that make up the batch, and a summary of each column in the section.

G/L Account	Account Description Explanation	Do Ty	Document	G/L Date	Co	Debit	Credit	Current Balance	LT	P C	Batch
	Colombian ECS Company				00080						
801110 BEAR	Bear Creek National Bank				00080	210,000					
		Balance	Forward			70,000					
	Colombian adjustment entry	JE	3077	6/30/05					AA	P	
	Brazil Expenses	JE	1066	6/30/05		7,000			AA	P	3496
	Account Activity June CO 80	JE	1027	6/30/05			14,000-		AA	P	2122
											1038
		Period Total				77,000	14,000-				
			Account Total			287,000	14,000-	273,000			
			Object Account Total			287,000	14,000-	273,000			
		Company Total	Posted			287,000	14,000-	273,000			
			Unposted								

From Date - 6/1-05
Thru Date - 6/30/05

Runtime Data Structures for Batch Applications

Batch applications use runtime data structures for the same purposes as for interactive applications. The runtime data structures provide computer memory buffers containing data that a batch application processes during execution.

There are four runtime data structures for batch applications: Business View Columns (BC), Processing Options (PO), System Variables (SV), and Report Variables (RV). The first three of these are identical to the same data structures discussed earlier for interactive applications.

Report Variables (RV)   The RV runtime data structure stores the values of report variables used in the batch application. Each column in a report has a corresponding RV data structure, and you can use it to modify or store data for the variable.

Hybrids of Interactive and Batch Applications

Hybrid applications are a combination of interactive and batch applications. These hybrid applications give users the ability to submit a request through an interactive application, and then launch a batch application to execute the request. You use hybrid applications in OneWorld to perform two-step operations such as submitting a journal entry to the general ledger.

The primary concern for development of hybrid applications is the security of critical tables in OneWorld (including general ledger balances, accounts receivable and payable, and fixed assets). Any changes requested by an employee are first screened and approved by an approval officer in the company, such as a comptroller, before the request is allowed to adjust the values in the critical tables.

The user request is stored in a document called a batch. A batch is created when an employee requests, through an interactive application, changes to the values in one of the critical tables. The batch is then submitted to an officer authorized to give final approval. Once the batch is approved, it is submitted to a batch application for updating the critical table.

NOTE

There are no special development tools for hybrid applications. You build hybrid applications by defining the roles of the interactive and batch applications.

Web Applications

Web applications are generated from interactive applications, enabling design and building of applications in FDA only. You create a web application by using a web generator that converts an interactive application, which is only executable through OneWorld, for use over the Web.

FDA is used to design and develop interactive and web applications because it provides three modes for developing an application. Mode 1 is the default mode for building interactive applications that execute in OneWorld. You use Mode 2 and Mode 3 to modify Mode 1 interactive applications for Java or HTML applications that execute over the Internet through a web browser.

After the interactive application is generated to a web application, that web application is stored in a database located on the Java Application Server (JAS) web server. The web generator knows where to store the new web application because the database on the web server is a fully qualified database data source.

The Object Librarian

You will use the Object Librarian application (P986101) throughout the development cycle to control development of objects in any OneWorld environment. Objects are the components that comprise OneWorld applications, and we describe them in the next Developer's Corner, titled "Are OneWorld Objects Based on Object-Oriented Technology?" The Object Librarian knows the location of objects and who has checked them out. It is the only entry point to the development toolset for modifying or creating objects.

DEFINITION

*In ActivEra terminology, the **Object Librarian** is an Activator that controls all OneWorld objects, and it is the entry point to the development toolset for them. The Object Librarian Activator manages the creation, development, and location of any object in OneWorld.*

As new objects are needed for a development project, you create them through the Object Librarian. When you need to modify them, you check the objects out from the Object Librarian to your workstation. And from the Object Librarian you can launch the appropriate development tool for the object. When the time comes to test the application you are modifying or creating, the Object Librarian can execute the application for testing without assigning the object to a menu. Finally, when you are finished with an object, you use Object Librarian to check the object back into the environment for others to modify or execute.

NOTE

You cannot create a table, application, business view, business function, or report without first creating the object in the Object Librarian (P986101). Object Librarian creates the necessary RDB and TAM specs for the object.

Because it is the single most used development tool in OneWorld, your knowledge of the Object Librarian will directly affect your proficiency as a developer. This section presents the essential topics.

Client Modifications Using OneWorld

Are OneWorld Objects Based on Object-Oriented Technology?

Object-oriented technology (OOT) is the industry standard for building today's applications. Applications built with OOT comprise many objects that perform one or more tasks. Objects based on OOT are self-contained entities that contain attributes, which are the properties of the objects. They also contain methods, which manipulate the objects' attributes. OOT objects support the following four principles of object-oriented technology:

- **Classes** A class is the design-time definition of an object, and the definition can only be modified during development time of the class. The definition contains all attributes and methods that make up the class, providing its features and functionality. As instances of a class are created during application execution, the definition for the class becomes the features and functionality of objects.

- **Polymorphism** Polymorphism allows the methods of an object to behave differently based on the type of object that invoked the method.

- **Encapsulation** Encapsulation hides the properties of objects and ensures that modifications of objects can only be performed through the use of the methods.

- **Inheritance** Inheritance allows a class to receive all or part of the attributes and methods of a parent class.

Based on this definition of OOT and this chapter's discussion of OneWorld objects, you can see that OneWorld objects are not OOT based. Experienced OOT application developers may be uncomfortable with this fact in view of OOT's widespread acceptance as a standard.

If OneWorld applications consist of objects that are not based on OOT, what are these entities and why are they called objects? The answer is quite simple: OneWorld objects are founded on *object-based technology (OBT)*, which is the ancestor of OOT.

164

Developer's Corner

NOTE

Everyday OneWorld applications are built using OBT objects. The OneWorld infrastructure that supports applications and the OneWorld environments is built using OOT objects.

Applications built with OBT, just like OOT-based applications, comprise many objects that perform one or more tasks. An OBT object, however, is a self-contained entity that contains a data structure representing the attributes of the object, and a set of functions used to manipulate the data structure. When you consider the definition and role of business functions, data structures, and business views, it makes sense to define OneWorld objects as OBT objects.

Now that you know OneWorld objects are OBT based, what are the advantages of using OBT objects over OOT objects? The answer is that OBT objects are highly reusable and easily maintained, and this results in higher productivity and efficiency. Modern ERP systems are very complex, so an efficient development environment ensures that a complex toolset does not further complicate your development project.

Object Reusability

You can define an object once and use it many times in more than one application. Although object reusability is touted as one of the main benefits of OOT, not all OOT-based objects are necessarily reusable. Small granular objects adapt more readily to reuse in an application than do large granular objects. For example, a general ledger report based on OOT has a low probability of being reused because its purpose is too specific to be adaptable throughout an entire system.

In contrast, OBT-based objects have a high degree of reusability because they are small granular objects. As a developer, you will more readily be able to use existing OBT objects in your projects, which will reduce the amount of time you spend in application development overall.

Developer's Corner

DEFINITION

Object granularity is the size and complexity of the object. Small granular objects are used to manipulate low-level entities such as dates and currencies. Large granular objects are used to manipulate high-level entities such as calendars and financial accounts.

Application Maintainability

You can easily modify the objects in an application to meet the requirements set by the development project. When you can quickly identify the spot in an application where change is needed so that it will meet the project requirements, your application is more easily maintained.

OOT increases the time you spend identifying the application's points of modification, because polymorphism and inheritance spread the features and functionality of an object throughout several classes. Therefore, the OOT-based application is less easily maintained.

Conversely, OBT encourages quicker identification of the application's points of modification, because the features and functionality of an object are contained within the object itself. OBT, coupled with OneWorld's well-defined interactive- and batch-application architecture, together create an environment in which you can quickly see the places where an application needs modification to meet requirements.

166

Object Naming Conventions

You'll use many object types in OneWorld to build applications for your users. Object naming conventions provide a standard for identifying and managing these objects throughout the OneWorld environment. In the Object Librarian, the object name is the unique identifier for all objects in OneWorld.

NOTE

Because it changes from release to release of OneWorld, it is important to occasionally review the object naming convention.

Table 4-1 displays the object naming convention for all objects in OneWorld. In the table, column one gives the full name of the object type, column two is the short name for the object type, and column three lists the standard format for names of these objects. In column three, *xxxx* is the system code; *yyy* is a next code; *zzzzzz* is a developer-assigned name; *eeeeeee* is the object name of an application; and *fffffff* is the object name of a table.

Object Type Long Description	Object Type	Object Name Format
Data Dictionary	DD	*xxxxdddd*
Tables	TBLE	F*xxxxyyy*
Business views	BSVW	V*fffffff*{A}
Applications	APPL	P*xxxxyyy*
NER-based business functions	BSFN	N*xxxxyyyy*
C-based business functions	BSFB	B*xxxxyyyy*
Data structures	DSTR	D*xxxxyyyy*{A}
Media object data structures	GT	Gt*xxxxyy*
Processing option data structures	PO	T*xxxxyyyy*
Reports	UBE	R*xxxxyyyy*
Forms		W*eeeeeeee*{A}

TABLE 4-1. Object Naming Convention for OneWorld

Supporting Object Librarian Tables

Five tables support the Object Librarian and store information for each object.

Object Librarian Master (F9860)

The Object Librarian Master table (F9860) contains the header information for each object in OneWorld. Every object in OneWorld is uniquely identified by the object name. The Object Librarian Master table includes the following information:

- Object name (for example, F0101 for the Address Book table's object name)

- Description

- System code (for example, system code 01 for all objects in the Address Book module)

- Object type (see Table 4-1)

Object Librarian Detail (F9861)

The Object Librarian Detail table (F9861) stores the location of all OneWorld objects on the corporate network, and the environment to which they're assigned. The table stores information on the checkout status of the object, and where it is currently located. The Object Librarian Detail table stores the following information:

- Client or server name

- Path code, such as DEVB733

- Check-in or checkout status code

- Software action request (SAR) number

NOTE

When you check an object out, the system copies the RDB specification that defines the object in Central Objects and translates it to TAM specifications on your client. When you check the object in, the system copies the TAM specification definition that you modified and translates it to the RDB specification in Central Objects to update the object.

One of the most useful data items in the Object Librarian Detail table is the SAR number, which is discussed in Chapter 8. The SAR number is useful for two purposes: tracking application defects and object identification in development projects. You assign a SAR number to application defects to track the status of the defect and to provide an identifier for the solution to the problem. In development projects, SAR numbers identify a group of common objects for a module or an application.

Object Librarian Function Detail (F9862)

The Object Librarian Function Detail table (F9862) stores one record for each BSFN. Since a BSFN can contain more than one function, the table maps the object name of the BSFN to the functions it contains, making it easy to find a given function in a set of BSFNs. The Object Librarian Function Detail table stores the following information:

- Object name

- Function name

- Description

Object Librarian Business Function Object Relationships (F9863)

The Object Librarian Business Object Relationships table (F9863) contains the dependencies for a C-based BSFN. These dependencies are used to ensure that all other header files referenced in the BSFN's header file are linked when the object is built during compile time.

C- and NER-based business functions and tables are the only objects in OneWorld with header files. These files contain information on how to properly call and communicate to the table or business function.

Form Information (F9865)

The Form Information table (F9865) identifies all the forms used within an interactive application; the table also identifies the online help file used for each form. As you add or delete forms from an application, the table is updated with information about them and their corresponding online help files. The Form Information table contains the following information:

- Form name

- Form ID

- Application ID

- Help filename

Supporting Applications

Several other supporting applications use the five Object Librarian tables for specific purposes. These supporting applications, discussed next, provide advanced functionality that is not present in the Object Librarian and help you find information on the state of all OneWorld objects in the system.

Business Function Search and Edit

The Business Function Search and Edit application provides an easy mechanism for finding a C- or NER-based function and the BSFN object to which it is assigned. For example, the Data Dictionary Glossary Item BSFN (B9200005) contains the functions Update Related Glossary Tables and Retrieve Error Message Info.

To access the Business Function Search and Edit application, follow these steps:

1. From the Object Librarian application (P986101), choose Function Search from the Form menu. The Business Function Search and Edit form appears, as shown in Figure 4-11.

2. Use the QBE line to find the function you need.

3. When your function is found, select it. The Business Function Source Librarian form appears. You can check the business function in or out from any environment in the Business Function Source Librarian form, and also launch the Business Function Design application (discussed in Chapter 13).

Promotion Manager

The Promotion Manager application (P98603), located on the Object Management menu (GH9081), allows you to search for objects by SAR, user ID, and workstation name. The Promotion Manager (Figure 4-12) provides real-time results that let you view the status of all objects for any environment.

TIP

If you don't know what objects you have checked out, you can use the Promotion Manager to identify those objects. This application is particularly useful if it has been a long time since you have done any object development.

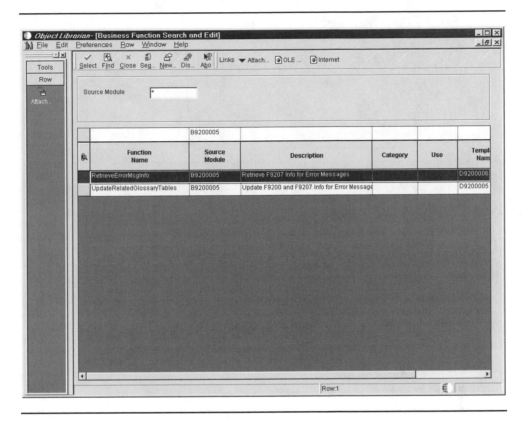

FIGURE 4-11.   Business Function Search and Edit form of the Object Librarian
application (P986101)

The Promotion Manager performs three functions for an object in OneWorld:
reviewing, promoting, and merging, as explained next.

Review   After you have searched for an object using the Promotion Manager, you
can use the Review function to inspect the object's record in the Object Librarian. To
review an object, select the item from the grid and choose Review from the Row menu.

Promote   The Promote row exit in Promotion Manager copies an object from one
path code to another. This is particularly useful for moving objects from the

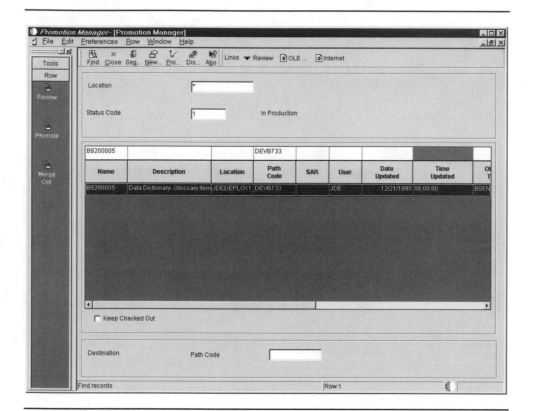

FIGURE 4-12.   Promotion Manager application (P98603)

development environment to the Conference Room Pilot environment for testing. To promote an object, fill in the destination path code at the bottom, select the object to promote, and choose Promote from the Row menu.

Merge   The Merge function in Promotion Manager provides developers and system administrators the ability to merge one or more objects with their respective objects in another environment. To merge an object into another environment, fill in the destination path code at the bottom, select the object to promote, and click the Merge Opt row exit.

Cross Reference Utility

The Cross Reference Utility application (P980011) is located in the Cross Application Development Tools menu (GH902). This application helps you find where an object is used throughout OneWorld, and view the relationships between that object and its supporting components.

N O T E

The Cross Reference files are not automatically built during a full install of OneWorld, nor are they rebuilt when objects are modified. To update or initialize the Cross Reference files, execute the All Objects version (XJDE0001) of the Built Cross Reference File batch application (R980011).

Here are the steps to search all the locations where an object is used:

1. Execute the Cross Reference Utility application (P980011) on the Cross Application Development Tools menu (GH902). The Cross Reference form appears, as shown in Figure 4-13.

2. Select the tab for the type of object you want to search for. The panel for that object type will appear. The panels for all object types are similar.

3. The Data Structure panel lists several choices for viewing the locations of data structures in OneWorld. Select one of the options, such as Everywhere A Data Structure Is Used. The next window lists the applicable locations where the data structure is used, as shown here:

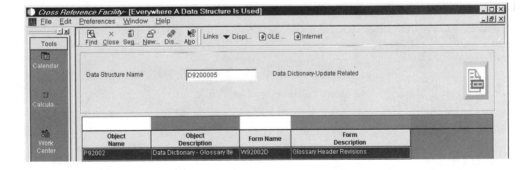

Checkout Log

Once you have created an object and checked it in for the first time, the Object Librarian logs all movement of the object. An object can be checked in, checked out, and promoted to another environment. All of this information is stored in the Checkout Log table (F9882) that exists in the system data source (SYSB733).

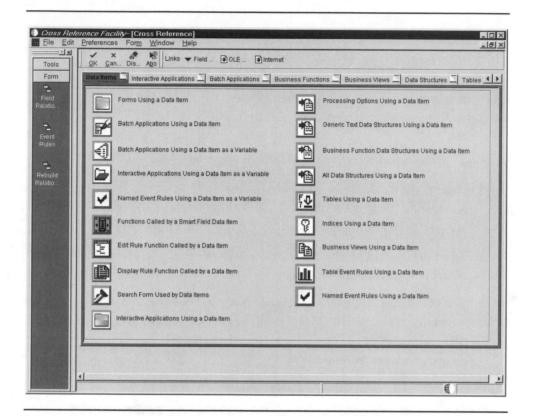

FIGURE 4-13. Cross Reference form of the Cross Reference Utility application (P980011)

To view the Checkout Log, double-click the Checkout Log application (P9882) on the Object Management menu (GH9081). The Work With Checkout Log form appears, as shown in Figure 4-14. Use the QBE line to find the object or objects for which you want to view the checkout status.

CAUTION

Execute the Purge Checkout Log batch application (R988200, version 002) on a regular basis to clean up outdated entries from the Checkout Log. If you neglect this task, the Checkout Log table (F9882) will grow to an excessive size.

Object Librarian Examples

The following sections show the most common uses of the Object Librarian. You will perform these tasks on a daily basis while developing applications.

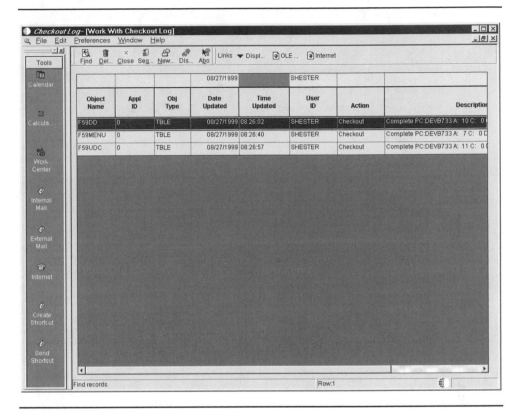

Object Name	Appl ID	Obj Type	Date Updated	Time Updated	User ID	Action	Description
			08/27/1999		SHESTER		
F59DD	0	TBLE	08/27/1999	08:26:02	SHESTER	Checkout	Complete PC:DEVB733 A: 10 C: 0
F59MENU	0	TBLE	08/27/1999	08:26:40	SHESTER	Checkout	Complete PC:DEVB733 A: 7 C: 0
F59UDC	0	TBLE	08/27/1999	08:26:57	SHESTER	Checkout	Complete PC:DEVB733 A: 11 C: 0

FIGURE 4-14.   Work With Checkout Log application (P9882)

N O T E

*To access the Object Librarian (P9860), type **OL** into the Fast Path box of OneWorld Explorer, or execute the application from the Cross Application Development Tools menu (GH902).*

Checking an Object In and Out

During a development project, checking objects in and out is a routine task that you will perform several times throughout a session. The checkout mechanism provides an efficient means of object management over a corporate network.

N O T E

You can modify an object only when it is checked out to your workstation. This ensures that modifications to an object occur in an orderly fashion.

When you check out an object, the TAM specs located on the local workstation are updated from the RDB specs on the enterprise server. After you have modified the object and checked it back in, the RDB specs on the enterprise server are updated with the TAM specs from your workstation.

The object's status code changes as you check the object in and out. This status code allows other developers in the organization to see who has objects checked out and the status of those objects. Here are the status codes for all objects:

Object Status Code	Description
1	In Production environment
2	In Test environment
3	In Development environment
4	Custom version
5	In use by vocabulary overrides

To check an object out, follow these steps:

1. Execute the Object Librarian application (P9860) to open the Work With Object Librarian form (Figure 4-15).

NOTE

If you are using the stand-alone version of OneWorld, skip to the next example in this section ("Forcing an Object Checkout").

2. Use the QBE line in the Work with Object Librarian form to find the object you need to modify.

3. Highlight the desired object and click the Select button. The Application Design Aid form appears, as shown in Figure 4-16.

4. Select the object to be modified, and click the Check Out row exit.

5. During the checkout process, a message form appears, prompting you to verify the action; click OK. Once the checkout process is finished, you can click the Design button and the system launches the appropriate design tool for that object.

6. Once you have the object checked out and you have clicked the Design button, the system will display the design form for the object, which is used to provide

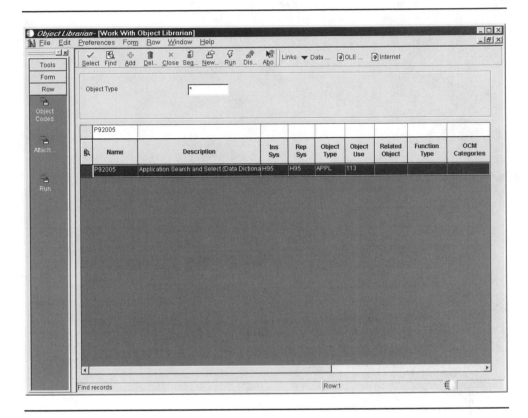

FIGURE 4-15. Work With Object Librarian form of the Object Librarian application (P9860)

further information of the object or launch the development tool for the object. For example, after you click the Design button for a business function object, the Business Function Design form appears, as shown in Figure 4-17. This form displays all the functions contained in the BSFN. If you want to modify the object, select the Edit menu item from the Form menu. The NER or C function tool will then appear and allow you to edit the function.

N O T E

All of the menu items that are found under the Form and Row menus for a form are also displayed in their respective exit bar. The exit bars are located to the left of the form, and they are sliding menus to provide you with quick access to links related to the form.

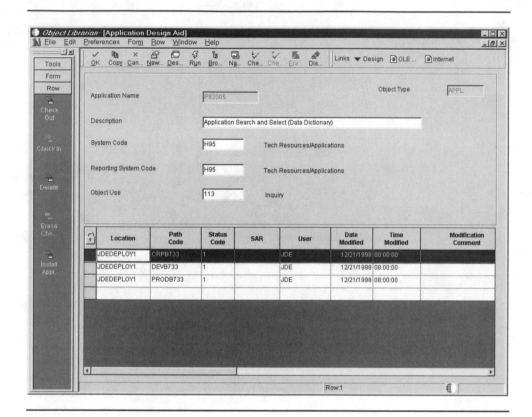

FIGURE 4-16. Application Design Aid form of the Object Librarian application (P9860)

NOTE

The checkout and check-in processes are identical for any object. When the Design button is clicked after the checkout process, however, the system displays the object's respective application design tool. For example, interactive applications are designed with FDA, batch applications are designed with RDA, tables are designed with TDA, and so on.

To check an object in, follow these steps:

1. Execute the Object Librarian application (P9860) to open the Work with Object Librarian form, shown earlier in Figure 4-15.

2. Use the QBE line on the Work With Object Librarian form to find the object you checked out.

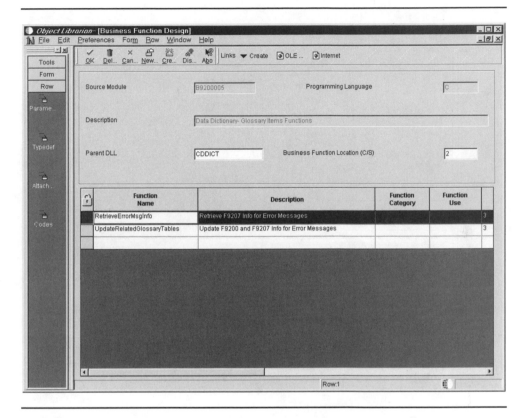

FIGURE 4-17. Business Function Design form of the Object Librarian application (P9860)

3. Highlight the desired object and click the Select button. The Application Design Aid form appears, as shown in Figure 4-16.

4. Select the object and click the Check In row exit. The Object Librarian Check In form appears, as shown in Figure 4-18.

5. Enter the SAR number for the object, and the environment—development (DEV733)—it needs to be checked into. If you need to keep the object checked out, select the Keep Checked Out check box.

N O T E

The check-in process is a single transaction. Therefore, if the process is interrupted, it will immediately terminate and roll back the transaction, allowing you to perform the check-in at a later time.

Client Modifications Using OneWorld

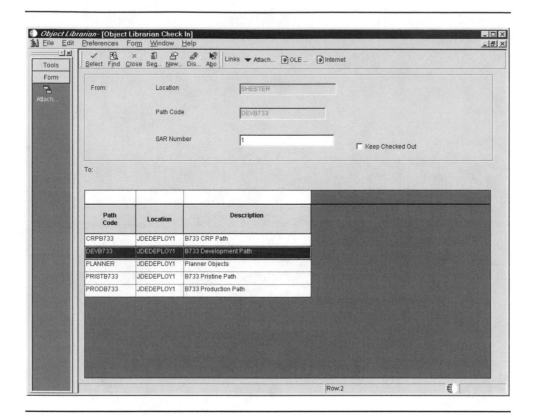

FIGURE 4-18.   Object Librarian Check In form of the Object Librarian application
(P9860)

Forcing an Object Checkout

When you develop applications on a stand-alone version of OneWorld, your client
workstation is not connected to any enterprise or deployment server. This prevents
the stand-alone version of OneWorld from having any access to RDB specs. Since the
checkout process includes translating the object to TAM specs from RDB specs, the
stand-alone version of OneWorld cannot check out objects as you normally would.
Therefore, you'll have to force the checkout of an object if you want to modify or view
it in the stand-alone version of OneWorld to avoid the translation of the object from
RDB to TAM specs.

N O T E

After you perform a forced checkout, the Object Librarian Detail table (F9861)
will be updated on your client, showing that you have the object checked out.

Another situation that requires a forced checkout is when the RDB specs on the enterprise server become corrupted or deleted. To recover the lost or damaged RDB specs for one or more objects, force an object checkout and then check the object back in from a machine that has a known good set of TAM specs.

N O T E

The opposite of forced object checkout is forced object check-in, discussed in a later example. Forced object check-in is nothing more than erasing the checkout record for the object.

Here are the steps to perform a forced object checkout.

1. Execute the Object Librarian application (P9860) to open the Work with Object Librarian form, shown earlier in Figure 4-15.

2. Use the QBE line of the Object Librarian application to find the object you need to check out.

3. Highlight the object and click the Select button. On the Application Design form, enter the following information into an empty row in the grid:

   - Location: *Your machine name*
   - Path Code: Type **DEMO** for the stand-alone version; or, if you are not using the stand-alone version, enter the name of the environment, such as **DEVEL**.
   - Status Code: 3

N O T E

To find the machine name of your workstation, select About OneWorld from the Help menu on OneWorld Explorer. When the dialog box appears, copy the name located in the Installed Location field to the Location field on the Application Design form.

4. Click OK to submit the change to the F9861 table.

5. Perform step 2 again, and the object's status code will show that you have the object checked out.

Client Modifications Using OneWorld

6. If you are not using the stand-alone version of OneWorld and you have finished with the object, check in the object you just modified, and your changes will be reflected in the RDB specs.

Creating and Deleting an Object

The following examples show you how to create and delete objects in OneWorld.

Creating an Object Following are the steps for creating an object.

1. Execute the Object Librarian application (P9860) to open the Work with Object Librarian form, shown earlier in Figure 4-15.

2. In the Object Type field, enter the type of object you want to create (see Table 4-1). For example, to create an interactive application, type **APPL** in the Object Type field.

3. Click the Add button. The Add Object form appears (Figure 4-19).

4. Fill in the following information on the Add Object form:

   - Object Name: See Table 4-1.

   - Description.

   - System Code: The code entered here will default into the Reporting System Code field.

   - Column Prefix: Only used for table objects.

   - Object Use: A UDC value that designates the use of the object.

   - Source Language: Only appears on the BSFN form.

   - SAR Number.

5. Click the OK button. The Application Design Aid form appears (shown earlier in Figure 4-16). Click the Design button on the form to begin definition of the newly created object.

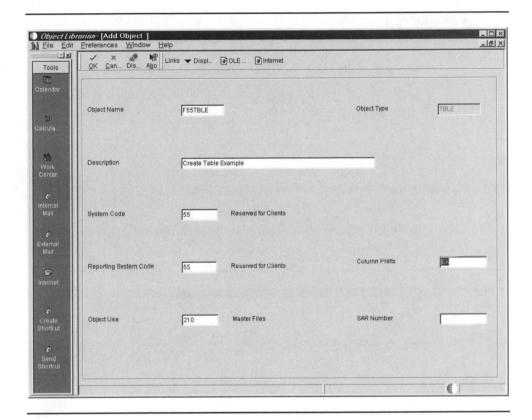

FIGURE 4-19.   Add Object form of the Object Librarian application (P9860)

Deleting an Object   Following are the steps for deleting an object.

CAUTION

Be careful when deleting an object; this change is permanent and cannot be undone.

NOTE

When deleting an object, you must first ensure that detail lines do not exist in the Application Design Aid form, as shown in Figure 4-16. Each detail line represents a checkout record for the object.

1. Execute the Object Librarian application (P9860) to open the Work with Object Librarian form, shown earlier in Figure 4-15.

2. Use the QBE line of the Object Librarian application to find the object you need to delete.

3. Highlight the object and click the Delete button.

NOTE

If the object exists on a server, you must provide a password to delete the object.

4. The Delete Object Specifications form appears, as shown in Figure 4-20. Click OK to verify that you want to delete the object.

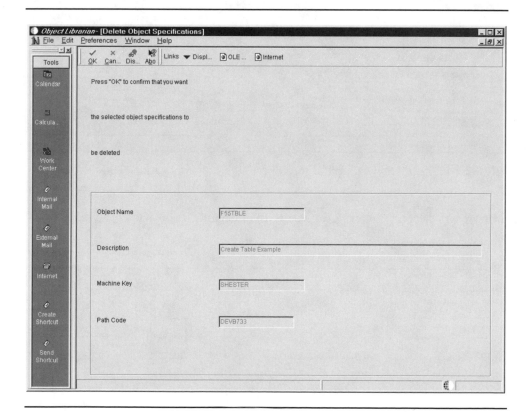

FIGURE 4-20.   Delete Object Specifications form of the Object Librarian application (P9860)

Erasing a Checkout Record

Sometimes you will not need to check an object back into the environment. For example, it may be that you have checked out an object to review another developer's work; or you may want to delete the changes you made previously; or you may be using the stand-alone version of OneWorld. Simply erasing the checkout record for the object will ensure that the object will not be checked back into the server.

N O T E

The stand-alone version of OneWorld does not contain any RDB specs. Since the check-in process includes translating the object to RDB specs from TAM specs, only the checkout record of an object can be erased in the stand-alone version of OneWorld.

To erase a checkout record, follow these steps:

1. Execute the Object Librarian application (P9860) to open the Work with Object Librarian form, shown earlier in Figure 4-15.

2. Use the QBE line of the Object Librarian application to find the object that contains the checkout record you want to erase.

3. Highlight the object and click the Select button. The Application Design Aid form appears (Figure 4-16).

4. Highlight the checkout record you want to erase, and click the Erase button.

Putting It All Together

This chapter's overview of application development in OneWorld will help decrease your project's overall development time and increase your productivity as a developer. As you can see, along with your primary job of designing and building OneWorld applications, you are also responsible for many other tasks in support of your development projects.

The OneWorld development cycle is very straightforward and contains no hidden secrets. The starting point for application development is the point where an object's dependencies do not affect it. Properly following the sequence of application development may be boring, but it gets better results.

To ensure that your development project does not suffer from unrealistically high expectations and demands, you need to properly analyze it. This analysis helps you measure the scope and complexity of the project from the outset, to encourage proper allocation of resources. Just as development tools are meant for specific purposes, so are the applications that you design and build. Spend the time to analyze your business requirements. Create the window and application navigation diagrams, which represent how the application meets and exceeds your requirements.

The Object Librarian is the single most important application in OneWorld that you will use to support your development projects. Get to know the features and functionality of the Object Librarian and its supporting applications. Your time and efforts in studying the Object Librarian will not go to waste.

CHAPTER 5

Form Design Aid

When developing in OneWorld, an important element of each project is to provide a way for the users to enter information interactively. J.D. Edwards provides the Form Design Aid (FDA) tool for creating interactive applications. Using the forms you design in FDA, the user can navigate through your application to view, add, change, and delete information.

FDA provides predefined forms to help you to create simple or complex applications that can tie to one or multiple tables. Your applications can be constructed of one or more forms and can call other applications, as well.

To describe how to use FDA to create the forms for your interactive applications, the following topics are discussed in this chapter:

- **Form Types**   There are seven different form types available in OneWorld. You need to understand the uses of each type so that you can choose the appropriate forms for your application.

- **Creating Forms**   You create forms using the FDA application. You can set various form properties and characteristics.

- **Adding Form Controls**   Once a form has been created, you'll add controls that let a user view data or interact with the form.

- **Modifying a Form's Grid**   You can also make changes to the form's grid, including adding columns and setting grid and grid column properties.

- **Overriding Data Dictionary Triggers**   You can override Data Dictionary item edits so that your form controls behave appropriately.

- **Changing the Data Structure of a Form**   If necessary, you can change a form's data structure to modify the way that it receives and passes values.

- **Designing a Form Layout**   Once controls are in place, you can move them around and change their size or location, as well as edit the grid on the form.

- **Creating Menu/Toolbar Exits**   An important part of application design is the creation of menu and toolbar exits, which (among other things) give you controls and events that create links between applications.

- **Creating a Sample Address Book Application**   The chapter ends by working through example of creating a functioning Address Book application.

Form Types

In OneWorld, an application is made up of one or more forms, each designed for a different purpose. Whether you're creating a new application or modifying an existing one, you need a thorough understanding of the types of forms and how they are used. Table 5-1 provides an overview of the form types. The last column, Change Data?, indicates whether the form is used to change data, although you can add ER to any form to allow data alteration.

The buttons on the forms work as follows:

- The Find button starts the query to the database and the load of the grid.

- The Select button processes the grid rows chosen by the user.

- The Add button is used to call another form in order to add new records

- The Copy button is used to call another form in order to paste information copied from the current form.

- The Delete button deletes the selected grid row.

- The Close button closes the form.

- The OK button saves the contents of the form to the database.

- The Cancel button causes the form to exit without saving any changes made.

Find/Browse Forms

Every application has a starting point, or a form that is the first form to appear when the user opens an application from a menu. The Find/Browse form, shown in Figure 5-1, is usually the entry to an application. Generally, it is used to view the contents of one table, although it can be used for more complex purposes. This form consists of a header and a grid with a Query By Example (QBE) line. In addition, it has a toolbar and pull-down menus.

The QBE line in a Find/Browse form allows users to enter their search specifications to narrow the amount of data that is displayed on the grid. Columns that are not in the business view do not have QBE capability and are grayed out in the QBE line. You can limit the use of the QBE line even further by creating an OCM mapping. This lets you limit the QBE capabilities for the table to allow only queries on key fields or

Form Type	Number of Business Views	Grid	Toolbar	Available Buttons	Change Data?
Find/Browse	One	Yes	Yes	Add, Close, Copy, Delete, Find, Select	No, except for deleting rows
Search & Select	One	Yes	Yes	Close, Find, Select	No
Fix/Inspect	One	No	Yes	OK, Cancel	Yes
Header/Detail	Two	Yes	Yes	OK, Find, Delete, Cancel	Yes, in header and grid
Headerless Detail	One	Yes	Yes	OK, Find, Delete, Cancel	Yes, in grid only
Parent/Child	One	Yes	Yes	Add, Close, Copy, Delete, Find, Select	No, except for deleting rows
Message Form	None	No	No	OK, Cancel	No

TABLE 5-1.   Form Properties

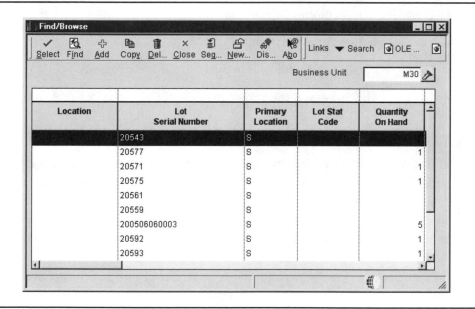

FIGURE 5-1.   A Find/Browse form in OneWorld

disallow QBE entirely. This also grays out the QBE Columns. For more information about OCM mappings, see Chapter 3.

Users can also use the Find/Browse form to search, view, and select multiple records within a grid. Users can exit the Find/Browse form to other forms within this or another application.

N O T E

To allow users to work with multiple records in a Find/Browse form's grid, you need to turn on the Multiple Select option in the form's grid properties. See the "Modifying Grid Properties" section, later in this chapter, for information about setting grid properties.

The standard buttons that will appear when you create a Find/Browse form are Find, Close, and Select. In addition, you can add Delete, Add, and Copy buttons to this form. For example, you may want to include a Delete button if the application does not contain a Headerless Detail form.

N O T E

You can add buttons to your forms by using the Menu/Toolbar Exits functionality. See "Creating Menu/Toolbar Exits," later in this chapter, for more information.

Search & Select Forms

A Search & Select form is designed to help the user find a value for a data item. This form displays values from the database in the grid. When a user chooses a value from the grid and clicks the Select button, that value is returned to the field on the preceding form. Data in a Search & Select form cannot be edited.

A Search & Select form, shown in Figure 5-2, looks similar to a Find/Browse form but has fewer features. For example, it doesn't have as many predefined buttons and it's not designed for anything other than selecting a value. The buttons on a Search & Select form are Find, Close, and Select. You can attach only one business view to this form type.

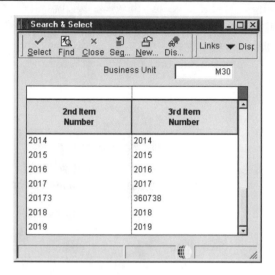

FIGURE 5-2. A Search & Select form in OneWorld

Fix/Inspect Forms

The Fix/Inspect form, shown in Figure 5-3, allows users to view, add, or update a record in a table. This form is usually called from a Find/Browse or a Headerless or Header/Detail form. To call the Fix/Inspect form from another form, a user typically clicks the Add or Copy button or selects a grid row and clicks the Select button.

Users can only modify one record at a time in Fix/Inspect forms. This form does not have a grid, and you can attach only one business view to it.

The Fix/Inspect form has two different modes, add and update, and will process differently depending on the selected mode. For example, if a Fix/Inspect form is called in update mode, it will load information from the database; but in add mode, it will not. This form automatically updates the database when the user clicks the OK button. The only other predefined button for this form is the Cancel button.

Header/Detail Forms

The Header/Detail form, shown in Figure 5-4, lets users view, add, change, or delete several records at a time. Like the Fix/Inspect form, the Header/Detail form can be in add or update mode. Header/Detail forms include an input-capable grid that allows the user to add or update records.

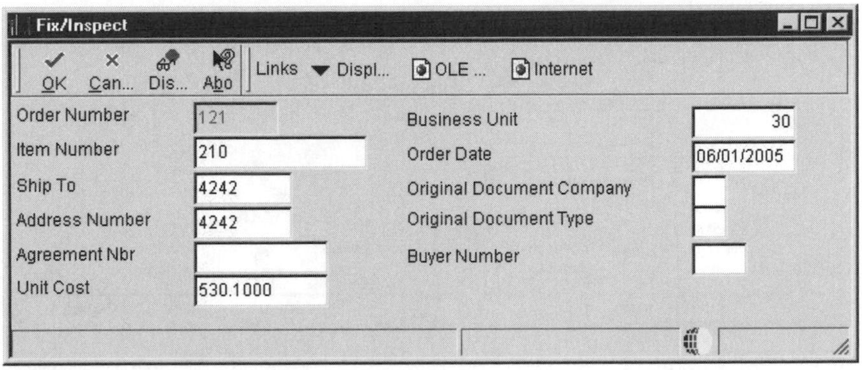

FIGURE 5-3. A Fix/Inspect form in OneWorld

This form is designed to be used with two tables that have a relationship of one header record to multiple detail records. For example, a sales order includes an order header record saved in one table, and multiple sales-order detail records that are saved in another table. You attach two business views to Header/Detail forms: one for the form and one for the grid, where the header view is attached to the form, and the detail view is attached to the grid.

The standard buttons that appear when you create a Header/Detail form are the OK and Cancel buttons. You can also add Copy, Delete, and Find buttons.

Headerless Detail Forms

The Headerless Detail form, shown in Figure 5-5, looks and acts like the Header/Detail form except that it is used with one table. The form shows information from only one business view. Headerless Detail forms include an input-capable grid that allows the user to add or update records. At the top, the form displays data that is common to all the records within the grid and is used to select records that will fill the grid.

The standard buttons that will appear when you create a Headerless Detail form are OK and Cancel. You can also add Copy, Delete, and Find buttons.

Parent/Child Browse Forms

A Parent/Child Browse form is similar to a Find/Browse form in that it is used to view data in a grid, but the Parent/Child Browse form displays the data hierarchically, as

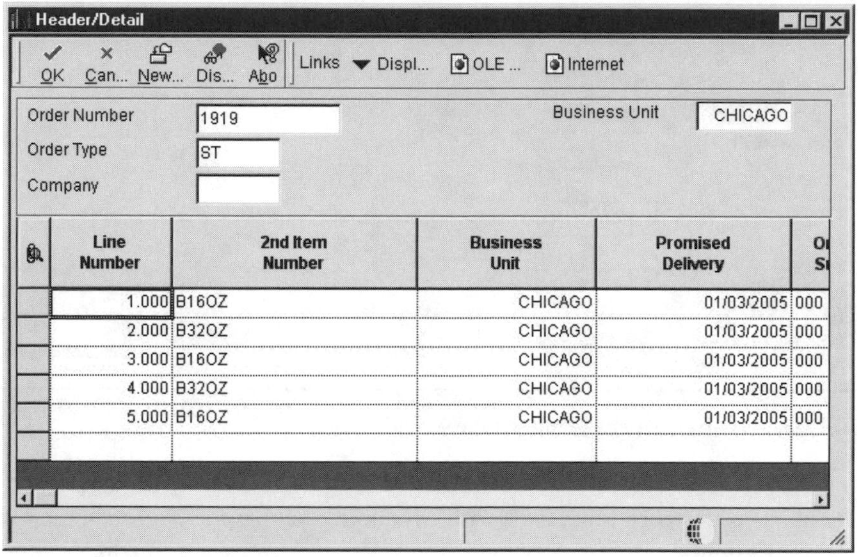

FIGURE 5-4. A Header/Detail form in OneWorld

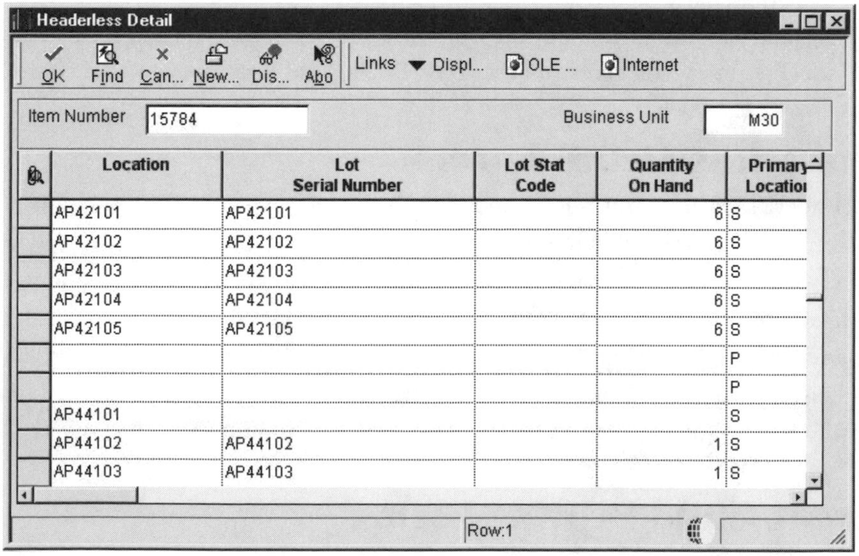

FIGURE 5-5. A Headerless Detail form in OneWorld

shown in Figure 5-6. A tree control on the left side of the form represents the parent-child relationship, with nodes that can be expanded to show the contents. The right side of the form presents a grid that displays additional information about the nodes in the tree control. You attach only one business view to this form type.

The standard buttons that will appear when you create a Parent/Child Browse form are Find, Close, and Select. You can add Add, Delete, and Copy buttons.

Message Forms

The Message form, shown in Figure 5-7, displays a message or requests action from the user. This is the only form type that doesn't use a business view. It's designed to pop up a dialog box to confirm a user's actions, such as deleting a record. You can add only static text and push-button controls to this form; typically, it has only OK and Cancel buttons.

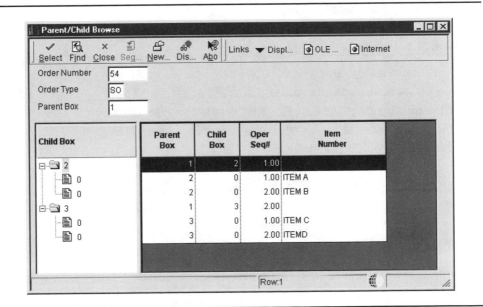

FIGURE 5-6. A Parent/Child Browse form in OneWorld

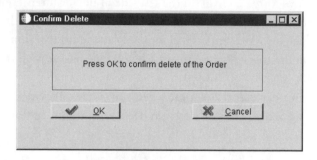

FIGURE 5-7.   A Message form in OneWorld

Creating Forms

Before you begin developing an application, you must decide what forms it will contain and how you want them to work together. You also need to establish the goal of the application in order to determine the steps you need to take before creating it. To help establish what the forms in your application will do, you should design application flow diagrams, as discussed in Chapter 4.

N O T E

Is your application going to use an existing table? If the table you want to use doesn't exist yet, that's a good sign you're getting a little ahead of yourself if you're already trying to design a form. First, you'll need to create the necessary data items, and then create the table and business view. See Chapter 11 for more information about Data Dictionary items and tables.

Here are the steps typically used to create a new application:

1. Plan the forms for the application.

2. Add an application object to the Object Librarian.

3. Create each form in the application.

4. Design each form by putting controls on the form.

5. Add logic using ER.

6. Test the application.

This section describes how to accomplish these steps in the OneWorld FDA application.

Planning Your Forms

Most OneWorld applications have a similar structure. In general, most applications start with a Find/Browse form, which calls either a Fix/Inspect or a Headerless Detail form. This sounds simple enough, but in practice it can become complicated.

Deciding Which Types of Forms to Create

The answers to the following questions will help you to design the forms for your application:

- Is your application going to change, add, or delete data in a table?

- Do you want users to be able to delete records on the form?

- Do you want to prompt users before they delete records? What about prompts for add and update operations?

- How is the information organized in the database? Is there a header file and a detail file? Is the information hierarchical in nature?

- If your application is going to alter data, do you want it to change one record at a time or multiple records at the same time?

- Do you want the data to appear in a tree format or only in the grid?

The answers to these questions will help you decide how many forms you need and how they should interact. For example, if you're going to change only one record at a time, you'll need to create a Fix/Inspect form. For changes to multiple table rows, you'll need to create a Header/Detail or Headerless Detail form. If the data is hierarchical in nature, you'll need a Parent/Child form. For viewing the data only, with no updates allowed, you'll need a Find/Browse form.

Developing a Form Naming Convention

Each form's name (its title) is very important because it should tell the user what the form is used for. You should use a consistent pattern for each form type so that users can quickly determine a form's purpose. OneWorld uses the following standards for its form names.

- Find/Browse or Parent/Child form names begin with "Work With," as in "Work With Address Book."

- Headerless and Header/Detail form names usually contain "Enter," as in "Enter Routing."

- Fix/Inspect forms usually end with the word "Revisions," as in "Item Master Revisions."

- Search & Select forms typically have the words "Search & Select" in the title.

- Message forms usually start with the word "Confirm," as in "Confirm Delete."

Choosing Business Views for Forms

Attaching a business view is simple, but deciding which business view to use might be more difficult. It's important to understand what a business view will do inside an application. The business view is the communication layer between your application and the database, controlling what information is fetched or updated in the database. If you have five items in the business view, only those five items will be fetched from the database.

You should decide which business views to use—or whether to create new ones—before you start creating forms. When you've decided which business views are needed, decide what information from the database will be displayed in the form. For example, if you want to display information from data items AAA and BBB from Table F550001, you need a business view that exists over Table F550001, such as V550001. Check the existing business views in the system to see if there is one that already contains the data items you need.

Choose carefully, because some business views contain many other data items besides the ones you need. If you attach this business view, you may compromise system performance because it will take longer to fetch those fields unused from the database. You may need to create a different, more appropriate business view for just this form.

NOTE

See Chapter 11 for information about how to create or modify business views.

Creating a OneWorld Object

When you create a new application, you must create a new object in the Object Librarian. If you are modifying an existing object, simply check out the application and click the Design button.

To create a new application object, follow these steps:

1. In OneWorld Explorer, type **OL** in the Fast Path box and press ENTER. The Work With Object Librarian form appears.

2. In the Object Librarian, type **APPL** in the Object Type field and click the Add button, as shown in Figure 5-8. The Add Object form appears.

3. Enter the application name in the Application Name field. The name usually follows the naming convention of P*XXX0000*, where P stands for program, *XXX* is the system code, and *0000* is a unique number. In our example, the application name is **P5510121**.

4. Enter a description of the application in the Description field. This can be anything you want, but be sure it is actually descriptive. In our example, the description is **Address Book**. Other examples of descriptions might be Customer Preference Search and Customer Preference Master.

5. Fill in the Product Code field. The product code value determines to which module the application is assigned. In our example, the product code is **55**. System codes are discussed in Chapter 4, and a list of them is provided in Appendix A.

6. Fill in the Product System Code field. This value is usually the same as product code value.

7. In the Object Use field, specify what this application will be used for. In our example, the code is **110**. The values for this field are defined in the user-defined code 98/FU. For applications, most of the time you'll type 110 (Video Programs), 310 (Browse Form), or 320 (Entry Form) in this information-only field.

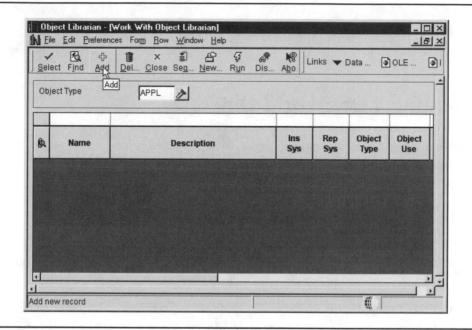

FIGURE 5-8. The Work With Object Librarian form

8. Type 1 as the SAR number or another number, as appropriate. A SAR number can be used for product control of objects inside OneWorld. See Chapter 4 for more information about SARs. Figure 5-9 shows the completed Add Object form.

9. Click the OK button in the Add Object form. The Application Design Aid form appears, as shown in Figure 5-10.

10. Click the Design button to begin creating the forms.

Creating a New Form

After you create the application object and click the Design button in the Object Librarian, the FDA application starts. To create a new form, follow these steps:

1. In FDA, select Form | Create and then choose a form type from the submenu, as shown in Figure 5-11. In this example, we are creating a Find/Browse form.

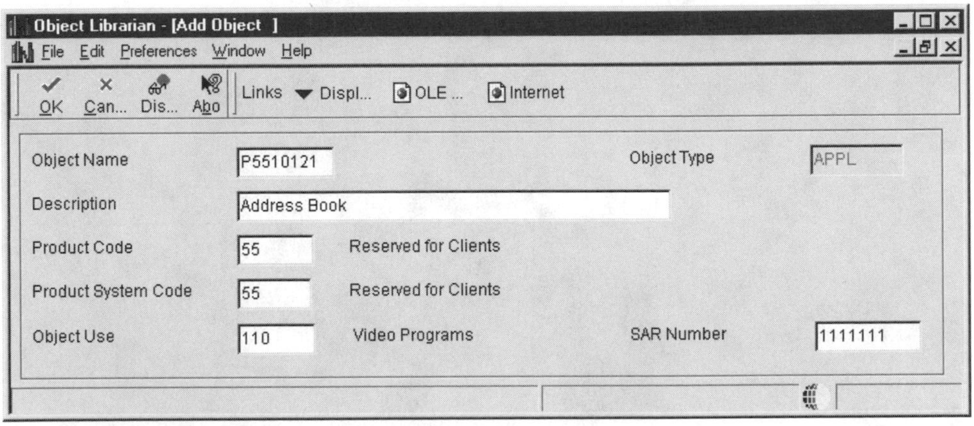

FIGURE 5-9. The Add Object form in the Object Librarian

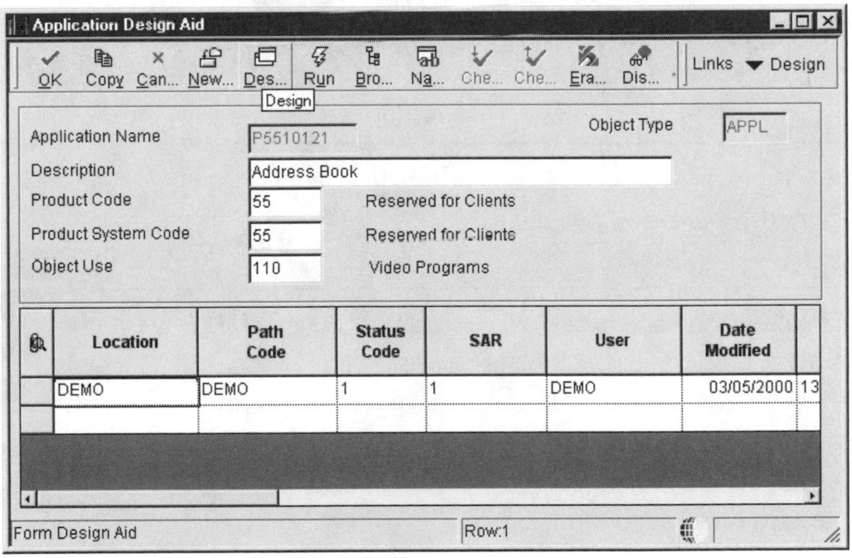

FIGURE 5-10. The Object Librarian record for an application object

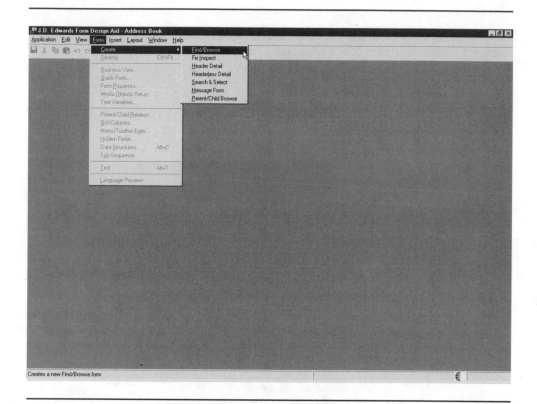

FIGURE 5-11.   Choosing to create a new form in FDA

N O T E

We will create sample Find/Browse and Fix/Inspect forms at the end of this chapter, in the "Creating a Sample Address Book Application" section.

2. The Form Properties dialog box appears, as shown in Figure 5-12. Enter a name for the form in the Title field. In the example, the form title is Work With Address Book.

3. Change the Style, Font, Options, and Wallpaper properties as desired. Form properties are discussed in detail in the next section.

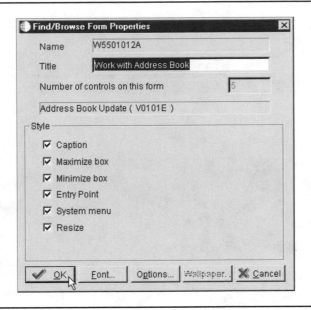

FIGURE 5-12. The Form Properties form

N O T E

You can modify form properties later on in the development process. To open the Form Properties form, either double-click on the form or choose Form | Form Properties.

4. Click OK to close the Form Properties form. The form appears in FDA, as shown in Figure 5-13.

5. Select Layout | Size To Guide. This assigns the standard 640 × 480 size to your form. The blue line surrounding the form represents the standard 640 × 480 size.

6. Click the form and select Form | Business View. The Individual Object Search and Select form appears.

7. Type the name of the business view, such as **V0101E**, that you want to attach to the form in the Object Name QBE line and click the Find button. Highlight the

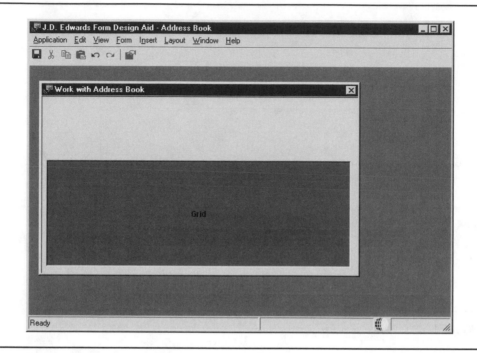

FIGURE 5-13.   A new form in FDA

row and click Select, as shown in Figure 5-14. If you're creating a Header/Detail form, click the grid and repeat this step to attach a business view to the grid.

TIP

If you're modifying an existing application and you need to see what business view is attached to a particular form, check the form's properties. The business view appears below the form name.

Setting Form Properties

Each form has properties that you configure depending on the form type and its role (see Figure 5-12, earlier in this chapter). Most of the options designate the way the form will display at runtime.

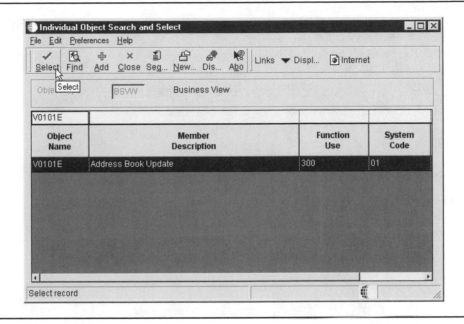

FIGURE 5-14. Attaching a business view to a new form in FDA

Style Properties

The Style section of the Form Properties form includes the properties listed in Table 5-2.

Form Property	Description
Caption	Displays the form name in the upper-left corner of the form.
Maximize Box	Maximizes the window at runtime.
Minimize Box	Minimizes the window at runtime.
Entry Point	Specifies the form you want to appear first if your application is run from a menu.
System Menu	Displays the system menu on the top of the form at runtime.
Resize	Allows the user to resize the window at runtime (if you turn off this property, the user won't be able to resize the application).
Transaction	Includes this window in the transaction processing (for information about transaction processing, see Chapter 16). Note that this property is only available for the Fix/Inspect, Headerless, and Header/Detail forms.

TABLE 5-2. Form Style Properties

CAUTION

You can have only one entry point per application. The Entry Point property is always enabled by default for the Find/Browse form. Other forms can also be designated as the entry point, such as a Headerless Detail form that contains a Find button. If you create a new form and turn on the Entry Point property, no other forms in the application can have this property enabled.

Font Properties

Click the Font button at the bottom of the Form Properties form to access the Font form, as shown in Figure 5-15. These properties control the font style and size of the grid columns on the form. Your choices here do not affect controls on the form.

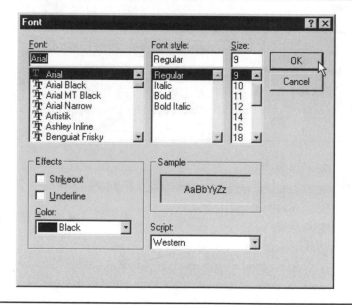

FIGURE 5-15.   The Font form

Options

Clicking the Options button at the bottom of the Form Properties brings up the Form Options form, as shown in Figure 5-16. This form contains the following options:

- **No Update on Business View** On a Fix/Inspect or Header/Detail form, this option prevents changes to form controls from being passed on to the database.

- **No Update on Grid Business View** On a Header/Detail or Headerless Detail form, this option prevents grid changes from being passed on to the grid in the database.

NOTE

A Find/Browse form cannot update data. Even if you disable a No Update option, the form won't update the database.

- **No Fetch on Form Business View** Prevents the form from fetching records when the form is loaded. This should be used only if you are going to fetch the data yourself.

- **No Fetch on Grid Business View** Prevents the form from fetching records when the Find button is clicked.

- **End Form on Add** Stops the form from exiting if the user adds a record and clicks OK. Use this option on a form in which the user will enter many records at one time, one after the other, and you don't want the form to exit after the OK button is clicked. For example, if a user clicks Add on the Find/Browse form and then enters a Fix/Inspect or a Headerless Detail form, the user can enter his or her information on that form. After clicking OK, the user will remain in the same form and can continue to enter other records.

CAUTION

Be careful when you select these options. The forms are predefined with the correct defaults. If you change these options, you may cause some problems inside your application, and these problems will be hard to track down.

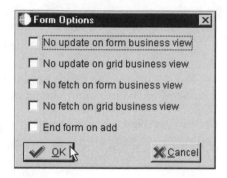

FIGURE 5-16. The Form Options form

Wallpaper

Clicking the Wallpaper button on the Form Properties form lets you change the background behind the controls on a form. If you choose tile, the wallpaper will be repeated across the form; otherwise, the image will be stretched to fit the form.

Deleting a Form

If you have a form in your application that you no longer need, you can delete it as easily as you inserted it into the application. Be very sure, however, that you want to delete the form, because you won't be able to recover your work after it's deleted.

To delete a form in FDA highlight the form itself and select Form | Destroy. You can also click the X button in the upper-right corner of the form. When the Close Window Request dialog box appears, click the Yes button to remove the form from the application.

CAUTION

After you delete a form, the only way to get it back is to exit the application without saving it, which will cause you to lose any other work you have done to the application.

Adding Form Controls

The controls you add to your forms are what users manipulate to view or change data and interact with the form. Although most controls are added to the form itself, you can add controls to the grid as well. Controls range from graphical controls, such as check boxes and radio buttons, to simple text.

Although one form can contain up to 250 controls, we recommend that you keep the number of controls on a form far below this maximum. Limiting the number of controls makes your form easier to manage. Sometimes this is hard to accomplish, however, especially if you're working with a large table.

You insert a control on a form by selecting it from the Insert menu, as shown in the following illustration. The available controls are described briefly in Table 5-3 and in more detail in the following sections.

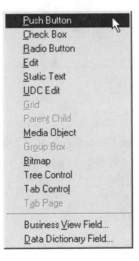

TIP

When you start adding controls to a form, the best place to start is with data fields. These are the controls that will contain the data you want to see on the form or in the grid. You can add any data item that is in the business view or any data item from the Data Dictionary as a control on the form.

Control	Description
Business View Field	A field that comes from the attached business view
Data Dictionary Field	A field not in the business view
Push Button	A button that executes events when clicked
Check Box	A control that the user can click to enter and remove a check mark to turn an item on or off
Radio Buttons	A group of controls from which the user can select only one
Edit	A control that allows the user to enter data
Static Text	A line of text on the form
UDC Edit	An edit control that has a relationship with a UDC table
Media Object	Text, an image, or an OLE object
Bitmap	A bitmap image on the form that can be clicked like a push button
Tree Control	A control that displays a parent-child relationship
Text Block	A control that contains text
Tab Control	A control that that can be added to create multiple panes (tabs) in the form

TABLE 5-3.   Form Control Types

All OneWorld controls have certain characteristics that are different from control to control, but they have common characteristics as well. For example, all controls can be placed on a form, and all controls are designed to hold or manipulate data. Some controls can have descriptions or data items associated with them, and all controls can have ER associated with them.

After you insert a control, you can specify its properties. There are three ways to access a control's properties:

- Double-click the control.

- Right-click the control and select Properties from the pop-up menu.

- Select the control and then choose Edit | Item Properties.

Some of the properties you specify for controls will apply to multiple controls. For example, the Tab Stop property allows you to specify where the users' cursors will appear when they enter a form and where it will go if they press the TAB key. The same is true with the Group property, which determines which control the cursor will enter when the user presses the arrow keys to navigate on the form. In addition to the properties displayed on the Properties form, the Control Options form allows additional properties to be set. To display this form, click the Options button.

Not all properties apply to every control. For example, you can't use the Invisible or Disabled properties on group boxes or bitmaps, but you can make business view fields invisible for data-filtering purposes.

N O T E

Any field you add to your form includes properties that you can modify. When the properties are changed, it affects the way the field can be employed by the user, as well as the field's role on the form. For example, you can disable a field so the user cannot change the value, or a field can be specified as a filter field, which will affect the way the grid is loaded. You can even hide fields.

Table 5-4 describes options that are common among controls. The properties specific to each control are discussed in the following sections.

N O T E

We will add controls to sample Find/Browse and Fix/Inspect forms at the end of this chapter, in the "Creating a Sample Address Book Application" section.

Adding Business View and Data Dictionary Fields

Many of the items you will add to the form and the grid will fall into two categories: business view fields and Data Dictionary fields. These two types of fields are basically the same—they both include the characteristics of the data item in the Data Dictionary. They can also include visual assists, as well as other attributes such as capital letters, text size, and formatting, if these attributes have been defined in the Data Dictionary. The difference is that business view fields have a relationship with the business view, and Data Dictionary fields do not. Business view fields are occasionally referred to as database fields, since the business view is tied to a table or tables. Business view fields are loaded by the application and can update the database, depending on the form type.

Fields from the business view can be used for several purposes. For example, business view fields can be used to display data, to allow users to change data, or to filter information.

Property	Use
Tab Stop	Allows the user to tab to the control instead of clicking it at runtime. You can change the tab sequence on the controls so the user can tab sequentially from one control to another (see the "Changing the Tab Sequence" section later this chapter).
Group	Allows the user to use the arrow keys to navigate through controls on a form. If this flag is turned on, it signals this control as the first in a group of controls. The user can then use the arrow keys instead of using the TAB key. When a different control with the Group property turned on is reached, that is the end of one group and the start of another.
Disabled	Prevents the user from modifying the control. You use the Disabled property when you want a field to be seen but not changed. For example, a generated sales order number that is created by the system shouldn't be changed by a user. Another example is a calculated value like a total, which can be viewed but not changed or even clicked on.
Visible	Makes a field visible or invisible. You can disable the Visible property to hide a control.
Clickable	Allows a user to click on a control. You use this property with Bitmap controls to treat a bitmap as a push button. This allows the user to click the bitmap, which will trigger a Button Clicked event.
Justification	Controls how information is displayed for the control, such as to the right, left, or centered.
Password	Treats the control like a password field. Anything the user types in this control will be displayed in asterisks (*) instead of the actual characters.
Read Only	Like the Disabled property, prevents the user from changing the control's value, but it will allow the user to click in the field. If the user clicks on the field, events like Row Is Entered will be triggered.
Do Not Clear After Add	If a form is in add mode and the user presses OK, then all the fields are cleared after a record is added to the database, unless this option is on.
Required Entry Field	This forces the user to enter a value in the control. If a value is not entered, then an error is automatically set.
Default Cursor On Add Mode	This designates the control as the initial cursor position in add mode.
Default Cursor On Update Mode	This designates the control as the initial cursor position in update mode.
No Display If Currency Is Off	This displays the control if currency processing is on, and hides it if it is off. Some fields should not be displayed unless multi-currency is on.

TABLE 5-4. General Control Properties

Adding a Single Business View Field

To insert a business view field on a form, follow these steps:

1. With your form open in the FDA, select Insert | Business View Field. The Select Database Column for Controls form appears, as shown in Figure 5-17.

2. In the Columns list box, find and select the database item (business view field) that you want to insert on your form, and then click the OK button.

3. Drag the outlined box onto the form and click once to place the control on the form.

4. Repeat steps 2 and 3 to select and place other business view fields on the form as needed.

5. When you have finished adding business view fields, click the Close button in the Select Database Column for Controls form to return to your form.

During design time, any business view field that you add to a form appears with a blue box; at runtime, the blue boxes are not visible.

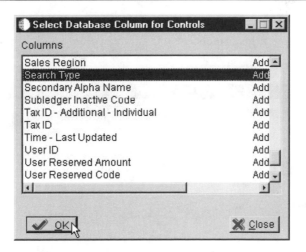

FIGURE 5-17. The Select Database Column for Controls form

Using Quick Form to Add Multiple Business View Fields

Instead of placing data items on the form one at a time, you can use a feature called Quick Form. The Quick Form tool allows you to quickly add business view data fields to a form (not to the grid). This is often the best choice when you are initially designing the form. After you use Quick Form, you can move the items to a more exact location.

CAUTION

We do not recommend you use Quick Form after you have added a large number of fields to a form, because it could relocate all of your fields.

To use Quick Form, follow these steps:

1. With your form open in FDA, select Form | Quick Form. The Quick Form Layout form appears, as shown in Figure 5-18.

2. In the Columns Per Row section, specify the number of columns you want on the form. Typically you will set this to 2, which will place two columns of controls on your form.

3. Select either Vertical Placement or Horizontal Placement. If you choose Vertical Placement, the fields you choose will fill one column and then start the next

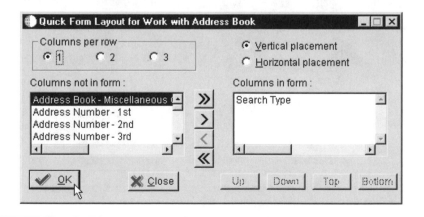

FIGURE 5-18.   The Quick Form Layout form

column. If you choose Horizontal Placement, the fields will be evenly distributed between the columns.

4. The fields displayed in Quick Form are from the business view. You can add as many fields as you want to the form from the business view. Click the right arrow button to move a field to the Columns in Form window.

5. Select and sort columns from the business view by clicking the arrow button to move fields from the left side to the right. Click the Up, Down, Top, and Bottom buttons to change the order.

6. Click OK to place the fields on the form.

7. Click Close when you are finished using Quick Form.

N O T E

If you add a lot of fields through Quick Form, you may need to resize the form or move and align fields to achieve the desired results.

Adding a Data Dictionary Field

Only business view fields update the database. Data Dictionary fields are also used to display and allow changes, but any information a user enters in these fields will not be added to the database. For example, if a user changes information in a business view field on a Fix/Inspect form and clicks OK, the data will be changed in the database. If the user changes data in a Data Dictionary field on a Fix/Inspect form and clicks OK, nothing will happen to the data (unless you added ER to specify otherwise, such as copying the Data Dictionary item to a business view field).

C A U T I O N

Do not add a data item from the Data Dictionary that is also in the business view. For example, if the data item ITM is in the business view, the form will not stop you from adding an ITM as a Data Dictionary field. However, although the form allows this addition, you'll want to avoid doing it because it can cause problems when you're reattaching business views and when the form loads data.

To add a Data Dictionary field to a form, follow these steps:

1. With your form open in the FDA, select Insert | Data Dictionary Field. The Data Dictionary Browser form appears, as shown in Figure 5-19.

2. Enter your search criteria and then press ENTER. In this example, we have entered AN8 as the alias to find in the Address Number field.

3. Select the desired Data Dictionary item, drag it to your form, and click once to place it.

During design time, the Data Dictionary fields appear with a yellow box; at runtime, the yellow boxes are not visible.

Modifying Business View and Data Dictionary Field Properties

A business view or Data Dictionary field on a form consists of two parts: the static text description and the edit control (the text box). You can change the properties of the

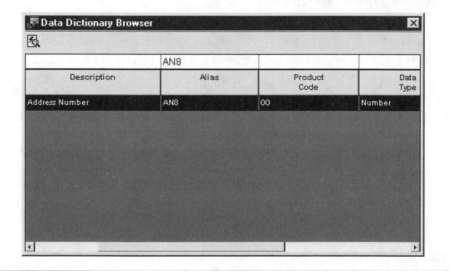

FIGURE 5-19. The Data Dictionary Browser form

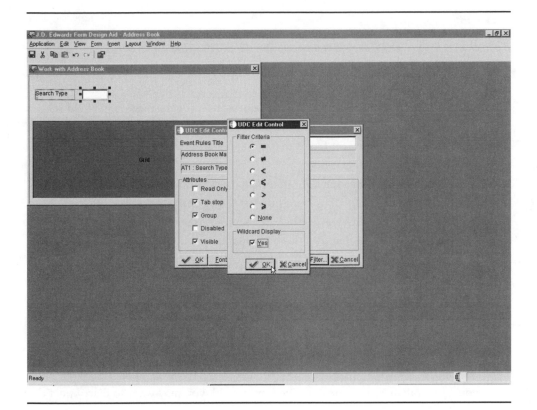

FIGURE 5-20. Modifying a business view field

field and also make it a filter field if it is a business view field. Figure 5-20 shows a
business view field, its properties, and the form for entering filter criteria.

To change the properties for either the text or the edit control, right-click the control
and select Properties from the pop-up menu. You may need to change the data item's
description if the Data Dictionary default is not sufficient. For example, sometimes the
field MCU is called Branch or Branch/Plant, or Depot or Cost Center. You can change
this description to suit your needs, and you can also change the description on the edit
control. Although the edit control's description is only visible in ER, you may need to
tweak it to make it unique, especially if you have many similar controls on the form.
Otherwise, it will be difficult to distinguish between them when you add ER code.
You can also set the other properties, as listed earlier in Table 5-4.

A filter field limits what is entered into the grid from the database. This field is
used in the same way that a QBE field is used. Since filter fields affect the loading of the
grid, a filter can only be used on forms that contain a grid (Fix/Inspect, Header/Detail,
Headerless Detail, or Search & Select).

To make the business view or Data Dictionary field a filter field, click the Filter
button in the Properties form. This brings up the Edit Control form (see Figure 5-20).
From the filter list, select the type of filter you want to use. For instance, with the =
filter specified, any value loaded into the grid must match the filter field exactly; if the
filter field were blank, any loaded record from the database would also need to have
the same field blank. If you want a blank to be treated as any value, click the Yes check
box in the Wildcard Display section. This causes an asterisk (*) to be displayed in the
control if it is blank.

Disconnecting Static Text from Business View or Data Dictionary Fields

After you add a business view or Data Dictionary field, you may want to disconnect the
static text from the edit control for several reasons:

- Because of space constraints

- To be able to move the two pieces separately

- To make a business view field invisible

To disconnect static text from controls, select the control and choose Edit |
Disconnect. You can now move the static text and the control separately. You can
also delete either one. If you want to make the field invisible, delete the text and make
the edit control invisible (by disabling its Visible property, as described in the
previous section).

Adding a Push Button

Users click a push-button control to execute the ER on the button. An example of a push button is an OK button on a Message form.

To add a push button on a form, simply select Insert | Push Button, drag the control onto the form, and click once to place it. After you insert the push button, you can set its properties by double-clicking it. This brings up the Push Button Properties form, as shown in Figure 5-21. Enter the name of the push button in the Title field. You will also want to add an ampersand symbol (&) in front of the letter that you want to use as the shortcut command key for the push button. You can set other properties as well, as listed earlier in Table 5-4. You can also change the font of the text displayed on the button by clicking the Font button in the Push Button Properties form and choosing the font you wish to use. Push buttons can be displayed on a form and clicked by the user, or you can make them hidden and use them as a subprocedure, as discussed in the following Developer's Corner, titled "Using a Push Button as a Subprocedure."

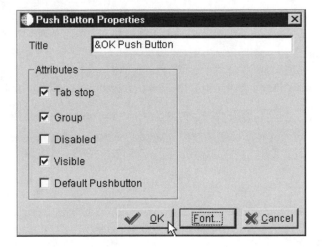

FIGURE 5-21. The Push Button Properties form

Developer's Corner

Using a Push Button as a Subprocedure

Many times when you are developing applications, it becomes necessary to have a subprocedure. A subprocedure could be a piece of ER that needs to be in many places inside the application. In the majority of the cases, you can build a business function. Any time you can create a function that does a calculation or only table I/O, we recommend you create a business function, but there will be some cases where you cannot use a business function. An example of when you cannot use a business function is when you are using a system function that is not available in a business function, such as manipulating the grid or tree controls and changes to controls. In these cases, the solution is to create a hidden push button and use that push button as a subprocedure.

An example of where you would use an invisible push button as a subprocedure is in grid-record processing. Suppose that your application calculates values that need the values of the grid fields. When the user changes one grid row, the other grid rows are updated. To update the grid, you need to loop through all the grid rows using the push-button system function and update the grid. If the grid needs to be updated on several events, it would be better to create one push button and execute this button on other events than to have the same logic on all controls.

Adding a push button to do this is the same as creating a push button for another purpose, except you make it invisible. Follow the steps as you would for a visible push button:

1. With your form open in FDA, select Insert | Push Button, drag the push button on the form and click once to place it.

2. Right-click the push button and select Event Rules.

3. On the Button Clicked event, add your ER logic from your subprocedure. When you have finished, save the ER by clicking OK.

4. Double-click the push button to display its properties.

5. Deselect the Visible check box so the push button will be hidden.

6. Go to any event that you want to execute this logic from and execute the push button by using the system function Press Button.

This button will not have parameters other than the normal variables inside ER, but it can help to speed up your coding time, as well as remove redundant code.

Adding a Check Box

You use check boxes to indicate whether a feature is enabled or disabled or when a data item has only two values. For example, if you have a business view field that has two possible values, you can create a check box that will hold the two values: 0 if unchecked or 1 if checked. The values can be anything you create, such as inbound or outbound. The check box control must be associated with a business view data item or a Data Dictionary item (see the "Associating Descriptions and Data Items with a Control" section later in this chapter).

To add a check box to a form, select Insert | Check Box, drag the control onto the form, and click once to place it. After you insert the check box, you can set its properties by double-clicking it. This brings up the Check Box Properties form, as shown in Figure 5-22. Fill in the Title field and the Checked and Un-Checked fields in the Value section to specify these values. You can set other properties as well, as listed earlier in Table 5-4.

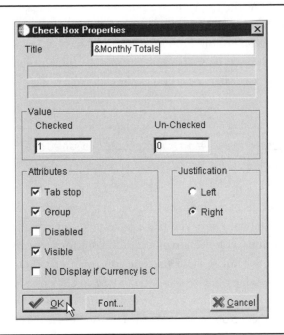

FIGURE 5-22. The Check Box Properties form

Adding Radio Buttons

You use radio buttons to give the user a selection of choices. Radio buttons got their name because they are similar to the buttons on a radio, where you push one button and the other button pops out, and only one button can be pushed in at a time. A radio button is similar to a check box but it can have one of multiple values. For example, if an item on your form can have one of three values, you might want to place three radio buttons to show these three values. When the user clicks one of the radio buttons, the item you have associated with it would then include the value you have assigned to this button. You can think of radio buttons as a group of controls that are treated as one. For example, if you want a group of radio buttons to change the value of the data item EV01, you would create as many radio buttons as you have values, and associate all the buttons with the data item EV01.

To add a radio button to a form, select Insert | Radio Button, drag the control to the form, and click once to place it on the form. Then double-click the control to display its properties, as shown in Figure 5-23. Enter a title for the radio button in the Title field. The title should be the value or a description of the value so the user knows what selecting that value means. Enter a value in the Value field. The Value field is used if the user selects this radio button. For example, if you have a 5 in the value and the user clicks the radio button, your associated item will have the value 5. Set other properties as desired (see Table 5-4, earlier in the chapter).

N O T E

You should never disable or make a radio button invisible. A disabled radio button can be very frustrating to the user.

Continue to insert as many radio buttons as you have values. When you place the values on the form, make sure you place them next to each other. After you have created the radio buttons, you need to associate the buttons to a Data Dictionary or database item so they will all be treated as one control. To do this, you need to select all the controls at the same time by using the mouse to click outside the controls, and then drag the mouse to create a box that will include all the controls. Then associate the group of controls to a data item. This process is described in the section "Associating Descriptions and Data Items with a Control," later in this chapter.

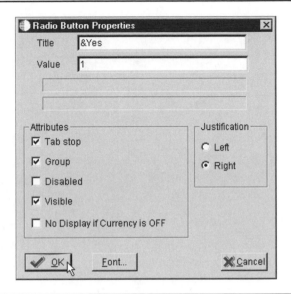

FIGURE 5-23. The Radio Button Properties form

Adding a Static Text Control

Static text controls are used as titles, headings, or instructions. Another term for static text is a *constant*. After you insert a static text control, you will see its text on the form. The user cannot change static text content at runtime.

To add a static text control, select Insert | Static Text, drag the control onto the form, and click once to place it. Then double-click the control to display its properties, as shown in Figure 5-24. In the Static Title field, enter the text for the control. Set other properties as necessary (see Table 5-4, earlier in the chapter).

Adding an Edit Control

Edit controls are generic input fields that have no associated text. You can associate edit controls with business view or Data Dictionary data items. For example, if you create an edit control and you want it to have the characteristics of a character data item, you would need to associate it with a character item from your business view or from the Data Dictionary.

Client Modifications Using OneWorld

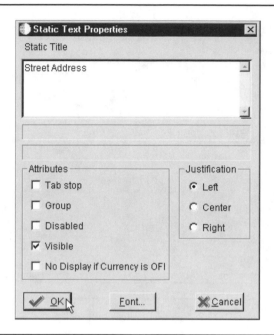

FIGURE 5-24.   The Static Text Properties form

To add an edit control, select Insert | Edit, drag the control onto the form, and click once to place it. Then double-click the control to display its properties, as shown in Figure 5-25. Fill in the Event Rules Title field. This will be the name of this control in the ER. The title should be a descriptive name.

Along with the properties listed earlier in Table 5-4, you can set the number of lines and scrolling for an edit control. If you want to limit the user to entering data on one line, choose Single in the Lines section. If you want the user to be able to enter multiple lines of information in the edit control, choose Multiple. For multiple-line edit controls, you can display a vertical scroll bar so the user can scroll through the text by selecting the Vertical option in the Vertical Scrolling section. To allow the form to display a scroll bar automatically, select the Auto Vertical option. In the Horizontal Scrolling section, you can choose Auto Horizontal or Horizontal to allow the user to scroll to the right or the left if the text is too large for the control.

You can also click the Font, Options, or Overrides button at the bottom of the Edit Control Properties form to change the font, set options, or override Data Dictionary

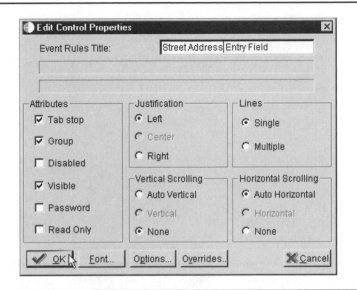

FIGURE 5-25.   The Edit Control Properties form

edits, respectively. Setting overrides is discussed in detail in the section "Overriding Data Dictionary Triggers," later in this chapter.

Adding a UDC Edit Control

A User-Defined Code (UDC) edit control allows users to enter specific values defined in an attached UDC table. This type of control is useful if you want the user to be able to select a value from a UDC table on a form. A UDC edit control automatically displays a visual assist flashlight button. The visual assist flashlight button calls the Search & Select form that is attached to the control to display a list of valid values for that control.

To add a UDC edit control, select Insert | UDC Edit, drag the control onto the form, and click once to place it. Then double-click the control to display its properties, as shown in Figure 5-26. Enter a title for the control in the Event Rules Title field. Choose any of the options described earlier in Table 5-4 to change the behavior of this control.

Client Modifications Using OneWorld

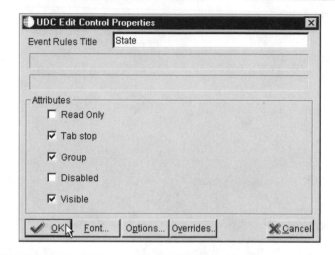

FIGURE 5-26. The UDC Edit Control Properties form

You can also click the Font, Options, or Overrides button at the bottom of the Edit Control Properties form to change the font, set options, or override Data Dictionary edits, respectively. Setting overrides is discussed in detail in the section "Overriding Data Dictionary Triggers," later in this chapter.

After you have created the UDC control, associate the control with a Data Dictionary or database item. This will attach a UDC table to this control only if the item has a UDC defined in the Data Dictionary. This process is described in the section "Associating Descriptions and Data Items with a Control," later in this chapter.

Adding a Media Object Control

Media object controls allow the user to enter lengthy text or attach images and OLE objects to a form. For example, you might use a media object to add an explanation to a form.

To add a media object control, select Insert | Media Object, drag the control onto the form, and click once to place it. Then double-click the control to display its properties, as shown in Figure 5-27.

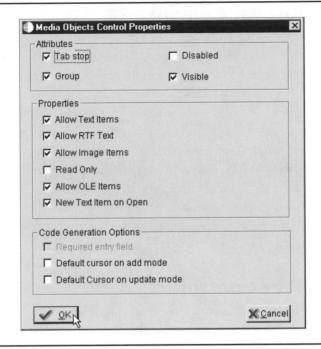

FIGURE 5-27. The Media Objects Control Properties form

Along with some of the properties listed earlier in Table 5-4, you can set the following properties and code-generation options for a media object control:

- Allow Text Items allows you to add text on this media item.

- Allow RTF Text allows the user to attach Rich Text Format (RTF) documents to the form.

- Allow Image Items allows the user to attach pictures to the form.

- Read Only prevents the user from modifying the media object.

- Allow OLE Items allows any OLE object to be attached to the form.

- New Text Item on Open adds a text item automatically.

- Required Entry Field requires the user to add a media object before clicking OK.

Adding a Bitmap Control

A bitmap can make your form more interesting by displaying a picture or a company logo, or by displaying wallpaper as background for your form. You can also create bitmaps that function as push buttons. For example, you could create a button that allows the user to choose a branch plant by clicking a bitmap that shows the state where the branch plant is located.

To add a bitmap control, select Insert | Bitmap, drag the control onto the form, and click once to place it. The Bitmap Properties form appears, as shown in Figure 5-28. Click the Find button to find the file you want to use for your bitmap control. The Bitmap Properties form displays the bitmap you have selected.

Choose the Clickable option to makes the bitmap work as a push button. If you want to the bitmap to serve as wallpaper, choose the Wallpaper option. For bitmap wallpaper, you can also choose the Tile option to repeat the bitmap.

Adding a Tree Control

A tree control looks very much like the tree control in OneWorld Explorer. The tree control contains nodes that can expand when the user clicks the plus sign next to a node or contract when the user clicks the minus sign next to a node. Sometimes, this is the best way to display data on a form. This is not the same thing as a Parent/Child Browse form, although it looks similar. A Parent/Child Browse form includes a grid

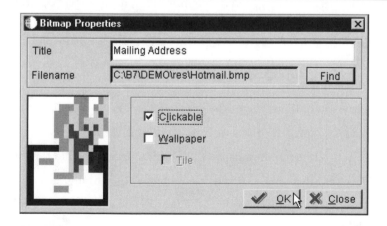

FIGURE 5-28.   The Bitmap Properties form

and tree control that are related. If you add a tree control to a form, there is no relationship to the grid or business view. If you want to use a tree control, you need to insert nodes by using system functions.

To add a tree control, select Insert | Tree Control, drag the control onto the form, and click once to place it. Then double-click the control to display its properties. The only property you enter for a tree control is its title, as shown here:

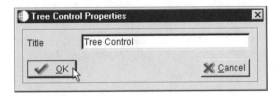

As shown in the following illustration, a tree control contains an item made up of other items. You can use system functions to change the folder icon to a different icon.

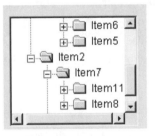

Adding a Group Box

A group box visually groups other controls together on the form by putting a box around them. This grouping is usually a logical grouping of controls. For example, you may add a group box around all header fields on a form. If you have a Fix/Inspect form with many form controls on it, you might want to group the controls by category. For example, all of the fields that deal with unit of measure will be in one group box and all of the fields that deal with cost will be in another group box. A group box has no effect on the form's logic but it helps the user view the data on a form.

To add a group box, select the controls you want to include in the group box by drawing a box around them with your mouse. You will notice that the box fits itself to the controls. You can adjust the sizing of the group box later. Then select Insert | Group Box.

Double-clicking the group box to access its properties is sometimes tricky, so you might want to hover the mouse over the group box and wait until the mouse changes to a box, and then either double–click or click once and then right-click and choose Properties. You can also click on it once and then choose Edit | Item Properties. This brings up the Group Box Properties form, as shown in Figure 5-29.

Enter a title for the group box in the Title field, if applicable. If you enter a title, it appears in the upper-left corner of the group box. If you do not enter a title, the group box will appear without a title. You can set other properties, but most of these are not useful for a group box. For example, an invisible group box isn't of much use. In addition, you probably won't need to add a tab stop to a group box or disable a group box.

Adding a Tab Control and Tab Pages

When you are developing a form, especially a form that contains a lot of information, you will realize that you are limited by the amount of real estate on a form. There is simply not enough room when you start adding control after control to a form. One solution is to add a tab control to a form. A tab control allows you to expand the amount of space within a form, because each new tab control you add contains a new space in which to add controls. On each tab control, you can add other form controls and treat each tab as a part of the form.

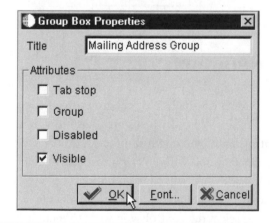

FIGURE 5-29. The Group Box Properties form

To add a tab control to a form, follow these steps:

1. With your form open in the FDA, select Insert | Tab Control. The Page Properties form appears.

2. Enter a descriptive name for the tab in the Page Title field, as shown in the following example. (Add only the controls that fit the tab name description to this tab.) You can also click the Event Rules button and add ER to the tab. Click the OK button to close the Page Properties form.

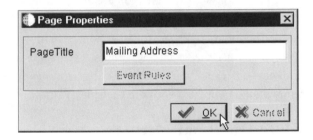

3. Position and resize the tab to the desired appearance. If you are adding a tab control to a Fix/Inspect form, your tab control will take up almost the entire form. If you are adding a tab control to a form with a grid, you will add the control to the top of the form above the grid.

4. After you have chosen the initial tab control, choose Insert | Tab Page to add more tab pages as needed.

Associating Descriptions and Data Items with a Control

FDA allows you to associate data items and descriptions with the controls. When you make an association, you create a relationship between a control and a description or an item. You can associate database items, Data Dictionary items, and descriptions with a control. Both the database and Data Dictionary items give the control the same characteristics as the item. You can think of associating a control as giving a control a data item's properties, such as size, formatting, and so on. Associating a data item is often necessary for certain controls like radio buttons or an edit control.

You may want to associate a Data Dictionary item with an edit control or radio button to give the control the correct visual assist or formatting style. You typically associate business view (database) items with radio buttons and check boxes, but you can also associate business view items with edit controls. The difference between creating an association between a Data Dictionary item and a database item is that the form will update the database with the associated item. For example, if you create an association for a check box with a database item, changing that check box will update the database.

If you associate a description with an item, you are adding a new control that has a relationship to the control you have associated. For example, if you associate a description with a Data Dictionary field, the Data Dictionary field will have a UDC associated with it. When you use the visual assist and select a value, the value will be put in the control; however, because you associated a description with the control, the associated description will be populated with the UDC description.

Associating Data Dictionary Items

To associate a database item, Data Dictionary item, or description with a control, first click on the control. For radio buttons, draw a box around them using your mouse. Then select Edit | Associate, choose the appropriate item from the submenu:

- If you're using a Data Dictionary item, find and select the item in the Data Dictionary Browser form, and then drag and drop this item onto the control you want to associate it with.

- If you select a database item, double-click the business view item in the Select Database Column for Controls form.

- If you select a description, place the Description field on the form by clicking the location in which you want to place the description. The field will now display the description for the UDC value selected.

Adding Event Rules to a Control

Events are actions that can take place on a form, such as the clicking of the OK button. Some events are part of the internal workings of a form, such as the loading of the grid. You use the ER language to code the logic instructions for a particular event, through the point-and-click ER Design tool. For example, when the user clicks the Find button, this causes the ER for the Find button to be executed. In addition, you can use ER to call another interactive application or batch application. You can create calculations and call business functions, as well as change the value of a control.

N O T E

It's very important to understand the flow of events in order to create applications. Since events are part of the internal workings of a form, you must understand the order in which the events occur before you'll know where to put ER. To review the general order of events, as well as what events occur on what forms, see Appendix B. Use the material in Appendix B to help plan where you need to add ER code in your forms.

Events occur at points where there is interaction between the user and the application, or between the application and the database. ER can affect the way the information is displayed or saved. For example, you can add appropriate ER code before a record is displayed in the grid, in the event called Write Grid Line Before. Event Rules are discussed in more detail in Chapter 7.

To add ER to a control, right-click the control and select Event Rules from the menu. Each control has events for entering a control, if it is exited, and if values have been changed.

Adding Text Variables to a Form

Text variables help you to avoid hard-coding values. You define your string as a text variable, and then you can assign the value to another variable. For example, if you want to add ER that display a message (for example, "ERROR") in a field, you could add in an assignment statement (discussed in Chapter 7) to do this, but it could never be translated. It is safer to create a text variable and assign your control the values of the text variable.

To add a text variable to a form, select Form | Text Variables. In the Text String field of the Text Variables form, select the last empty row and enter the text string you want to use. Tab to the next row to add another text variable, as shown in the example in Figure 5-30. Click OK to save the text variable and add it to the form.

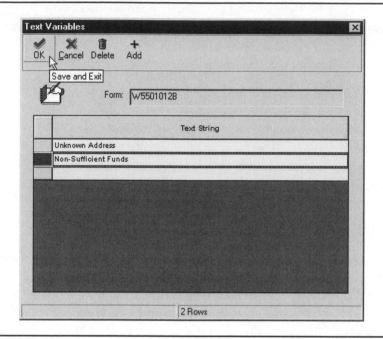

FIGURE 5-30.   The Text Variables form

Changing the Tab Sequence

The tab sequence allows the user to navigate through the form's controls by tabbing instead of clicking on each individual control. We suggest you change the tab sequence on every form that you create; otherwise, the cursor might end up at an odd location when the user enters a form. Usually, the tab sequence starts at the form's upper-left corner and travels down the first column of controls, then to the top of the next column. Change the tab sequence so that the cursor travels through all the controls and the grid in a logical manner.

To change the tab sequence, select Form | Tab Sequence. The system displays the current tab control order in each control, as shown in Figure 5-31. The 1 is the first tab stop, which is where the cursor will be when the user enters the form. Select the

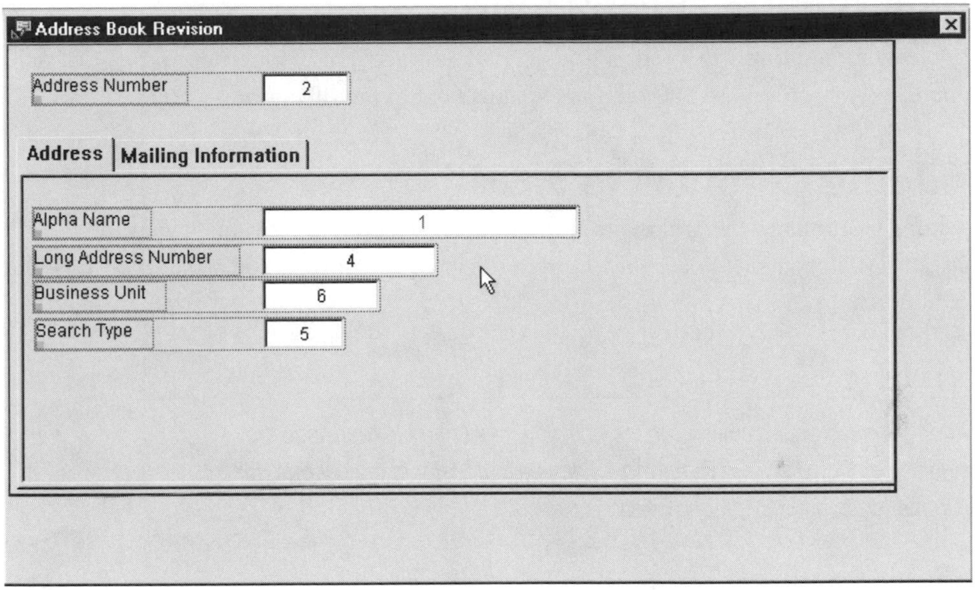

FIGURE 5-31.   The tab sequence displayed on the form

controls in the order in which you want the cursor to move around on the form. The system renumbers the tab-control sequence. When you have finished, select Form | Tab Sequence again to hide the tab sequence.

The number 1 tab stop is where the cursor will go unless you specify the initial location of the cursor in add or update mode. To override where a cursor will default, you simply follow these instructions:

1. Click the control that you want the cursor to default to.

2. Double-click the control to bring up its properties.

3. Click the Options button.

4. Turn on one or both of the following properties:

   - Default Cursor On Add Mode
   - Default Cursor On Update Mode

5. Click OK.

Modifying a Form's Grid

You can add columns to a form's grid, as well as modify the properties of the grid itself and the grid's columns. This section explains how to modify a grid.

Adding Columns to a Grid

Adding columns to the grid is simply a matter of selecting the business view items or Data Dictionary items you want to add to the grid. You cannot add special controls like radio buttons and check boxes to grids.

NOTE

After you have added columns to the grid, you might need to rearrange the columns in the grid. See "Designing a Form Layout," later in the chapter, for information about moving and deleting columns.

Adding a Business View Column

To add a business view column to the grid, follow these steps:

1. Click on the grid and select Form | Grid Columns. The Grid Column Layout form appears, as shown in Figure 5-32.

2. You can add some or all fields to the grid from the attached business view. Click the right-arrow button to move one column to the grid, or click the double right-arrow button to move all of the columns to the grid.

3. To sort the columns, click the Data Sort button. The Select Grid Row Sort Order form appears, as shown in Figure 5-33. You can click the arrow buttons to move columns into the order in which you want the columns to be displayed.

4. Click OK when you have finished.

CAUTION

Always match your grid sort to an existing key. If a key does not match, it could degrade performance.

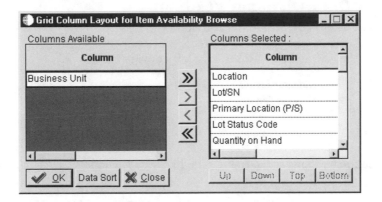

FIGURE 5-32.   The Grid Column Layout form

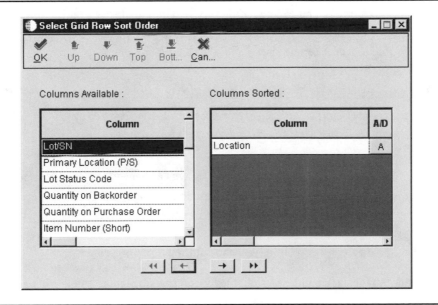

FIGURE 5-33.   The Select Grid Row Sort Order form

Adding a Data Dictionary Column

To add a Data Dictionary item to the grid, follow these steps:

1. Click the grid and select Insert | Data Dictionary Field.

2. In the Data Dictionary Browser form, find and select the item you want to add to the grid.

3. Drag and drop the item onto the grid.

Data Dictionary items added to the grid, like Data Dictionary fields on a form, will not be automatically updated to the table through the business view.

Modifying Grid Properties

You can modify the properties that control the way the grid will be viewed at runtime, as well as set user-interaction properties. You may want to modify the grid properties to change the look and feel of a grid. Some applications will look better without lines in the grid, for example. You can also hide the QBE line to ensure that the user only uses filter fields on the form, which can help improve performance because the user will not be able to select certain data.

N O T E

The Headerless Detail form has certain grid properties enabled and disabled by default. JDE strongly recommends that you not change those properties.

You can access the Grid Properties form, shown in Figure 5-34, in the same ways that you display a control's properties: double-click the grid, right-click the grid and then select Properties from the pop-up menu, or select the grid and then select Edit | Item Properties.

In the Grid Preferences section, you can set the following properties:

- Hide Row Headers hides a clickable button that appears to the left of each row on a Header/Detail form or a Headerless Detail form.

- Hide Row Lines hides the lines between grid rows.

- Hide Column Lines hides the lines between grid columns.

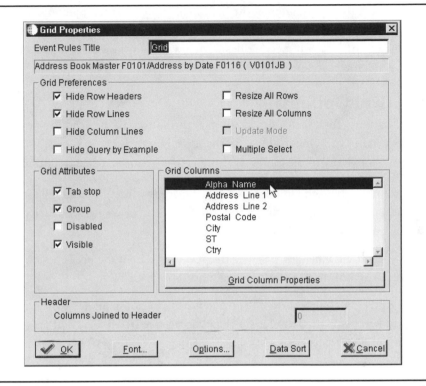

FIGURE 5-34. The Grid Properties form

- Hide Query By Example hides the QBE line.

- Resize All Rows allows the user to resize the grid rows.

- Resize All Columns allows the user to resize the columns.

- Update Mode allows the grid to update the database.

- Multiple Select allows the user to select multiple grid rows at one time.

The four properties listed in the Grid Attributes section work in the same way as the corresponding properties for controls (see Table 5-4, earlier in the chapter). The Grid Columns section allows you to set properties for specific columns, as described in the upcoming "Modifying Grid Column Properties" section.

You can click the Font button at the bottom of the form to set the font size and style of grid. Clicking the Data Sort button lets you specify how the grid will be sorted. The Options button lets you specify rules for the way the grid will function, as explained in the next section.

Setting Grid Options

To set grid options, click the Options button at the bottom of the Grid Properties form. This brings up the Grid Options form, as shown in Figure 5-35.

You can choose any of the following options to override the default options:

- **Automatically Find On Entry**   Loads the grid without the user clicking the Find button. Use this with caution, because it can cause performance problems if the grid takes a long time to load.

- **Auto Find On Changes**   Causes the grid to update if the user opens a different form in add or update mode from a Find/Browse form.

- **No Adds On Update Grid**   Prevents users from adding new records if they are in update mode on a Headerless Detail or Header/Detail form and only allows them to do updates.

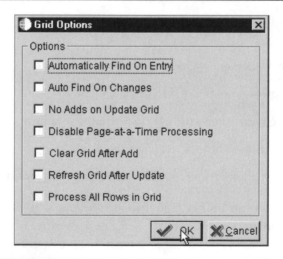

FIGURE 5-35.   The Grid Options form

- **Disable Page-at-a-Time Processing**   Turns off the option for the grid to load only two pages of information at one time. If your application needs to load all the records at one time, select this option.

- **Clear Grid After Add**   Clears the grid when the user clicks OK in add mode.

- **Refresh Grid After Update**   Reloads the grid in update mode on a Headerless Detail or Header/Detail form.

- **Process All Rows in Grid**   Causes the form to process all records even if they were not changed, if you are in update mode on a Headerless Detail or Header/Detail form. For performance reasons, this option should only be used if absolutely necessary.

Modifying Grid Column Properties

Grid column properties are the characteristics of any column in the grid. They control the description of the column, as well as how it interacts with the user. For each grid column, you can change the column's description or how it can be used at runtime.

To set column properties, from the Grid Properties form, select the grid column from the Grid Columns list and click the Grid Column Properties button. This brings up the Grid Column Properties form, as shown in Figure 5-36.

If you need to change the grid column heading, enter the new heading in the Column Heading 1 and Column Heading 2 fields. The default column heading comes from the Data Dictionary.

In the Attributes section, you can choose one or more of the following options:

- **Visible**   Shows the column in the grid. You disable the Visible property to make a column invisible. For example, you might want to hide a column that will be used for calculations or processing.

- **Disable Input**   Prevents the user from making changes to this field.

- **Disable QBE**   Disables QBE, which can speed up performance.

In the SORT Order section, you can choose either Ascending or Descending to specify the sort order of data. In the Display Style section you can choose either Default or Check Box to specify the display style.

The Overrides button allows you to override the Data Dictionary, as explained in the section "Overriding Data Dictionary Triggers," later in this chapter. Clicking the

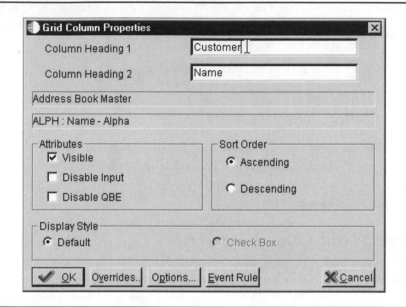

FIGURE 5-36. The Grid Column Properties form

Options button brings up a form that allows you to change how this field can be used. The Event Rules button lets you add ER logic to this column.

Setting Parent/Child Grid Properties

When you create a Parent/Child Browse form, you must specify which field you want displayed in the tree control. You also need to create a mapping between fields.

A Parent/Child grid is made up of two parts: the tree control and the grid columns. The tree control displays the contents of one column. You need to specify which column to display. To specify the field in the grid to be displayed in the tree structure, follow these steps.

1. Double-click the grid to open the Parent/Child Control Properties form, as shown in Figure 5-37.

2. In the Parent/Child Columns list, select the field that you want to display in the tree control. This can be any item in the grid.

3. Click the Move Column to Tree check box beneath the list.

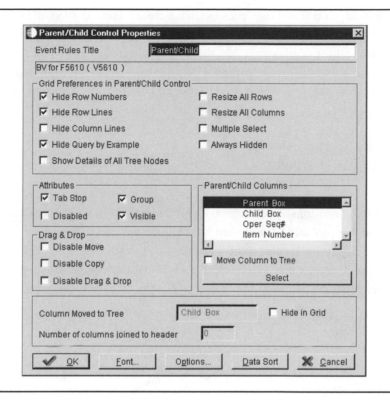

FIGURE 5-37. The Parent/Child Control Properties form

4. If you want this item to be only in the tree and not in the regular grid, click the Hide in Grid check box.

T I P

You can change the default bitmaps displayed in the tree structure by using the Set Bitmap Scheme system function. System functions are discussed in Chapter 7.

Since the database table that you will be using will have a parent-child relationship, you need to describe this relationship to the grid. For example, if your table has a relationship in which there are parent and child boxes, you need to map the parent item to the child item. This relationship will be used by the tree control when the user

Client Modifications Using OneWorld

clicks the parent control and then tries to fetch a child record. If a record is found, the child record becomes a parent record.

For example, in the following table, there are two records, where box A is the parent of box B, and box B is the parent of box C. So box B is a parent in one case and a child in another case. You would need to tell the form to map the Parent Box item to the Child Box item.

Parent Box	Child Box
Box A	Box B
Box B	Box C

To create the relationship, click on the grid and select Form | Parent/Child Relation. The Parent/Child Relationship form appears, as shown in Figure 5-38. This allows you to map the relationship between the parent and child. The columns on the left display the data item that is the parent, and the column on the left shows the child record. By clicking the arrow button, you can map the child to the parent.

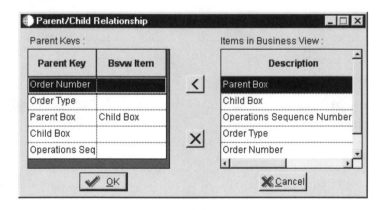

FIGURE 5-38. The Parent/Child Relationship form

NOTE

You can have a relationship that involves more that one item. For example, you could have parent and children orders. In this case, you would need to map Parent Order Number to Child Order Number, and Parent Order Type to Child Order Type. Another example is parent item and branch could be mapped to child item and child branch.

Overriding Data Dictionary Triggers

When a Data Dictionary item is created, it has many formats and edits defined. For example, you can specify that the Data Dictionary item is always in capital letters or only certain values are correct from the item. When you add a control that has a data item to a form or grid, the control inherits these traits.

Sometimes, you will want to disable or override the Data Dictionary edits so that the control will act as you want it to. For example, you may want to keep a control from validating against a UDC, or you might want it to validate against a different UDC. If you are using a Master Business Function (see Chapter 13 for information about business functions) that will be performing data edits, you could disable the editing on a grid row, so the validation is not done twice. You can override almost all Data Dictionary editing for a form, a control, or a grid.

CAUTION

If you disable Data Dictionary editing, you could cause the data to become corrupt. Data Dictionary edits are designed to ensure that only correct data is added to the database. Be careful when disabling or changing Data Dictionary edits.

You can disable Data Dictionary triggers through the Data Dictionary Overrides form, as shown in Figure 5-39. To access this form, open the Properties form for the form, grid, or control (by double-clicking or right-clicking and choosing Properties, and click the Override button.

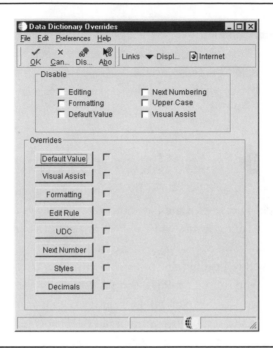

FIGURE 5-39.   The Data Dictionary Overrides form

From this form, you can disable and override Data Dictionary edits, as explained in this section.

Disabling Data Dictionary Edits

The top half of the Data Dictionary Override form lists edits you can disable. Simply select the check box next to any editing you do not want to do. Choose any of the following options:

- **Editing**   Disables any UDC editing and edit rule triggers that were set up for this item

- **Formatting**   Disables any formatting on the control

- **Default Value**   Prevents a default value from being used

- **Next Numbering**   Prevents an item from having a next number

- **Upper Case**   Turns off any case validation

- **Visual Assist**   Prevents the display of a visual assist

Overriding Data Dictionary Edits

The bottom half of the Data Dictionary Overrides form allows you to override the way a control is defined to work in the Data Dictionary. You can override the following triggers:

- Default Value allows you to specify a different default value. If the control is blank, the value you define will be used.

- Visual Assist allows you to change the type of visual assist used. You can even specify a form created inside the current application or another application.

- Formatting allows you to change the type of formatting done on a field.

- Edit Rule allows you to override the editing done on a field.

- UDC overrides the UDC table that is used to validate this record.

- Next Number allows you to change the next number code for this item.

- Styles allows you to override blank and uppercase processing.

- Decimals allows you to change the number of decimal places.

Overriding a Default Value Trigger

If a default value is not specified in the Data Dictionary, or if you want to change the default, you can override it in FDA. For example, you may need a form control to use a default of 100 instead of the Data Dictionary default of 1. To override the default value, click the Default Value button on the Data Dictionary Overrides form. On the Override Default Value form, choose either None, to specify that no default value be used, or Override Default Value to use another default value.

Overriding a Visual Assist Trigger

The visual assist that is defined in Data Dictionary may not be appropriate for the form you are working on. By overriding the Data Dictionary, you can force the controls visual assist to execute a Search & Select form that is different from the form defined in the Data Dictionary.

To override the visual assist, click the Visual Assist button on the Data Dictionary Overrides form. On the Override Visual Assist form, choose one of the following options:

- **None**   Prevents the display of a visual assist

- **Calculator**   Displays a small calculator that the user can use to return a value to this control

- **Calendar**   Displays a small calendar that allows the user to select a date

- **Search Form**   Displays a Search & Select form that you specify

Overriding a Formatting Trigger

Controls that allow the user to enter information can have a trigger on them that will do formatting. This formatting can be simple, such as filling the right or left with blank characters, or it can be more complex, such as formatting that needs to be done inside a business function. In the Data Dictionary, you can specify how to format an item, but you can override this formatting in FDA.

To override the formatting, click the Formatting button on the Data Dictionary Overrides form, shown here:

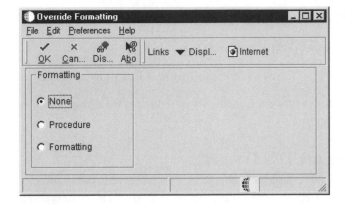

Choose one of the following options:

- **None**   Suppresses any special formatting.

- **Procedure**   Calls a business function to do the formatting.

- **Formatting**   Allows you to specify special formatting as defined in UDC 98/DR.

Overriding an Edit Rule Trigger

A data item can have an edit rule defined to ensure that users can only add a valid value. You may need to change or remove this validation on your form. (For more information about edit rules, see Chapter 11.)

To override the edit rule, click the Edit Rule button on the Data Dictionary Overrides form, shown here:

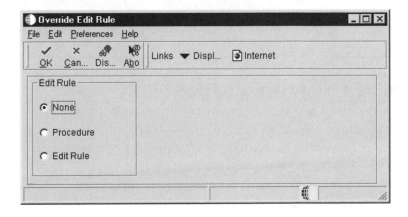

Choose one of the following options:

- **None**   Specifies that no edit rule be used.

- **Procedure**   Allows you to call a business function.

- **Edit Rule**   Allows you to specify an edit rule from the list available on the visual assist.

Overriding a UDC Trigger

You can define a UDC table for a data item. This can enable data validation, as well as allow you to return description for the given value. If a UDC table is defined for an item, the only valid values are the values defined inside the table. You can override the Data Dictionary so that it does not perform a UDC validation, or you can override the UDC table and specify one of your own. For more information about UDCs see Chapter 11.

To override the UDC trigger, click the UDC button on the Data Dictionary Overrides form. On the Override UDC form, you can choose None so that a UDC table is not used. Alternatively, you can choose Override UDC, which allows you to tell the tool to compare any value added to this field to a UDC that you define.

Overriding a Next Number Trigger

A data item can have a next number generated automatically. The next number is defined by a product code and an index. Next Numbers are discussed in Chapter 11.

To override the next number definition, click the Next Number button on the Data Dictionary Overrides form. On the Override Next Number form, you can choose None, so that no next number is generated. To add a system code and index so the next number will pulled from another location, select Override.

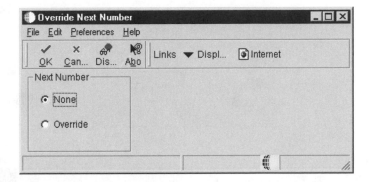

Overriding a Styles Trigger

To override the Data Dictionary styles, click the Styles button on the Data Dictionary Overrides form, shown here:

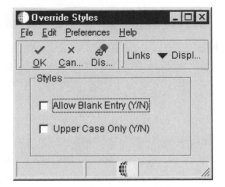

Select one of the available options:

- **Allow Blank Entry (Y/N)**   Lets the user leave this field blank. Some fields, such as a key field, shouldn't be blank.

- **Upper Case Only (Y/N)**   Causes the form to make the field uppercase.

Overriding a Decimal Trigger

Data items that are numbers have a set number of decimal places. You can override the number of decimal places to change them or hide them. To override the decimal display, click the Decimals button on the Data Dictionary Overrides form. On the Override Display form, shown in the following illustration, fill in the Display Decimals field. This will cause more or fewer decimals to be displayed on the form.

Client Modifications Using OneWorld

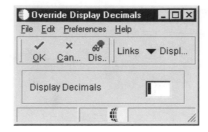

CAUTION

Be careful when you are overriding decimal places. If the number you enter is too large, the form might allow the user to enter a number to more decimal places than will be saved in the database.

Changing the Data Structure of a Form

Each form contains a data structure that allows it to pass values to and from it. For example, the data structure is used to pass information to a Header/Detail from a Find/Browse form or to pass the response from a Message form back to the calling application.

As you will learn in Chapter 7, ER has a function called a Form Interconnect (FI), which is used to call another form. The data structure for the called form determines what parameters can be passed to the form within the FI (such as information used to load the grid or form, as well as additional flags used for processing). For example, you may need information calculated from a Find/Browse form inside a Fix/Inspect form. By adding an additional parameter to the data structure, you can pass this calculated information into the Fix/Inspect form.

NOTE

The "Creating a Sample Address Book Application" section, later in this chapter, demonstrates how to call another form using Form Interconnect.

By default, the data structure is the key of the business view you attached to the form. To change a form's data structure to include additional fields from the business view or any data item, from FDA, click the form you want to change and select Form | Data Structure. The Form Data Structure form appears, as shown in Figure 5-40. You can add

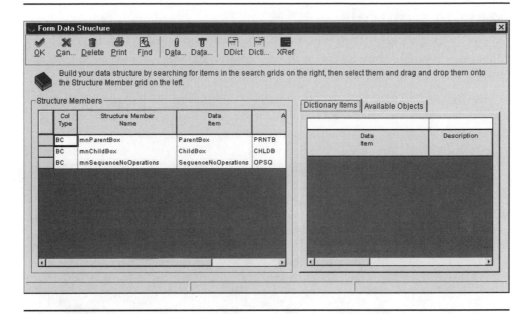

FIGURE 5-40. The Form Data Structure form

or delete data structure items. To add an item, find and select it from the Dictionary Items of Available Objects tab of the window on the right and drag it to the Structure Members window on the left.

NOTE

If you delete items from the form's data structure, consider that they may be used in the form's ER. Be sure to remove or edit any affected ER before you delete the data structure member.

Designing a Form Layout

FDA includes features that help you refine the look of your forms. For example, you might want to move controls around on the form to group them in a more logical order, or you might want to resize controls and grid columns. In this section, we describe several features that will help you refine your form layout.

Moving Controls

When you are designing a form in FDA, you can move a control simply by dragging it into its new position. Move the cursor over the control, and the cursor will change to the hollow-square design tool. Then click and hold the mouse button while dragging the control to the desired position, as shown in the following illustration. If you are trying to move a data item that has an edit control and text, click between the text and control to move both. Release the mouse button to drop the control into its new location.

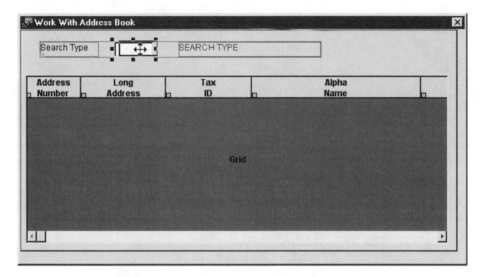

If you want to move a Data Dictionary or business view field, trying to click in the correct place so that the edit control and the text description move together can be frustrating. The easy way to move any set of controls that you want to keep together is to move them as a group. To move a group of controls, follow these steps:

1. Move the cursor outside the group of controls you want to move and click. The cursor changes to the pencil design tool.

2. Drag the mouse to the opposite corner of the group of controls. As you drag the mouse, a rectangle surrounds all of the controls you want to move.

3. Release the mouse button. A gray box surrounds the chosen group of controls.

4. Move the cursor over the chosen group of controls. The cursor changes to the hollow square design tool.

5. Click and hold the mouse button while dragging the group of controls to the desired location, as shown in the following illustration. Release the mouse button.

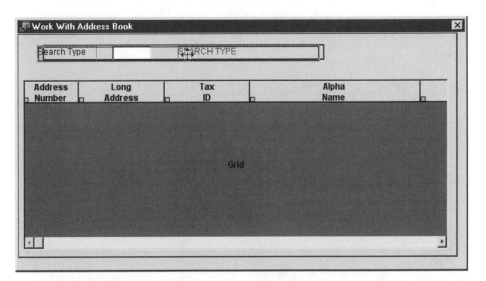

Moving and Deleting Grid Columns

While designing your form, you might need to rearrange the columns in the grid. To do this, just click the grid column you want to move, press the CTRL key, and use the arrow keys to move the field. For example, press the RIGHT ARROW key to move the field to the right.

If you want to delete a column from a grid, click the column and press the DELETE key. Alternatively, you can click the grid column and select Edit | Delete.

Resizing Grids and Controls

You can resize individual controls, the grid, or the form itself. With the mouse, you can drag an item to resize it. For more precise sizing and positioning of controls, you can use the Size command.

T I P

In general, you want to make your grid as large as your form will allow. This allows the user to see as many rows and columns as possible.

Resizing Controls Using the Mouse

To resize a control, the grid, or the form, select the item you want to resize. Handles appear on the control as small black boxes, as shown in the following illustration. Move the cursor over one of the handles. The cursor changes to the filled-square design tool.

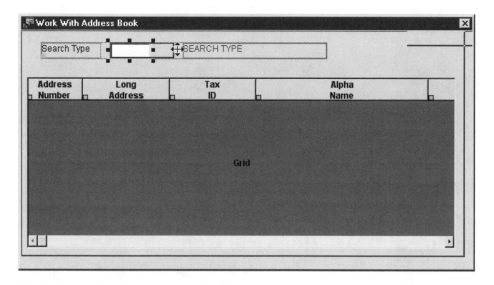

Drag a handle to resize the item as follows:

- To change the width of the item, drag the handle on the left or right.

- To change the height of the item, drag the handle on the top or bottom.

- To change both the width and the height of the item, drag the handle at the corner.

Sizing and Placing a Control Using the Size Command

When you are adding controls to forms, it is much easier to make a control an exact size using the Size command than it is to try and drag the control to a certain size. To use this command, select the desired control (small black boxes appear around the control) and choose Layout | Size. This brings up the Resize Control form, as shown in Figure 5-41.

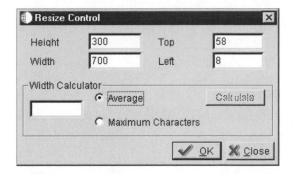

FIGURE 5-41.   The Resize Control form

In this form, you can specify the size and position of the control in several ways:

- Enter the desired size, in pixels, in the Height and Width fields.

- To have the tool calculate the width of a control, enter the number of characters in the Width Calculator field, and then choose either Average or Maximum Characters. Click the Calculate button. The new width, in pixels, appears in the Width field.

- To give the exact position of the control, enter the size, in pixels, in the Top and Left fields.

Click OK if the control is the size you want. The Resize Control form will remain open for more changes. Click Close when the control is the size you want.

Using Cut, Copy, and Paste

FDA allows you to cut, copy, and paste controls within a form. Select the desired control or group of controls and choose Edit | Copy or Edit | Cut. Choose the form on which you want to paste the control or group of controls and select Edit | Paste. Move the outline of the controls to the specific location on the form. Click once to place the controls on the form.

Client Modifications Using OneWorld

NOTE

You can also use CTRL-X to cut, CTRL-C to copy, and CTRL-V to paste controls to perform these functions

Aligning Controls

It can be frustrating to align controls on a form. FDA provides some tools to make aligning controls on your form easier. You can align a group of controls or use the alignment grid to align controls.

Aligning a Group of Controls

To align a group of controls on the form, choose the group of controls you wish to align. Then click the control within the group against which you wish to align the group of controls. Select Layout | Align. From the submenu, choose one of the following options:

- **Left**   Aligns a group of controls vertically with the left edge of the chosen control.

- **Horiz. Center**   Centers a group of controls horizontally in relation to the chosen control.

- **Right**   Aligns a group of controls vertically with the right edge of the chosen control.

- **Top**   Aligns a group of controls horizontally with the top edge of the chosen control.

- **Vert. Center**   Centers a group of controls vertically in relation to the chosen control.

- **Bottom**   Aligns a group of controls horizontally with the bottom edge of the chosen control.

- **Align Database**   Aligns the text and edit controls inside the selected group of controls.

Using an Alignment Grid to Align Controls

To use an alignment grid, select Layout | Grid Alignment to display the Grid Alignment form, as shown in Figure 5-42. To define the grid spacing, fill in the Horizontal and

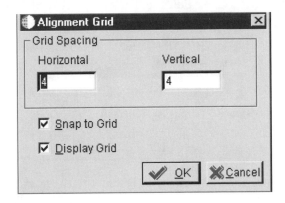

FIGURE 5-42.   The Alignment Grid form

Vertical fields. The Snap to Grid option makes it easy to align items on your form. When you move a control on a form with the Snap to Grid turned on, the control will align with the closest vertical or horizontal grid line.

With the Display Grid option turned on, you will see little dots on the form. The little dots represent grid lines for alignment. The placement of the dots is determined by the grid spacing values you entered in the Horizontal and Vertical fields. If you have it set to a high number, the dots will be spread far apart. If the number is small, the dots appear closer together. Using both the Snap to Grid and Display Grid options will help you get your controls lined up as well as uniform.

CAUTION

If you are modifying a form, be careful not to move controls if they were aligned previously, or you may need to realign all of the controls in the form. The grid that is displayed changes slightly each time the form is entered, so the grid might not be in the exact same position and size as it was when the controls were aligned. If you move controls, be sure they are all aligned when you have finished.

Using Undo and Redo

Undo allows you to undo the last action taken on a form. Redo allows you to add the last action back to the form. You can also control the undo depth, which determines how many actions you can undo.

To set the undo depth, choose Edit | Set Undo Depth. Enter the number of actions you want the system to undo, as shown here:

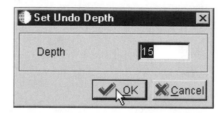

NOTE

You will want to keep the undo depth to a minimum. The undo function takes up buffer memory that can lead to performance issues. Normally, you will want to have it set to a depth of 15 to 25.

To undo a change, select Edit | Undo. To reapply a change, select Edit | Redo.

Testing and Previewing the Form

Testing the form allows you to quickly see how the form will look at runtime without leaving the FDA tool. You can see the form and click on its controls. This will help you to make sure your form looks correct. You can also preview the form in other languages and display forms from the Object Librarian.

Testing the Form

To test your form from FDA, select Form | Test. The form appears as it will look in the working application. To return to design mode, click Close or Cancel on the form.

Previewing the Form in other Languages

Previewing the form in other languages allows you to see quickly how your form will look in other languages. To preview the form, select Form | Language Preview. On the Language Preview form, choose the language you want the form displayed in, as shown here, and click OK.

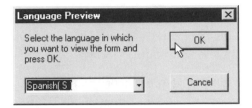

Displaying Forms from the Object Librarian

The Object Librarian offers you a quick way to view the forms in your application.
Follow these steps to display your form:

1. From the Object Librarian, select the desired application from the grid and click
   Select, as shown in Figure 5-43.

2. From Application Design Aid, select Form | Named Forms. The Work With
   Forms form appears.

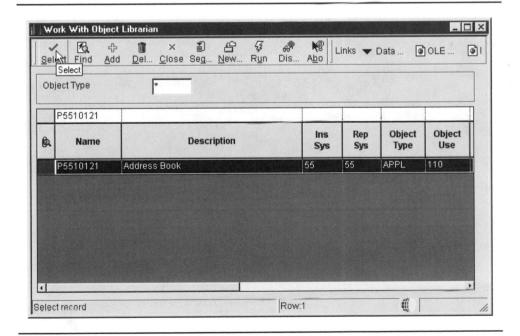

FIGURE 5-43.   Selecting an interactive application in the Object Librarian

3. In the View section on the right side of the form, select either the Checked-In Forms option or the Local Forms option. The Work With Forms form shows a list of the forms in the application, as shown in Figure 5-44.

4. Select one of the forms to view or change more detailed data about the form by double-clicking the grid row. This brings up the Form Information Revisions form shown in Figure 5-45.

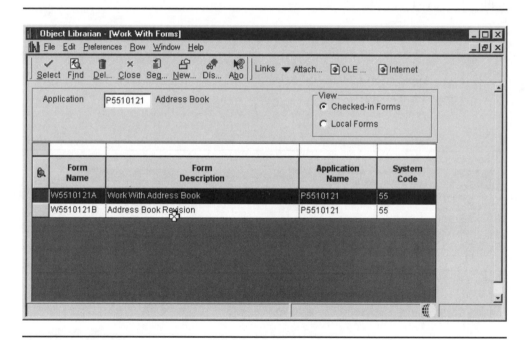

FIGURE 5-44. The Work With Forms form in the Object Librarian

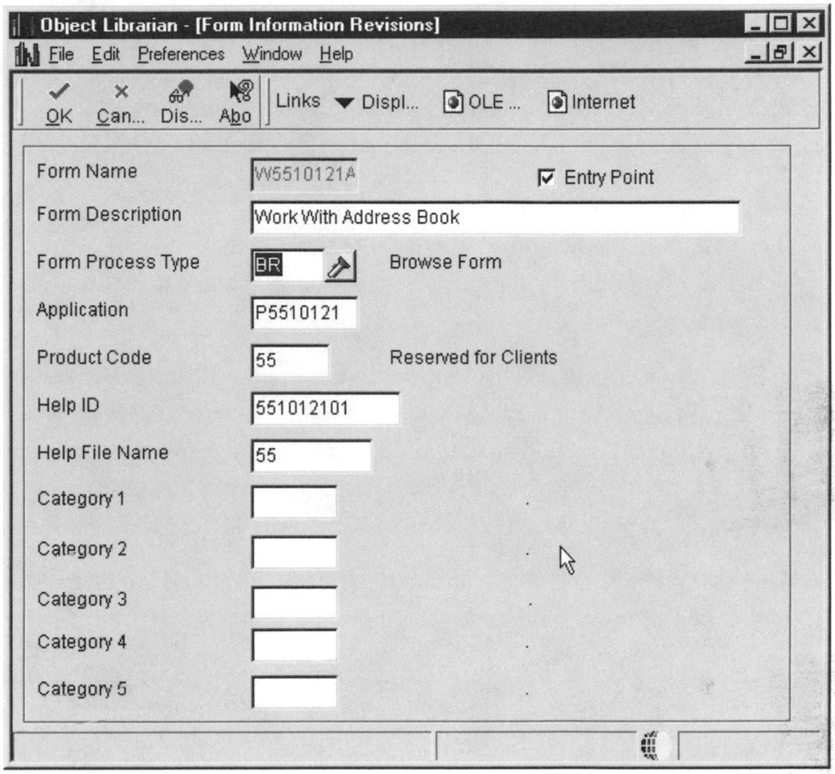

FIGURE 5-45.   The Form Information Revisions form

Throughout this chapter we have discussed different form types and controls that can be added to these forms, but to understand the best way to design your form, see the following Developer's Corner, titled "Laying Out Your Form."

Laying Out Your Form

Sometimes, the hardest part of creating a form is deciding how to make your form easier for the user to view and use. Here are a few tips that will make working with your form easier:

- Try to maximize the grid size. The more records that you can see in the grid, the better. Maximizing the grid size also allows the user to see and modify more information.

- If there are a large number of header fields on your form, you might consider adding a tab control to allow logical grouping of the data as well as add extra room. A tab control allows you to create a tab for different groupings of controls. For example, you could add a tab that contains information that deals with units of measure and another tab that deals with currency information.

- Use group boxes to logically group data. If you group information using boxes, it will be easier for the user to see information.

- If you need to fit "just one more field" onto a form, you can change the alignment grid size. To do this, select Layout | Grid Alignment. Changing the Horizontal and Vertical settings to be 2, or even 1, will allow you to put more controls onto a form.

- If you have run out of options and you still need to display more information, you can expand the form size to be larger than the blue line. We do not recommend that you do this, because some monitors will not be able to display the entire form. However, if you are doing custom work and you know that all the monitors will be a certain size, you can break this rule.

Creating Menu/Toolbar Exits

Menu and toolbar exits are an important part of application development. FDA allows you to add predefined and custom menu items and toolbar items to a form through the Menu/Toolbar Exit feature. Using this feature allows you to create two items:

- A menu category, which is simply the title of a pull-down menu

- A form exit, which is an option on that menu or on the toolbar

Form exits, also referred to as toolbar buttons or menu items, can actually do anything that you tell them to do in the event. For example, the exit you create could take the user to a different application, or it could launch a report. It could also start processing on the form that does not call another form or report, in the same way that a push button works.

NOTE

We recommend that you use a Menu/Toolbar Exit instead of a push button to add logic to your applications (except on a Message form). If you add a push button to your form, it clutters the form and takes up room. A Menu/Toolbar Exit allows you to have the same logic in a pull-down menu, an exit bar, or a toolbar of an application.

When you create a Menu/Toolbar Exit, it can be displayed in three places: the pull-down menu, the exit bar, or the toolbar.

OneWorld provides several predefined exits and menus. For example, the buttons for Find, OK, Select, Cancel, Close, and Delete are predefined in OneWorld. On Headerless Detail and Header/Detail forms, the OK and Cancel exits are predefined. Similarly, on Find/Browse forms, the Select and Close exits are predefined. You may need to add other predefined exits to your form such as a Find button to a Headerless Detail form or a Delete button to a Find/Browse form. OneWorld also provides predefined menu categories that you can use on your forms.

Adding a Menu Category to a Menu/Toolbar Exit

When you start adding menu categories to the Menu/Toolbar Exit of a form, you need to determine what you want to happen on each menu. OneWorld has three predefined pull-down menu titles that you can use: Form, Row, and Report. The Form menu should contain any exit or processing that applies to the entire form, such as an exit to another form that does not require the user to select a grid row. An exit that exists in a Row menu requires the user to select a grid row before it can be used. The Report menu is provided if you want to add report exits to your form. If you need to define additional menu custom menus, you can do that as well.

Creating a Predefined Menu Category

To use the Form, Row, or Report menu category and add a form exit to your form, follow these steps:

1. In FDA with your form open, select Form | Menu/Toolbar Exits. The Menu/Toolbar Exits form appears, as shown in Figure 5-46.

2. On the Menu/Toolbar Exits form, click the Add button. The Exit Properties form appears, as shown in Figure 5-47.

3. From the Class drop-down list, select Form, Row, or Report. Click the OK button.

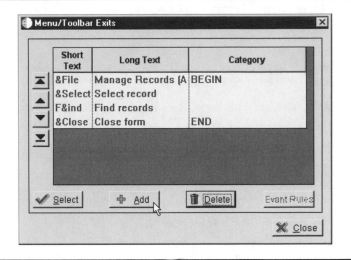

FIGURE 5-46.   The Menu/Toolbar Exits form

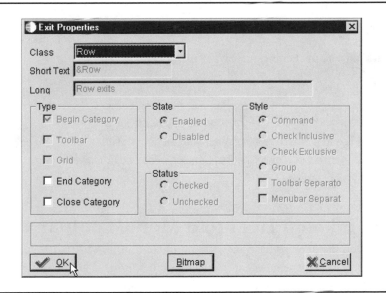

FIGURE 5-47.   The Exit Properties form

Creating a Custom Menu Category

You can also create your own custom menu category. To create a custom menu category, follow these steps:

1. In FDA with your form open, select Form | Menu/Toolbar Exits.

2. On the Menu/Toolbar Exits form, click the Add button. The Exit Properties form appears.

3. From the Class drop-down list, select User Defined. Any custom menu or exit is in the User Defined class.

4. In the Short Text field, enter a name for the menu category, such as **&View** for a menu that will contain items dealing with the view of the form. This name appears on the pull-down menu and exit bar. You use an ampersand (&) to define the shortcut key for that menu item. For example, a user can press ALT-V to select the View menu.

5. In the Long field, enter a more descriptive name for the category, such as **Form View**.

6. In the Type section, select the Begin Category check box.

7. Click OK. Your menu category has now been created.

N O T E

When you create a custom menu category, you need to select the Begin Category check box to tell the form that it is a menu category, not an exit. Every Begin Category needs a matching End Category. The End Category is discussed in the next section.

Adding a Menu Item to a Menu/Toolbar Exit

You can also add menu items (also called exits) to your form. A menu item acts like a push button or a user-triggered event that calls another form, calls a report, or performs any other processing. You can use the predefined menu items or create your own.

Adding a Predefined Menu Item

To use a predefined menu item, follow these steps:

1. In FDA with your form open, select Form | Menu/Toolbar Exits.

2. On the Menu/Toolbar Exits form, click the Add button. The Exit Properties form appears.

3. From the Class drop-down list, select the button you want to add, such as Delete. Click the OK button.

Creating a Custom Menu Item

To create your own menu items, follow these steps:

1. In FDA with your form open, select Form | Menu/Toolbar Exits.

2. On the Menu/Toolbar Exits form, click the Add button. The Exit Properties form appears.

3. From the Class drop-down list, select User Defined.

4. Enter in a name for the menu item, such as **&A/B Revisions** or **&Item Master**, in the Short Text field. This name appears on the pull-down menu and exit bar.

5. In the Long field, enter a more descriptive name, such as **Address Book Revisions**.

6. Select any of the following options:

   - **Begin Category**   Makes this menu item a menu within a menu.
   - **Toolbar**   Makes the menu item a button on the toolbar.
   - **Grid**   Displays the menu item on the pop-up menu that appears when the user right-clicks the grid.
   - **End Category**   Indicates that this is the last item in the category for this pull-down menu.
   - **Close Category**   Closes the Begin Category for menus within menus.

7. Figure 5-48 shows an example of a completed Exit Properties form for a menu item. Click OK to save this menu item.

8. Repeat steps 2 through 7 to add as many menu items as you need for this menu. Figure 5-49 shows a Menu/Toolbar Exits form with menu categories and items added.

9. When you have finished, click the Close button.

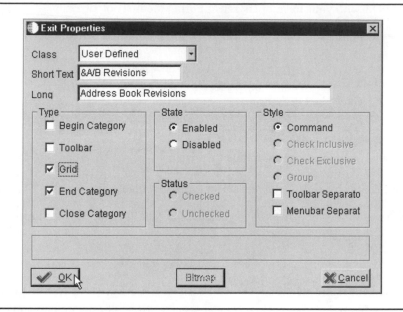

FIGURE 5-48.   Creating a custom menu item

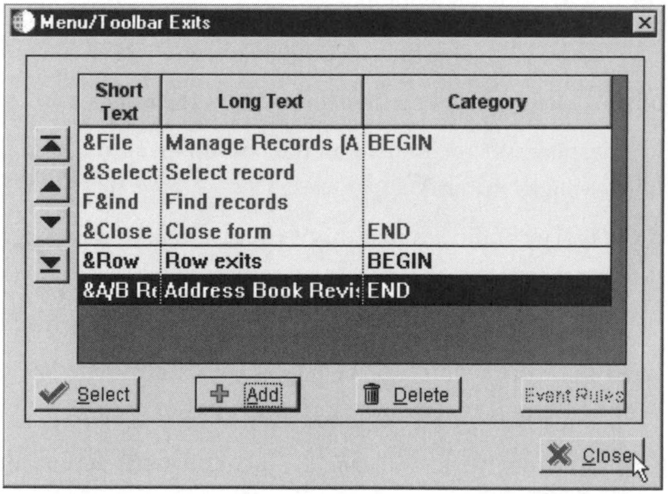

FIGURE 5-49.   Adding Menu/Toolbar Exits

Creating a Sample Address Book Application

At this point, we have discussed the types and components of forms and how to create forms in FDA, as well as how to create menu and toolbar exits. Now you will see how it all works by creating simple Find/Browse and Fix/Inspect forms for an Address Book application.

N O T E

Refer to the earlier sections in this chapter for illustrations and details about the steps in the processes.

Creating the Find/Browse Form

As discussed earlier, a Find/Browse form is the entry point for most applications. In the following steps, you will create the application object, specify the form types, and add controls.

1. In OneWorld Explorer, type **OL** in the Fast Path box. The Work With Object Librarian form appears.

2. In the Object Type field, type **APPL** and click the Add button. The Add Object form appears.

3. In the Object Name name field, type **P5510121**. In the Description field, type **Address Book**. In the Product Code field, type **55**. In the Product System Code field, type **55**. In the Object Use field, type **110**. Click the OK button. The Application Design Aid form appears.

4. Click the Design button. The FDA application starts.

5. Select Form | Create | Find/Browse. FDA creates the form and displays the Find/Browse Form Properties form.

6. Type **Work with Address Book** in the Title field and click OK.

7. Select Layout | Size to Guide to size the form to the 640 × 480 standard window size.

8. Select Form | Business View. The Individual Object Search and Select form appears.

9. Type **V0101E** in the Object Name QBE line and click the Find button.

10. Highlight the row and click Select. The system attaches the Address Book Update (V0101E) business view to the form.

11. Select Insert | Business View Field. The Select Database Column for Controls form appears.

12. Highlight Search Type and click the OK button.

13. Drag the outlined box to the top of the form and click once to place the control on the form.

14. Click the Close button on the Select Database Column for Controls form to return to your Work with Address Book form.

15. Place the business view field control on the top-left side of the form, as shown in Figure 5-50. This control is now on the form but it is not doing anything yet. We need to make this a filter field so that it will control the data that is loaded into the grid.

16. Double-click the edit control. The Edit Control Properties form appears.

17. Click the Filter button. The Edit Control form appears.

18. Choose = (equal to) from the Filter Criteria section, and select Yes in the Wildcard Display section. Click the OK button, and then click the OK button on the Edit Control Properties form.

19. Click the grid on the form and select Form | Grid Columns. The Grid Column Layout for Address Book Update form appears.

20. In the Columns Available list on the left side of the form, select Address Number, Alpha Name, Long Address, and Search Type. Click the right-arrow button after highlighting each field to move it to the Columns Selected list on the right side of the form. Click the OK button to place the columns on the grid.

21. Click the Close button. The Select Grid Row Sort Order form appears.

22. Highlight the Address Number column and click the right-arrow button to select Address Number as the column to sort the grid. Click the OK button.

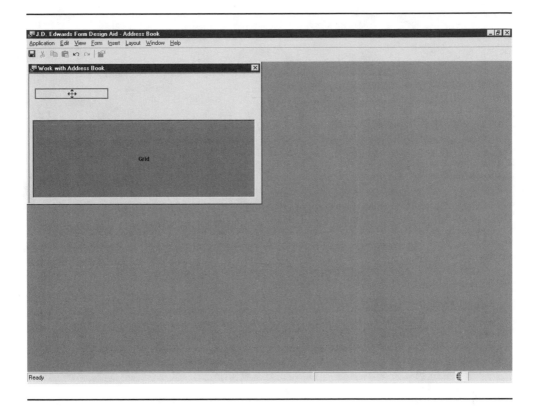

FIGURE 5-50. Placing a business view field on the form

Your form should look like the one shown in Figure 5-51. We have just created the Find/Browse form. When the user clicks the Find button, it will load the grid with information from the business view V0101E. If the user enters a value in the Search Type field, it will filter the data that appears in the grid using that column.

Creating a Fix/Inspect Form

Now we need to create the Fix/Inspect form that will allow users to modify and add data. Follow these steps to create the form:

1. In FDA, select Form | Create | Fix/Inspect. FDA creates a Fix/Inspect form and displays the Fix/Inspect Form Properties form.

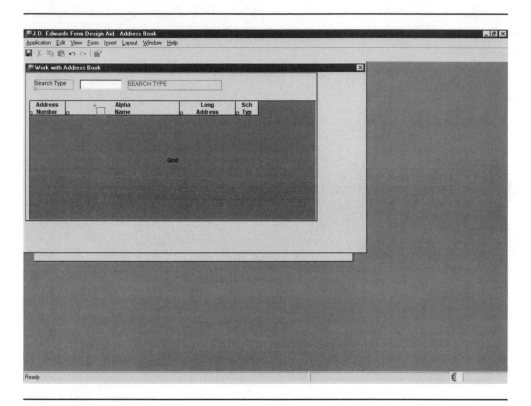

FIGURE 5-51. The sample Work with Address Book form with the columns placed in the grid

2. Type **Address Book Revisions** in the Title field, as shown in Figure 5-52, and click the OK button.

3. Select Layout | Size to Guide.

4. Select Form | Business View. The Individual Object Search and Select form appears.

5. Type **V0101E** in the Object Name and click Find.

6. Highlight the business view and click Select. The system attaches the Address Book Update (V0101E) business view to the form.

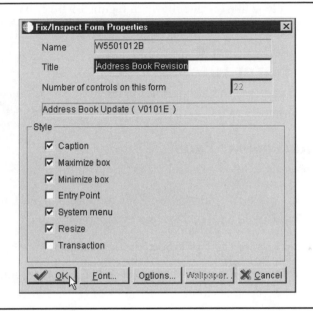

FIGURE 5-52.   The Fix/Inspect Form Properties form

NOTE

In this example, we are using the same business view as the Find/Browse form because we need the same data. This is not always the case. You can, and probably will, have different business views for different forms In the same application.

7. To add all of the controls to this form quickly, select Form | Quick Form. The Quick Form Layout for Address Book Revision form appears.

8. In the Columns Not in Form list on the left side of the form, select Name-Alpha, Secondary Alpha Name, Long Address Number, Business Unit, and Search Type. Click the right-arrow button after highlighting each field to move the fields to the Columns in Form list on the right side of the form. Click the OK button to place the controls on the form.

9. Click the Close button to return to the Address Book Revision form.

Your form should look like the one shown in Figure 5-53. We have now completed the Address Book Revisions form.

Creating a Form Interconnect

Now we need to connect the Find/Browse form to the Fix/Inspect form. To do this, you must return to the original form.

Adding Menu/Toolbar Exits

Follow these steps to create the menu and toolbar exits for the form:

1. In FDA, select the Work with Address Book form and choose Form |
   Menu/Toolbar Exits. The Menu/Toolbar Exits form appears

2. Click the Add button. The Exit Properties form appears.

3. Choose Row from the Class drop-down list and click the OK button. You return to the Menu/Toolbar Exits form.

4. Click the Add button.

5. On the Exit Properties form, choose the End Category and Grid options in the Type section. In the Short Text field, type **A/B &Revision**. In the Long field, type **Address Book Revision**. Click the OK button.

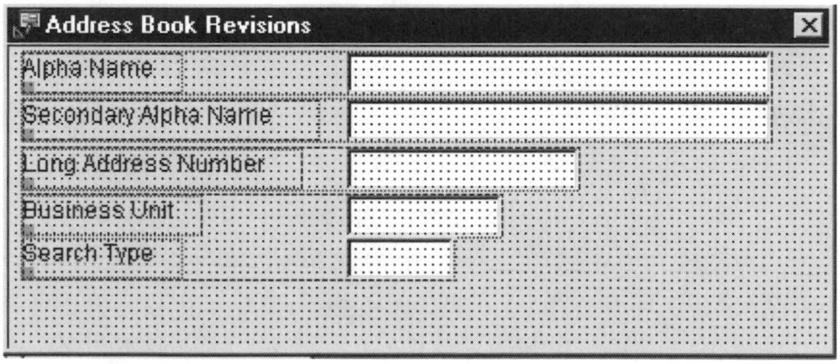

FIGURE 5-53. The sample Address Book Revisions form with the controls placed in the form

This adds an item to the menu that will call the other form. You may receive a window telling you to save before adding ER. If this happens, click Cancel, and then save the application and reenter the Menu/Toolbar Exits form.

Adding Event Rules

We now need to add Event Rules to call the other form and pass parameters from the Find/Browse form to the Fix/Inspect form. Follow these steps to continue:

1. On the Menu/Toolbar Exits form, highlight the Address Book Revision row and click the Event Rules button, as shown in Figure 5-54.

2. Choose the Button Clicked event from the drop-down menu to specify that you want the ER to occur when the user clicks the A/B Revisions menu item.

3. Select Insert | Form Interconnect. The Work With Applications form appears.

4. Type **P550101** in the Object Name QBE line and click the Find button.

5. Highlight the row and click the Select button to select application P550101, which is the form you are currently designing. You can call forms in the

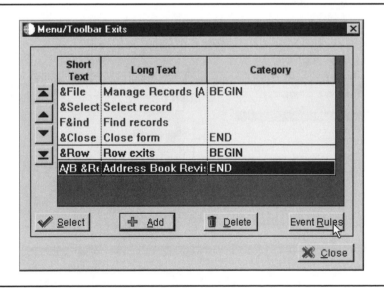

FIGURE 5-54. Adding ER to a menu item

application you are working on or forms in other applications. The Work With Forms form appears.

6. Highlight the row with Address Book Revision in the Description column and click the Select button. The Form Interconnections form appears.

7. In the Available Objects list on the left side of the form, select GC AddressNumber and click the right-arrow button to move it to the Data Structure list on the right side of the form. Click the directional arrow in the Dir column until it points to both the Value and the Data Item columns, as shown in Figure 5-55. Then click the OK button.

8. Select File | Save, and then choose File | Exit.

9. Click the Close button on the Menu/Toolbar Exits form.

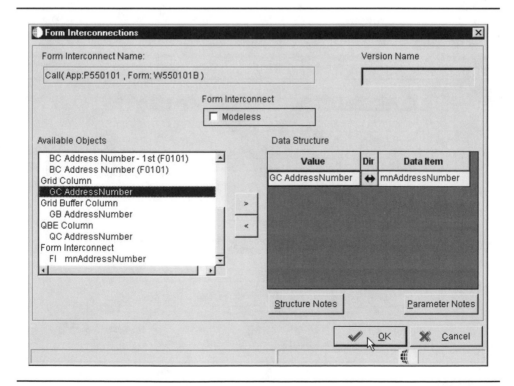

FIGURE 5-55. The Form Interconnections form

Saving and Running the Application

Now it's time to save and test the sample application.

1. In FDA, select Application | Save, and then click the OK button when prompted.

2. Select Application | Exit.

3. In the Object Librarian, select Form | Run. Your application appears.

Congratulations! You have created your first OneWorld application! By now, you should see the potential of using the OneWorld tools for creating your interactive applications.

When creating applications in OneWorld, occasionally you will need to tweak your applications to improve performance. This is discussed in the following Developer's Corner, titled "Performance Techniques for Forms."

Client Modifications Using OneWorld

Performance Techniques for Forms

In some cases, you may run into the problem of an application's performance being too slow. "Too slow" is, of course, a relative term. Too slow might be 2 seconds or 25 seconds. You also need to understand the difference between actual performance and perceived performance.

Even if you cannot make an application faster, you may be able to make it seem faster to the user. For example, you can put ER in events like the Row Is Exited and Changed - Async event and the Post OK Button is Clicked event, which will make it appear as if the application is running faster, when it is actually performing at the same speed. This allows the user to do other things in the meantime. However, be careful if you put logic in a Post OK Button is Clicked event, because if there are any errors in what the user entered, the user will not be able to see and correct them.

If it takes too much time to load the grid when the user clicks the Find button, there are a few things you can do:

- Use the minimum number of controls in your business views. The more data the form needs to load, the slower it will work. Fewer columns in your business view will reduce the time it takes to bring up your form.

- Use a business function to cache data in memory, or to store data, instead of using a temporary worktable. (Cache is described in Chapter 17). A work file takes more time because it is being written to hard disk and travels over the network, where cache is in RAM and can be mapped to run on your client machine.

- The sort order in your grid (in a Find/Browse, Headerless Detail, or Header/Detail form) should match, at least partially, the index in the OneWorld table (from the beginning of the index, in the same order). To see which the indexes are on a form, look at the table that the business view is associated with.

- Try not to filter records from the database on your own. In other words, don't fetch all the records in the table and suppress the record from being inserted into the grid after it is fetched.. What you can do is create a business view field in the header that is hidden and make it a filter field. In your ER, you can load a value, and the form will filter the information for you.

- Make sure you map business functions, especially Master Business Functions, to run on the server if possible. If there is a lot of I/O inside a function and it is mapped to run on the server, it will run faster because the database I/O will take less time.

Putting It All Together

In this chapter, we showed you how you can quickly and easily create applications by using the Forms Design Aid (FDA) tool. By following the guidelines described in this chapter, you will be able to create your own OneWorld applications successfully.

We started by explaining the different types of forms and the differences between these form types. We then discussed different types of controls and how you can use them to display information. We also showed you how to add controls to a form. Additionally, we walked you through the process of adding Menu/Toolbar Exits to your forms. We finished off this chapter with an example of creating a simple Address Book application.

CHAPTER 6

Report Design Aid

Overview of Report and Batch Applications

Report Section Types and Fields

Creating Reports

Viewing and Modifying Reports

Submitting a Report from OneWorld Explorer

Putting It All Together

In older accounting and manufacturing systems, batch applications were defined by a single file that executed from the first line to the last line of the file. The logic flow was straightforward, and programmers had total control over the execution. However, creating different versions and upgrading these older applications was very difficult. To produce another version, programmers needed to copy an existing application and modify it. Also, the older batch applications were usually specific to the current release of the system. When the system was upgraded, most of the applications had to be rewritten because some of the statements in them became obsolete.

OneWorld's approach provides programmers with greater control and flexibility for developing report and batch applications. Versioning and upgrading are easy, because the system has built-in capabilities for versioning control.

You create and modify report and batch applications in OneWorld in the Report Design Aid (RDA) application. RDA is a state-of-the-art, report-writing application that is integrated into OneWorld. With RDA, you can produce powerful report and batch applications.

To describe how to use RDA for your report and batch application needs, the following topics are discussed in this chapter:

- **Overview of Report and Batch Applications**   The overview explains how event-driven programming works for report and batch applications. It also describes the components of report and batch applications.

- **Report Section Types and Fields**   Reports are composed of various sections, which, in turn, consist of fields. This section describes the types of sections and fields that can be in report and batch applications.

- **Creating Reports**   This section covers the steps for creating a report from scratch with RDA. You will learn how to use the features and functions of RDA.

- **Viewing and Modifying Reports**   After you have created your report, you can view and modify it in RDA. This section describes how to change your report's properties and view it in different ways.

- **Submitting a Report from OneWorld Explorer**   After you have developed your report, you will need to execute it. This section describes how to submit a report from OneWorld Explorer.

NOTE

In OneWorld, the differences between the report and batch applications have been minimized, and the two are almost identical. Therefore, in this book, and especially this chapter, the two terms are used interchangeably.

Overview of Report and Batch Applications

The primary difference between batch and interactive applications is that batch applications do not require user input during execution, while interactive applications do. Once a batch application starts execution, it does not stop processing until the end of the code in the application is reached. Therefore, your only chance to interact with a report or batch application is before it is executed. Before executing a report or batch application, you can make the following changes:

- You can change the processing options to enable certain features in the batch application, such as to have it run in proof or final mode.

- You can modify the settings for the data selection for a report to limit the number of records that the application executes.

- You can modify the data sequencing of a report to change the order of the data in the output medium.

DEFINITION

*The **output media** for a report are the types of output that the application provides. For report applications, the output media can be an Adobe PDF file, hard copy from a printer, or a flat file that is formatted as comma-separated values (CSVs).*

The core difference between report and batch applications in OneWorld and the same applications in older financial and manufacturing systems is that OneWorld applications use event-driven programming.

Event-Driven Programming

Event-driven programming is a paradigm for applications that allow the system to execute the application, and then stop periodically to execute code that is embedded in events in the application. The events are generated by different actions that occur on objects in the application, such as a report variable in a batch application.

NOTE

For interactive applications, events are generated by the applications as users interact with them, such as when buttons are clicked. The GUI runtime engine processes interactive applications. The processing of interactive applications is discussed in Chapter 5.

The system uses a runtime engine, called a *Universal Batch Engine (UBE)*, to execute the application. This runtime engine has total control over the application. When the UBE detects that an event has occurred, it executes the code written for that event in the application. Using this approach, the focus changes from line-by-line execution, which occurred in older applications, to event-by-event execution.

DEFINITION

*The **Universal Batch Engine (UBE)** is a system-level process that executes report and batch applications in OneWorld. When developers refer to a UBE, in most cases, they are actually referring to an application that is processed by the UBE.*

The UBE processes the code in the events of reports and batch applications as it processes the objects. As the UBE processes each object, it changes execution to the ER code that you embedded into the event of that object. For example, you may place ER code into an event when the object is created, before the object is exported to the output medium, and before the object has completely finished processing in the report.

The key to understanding how the UBE processes each object in a report is how it exports a report to an output medium. The UBE exports objects in a report in order of sections and fields. First, the UBE processes all sections in the report from the top down, such as report header section, page header section, group section, page footer section, and report footer section. Second, when the UBE processes a section, it processes all fields in that section from left to right.

When the UBE processes a section, all of the events related to it are executed as they occur. In general, the events for a section occur when the section is initialized in memory, before the section is exported to the output medium, after the section is exported to the output medium, and before the memory the section occupied is released. The same processing occurs for the fields in the section. Report sections and fields are discussed in more detail in "Report Section Types and Fields," later in this chapter.

N O T E

The UBE for OneWorld clients on the network is built into the OneWorld Explorer application (OWEXPLORE.EXE). For servers, the Type 2 JDENET kernel is the dedicated process that comprises the UBE, as discussed in Chapter 15.

Batch Application Components

Like OneWorld interactive applications, report and batch applications are object based. The major components and objects that make up a report are the report object, report versions, and report sections.

Report Object

Report applications have their own object definition that is managed by the Object Librarian. When you need to create a new report application, you first need to define the object so that the system can maintain information on its location, title, and product code. Whenever you need to modify the batch application, you use the Object Librarian to check out and check in the report object from the system and to modify it.

D E F I N I T I O N

*The **report object** contains the master specifications for the report application. The master specifications define how the report sorts, sequences, presents, and calculates information for the output media of the report application.*

To modify the report object, you launch the Report Design Aid (RDA) application from either the Object Librarian application (P9860) or OneWorld Explorer, and make the changes in RDA. After you make changes to the report object and check it in, the master specifications of the report application are modified.

Batch Versions

To execute a batch application, you must attach a version to it in order to submit the application to the UBE for processing. The batch version is a copy of the report object, and you use it to modify the specifications of the report object to suit your needs. The advantage to this is that you can tailor the report version without violating the integrity of the report object for other users.

You can override four properties in a batch version: processing options, data selection, data sequencing, and the object specifications. Overriding the processing options allows you to create versions of a report object that allow you to change its behavior. For example, you can have one version of the Print Invoices application (R42565) that prints the invoice and modifies the next status code for the items attached to the sales order, and another version that does nothing more than print a proof of the invoice without modifying any values in the sales order. Processing options are further discussed in Chapter 12.

Versions also allow you to override the data selection and sequencing of the report without modifying the report object. This is particularly useful in cases in which you want a set of report versions for each business unit in the company to make it easier for employees in the company to use the report. Versions are further discussed in Chapter 10.

Report Sections

Report and batch applications in OneWorld are comprised of one or more sections. Sections are the building blocks for report and batch applications, analogous to the forms that make up interactive applications. You use sections to group common fields in the report into logical segments, and make them easier to build and modify. Report sections and fields are described in more detail in the next section.

Report Section Types and Fields

Reports can be composed of various header, detail, and footer sections. A header section is typically used for presenting information from the parent table for a set of tables that have a parent-child relationship. A detail section presents information from the child tables. For example, in a sales-order report, the header section might contain header information, the detail section may include the detail lines that are attached to the sales order, and the footer section could be used for grand totaling and notes about the report in general.

Types of Report Sections

Seven types of major sections can be used for a report or batch application: report header, report footer, page header, page footer, group, columnar, and tabular. Figure 6-1 shows an example of a report with four sections: report header, page header, columnar, and page footer. The report header and footer contain a statement of confidentiality; the page header section summarizes the date, time, and name of the report; and the columnar section contains the primary information of the report.

Also shown in Figure 6-1 are the report constants and variables in the sections, which make up all of the individual fields in any section of a report. In this example, the report constants are the column headings in the columnar section, the name of a company in the page header section, and the statement of confidentiality in the report header and footer sections. The report variables are the fields that compose all of the

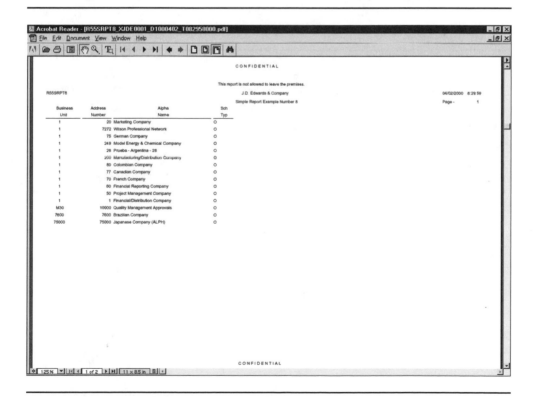

FIGURE 6-1.   A report with four sections

Client Modifications Using OneWorld

rows in the main portion of the columnar section, and the date and time in the page header section.

All sections are grouped into two major categories: level 1 and level 2. Level-1 sections are independent sections that do not require the existence of another section. Group, columnar, and tabular sections are level-1 sections, which contain the main content of the report. Level-2 sections are dependent sections that require the existence and data of a level-1 section. Headers and footers are level-2 sections.

Each section type has one or more special characteristics for specific uses in reports. Table 6-1 lists the major report sections and summarizes their characteristics, and the following sections describe the section types in more detail.

NOTE

Refer to Appendix C for a complete description of all of the types of report sections and their characteristics.

Section Properties	Report Header	Page Header	Group	Columnar	Tabular	Page Footer	Report Footer
Independent section (level 1)	No	No	Yes	Yes	Yes	No	No
Dependent section (level 2)	Yes	Yes	No	No	No	Yes	Yes
Assigned a business view	No	No	Yes	Yes	Yes	No	No
Free-form layout	No	No	Yes	No	No	No	No
Column-style layout	No	No	No	Yes	Yes	No	No
Used as a conditional section	No	No	Yes	Yes	No	No	No
Used as a subsection join section	No	No	Yes	Yes	No	No	No
Used as a level-break header	No	No	Yes	No	No	No	No
Used as a level-break footer	No	No	Yes	Yes	No	No	No
Able to format headers and footers	No	No	Yes	Yes	No	No	No
Implicit totaling on level break	No	No	No	No	Yes	No	No
Auto-generation of grand totals	No	No	No	No	Yes	No	No
Data selection at the column level	No	No	No	No	Yes	No	No
Auto-population of descriptions	No	No	No	No	Yes	No	No
Drill-down capability	No	No	No	No	Yes	No	No

TABLE 6-1. Properties of Sections in Report and Batch Applications

Report Header and Report Footer Sections

A report has a single report header section and a single report footer section, which are used as the entry and exit points for the report, respectively. The primary purpose of the report header section is to provide useful information to the users of the report, such as the name and address of the company. The report footer section is intended to provide last-minute information to the users of the report, such as a statement of confidentiality. The system does not populate any information in the report header or report footer sections, because they are used to provide information that is unique to your company.

The event sequence for a report header section is shown in Figure 6-2. The report footer section has the same events, except that they begin from the previous section and end with the end of the report. The events in the report header and footer sections execute once, because these sections are only executed once in a report.

The Initialize Report Header or Initialize Report Footer event is executed immediately after the report header or report footer section is initialized in the system. The flow of execution then proceeds to the Do Section event, which is executed before the UBE prints the constants and variables to the output medium of the report. The After Last Object Is Printed event is executed when all of the output has been printed to the output medium. The End Report Header or End Report Footer event is executed when the execution of the report header section or report footer section has ended.

T I P

Typically, you will only need to insert lines of ER code into the report header section to set global variables used by the report. For a report footer section, you might need to insert lines of ER code to clear any temporary files or tables. You should place any lines of ER code into the Do Section event of the report header or report footer section.

Page Header and Page Footer Sections

The page header section is executed every time a new page is created for the PDF file or hard copy of the report. If a report header section does not exist in the current report, the page header section is the first section to execute. The primary purpose of the page header section is to provide useful information to the users of the report, such as the report name, date, time, and company name. If you do not modify anything in this section, the system automatically supplies the information for you.

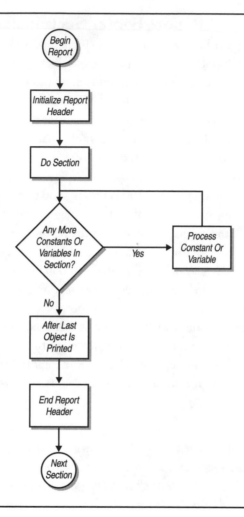

FIGURE 6-2. The event sequence for a report header section

RDA will always include the page header section in any report or batch application that you create. We strongly encourage you to include this section in your report, because it provides essential information about the report's purpose and when the report was processed.

The page footer section is executed every time the end of a page has been reached. The page footer section can be used to provide additional information to the users of the report, such as a statement of the report's purpose. The system does not populate any information in the page footer section, because it is intended to provide the information that is unique to your company.

The event sequence for a page header section is shown in Figure 6-3. Page footer sections have the same events as page header sections. The Initialize Page Header or Initialize Page Footer event is executed immediately after section is initialized in the system. The flow of execution then proceeds to the Do Section event that is executed before the UBE prints the constants and variables to the output medium of the report. The After Last Object Is Printed event is executed when all of the output has been printed to the output medium. The End Page Header or End Page Footer event is executed when processing of the current section has ended.

N O T E

The Initialize Page Header and Initialize Page Footer events are called only once. If you need to execute logic in the page header section or page footer section every time that the section is executed or after a new page is created, insert your code into the Refresh Section event for the sections.

Group and Columnar Sections

Group sections are independent sections that display the main content of the report. The group section has a free-form layout that allows you to define the location of fields anywhere within the section. Group sections are typically used for second-level sections, such as level breaks for header and footer sections. Level-break header and level-break footer sections are group and columnar sections that are processed when specific data in the previous and current records is different. These types of sections are used to segregate large amounts of data into smaller, more intelligible and logical groups.

In the example shown in Figure 6-4, the data in the group section is arranged into five lines of data that have no column order. In the illustration, the information in the group section is sequenced in the common mailing address order for better readability. The page header section is also a group section that displays general information (such as title, date, time, and page number) about the report in a row format.

Some of the other uses for group sections are as subsection joins and conditional sections. Subsection joins are used in cases in which the data exists in two tables, and

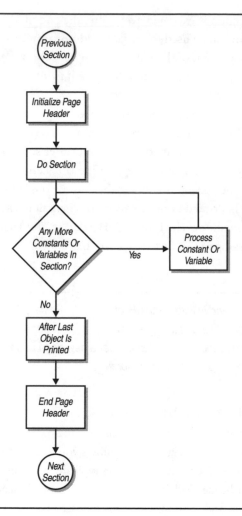

FIGURE 6-3. The event sequence for a page header section

the relationship between the tables is either parent-child or one-to-many. The subsection join allows the report to display information from both tables. Conditional sections are used in cases in which processing of a section is dependent on one or more situations. When a section is defined as a conditional section, the system will only execute it when it is explicitly called by a system function.

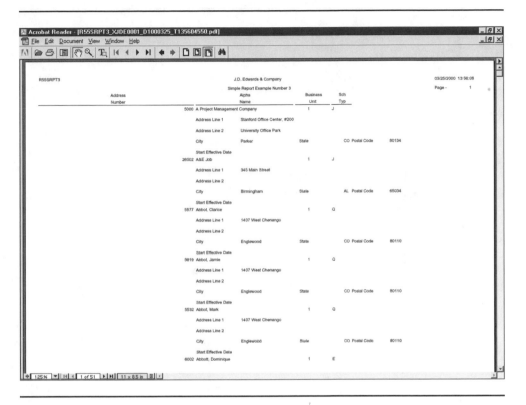

FIGURE 6-4. A group section in a report application

NOTE

Subsection joins can be viewed as the logical equivalent of the header detail forms for interactive applications. Both subsection joins and Header Detail forms require the use of two business views in order to present data.

A columnar section displays the main content of the report in a column format. The data in this section is directly tied to the column heading that it resides under, so it has a fixed format. Columnar sections are useful in financial reporting, inventory reporting, and various status reports. In the example shown in Figure 6-5, the data in the columnar section is arranged into nine columns of data, where each row in the

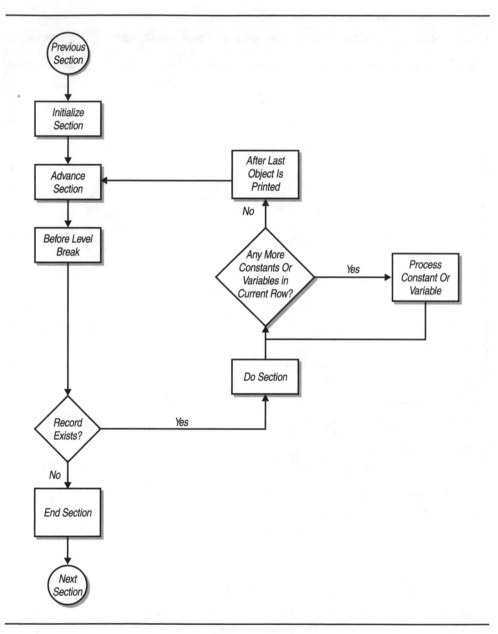

FIGURE 6-5.   The event sequence for group and columnar sections

section represents one record fetched from the database. Columnar sections are typically used for level-break footers, but they can also serve as conditional and subsection join sections in reports.

The event sequence for group sections and columnar sections, shown in Figure 6-6, is the same. The Initialize Section event is executed immediately after the group or columnar section is initialized in the system. The Advance event is executed each time the system retrieves a record from the business view that is assigned to the group or columnar section. The flow of execution then proceeds to the Do Section event that is executed before the UBE prints the constants and variables to the output medium of the report. The After Last Object Is Printed event is executed when all of the output

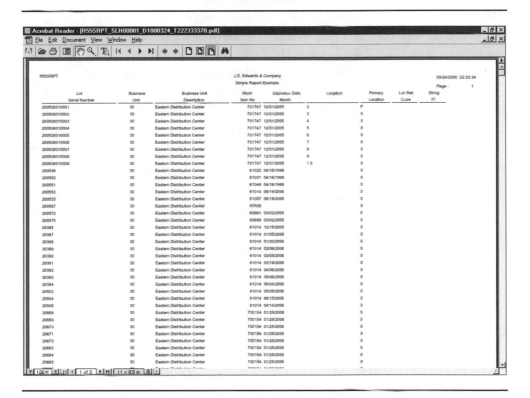

FIGURE 6-6.   The event sequence for group and columnar sections

has been printed to the output medium. The End Section event is executed when the last record is fetched from the database.

T I P

If you need to insert ER logic into a group or columnar section, you will typically insert it into the section's Do Section event. This event is used to perform any last-second processing of data before it is written to the output medium of the report.

Tabular Section

The tabular section is an independent section that displays the main content of the report in a column and row format. The data in this section is formatted down to a cell in the section. This flexibility makes tabular sections the ideal choice for financial reporting that requires multiple levels of totaling along columns and rows.

In the example shown in Figure 6-7, the financial information for a particular general ledger account in the tabular section is presented in Prior Year End Balance, Period Activity, YTD Current Period, and Current Total columns. The value in the Current Total column is the sum of the prior year-end balance and the year-to-date current period for a row. The Company, Object Account, and Subsidiary columns are defined as level breaks, so their data is not included in the totals.

Tabular sections have the following advantages over the other section types, especially group and columnar sections, for financial reporting:

- Tabular sections require fewer lines of ER code to write, because you can define column and row totaling without entering a single line of code. Many totaling and formatting features are built into them. Tabular sections automatically embed totaling for every level break, giving you the flexibility to include intermediate and grand totaling in your report.

- Tabular sections reduce the number of sections required in a report, because they have level breaks built into them. For group and columnar sections, you need to define and design any level breaks. Therefore, a single tabular section can do the work of at least two columnar or group sections. A tabular section automatically adjusts itself for any changes in totaling levels, but a group or

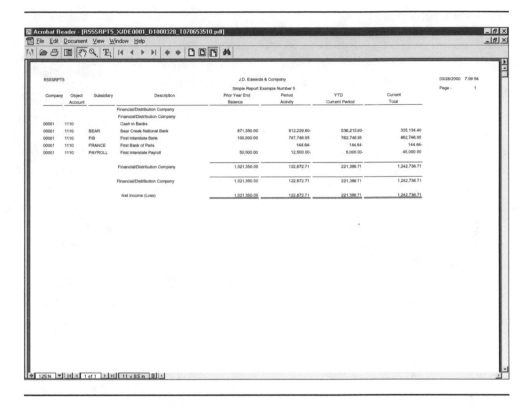

FIGURE 6-7. A tabular section in a report application

columnar section cannot make such an adjustment. You must modify the level breaks that are attached to group and columnar sections in order for changes to take place.

- Tabular sections process the automatic assignment of descriptions. As the tabular section processes each row of data in the report, it retrieves any descriptions that are required, such as the name of an account.

- Tabular sections can use smart fields, which automatically calculate balances without coding. Smart fields are special data dictionary items that have a business function attached to them. The business functions are executed to calculate the value for their smart fields.

Smart fields *are data items with business functions attached to them. They can only be used in tabular sections of batch applications. They are normally used to calculate balances, such as year-to-date and current periods.*

The event sequence for tabular sections, shown in Figure 6-8, is unique because of the automatic totaling and level breaking. The Initialize Section event is executed immediately after the tabular section is initialized in the system. The Advance event is executed each time the system retrieves a record from the business view that is assigned to the tabular section. If the record generates a level break, the Column Inclusion event is executed for each cell in the current row of the section. At this point, the Do Tabular Level Break and the Do Section events are executed to process the level breaking and totaling for the section. After all of the report constants and variables are exported to the output medium of the report, the After Last Object Is Printed event is executed. When the system detects that a last record has been fetched from the database, the End Section event is executed to perform any last-minute level breaking and grand totaling for the section, and it cleans up any other required processing for the section.

If you insert the ER logic into the Do Section for report variables in tabular sections, it will not affect the variable, because the event is used for processing the level break that is defined for the section. The Column Inclusion event for a cell in a tabular section is the event in which you will normally insert ER logic.

Section Fields

A field is used to contain a single unit of information for a report section. The total of all of the fields in a section represents the logical grouping of information for the section, such as address information for companies or account balance information from the general ledger. The fields of the section originate from either report constants or report variables.

Report constants are static fields that display text. The events for a report constant are executed before and after the values in the constant are exported to the output medium of the report. You typically use report constants to display the name of a company, title of the report, notes, and the confidentiality statement.

Client Modifications Using OneWorld

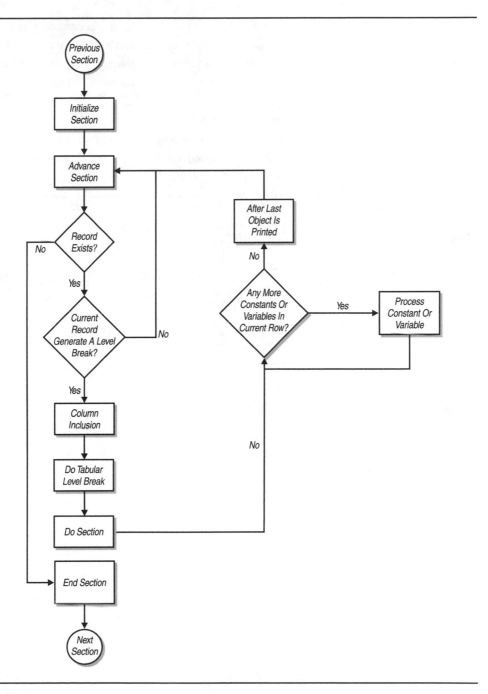

FIGURE 6-8. The event sequence for a tabular section

Report variables are fields that contain variable information that is defined while the report is executed. Report variables can be either alphanumeric or numeric. Alphanumeric variables contain alphabetic and numeric information, such as the name of a general ledger account. Numeric variables contain only numeric information, such as a grand total for a column.

The events for report variables are executed before and after the values in the constant are exported to the output medium of the report. The event sequence for report constants is shown in Figure 6-9. The sequence for report variable events is

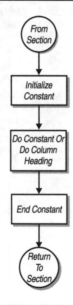

FIGURE 6-9.   The event sequence for report constants

similar. The Initialize Constant or Initialize Variable event is executed immediately after the report constant or variable is initialized in the system. The flow of execution then proceeds to the Do Constant or Do Variable event, which is executed before the UBE prints the constants and variables to the output medium of the report. The End Constant or End Variable event is executed when the value of the report constant or variable has been exported to the output medium.

Before we proceed to the next section on creating reports in OneWorld, we want to shift gears for a moment and discuss design techniques for reports. This topic, discussed in the following Developer's Corner, "Design Techniques for Reports," is important because it will give you the information you need to design professional and effective reports.

Client Modifications Using OneWorld

Design Techniques for Reports

The primary purpose of reports is to provide appropriate and accurate information to help business managers and executives make critical decisions regarding their business operations and profitability. For example, reports may be designed to show the current profitability of a company; a company's daily activity of operations; or how a product line has performed in the marketplace by region, salesman, and business unit. The quality of the information in a report is the dominant factor that determines the usefulness of a report. The better the quality of the information, the more useful the report is for assisting people in making decisions or taking action.

Asking the following questions will provide you with some guidelines for designing a report:

Design Question	Purpose
Who is the target audience for the report?	You need to decide if the report will be used for internal purposes, such as age trial balance, or for external purposes, such as invoices and delinquency letters. This is important because reports for internal purposes do not need to look as good as reports sent to suppliers and customers.
What is the purpose for the report?	A report with a well-defined purpose for its users is the most effective one and the easiest to design and construct.
What actionable event is generated by the report?	Effective reports usually generate action by one or more users. For example, invoices generate an action event by notifying the recipients that they owe money to your company.
What information is the report to provide?	The answers to this question provide the content that is displayed in the report.
Is a sample or existing report available in OneWorld?	If a similar report is in OneWorld, using it as the basis for your report will reduce the amount of design work you need to do to lay out the report.
How should the information in the report be segmented?	The answer to this question will help you divide the report into sections.
What OneWorld tables will the data come from?	The answer to this question will help you determine which records to include in your report.
Have the fields on the report been defined?	The earlier the fields are defined, the faster the report can be built.

Once you have answered these questions, you can proceed with designing your report or batch application. The first step is to lay out the information and group-related pieces of information in the report. Constructing a prototype report in Microsoft Word or Excel can help you with this task, and you will be able to present the initial report design to the users. This will provide them with the opportunity to examine the report and provide any further comments or suggestions.

An example of a report prototype in Microsoft Word is shown in Figure 6-10. The prototype is a design layout of a sales-quote document that will eventually become a version of the Print Invoices batch application (R42565). The purpose of the report is to issue quotes to potential customers. This prototype groups all of the information in the report into related sections. A developer can decompose the prototype into report sections, variables, and constants.

NOTE

The users determine the quality of the information in a report because they determine the usefulness of a report. This is the primary reason why report construction is a very tedious and time-consuming task. It usually takes several design and construction iterations before your users find the report useful.

ACME MOTOR COMPANY
QUOTATION

		Page Number 1
Quoted To ABC Inc	Ship To ABC Inc	Date 8/26/02
5555 Secor Rd.	5555 Secor Rd.	Installed by Acme Equipment
Toledo OH 43623	Toledo OH 43623	Customer 50516
		Quote Number - **864** QO
		Your Salesperson John Doe
		E-Mail Address johndoe@acmemotor.com

Promised Delivery:	Customer P.O. 123456-7	Ship: Deliver to North	Customer Contact Jane Doe
3-4 weeks	FOB	Inst: Dock	Phone (999) 999-9999
End Customer			Fax (999) 999-9999

Ln No	Description	Item Number	UM	Quantity	Price	Extended Price
1	4x4 Truck with Snow Plow	QUOTE	EA	1	$3,000.00	$3,000.00
	Snow Plow					
	4x4 Custom Mounting					
	Plow lights					
					Sales Tax	**TOTAL COST**
	Terms Net 10 Days		Tax Rate 0%			$3,000.00

Agreements are contingent upon strikes, accidents and all other delays unavoidable or beyond our control. Not subject to cancellation without prior consent. Prices subject to all existing Federal and State taxes unless otherwise specified. We are not responsible for property of others, for losses from fire, theft or damage while in our possession. Any changes in the above specifications that involve additional cost will only be made upon written order, and an extra charge will be added. A 50% deposit is required for all custom ordered equipment.

THIS QUOTATION IS VALID FOR THIRTY DAYS

ALL CANCELLED ORDERS ARE SUBJECT TO A 30% RE-STOCKING CHARGE

_____   _____
Customer Signature   Date

FIGURE 6-10. A report prototype developed in Microsoft Word

Creating Reports

You use the RDA application to create and modify all report and batch applications in OneWorld. The RDA is a WYSIWYG (What You See Is What You Get) interface, which allows you to create and modify your report in the manner in which you would view it from the output media. With RDA's drag-and-drop functionality, you can place fields and other objects in your reports without leaving the tool.

To increase the usability of RDA for your reports, the Report Design Director (RDD) guides you through the initial construction of your report or batch application. The RDD allows you to build reports ranging from simple tables of records to complex financial reports with subtotaling and grand totaling. In this chapter, we will create a simple report to demonstrate how to use RDA.

Creating a Report Object

The first step in constructing a new report application is to define its report object. In OneWorld, you can create a report object through the Object Librarian, or you can create a report object in the RDA tool itself.

Creating a Report Object Through the Object Librarian

The technique for creating a report object by using the Object Librarian application (P9860) is the typical one that you use to create all other objects in the system. Following are the steps required to create a report object:

1. From OneWorld Explorer, type **OL** into the Fast Path box and press ENTER. The Work With Object Librarian form appears, as shown in Figure 6-11.

2. In the Work With Object Librarian form, type **UBE** into the Object Type field, press ENTER, and then click the Add button. The Add Object form appears, as shown in Figure 6-12.

3. In the Object Name field, enter **R55SRPT**. The object name is a unique identifier for the report object, and it appears in the upper-left corner of the header for the report.

4. In the Description field, enter **Simple Report Example**. The description is the title of the report that is positioned in the center of the page header section.

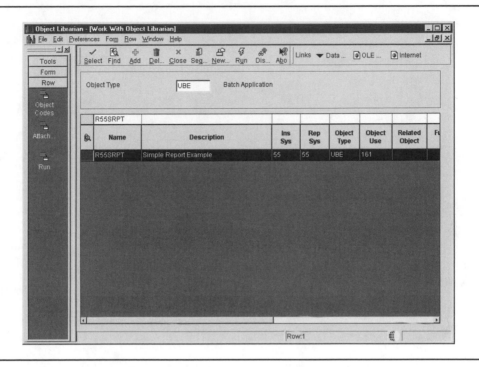

FIGURE 6-11. The Work With Object Librarian form

5. In the Product Code field, type **55**. The product code value determines to which module the report is assigned.

6. In the Product System Code field, type **55**. This value is the same as the product code value.

7. In the Object Use field, type **161**. For reports, the Object Use field needs to contain the value 161. The values for this field are defined in the user-defined code 98/FU.

8. In the SAR Number field, type **1**. The SAR number is the unique value that you use for project control of all modifications to objects in OneWorld.

9. Select the Auto-Create Version check box. When the Auto-Create Version option is selected, the system automatically creates a version for the report object. This feature saves you the work of creating a version later.

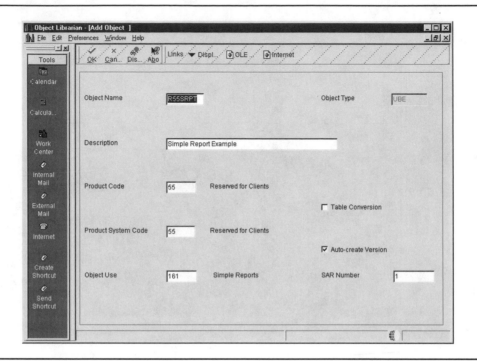

FIGURE 6-12. The Add Object form in the Object Librarian

10. When you've finished entering data into the Add Object form, click the Add button. The Batch Application Librarian form appears, as shown in Figure 6-13.

11. In the Batch Application Librarian form, click the Design button to design the report. The system launches the RDA application. You can then proceed to create your report, as described in "Creating a Simple Report with the Report Design Director" section.

Creating a Report Object Through RDA

Instead of using the Object Librarian, you can launch the RDA application and define a new report object directly in RDA. This offers a convenient method for creating report objects. To create a report object through the RDA application, follow these steps:

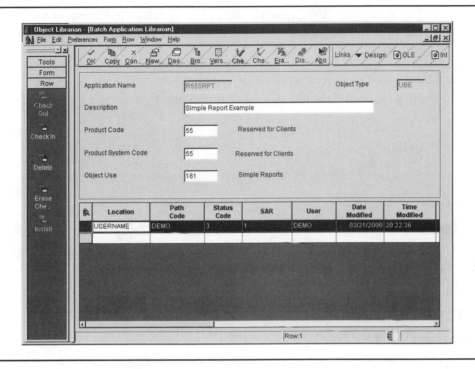

FIGURE 6-13. The Batch Application Librarian form in the Object Librarian

1. From the OneWorld Explorer, select Tools | Report Design to launch the RDA application.

2. In RDA, select Report | New to create a new report. The Create New Report form appears, as shown here:

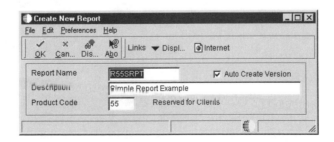

3. In the Object Name field, type **R55SRPT**. The object name is a unique identifier for the report object, and it appears in the upper-left corner of the header for the report.

4. In the Description field, type **Simple Report Example**. The value in the Description field is the title that is positioned in the center of the page header section for the report.

5. In the Product Code field, type 55. The product code assigns the report to a module, and the report is displayed in the RDA application.

N O T E

The other fields that appear in the Object Librarian Add Object form, described in the previous section, are still applicable. However, those fields are assigned values automatically by the RDA application.

Creating a Simple Report with the Report Design Director

After you've defined the report object, RDA immediately starts the Report Design Director (RDD) to assist you in designing a report. The RDD leads you through several steps that ask you a few questions about the layout and design of your report. The RDD will then build the report based on the answers that you have provided and display the design layout of the report in RDA. In this way, the RDD gives you a jump-start on designing and building your reports.

N O T E

You can design your report without the assistance of the RDD. To dismiss the RDD, click the Cancel button in any of the RDD forms.

While the RDD is running, you will see the Navigation Assistant on your desktop, as shown in the next illustration. The Navigation Assistant shows where you are in the process of creating the report. The arrow icon next to a step indicates your current location in the RDD, a dull red circle icon represents the steps you have already completed, and a three-dimensional red button indicates the RDD steps you have

not yet viewed. You can click on any step in the Navigation Assistant to jump forward
or backward to a form in the RDD at any time.

Defining the Sections for the Report

The first form in the RDD allows you select which sections you want in your report.
In this example, you will use page header and columnar sections. (The report section
types were described in "Types of Report Sections," earlier in this chapter.)

From the RDD's Welcome form, shown in Figure 6-14, select the Page Header
check box and the Columnar radio button to include those sections in the report. Click
the Next button.

The Page Header Details form appears, as shown in Figure 6-15. (If you did not
choose to include a page header section, the RDD will proceed to the business view
selection step.) By default, the page header section fields include the object name,
title, date, time company name, and page number of the report. Click the Next button
to continue.

Selecting a Business View for the Section

Like its form counterpart in an interactive application, a business view is the link
between the database and a section in the report. A business view defines the
tables and their columns that are available in the section, and makes the columns
available for use as fields in the section. You can only assign a business view to
level-1 sections (group, columnar, and tabular).

NOTE

Group, columnar, and tabular sections are not required to have a business view.
Level-1 sections that do not have business views are typically used for batch
and subsystem applications.

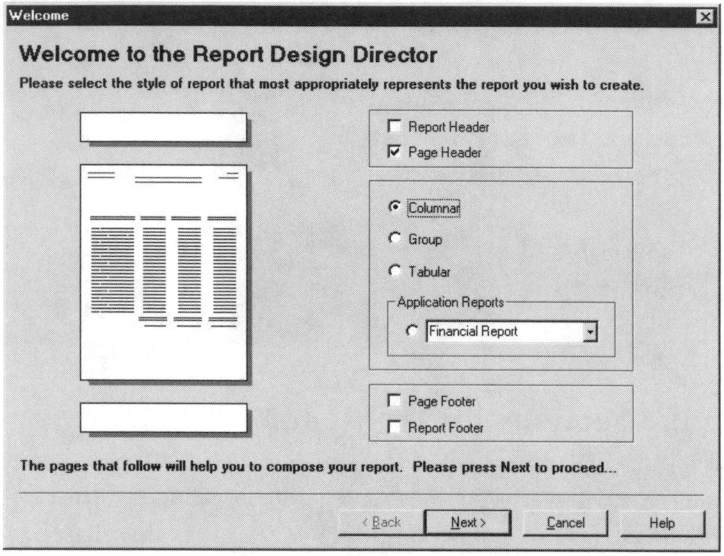

FIGURE 6-14. The RDD Welcome form

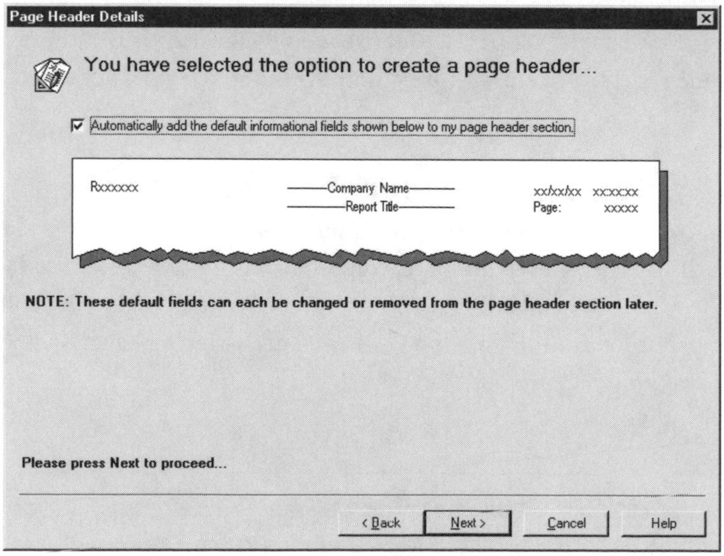

FIGURE 6-15. The RDD Page Header Details form

Using a business view for a section improves the performance of the section, because it only uses the columns and tables that it needs. You can also combine data from multiple tables into a single business view that a section can use. In this example, you will use a business view that is a join of two tables.

From the Business View Selection Options form, shown in Figure 6-16, choose the option that allows the RDD to help you find a business view, and then click the Next button.

The Favorite Business Views form appears, as shown in Figure 6-17. For this example, select the Item Location / Lot Join business view (V41021Y) for the columnar section of the report. Click the Next button.

Defining the Fields from the Business View for the Section

Now that you have the connection between the database and the section, you can select the columns from the business view that you want in your report. If you need more columns in your report, you can go back to the previous step to select another business view, or you can wait until the report is generated and add the fields directly from the data dictionary.

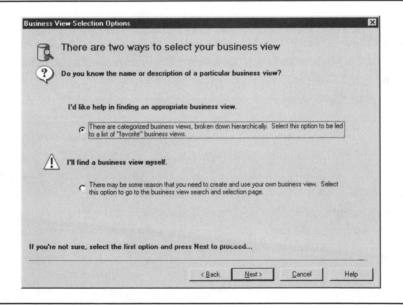

FIGURE 6-16. The RDD Business View Selection Options form

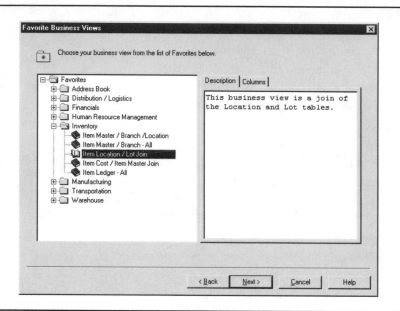

FIGURE 6-17.   The RDD Favorite Business Views form

In the Section Layout form, shown in Figure 6-18, the Available Business View Columns window lists all of the data items in the business view. To select a data item for the report, highlight it and click the single arrow that points to the right. The data item will be listed in the Select Columns window. If you want to use all of the columns that are listed in the Available Business View Columns window, click the double-arrow button that points to the right.

If you do not want a data item in the Selected Columns window, highlight it and click the single arrow that points to the left. If you need to remove all of the columns that are listed in the Selected Columns window, click the double-arrow button that points to the left.

For this example, select the CostCenter and Lot columns by highlighting them in the Available Columns list and clicking the single right-pointing arrow button. They will be listed in the Select Columns window.

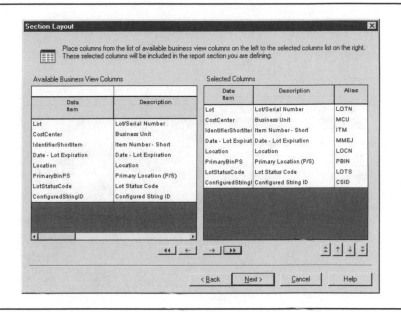

FIGURE 6-18.   The RDD Section Layout form

Defining the Data Sequence of the Report

For most reports, the order of the data that is retrieved from the database needs to be in a specific format. In the Section Data Sequencing form, shown in Figure 6-19, you define the data sequence for the section or report.

The Available Columns window lists all of the data items in the business view that are available for sequencing in the report. You can define the data sequence by any of the columns in the tables that the business view uses. This allows you to sequence your data by a column that is or is not defined in the business view.

To select a data item for sequencing, highlight it in the Available Columns list and click the single arrow that points to the right to move the item to the Select Columns window. If you need to use all of the columns that are listed, click the double-arrow button that points to the right.

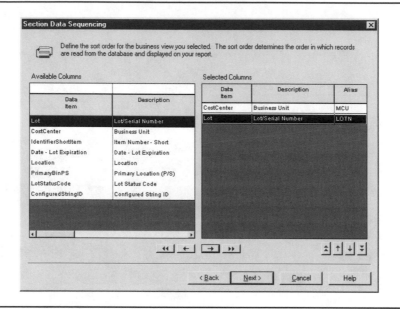

FIGURE 6-19.   The RDD Section Data Sequencing form

If you do not want a data item in the Selected Columns window, highlight it and click the single arrow that points to the left. To remove all of the columns that are listed in the Selected Columns window, click the double-arrow button that points to the left.

After you have selected the columns that control the sequence of the report, you need to define how the selected columns order the data. You do this by arranging the order of the columns listed in the Selected Columns window. You modify the order of the Selected Columns items by clicking the up and down arrow buttons below the window, as follows:

- To move a column up in the order of the sequence, highlight it and click the single up-arrow button.

- To move a column down in the order of the sequence, highlight it and click the single down-arrow button.

- To move a column to the top of the order, highlight it and click the double up-arrow button.

- To move a column to the bottom of the order, highlight it and click the double down-arrow button.

For this example, the CostCenter column is listed above the Lot column in the Selected Columns window.

After you have finished defining the layout of the section for the report, click the Next button.

Defining the Sort Properties of the Report

The sort properties of a report control the sequencing order and where level and page breaks occur in the report. In the Define Sort Properties form, shown in Figure 6-20, you define the sort properties for each data item in the Sort Columns grid.

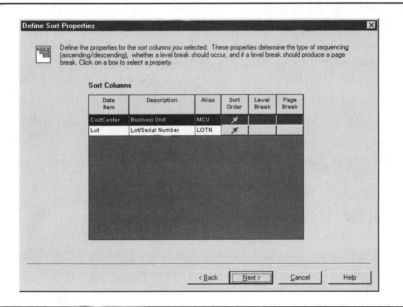

FIGURE 6-20.   The RDD Define Sort Properties form

For every data item in the Sort Columns grid, complete the following fields to further sort the data in the report:

- The Sort Order property for a data item defines the order in which the data is presented in the report, in either ascending or descending sequence. It is graphically denoted by an arrow button (the Sort Order button) that points up for ascending order or down for descending order. Click the button, and the system will change the order from ascending to descending, and vice versa.

- The Level Break property defines the data items that are used for level breaking. Level breaking allows you to group related records by a common value in a field, such as zip code or area code. To add a level break, click the Level Break button for the data item, and the system will place a check mark on the button. The check mark denotes that the data item is defined as a level break.

- The Page Break property forces a page break when the data item's value changes during processing. The data item must also include a level break in order for it to force page breaks. To add a page break, click the Page Break button for the data item, and the system will place a check mark on the button. The check mark denotes that a page break will occur every time the value in the data item changes in the report.

For this example, both columns will be sorted in ascending order and no level breaks or page breaks will be used.

When you have finished defining the sort properties of the columns, click the Next button.

Defining the Data Selection for the Section

The data selection step of the RDD allows you to filter records that come from the database. In the Section Data Selection form, shown in Figure 6-21, you define a set of criteria that the RDD uses to extract the records you want your report to process. Using data selection improves the performance of your report during execution, because the report only processes the records it needs to.

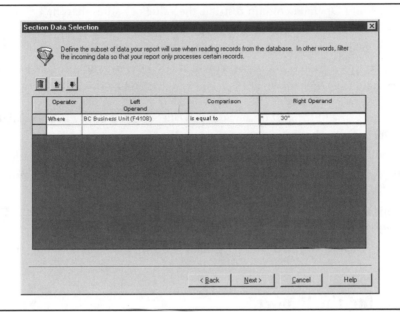

FIGURE 6-21.   The RDD Section Data Selection form

In the grid of the Section Data Selection window, you build the SQL Where clause that filters the data that will appear in the section of the report. To do this, define the following columns in the grid:

- The Operator column in the first row of the grid must contain a Where statement. Subsequent cells in other rows of the grid will provide you with And and Or statements to further define your data selection criteria.

- The Left Operand column lists all of the items that are available for your criteria.

- The Comparison column compares the values in the Left Operand and Right Operand columns according to your criteria. The valid comparisons are is equal to, is greater than, is greater than or equal to, is less than, is less than or equal to, and is not equal to.

- The Right Operand column restricts the value or values that the Left Operand can have. This can include assigning the Right Operand to a literal value, null, zero, blank, column in a business view (BC), form interconnect value (FI), processing option (PO), report constant (RC), report variable (RV), system variable (SV), system value (SL), and variable (VA).

To delete a row in the grid of the Section Data Selection dialog box, highlight the row and click the Garbage Can button.

To modify the order of rows in the grid of the Section Data Selection dialog box, highlight the row and click the up arrow button or down arrow button to move the row up or down in the grid, respectively.

For this example, the Where clause is Where BC Business Unit (F4108) is equal to "30".

When you have finished defining the data selection for the report, click the Next button.

Generating the Report

At this point, you have performed all of the RDD steps for defining your report. The RDD displays the Finish form, as shown in Figure 6-22.

After you click the Finish button on the form, RDD processes your responses to its questions and generates the report. When the RDD has finished generating the report, you will see the design layout of the report in RDA.

CAUTION

Once you click the Finish button on the Finish form of the RDD, you will not be able to access some of the RDD panels for this report. If you want to add another section in your report, you will need to add it manually by using the menus in the RDA application. To avoid extra work, before you click the Finish button, review the choices you made. You can use the Navigation Assistant and the Back and Next buttons in the RDD forms to check that you have defined your report properly.

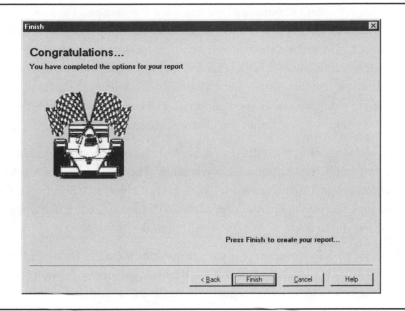

FIGURE 6-22.   The RDD Finish form

Viewing and Modifying Reports

In RDA, you can view and modify every constant, variable, section, and other properties of your report. The RDA includes Report, Preview, Attachments, and Column tabs that allow you to work with your report's design. To assist you in viewing and modifying your report in RDA, there are several dockable toolbars available:

- The File toolbar includes the standard New, Open, Save, Cut, Copy, Paste, and Undo buttons, which perform the same functions that are available in all Windows-based applications. The toolbar also has an Item Properties button, which allows you to view the property of a selected report constant or variable.

- The View toolbar contains the Business View Browser and Data Dictionary Browser buttons that you use to select a data item from the business view of the section and from the data dictionary itself, respectively. The Refresh Preview Window button forces RDA to execute the report again so you can preview it in the Preview tab. The Switch View Mode button switches the view mode from design to print preview in the Report tab. The Hide/Show Invisible Sections button either hides or shows the hidden sections in a report.

- The Section toolbar includes the Create Columnar Section, Create Group Section, and Create Tabular Section buttons. The Select Business View button lets you assign a business view to your section. The Quick Section button launches the Section Layout form of the RDD (shown earlier in Figure 6-18) to allow you to select or deselect a field from the business view of the section.

- The Insert toolbar contains the Constant, Alpha Variable, Numeric Variable, Date Variable, and Smart Field buttons. By clicking one of the buttons, you can insert a new field into your report. The Smart Field button is only available for tabular sections.

- The Tabular toolbar is activated only when you are working in a tabular section. You can use it to edit all of the properties that you can modify when you are designing and modifying a tabular section. The Tabular toolbar includes Data Selection, Define Calculation, Inclusion Event Rule, Column Detail, Modify Row Data Selection, Modify Row Calculation, Add Row Data, Create Calculation Row, Underline Row, Create Constant Row, Sum Row, and Change To/From Cell Mode buttons.

- The Layout toolbar contains the alignment buttons that allow you to modify the alignment of report constants and variables in a report. The toolbar is inactive until you select one or more fields for alignment. The Layout toolbar includes Align Left, Align Right, Align Center, Align Top, Align Center, and Align Bottom buttons.

Changing Report Properties

In RDA, you can view and modify the properties for report constants, variables, and sections, as well as for the report itself. You can change characteristics such as the name, description, and font of report items. Sections in a report can have their own data sequencing and data selection.

NOTE

When you have finished viewing and modifying report properties in the appropriate form, click the OK button to save your changes and exit the form. If you click the Cancel button, you will exit the form without saving the modifications you made to the properties of the report item.

Modifying a Report Constant

To view or modify the properties of a constant in the report, select the report constant in the Report tab, right-click, and choose Properties from the pop-up menu, as shown in Figure 6-23.

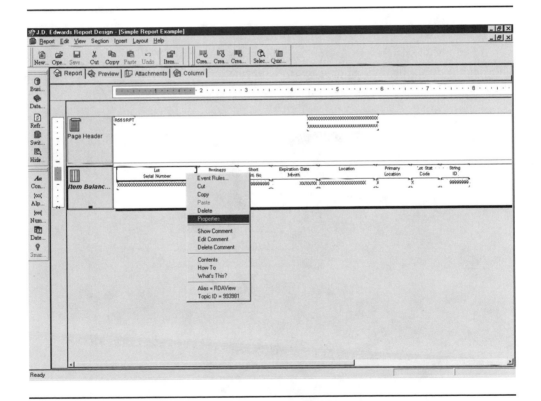

FIGURE 6-23. Choosing Properties for a constant in the Report tab

You will see the Column Heading Properties form, which contains the following tabs:

- The General tab, shown in Figure 6-24, contains the name and heading for the constant. This information will appear on the report.

- The Font/Color tab, shown in Figure 6-25, lets you change the font and color settings for the report constant. As you select a different font, color, style, and size, a preview of your changes appears in the Sample box. If you are not satisfied with the current settings of the font and color for the constant, click the Defaults button to reset them to their original values.

- The Style tab, shown in Figure 6-26, lets you place graphics around the report constant, place a rectangular box around the constant, or underline and overline the constant.

- The Advanced tab, shown in Figure 6-27, includes the Visual option, which allows you to hide or show the constant on the report.

If you need assistance while you are editing the properties for the constant, click the Help button. The online help provides information about the different options in the Column Heading Properties form.

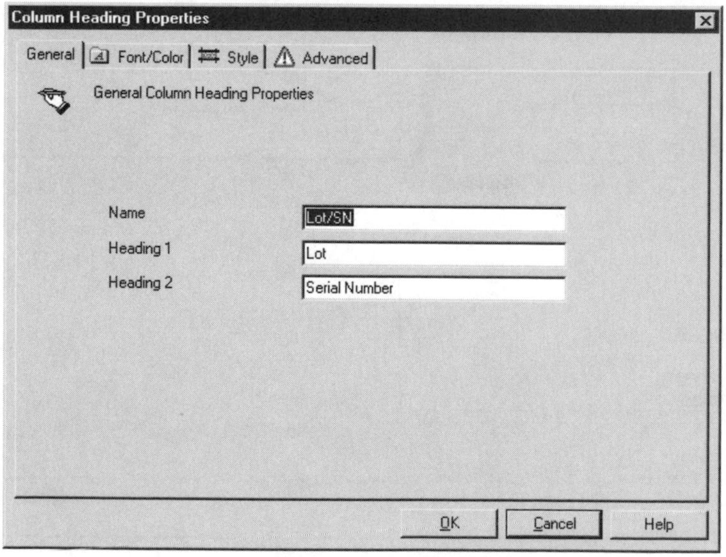

FIGURE 6-24. The General tab of the Column Headings Properties form

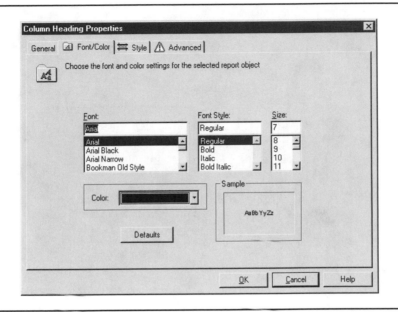

FIGURE 6-25. The Font/Color tab of the Column Headings Properties form

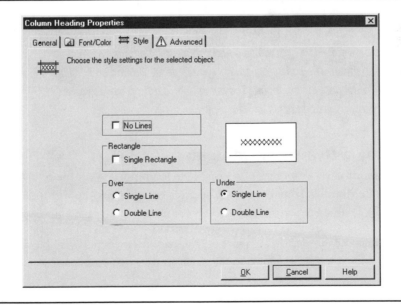

FIGURE 6-26. The Style tab of the Column Headings Properties form

Client Modifications Using OneWorld

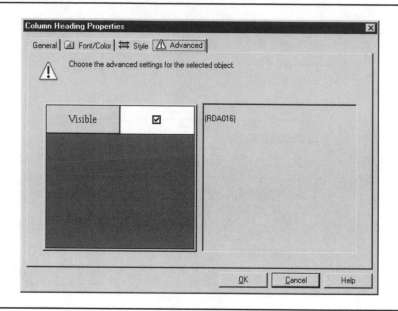

FIGURE 6-27. The Advanced tab of the Column Headings Properties form

TIP

For all report constants and variables in the Report tab of RDA, you can assign a comment to the field. Right-click the field and choose the Comment menu item from the pop-up menu. The comments are only available for viewing and editing in RDA; they do not print in your report. The comments feature provides you with the ability to write design notes into the report.

Modifying a Report Variable in a Report

To view or modify the properties of a variable in the report, select the report variable in the Report tab, right-click, and choose Properties from the pop-up menu. You will see the Column Variable Properties form, which contains the following tabs:

- The General tab, shown in Figure 6-28, associates the report variable with the data item and table that is defined in the business view that is assigned to the section.

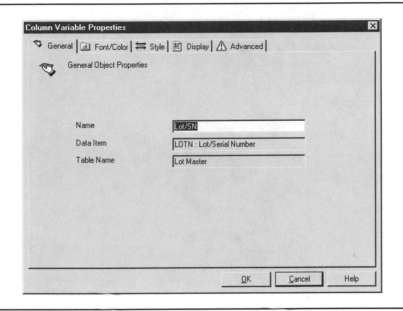

FIGURE 6-28.   The General tab of the Column Variable Properties form

- The Font/Color tab lets you change the font and color settings for the report constant. It is identical to the same tab in the Column Heading Properties form (shown earlier in Figure 6-25).

- The Style tab lets you place graphics around the report variable, place a rectangular box around the variable, or underline and overline the variable. It is identical to the same tab in the Column Headings Properties form (shown earlier in Figure 6-26).

- The Display tab, shown in Figure 6-29, allows you to set the justification and length of the value printed on the report for the report variable.

- The Advanced tab, shown in Figure 6-30, contains four options. The Visible option allows you to hide or show the variable on the report. The Suppress At Totals option prevents the variable from being printed on total lines for a report. The Print On Change Only option prints the variable on the report only when its value changes. The Global Variable option makes the variable available for use in all sections of the report.

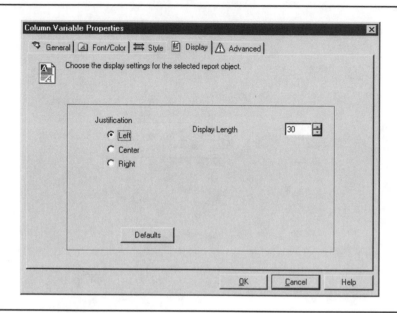

FIGURE 6-29.   The Display tab of the Column Variable Properties form

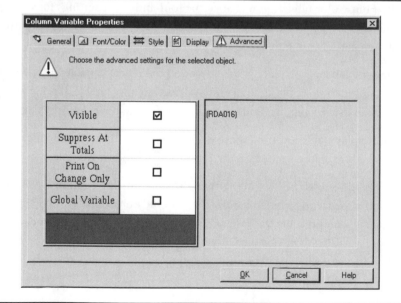

FIGURE 6-30.   The Advanced tab of the Column Variable Properties form

Changing Section Properties

You may need to change the properties of a section in a report. For example, you may want to change the name of the section, disable fields that are within it, or turn on certain advanced features. To view or modify the properties of a section in the report, select the report section in the Report tab, right-click, and choose Properties from the pop-up menu. You will see the Columnar Section dialog box, which has the following tabs:

- The General tab, shown in Figure 6-31, provides a description of the section and the business view that is assigned to it.

- The Font/Color tab is identical to the same tab in the Column Heading Properties and Column Variable Properties forms (see Figure 6-25, earlier in the chapter), except that it also contains the Apply Settings To All Objects option. That option allows you to assign the same font and color values to all of the fields attached to the section.

- The Fields tab, shown in Figure 6-32, lists all of the report constants and variables in the section. You can select any variable or constant in the grid and click the Field Properties button to access the report variable or constant properties, as described in the previous sections.

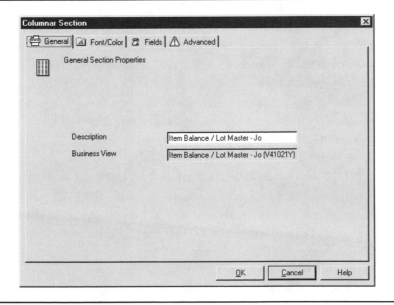

FIGURE 6-31. The General tab of the Columnar Section form

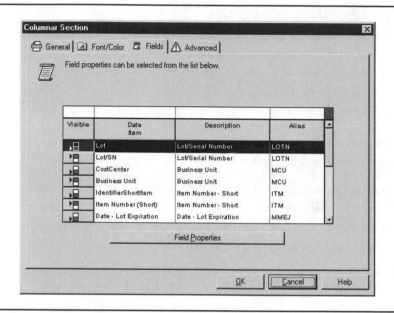

FIGURE 6-32. The Fields tab of the Columnar Section form

- The Advanced tab, shown in Figure 6-33, includes five options. The Visible option hides the section from the report that is generated. If the Absolute Position option is enabled, the section truncates the value when it exceeds the maximum length of the variable. Otherwise, the section wraps the characters to another line in the variable. The Conditional option ensures that the section is only processed when it is explicitly called. The Page Break After option forces a page break after the section has finished processing. The Reprint At Page Break option reprints the section each time a page break occurs.

Modifying the Data Sequence of a Section in a Report

You can assign different data sequences to specific report sections. To view or modify the data sequence of a section in the report, select the report section in the Report tab, right-click, and select Define Data Sequence from the pop-up menu.

The Data Sequencing form that appears has two tabs: Section Data Sequencing and Define Sort Properties. These tabs have the same data-sequencing and data-sorting options as the RDD's Section Data Sequencing and Define Sort Properties forms (see Figures 6-19 and 6-20, earlier in this chapter). See "Defining the Data Sequence of the Report" and

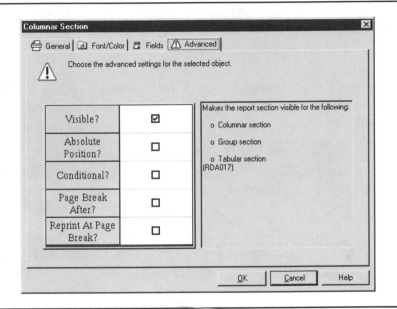

FIGURE 6-33.   The Advanced tab of the Columnar Section form

"Defining the Sort Properties of the Report," earlier in this chapter, for details on how to specify the column sequence and sort order for the section.

Modifying the Data Selection of a Section in a Report

You can also assign different data selections for specific sections in a report. To view or modify the data selection of a section in the report, select the report section in the Report tab, right-click, and select Define Data Selection from the pop-up menu.

The Data Selection tab that appears has a Section Data Selection tab. This tab has the same data-selection options as the RDD's Section Data Selection form (See Figure 6-21, earlier in this chapter). See "Defining the Data Selection for the Section," earlier in this chapter, for details on specifying the data selection for the section.

Modifying the Properties of a Report

By changing report properties, you can change the name of the report, disable sections in the report, or turn on certain advanced features. To set report properties, in the Report tab, select the Report | Properties menu item. The Properties form for the report appears. This form has five tabs with options that you can set for the report's properties.

Report Properties   The Report Properties tab, shown in Figure 6-34, contains the following properties:

- The Report Name field contains the object name of the report.

- The Version Name field displays which version or object you are modifying in RDA. If you are modifying a version of a report, the version name of the report is displayed. Otherwise, the field contains the value template, and it denotes that you are modifying the report object.

- The Processing Options field displays the name of the processing option template that is assigned to the report.

- The Totaling property options are Print Totals Only or Print Grand Totals. The Print Totals Only option changes the output of the report to display a summary report with totals only. The Print Grand Totals option changes the output of the report to allow grand total printing at the end of it.

- The Suppress All Output option prevents any output for the report.

- The Limit Number Of Primary Table Rows option restricts the number of records that the report is allowed to process at any time.

Font and Color Properties   The Font/Color tab contains the same properties as the corresponding tabs in the Column Heading Properties, Column Variable Properties, and Columnar Section forms (see Figure 6-25, earlier in the chapter). It also includes the Apply Settings To All Objects option. When you choose this option, RDA applies the font, color and style settings defined in this tab to all of the report constants and variables in the report.

Cover Page Options   The Cover Page Options tab, shown in Figure 6-35, allows you to print a cover page when you print the report. When you choose the Print Cover Page option, RDA allows you to select any report and section properties to be printed on the cover page of the report. The cover page identifies the properties that the report used during processing, and it is handy for troubleshooting problems with your reports.

Decimal Scaling Settings   The Decimal Scaling tab, shown in Figure 6-36, allows you to scale the numeric values that are used in your reports. This is very useful in cases in which the numeric values in your report are very large, and you need to scale the values to make them easier to read in the report.

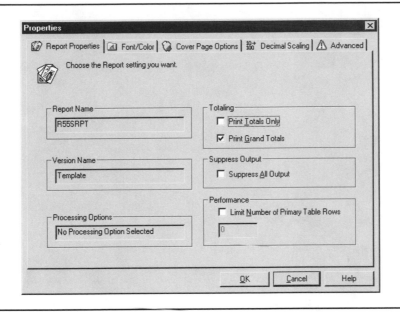

FIGURE 6-34. The Report Properties tab of the Properties form

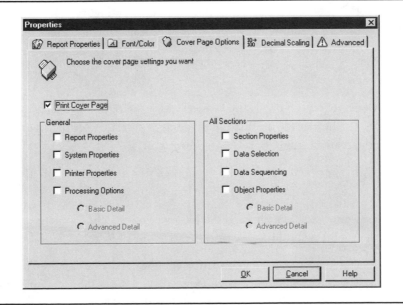

FIGURE 6-35. The Cover Page Options tab of the Properties form

Client Modifications Using OneWorld

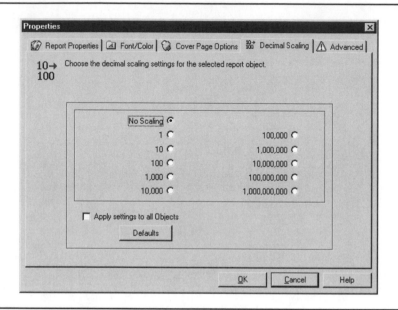

FIGURE 6-36. The Decimal Scaling tab of the Properties form

Advanced Report Properties The Advanced tab, shown in Figure 6-37, lets you set advanced properties for your report application. The following options are available:

- The Subsystem check box allows you to define the report application as a subsystem job.

- The Generate button builds the header file for the report data structure for the report. The header file is placed in the Include directory for the environment in which you are creating or modifying the report.

- The Wait Time field sets the amount of time that must pass before the report application is executed again (in milliseconds).

- The Custom check box for Paper Size allows you to define a custom paper size that the report will print.

- The Enabled check box for Transaction Processing defines that the report is enabled for transaction processing. (See Chapter 16 for information about using transaction processing in report and batch applications.)

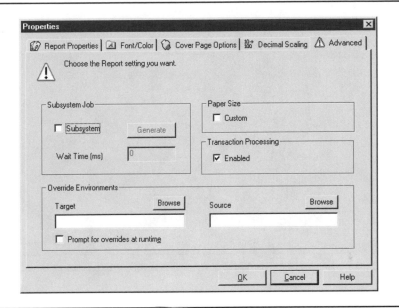

FIGURE 6-37. The Advanced tab of the Properties form

- The Override Environments section of the Advanced tab allows users to override the setting for the database and environment that the report uses during processing.

Modifying the Printer Setup for a Report

For some reports, you need to assign a specific printer or paper size, such as for payroll checks. To embed printer-specific information into a report, you can modify the report's printer setup properties to accommodate your requirements.

To modify the printer setup properties, in the Report tab, select the Report | Print Setup menu item. The Printer Setup form for the report appears, as shown in Figure 6-38. This form allows you to define the following printer setup options for the report:

- The OneWorld Printer section allows you to define the specific printer that the report application will print to. You can also force the report to always export the data processed in the report to a CSV text file.

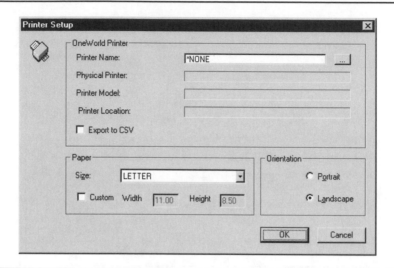

FIGURE 6-38.   The Printer Setup form

- The Paper section allows you to define the paper size for the report. If you chose the Custom option for Paper Size in the Advanced tab of the Properties form (described in the previous section), you also need to define the custom paper size for the report here.

- The Orientation section gives you a choice between landscape or portrait for the printed page orientation.

Viewing Report Elements

In RDA, you can view your report in tree format, view the ER code for the report, see all of the columns in a section's business view, or browse through the data dictionary. You can also set user options for the way that RDA displays your reports.

Viewing the Report Tree for a Report

Examining your report in the Report Tree view offers you a different perspective of it. This view logically organizes the report in a parent-child relationship. The top of the tree is the report object itself. When you expand other areas of the tree, the sections that are assigned to the report are displayed. When you expand the sections of the report in the tree, you see the dependent sections that are assigned to the report, as well as its report constants and variables.

The importance of the Report Tree view becomes obvious when you realize how it organizes the objects in your report. The information is presented in the manner that the UBE will process it. As explained in "Overview of Report and Batch Applications," earlier in this chapter, report applications are processed by the UBE from the top to the bottom for sections, and from left to right for the fields within the section. Therefore, as you view your report in the Report Tree view, you are viewing the processing order of the sections and fields in the report.

T I P

If you need to know the execution order of sections in a report or batch application, examine your report in the Report Tree view. This view shows the execution order of the UBE when it processes your report.

To examine the layout of your report in the Report Tree view, in the RDA application, select the View | Report Tree menu item. The Report Tree view appears, as shown in Figure 6-39. The top of the tree is the overall report, and the sections of the report are listed beneath it. In the example shown in Figure 6-40, the tree shows all of the components assigned to the Simple Report Example application (R55SRPT).

Viewing the Event Rules for a Report Using BrowsER

The BrowsER view allows you to examine only the ER code of a report or batch application. This view offers an efficient alternative to using the "hunt-and-peck" method of examining code for different objects and events in the report object or version. The BrowsER dialog box offers you more flexibility because it allows you to perform a global search for all ER code in the report object or version.

To examine the layout of your report in the BrowsER view, in RDA, select the View | BrowsER menu item. The BrowsER view for the report appears, as shown in Figure 6-40.

The BrowsER view provides more information than its Report Tree view counterpart. The BrowsER view includes the section type for each section in the report, the type of field located on the report, and any ER code attached to an event of a component in the report.

To adjust the BrowsER view, right-click to display the pop-up menu. In the example shown in Figure 6-40, the Show Object IDs option is selected, which shows that the

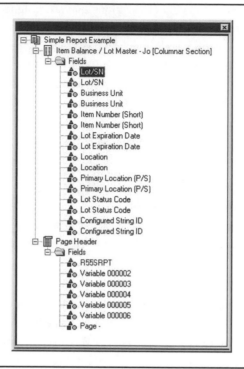

FIGURE 6-39. The Report Tree view in RDA

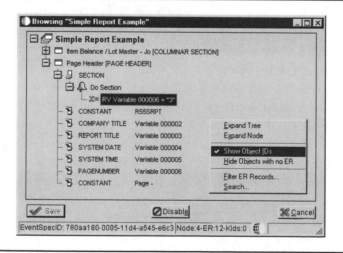

FIGURE 6-40. The BrowsER view in RDA

report variable 000006 contains an assignment of 3 in the Do Section event of the page header section. The BrowsER view pop-up menu contains the following options:

- The Expand Tree option expands all of the nodes in the tree.

- The Expand Node option expands (or collapses) a node. You can perform the same function by clicking the plus or minus button to the left of a component.

- The Show Object IDs option provides the identification number for the component or ER line that is in the TAM specs for the report application. The object ID is shown in the status bar for the BrowsER view.

- The Hide Objects With No ER option removes all components in the report that do not have any ER code in their events.

- The Filter ER Records option allows you to filter the lines of ER displayed in the BrowsER view. You can filter the lines of ER by comments, field assignments, system functions, and so on.

- The Search option allows you to find one or more words in the BrowsER view. You can search for strings in the names of objects and in the lines of ER code in the report.

Viewing the Business View Columns for a Report

The Business View Columns Browser view lists all of the columns that are in the business view for the section that you are currently modifying. This view allows you to select a data item and drag it to add it to a section.

To see the Business View Columns Browser view, in RDA, select the View | Business View Columns Browser menu item. The Business View Columns Browser view for the report appears, as shown here:

BSVW: V41021Y - Item Balance / Lot Master - Jo

Data Item	Description	Alias	Table Name
Lot	Lot/Serial Number	LOTN	F4108
CostCenter	Business Unit	MCU	F4108
IdentifierShortItem	Item Number - Shor	ITM	F4108
Date - Lot Expiratio	Date - Lot Expiratio	MMEJ	F4108
Location	Location	LOCN	F41021
PrimaryBinPS	Primary Location (F	PBIN	F41021
LotStatusCode	Lot Status Code	LOTS	F41021
ConfiguredStringID	Configured String II	CSID	F41021

Client Modifications Using OneWorld

The Business View Columns Browser view shows the column's data item name, description, alias, and table that it is assigned. You can select a column in the view and drag and drop the column onto the section.

Viewing the Data Dictionary Browser

For situations in which the required data item does not exist in the business view, it is sometimes easier to add a data item from the data dictionary instead of modifying the business view. The Data Dictionary Browser view allows you to search for a data item using the QBE line. When you find the data item that you need, you can drag it onto a section.

To use the Data Dictionary Browser, in RDA, select the View | Data Dictionary Browser menu item. The Data Dictionary Browser view for the report appears, as shown here:

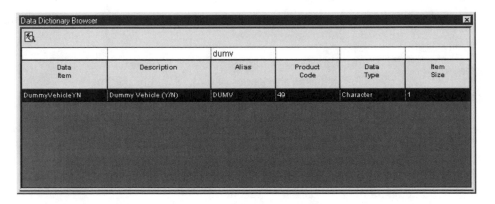

In the Data Dictionary Browser view, you can search for any data item in the data dictionary. To add a data item to your report, drag and drop it onto the section.

Viewing and Modifying the User Options for RDA

RDA provides a set of options that allow you to customize the look and feel of the RDA application. This is particularly useful for hiding or showing certain elements of RDA. For example, you can enable or disable tabs, rulers, and the Navigation Assistant.

To customize RDA to meet your needs as you are modifying reports, select the View | User Options menu item. The User Options form appears, as shown in Figure 6-41.

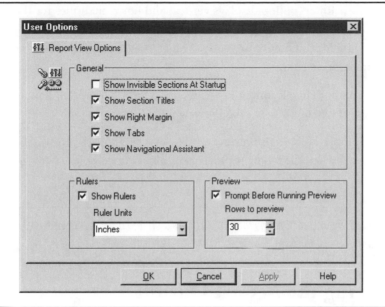

FIGURE 6-41.   The User Options form

Choose one or more of the following options to change the look and feel of RDA.

- The Show Invisible Sections at Startup option shows all hidden sections in the report when it is displayed.

- The Show Section Titles option displays the name of the section on the left side of the report when viewed on the Report tab of RDA.

- The Show Right Margin option has RDA display the right margin of the report on the Report tab.

- The Show Tabs option enables or disables the Report, Preview, Attachments, and Column tabs in RDA.

- The Show Navigation Assistant option displays the Navigation Assistant when you are creating a report with the RDD.

- The Show Rulers option displays vertical and horizontal rules for the report. If you highlight any report constant or variable in the report, the rulers will display their position on the report. You can set the ruler units to inches, centimeters, or points.

- The Prompt Before Running Preview option has RDA prompt you to preview the report when you select the Preview tab.

- The Number of Rows to Preview option sets the number of rows that are processed when the report is previewed in the Preview tab.

N O T E

The Apply button in the User Options form allows you to set the options that you modified before you exit the form.

Previewing the Report Output

The Preview tab in RDA allows you to see what your report will look like before you print it. This feature saves you time in the design, modify, and test cycles of report and batch application development.

To preview a report in RDA, click the Preview tab for the report you are designing. As RDA processes the records for the report preview, it reports the current status of the processing. When RDA has finished processing the records for the report, the Preview tab will display the report, as shown in Figure 6-42.

N O T E

Two User Options settings affect preview processing, as described in the previous section. If the Prompt Before Running Preview option is selected, you will be prompted to confirm that you want to preview the report. Also, RDA will only process the number of records set by the Rows To Preview option.

Creating Notes for Your Report

The Attachments tab allows you to attach media objects to the report you are currently designing. The attachment can contain text, images, OneWorld shortcuts, and any file through the use of OLE. The information in the Attachments tab is only viewable in RDA, and it cannot be printed to another report.

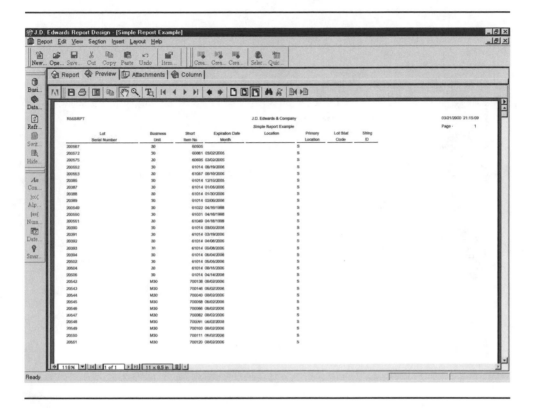

FIGURE 6-42. The Preview tab showing the Simple Report Example application

To edit the information in the Attachments tab of a report, click the Attachments tab for the report you are designing in RDA. The attachment for the report is displayed, as shown in Figure 6-43.

The Attachments tab provides you with the same editor that is available for attachments in OneWorld. The editor is useful for writing design notes and documentation for the report you are designing.

Reviewing the Properties of Section Columns

The Column tab in RDA allows you to view all of the properties of columns in a section. The information in the Column tab includes the data item type of the column, column heading description, and the length of the field. The Column tab is very useful in situations in which the formatting of the fields in the report is inconsistent.

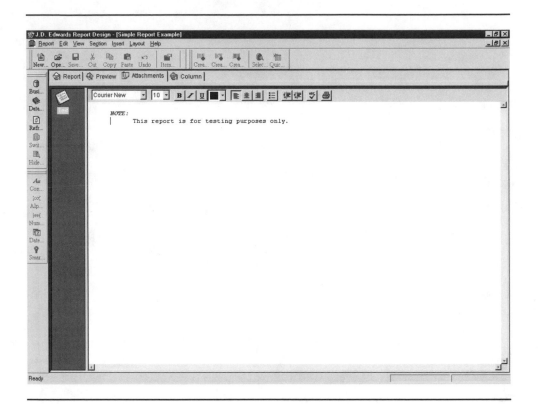

FIGURE 6-43.   The Attachments tab for the Simple Report Example application

To view the properties of the columns in the report, click the Column tab for the report you are designing in RDA. A summary of all column properties in the report is displayed, as shown in Figure 6-44. Information such as the font, font size, display length, justification, and so on, appears on this tab.

Submitting a Report from OneWorld Explorer

After you have viewed and modified various objects in your report, you will need to execute it by submitting it to the UBE. First, you must select a version of the report you want to process. The system combines the report version you selected with its object to create the report, and then the system issues the report to the UBE for execution.

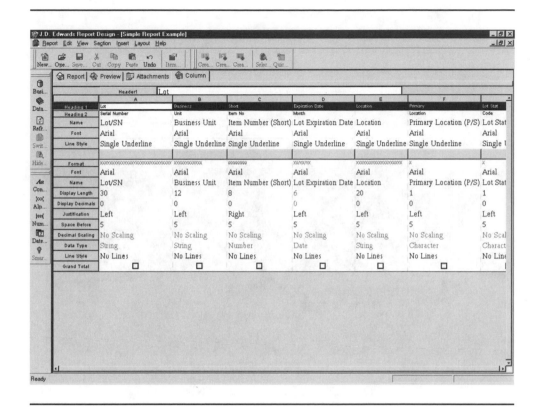

FIGURE 6-44. The Column tab of the RDA application for the Simple Report Example application

NOTE

If you selected the Auto-Create Version when you created the report object in the Object Librarian application (P9860), you will notice that the system created a XJDE0001 version for you. This feature is very useful in reducing the time it takes from report object creation to its eventual execution.

To submit the report from OneWorld Explorer, perform the following steps:

1. Select the Tools | Report Versions menu item.

2. The Work With Batch Versions form of the Batch Versions application (P98305) appears, as shown in Figure 6-45. Type the object name of the report

Client Modifications Using OneWorld

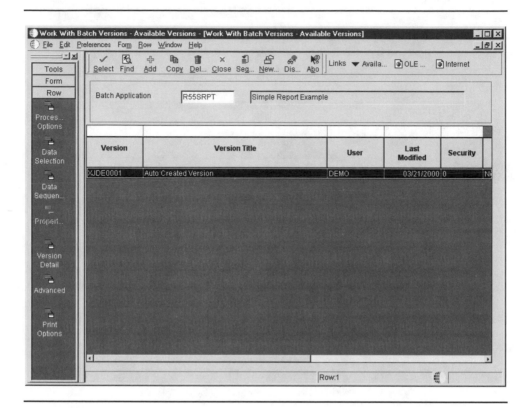

FIGURE 6-45.   The Work With Batch Versions form of the Batch Versions application for the Simple Report Example application

into the Batch Application field. In this example, the value **R55SRPT** is entered into the field.

3. Click the Find button to show all of the versions for the report. As shown in Figure 6-45, RDA defined an Auto Created Version for the report, because the Auto Create Version check box was enabled during creation of the report object.

4. To initiate the execution of the report, highlight the version and click the Select button. The system displays the Version Prompting form of the Work With Batch Versions application, as shown in Figure 6-46.

5. If you need to override the execution location or enable logging of the report, click the Advanced button. The Advanced Version Prompting form appears, as

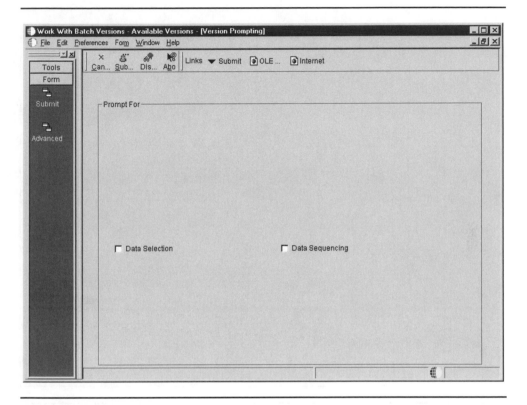

FIGURE 6-46. The Version Prompting form of the Work With Batch Versions application for the Simple Report Example application

shown in Figure 6-47. This form contains the following options for advanced application-processing features:

- The Override Location option allows you to override the location of execution for the report application. After you click the OK button, the system will prompt you to select a machine to execute the report application. This option is particularly useful when you want to test your modifications to a report locally.

- The Logging option sets the UBE to write log messages to the JDE.LOG file.

- The Tracing option sets the UBE to write tracing messages to the JDEDEBUG.LOG file.

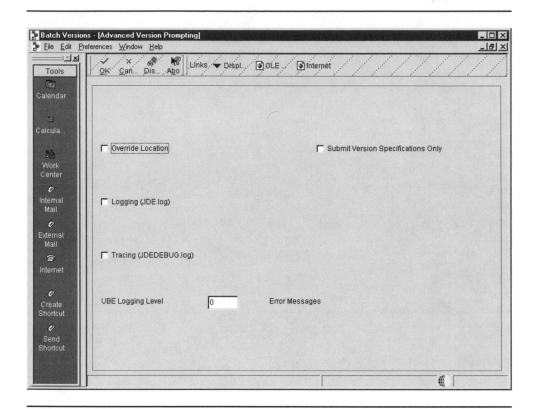

FIGURE 6-47. The Advanced Version Prompting form of the Batch Versions application for the Simple Report Example application

- The Submit Version Specifications Only option moves the report to an enterprise server, without processing it. This field requires that you enable the Override Location option so that you can select the enterprise server to receive the report application.

- The UBE Logging Level setting indicates the trace level for logging to the JDEDEBUG.LOG file. The types of messaging that are available are Error (0), Informative (1), Section Level (2), Object Level (3), ER Level (4), SQL (5), and UBE Function (6).

6. Click the Submit button to submit the report without making any changes to the Data Selection and Data Sequencing parameters. The Report Output Destination form of the Work With Batch Versions application appears, as shown in Figure 6-48.

7. The system executes the report. When the system has finished processing the report, the output of the report is displayed, as shown in Figure 6-49.

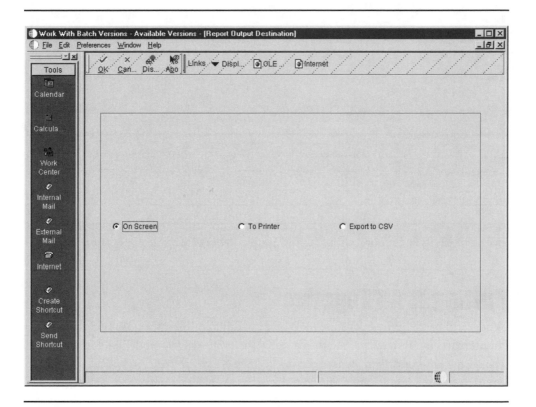

FIGURE 6-48. The Report Output Destination form of the Batch Versions application for the Simple Report Example application

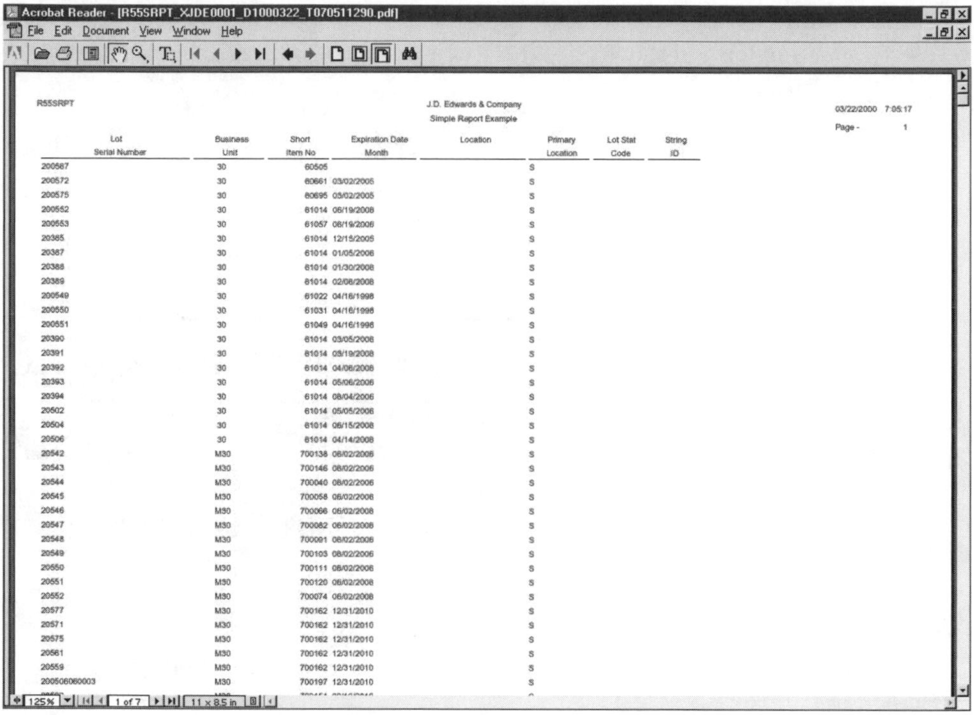

R55SRPT

J.D. Edwards & Company
Simple Report Example

03/22/2000 7:05:17
Page - 1

Lot Serial Number	Business Unit	Short Item No	Expiration Date Month	Location	Primary Location	Lot Stat Code	String ID
200567	30	60505			S		
200572	30	60661	03/02/2005		S		
200575	30	60695	03/02/2005		S		
200552	30	61014	06/19/2008		S		
200553	30	61057	06/19/2006		S		
20385	30	61014	12/15/2005		S		
20387	30	61014	01/05/2006		S		
20388	30	61014	01/30/2008		S		
20389	30	61014	02/06/2008		S		
200549	30	61022	04/16/1998		S		
200550	30	61031	04/16/1998		S		
200551	30	61049	04/16/1996		S		
20390	30	61014	03/05/2006		S		
20391	30	61014	03/19/2008		S		
20392	30	61014	04/06/2008		S		
20393	30	61014	05/06/2006		S		
20394	30	61014	08/04/2006		S		
20502	30	61014	05/05/2006		S		
20504	30	61014	06/15/2008		S		
20506	30	61014	04/14/2008		S		
20542	M30	700138	06/02/2006		S		
20543	M30	700146	08/02/2006		S		
20544	M30	700040	08/02/2006		S		
20545	M30	700058	06/02/2006		S		
20546	M30	700066	06/02/2008		S		
20547	M30	700082	06/02/2008		S		
20548	M30	700091	06/02/2006		S		
20549	M30	700103	08/02/2006		S		
20550	M30	700111	08/02/2006		S		
20551	M30	700120	06/02/2008		S		
20552	M30	700074	06/02/2008		S		
20577	M30	700162	12/31/2010		S		
20571	M30	700162	12/31/2010		S		
20575	M30	700162	12/31/2010		S		
20561	M30	700162	12/31/2010		S		
20559	M30	700162	12/31/2010		S		
200506060003	M30	700197	12/31/2010		S		

FIGURE 6-49. The report output for the Simple Report Example application

Putting It All Together

Report and batch applications in OneWorld are different than their WorldSoftware counterparts by design, because they employ the event-driven model for applications. The events are not driven by user actions, as they are in interactive applications. In report and batch applications, the UBE processes events as it processes each object in the report.

One of the useful aspects of creating reports in OneWorld is that they can be exported to many output mediums: Adobe PDF files, hardcopies from a printer, or CSV files. This provides you with the ability to switch output medium for data collection or reporting at any time.

The focus of this chapter is on creating a single report and modifying it through one of its versions. The examples provided you with a detailed view of how to modify and create reports in RDA. Also, it allowed you to see how one report can meet the needs of all employees in a company by creating a modified version of it.

The information in this chapter provides you with a foundation for other topics related to batch applications—in particular, how batch applications are used in interoperability (Chapter 14) and transaction processing (Chapter 16).

Client Modifications Using OneWorld

CHAPTER 7

One Common Language: Event Rules

All the OneWorld tools for application development utilize a common language, called Event Rules. You code this language through a convenient point-and-click user interface. Event Rules—ER for short—can be used on any event within an application, batch application, database trigger, or Named Event Rule (NER). This allows you to call business functions, applications, and reports, and to manipulate data to produce the needed results. Like other programming languages, you can use variables and typical programming elements to code your logic.

This chapter covers the following topics about Event Rules:

- **OneWorld's Event Rules Language**   The overview section explains the fundamentals of Event Rules. We'll discuss each object that can use ER, and introduce the components used to create them.

- **Variables**   Variables are one of the basic building blocks of Event Rules. This section explains how to assign values to variables, and how to create calculations using variables.

- **If Statements and While Loops**   These components—Event Rules If statements and While loops—are another basic building block of ER. We'll show you how to set up conditional statements and loops in your code.

- **System Functions**   The system functions components of Event Rules are provided by J.D. Edwards. These functions enable you to perform specialized modifications and calculations in forms and batch applications.

- **Business Functions**   Business functions, too, can be used inside ER. We'll show you how to choose business functions, and how to hook up functions written in C as well as Named Event Rules.

- **Table I/O**   As you develop logic using Event Rules, you'll probably need to do table input and output. This section explains how to fetch, insert, update, and delete records from tables using ER.

- **Calling Forms and Sections**   Many forms and reports call other forms and reports to meet business needs. This section explains the simple process of connecting applications and batch applications using ER.

- **Event Rules Examples and Tips**   To put in practice all the information discussed in the chapter, we'll walk through an example using Event Rules.

OneWorld's Event Rules Language

As discussed in Chapters 4 and 5, applications and reports are event driven. Events occur when the user enters a form, clicks on the grid, tabs out of a field, clicks a button, or exits the form. Some events occur without the user's doing anything. For example, events occur when the form or report processes data by fetching information, or before and after the application displays grid rows. Events also occur when a form or report is started by a user or another application, report, or function.

DEFINITION

*An **event**, to a OneWorld developer, is any specific action the user triggers while interacting with the form, or that the form or report triggers while interacting with the database or other objects.*

As implied by the words used in the name Event Rules, you enter the Event Rules for an event; and these rules are executed when the event is triggered by the user, application, or report. For example, the event called Button Pressed occurs when a user clicks a button on a form inside an application. If you create Event Rules on this event, they will be executed when the user clicks this button. In other words, you can enter logic (Event Rules) on an event (Button Pressed).

All OneWorld objects that use Event Rules will use the same ER interface and have basically the same functionality. However, there are some differences in ER for the various OneWorld objects. For example, if you are creating or changing ER for an application, you use a particular set of system functions that are different from the ER for a report.

NOTE

It's in your best interest to design in advance what you want done by your application or report, and then plot out the content and location of your logic inside the application or batch application. If you start adding and changing ER without knowing exactly what results you want, you'll likely have to backtrack and make corrections. For example, if you add logic to the wrong event, you'll have to re-create the logic in a new location. Be sure you understand the flow of events as described in Appendix B.

Client Modifications Using OneWorld

Objects That Use Event Rules

As mentioned, Event Rules can be used in interactive and batch applications. In addition, you can add ER to table triggers, and to business functions that use Named Event Rules (Named ER or NER, for short). In general, there are three ways to access Event Rules on an application or report. First, select where you want to modify the Event Rules, and then do one of the following:

- Right-click and select Event Rules from the pop-up menu.

- Press CTRL-R.

- Select Form | Event Rules.

That is the general way to access Event Rules, but each object is different. Let's take a look at the slightly different processes for accessing the ER in each object.

Accessing Application Event Rules

To access Event Rules for an application, you must first check out the application and select Design in the Object Librarian. In Forms Design Aid (FDA), select the form on which you want to add or change the Event Rules. Application events occur on any input-capable control, on the grid, and on the form itself, so finding the event that you want to modify may require some searching. For example, if you want to change the way the grid is being updated, you might need to change ER on the form event Grid Record Is Fetched or Write Grid Line Before, or even on the Find button.

CAUTION

If two people check out the same object, modify it, and check it back in, only the changes made by the second person to check in the object will be saved. The first person's changes will be lost. OneWorld will not merge the ER; the last check-in overwrites all previous check-ins. This is true even if the programmers are working on separate forms inside the same application. We recommend that you carefully coordinate modifications, making sure that an object is altered and checked back in before another person checks it out again.

Controls, Grids, and Forms   Here's how to access Event Rules for controls, grids, and forms:

- For a control, right-click the control and choose Event Rules from the pop-up menu.

- For the grid, right-click anywhere in the grid and choose Event Rules from the pop-up menu.

- For the form, right-click some part of the form that does not contain a control or grid. Then choose Event Rules from the pop-up menu.

Menu/Toolbar Exits, Hidden Fields, and Push Buttons   You can also add Event Rules to menu/toolbar exits, hidden fields, and push buttons. (These controls are discussed in Chapter 5.) To access Event Rules for menus and toolbar exits in FDA, follow these steps:

1. Select Form | Menu/Toolbar Exits.

2. Select the toolbar exit you want to modify.

3. Click the Event Rules button.

To access Event Rules for hidden fields or hidden push buttons:

1. Select Form | Hidden Fields.

2. Select the hidden field that you want to modify.

3. Click the Event Rules button.

Accessing Batch Process Event Rules

Getting to the ER for a batch application (discussed in Chapter 6) is slightly different than for an interactive application. First check out the batch application and go into Report Design Aid.

Usually, you add or modify ER for reports at the section level. To access the ER for a section, follow these steps:

1. Select the section you want to modify.

2. Right-click a blank area of the section.

3. Select Event Rules from the pop-up menu.

Occasionally, events are assigned to the fields that are placed inside a section (although these are rarely used). To access these Event Rules, right-click the field and choose Event Rules from the pop-up menu.

ER can also be attached to events on the report itself. To get to these events:

1. Click the parent node in the tree view. In Figure 7-1, the parent node is called Order Information.

2. Select Edit | Event Rules.

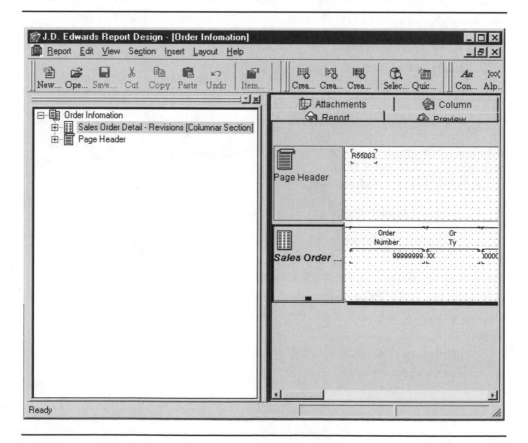

FIGURE 7-1.   Selecting the parent node for the report to get to the report's ER

Event Rules Attached to a Table Trigger

Event Rules added to a table are called *table triggers*. To access Event Rules for a table, in the Object Librarian select and check out the table. Select Form | Table ER, as shown in Figure 7-2. This displays the Event Rules Design form, on which you add Event Rules to occur anytime a certain database operation is triggered. For example, you can add ER that deletes data from a particular file whenever a record is deleted inside the table. (You'll see much more of the Event Rules Design form later in the chapter.)

N O T E

Be very careful when adding table triggers because they will be executed every time the table operation is triggered. For example, if Event Rules are added to the Fetch event and this logic is only needed once in every 1,000 table hits, then, for the other 999 fetches, the logic is just wasted processing time.

Client Modifications Using OneWorld

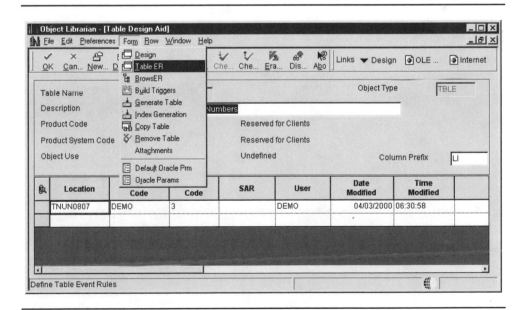

FIGURE 7-2. Selecting Form | Table ER to add Event Rules for a table

Event Rules Inside a Named Event Rule

A Named Event Rule (NER) is a business function that is coded by using Event Rules. (NERs are discussed in detail in Chapter 13.) Using NERs can be an easy and quick way to create reusable ER. With a NER, you can call the same functionality in any interactive or batch application, or even inside another NER. Read the Developer's Corner, "When to Create a NER," for additional instructions on when to use a NER.

Once the NER is created, follow the these steps to add or modify it:

1. In Object Librarian, find and select the function you want to modify.

2. Click the Design button.

3. Select the function you want to modify by clicking the grid row.

4. Select Form | Edit.

When to Create a NER

A large part of application development involves retrieving and manipulating data from tables, or standard calculation and/or formatting of data. It's very tempting to program these operations using table I/O or logic whenever you need it, whether it's inside an application or a UBE. Although this method will work, it can cause problems with program maintenance and it can affect application performance. One solution to this is to create a NER for your logic instead.

In general, you always want to try and reduce the amount of redundant code among related applications. When you need to access a table in the same way from three different applications or from two different sections inside a UBE, that may be a good time to create a NER. Another candidate for NERs is for formatting data that needs to be displayed. Sometimes an item inside an application needs to do a calculation (unit of measure, for instance) before displaying data, and this calculation logic will exist in multiple locations inside many reports or applications. It's best to create a NER to perform this logic, ensuring consistency and accuracy and reducing maintenance time. If there is an error in your calculation, you'll only need to fix the logic once rather than in every location where it's used.

The second reason to create a NER is to improve performance. Fetching from the database is faster if the function doing the fetching is on the same server as the data. When an application has to send a request from the client to the server to get the information, performance will take a hit. This is magnified if you're fetching from several different files. We have worked in development environments that do not allow table I/O inside applications at all, requiring that programmers do this in NERs instead.

Creating a NER does take a little more programming time up front to create the objects needed (such as data structures), but using NERs can save you time in the long run. They give you more flexibility from a CNC standpoint, as well as saving debugging time.

The Event Rules Design Tool

This section discusses use of the Event Rules Design tool to create and modify ER. To bring up the Event Rules Design interface, follow the instructions discussed in the earlier section "Objects That Use Event Rules." Here's the window you'll see:

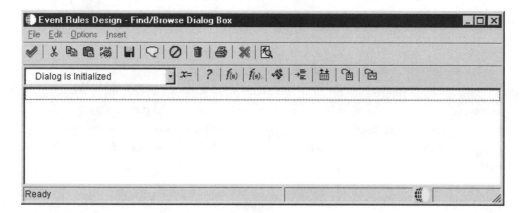

The Event Rules Design form has three main elements: the toolbar, the code pane, and the event list.

ER Design Window Toolbar

The buttons in the ER Design window's toolbar allow you to add or modify ER. There are buttons for creating and assigning variables, calling business functions, creating form and report interconnections, adding logic, and—everyone's favorite—adding comments. Table 7-1 describes the function of each button, and you'll get more acquainted with them as you work through the chapter.

Icon	Name	Description
✔	OK	Save and exit from ER.
✂ 📋 📋 📋	Cut, Copy, and Paste	ER editing operations: cut, copy, paste, and paste options. Paste options allow you to specify whether you want comments placed before and after the code you paste. This is helpful if you are pasting a large amount of code and you want to know where it starts and finishes.

TABLE 7-1. Toolbar Buttons in Event Rules Design Interface

Icon	Name	Description
🗑	Delete	Delete the line.
⊘	Disable	Disable the line.
✖	Cancel	Leave ER without saving.
💾	Save	Save ER and continue processing.
$f(\text{B})$	Business Function	Call a business function (C or NER).
$f(\text{S})$	System Function	Call a system function.
🔍	Find	Find a word or phrase inside the code.
⬆	Table I/O	Perform a database operation.
❖	Variables	Create a variable.
💬	Comment	Add a comment to the ER code.
🖨	Print	Print the Event Rules.
$x=$	Assignment	Assign a value to a variable.
📋	Form Interconnect	Call another form or application from this form.
📋	Report Interconnect	Call a report.
?	If/While	Create an If statement or a While loop.
⬦	Else	Restore a previously deleted Else statement for an existing If statement.

Client Modifications Using OneWorld

TABLE 7-1. Toolbar Buttons in Event Rules Design Interface *(continued)*

Event List

The drop-down list of events (shown open just below) contains all the events available for use with the selected object. This list is dynamic and changes when you click a control or the grid or some other part of a form, or inside another object such as a NER or batch application. Here is the Event List for a find/browse form:

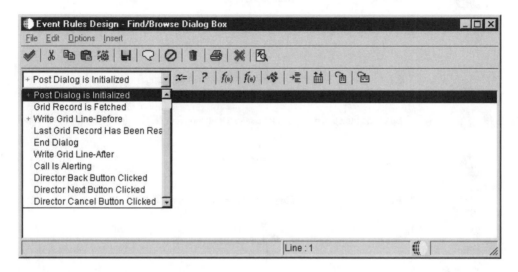

When you attach ER to an event, a green plus sign appears next to that event in the list. To add or modify ER for an event, simply select it in the list. Any existing ER for the selected event appears in the code pane.

Code Pane

The large area in the main part of the Event Rules Design window is the code pane, which displays Event Rules that have been added to the selected event. By double-clicking a line of code, you can modify it. If you click a line and then click one of the buttons that will add code previously described in Table 7-1, your new line of code is inserted below the line you are currently on.

You can also drag and drop lines of ER to new locations. Although this is much easier than re-creating the line of code, using drag-and-drop to move code can cause execution errors. For example, you might put an Else before an If, or an End If in a spot where it shouldn't be. You can also cause problems by deleting an End If statement by mistake instead of an If statement. Deleting the If statement also deletes the End If, but deleting the End If alone will leave an orphaned If. The ER interface will respond with validation errors. So be careful when dragging and dropping lines of code.

Variables

Variables of one type or another are used in almost every line of Event Rules. They are the grid columns, form controls, report variables, system values, data structure elements, processing option fields, and other elements used throughout the ER of OneWorld applications.

Application and Report Variables

When creating an interactive or batch application, you add fields by attaching business views and adding controls to the form, grid, or section. By doing this you are creating variables for use within your Event Rules. Variables of this type are usually referred to by two-letter abbreviations representing the object type. For example, business view controls are BC fields. Variables are populated at various times and used in various system functions inside ER. Table 7-2 describes the types of variables available in interactive applications.

Table 7-3 lists the variables that are used inside batch applications. These variables are similar to those found in FDA.

Variable Name	Abbreviation	Description
Business View Column	BC	An element inside the business view that is attached to the form. All columns inside the business view are listed as available variables, even if they are not placed on the grid or form.
Grid Column	GC	Any column inserted inside the grid. These columns might come from the business view, or they might come from a Data Dictionary item. They may or may not be hidden.
Grid Buffer Column	GB	Copies of the GC fields, but the form does not load them; they are used by the programmer in grid manipulation.
QBE Column	QC	The columns located in the QBE line of the application.
Form Column	FC	Any field inserted into the form itself. This could be a business view or any other Data Dictionary field.
Hypercontrol	HC	The members of the hypercontrol. These cannot be assigned values but are used in certain system functions.
Processing Option	PO	All fields inside any Processing Option template that may be attached to this form. For more information on processing options, see Chapter 12.
System Variable	SV	Variables provided by the system, such as Form_Mode.
User Variables	VA	User-defined variables.

TABLE 7-2. Variables Available in FDA

Variable Name	Abbreviation	Description
Business View Column	BC	Elements inside the section business view. All columns inside the business view are listed even if they are not placed in or visible on the section.
Processing Option	PO	All fields inside the PO template that is attached to this UBE.
System Variable	SV	Variables provided by the system.
Report Constant	RC	Constants that were placed in the section.
UBE Interconnect	RI	Report interconnect; these are the elements of the report data structure.
Report Section	RS	All the sections inside the report.
Report Variable	RV	Variables placed on the section using Data Dictionary items that are not in the business view.
User Variables	VA	Variables created by the programmer; see "User-Defined Variables."

TABLE 7-3.   Variables Available in RDA

Table 7-4 lists the variables that are available for use in Table Event Rules (TER). As you can see, there aren't many. The only types of variables you can use in TER are those you have created and the ones that appear as table columns.

Table 7-5 describes the two types of variables used inside Named Event Rules.

User-Defined Variables

In addition to the variables provided with the table, NER, application, or report, you can create user-defined variables. Since these variables aren't displayed on a form or a report, they can only be assigned values and used inside your Event Rules.

Variable Name	Abbreviation	Description
Table Column	TK	All the columns that are inside the table.
User Variables	VA	Variables created by the programmer; see "User-Defined Variables."

TABLE 7-4.   Variables Available in TER

Variable Name	Abbreviation	Description
Business Function Column	BF	All the elements that are part of the data structure attached to this function.
User Variables	VA	Variables created by the programmer; see the "User-Defined Variables" section.

TABLE 7-5.   Variables Available in NER

DEFINITION

User-defined variables are variables that can only be used in the ER where you created them.

User-defined variables are very easy to create; you simply give the variable a name and specify a Data Dictionary item after which you want to pattern your item. You can deploy a user-defined variable whenever you need to make a flag or store a value. For example, say you have a loop in your code that you want to loop 10 times only; you may need to create a variable that will be used as a counter; or, when fetching from a table, you might want a variable to receive the value that will be returned.

Here are the steps for creating your own user-defined variables:

1. Click the Variable button in the Event Rules Design toolbar (see Table 7-1). This brings you to the form displayed in Figure 7-3.

2. Type the name of the new variable into the first field. Naming conventions are discussed in the next section, "Variable Names."

3. Type the alias of a data dictionary item in the edit control inside the Data Dictionary group box. The alias is a short description of the data item. In this example, we are using PQTY. Your variable will include the characteristics of this data item.

TIP

If you don't know the alias of the data item for your variable, you can look it up in the Data Dictionary (see Chapter 2).

Client Modifications Using OneWorld

4. Select one of the variable scopes, Form or Event, as described later in "Variable Scope."

5. Click the Add button to create your variable.

6. Add other variables as needed. When you're ready to return to the Event Rules Design interface, click OK.

Now let's take a closer look at the information you provide when you add a user-defined variable: the variable name, scope, and Data Dictionary item.

Variable Names

The variable name can be anything you want, but we recommend that you follow a naming convention. For example, you might want to add the Data Dictionary alias to

FIGURE 7-3. User-Defined Variables form

the end of names, as in mnItemNumber_ITM. By adding the alias to the end of the variable, you will always know what data item was used when the variable was created. Make sure your variable name is descriptive; for example, if you have multiple items that are all numbers, make sure you give the variable a descriptive name such as mnParentItemNumber_ITM, or mnInventoryItemNumber_ITM.

The two characters, *mn*, at the front of the variable name mnItemNumber_ITM are an example of a naming scheme known as *Hungarian notation*. You can add this one- or two-character prefix to identify the class or usage of the variable. In this case, *mn* stands for *math numeric;* other indicators are *sz* for a null-terminated string, *c* for character, and *jd* for Julian date. There is no "standard" Hungarian notation; the point is to create a consistent system. For a full list of recommended prefixes, see Chapter 13.

Try to avoid giving variables vague names such as Number, String, or Flag; use specific names such as cCartonInvalidFlag_EV01 instead. When you establish a naming standard, make it easy to recognize the use and type of each variable; this helps anyone reading the code. Like most programming languages, ER does not allow you to include spaces or special characters such as asterisks and hyphens in variable names.

Variable Scope

When you define the scope of the variable, you are telling the application where this variable can be used inside your ER. If you want a variable to be used the entire time a form is active, you'll select Form as the scope. If your variable will only be used inside one event, you can select Event as the scope. An Event-level variable can only be used inside the event where it's created. After all processing is finished in the event, the variable is no longer valid (it is "out of scope"). The next time you enter this event, the variable does not retain the previous value.

Variables used in a report have three levels for scope: Report, Section, and Event. If a variable has Report scope, it can be used inside the Event Rules of any event in any section of a report. With Section scope, it can be used in any event inside the section where it was created. A variable with Event scope can only be used in the event where it was created.

N O T E

You could create a variable in an event with the same name as a variable in another event, as long as the scope for both variables is Event. This creates two separate variables.

When creating a variable inside an interactive or batch application, you can make the variable's scope either Event or Form/Report. Choose the Form/Report scope *only* if you need to use the variable in other events, or if you need the variable to retain its value until the next time the event is hit.

For simple loop counters or temporary storage of a value between different ER lines, use the Event scope. If you give every variable the Form/Report scope, it's likely to become difficult to discern the purpose of each variable. By using a smaller scope for the majority of your variables, you reduce the number of variables on each event.

The scope is appended as a prefix in the list of available events. For example, the variable mnTotalQuantity, given an Event scope, appears as user variable VA evt_mnTotalQuantity. The "evt" portion indicates the scope.

NOTE

For Named Event Rules you can only create Event-level variables.

Grid Variables   In FDA, you have an additional option: You can make a variable a *grid variable*. Enabling the Grid Variable option (shown earlier in Figure 7-3) adds the variable to the grid row. In other words, it creates this same variable on every grid row. You can think of it as an invisible grid column. For example, if you have three grid rows on your form, each grid row will contain a grid variable, and each of these variables can have a different value. When the user selects that grid row, the grid variable associated with that grid row will be available.

Associated Data Item

After you define the name and scope of the variable, you must associate it with a data item. The variable you create will inherit the properties of the associated data item.

You should use the same data item as what you will be loading into this variable. For example, in Figure 7-3, we associated the data item PQTY to our variable. Therefore, the variable will include all the characteristics of PQTY, including the field size (length 15). In some cases, however, you'll need to assign a generic data item for a flag or a calculation. OneWorld provides the data items listed in Table 7-6 for you to use as generic variables.

Variable Assignment

Now that you know about the types of variables you can use in a OneWorld object, we'll examine the process of assigning values to them. During the processing of a J.D. Edwards

Type of Variable	DD Item	Description
Character	EV01	For simple flags or a character.
Math numeric	MN29D9	This is a number with length 29 and 9 decimal places. It can be used for calculations.
Integer	INT01	Creates an integer for counter variables.
Long integer	GENLNG	Creates a long integer that can be used for cache handles or other values.

TABLE 7-6.   Generic Data Dictionary Items

form or report, some of these variables, such as business view columns or grid columns, may be populated automatically by the form or report. In the case of the user-defined variables or Grid Buffer (GB) fields, the programmer must populate the variables. In either case, you may need to change the value of a variable inside your Event Rules. To do this, you'll use an assignment statement or OneWorld's Expression Manager.

Assignment Statements

An assignment statement is line of code with an "equals" statement in it; for example: szCostCenterSave_MCU = szBranchPlant

To create an assignment statement, click the *x=* (Assignment) button in the Event Rules Design window; or double-click one of the assignment statements in the code pane. This brings up the following Assignment form, in which you'll assign a value to a variable. The value can be a literal value, the value of another variable, or the result of a calculation.

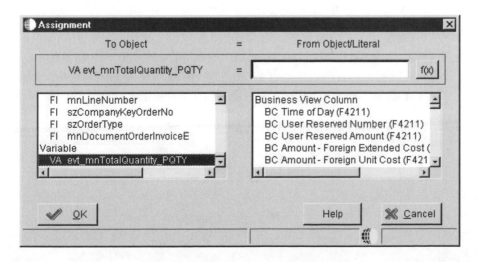

Client Modifications Using OneWorld

To assign a literal value to the variable, follow these steps.

1. Click the *x=* button on the Event Rules Design toolbar.

2. In the Assignment form, click to select the variable in the list on the left. The variable will appear on the left-hand side of the assignment field (To Object) just above the list box.

3. In the blank box to the right of the selected variable (From Object/Literal), type a literal value, such as **10** for an integer, or **car** for a string. Obviously, the literal value must match the data type of the variable. For instance, you cannot assign a "cat" to a math numeric variable.

4. Click OK to process the assignment and return to the Event Rules Design interface.

Although the form should initialize the variables to a zero or blank value, if you are using these variables multiple times you may need to initialize them yourself. To initialize a variable, assign the variable a value of 0 or blank before you start to use the variable. The can be done as the beginning of ER code for an event.

To assign a variable the value of another variable:

1. Click the *x=* button on the Event Rules Design toolbar.

2. In the Assignment form, click to select the variable in the list box on the left. The variable will appear on the left-hand side of the assignment field ("To Object") just above the list box.

Notice that the list of variables in the right-hand list box has changed. OneWorld displays only variables of the same type for assignment to another variable. For example, you cannot assign a string to a math numeric.

3. In the right-hand list box, select the variable whose value you want to assign to the selected variable on the left (To Object). The variable will appear on the right-hand side of the assignment field (From Object/Literal) just above the list box.

4. Click OK to process the assignment and return to the Event Rules Design interface.

The Expression Manager

The majority of your variable assignments will be done using a literal value or a straight assignment of another variable's value, but in some cases you'll need to manipulate data to get the desired results. OneWorld allows you to make calculations using variables and literal values. To do this, enter the Assignment screen and click the f(x) button next to the From Object/Literal blank box. This brings up the Expression Manager, shown in Figure 7-4.

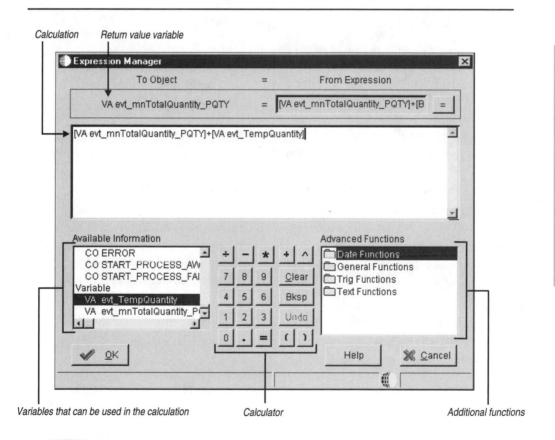

FIGURE 7-4. Adding in a calculation using functions and variables in the Expression Manager

The Expression Manager window has several parts. The large pane in the center displays the calculation that you are creating. At the bottom left, the Available Information list box displays all the variables that you can use. Next to this is the keypad of a calculator. On the bottom right is the Advanced Functions list.

Let's say you need to add two variables; perform the following steps:

1. Click the *x=* button in the Event Rules Design toolbar.

2. In the Assignment form, click to select the To Object variable (on the left) into which you want to put the sum of the two variables.

3. Click the f(x) button to open the Expression Manager.

4. In the Available Information list box, click the first variable you want to add.

5. Click the plus key in the calculator.

6. In the Available Information box, click the second variable you want to add.

7. Notice that all your calculation elements are displayed in the center pane. Click OK to save your calculation. This will return you to Event Rules Design.

Using Advanced Functions in Expression Manager

As you can see, you can easily create basic mathematical functions (add and subtract, divide and multiply) using the variables and the calculator in the Expression Manager. But not all your calculations will be this simple. To create more complex calculations, use the advanced functions provided in the Expression Manager.

The advanced functions (see Table 7-7) are divided into categories: Date, General, Trig, and Text. To see a brief definition of the functions in each category, click the category folder and then click a function. The bottom of the form below the push button will display a brief description of the function and the parameters it requires if you click on the system function.

- Date functions perform basic date manipulations. These functions make programming much easier for advancing dates and calculating the time between two dates.

- General and Trig functions perform math manipulations, such as rounding and taking the cosine of a number.

- Text functions help you manipulate strings, performing operations such as padding the left-hand side of a string or converting a string to upper- or lowercase.

Date Functions	General Functions	Trig Functions	Text Functions
add_days	abs	acos	concat
add_months	ceil	asin	indent
days_between	exp	atan2	length
date_day	floor	atan	lower
date_month	pow	cos	lpad
date_year	pow10	cosh	ltrip
date_today	round	log	rpad
last_day	sign	log10	rtrim
months_between	sqrt	sin	substr
next_day		sinh	upper
		tan	
		tanh	

TABLE 7-7. Expression Manager Advanced Functions

Using these advanced functions is easy. For example, here are the steps to concatenate two strings:

1. Click the *x=* button in the Event Rules Design toolbar.

2. In the Assignment form, click to select the variable on the left (To Object) into which you want to put the concatenated string.

3. Click the f(x) button to open the Expression Manager.

4. In the tree structure in the Advanced Functions box, click to open the Text Functions folder. Select Concat.

5. In the center pane, your cursor is now positioned inside the parentheses following the concat function. In the Available Information list box, double-click the first string you want to concatenate. The variable is inserted inside the function. (See Figure 7-5.) The variable name appears in the brackets, and the cursor moves to the next position.

6. In the Available Information box, double-click the second string to be concatenated. This places the string inside the function, in the second set of brackets. See Figure 7-5.

7. Click OK to save your expression. You will be returned to the Event Rules Design form, and a new line of code will be added containing your new expression.

CAUTION

We suggest you avoid inserting a variable name into the expression by typing it in. Instead, you should double-click the variable name in the Available Information list. Typing it in leaves room for mistakes that will be very hard to find later.

Also, don't nest too many of these advanced functions together; you may get unpredictable results (for example, inside one assignment you can create a substring of a substring). It's better to do it in two separate statements.

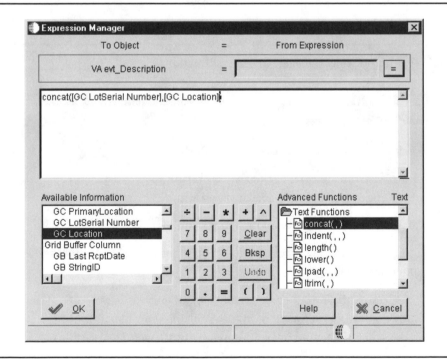

FIGURE 7-5. Using Expression Manager to concatenate two strings together

If Statements and While Loops

Although you use the same application—the Criteria Design form—to create If statements and While loops, their functionality is very different.

If Statements

The If statement creates an If, Else, End If skeleton that you then use to code your application. You can nest If statements (placing an If statement inside an If statement), and you can have multiple parts of If statements joined together by Ands and Ors. For example, you can use an If statement to validate whether the values in any key fields have changed. In Figure 7-6, the If statement is displayed.

Client Modifications Using OneWorld

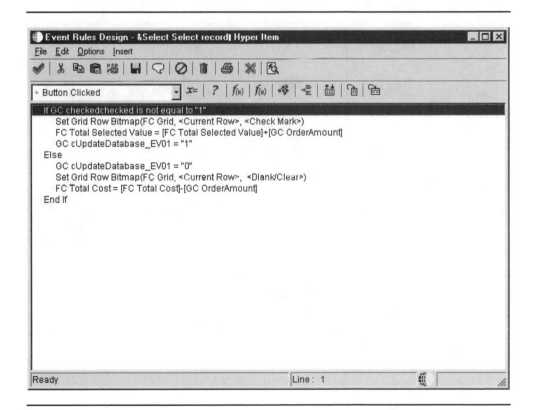

FIGURE 7-6. An If statement inside ER code for comparing values in columns

In these next steps, you'll create an If statement with two lines that compare the Item Number and the Branch fields to two user-created variables.

To create an If statement, follow these steps:

1. In the Event Rules Design interface, click the ? button in the toolbar. This displays the Criteria Design form, which is used to create both If and While statements.

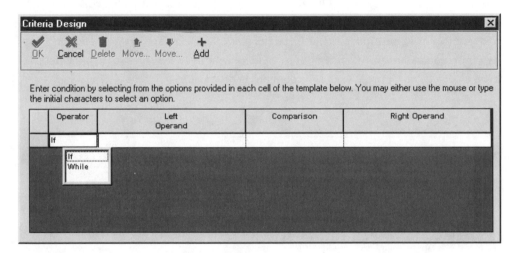

2. In the Operator column, click the cell that contains the word "If."

CAUTION

If you create an If statement and you need to change it to a While statement, you must delete the statement and re-create it. You cannot change an If statement to a While statement.

3. Click the adjacent cell in the Left Operand column, which is empty. From the list that appears (as shown on the next page), select a variable to insert (szCostCenter) in the Left Operand column; this is the variable to which you want to make a comparison.

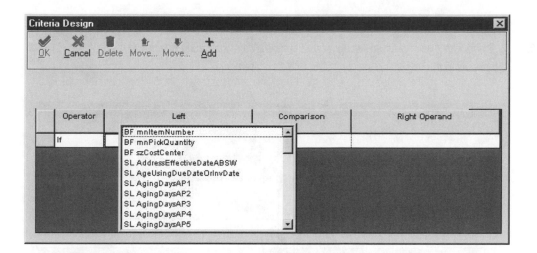

4. Use the Comparison column to specify what kind of comparison you want to make. This compares the variable in the Left Operand column to the variable you'll insert in the Right Operand column. In this example, we chose "is not equal to." Your choices of Comparison operations that appear in the list box are

- is equal to
- is greater than
- is greater than or equal to
- is less than
- is less than or equal to
- is not equal to

5. Next, in the Right Operand column, insert the value to which you want to compare your variable (the Left Operand). This is described in the following section, "If Statement and While Loop Comparisons." In this example, you're going to compare one variable (szCostCenter) to another variable (szCostCenterSave_MCU).

6. To add a second line to your If statement, click the Operator column again, below the If statement you just added. Insert an And or an Or statement by selecting it from the list that appears, as shown next.

CAUTION

Working with And and Or statements can be tricky. Make sure you understand the details in the upcoming section, "And and Or Statements."

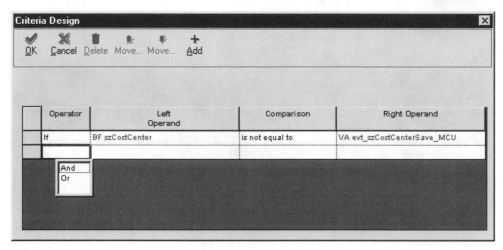

7. As you did in steps 3–5, insert the variable in the Left Operand column, the comparison in the Comparison column, and the value to compare to in the Right Operand column.

8. Repeat steps 6 and 7 if you need to add additional And or Or statements.

9. Click OK to save the If statement. Here's what a finished If statement looks like in the Criteria Design form:

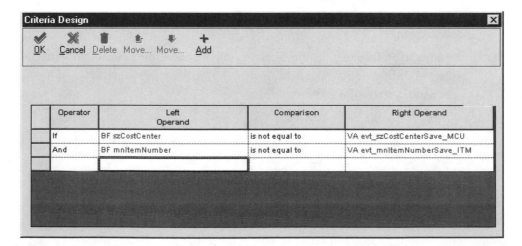

N O T E

When you create an If statement, you automatically get an Else statement. Often you won't need an Else condition in the code, so you can delete it. If you find later that you need it, you can restore it. Just click the If statement in the code pane and then click the Else button in the Event Rules Design toolbar. The Else statement is inserted after the If statement, and then you can drag the Else to the appropriate location in your code.

If Statement and While Loop Comparisons

When creating an If statement, you will be comparing a variable in the left operand to a value or a set of values in the right operand. You can compare your left operand variable to another variable or to a literal value or system value. You can use the system values <Zero>, <Blank>, and <Null> instead of typing in a value. (Note that Blank and Null are different values.) In addition, OneWorld allows you to enter a literal. When creating an If statement, if you click the Literal item from the list box of the right operand, the Range of Values form (see Figure 7-7) is displayed.

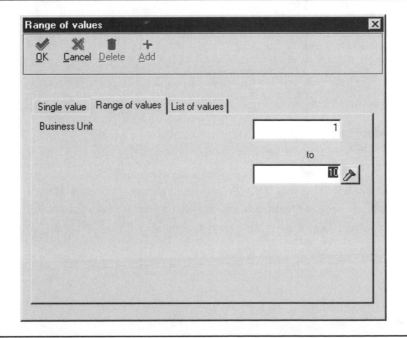

FIGURE 7-7.   Inside an If statement, you can compare a variable to a single literal value, a range of literal values, or a list of literal values

As you can see, this form has three tabs: Single Value, Range of Values, and List of Values.

- The Single Value tab allows you to type in a single, literal value. For example, you might use a single value if you want to make sure a percentage value is not greater than 100.

- The Range of Values tab allows you to type in an upper and a lower bound for a comparison. For example, you could specify that a certain value must be in the range 0 to 100.

- The List of Values tab allows you to type in a number of values to compare against. For example, you could specify that the Branch variable must not be equal to Boston or Atlanta.

You can also create range and list values by using multiple lines inside an If statement, but using the Range of Values form is typically much easier.

And and Or Statements

In OneWorld If statements, Ands have precedence over Ors. For example, the following statement:

```
IF     Quantity is equal to 5
And    Branch is equal to "Boston"
Or     Branch is equal to "Denver"
```

would be interpreted as

```
IF     (Quantity is equal to 5
And    Branch is equal to "Boston")
Or     Branch is equal to "Denver"
```

So if the branch value was "Denver," it would always go into the If statement regardless of the value of Quantity—which may or may not be what you want to happen. If you're in doubt about how an If statement will be interpreted, you should nest multiple If statements as shown in the following example. Here we have two If statements, one inside the other:

```
IF    Quantity is equal to 5
   IF     Branch is equal to "Boston"
   Or     Branch is equal to "Denver"
```

While Loops

The second programming element available to you in the Criteria Design form is the While statement. Using this element, you can create a loop in your code that will execute until the statement is false. The While statement can be used to fetch all the records in a file or to get all or any specified number of records in a grid.

To create a new While loop, follow these steps:

1. In the Event Rules Design window, click the ? button.

2. When the Criteria Design form appears, change the If to a While. Click the If cell in the Operator column and change it to While.

3. Create a While statement as you did for the If statement, following steps 3 through 8 as described for creating the If statements.

4. Click OK to save the While statement.

Here's an example of a While loop in the Criteria Design form:

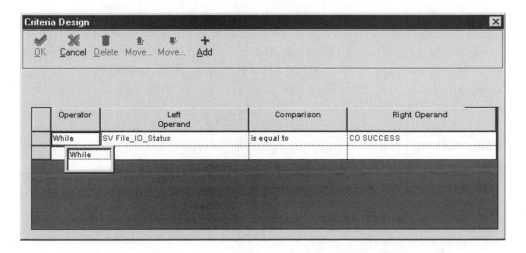

Client Modifications Using OneWorld

While statements can be nested; you can have a While loop inside another While loop. Here's a completed While statement inside Event Rules code:

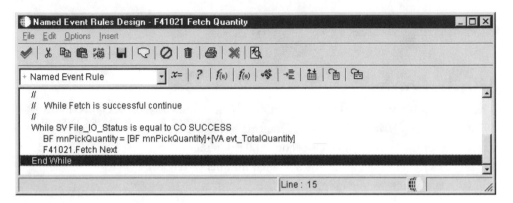

System Functions

System functions are components provided by OneWorld that you can use inside of your Event Rules code. These functions will be used to send messages, hide and show fields, or change the way a form or report will process. For example, system functions allow you to insert data into and get information from a grid.

System function use parameters, or arguments that are passed in or out of the function. When calling a system function you will need to map the system function's parameters to variables or assign a literal value to each parameter. The system function will use the value that was passed into each parameter. For example, if want to disable a field in a grid, you will need to pass the system function information, such as which row and column you want to disable. In addition, a function may change the value of a variable that was mapped. This will happen if you call a system function Get Max Grid Rows. This function will return the total number of grid rows into a variable that you have mapped to its Row parameter.

The types of system functions that you can use in Event Rules will depend on the OneWorld object you're working with. For example, applications will have the largest number of available system functions because of user interaction, and NERs will have the fewest. System functions, unlike business functions, do not have source code that you can view or modify. System functions cover a wide variety of topics. Appendix E lists all the system functions that are appropriate for each of the OneWorld objects. To use system functions, click the $f(s)$ button in the Event Rules Design window, which will open the form shown in Figure 7-8. This form allows you to view and select from all the system functions available in OneWorld.

To select and assign a system function, perform the following steps:

1. In the Event Rules Design interface, click the *f*(s) (System Function) button. The System Functions form is displayed.

2. The form opens on the Function Selection tab. On that tab, go to the tree control and find the category of function you want to use. Click a folder that contains the category to see the functions in that category, and then select the function by double-clicking the function name. This changes the form to the Parameter Mapping Tab.

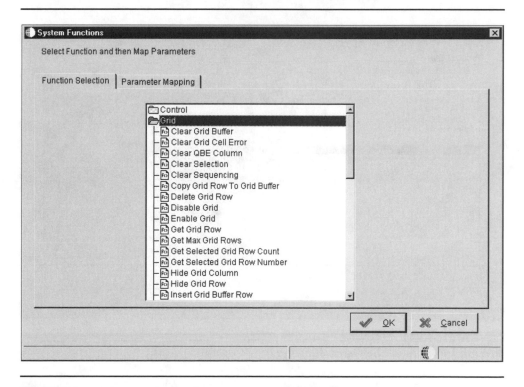

FIGURE 7-8.   Selecting system functions in Event Rules Design

Client Modifications Using OneWorld

3. A list of parameters for the function is displayed on the right. Map these parameters to your variables by clicking a parameter and then double-clicking a variable in the Available Objects list. You also can click the variable and then click the > button to send it to the Parameters column. For some parameters, you will also be able to map system values, literal values, or form controls. In Figure 7-9, Hide Control is being selected from the Control list and the OK button is mapped to the Control parameter.

4. After mapping all elements of the function, click OK to save the system function call.

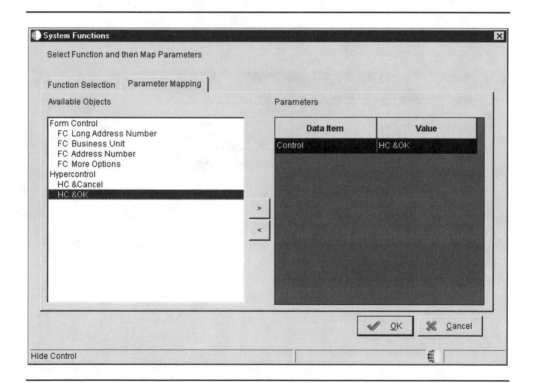

FIGURE 7-9. Using the system function Hide Control

In some cases, you'll have access to system functions that are not valid for a particular event and will not work. For example, inside a form you can select a system function for a tree control, even if you don't have a tree control on your form. When this happens, the Available Objects list might be blank whey you try to map certain parameters. This is a good indication that you cannot use the system function on this form or event. For example, if you're using the system function Insert Grid Buffer Row on a Fix/Inspect form, you won't have a Grid object in the Available Objects list to map to the Grid parameter.

Business Functions

Calling business functions is an important part of the logic you add in Event Rules. To communicate between the business functions and the calling application, OneWorld uses a data structure whose parameters direct data either into or out of the business function.

These business functions give you a great deal of flexibility in the manipulation of your OneWorld data. You can create business functions using either the C programming language or ER, depending on the purpose of the function. (For more information on creating business functions, see Chapter 13.)

Using a business function inside of Event Rules involves two steps: choosing the business function, and mapping variables to the business function's parameters. Every business function has a data structure attached to it, and this data structure will contain the business function parameters. As with system functions, you can map variables or literal values to the business functions parameters.

Finding the Correct Business Function

Many times the hardest part of using a business function is finding the appropriate one to use. To see the available business functions, click the $f(\textsc{b})$ button in the toolbar of the Event Rules Design window. This displays the Business Function Search form shown in Figure 7-10.

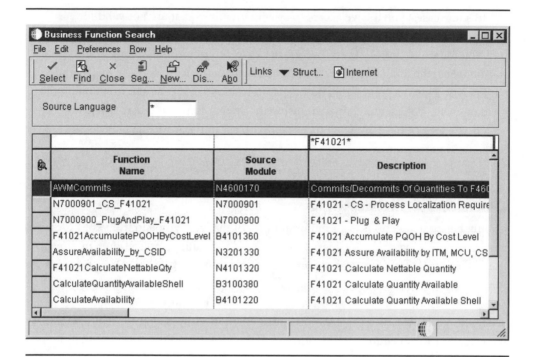

FIGURE 7-10. Business Function Search form

To pick a function, you can type the name of the function's source file into the QBE line above the Source Module column. Alternatively, if you know the name of the function or its description, you can type either one into the QBE line above the Function Name or Description column.

If you don't know the function's name, you can search for it using the QBE line. Here are some tips for searching:

- Most OneWorld business functions follow the naming convention *filename*, *verb*, *description* (for example, F4101 Get Item Master Row, where F4101 is the filename, Get is the verb, and Item Master Row is the description [object of the verb]). So, to find all functions that refer to the Item Master, you could enter F4101* or *Item* in the QBE line above the Description column. Be prepared to look through a large list of functions if you don't refine your search. (This is a good example of the importance of naming standards when creating business functions.)

- Another way to find a business function is to search by system codes. Each business function that is created is given a system code to identify what application group it belongs to. For example, you could type 40 in the System QBE field to view a list of all the business functions for the Distribution system. A complete list of system codes is provided in Appendix A.

Although there's no search method that is completely comprehensive, by limiting your search you'll be able to find a collection of functions that might meet your needs. After you select the function you want to use, the system displays the Business Functions form, in which you map the function's parameters. Some business functions include notes that you can read to help you decide whether the selected function will suit your needs and how to use the function. These notes are available through the Business Function Notes, Structure Notes, and Parameter Notes buttons on the Business Functions form.

Mapping the Function's Parameters

When business functions are created, the programmer attaches a data structure to the function. This data structure is how the business function communicates with your ER. Having selected your business function, you're ready to map parameters to it.

Here are the steps for calling a business function inside of Event Rules code:

1. Click the ƒ(B) (Business Function) button in the Event Rules Design toolbar.

2. In the Business Function Search form, select the business function you want. The Business Functions window appears, with the selected business function reflected in the description lines at the top.

3. In the Data Structure box on the right, click the parameter you want to map. You can click either the Value or the Data Item column.

4. In the Available Objects list box on the left, double-click the parameter you want to map. Or you can click <Literal> under Special Values at the top of the list, and a form appears allowing you to type a value into the Single Value field. The Value column on the right will now be populated with the name of the variable you selected or the value you entered.

5. Click the button in the Dir (Direction) column of the Data Sturcture box to pass this variable either into or out of the business function. If you choose the bidirectional arrow, the data will flow in both directions. This is discussed in the following section, "Choosing Data Flow Direction."

6. Repeat steps 3 through 5 for each parameter of the business function.

7. Click OK to save this connection for the business function.

Choosing Data Flow Direction

When you're hooking up a business function, you'll be able to pass variables from your ER to the business function data structure. By setting the direction using the arrow buttons in the Data Structure box, you tell the ER which direction you want the data to flow. If the arrow is pointing to your variable, the business function can change the value of your variable. If the arrow points to the business function data structure, the system passes the value into the function. A bidirectional (double-headed) arrow allows the data to be passed into and out of the function.

Figure 7-11 shows an example of parameter mapping for the function F41021, Fetch Item Quantity, which exists in the source file B5600001. The F41021, Fetch Item Quantity function has a few parameters, and they're all used. Not all parameters in all functions need to be used, however. Some functions have a long list of parameters; depending on the function's usage, only a few of the parameters are needed. As you can see in Figure 7-11, some of the parameters are passing data in and some are passing data out.

NOTE

Occasionally you will not be able to change the direction of the data flow arrow. The direction of the arrow can be forced a certain way when the data structure is created. This is done so that when this function is used in Event Rules code the direction of the arrow will be the correct.

Unused parameters should be marked by changing the direction column to Not Used (a circle with a line through it). This is the default state for the direction column and causes data not to be passed in either direction.

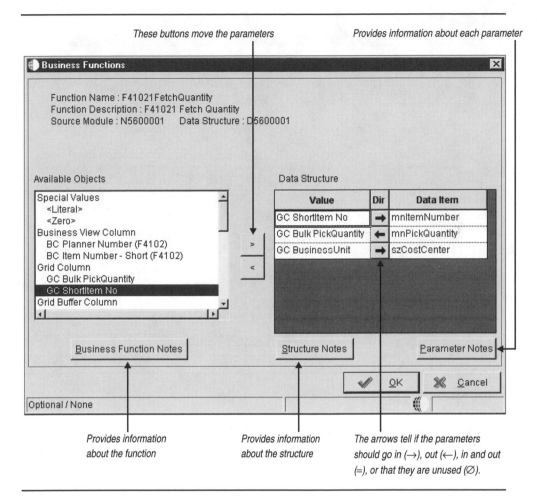

These buttons move the parameters

Provides information about each parameter

Provides information about the function

Provides information about the structure

The arrows tell if the parameters should go in (→), out (←), in and out (=), or that they are unused (∅).

Client Modifications Using OneWorld

FIGURE 7-11. Mapping parameters from ER to a business function

Table I/O

When you work with ER, you'll often need to get or modify data in a table. OneWorld Event Rules provide functions for fetching, updating, and deleting records in a table or through a business view. To get to these functions, click the Table I/O button in the Event Rules Design toolbar (see Table 7-1, earlier in this chapter). The system displays the first screen of the TableIO Director, shown in Figure 7-12.

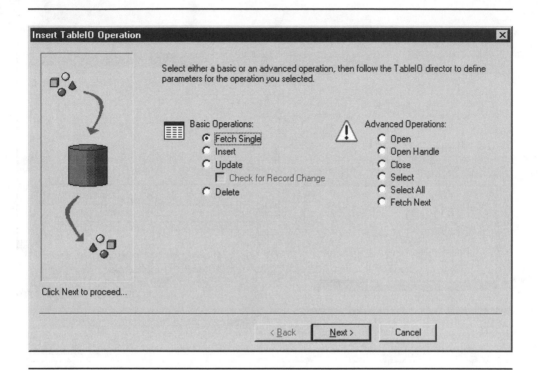

FIGURE 7-12. The Table I/O form

Table I/O functions are divided into basic and advanced operations. The items in the Basic Operations list are stand-alone functions. For example, if you want to simply fetch one record, you can create one line of basic ER that will do that. On the other hand, to fetch all records that match certain criteria, you'd use items in the Advanced Operations list.

Basic I/O Functions

The basic functions of table I/O are fetch, insert, update, and delete. These functions are designed to execute simple I/O operations and they all follow the same logic.

One of the most important parts of doing table I/O is mapping your variables to the table fields. There are two types of table fields: key fields and nonkey fields.

Most tables have more than one key, and table I/O allows you to change the key that will be used. Basic table I/O operations only allow you to do selection on the fields that are part of the key, so you would need to change to one that matches your selection needs. To change the key, use the Index pull-down menu. The key fields are marked with an asterisk to the left of the column name. The nonkey fields, which do not have an asterisk, can be returned to you by mapping a variable to the correct database field. In other words if there is an asterisk next to the value, it will be used in the record selection if a value is passed into this field for the basic operations.

In some cases you will not be able to do a fetch because your fetch does not match any index. In these cases, you will need to use the Select statement discussed in the upcoming "Advanced Operations in Table I/O" section. In addition, update and delete can affect multiple rows inside a table. If you are updating the table or deleting a record, ensure that you get the correct row and no others by using the full primary unique key to do the operation.

To illustrate this point, we will walk through a simple fetch of a record from the F41021 file as follows:

1. First, in the TableIO Director, select the database operation you want to perform. In this example, choose Fetch Single. Click the Next button.

2. At this point, the Data Source form appears and allows you to find and select the table (in the Tables tab) from which you will fetch records. You can also select a business view in the Business Views tab. (The Handles tab will be discussed in a later section.) In Figure 7-13, we have selected table F41021. Click the Next button to proceed.

3. After selecting the table, a Mapping form is displayed (similar to the one in Figure 7-14). You use this form to map your variables to the correct table columns. First map the key fields. To do this, click on the Mapping column across from the table field you want to map. Then double-click the appropriate variable using the tree control on the left side of form. The variable name will then be displayed in the Mapping column.

4. After setting the columns for mapping, select the comparison operation for each column. Click the button in the Operation column to cycle through the options, which include =, <, >, and several other comparison operators.

5. The fields that you want to return can be mapped as shown in Figure 7-14. Do this as described in step 3. Click Finish when you're done.

At this point you have designed this fetch operation to return the quantity from the F41021 table by selecting the record that matches the item and quantity by mapping the key fields. When the matching record is fetched, it will return the values into the variable as you have mapped.

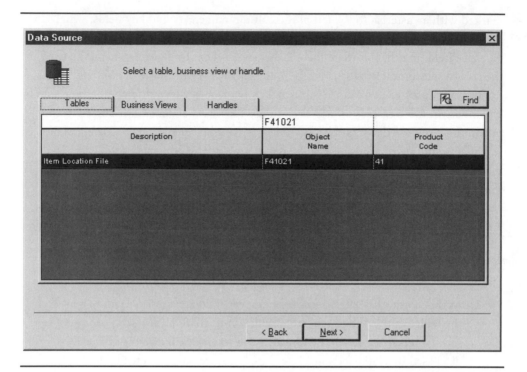

FIGURE 7-13. Selecting a table in which to insert, update, delete, or fetch records

Checking for Success In your ER, you can check to see whether a mapped database operation was successful. To do this, create an If statement using the SV File_IO_Status variable. The SV value is changed by the system after you do a database operation. Here is an example of such an If statement:

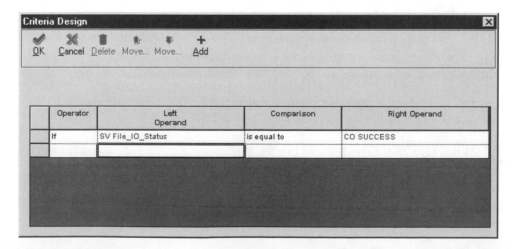

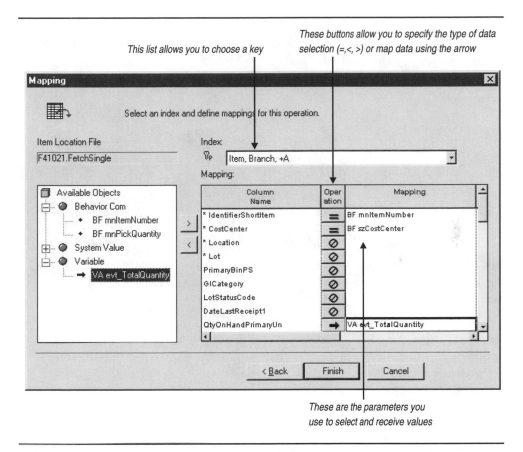

FIGURE 7-14. The mapping between ER variables and table columns for the Fetch Single operation

By adding an If statement, you can add conditional logic based on the outcome of a database operation. For example, if the statement is not successful, you may need to set an error (a system function). To do this you would need to add a line of code by selecting the system function button (shown earlier in Table 7-1) and choosing the appropriate system function (Set Grid Cell Error, Set Control Error, or Set NER Error). In addition, you may add logic dependent on a success or failure into the code, such as additional fetches or business function calls.

Advanced Operations in Table I/O

The advanced operations in table I/O are functions that require you to do a little more setup, but these functions are also more powerful than the basic functions. For example, you can fetch all records in a table that match your specified criteria.

Advanced functions allow you to open and close a table, and select and fetch records. You can also open a table multiple times. In addition, you can use separate handles, as discussed later in "Multiple Table Handles."

When using the advanced functions to work with tables, you'll follow this basic logic:

1. Open the table.

2. Select the records.

3. Fetch the records (loop).

4. Close the table.

You don't always have to open and close a table explicitly, but some programmers like to use these functions so they know when a table has been opened and closed. If you don't open and close the table explicitly, your ER will do it for you.

Single Table Access

When you want to fetch one record at a time from only one table, follow the steps in this section.

To open or close the table, follow these steps:

1. In the Event Rules Design toolbar, click the Table I/O button. The first page of the TableIO Director appears,

2. To open the table, click the Open radio button; or, for a table close operation click the Close button. Click Next to proceed.

3. In the Data Source page, select the table or business view you want to open. In most cases, you'll be selecting a table or a business view over one table. However, when you need to do a join between two tables you'll need to use a business view.

4. Click the Finish button.

Next, you'll select records in the table, as follows:

1. In the ER Design toolbar, click the Table I/O button to open the Table I/O Director.

2. Click the Select radio button in the Advanced Operations list, and click Next to proceed.

3. In The Data Source page, select the table or business view from which you want to select records. Click Next to proceed to the Mapping page.

4. Map the selection criteria by clicking the table field you want to map and then double-clicking the variables from the available object tree control. Set the comparison operation for each variable by clicking the buttons in the Operation column. In the Mapping page in Figure 7-15, we are selecting from the F41021 table, fetching all the records that match the item number and cost center.

NOTE

When mapping selection criteria, you can choose key fields that will be used as your sort order. Unlike a Fetch Single operation, you aren't limited to using the key fields for your selection; but if you don't, it could negatively affect your application performance.

5. Click Finish when you're done.

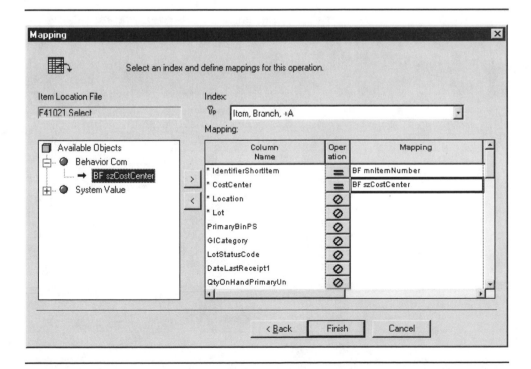

Client Modifications Using OneWorld

FIGURE 7-15. An example of a Select statement setup in the Table I/O Director's Mapping page

So far, you have selected records, but you haven't yet fetched them. The Fetch Next function fetches the first record in the selection, the first time the function is called. Subsequent calls will fetch the next record that matches your selection criteria. To perform a fetch, follow these steps:

1. Click the Table I/O button in the ER Design toolbar, and select the Fetch Next radio button in the first page of the TableIO Director. Click Next.

2. Select the same table or view that was chosen for the Select operation. Click Next.

3. Map the table elements to the variables that will be returned from the fetch. Notice that all mapped variables will have a directional arrow, even if they are key fields (as shown for the Total Quantity variable in Figure 7-16).

4. Click Finish when you're done.

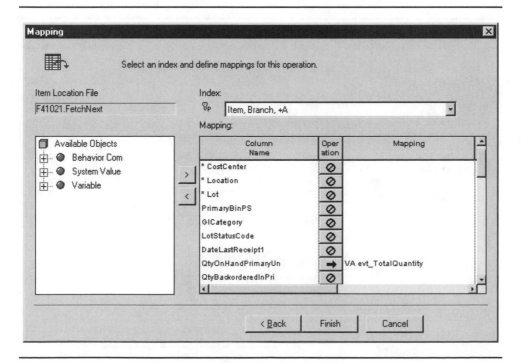

FIGURE 7-16. The Fetch Next function setup. This example will return QtyOnHandPrimaryUn into the Total Quantity variable for the first selected record.

In most cases, in addition to a Select statement and a Fetch Next, you will also need to create a While loop like the one in Figure 7-17, that loops through all records in the table until the fetch fails. Using a loop like this will process all the records that match your search criteria. In this example, we are using a Named Event Rules business function to do the table processing. It is a good idea to do this, as explained in the Developers Corner, "When to Create a NER," at the beginning of this chapter.

Multiple Table Handles

Most of the time you can do database operations without using *database handles* (a variable that allow you to keep track of a specific occurrence of table or business view operation). There are three cases in which you would need to use database handles:

- If you need to open multiple occurrences of the same table or business view

- If you need to open a table in an environment other that the one you logged into

- If you need to pass a handle into a form or business view so that you don't open a the table or business view more than once

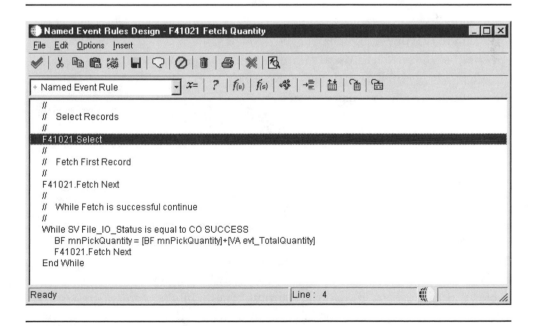

FIGURE 7-17.   While loop used for the Fetch Next function

An example would be when you need to loop through a table to fetch information without losing your positioning for the original fetch. To do this, you'll need to use multiple database handles.

NOTE

For more information about multiple database handles, look at the OneWorld online help for Table I/O Data items.

Using database handles is almost the same as setting up fetches, except that you use a specific handle for fetching the records instead of specifying the table every time. You have to create data items with certain characteristics specifically for use in the ER. To see examples of this technique, look up data items such as HV3002W or HF9001 in the Data Dictionary. The edit rule for these data items specifies the table or business view that is used with this data item. The HV3002W data item fetches from the business view V3002W, which is defined in the edit rule of that data item. Figure 7-18 shows an example of a handle data item.

To use table handles, you first need to create a variable(s) for each handle. The handle variable will be of the same type of data item you created for the table in the Data Dictionary. Generally, it's helpful to name handles for the same table sequentially; for example HV3002W1, HV3002W2, and so on. If you need guidance on creating variables, see the section on User-Defined Variables in this chapter.

After you've created the data item and variables for each handle you need, follow these general steps for every handle you use:

1. Open the handle.

2. Select the records.

3. Fetch information.

4. Close the handle.

To open a handle, specify the correct environment for it; this will probably be the Login Environment System Value (SL). Since the data item states what table or business view will be used, there's no need to specify it here. You can then use the Table I/O Select function to select the matching records. In single-table access, you pick a table or business view to select with—in this case, the handle you created. You can then fetch, update, or delete, using your table handle.

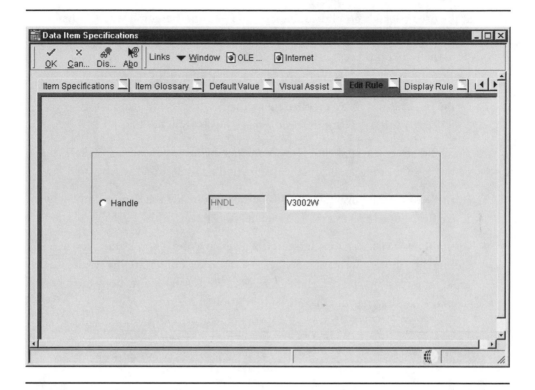

FIGURE 7-18. Edit rule for a handle data item

CAUTION

Handles cannot be used if you are doing transaction processing. For more information on transaction processing, see Chapter 16.

Calling Forms and Sections

Interactive or batch applications typically call other interactive or batch applications. This section explains the easy process of calling these objects in ER.

Calling Applications

The Form Interconnect button on the Event Rules Design toolbar (see Table 7-1, earlier in the chapter) displays a form that helps you connect the calling form to another form. In the application, you would normally call a form from a menu or toolbar exit, in which the user selects a grid line or chooses to go to another application. Whether you call a form inside another application, or call a form inside the currently open application, the hookup process is the same.

The following steps show you how to call an application's form.

1. In the Event Rules Design toolbar, click the Form Interconnect button. The Work With Applications form appears next (Figure 7-19).

2. Find and select the application that contains the form you want to call. If you're calling a form in the application you're in, find and select the current application.

3. In the Work With Forms screen, select the form inside the application you want to call by double-clicking the form name.

4. In the Work With Versions form, select a version of the application you are calling. For more information about versions, see Chapter 10. If you don't need to select a version, you can click Close. The Form Interconnections form is now displayed, reflecting your specified application at the top.

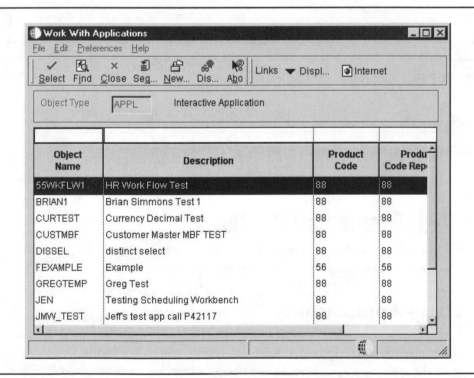

FIGURE 7-19.   The Work With Applications form, for calling a form from another form

5. In the Form Interconnections form for your selected application, form, and version (see Figure 7-20), map the parameters for the form call. This form contains all the parameters of the data structure for the form you are calling. You'll need to map the necessary variables, or assign literal values to the parameters by clicking the <Literal> option at the top of the Available Objects box. The mapping of parameters is similar to calling a business function.

6. If you didn't select a form version, the Version Name field in the top-right corner is blank. If this form is in the current application, you might want to click the field and insert the form's System Value for the version name.

7. The Modeless check box allows you to designate that the called form doesn't have to be closed before you close the current (calling) form. In most cases you'll want to leave the Modeless option disabled, to force the user to close the called

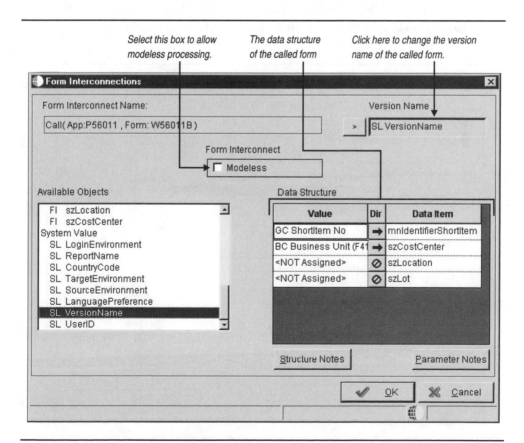

FIGURE 7-20. Mapping of variables and literal values for calling the form

form before they can process their changes and close the current form. For more information on modeless processing and interactive applications, see Chapter 8.

8. Click OK to save the form interconnection.

Calling Batch Applications

The process for calling a batch application is slightly different from calling a form. When you call a section in a batch application, you use a system function; if you call another batch application, you use the Report Interconnect button on the ER Design toolbar (see Table 7-1 earlier in the chapter).

Here are the steps to call a section within the batch application you are currently in:

1. In the ER Design toolbar, click the *f*(s) (System Functions) button.

2. In the Function Selection Tab under the Section category, select the system function called Do Custom Section. This is shown in Figure 7-21.

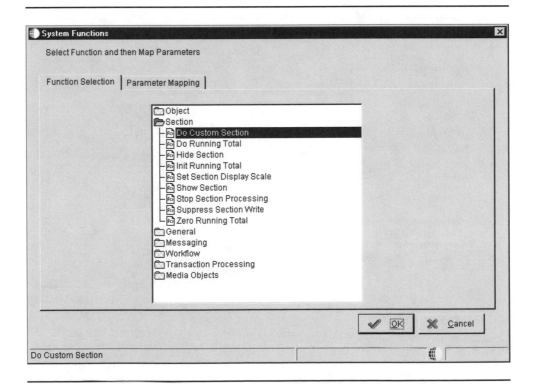

FIGURE 7-21.   The Do Custom Section system function

3. Now select the section inside your report that you want to call. For example, if want to call the section Totals, map the Totals section to the Section Parameter.

4. Click OK.

To call a batch application other than the one currently open, the Event Rules are different. Follow these steps:

1. In the Event Rules Design toolbar, click the Report Interconnect button.

2. After you click the button, you'll be prompted to select the batch application you want to call. To do this, enter the name of the batch application you want to call and press Find. Then double-click the batch application in the grid to select it.

3. You are then prompted to select a version you want to call. You must select a version you want to run, but you can change that version in the next form if necessary. To select a version, double-click the version in the grid.

Once you've selected a batch application and version, the system displays the UBE Interconnections form shown in Figure 7-22. Here you can configure the processing of the batch application you are calling. There's a Version Name field in the top-right corner; we recommend that you do not hard-code this to a specific version. Instead, pass processing option values to this batch application, as shown in the next step. (For details on processing options, see Chapter 12.)

4. There are two options for specifying the way this called batch application will process.

- Choose the Transaction Processing option (the Include in Transaction check box) if you want the called batch application to be included in the calling report's transaction processing. (For more information on transaction processing see Chapter 16.)

- The Run Process Asynchronous option allows you to run the batch application asynchronously, which means both reports will run at the same time. If you don't enable this option, the calling report will wait to continue until after the called report has finished processing. Unless you are sure about running the second report asynchronously, do not enable this option.

5. Finally, designate the data structure values you want passed into the batch application. Note that some batch applications might not have a data structure. Mapping a batch application data structure is similar to mapping a business function.

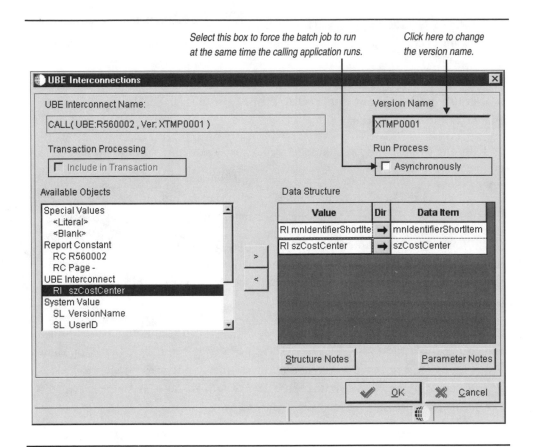

FIGURE 7-22. This form allows you to call a batch application

The Structure Notes and Parameter Notes buttons at the bottom of the UBE Interconnections form can be used to help you hook up your batch application. To view the Structure notes, just click the button. You'll need to select a parameter before clicking the Parameter Notes button.

Event Rules Examples and Tips

To help you understand everything described in this chapter, we'll walk through an example. But first, here are a couple of topics that will help you when creating Event Rules in your own projects.

Cutting and Pasting Code

When you create ER, like all good programmers you'll be copying and pasting code. As you use this technique to speed up your ER programming tasks, there are a few things you should be careful about.

When you cut and paste code, you are making the assumption that your variables in the source destination will be exactly the same. The variables mapped in the business functions and system functions that you called might not have the same variable names, however, as the ones that exist in the location where you pasted your code. This can cause problems, such as the ER not validating, or variables inside of business functions being left blank.

Also, be very careful with If statements and While loops. Don't neglect to include the beginning and ending of these statements when you cut. This, too, can also cause validation errors or even corrupt your ER.

CAUTION

If you run into problems after you paste a chunk of code, it's in your best interest to double-click each line of the pasted code and then click OK. This will cause ER to reset each line.

Troubleshooting Event Rules

After creating Event Rules, you may want to run—or in some cases will be forced to run—ER validation. For example, when you save an application in FDA, the system runs a validation of your ER code. Likewise, when you create a NER, the system will validate when you build the function. In addition, when you add ER in RDA, you can run a validation on your own by choosing Validate Event Rules from the Report menu.

Quite a few things can cause errors in your Event Rules, but most are easy to fix. Some you can even ignore.

- **Deleting link/spec records for nonexistent section/object**   You may get this error if you deleted all the logic from an event. This error is just telling you that ER existed on an event but doesn't any longer.

- **NO Event Rule specifications exist**   You'll probably get this error the first time you validate ER on a new application. The message simply says that there is no ER yet.

Some errors are more serious and may be a little harder to correct. The following error is common if you're doing substantial development and parameters are changing a lot within business functions:

```
/* CER WARNING #2005 : Datastructure parameter count mismatch */
       Function Name: S10_0_13
       Function Description: ER for R56001
       Section: S10 - Get Item Information
       Event: 13 - Do Section
       Seq #: 23
       Line #: 21
       Line Text: GetItemInformation
       /* Additional unmapped elements exist in structure D5600001 */
```

As you can see, this error gives you a little information about how to fix the problem. Here, it tells you that the elements of D5600001 are not mapped correctly. It also gives the line number (21) and the erroneous event (Do Section). This error occurs because the function GetItemInformation has changed but the ER has not been changed. To fix this omission, you'd go to the Do Section in the batch application and double-click line 21, which should be the GetItemInformation function just described.

Event Rules Example

To put everything together, we'll demonstrate how two different OneWorld objects, both using ER, work together. Using ER inside a Named Event Rule and in an application, we'll loop through the records in the F41021 table and calculate a value for Total Quantity On Hand. After the quantity is totaled in the function, we'll call this function from another location.

The first thing we do is add logic to our NER. You could add this logic directly into your application on the Write Grid Line Before event, if you prefer. Creating this logic inside the business function is better, because you can use Object Configuration Manager (OCM) to map the business function to the server to improve performance. For information about OCM, see Chapter 3.

The business function we work with here includes a data structure with three variables: Item, Branch, and Quantity.

1. Inside the NER, we need to add logic to fetch all the records that match the F41021. First, we create a variable using the Variables button in the ER Design toolbar. This displays the Variables form shown in Figure 7-23.

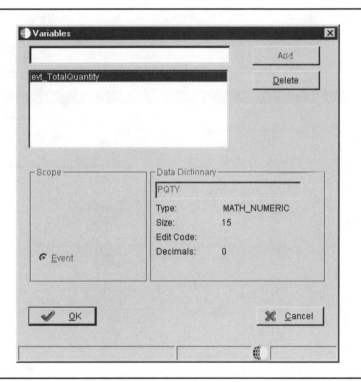

FIGURE 7-23. Creating a variable to return a value

2. Use the advanced Table I/O function, Select, to select records using the values passed to table F41021, and map the correct variables (see Figure 7-24).

3. After the Select operation, you need to fetch the record using another advanced Table I/O function, Fetch Next. In Figure 7-25, the variable is mapped to get the value of what was fetched.

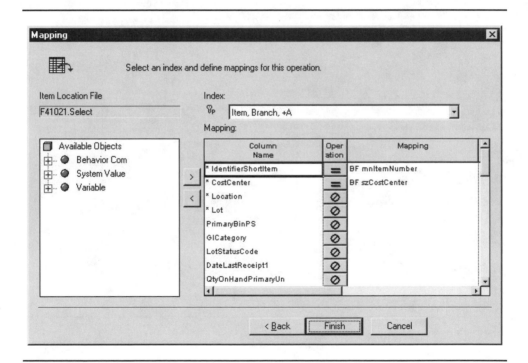

FIGURE 7-24. Mapping the Select statement

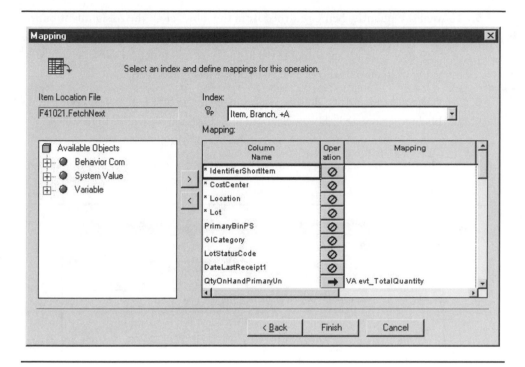

FIGURE 7-25. Fetch Next code to retrieve values from the F41021 table

4. Click the If/While button in the ER Design toolbar. Create a While loop and have it loop until the SV File I/O status is invalid, as shown here:

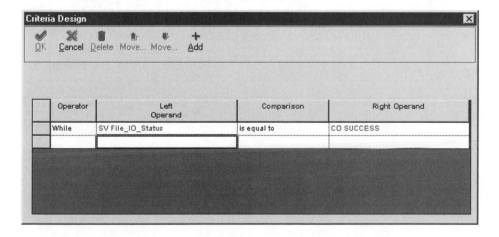

5. To total the quantity being returned from the table, click the Assignment button in the ER Design toolbar and then click the *f*(x) button in the Assignment form. In the Expression Manager, specify that the business function variable will be the value of itself plus the variable, as shown in Figure 7-26.

6. Fetch the next record. To do this, copy and paste the first Fetch Next code. After all this logic is created, the code should look like that shown in Figure 7-27.

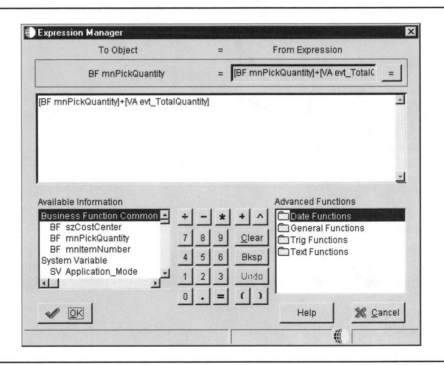

FIGURE 7-26.   Calculation using the Assignment button

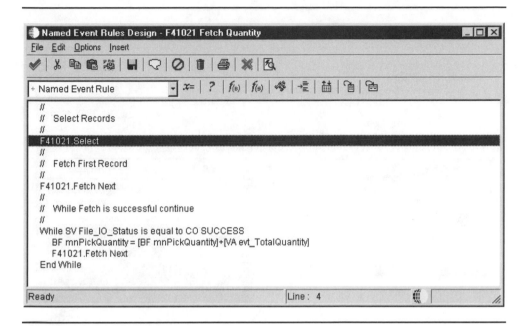

FIGURE 7-27. Code for fetching the next record

7. After the NER is created, we can call it from the application that wants the information. Inside the application on the Write Grid Line-Before event, we add a call to the business function by clicking the f(B) button on the ER Design toolbar, as shown here:

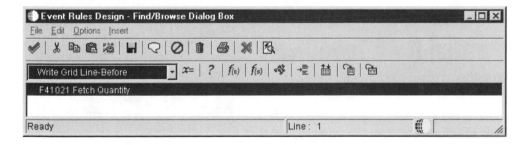

and then mapping parameters, as shown here in Figure 7-28. We chose the Write Grid Line-Before event because it allows the grid value to be changed and can be viewed by the user.

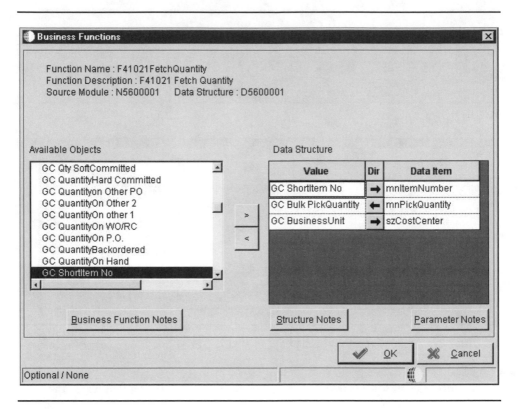

FIGURE 7-28.   Business function mapping

Putting It All Together

Whether you are creating a new object inside OneWorld or modifying existing code, you need to understand how to use Event Rules and how they work together to form the logic of your OneWorld application. In this chapter we discussed several parts of Event Rule coding, from If statements and While loops to table I/O. In most cases you'll be using all the ER explained in this chapter to code your applications.

We also discussed the use of system functions and business functions that can add flexibility to your applications. In addition, in the Developers Corner, "When to Create a NER," we spoke about using NER to remove redundant code and make your applications more modular and flexible.

Take the time to design in advance what you want your applications to do before you begin writing their Event Rules. It will save you time in the long run. By using Event Rules in your applications, you'll be able to create business logic to meet your business needs.

Client Modifications Using OneWorld

CHAPTER 8

OneWorld Modification Guidelines

Powerful and flexible it may be, but OneWorld, like other ERP packages, may not meet all of your company's business requirements. Your enterprise may need to configure its business processes to adapt to OneWorld's functionality, or you may have to modify OneWorld to match your company's business processes. Most likely, they'll meet somewhere in the middle. One way or another, however, to get OneWorld to function as your enterprise needs it to, you'll have to make some modifications to the standard OneWorld applications. Once those applications are customized and in place, new releases of OneWorld will come along and you'll want to incorporate new features and functionality or apply interim updates. It's important to prepare for the effects of upgrades. Knowing the consequences of modifying OneWorld applications will help you decide when it's appropriate to make those modifications.

OneWorld offers a number of tools that help you create new applications and make modifications to existing applications. In this chapter, we'll discuss the recommended guidelines for modifying OneWorld objects, as follows:

- **General Guidelines for Modifying OneWorld Software**   There are guidelines for modification in OneWorld that are common across all OneWorld objects. This section explains them, and also explains terms used in the chapter.

- **Interactive Application Modifications**   Modifications made to interactive applications can sometimes be affected during an upgrade; we will discuss guidelines specific to interactive applications.

- **Batch Application Modifications**   Guidelines specific to batch applications are discussed in this section.

- **Version Modifications**   Since versions are used in both interactive and batch applications, it is necessary to understand how new and modified versions will be changed after an upgrade.

- **Business Function Modifications**   Modifications made to business functions can sometimes be replaced during an upgrade; we'll describe the circumstances in which this can happen and tips to help you avoid losing your code.

- **Event Rules Modifications**   Event Rules can be added to most objects inside OneWorld. An upgrade could cause your ER to be moved and disabled or replaced.

- **Table Specification Modifications**   OneWorld allows modifications to a table's columns and indices; an upgrade can affect your modifications.

- **Business View Modifications**   This section describes how modifications made to business views can be affected during an upgrade.

- **Data Structure Modifications**   We will conclude with a discussion of how an upgrade impacts data structure modifications.

General Guidelines for Modifying OneWorld Software

Before you alter anything in OneWorld, it's important to begin with an understanding of the general modification guidelines. Following these guidelines will decrease the changes you must make to the software after you upgrade OneWorld.

Your modifications to OneWorld applications are handled in one of three ways at upgrade time: they are *preserved*, *replaced*, or *changed*.

- *Preserved* means that during an upgrade, OneWorld automatically merges your modifications with the new J.D. Edwards OneWorld specifications. You do not lose your modifications. If there is a conflict between your specifications and J.D. Edwards, the upgrade uses your specifications. If there is no conflict, the upgrade merges the two.

- *Replaced* means the upgrade does not merge the modifications you have made to your OneWorld objects. The J.D. Edwards upgrade replaces your modifications, which makes it necessary for you to reapply your customizations after the upgrade is done. This takes time, especially if you have made significant modifications to your OneWorld environment.

- *Changed* means your modifications need to be reenabled after the upgrade is finished. Your modifications are disabled during the upgrade, and you must implement them again after the upgrade.

Certain general guidelines apply to all OneWorld objects that you add or change:

- *When adding new objects in Object Librarian, you should use system codes 55xx through 59xx.* OneWorld reserves these system codes for client use, as part of the categorization of application groups. When OneWorld encounters these system codes, it does not replace your objects with J.D. Edwards objects. Because these system codes are reserved for client use, objects using these system codes will not be delivered in later releases.

- *Avoid creating new version names that start with ZJDE or XJDE.* These prefixes are reserved for standard version templates. If you use them for your custom versions, you run the risk of their being overwritten by a standard version of the same name during an upgrade.

In addition to these general technical considerations, it's also to your company's advantage to put some other controls in place. For example, it's a good idea to document any modifications you make to OneWorld, to make it easier to reenable them after an upgrade has replaced or changed them. You should also consider implementing development standards in your organization. Following these standards allows your customizations to be more easily maintained and upgraded.

OneWorld is a very flexible product, and many modifications can be made without changing the application. This will be discussed in the following Developer's Corner, titled "Modeless Mods: Changing Applications Without Changing Code."

Developer's Corner

Modeless Mods: Changing Applications Without Changing Code

OneWorld includes other means of modifying applications without changing the code. Unofficially, these modifications are called "modeless mods." Most of the time, users can make these changes without a developer's assistance. Generally, the changes are not affected by an upgrade.

Here are examples of ways to configure your system without modifying code: user overrides on a grid, User Defined Codes (UDC), added or revised menus, configured processing options, Data Dictionary modifications

You can configure the grid to look exactly as you want it, without altering the code. In fact, every user can configure the grid to his or her liking. To do this, right-click the grid and choose Format from the pop-up menu, to create a new grid format or revise an existing format. Then go to menu GH9011, choose the User Overrides application (P98950), and copy this format to other users on the system.

You can also change the User Defined Codes (UDC) table inside of OneWorld. A UDC table allows you to enter a list of values that match a system code and UDC code. UDC tables are used in many Data Dictionary items to display allowed values as well as some simple setup. For example, if you want to process certain orders differently from others, you can create alternate order types in the Order Type UDC table. By using the custom order type inside your applications and versions, you can do alternate processing without having to modify code. (To add or review UDC tables, enter **UDC** in the Fast Path and press ENTER.)

You can also add or revise menus to give users fast access to applications and reports, as well as the ability to configure their own personal menus. For example, if a group of users only access certain applications, you can create a menu that lists just these applications. In addition, a user can create a personal menu. (To access the application for changing menus, enter **Menus** in the Fast Path and press ENTER.)

In the chapter on processing options (Chapter 12), we'll examine the process of changing processing options. It's a very powerful way to configure your system and involves creating new versions of the interactive and batch applications. This capability is one of the strengths of J.D. Edwards software.

Finally, you can modify Data Dictionary attributes, including an item's visual assist or the glossary. We strongly discourage changing the size or type of the data item, however; this can have drastic effects on applications and the database that stores these values.

Interactive Application Modifications

Interactive applications are defined as object type APPL within Object Librarian. You can make various modifications to this object type that will be preserved during an upgrade.

You have two choices when you know a OneWorld application will not meet your needs: you can modify it, or you can create a new application. Your decision will be based on a comparison of the changes you plan to make to the standard application versus the enhancements that may be included in the next OneWorld release. For example, if you need only minor changes to a form and you also expect substantial changes to the same form in the next software release, you're better off modifying the existing application. This means your enterprise only has to ensure that the minor modifications are still functional after the update, rather than having to implement all the new functionality included in the new release.

For example, suppose you need to add a control to a form—a minor change and easy to do. Or suppose you want to add an exit from one form to another form. In both cases, modifying the existing form is a better choice than creating a new one. But when you need to do major surgery on a form, such as removing ER code or changing the form's business view, it's wise to copy the existing application and make your own, using a system code in the range 55*xx* through 59*xx*.

When you copy an existing application and modify this copy, you won't lose your changes during an upgrade—but you also won't get any updates during the upgrade. Let's say you've copied application P4101 to P554101; your customized P554101 will be protected during a OneWorld upgrade. But your P554101 custom application also won't receive any bug fixes or enhancements made to P4101 during an upgrade. Be sure to maintain the documentation for your copied application. That documentation will be important if you need to change your custom application to match an upgraded OneWorld application, or if you have to recopy it and again implement the modifications.

Interactive Application Modifications Preserved

The modifications to an interactive application that are preserved during an upgrade include the following:

- **New applications assigned system codes 55*xx* through 59*xx*, created from scratch or by copying an existing application**   Since the new application object is custom at upgrade time, it will be preserved in its entirety.

- **New form controls added to existing forms within an application** If J.D. Edwards places a control in the same location on the form, both controls might be displayed on top of each other. After the upgrade, you'll need to rearrange the controls using the Form Design Aid.

- **Changes to form and grid control properties, options, text, overrides, and filters** Your custom setting will take precedence over the J.D. Edwards settings.

- **New menu/toolbar exits** Any menu or toolbar exit you add to an existing form will be preserved.

- **Existing controls that have been hidden** Bear in mind that ER logic previously disabled or newly coded by J.D. Edwards in the upgraded version may show the control that you wish to hide.

- **Modified tab sequences** New OneWorld controls are moved to the end of your custom tab sequence after an upgrade, so you should recheck the tab sequences in any forms you have modified.

C A U T I O N

Do not delete form controls, grid columns, or hypercontrols in current OneWorld applications; instead, disable or hide them. If you delete these objects, it could affect important functionality within an application, such as calculations that use a form control to store a value.

Interactive Application Modifications Replaced

In contrast to the long list of modifications that are preserved in an interactive application during an upgrade, only two things are not preserved:

- **New forms in an existing OneWorld interactive application** To handle this situation, you can copy the existing application and give it a new name (using system codes 55*xx* through 59*xx*). You can then add the form to this new application.

- **Existing forms that have been deleted from an interactive application** If you don't want a particular form to be used, you should remove the menu/toolbar exits that call this form, or implement security so that a user won't be able to access the form.

Batch Application Modifications

The guidelines for modifications to batch applications (object type UBE) are similar to those for interactive applications. In addition, you have the opportunity to customize at the batch application's version level, as well as the batch application itself.

N O T E

Batch applications have an important relationship with versions in the context of OneWorld. We'll discuss guidelines for modifying batch application objects first, and then modifications at the version level.

Batch Application Modifications Preserved

As you do for interactive applications, you must decide if your enterprise is better off modifying an existing report, creating a new report from scratch, or copying and then modifying an existing report. Here, also, make an evaluation based on the level of changes you have to make to the standard application versus the enhancements you expect to be included in the next release. You should also consider whether to modify the batch application's object itself or just the version.

OneWorld preserves the following modifications to batch applications during an upgrade:

- **New batch applications assigned to system codes 55xx through 59xx, created from scratch or by copying an existing batch application**   At upgrade time, this object will not be modified.

- **New section objects**   Section objects include constants, alpha variables, numeric variables, date variables, runtime variables, database variables, and Data Dictionary variables. This refers to objects inside a section, not to a section itself.

- **Existing section controls that have been hidden**   Bear in mind that ER logic previously disabled or newly coded by J.D. Edwards may show the control after the upgrade.

- **Existing section objects that have been deleted**   It's not a good idea to delete section objects in J.D. Edwards applications because a control may be used behind the scenes as a variable or in calculations.

Batch Application Modifications Replaced

The following modifications made to batch applications will be replaced during an upgrade:

- **New sections in a OneWorld batch application**   Since these sections will not be preserved, an alternative approach is to add the logic to a custom batch application or business function. You can then insert a call to your custom object from the existing OneWorld batch application using Event Rules. That new object won't be replaced during the upgrade, so you can easily re-add the ER that was appended to the OneWorld batch application.

- **Existing sections that have been deleted**   You're better off making the report section conditional and turning off the visible property.

Version Modifications

When applications or reports are set up for your business, one of the first things to be added by the users and application developers will be new versions of these applications. During creation of a new version or modification of an existing version, you have the opportunity to change processing options. For a batch application, you also can change the data selection, sequencing, and even the report's design and Event Rules.

You can change versions freely to suit the needs of your enterprise, but it is important to create new versions of an interactive or batch application rather than modifying the J.D. Edwards (JDE) versions. Use caution when naming copied versions, to prevent your copies from being overwritten during an upgrade. For more information about creating and modifying versions, see Chapter 10.

Interactive Version Modifications Preserved

Interactive applications that include processing option templates must have versions attached to them, and you can change the processing option values for each version. When you create a new version, your non-JDE version is called a custom version. OneWorld preserves the following modifications to your custom versions during an upgrade:

- **Custom versions that do not use the prefixes XJDE and ZJDE**

- **Processing option values for custom versions** Values are brought forward to the new version but are not edited, which means that the upgraded version might contain invalid values for processing options. If this is the case, a warning will appear when a user works with the processing option values. You can revise the values in the new version to be valid.

- **Non-JDE version properties** These are the properties assigned to the version, such as security and the version description.

Batch Version Modifications Preserved

Batch applications, too, can have processing option templates attached. In addition to changing these processing options, you can modify the data selection and sort, the report layout, database output, and Event Rules at the version level. OneWorld preserves the following modifications to batch versions during an upgrade:

- **All versions that are created for new batch applications in system codes 55xx through 59xx**

- **Non-JDE versions that do not use the prefixes XJDE and ZJDE**

- **Processing option values for custom versions** Values are brought forward to the new version but are not edited, which means an upgraded version might contain invalid processing option values. If this is the case, a warning will appear when a user works with the processing option values. You can revise the values in the new version to be valid.

- **Non-JDE version properties** These are the properties assigned to the version, such as security and the version description.

- **Section layout modifications** These are changes such as moving a column on a report to a new location.

- **Section data selection and sort**

Version Modifications Replaced

OneWorld replaces the following modifications in both batch and interactive versions during an upgrade:

- **Any version whose name starts with ZJDE or XJDE runs the risk of being overwritten, because J.D. Edwards names all of its versions with these prefixes**   At upgrade time, if new versions are being delivered and they start with XJDE or ZJDE, or if you modified the versions starting with XJDE or ZJDE, they could be overridden.

- **Event Rules modifications**   Any modifications that you add to the ER in a custom version of a OneWorld batch application will not be reconciled with the ER of the original OneWorld batch application.

Although it's best to use custom versions rather than changing existing versions, sometimes you have no option but to modify the JDE version. This can happen, for instance, when a version is hard-coded in a row or form exit. In these cases, it is easier to change the processing option than it is to change the call to the application. This is another example of the importance of documenting changes so that an upgrade will go smoothly.

Business Function Modifications

Business functions (object type BSFN) have some of the most demanding modification rules of any OneWorld object, because all modifications that you make to a business function will be lost at upgrade time. If you need to add extensive modifications to a business function, consider creating an entirely new (custom) business function and use it in place of the J.D. Edwards function. Bear in mind that your custom modification will not be upgraded, and so the custom function will not receive any bug fixes or enhancements during the upgrade.

You have two additional options when modifying a business function:

- *If you just need to add code to the beginning or end of an exiting OneWorld function, you can create a custom "wrapper" function that calls the existing OneWorld function.* The wrapper function will call the OneWorld function and will contain your new logic as well. You can add logic to your custom function before or after the call to the OneWorld function.

- *If you need to add logic to the middle of a OneWorld function, it's to your advantage to create a custom function and add your logic to it.* Then insert a call to your custom business function from the existing OneWorld function. During an upgrade, you'll lose your changes to the OneWorld function, but your documentation of the changes will help you restore the call to the custom function after the upgrade.

Business Function Modifications Preserved

Only new (custom) business functions, and C or NER business functions, are preserved at upgrade time—as long as you create them with system codes 55*xx* through 59*xx*. For any custom business functions you create, you must also create a new (custom) parent DLL to store the modifications. To do this, add a new object of type BL in Object Librarian, and then configure any custom functions to use this DLL. If you need to review business function concepts, see Chapter 13.

Always use the standard API (jdeCallObject) to call other business functions from within your custom business functions. Failure to follow these standards guarantees you'll have problems. For example, if you don't use the standard API to call other J.D. Edwards business functions, they may be in a different DLL after your upgrade, and, therefore, your business functions may not work. During the upgrade process, your parent DLL for custom business functions may be lost, but it's regenerated when you rebuild your package.

NOTE

Always remember—if you don't want to lose changes to your business functions, make sure you create custom functions that use system codes 55xx through 59xx.

Event Rules Modifications

Event Rules are in almost any object you can define in Object Librarian (except for C business functions and data structures). All modifications you make to Event Rules will be saved at update time. They may, however, be moved and/or disabled.

ER Modifications Preserved

Any Event Rules you add to a custom table or application will be preserved at update time. In other words, any ER you add to any object that has a system code of 55*xx* through 59*xx* will be preserved.

Any Event Rules you add to a OneWorld application event that has no existing ER will also be preserved.

T I P

When you need to add extensive logic and if this logic can be added to a business function (that is, it doesn't need FDA or RDA system functions), we suggest you use a function rather than add substantial ER code to an existing application or report. After you create the business function, you can then add a call to this function inside the OneWorld application. As always, make sure to document your changes so that you can implement them again after an upgrade.

ER Modifications Changed

Any Event Rules you add to a OneWorld event that contains existing ER will be disabled during an upgrade and moved to the end of the event, as shown in Figure 8-1. After the upgrade, you'll need to reenable and reposition any ER code that you've added to a OneWorld interactive or batch application. Chapter 7 explains how to enable and disable code.

As with any change to an application, be sure to document your modifications, so at upgrade time you'll know what you modified and why.

Table Specification Modifications

A table in OneWorld is made up of two parts: the table specification, defined as an object type TBLE within Object Librarian, and the data inside a database. This section discusses modifications to table specifications, not the table data. To save table data during an

Client Modifications Using OneWorld

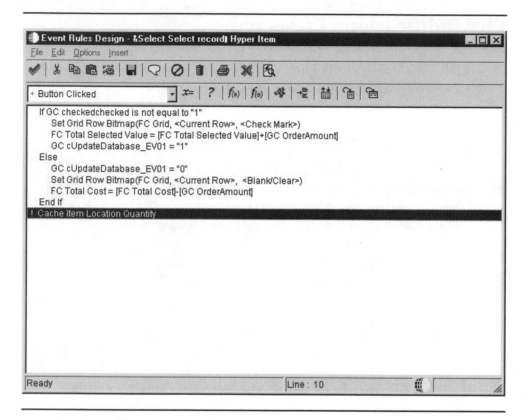

FIGURE 8-1. Disabled code inside an event

upgrade, be sure to back up your database. After the upgrade, you may need to use the OneWorld Table Conversion tool (Chapter 9) if the table format has been revised.

As with the other objects discussed in this chapter, you can modify existing JDE tables as well as create your own custom tables. When modifying a table's specification, you can change two things: the table columns and the table's indexes. You should avoid changing the table columns unless it is a custom table.

Table Modifications Preserved

At upgrade time, any new (custom) tables you created are preserved. Changes that you make to JDE tables may be replaced during an upgrade. Tables will be preserved in the following situations:

- **New (custom) tables** Any table in system code range 55*xx* through 59*xx* will be preserved. This includes tag files. For more information on tag files, see the following section on replaced modifications.

- **Added indexes** Your custom table indexes will be preserved.

If OneWorld replaces an index with a new index during the upgrade, your custom index will be moved down in the table order. For example, if you've added a third index to a table and OneWorld delivers another index with the upgrade, the OneWorld index becomes the third index and your custom index becomes the fourth index.

This arrangement has an impact on C business function code as well as system-generated objects with C components, such as table .h files, Named Event Rules, .c files, and .h files. These compiled objects use indexes for database manipulations. So when an index gets moved down, the index number changes. If you've follow standards, however, and have used the generated index names instead of numbers, you'll only need to rebuild the functions. On the other hand, if you've used the index numbers instead of names, you may need to modify the business functions.

Table Modifications Replaced

An upgrade replaces any ER that you've added to an existing table, or to a noncustom table (a table you did not create). Also, any index or column that you have modified or deleted will be replaced by the upgrade.

T I P

Rather than adding a new column to an existing table, consider creating a new tag file and name it using system codes 55xx through 59xx. A tag file is simply a new table that contains the additional fields needed in the table. The tag file usually contains the primary unique key from the original table, and the new columns. For example, the F4102 table (Item Master) contains a unique key that is made up of the items ITM and MCU. If you need to add an additional field to this table, such as 55XYZ, you could create a new table called F554102. Then, every time you update or fetch from the F4102 table, you can update or fetch from the F554102 table as well.

The following parts of a table specification will be replaced during an upgrade:

- **A new column in a OneWorld table**   The new column will be removed.

- **A modified column in a OneWorld table**   An upgrade replaces any modified columns with their original definition, which will cause the physical table to be regenerated. Therefore, the data will be lost.

- **A deleted column in a OneWorld table**   An upgrade replaces any columns you have deleted.

- **A deleted index in a OneWorld Table**   The upgrade process re-creates indexes you've deleted.

- **A modified index in a OneWorld table**   Any indexes you've modified are returned to their original state.

Business View Modifications

Business views play a very important role in communication between OneWorld applications and OneWorld tables. When you modify a business view—or, more importantly, when you delete columns from a business view—you can cause problems in your applications. These fields in the business view may be displayed on a form, used in calculations, or used to update the database; if you remove them, you'll get unpredictable results. If you need to hide a column, do so at the application design level using either Form Design Aid or Report Design Aid (see Chapters 5 and 6).

Deleting columns from a business view gives you no significant performance gain, and the disadvantages far outweigh the advantages.

Business View Modifications Preserved

Like other modified objects, any custom business view that you create will be preserved during an upgrade. (Be sure to use system codes 55*xx* through 59*xx* for your new business views.)

Table columns and joins to new tables that you add to a business view will be preserved at upgrade time, too, as will any columns added or tables joined to a OneWorld business view.

T I P

Although your modified business view is preserved, you may get unexpected results if J.D. Edwards changes a business view by appending another table. So if you need a business view for a custom application, it's best to create a new business view rather than modify an existing OneWorld business view. That gives you complete control over your business view, and you don't need to worry about the effects of an upgrade.

Business View Modifications Replaced

An upgrade replaces any tables, columns, and joins that you have deleted in a J.D. Edwards business view, as follows:

- If your business view contains multiple tables and you removed one table, an upgrade replaces the deleted table.

- If you deleted any columns from a business view, an upgrade replaces them.

- Any modification or deletions of joins in a OneWorld business view will be replaced during the upgrade. This includes the operator functions =, <, >, <=, and >=; and the join types Simple, Left Outer, Right, and Outer, as well as the items that are joined.

Data Structure Modifications

OneWorld data structures can be used for business functions as well as processing option templates. Data structures also exist in batch and interactive applications. None of the modifications you make to OneWorld data structures are preserved at upgrade time. However, all new (custom) data structures that you create will be preserved.

Data Structure Modifications Preserved

In general, the only data structure modifications that OneWorld preserves during an upgrade are those made to new (custom) data structures that you create. Any modifications you make to the following data structures will be preserved during the upgrade:

- Any custom business function data structure

- Any custom processing option template

- Any custom media object data structure

- Any custom form data structure

- Any custom report data structure

Data Structure Modifications Replaced

During an upgrade, both business function data structures and media object data structures will be replaced. Therefore, be sure to document any modifications you make to these data structure types. The following data structures will be replaced during an upgrade:

- **Elements added to a OneWorld data structure**   The upgrade will remove any custom elements you have added to the existing data structure.

- **Modifications to an existing data structure**   The upgrade will restore the original design of the data structure.

- **Elements deleted from an existing data structure**   The upgrade will replace any elements you have deleted.

- **Modified tabs**   The upgrade will replace any tab changes on a processing options template.

- **Tabs, comments, or data items added to an existing processing option data structure** The upgrade will remove any custom elements you have added to the existing template.

- **Modified tabs, comments, or data items in a processing option data structure** The upgrade will restore the original design of the template.

- **Deleted tabs, comments, or data items in a processing option data structure** The upgrade will replace any elements you have deleted.

Putting It All Together

Before you modify any object within OneWorld, you should consider the implications of a software upgrade. The topics we discussed in this chapter really come down to the same set of decisions: How extensive will your changes be? If they're minor and will be preserved as described in this chapter, then modifying the software might be the right way to go. Even if you need to make substantial modifications, as long as they meet the guidelines above, you'll be able to save your work at upgrade time. Another option is to create custom objects using system codes 55xx through 59xx, which will be preserved during an upgrade. If you decide to create copies of the OneWorld objects, be aware that there's a trade-off here: The copies will not receive bug fixes and enhancements during a normal software upgrade. You may need to update your object afterward, or even recopy it and introduce your changes all over again.

Understanding the modification guidelines discussed in this chapter will help you make informed decisions about changing your OneWorld environment. And here's one last reminder of the importance of documenting any and all changes to the software. Your documentation will help you create modifications and customizations that will make it smoothly through an upgrade.

Client Modifications Using OneWorld

CHAPTER 9

Development Environment Tools

Universal Table Browser (UTB)

Debugging Tools

Table Conversion Tool

Putting It All Together

In previous chapters you've studied OneWorld's Forms Design Aid (Chapter 5), Report Design Aid (Chapter 6), and other tools with which you create new objects for applications in OneWorld. These objects include tables, business functions, business views, and more. In addition to these object creation tools, OneWorld provides a number of other vital utilities for viewing and maintaining the data in tables, debugging your applications, and converting table data for OneWorld use.

- **Universal Table Browser (UTB)**   This chapter starts with a discussion of the Universal Table Browser—your window into the data inside any OneWorld table—for purposes of analysis, troubleshooting, and debugging.

- **Debugging Tools**   Next we'll look at how to view Event Rules (ER) code and how to enable a log file, and discuss various tools for debugging ER code and programs written in C.

- **Table Conversion Tool**   We'll finish up with a description and example of the table conversion tool, which helps you convert data from other formats and locations.

Universal Table Browser (UTB)

When you test your applications or are trying to pinpoint where problems exist, it's very helpful to look at the information directly inside the tables. This is usually done before you do any debugging. By looking into the tables, you can sometimes learn where your application isn't functioning correctly.

It's not always convenient to select and view data with the tools provided by Oracle or Access, or whatever database you're using; you might not even have access to these database tools. You might not know what kind of database is used, since OneWorld is designed to work with many databases. The Universal Table Browser (UTB) is your answer; it lets you view data inside any table that was created in OneWorld, no matter what type of database the table resides in, on any machine known to OneWorld.

To view a table, you must know only two things: its name and its data source. The table's name is its Object Librarian name, such as F0101 or F55002. The data source tells UTB where in a particular type of database (Oracle, Access, and so on) the table resides. (Data sources are discussed in Chapter 2.) Most of the time, you'll use the default data source, which is defined for the table using Object Configuration Manager (OCM) as described in Chapter 3. Since a table may exist in two different data sources, UTB lets you view the data in either data source. For example, if you're signed into one environment, which has a default data source of Local, you can use UTB to view data in another data source on the server.

The UTB interface is illustrated by the form in Figure 9-1. Most parts of the interface are intuitive and easy to use. The Find button on the toolbar loads data into the grid. In the QBE line (the row above the grid column titles), you can restrict the amount of information displayed. For instance, in Figure 9-1 we are comparing against M30, which causes the form to select only records that have M30 in the MCU (alias) field. You can refine your search using logical operators (>, <, and ! for not equal) in front of the QBE value; for instance, enter **>M30** to view all records with a Cost Center value greater than M30.

Working with the UTB is a simple matter of activating the tool, choosing your table, and understanding what is displayed.

Launching UTB

There are a couple of ways to start the UTB. You can type **UTB** in the Fast Path box in OneWorld Explorer and press ENTER. Or you can choose Universal Table from menu GH902. This brings up the Universal Table Browser form. Now you need to select a table to browse.

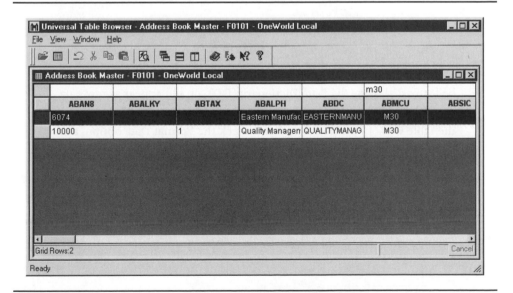

FIGURE 9-1.   The F0101 table viewed inside Universal Table Browser (UTB)

Choosing a Table to View

After you are in UTB, the next step is to open a table. To choose a table, follow these steps:

1. In UTB, select Open Table from the Form menu. This brings up the Table and Data Source Selection form.

2. In the Table and Data Source Selection form, enter the table name and tab out of this field.

3. The default data source in now displayed for this table. In the following illustration, we entered the name of the Address Book table (F0101), and its displayed data source is OneWorld Local. This default data source is where you'll view the data used by your applications or reports. If you want to change this data source, click the flashlight button beside the Data Source field and select a different data source.

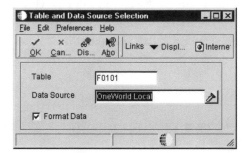

4. Use the Format Data check box to designate whether the displayed data will be formatted using the Data Dictionary (DD), or will appear as raw data. For example, a field might have two decimal places inside the DD but be saved in the table without the decimal. If you check the Format Data option, the number will be displayed with the decimal places, such as 20.51. Without this option enabled, you'll see 2051.

NOTE

We recommend you leave the Format Data option enabled.

5. After entering the table name and determining the data source, click OK in the toolbar. The system displays a form with your table's name and description in the title.

UTB allows you to have more than one Table and Data Source Selection window open so that you can look at multiple tables. Simply repeat the proceding steps to open additional windows.

Viewing Data in the Table

In the UTB window, each row in the table grid contains an entire row from the table. The column titles in the grid are the actual table field names, which consist of the DD alias plus a prefix. In Figure 9-1, for example, the field MCU in the F0101 table is called ABMCU, where AB is a prefix assigned to every field in the table. By using the field's alias (MCU), you can look it up in the DD to determine its use. Or you can simply right-click the column within the UTB, and select Column Properties to view information about the field (see Figure 9-2).

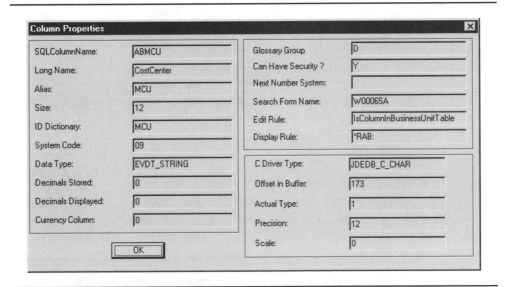

FIGURE 9-2. Column properties shown in UTB for the ABMCU column

Debugging Tools

There are three ways to debug your OneWorld application or report when it's not working correctly:

- Turn on a log that will print to a file every time the application does anything.

- Debug the Event Rules code using the OneWorld Debugger tool.

- If the code you want to debug is compiled, such as a business function or database trigger, you can debug the code using Microsoft Visual C++.

This section examines each of these debugging methods. But first, let's take a look at OneWorld's Event Rules Browser, your window into the Event Rules that make your application run. The Event Rules Browser allows you to view the code inside an interactive or batch application to determine where to start your debugging efforts.

Event Rules Browser

When you need to see the Event Rules (ER) of an application or report, getting into the design tool and methodically searching for each event isn't a very easy or practical solution. Fortunately, OneWorld provides a tool—the Event Rules Browser—that allows you to view all the events and ER inside an application.

To access the ER Browser, follow these steps:

1. From the Object Librarian, select the application or report that you want to examine.

NOTE

It's not required that you check out the object before you can browse the ER. However, if the object has changed since your last install or checkout, you should check it out to get the latest code on your machine before you browse the object's ER.

2. In the Application Design Aid or the Batch Application Librarian form, select BrowsER from the Form menu. The Browsing window appears, as shown in Figure 9-3.

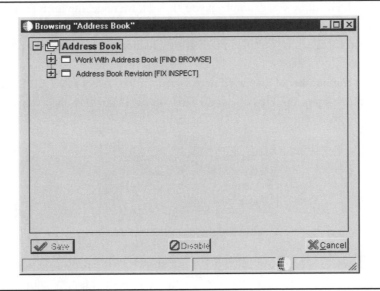

FIGURE 9-3.   The ER Browser

3. In the tree control, you can expand each node by clicking the plus and minus
    icons beside the node name. This lets you view the forms, variables, and ER in
    the application.

Configuring the ER Browser

By using options inside the ER Browser itself, you can configure the appearance of the
Browsing window. Right-click on the form to see a pop-up menu with these options:

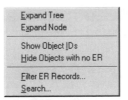

Use the Expand Node to expand a single node, and Expand Tree to expand every
node in the tree. The Show Object IDs option lets you enable a display of the object ID at

the bottom of the window. For example, if you click a form node, the form number is displayed. The next option, Hide Objects With No ER, lets you show only those nodes that have associated ER. Turning on this option greatly reduces the number of nodes in the tree structure.

To reduce the number of displayed nodes even further, select Filter ER Records on the Browsing window's pop-up. This opens the Show Event dialog box shown here:

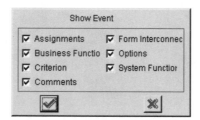

This form allows you to choose the types of ER shown in the Browsing window. For example, if you only want to see business function ER inside this application, you would deselect all the check boxes except Business Functions.

TIP

If you need to review the different types of Event Rules, see Chapter 7.

The final configuration option for the ER Browser is the Search option. This is a powerful tool that can help you find a specific line of ER. When you select this option on the pop-up, you'll see a Find dialog box shown here:

This Find dialog box works just like similar ones in other Windows applications; simply enter your search criteria and click Find Next. ER Browser can be a valuable tool to search through your code; but in some cases, you may want to search your code outside of OneWorld or mark your code. This is discussed in the following Developer's Corner, titled "Using Print To File to Find and Examine ER."

Developer's Corner

Using Print To File to Find and Examine ER

It can sometimes be very difficult to locate the exact event you need when you're searching for a specific line of code in Event Rules. The ER Browser is helpful, but it doesn't allow you to mark the line of code. The Print To File function within the ER Design interface comes in handy for this task.

Inside any object that uses ER, there is an option to print a hard copy of the ER code. Likewise, you can print your ER to a file. This lets you browse the ER using Notepad or any other word processing program. This way, you can search for specific text, which helps you find out what event is calling a particular function or using a particular variable.

To print to a file, follow these steps:

1. Check out the object from Object Librarian, and click the Design button.

2. Select the form or report you want to work with, and then right-click the form and select Event Rules. (See Chapter 7 for more information about working with Event Rules.)

3. Select File | Print.

4. When the Print dialog box appears, select the File radio button.

5. Click the ... button across from the File button, and select a location and name for the file you want to print. We suggest you name the file after the application or report, something like P550001er.txt.

6. Change the Print Scope to be Report for a batch application, or Application if you are in FDA; then click OK.

7. Open any word processing program, such as Notepad or Word Pad, and open the file you just printed. Now search through it like any other text document.

Printing your ER to a file allows you to use the Find and Find Next commands in your word processing program, to quickly find the place in your ER that you need to examine. You won't be able to change the ER code, but you'll be able to quickly find logic and highlight this ER. After you find the event, you can go back into OneWorld and modify or change the logic.

Debug Log File

Sometimes, looking at the ER code won't help you find the problem, and you'll need to debug the application or report instead. You may not even know where to start looking for the problem. OneWorld provides a log file, Jdedebug.log, that you can generate to give you information about how the application is processing. This log file contains information about system functions, business functions, and forms and reports being called, as well as all database calls. Jdedebug.log can be of substantial value because it tells you the order of what was called, and it tells you whether or not the functions returned errors.

Jde.ini File Changes for Debugging Purposes

Before you can write a log file, you need to make two changes to your Jde.ini file to activate—or turn on—the debug log file. Follow these steps:

1. Open Jde.ini from Notepad. Your .ini file should be in the Windows directory for Win95 or Win98, or the winnt directory if you're running NT.

2. Find the DEBUG section of the Jde.ini file.

3. Change the Output designation to FILE instead of NONE, as shown in the following excerpt from Jde.ini. This tells OneWorld that you want it to produce a debug log file.

```
 [DEBUG]
TAMMultiUserOn=0
Output=FILE
ServerLog=0
LEVEL=BSFN,EVENTS
;BSFN,EVENTS,SF_CONTROL,SF_GRID,SF_PARENT_CHILD,SF_GENERAL,
SF_MESSAGING,SF_WORKFLOW,SF_WORKFLOW_ADMIN,SF_MEDIA_OBJ
DebugFile=c:\jdedebug.log
JobFile=c:\jde.log
Frequency=10000
RepTrace=0
```

4. The LEVEL field tells OneWorld what you want to see in the log file. For now, the BSFN and EVENTS levels are sufficient. You can add other types of messages to the log file, if you wish, choosing from the list below the LEVEL field. This includes SF_PARENT_CHILD and SF_MESSAGING. For details about the Jde.ini file, see Appendix F.

NOTE

You can also change the location of the Jdedebug.log file, but we recommend you leave it in the root directory.

5. After you have changed your DEBUG settings in Jde.ini, find the section titled UBE.

6. Change the UBEDebugLevel to a number between 0 and 6, where 6 gives you the most information and 0 gives you no information. We suggest you set this to 6.

```
[UBE]
UBEDebugLevel=6
UBESaveLogFile=0
UBEFont_FaceName=Times New Roman
UBEFont_PointSize=8
```

7. Save and exit your Jde.ini file.

CAUTION

After you activate the Jdedebug.log file, OneWorld will add a large number of lines to your log file. This file can get very large and may slow down processing time. Therefore, we suggest that you only activate the log file when it's needed. As soon as you've finished with it, deactivate debugging by changing Output back to NONE in the DEBUG section of the Jde.ini file.

Viewing the Log File

After you activate the debug log, every action you perform in OneWorld will be logged inside the Jdedebug.log file. To view the log, simply open Jdedebug.log in Notepad or another text editor. The log file will be stored in the location that is set in the Jde.ini file.

We'll show you how to use Jdedebug.log at the end of this section, in "Example: Debugging an Application."

OneWorld Debugger

You already know that interactive and batch applications in OneWorld use the Event Rules (ER) language. After you've added ER to your application, you may find some bugs that need fixing. OneWorld's Debugger tool helps you step through the ER to find these errors.

Using OneWorld Debugger involves several steps. First, of course, you have to build the application for debugging. Then you set breakpoints; and, finally, you launch your application.

DEFINITION

*A **breakpoint** is a spot in the code where you want the Debugger to stop so you can observe the action.*

NOTE

You can use the OneWorld Debugger only on the client machine. You cannot debug an application that runs on a server. Furthermore, OneWorld Debugger only works on interactive and batch applications, not on Named Event Rules or business functions written in C.

Building an Object for Debugging

Before you can debug your application, you need to build it with debug information. To do this, follow these steps:

1. In the One World Explorer window, type **Debug** in the Fast Path box and press ENTER. The system displays menu GH902, as shown in Figure 9-4.

2. Double-click the Debug Application item to bring up the Event Rules Debugger form (Figure 9-5).

3. In the lower-left part of the form is the Object Browse window, which contains three tabs: one for applications (APPL), one for batch applications (UBEs), and one for table conversions (TC). Open the tab for the type of object you want to debug. In the Object Name QBE column, type the name of the object you want to debug and press ENTER to find it.

4. Double-click the grid row containing your object in the Object Browse window. This builds the debug information. It also displays the object in the Applications window (top left).

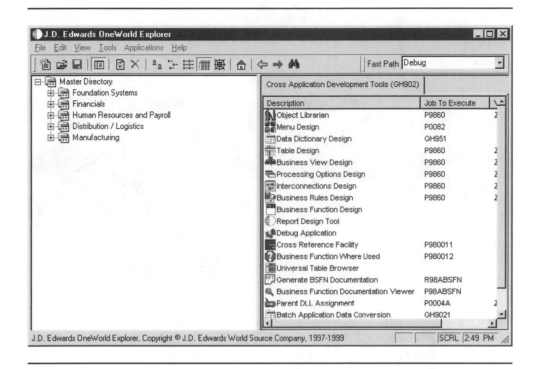

FIGURE 9-4. Cross Application Development Tools menu GH902

5. Any time you modify your application in any way, you must rebuild the object before you can debug it. Do this by selecting your application or report in the Applications window and clicking the Rebuild button.

N O T E

You can add more than one application to the Debugger at a time. You'll do this when one application calls another application.

Setting a Breakpoint

The next step in debugging your application is to set a breakpoint. For example, let's say you're debugging code added to events in your application; you can place a breakpoint on any line of code in an event so the Debugger will pause there and let you examine the

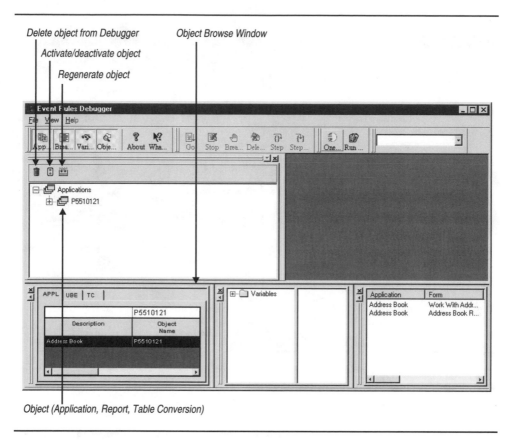

FIGURE 9-5. The Event Rules Debugger form

processing. To review a list of events, see Appendixes B and C. It's also a good idea to set a breakpoint at the location where you want to start debugging.

After you've generated your application, follow these steps to set breakpoints:

1. In the tree control at the top left of the Debugger, find the event that contains the ER on which you want to set the breakpoint.

2. After you've selected the event, the ER code will appear in the window at the top right of the Debugger form. To set (or remove) a breakpoint on any line of code, double-click that line. You can also press F9 or the toolbar buttons to set and remove breakpoints. In Figure 9-6 we have placed a breakpoint on the Button Clicked event.

3. Repeat steps 1 and 2 to add more breakpoints to your application as needed.

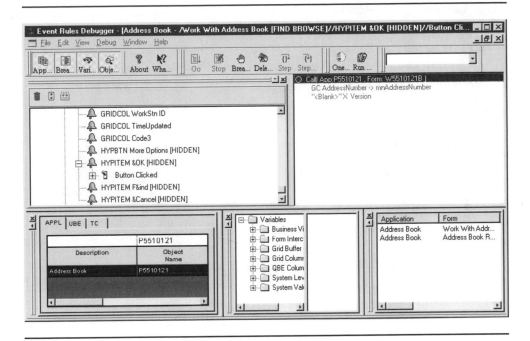

FIGURE 9-6. Breakpoint is set on the Button Clicked event

Debugging Your Application

The Debugger provides a number of operations useful in debugging your ER code. You can step through the code one line at a time, or you can "step into" lines of code. (For example, if you're on a line of code that calls another form, you can step into the code for that called form.) You can also look at the value of any variable.

In the toolbar of the ER Debugger, the Go button runs the application until it hits the next breakpoint. The Stop button stops the Debugger. The Break button inserts or removes a breakpoint. The Delete Breakpoint button deletes a breakpoint. The Step button steps you forward to the next line of code in this event; if the next line is the last line in this event, Step takes you into the first line of code in the next event. The OneWorld button opens up Microsoft Visual C++ for debugging business functions using Oexplorer.exe, and the Run LaunchUBE button opens up Microsoft Visual C++ to debug business functions using LaunchUBE.exe. Debugging Business Functions will be discussed in the next section, "Microsoft Visual C++." The input-capable control on the far right allows you to enter text and press F3 to find code with the text you typed in.

To debug your application, leave the Debugger running and then run the application in OneWorld as you normally would. When you get to one of your set breakpoints in the code, the Debugger application appears on top of your application. At this point you can step to the next breakpoint, step into another event, or click Go.

As mentioned, you can also look at variables within the Debugger. Use the variable tree control (lower-middle window), and select the variables you want to look at.

We'll walk through a debugging operation later, in "Example: Debugging an Application."

Microsoft Visual C++

The ER Debugger is a good way to debug batch and interactive applications, but you need help from a different source when you need to examine a business function written in C or a Named Event Rule. For finding the errors in these elements, you need the debugger in Microsoft Visual C++.

Don't be intimidated by the "C++"; "Visual C++" is just the name of the Microsoft product that you'll be using. Debugging a business function is different from debugging an application because a business function is compiled into a DLL (Dynamic Link Library), and you use this DLL for debugging. It's far less technical than it sounds—if you follow the techniques described in this section, you'll quickly master the process of debugging a program written in C.

For more information about the debugger in Visual C++, go to the online help and tutorials provided by Microsoft.

N O T E

The techniques described here are applicable only to business functions and Named Event Rules (NER) on a local machine. Debugging on the server may require a different tool.

The examples in this section employ the same concepts discussed earlier for debugging an application. Here, too, you'll learn how to set breakpoints, step through code, step into code, and run code. In addition, we'll look at how to view data and even change it inside the code.

To start the process of debugging a business function using Microsoft Visual C++, use any of these methods:

- Run OneWorld by launching it inside Microsoft Visual C++.

- Attach Microsoft Visual C++ to OneWorld if it is already running.

- Step into the C code from inside the Event Rules Debugger, which will start Microsoft Visual C++. This technique is used in the example at the end of this section.

Setting Up a Workspace in Visual C++

If you're going to be debugging a lot of C code, doing it using Microsoft Visual C++ is likely to be quicker and easier, but it requires a little advance setup on your part. First, you need to tell Visual C++ what executable you want to use, as well as what DLLs you will be debugging. The executable is important because it sets up a *workspace* in which to debug the code. The executable you'll use in this case is Oexplore.exe, for both interactive and batch applications.

To set up a workspace in Microsoft Visual C++, follow these steps:

1. Click the Start button in Windows, and choose Microsoft Visual C++.

2. In Microsoft Visual C++, select the File menu and choose Open Workspace. The Open Workspace form appears.

3. Choose Oexplore.exe as your workspace. In the Files Of Type field, select the Executable Files (.exe) option, as shown in the following illustration. The Oexplore.exe should be in your B7\System\Bin32 directory. When you've designated the .exe file, click Open. This tells Microsoft Visual C++ which executable you want to use.

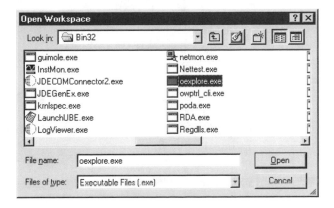

4. Now specify the DLLs you'll be using. From the Project menu, choose Settings. The Project Settings window appears (Figure 9-7). Open the Debug tab, and change the Category to Additional DLLs.

Client Modifications Using OneWorld

5. Next, add the DLL(s) you want to debug. In this example, we use Callbsfn.dll (see Figure 9-7).

   The DLL you use will be either a specific one that your company uses for this purpose, or a J.D. Edwards DLL (such as Cdist.dll for distribution or Cfin.dll for financials). To find out which DLL contains the business function you want to debug, look for the function in the Object Librarian's Parent DLL for the function. Click OK when you've finished.

6. Select File | Save Workspace.

NOTE

Before you can debug a business function, it must be built on the client machine. For information on building functions, see Chapter 13.

Setting Breakpoints in Visual C++

Now your workspace is set up, and the next step is to set breakpoints. Doing this in Visual C++ is similar to the process you use in the Event Rules Debugger: You simply

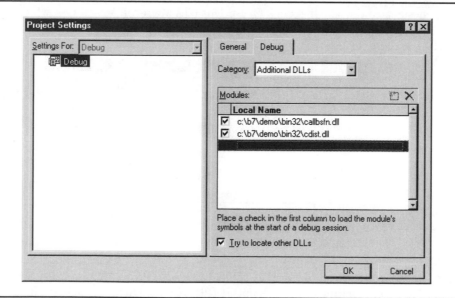

FIGURE 9-7. Specifying and adding DLLs for the debug operation

open the code that you want to debug, find the line on which to set a breakpoint, and set the breakpoint. Here are the steps:

1. Select File | Open. (*Don't* select Open Workspace.) An Open dialog box appears.

2. Open the source file for the function to be debugged. The source file should be in the directory B7/*environment*/source, where *environment* will be DEMO, DEV733, or something similar.

3. In this example, we'll place a breakpoint at the top of the code. To do this, press F9 or click the toolbar icon that looks like a hand. A red dot appears next to the line of code, indicating that the breakpoint is set, as shown in Figure 9-8.

4. Save your workspace again, with File | Save Workspace.

Debugging a Business Function in Visual C++

At this point, you can run your application for debugging. As mentioned earlier in this section, you have two options for this step: If OneWorld is running, you can do an

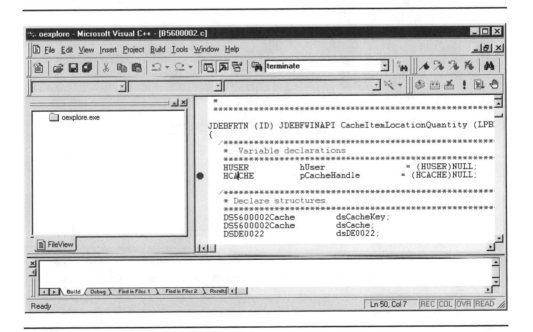

FIGURE 9-8. Setting a breakpoint in Visual C++

Attach To Process command to start debugging. If OneWorld is not running, you can start it from Microsoft Visual C++.

First let's walk through the steps to start debugging a business function with OneWorld already running. You need to attach the Visual C++ debugger to the OneWorld executable.

1. In Microsoft Visual C++, select Build | Start Debug and choose Attach To Process.

2. In the Attach To Process window, choose OEXPLORE, as shown here:

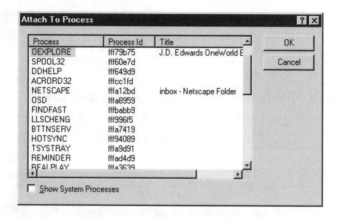

3. At this point, you may see the window shown in the following illustration. Don't worry about this message; you're not debugging OneWorld. You're debugging the DLLs that contain the business function. Click OK to continue.

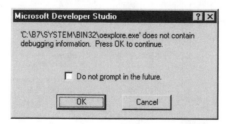

4. You may get a pop-up window saying a DLL does not contain debug information. This means you have not built any functions in this DLL, but you attached the DLL in the Project Settings. You'll need to stop debugging and rebuild the function you want to debug.

5. At this point, you are in OneWorld. Run your application, and it should stop on your breakpoint.

6. To stop the Visual C++ debugger, first exit OneWorld as you normally would. This will stop the debugger. Then exit Visual C++.

N O T E

While debugging using Microsoft Visual C++, you can stop the debugger inside Microsoft Visual C++ from the Debug menu by selecting Stop Debugging. This is a somewhat ungraceful way of stopping debugging, because not only does it stop Visual C++ debugger, it also stops the execution of OneWorld and any processes OneWorld is running on the client machine. Try to avoid doing this, if possible. Stopping the debugger could stop a process in the middle of an action, which could corrupt data.

Launching OneWorld from Visual C++

If you want to debug a business function and OneWorld is not running, you can launch OneWorld from Microsoft Visual C++. Follow these steps:

1. From Visual C++, open your Oexplore workspace as described earlier (in "Setting Up a Workspace in Visual C++").

2. Select Build | Start Debug, and choose Go.

3. At this point, you're running OneWorld. Run your application, and the debugger should stop on your breakpoints.

4. To stop the debugger, exit OneWorld as you normally would.

Example: Debugging an Application

You've seen in this section that there are several ways and means to debug your OneWorld applications. In this example, we'll debug an application using several tools: looking at the Jdedebug.log file, the Event Rules Debugger, and Microsoft Visual C++.

In most cases, you won't require all the tools at the same time; typically, you'll only use one. For example, if you're trying to find an error in an application, you won't need Visual C++. Sometimes, however, you'll need all three tools working together to examine and fix an application that isn't running correctly. For instance, your problem may be occurring in either the business function or the application, so you'd need to debug both at the same time. Our example application has two forms: the first form calls the second form, and the second form calls a business function.

This example demonstrates the rare case when you employ the debug log, the ER Debugger, and Microsoft Visual C++ at the same time. In addition, you'll see that debugging a business function in this way means you don't need to do all the workspace setup outlined in the preceding section. The Event Rules Debugger does it for you.

1. Activate the Jdedebug log file, as described in "Jde.ini File Changes for Debugging Purposes," earlier in the chapter.

2. In OneWorld Explorer, type **Debug** in the Fast Path and press ENTER.

3. Select Debug Application from the menu on the right.

4. Build the application you want to debug. This is explained earlier in the section "Building an Object for Debugging."

5. Place breakpoints in the event you want to debug. This is explained earlier in the section "Setting a Breakpoint."

6. As shown earlier in Figure 9-6, we set a breakpoint on the ER that calls the other form. This is the Button Clicked event on the Select button.

7. Now start the application from the OneWorld Explorer menu or Object Librarian.

8. In the application, click Find on the Work With Address Book form. In the Jdedebug.log, you'll see that the application is executing a fetch to the F0101 table. You can see the Select statement in the following excerpt from the Jdedebug.log:

```
Apr 04 02:21:28 ** 4294173777/4294433917 Entering
JDB_SetSequencing
Apr 04 02:21:28 ** 4294173777/4294433917 Entering
JDB_SelectKeyed
Apr 04 02:21:30 ** 4294173777/4294433917 SELECT ABAN8, ABALKY,
ABTAX, ABALPH, ABDC, ABMCU, ABSIC, ABLNGP, ABAT1, ABCM, ABTAXC,
```

```
ABAT2, ABATP, ABATR, ABATPR, ABAB3, ABATE, ABSBLI, ABEFTB, ABAN81,
ABAN82, ABAN83, ABAN84, ABAN86, ABAN85, ABAC01, ABAC02, ABAC03,
ABAC04, ABAC05, ABAC06, ABAC07, ABAC08, ABAC09, ABAC10, ABAC11,
ABAC12, ABAC13, ABAC14, ABAC15, ABAC16, ABAC17, ABAC18, ABAC19,
ABAC20, ABAC21, ABAC22, ABAC23, ABAC24, ABAC25, ABAC26, ABAC27,
ABAC28, ABAC29, ABAC30, ABTXCT, ABTX2, ABALP1, ABURCD, ABURDT,
ABURAT, ABURAB, ABURRF, ABUSER, ABPID, ABUPMJ, ABJOBN, ABUPMT
FROM F0101  ORDER BY ABAN8 ASC
Apr 04 02:21:32 ** 4294173777/4294433917 Entering JDB_Fetch
```

9. In the Work With Address Book form, select a grid row.

10. After you click Select, the Event Rules Debugger goes to work and stops on the line of ER where you placed the breakpoint, as shown here:

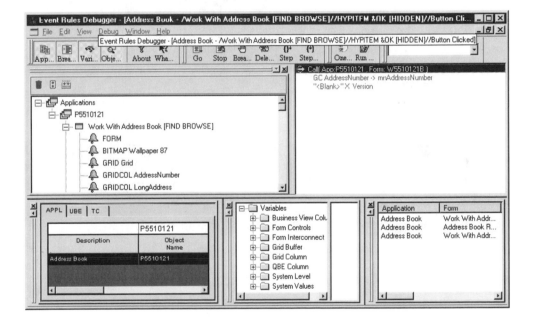

Client Modifications Using OneWorld

11. Click the Step Into button.

12. This stops at the next line of ER code, which happens to be in the Post Dialog Is Initialized event in the form that was called.

13. This form is calling an NER business function. Click Step Into again, and Microsoft Visual C++ opens (Figure 9-9). At this point you can step through your C code. Then press F5 to go to the next breakpoint.

14. When you've finished debugging the application, exit OneWorld, as you normally would.

N O T E

While debugging with Microsoft Visual C++, you may at some point enter assembly code. This is okay; just close the window and press F5.

Using the ER Debugger and Microsoft C++ can help meet all of your debugging needs, but there are two more ways to debug your applications that are discussed in the following Developer's Corner, titled "Other Debugging Tools: M & D Debug and Write to JDE Log."

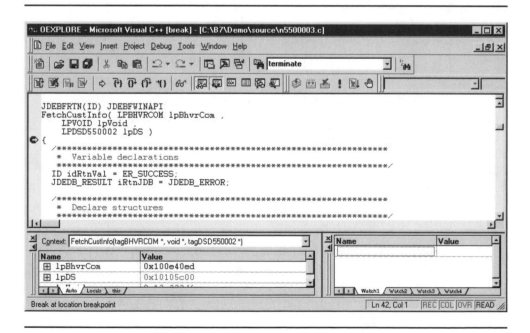

FIGURE 9-9.   Stepping inside Microsoft Visual C++ to debug a business function

Other Debugging Tools: M & D Debug and Write to JDE Log

The Jdedebug.log, ER Debugger, and Visual C++ are complex and flexible tools, great for stepping through code to find a problem. But sometimes you'll just want a "quick-and-dirty" utility to get some feedback from your application or report.

M & D Debug

When you just want a fast peek at the value of a field, or some confirmation that an event is successfully being triggered, try M & D Debug, a very, very simple business function. All it does is pop up a window that displays the values you pass to it. Let's say you just want to see the values that are inside certain fields at run time; call M & D Debug and it will show you a window with these values. This handy tool can be used for many purposes—in addition to displaying values, you can use it to temporarily stop your application.

All you need to do is call the M & D Debug business function from inside your ER (the source file is md_debug). When you call it, pass in the values you want, and they'll be displayed in the pop-up window shown here:

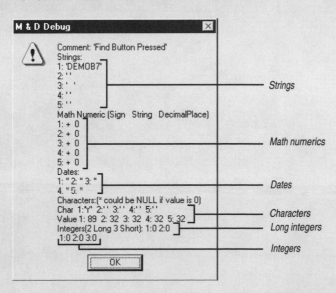

461

The M & D Debug function's parameters are divided into seven parts, which you can use as desired. You can pass as many of these parameters as you like, and you can call M & D Debug from any object that contains ER.

CAUTION

Although M & D Debug is easy to use, it's also easy to forget about. Do not check in an object that contains an M & D Debug function. Having an M & D Debug box pop up will be quite an unwelcome surprise to a user. But of far more consequence is a report's hitting an M & D Debug function when the report is running on the server; it can hang up the kernel. Make sure you remove all M & D Debug functions when you've finished with them.

Write To JDE Log

Another helpful function, Write To JDE Log (B0900102), will write to the Jdedebug.log file. You can use this function in the same way you use M & D Debug, except Write To JDE Log will write to the Jdedebug.log file rather than popping up a window. This function is valuable when you need to debug an application running on the server.

Table Conversion Tool

The Table Conversion tool in OneWorld offers a very effective way of changing data, allowing you to quickly convert data between different tables and different formats. Table Conversion is helpful when you are upgrading or changing environments, as well as manipulating data located outside of OneWorld.

This section explains the types of data that can be processed with the Table Conversion tool, as well as the types of data conversion objects. We'll also walk through an example of its use.

Data Formats and Environments

The Table Conversion program converts data from one format and environment to another format and environment. Table Conversion can receive and convert data in several ways. It can

- Convert data to or from a file inside OneWorld.

- Convert data to or from a table outside OneWorld.

- Receive information to or from a business view.

- Convert data to or from a flat file.

You can mix and match any of these types of conversions. For example, you might convert data from a flat file to a OneWorld table. You can also create joined business views to pull data from several tables at the same time.

Data can come from any database, even from a table not defined inside Object Librarian. The table does, however, have to be in a OneWorld-supported database (such as Oracle, Access, AS/400, or SQL Server). If you're planning to use a table that is outside OneWorld (a "foreign" table), you must define this table by creating a special data source and environment. You'll see how to do this in the example at the end of this section.

In addition to converting different types of data, you can also convert data between environments. There are three environments involved during the processing of a table conversion: the sign-on environment, the input environment, and the output environment. For example, a large amount of data inside a table may need to be converted between environment Dev731 and Dev732, but you are signed on to a third environment. The specifications for your table conversion will be saved in your sign-on environment;

the data will be loaded from Dev731; and the data will be copied to Dev732. Of course, any table involved must be defined in the environment that you choose.

Table Conversion Types

Table conversion is very similar to a report or batch application. In fact, when you create a table conversion object in OneWorld, you create a UBE object that is defined as a table conversion. The Table Conversion tool offers four different types of conversions:

- **Data Conversion** This is the most prevalent and effective table conversion. It allows you to move data from an input table using logic that you define.

- **Data Copy** This allows you to convert data between tables, or from one data source and environment to another data source and environment.

- **Data Copy With Table Input** Similar to a Data Copy conversion, the Data Copy With Table Input conversion gives you the added flexibility of using an input table that provides information about the type of copy needed.

- **Batch Delete** This conversion deletes records from a table.

All four table conversion types follow the same event flow:

1. **Process Begin** This event happens only once; you add logic that is common across all records processed during the conversion.

2. **Row Fetched or Format Fetched** These events occur each time a record is fetched from either a table (row fetched) or flat file (format fetched). You can add logic to these events, as well as set up mappings between your input and output data sources.

3. **Data Changed** If you're doing any kind of data sequencing in your table conversion, the Data Changed event is triggered when any field in the data sequence changes. Although this is not as configurable as a level break inside a

normal batch application, you can use Data Changed events to group records together if you add the logic to do so.

4. **Process End**   This event is called only once, at the end of the table conversion, to do any processing that occurs after all the records are converted to the new location.

Example: Converting a Foreign Table to OneWorld

To better understand how to use a table conversion, let's walk through a typical utilization of this tool. We'll pull data from a database outside of OneWorld (a foreign table) and use it to populate a table inside OneWorld. There are two steps to this process:

- Set up a data source and environment for our foreign table.

- Set up a mapping of the import table to the export table.

The data source in our example is a standard ODBC data source, which will be used by the Table Conversion program to access the foreign table; setup of an ODBC data source is done outside of OneWorld. The ODBC Data source connects to the foreign database. After it's created, we need to tell OneWorld to use this data source. This is done by creating two objects: the OneWorld data source and the OneWorld environment.

When you create the OneWorld data source, you tell it what ODBC data source you want to use. When you create the environment, you tell it what OneWorld data source to use for a specific table. This is accomplished by setting up an Object Configuration Mapping (OCM) record. The data source, environment, and OCM mapping together allow your table conversion to fetch from a foreign table.

Once the data source, environment, and OCM mapping are established, we'll create and run a table conversion (TC) to convert the data from the foreign table to a OneWorld table.

Setting Up a Foreign Table

For this exercise, we assume you already have a database with a table inside it. The table used in this example will be in a Microsoft Access database. To use this table, we have to

- Add a new ODBC data source to the client machine.

- Create a OneWorld environment for the data source.

- Create a OneWorld data source.

- Create an OCM mapping.

Before creating an ODBC data source, talk to someone who's an expert on the database in question. In our example, we created a new system Access data source on our client machine. Follow these steps to create your data source:

1. In Windows, go to the Control Panel and select ODBC Data Sources.

2. In the ODBC Data Source Administrator, open the System DSN tab:

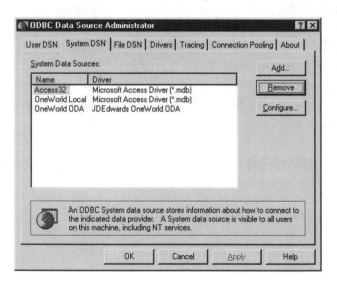

3. Click the Add button.

4. In the Create New Data Source dialog box, double-click to select Microsoft Access Driver:

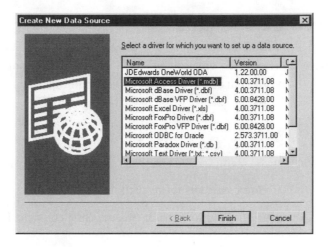

5. In the ODBC Microsoft Access Setup dialog box:

   • Enter a name for the data source, *and remember this name*. You'll use it later.

   • Enter a description for the data source.

   • Click the Select button to find your database. Your database should now be displayed in the Database box.

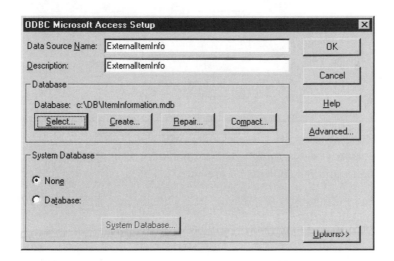

6. Click OK in the upper right-hand corner of the form to save your new ODBC data source.

Adding a New Environment

You've just added a new ODBC data source, but OneWorld still doesn't recognize this database. You have to create a new environment and OneWorld data source. (An ODBC data source and a OneWorld data source are two different things.) To add a new environment, follow these steps:

1. Log on to OneWorld.

2. In the Environments menu (GH9053), select Environment Master.

3. In the Work With Environments form, click Add.

4. When the Environment Revisions dialog box appears, enter the following, as illustrated here:

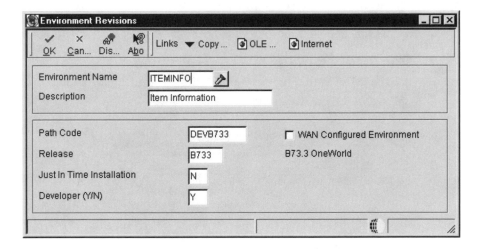

- A name and description for your new environment. Choose a descriptive name, and remember it for use later.

- A path code. This must be the path code that you'll use when you sign on to OneWorld.

- The number of release you're using, such as B733.

- N to disable Just In Time Installation (JITI), which is needed only for OneWorld tables, not foreign tables.

- **Y** for Developer. (This field is reserved for future use and is always set to Y.)

5. Click OK when you've finished.

Adding a New OneWorld Data Source

With your new environment all set up, you now create a new OneWorld data source:

1. In the System Administration Tools menu (GH9011), select Database Data Sources.

2. In the Machine Search & Select form, select your current machine name and data source, because it will be used by OneWorld when looking for data sources on this machine. (For more about data sources, see Chapter 2.)

3. Click Add.

4. In the Data Source Revisions dialog box (Figure 9-10), enter the following:

   - A new data source name, which you'll need for a later step.

   - **A** in the Data Source Type (for Access) field.

   - **Jdbodbc.dll** in the DLL Name field. This DLL, provided by J.D.Edwards, is used by OneWorld when accessing the ODBC data source we created.

   - The *exact* name of the ODBC data source, in the Database Name field (accuracy is very important here).

   - The server name and platform.

   - A check mark in the OCM Data Source check box.

5. When you've finished, click OK.

Adding an OCM Mapping

The final setup step is to add the Object Configuration Manager (OCM) mapping that ties everything together. In the following steps, we create a default OCM mapping for any table in the environment that uses the OneWorld data source, which will use the ODBC data source, which will use your database.

1. In OneWorld Explorer, type **OCM** in the Fast Path and press ENTER.

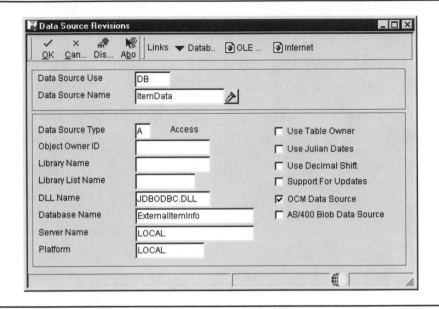

FIGURE 9-10. Adding a OneWorld data source for the foreign table

2. On the Machine Search and Select form, select the machine and data source you are currently using. This will be the same machine/data source combination you used in the foregoing procedure for adding a new data source.

3. In the Work With Object Mappings form that appears, click Add.

4. In the Object Mapping Revisions form, enter the following, as illustrated next:

- The name of your environment, in the Environment Name field.

- **DEFAULT** in the Object Name field.

- The name of the OneWorld data source you created, in the Primary Data Source field.

- ***Public** in the User field. This ensures that anyone who uses your environment will use the correct data source.

- **TBLE** as the Object Type.

- **P** (for primary), in the Data Source Mode field.
- **1** in the Allow QBE field, to ensures that QBE will be used when this data source is accessed.

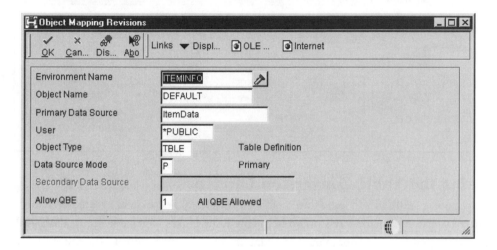

5. Click OK when you've finished. You will now be returned to the Work With Mappings form.

6. You're almost done. The OCM mapping must be activated—don't forget to do this. From the Work With Mappings form, find the OCM mapping you just created and select it. From the Row menu, select Change Status. The row should now be active (AV).

Creating the Table Conversion Object

With all the parts in place, now you can create the table conversion object. This works much like creating a batch application: Create a UBE object in Object Librarian, choose the Table Conversion option, and then step through a director to create the table conversion.

1. Go to Object Librarian.

2. In the Object Type field, type **UBE** and click Add.

3. Enter the Object Name, Description, and System Code.

4. Select the Table Conversion check box, and click OK. The finished table conversion object is shown here:

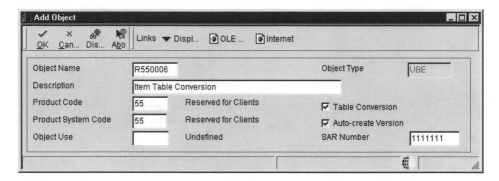

Using the Table Conversion Director

Now you're ready to add logic to the table conversion object you've created. When you enter Design, a director starts up, to help you easily create your table conversion. As part of the table conversion, you'll map data from your input table to the output table. By mapping the data, you tell the table conversion how to copy the information from the input table to the output table.

This next example simply maps input data from the input file to the output file; but, of course, you're not limited to this use of the Table Conversion tool. On the mapping form described in step 10 of this example, you can map other fields, such as system values and literals, to your output columns; you can even add calculations. We'll take a closer look at this after the example.

Here are the steps to processing the table conversion:

1. From Object Librarian, click Design.

2. This opens the director that will walk you through creation of the table conversion. In the first page, select Data Conversion. An explanation of the selected conversion type appears in the box beneath the list of options, as shown in Figure 9-11. Click Next to proceed.

3. In the next page of the TC director, you can add processing options and a data structure to your table conversion. We won't be adding these in this example,

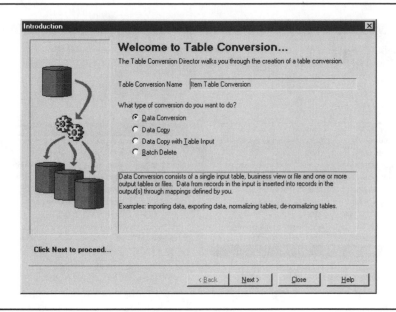

Introduction

Welcome to Table Conversion...

The Table Conversion Director walks you through the creation of a table conversion.

Table Conversion Name   Item Table Conversion

What type of conversion do you want to do?

- ⊙ Data Conversion
- ○ Data Copy
- ○ Data Copy with Table Input
- ○ Batch Delete

Data Conversion consists of a single input table, business view or file and one or more output tables or files. Data from records in the input is inserted into records in the output(s) through mappings defined by you.

Examples: importing data, exporting data, normalizing tables, de-normalizing tables.

Click Next to proceed...

< Back   Next >   Close   Help

FIGURE 9-11.   Selecting the table conversion type

however, so click Next to move on. (For more information on data structures and processing options, see Chapters 5 and 12.)

4. In the next page (Figure 9-12), choose an environment for your input and output data. In this example, we're creating an environment for input data, so we select that environment (ITEMINFO) in the list on the left. Leave the output environment designated as <LOGIN ENV> (the login environment). By doing this, you will use your foreign table to load a table in OneWorld.

5. Click Next to move to the Select Input page. Here you select a table from the database. If you've done your setup correctly, the Foreign Table tab displays the tables inside the database. Since there is only one table (Products) inside this database, double-click to select it (Figure 9-13). At this point, you could also select any other table, business view, or flat file for your table conversion. You can even select a flat file.

Client Modifications Using OneWorld

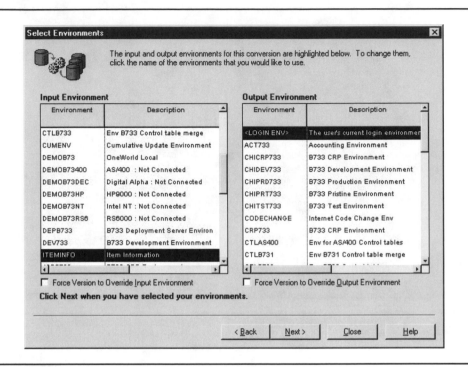

FIGURE 9-12.   Mapping the environment used for input and output

6. Click Next. The next page allows you to do data sequencing. You won't do this in this example, so click Next to move on.

7. The next page allows you to do data selection. In this case, you'll use all the data in the table, so you don't need to specify data selection. Click Next.

8. Now you'll select the output table. Here you'll be mapping to OneWorld table F55003, so select this table. Again, depending on the type of environment and your needs for this table conversion, you can continue to choose tables, a foreign table, or a text file (flat file).

9. Click Next again, and you'll come to the Table Options page (Figure 9-14). This form offers you three overrides:

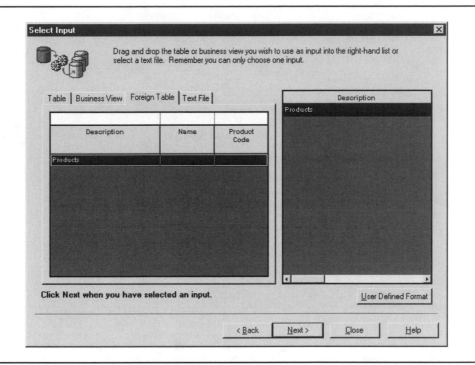

FIGURE 9-13. Selecting an input table

- *You can turn off currency triggers.* We recommend that you leave the currency triggers *on.* This is safer, because OneWorld will do some currency processing for you.

- *You can clear your output table.* Although this can be a very useful feature, be cautious about using it, because it will wipe out any data in the output table.

- *You can disable row-by-row processing.* Row-by-row processing means you get one row at a time. If you disable this option (by deselecting the check box), OneWorld copies multiple rows at the same time. This is a faster way to do table conversion, but it can cause problems if you have logic that is different from row to row.

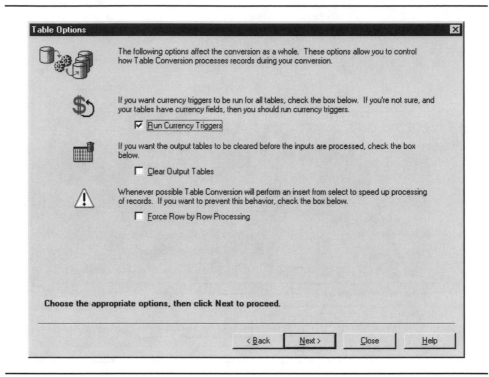

FIGURE 9-14. The Table Options form

10. Clicking the Next button brings you to the Mapping form, shown in Figure 9-15. For now, we will drag and drop fields from the foreign table on the left-hand side of the screen to the right-hand side. By doing this, we will map fields from our input file (Product Name, Product ID, Units In Stock, Supplier ID) to specific fields in the output file (Description, Item Number, Quantity, Address Number). You can see that the name of the input file fields are now in the Mapping Column.

11. Click Next to continue to the Error Logging form, and click Next again. We won't set up error logging for this conversion.

12. Click Finish to complete the TC director.

13. Now you can run the table conversion from the versions list just like any other batch application.

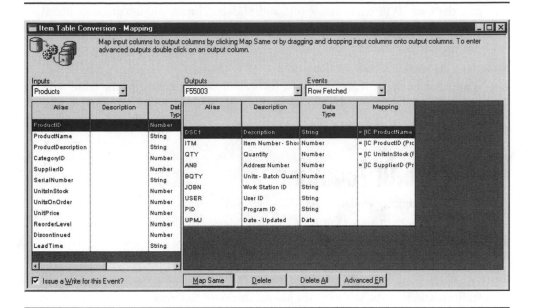

FIGURE 9-15. The Mapping form, in which you can map parameters and add logic

As discussed in the beginning of this section, you aren't limited to mapping columns from the input file to the output file. To map another object, you'd double-click the output column to get a form like the one shown here:

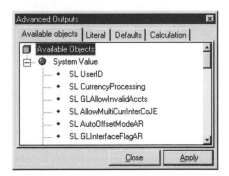

Use this form when your needs go beyond simply mapping fields from the input file to the output file. The four tabs on this form allow you to pass other data. In the first tab, you can select system values to pass to the output column; for instance, you

can pass the user ID or report name into audit fields. The second tab presents literal values; the third tab lets you enable the Data Dictionary default value for a column; and the last tab lets you add in a calculation. The Expression Manager, discussed in Chapter 7, is used to define a calculation.

In addition to the advanced outputs, you can also add ER code to the table conversion. You initiate this process by clicking the Advanced ER button in the Mapping form.

Putting It All Together

This important chapter explains OneWorld's development environment tools that allow you to view data and Event Rules, convert data, and debug applications and functions. Each of the tools discussed in this chapter is used for a specific purpose. When you need to view data, use the Universal Table Browser (UTB). The Event Rules Browser helps you see into Event Rules and even filter the code you view. To debug applications and reports, you have the use of OneWorld's Event Rules Debugger and the Jdedebug.log file. Similarly, business functions and Named Event Rules can be debugged using Microsoft Visual C++. And, finally, the Table Conversion utility helps you convert data from a different location.

Your knowledge of these tools will enable you to meet business needs by converting data and quickly finding bugs in applications. Add them to your arsenal for attacking problems and finding solutions.

CHAPTER 10

Versions

I n OneWorld, a version is a named configuration of an application, which can be made up of three components: processing options, data selection, and data sequencing. Versions are an important part of OneWorld applications because they allow users to configure applications to meet their needs. For example, one report can be used for two purposes by simply creating two versions of the same report. By creating multiple versions of the same application, you can provide multiple business solutions without needing to change any code.

You can create versions for interactive or batch applications. Both interactive and batch applications can have processing options that can be defined by the user. Batch versions also allow the users to select the data they wish to process and to choose the sort order for the data.

By using the different components of a version (processing options, data selection, and data sequencing), you can create numerous configurations of your applications. After you create a version of an interactive or batch application, it can be executed from a menu or from a different application.

To help you understand how to create and maintain versions, this chapter discusses the following topics:

- **Overview of Versions**   The overview describes how versions are used for interactive and batch applications and naming standards for versions.

- **Creating Interactive Application Versions**   For interactive applications, versions are used to create a named configuration of a set of processing options.

- **Creating Batch Application Versions**   For batch applications, versions are used to specify data selection and sequencing, as well as to create processing options.

Overview of Versions

A version is a named set of processing options, data selection, and sequencing that is tied to a specific interactive or batch application. You can use versions for a number of purposes, but their basic function is to tell the application what you want it to do and what data you want it to process.

Client Modifications Using OneWorld

DEFINITION

Processing options *allow users to pass values into an application or a report, so that they can change the way that information is displayed or processed based on their requirements. Processing options are used to pass default values, processing information, or display rules into an application or report.*

By simply setting up versions, you have the ability to change the way that the program will run. For example, you might use the same report for weekly and monthly processing, but you need the monthly processing report to use a different data set and process the data in a slightly different way. You could create Version1 for weekly processing and Version2 for monthly processing. As another example, suppose that two departments in your organization have different sales-order types. To handle the sales-order processing needs of both departments with a single application, you could create one version of the Sales Order Entry application for Department A and another version for Department B.

Versions for Batch and Interactive Applications

You create and maintain batch and interactive application versions somewhat differently. A batch application version follows the same basic creation and maintenance rules as other OneWorld objects. After you create a batch application version, you need to check it in before anyone else can use it. If you want to modify it, you need to check it out. Interactive application versions only need to be created on one machine, and anyone can use them.

Processing options can be set for versions of both interactive and batch applications, as long as there is a set of processing options attached to the application. If you are working with an interactive application that does not have processing options attached, there is no need for a version; in fact, you will not be able to create one. (For information about creating processing options, see Chapter 12.)

NOTE

If an application is run from the Object Librarian, it is executed without a version, so it does not contain processing options.

If you create a batch application, you must create a version for it before you can run it. Even if there are no processing options attached and it does not contain data selection or sorting, you still need to create a version. In other words, you cannot run a batch application without a version.

When menus are created, interactive or batch applications can be added as menu items. At the time you are creating a menu, you can specify a version as well as the application. This allows you to have multiple versions of the same application listed on the same menu. Figure 10-1 shows an example of a standard OneWorld menu that includes versions. In this example, both versions are named TMP0001.

This chapter describes how to create and configure versions. For a description of when to create versions see the Developer's Corner, titled "How Should I Use Versions?" at the end of this chapter.

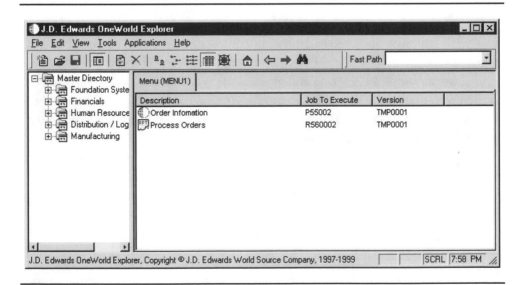

FIGURE 10-1. A OneWorld Explorer menu displaying application versions

Naming Standards for Versions

J.D. Edwards names its versions using the naming standard ZJDE*XXXX* and XJDE*XXXX*. The Z stands for an interactive application. An X is used for batch applications. The JDE part of the name indicates that it is a version created by J.D. Edwards, and *XXXX* is the sequence number for the version. For example, versions named ZJDE0001 and ZJDE0002 are attached to interactive applications, and versions named XJDE0001 and XJDE0002 are attached to batch applications.

We suggest that you follow a version naming standard similar to that used for the J.D. Edwards versions. Use the format *XXXXYYYY*, where *XXXX* is a three- or four-letter description of your company and *YYYY* is a number. Using Z to represent interactive applications and X for batch applications is optional. However, you should never name your versions starting with ZJDE or XJDE, because these prefixes are reserved for J.D. Edwards. If you use the reserved prefixes, you risk losing your version during an upgrade. (For more information about upgrades, see Chapter 8.)

The name of a version needs to be unique to its application, but it does not need to be unique across all applications. For example, Application A and Application B can both have versions named TEMP0001, but Application A cannot have two versions called TEMP0001.

CAUTION

You shouldn't change any of the J.D. Edwards versions. If you want to modify a J.D. Edwards version, you should copy the version and make your changes to the copy.

Creating Interactive Application Versions

You use versions for interactive applications only to create a named configuration of a set of processing options. This section explains how to create, copy, and change interactive application versions.

NOTE

You can add versions to an interactive application only if there are processing options attached to the application.

Creating a New Version for an Interactive Application

When you create a new version for an interactive application, you specify a description for the version. You can also set processing options and a security level for the version.

You give the version a specific description to indicate why you created the version and when it is appropriate to use it. Generally, the description contains the application name followed by its purpose. For example, a version for the application named Order Information that will be used for orders of type S4 might have the description "Order Information, Order Type S4."

Prompting options tell the system what to do when the user runs this version of the application. The three prompting options are described in Table 10-1.

The five levels of security you can add to a version are listed in Table 10-2. When a version is created or modified, the user that changed or created this version is the "Last Modified User." The security of a version can exclude users from making certain modifications to a version.

Code	Description	Use
Blank	No processing options	If you use this option and there are processing options attached to the application, the processing options will be ignored.
1	Blind execution	Use this option when you have set the processing options and the user will not be changing them often. This will run the application using the values you set for the processing options.
2	Prompt for values	Use this option if the user will need to change the processing options frequently. This option causes the processing options to appear every time the application is executed.

TABLE 10-1.   Version Prompting Options

Code	Description	Explanation
0	No Security	The default (and lowest) security level; anyone can modify this version.
1	Medium Security	Anyone can copy, transfer, install, or run this version, but the Last Modified User can design or change processing option values, check the version in or out, and transfer or delete the version.
2	Medium to Full Security	Anyone can install or copy this version, but only the Last Modified User can modify it.
3	Full Security	Not used in OneWorld.
4	Medium Security Extended	In addition to the security privileges described in Medium Security, the Last Modified User can modify a version, including changing runtime processing options and data selection.

TABLE 10-2.   Levels of Security

To create a new version for an interactive application, follow these steps:

1. In OneWorld Explorer, type **IV** in the Fast Path field, as shown here, and press ENTER. IV stands for Interactive Versions. The Work With Interactive Versions form appears.

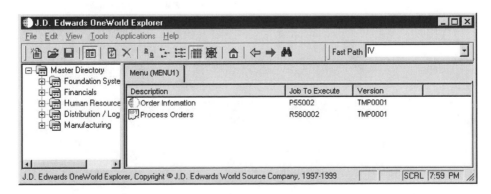

Client Modifications Using OneWorld

2. In the Interactive Application field, enter the name of the interactive application for which you want to create a version. In this example, we will create a new version for the Order Information application (P55002).

3. Click the Find button. If any versions have been created for this application, they will be displayed in the grid.

4. Click the Add button to create a new version. The Version Add form appears.

5. Enter a name for the version in the Version field, according to the naming conventions. In this example, we are naming our version **ZTMP0002**.

6. Enter a version description in the Version Title field. The description for this example is **Order Information, Order Type S4**.

7. Type **1** (for blind execution) in the Prompting Options field.

8. In the Security field, type **0** (no security) for the level of security for this version. Figure 10-2 shows the completed Version Add form.

9. Click the OK button.

You have now created a version of an application that can be used in a menu or from another application. You can modify this version's processing options by using the techniques described in the "Changing a Version's Processing Options" section, later in this chapter.

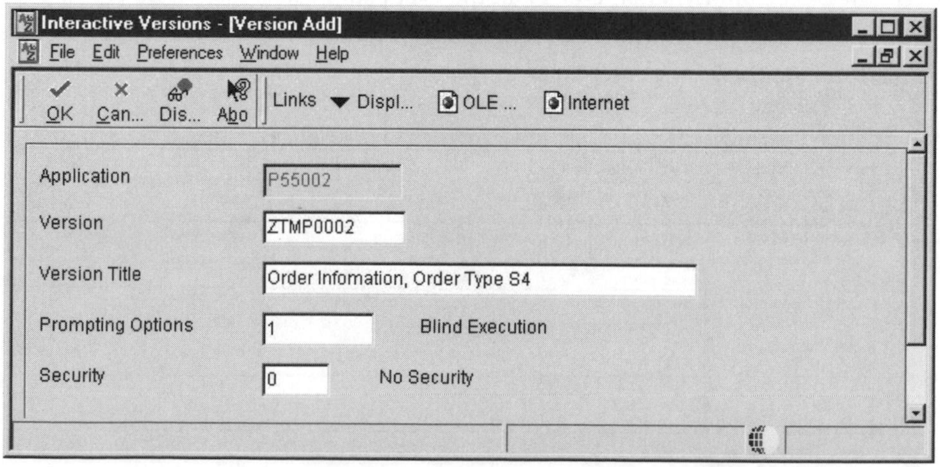

FIGURE 10-2. The Version Add form for an interactive application version

Copying a Version for an Interactive Application

Although you can always create a new version from scratch, sometimes it is easier to start from a copy of one of the existing versions. Some applications have multiple tabs of processing options, and you may only want to change a few processing options for the new version. For example, the Sales Order Entry application (P4210) has more than 75 processing options on 15 tabs. Rather than setting up all these processing options in a new version, you can simply copy an existing version and change only the processing options that should be different for the version.

To copy a version, perform the following steps:

1. In OneWorld Explorer, type **IV** in the Fast Path field and press ENTER.

2. On the Work With Interactive Versions form, enter the name of the application in the Interactive Application field. In our example, we are using application **P55002**.

3. Click the Find button. The versions that have been created for this application will be displayed in the grid.

4. Select the grid row that contains the version you want to copy and click the Copy button. In this example, we are copying the ZTMP0002 version of the Order Information application, as shown in Figure 10-3. The Version Copy form appears.

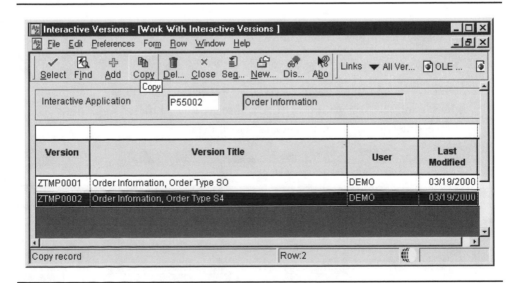

FIGURE 10-3. Selecting a version to copy on the Work With Interactive Versions form

5. Enter the new version's name and description. In this example, we are naming the version **ZTMP0003** and giving it the title **Order Processing, Order Type S1**, as shown here:

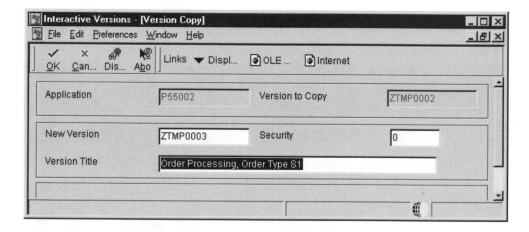

6. Click the OK button.

Changing a Version's Processing Options

A version's processing options are passed into the application when the version is executed. After you've created a version, you may need to reconfigure its processing options.

To change a version's processing options, follow these steps:

1. In OneWorld Explorer, type **IV** in the Fast Path field and press ENTER.

2. On the Work With Interactive Versions form, select the grid row that contains the version that you want to change and select Row | Processing Options. The Processing Options form appears, as shown here:

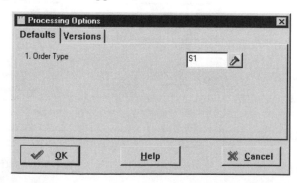

3. Change the processing options as desired. In the preceding screen example, there is only one processing option, but your applications may have numerous processing options.

4. After you have changed the processing options, click the OK button to save your changes.

Creating Batch Application Versions

For batch application versions, you need to specify data selection and sequencing, as well as create processing options. This section explains how to create, copy, and change batch application versions.

Creating a New Version for a Batch Application

When creating a version of a batch application, you need to specify a name, a description, prompting options, and security. A good description is important (although you can also add a lengthy description in the Version Detail field when you create the version). In general, the description should contain the application name followed by a purpose, such as "Item Quantity, Branch 154."

To create a new version for a batch application, follow these steps.

1. In OneWorld Explorer, type **BV** in the Fast Path field and press ENTER. BV stands for Batch Versions. Alternatively, from the Object Librarian, select the report you want to modify and select Form | Versions List. The Work With Batch Versions form appears.

2. Enter the name of the batch application for which you want to create a version. In this example, we will create a new version for the Item Quantity application (**R560002**).

3. Click the Find button. If any versions have been created for this batch application, they will be displayed in the grid.

4. Click the Add button to create a new version. The Version Add form appears.

5. In the Version field, enter a name for the version. In our example, we are naming the version **XTMP0003**.

6. Enter a description of the version in the Version Title field. In our example, we used the title **Item Quantity, Branch 154**.

7. In the Prompting Options field, enter the type of prompting for processing options you want the system to perform (see Table 10-1 for the valid values for this field). In our example, this field is disabled because the version does not contain processing options.

8. In the Security field, enter the level of security for this version (see Table 10-1 for the valid values for this field). In our example, we are using a level of 0 (no security).

9. The Job Queue field tells the server which job queue this version will be placed in. To see which queues are available, use the visual assist. If you leave this field blank (as in our example), the default queue will be used.

10. The Version Detail field allows you to enter a lengthy description of this version if necessary. This can be useful if you have several versions that are similar. In our example, we added the detail "This version is configured for Branch/Plant 154."

11. If you want the version to print a cover page before the report prints, select the Print Cover Page check box. This option is not selected in our example. Figure 10-4 shows the completed Version Add form.

12. Click the OK button.

You have now created a version of a batch application that can be used in a menu or in another application. You can change this version's processing options as described in the "Configuring a Version for a Batch Application" section, later in this chapter.

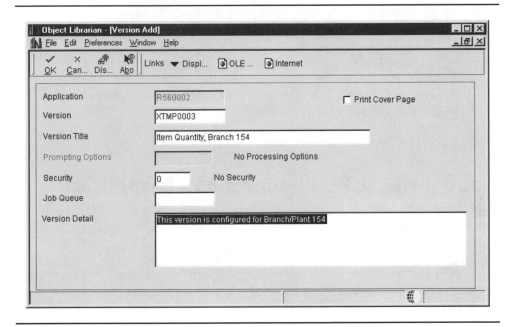

FIGURE 10-4. The Version Add form for a batch application version

Client Modifications Using OneWorld

Copying a Version for a Batch Application

Although you can create new versions from scratch, sometimes it is easier to start from a copy of an existing version. To copy a version, perform the following steps:

1. In OneWorld Explorer, type **BV** in the Fast Path field and press ENTER.

2. On the Work With Batch Versions form, enter the name of the batch application in the Batch Application field. In our example, we are using application **R56002**.

3. Click the Find button. The versions that have been created for this application will be displayed in the grid.

4. Select the grid row that contains the version you want to copy and click the Copy button. In this example, we are copying the XTMP0003 version of the Item Quantity application. The Version Copy form appears.

5. Enter the new version's name and description. In this example, we are naming the version **XTMP0004** and giving it the title **Item Quantity, Branch 160**, as shown in Figure 10-5.

6. Click the OK button.

Configuring a Version for a Batch Application

After you have created, copied, or changed a version, you will need to configure its processing options, data selection, and data sequencing.

N O T E

For details on data selection and data sequencing in batch applications, see Chapter 6.

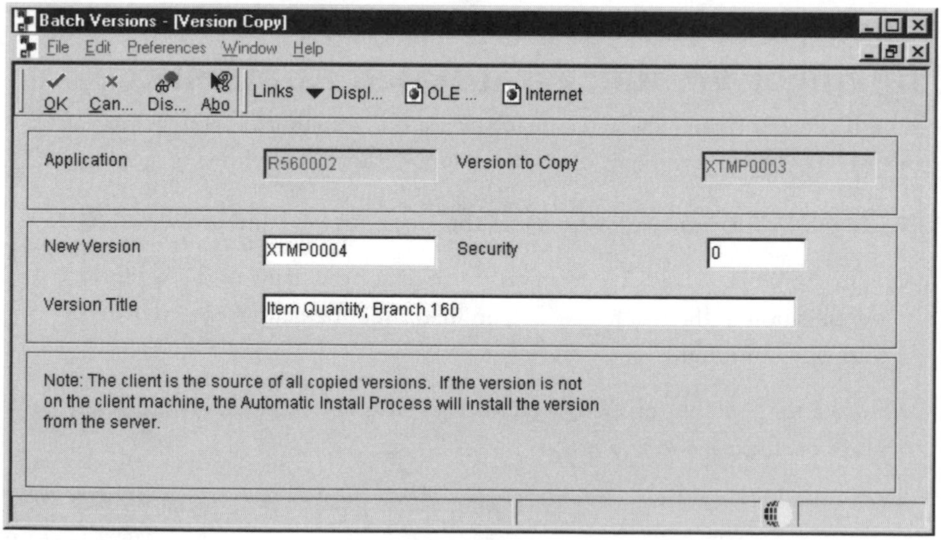

Batch Versions - [Version Copy]		
File Edit Preferences Window Help		
✓ ✗ 👓 📖 Links ▼ Displ... ▣ OLE ... ▣ Internet		
OK Can... Dis... Abo		

Application	R560002	Version to Copy	XTMP0003
New Version	XTMP0004	Security	0
Version Title	Item Quantity, Branch 160		

Note: The client is the source of all copied versions. If the version is not on the client machine, the Automatic Install Process will install the version from the server.

FIGURE 10-5. The Version Copy form for a batch application version

Configuring Processing Options

If processing options are attached to your batch application, you need to configure them to suit your needs. You follow the same procedure to configure processing options for batch application versions as you do for interactive application versions.

N O T E

Before you can change a version, it needs to be checked out. This procedure is described in the "Checking Versions In and Out" section, later in this chapter.

To change a version's processing options, follow these steps:

1. In OneWorld Explorer, type **BV** in the Fast Path field and press ENTER.

2. On the Work With Batch Versions form, select the grid row that contains the version that you want to change and select Row | Processing Options. If there are no processing options attached to this batch application, you will see the message shown in the following illustration. Otherwise, the Processing Options form will appear.

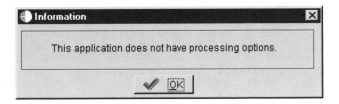

3. Change the processing options to meet your needs.

4. After you have changed the processing options, click the OK button to save your changes.

Setting Up Data Selection

An important part of creating a version for a batch application is data selection. You select data to limit the number of records that your application will use at runtime. For example, suppose your application is running against the Item Branch table (F4102), which contains a large number of records. You may need to process only some of the items, such as those in your branch. By using data selection, you can limit the amount of data that is processed.

Think of data selection as a Select statement or a Where clause inside a database. You can perform data selections against only one business view that the batch application is using. More specifically, it will be the business view of the first nonconditional section with a business view, inside the batch application. The basic idea is to limit the amount of data that this batch application will be processing.

Data selection involves comparing a field in your business view to a value. You have four basic choices for comparison:

- A literal value

- A constant

- A different field in the business view

- A column in the batch application's data structure

If you choose literal (a value that you will type in), you will see a form like the one shown in Figure 10-6. This form has three tabs that allow you to enter a literal value in three different ways:

- The Single Value tab allows you to add one value. For example, if you want to match your branch to 160, you can define it on the Single Value tab.

- The Range of Values tab allows you to enter two values: a from value and a through value. For example, if you want to include all dates in the range of 1/1/00 to 5/1/00, you use the Range of Values tab.

- The List of Values tab allows you to enter multiple items to compare against. For example, if you want to match any of the branches 160, 170, or 180, you use the List of Values tab.

Instead of entering a literal value, you can use a constant for comparison. These constants are <Blank>, <NULL>, and <ZERO>. For example, you could specify data selection as all locations not equal to <Blank>.

Finally, you can compare data items to another column in the business view or to a column in the batch application's data structure. For example, if one batch application is calling another batch application, you would pass values using the data structure of the application being called. You could then use these values in data selection.

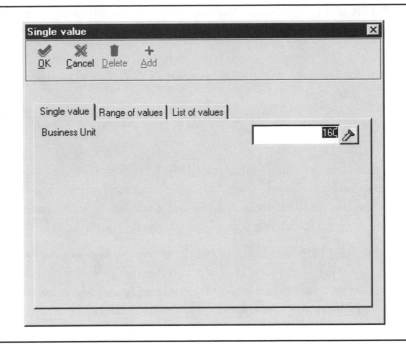

FIGURE 10-6.   The Single Value tab used for data selection

CAUTION

If you do not limit the data selection correctly, it could cause your batch application to be very large; take a long time to run; or, even worse, update data that you do not want to be updated. It is very important that you select only the records that you want to process.

To add data selection to the version, follow these steps:

1. In OneWorld Explorer, type **BV** in the Fast Path field and press ENTER.

2. On the Work With Batch Versions form, enter the name of the batch application in the Batch Application field.

3. Click the Find button. The versions that have been created for this batch application will be displayed in the grid.

4. Select the grid row that contains the version that you want to change and select Form | Data Selection. The Data Selection form appears, as shown in Figure 10-7.

5. Click in the Left Operand column (to the right of the Where column). The system displays a list of every data item within the business view used by the batch application.

6. Select a data item by double-clicking it. In our example, we will use the BC Business Unit (F41021).

7. The Comparison column allows you to specify a comparison operator. The comparison operators are is equal to, is greater than, is greater than or equal to, is less than, is less than or equal to, and is not equal to. Choose one by double-clicking it. This example uses the is equal to operator.

8. Click the Right Operand column, and the system displays a list of every value you can use in the comparison. Select the value that you want to compare the first value to. In our example, we are comparing against a literal value of 160 by selecting a literal from the list and using the Single Value tab.

9. After you finish the line, you can add more lines. Click the leftmost column beneath the line you just added and select either And or Or, as shown in Figure 10-8. As in other programming languages, And statements have precedence over Or statements.

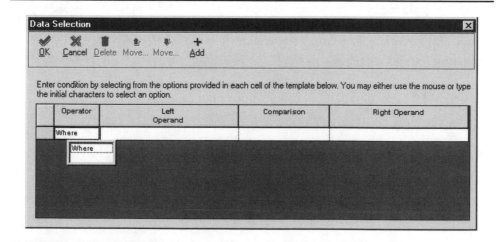

FIGURE 10-7.   The Data Selection form

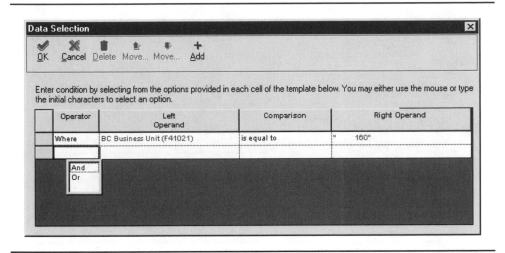

FIGURE 10-8. Adding a new line

NOTE

If you use the List of Values tab, as described earlier, you may not need to use the Or operator. For example, instead of entering **Branch is equal to "160" Or Branch is equal to "170,"** *you could enter the statement* **Branch is equal to LIST***, where the list includes 160 and 170.*

10. Fill in the columns for the next line. In this example, we created a Select statement. This statement will cause the batch application to process only records that are in Branch 160 and have a quantity not equal to zero. Figure 10-9 shows the finished Data Selection form.

11. When you have finished adding lines, click the OK button.

Data Sequencing

In addition to changing the records that will be processed, you can also change the order in which the records will be processed. Specifying the data sequence is most useful with reports that produce output. For example, if you have a report that displays information in Branch, Item sequence, you may need to modify it to display information in Item, Branch sequence instead.

Client Modifications Using OneWorld

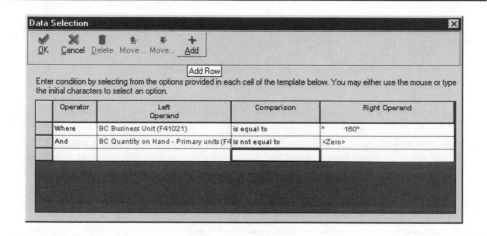

FIGURE 10-9. The Data Selection form with Where and And statements

CAUTION

In most batch applications you can change data sequencing, if necessary. However, in some cases, such a change can drastically affect the report's processing. For example, if you change the date order in an application that needs the date order for reporting purposes, the report might not process correctly. Also, changing the data selection to a sequencing that does not match an index on the table could cause performance problems. To find the indexes defined on a table, review the table in the Object Librarian.

To change a version's sequencing, follow these steps:

1. In OneWorld Explorer, type **BV** in the Fast Path field and press ENTER.

2. On the Work With Batch Versions form, enter the name of the batch application in the Batch Application field.

3. Click the Find button. The versions that have been created for this batch application will be displayed in the grid.

4. Select the grid row that contains the version that you want to change and select Row | Data Selection. The Section Data Sequencing form appears, as shown in Figure 10-10. The default sequencing order is what was set up originally.

5. Change the sequencing order, the type of sequencing (ascending or descending), and the page breaks, as follows:

   - To add or remove columns from the sequencing, use the left and right arrows.

   - To change the sequencing from ascending to descending or vice versa, click the A/D column.

   - To add a page break (allowable on certain fields, such as level-break fields), double-click the P/B column. This will cause the report to start a new page if the values in this field change.

6. Click the OK button.

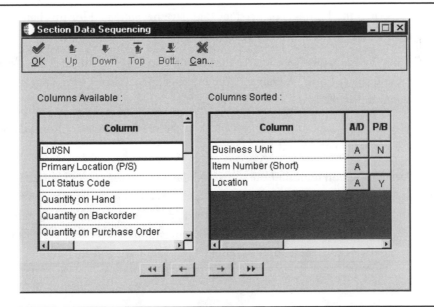

FIGURE 10-10. The Section Data Sequencing form

Checking Versions In and Out

You need to check in any version if you want to save the version or to allow it to be used by others. In addition, you need to check out any version that you want to modify. Instead of checking a version in or out through the Object Librarian, you check them in through the Advanced option of the Batch Versions application.

NOTE

If you just want to use a version, OneWorld will install this version on your computer when you run this version of the batch application for the first time.

To check in or check out a version, follow these steps:

1. In OneWorld Explorer, type **BV** in the Fast Path field and press ENTER.

2. On the Work With Batch Versions form, enter the name of the batch application in the Batch Application field.

3. Click the Find button. The versions that have been created for this batch application will be displayed in the grid.

4. Select the grid row that contains the version that you want to check in or check out and select Form | Advanced. The Advanced Operations form appears, as shown in Figure 10-11.

5. Select Row | Check In Version to check in the version, or select Row | Check Out version to check out the version.

The Design Version option of the Advanced Operations form's Row menu lets you change the version in the same way that you modify the batch application from the Object Librarian. Choosing this option opens the Report Design Aid (RDA) application. In essence, you are making a copy of the batch application. However, a better approach is to make a copy of the batch application in Object Librarian and then modify it

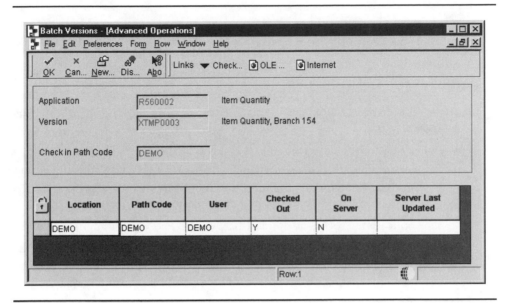

FIGURE 10-11. The Advanced Operations form

through RDA (see Chapter 6 for details on using RDA). Copying and modifying the batch application makes it easier to maintain and upgrade.

After you change the version, you have marked this version as changed and essentially disconnected the version from the actual batch application. This is because any change you make to the actual batch application in the Object Librarian will not be reflected in the version you have changed. In other words, if you change the design of a version, and at a later point you want to change the batch application's design or logic so all versions will be changed as well, the version you changed will not be updated.

How Should I Use Versions?

At this point, you should understand how to create and maintain versions, but you still may want some guidance on how to use versions to meet the needs of the users and make your job easier. As explained in this chapter, versions are made up of three main parts: processing options, data selection, and sort capabilities. When you create new applications, be sure you design them to take advantage of these three parts.

Processing options are discussed in detail in Chapter 12, so we will just mention a few key points here. For your applications, you should create processing options that are well organized and intuitive. In addition, you need to know how the users intend to use the application. Processing options that are attached to your application and used in a version should be designed so that users can easily understand and configure the application to meet their specific business needs. Your applications will be most flexible and effective if their design takes into consideration who will configure the processing options.

As discussed earlier in this chapter, in a batch application, a version's data selection and sort capabilities apply to the first nonconditional section in the report. Make sure your batch application is structured in such a way that you allow the correct business view to be used. For example, if you are creating a report that will display inventory information, make sure the first nonconditional section contains a business view of the inventory file, not some other table you happen to be using. If that business view is not useful, the version may not be useful either. For more information about creating batch applications, see Chapter 6.

Developer's Corner

In determining how many versions of an application you should create, you need to understand what the end users need. What will the users be doing with this application? If they will use it for only one purpose, such as to generate an end-of-day report that only one user will run, chances are you need only one version of your application. But if the application offers multiple uses, such as to process both new orders and returned orders, you may need multiple versions with different configurations of processing options. Does the user need several reports that will display different data? If so, instead of having one version that the users must change each time they run a report, it might make more sense to create multiple versions using different data selection for each version.

We have discussed some tips for designing applications that will use versions effectively, but you should also understand how to best use versions of existing applications. You may need to call these existing applications from a menu or from another application. Before you create a new version of an application, be sure you understand how the application works. By changing the processing options, you can drastically change how an application will process. For example, changing a processing option to update an order to a different status or include foreign currency can affect your processing. Make sure the versions of the application you create will do only what you want them to do.

If you are creating a version of an existing J.D. Edwards application, a good starting point is to copy the J.D. Edwards version instead of creating your own version from scratch. Some applications have pages and pages of processing options, and it is difficult to set up the version correctly. To reduce the chances for error, copy the version that already exists and modify only the fields you need to change.

Putting It All Together

Versions are an important part of OneWorld software. Versions add flexibility to any OneWorld applications you might create, and an understanding of how to create and maintain versions is essential. You can use versions for a number of purposes, but the most important goal is to create versions that match your users' needs.

In this chapter, you learned how to create and copy versions. When you are creating versions, be sure to give them good descriptions so you will know what each version is used for. Also, be sure not to name any of your versions starting with the letters *ZJDE* or *XJDE*, because you could lose them when the software is upgraded.

When creating versions for batch applications, limit your data selection to process only the records you want. If you don't do this, you could update records you didn't expect to update.

PART III

Advanced Application Development

CHAPTER 11

Generic Application Development

User-Defined Codes (UDCs)

Next Numbers

Data Dictionary Items

Tables

Business Views

Menus

Putting It All Together

The previous chapters provided information on how to create and modify interactive (Chapter 5) and batch applications (Chapter 6) in OneWorld. The focus of those chapters was to provide a picture of the overall process of building applications with the design tools. We intentionally did not discuss the technical details and the supporting components of applications in those chapters.

In this chapter, we are moving the discussion from the applications to the supporting objects that make up applications. Ingeniously, OneWorld uses the same objects for interactive and batch applications. This approach has a couple of advantages: objects are generic and have a high degree of reusability, and your ability to design and construct any OneWorld application is increased because all of the components that comprise applications are identical.

Figure 11-1 provides you with a block diagram showing how applications are used and what objects comprise them. The diagram starts at the top with the OneWorld Explorer that all users and developers interact with for any OneWorld session, and proceeds down to the lowest objects that are used in an application.

As you can see in Figure 11-1, OneWorld Explorer uses menus to launch interactive and batch applications. The interactive and batch applications can interact with one of the following objects: C- and NER-based business functions; business views; tables; and other interactive and batch applications. These objects interact with tables that store application and system data for OneWorld, and the tables are composed of data items that originate from the Data Dictionary. The Data Dictionary contains data items that all of the other objects use, and some of these data items may use the User-Defined Code or next-number facilities.

To illustrate how objects in Figure 11-1 support an application, we focus most of the examples in this chapter mainly on the construction of a single example application, which is called Supplier's Delivery Quality. The advantage to this approach is that you can see, from the ground up, how an application is built and made available to users in OneWorld Explorer. We present the objects and their examples in the reverse order of Figure 11-1, since application construction in OneWorld starts at the Data Dictionary and builds up.

The objects that we discuss in this chapter are outlined here:

- **User-Defined Codes (UDCs)**   UDCs are a set of valid values that are assigned to data items. From a user's perspective, they provide a user-friendly list of valid values for a field in an application. From a developer's perspective, they are an alternative to creating a separate table to store valid attribute values for an

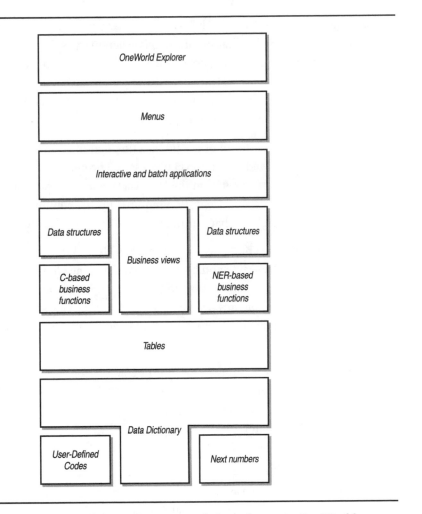

FIGURE 11-1. Block diagram of the applications and their objects in OneWorld

attribute in a table. For example, a UDC is assigned to the State or Province data item (ADDS) to provide a list of valid values for the data item.

- **Next Numbers** The next-number facility stores the next valid number for a particular data item. As new instances of a data item are generated, the next-number facility generates numbers for the new instances. For example, a common use for next numbers is to supply unique numbers for consecutive documents, such as sales orders and purchase contracts.

- **Data Dictionary Items**   The Data Dictionary manages all data items for OneWorld. One key feature of the Data Dictionary is that it is dynamic, so all changes you make to a data item are reflected immediately throughout all applications that use it. Data items can dynamically change on the fly their presentation on reports and forms, data validation, row and column descriptions, and field-level help.

- **Tables**   Tables store all of the information that is generated in OneWorld by applications and system-level processes. The columns of the tables are composed of data items from the Data Dictionary. The advantage of using data items is that there is no definition required for the columns in the table because the data item embeds that information through the Data Dictionary.

- **Business Views**   Business views provide a view of one or more tables in a database for interactive and batch applications. The view defines the columns that are used by an application and maps the application fields to columns in the tables it manipulates. OneWorld uses business views to generate the SQL statements that are issued to valid OneWorld databases.

- **Menus**   Menus are used in OneWorld Explorer to provide users with an entry point for executing batch and interactive applications. Menus that launch applications are displayed in the right panel of OneWorld Explorer, whereas menus that point to other menus are displayed in the left panel of OneWorld Explorer.

NOTE

As you can see, not all of the objects shown in Figure 11-1 are discussed in this chapter. The other objects shown in Figure 11-1 but not discussed in this chapter will be presented in Chapter 13.

As stated earlier, most of the examples in this chapter are focused on the construction of the Supplier's Delivery Quality application, the purpose of which is to assist a business in selecting the most reliable delivery method. For example, if someone in the company needs to make an order for a pending deadline, the Supplier's Delivery Quality application can be used to select the supplier with the best delivery time and quality. The Supplier's Delivery Quality application tracks the number of days it takes to deliver material and the material quality of the package upon receipt for a specific delivery. There are two types of deliveries that will be tracked: normal and rush.

User-Defined Codes (UDCs)

User-Defined Codes are used to assign a list of valid values for a field. UDCs can be viewed as an alternative to creating a separate table to store valid values for a column in a table. The advantages of using UDCs in your application are these:

- They reduce the number of tables that you have to create for applications.

- The system automatically validates any field that is assigned a UDC every time a user enters data in the field.

- They allow your users to search for a valid UDC value for a field by using a search and select form.

A good example of a typical use for UDCs is the Address Book's Search Type data item (AT1). This data item uses a UDC (01/ST) that defines the type of entity that the Address Book entry is, such as an employee (E), supplier (V), or customer (C). OneWorld comes preloaded with a standard set of values for UDC 01/ST, but you can add a new UDC value at any time, such as guest (GU), to create a new entity for the Address Book.

UDCs are stored in the User-Defined Code Types (F0004) and the User-Defined Codes (F0005) tables. The User-Defined Code Types table (F0004) stores the definition of the UDC, and the User-Defined Codes table (F0005) stores the list of values that are assigned for the particular UDC definition. For example, the Address Book's Search Type data item (AT1) stores the definition of its UDC (01/ST) in the User-Defined Code Types table (F0004), and the values for its UDC, such as V, C, and E, in the User-Defined Codes table (F0005).

If you are a developer, implementing UDCs can greatly enhance your applications. UDCs are used in situations where two descriptions for the UDC are the only information that is needed. For example, the UDC values for 01/ST assign a description to a code, such as "employee" to the code "E." If more information is required to be stored for the UDC 01/ST than another description, then it cannot be implemented as a UDC because no other fields are available—you will need to implement it in a separate table.

As simple as the definition of UDCs is, however, there are subtle nuances with UDCs that can be confusing during the design and implementation phases of your applications. The nuances involve soft-coded and hard-coded UDCs. The differences between them are not very obvious, and they are just different enough to trip you up when you are trying to determine where to use them.

Soft-Coded UDCs

Soft-coded UDCs are intended to be modified by end users in order to group records in a table for searching, sorting, and reporting. The meanings and valid values of the UDCs are determined by the users, allowing them to soft-code functionality into various applications. Also, as business requirements change, the users can also change the UDC values to meet their needs with no impact on the system or applications.

In your development projects, you can provide soft-coded UDCs in your tables to give users the ability to categorize records within a table. You implement soft-coded UDCs by adding several data items that are assigned UDCs, and then make them available for modification and use in one or more applications.

NOTE

Soft-coded UDCs are not used by applications and system-level processes, because their main purpose is to group and categorize records in a table for users. This allows your users to select and sequence records in interactive and batch applications.

For example, all Address Book entries have 30 category codes available for definition, as shown in Figure 11-2. None of the 30 category codes have any purpose in the system or application—they simply provide 30 different ways to categorize Address Book data, such as by region, division, product line, salesman, and so on. The Address Book table (F0101) stores the 30 category codes as data items AC01 through AC30, and they are assigned UDC 01/01 through 01/30, respectively. Category Code 01 (AC01) is assigned to UDC 01/01, Category Code 02 (AC02) is assigned to UDC 01/02, and so on.

Hard-Coded UDCs

Hard-coded UDCs are not intended for use by end users—they are designed for use in applications and system processes for OneWorld. Changing the value of a hard-coded UDC can have a dramatic effect on OneWorld, because it can change the configuration of the system.

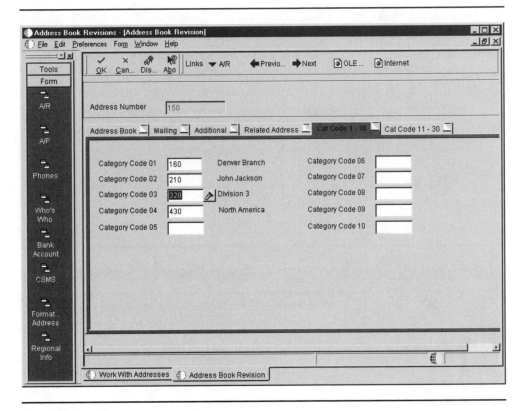

FIGURE 11-2. First ten category codes for Address Book entries

NOTE

Hard-coded UDCs are defined by having their Hard Coded field set to Y. The value is hard-coded because various applications and system processes in OneWorld use it.

In your development projects, you use hard-coded UDCs in situations in which configurable business processes and system applications are required. Each UDC value changes the features and functionality of one or more applications and system processes. Thus, you can avoid creating a single application for each business process, and instead integrate related processes into a single application. The end result is one application that can perform more than one task by changing its UDC value. Ultimately, this technique reduces the amount of code that needs to be maintained over the lifetime of an application.

Advanced Application Development

For example, the General Accounting Constants application (P0000) contains a set of data items that configure the financial modules for OneWorld. The Multi-Currency Conversion data item (CRYR), shown in Figure 11-3, is assigned the UDC H00/CR. Each value for H00/CR modifies the features and functionality of the various financial applications and system processes. The UDC values for the Multi-Currency Conversion data item (CRYR) are N for not enabling multi-currency conversion in the system, Y for enabling multiplier-based currency conversion (Y) in the system, and Z for enabling divisor-based currency conversion (Z) in the system.

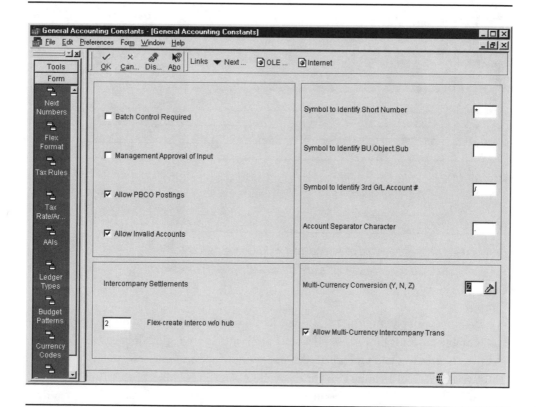

FIGURE 11-3.   Hard-coded UDC example in the General Accounting Constants application (P0000)

Creating User-Defined Codes

The examples for this section take you through the common tasks involved in creating UDCs: creating a new UDC type and adding valid values to an existing UDC. Whether you are defining soft- or hard-coded UDCs, the steps required to build them are the same. These examples build UDCs that are used for the Supplier's Delivery Quality application, which is the main example in this chapter.

NOTE

The SLH product code is for prototyping purposes and is used throughout the examples in this chapter. You must add the SLH value in the UDC 98/SY for the later examples to work, or you will need to use another product code when building your applications.

Creating a Code Type

If there is not an existing UDC defined for your development project, you will need to create a code type. The new code type for the Supplier's Delivery Quality application is MQ, which stands for "material quality." To create the MQ code type, complete the following steps:

1. Type **UDC** into the Fast Path box and press ENTER. The Work With User Defined Codes form (P0004A) appears, as shown in Figure 11-4.

2. From the Form menu, choose Code Types. The system displays the Work With User Defined Code Types form, as shown in Figure 11-5.

3. To create a new code type for system code SLH, type **SLH** into the System Code field, and click the Add button. The User Defined Code Types form will appear, as shown here:

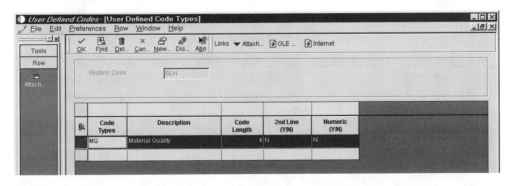

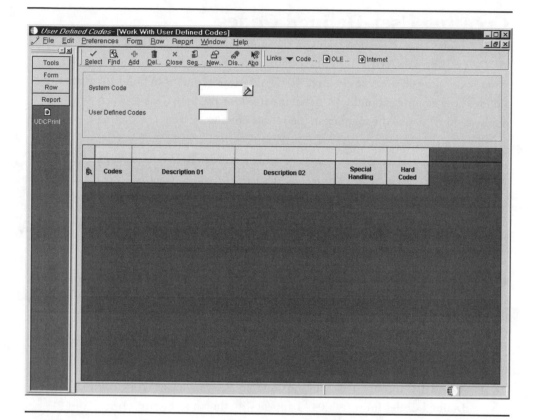

FIGURE 11-4.   The Work With User Defined Codes application (P0004A)

4. Enter the new code type on the last line of the grid. For this example, the following values have been entered into the grid line:

Field	Value	Description
Code Types	MQ	An alphanumeric value that defines a UDC code for a particular Product Code.
Description	Material Quality	A meaningful name for the UDC.
Code Length	4	The maximum length for UDC values assigned to this UDC code.
2nd Line	N	This enables (Y) or disables (N) the use of the second description for a UDC value.
Numeric	N	This determines whether the UDC values assigned to this UDC are numeric (Y) or alphanumeric (N).

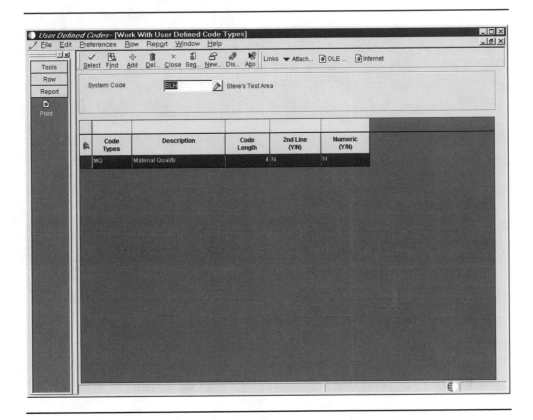

FIGURE 11-5. The Work With User Defined Code Types form of the Work With User Defined Codes application (P0004A)

5. Click the OK button. The system returns to the Work With User Defined Code Types form (see Figure 11-5). To verify that the code type was saved to the database, click the Find button.

6. Click the Close button when you have finished. The system returns to the Work With User Defined Codes form.

Creating a UDC

Any time you need to add a new value to a UDC, you first need to create a UDC for a specific code type. This example adds three values—Good, Fair, and Poor—to the MQ UDC that you created in the previous steps.

N O T E

When creating UDC values, it is useful to keep in mind that the system will sort the values in alphanumeric order. Therefore, the UDC values for this example will sort Fair, Good, and Poor, even though the values are entered Good, Fair, and Poor.

To create a UDC, complete the following steps:

1. Type **UDC** into the Fast Path box. The Work With User Defined Codes form (P0004A) appears, as shown earlier in Figure 11-4.

2. Type the following information into the fields on the form:

Field	Value	Description
System Code	SLH	The module that the UDC code is assigned to
User Defined Codes	MQ	The value of the UDC code that was created in the preceding example

3. Click the Add button and the User Defined Codes form appears, as shown in Figure 11-6.

4. Enter the following information in the grid in Figure 11-6:

Codes	Description 1	Hard Coded
GOOD	Good Quality	N
FAIR	Fair Quality	N
POOR	Poor Quality	N

N O T E

The Hard Coded column defines the UDC value as a hard-coded UDC when the value in the column is equal to Y. Currently in OneWorld, the Hard Coded field is for informational purposes only, and no system validation processing is performed on hard-coded UDCs.

5. Click the OK button. The system returns to the Work With User Defined Codes form. To verify that your UDC was saved, click the Find button. The UDC you added will appear in the grid.

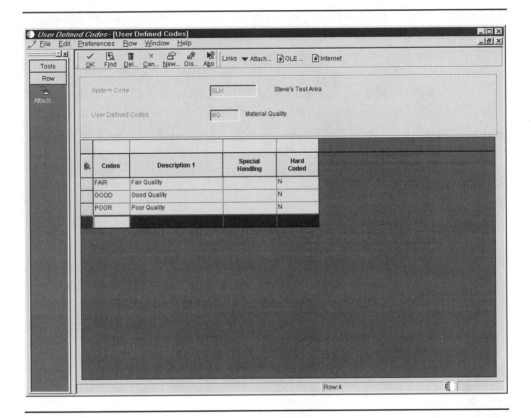

FIGURE 11-6. The User Defined Codes form of the Work With User Defined Codes application (P0004A)

N O T E

The Special Handling field on the User Defined Codes form is available for developers to define special processing requirements. Any processing that is dependent on the Special Handling field has to be written into your applications. A common use for the Special Handling field is language-preference descriptions.

Next Numbers

Most companies generate numerous documents, such as sales and purchase orders, over a period of time. In order for these documents to be uniquely identified in the system, the next-number facility in OneWorld is used to assign a value to a field on the document. The next-number facility controls the automatic assignment of numbers to identify every document or record in a table uniquely. Every time a new record is created or a new document is generated, the next-number facility assigns the next available number to that record.

A good example of using next numbers in OneWorld is the Address Book Number data item (AN8). The data item is used to store a unique number that identifies a particular entry in the Address Book Master table (F0101). The Address Book Number data item (AN8) is assigned the next-number value 01/1, and the next-number facility maintains this next-number value for it. As shown in Figure 11-7, the Address Book Number data item (AN8) is assigned its next-number value in the Next Number panel of the Work With Data Dictionary Items application (P92001).

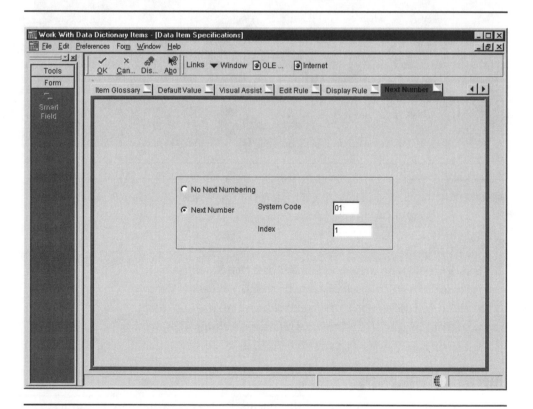

FIGURE 11-7. The Next Number panel of the Work With Data Dictionary Items application (P92001)

There are two types of next numbers in OneWorld: standard and company/fiscal year numbers. Standard next numbering uses the Next Numbers table (F0002) to assign a unique value for any table or document in a particular system. Company/fiscal year next numbering uses the Next Numbers by Company/Fiscal Year table (F00021) to assign a unique value for a document within a specific company and fiscal year combination.

CAUTION

Do not change any of the next numbers in the F0002 and F00021 tables. The next-number facility will not be able to guarantee unique values, because it is only concerned with assigning the next number for a value.

Next numbers are stored in both tables by system or product code, and there are ten next numbers available for each one of them. Therefore, for any system code, you can only have ten Data Dictionary items that use next numbering. If you need more than ten numbers for a particular system or product code, you will need to create your own next-numbering facility.

Not only does the next-numbering facility provide unique numbers for various documents and tables, it also lowers the likelihood of transposing one number with another by assigning a check digit to the next number. To provide numbers that cannot be transposed with a previously assigned value, the modulus 11 algorithm is used to assign the next unique value.

Assigning Next Numbers

The following example shows you how to assign next numbers to an existing product code. As mentioned previously, each product code in OneWorld can support up to ten next numbers.

To assign next numbers to a product code, complete the following steps:

1. Type NN into the Fast Path box and press ENTER. The Work With Next Numbers form (P0002) appears, as shown in Figure 11-8.

2. To add a set of available next numbers for system code 55, click the Add button. Otherwise, double-click an existing system code to add a next number to it. The Set Up Next Numbers by System form appears, as shown in Figure 11-9.

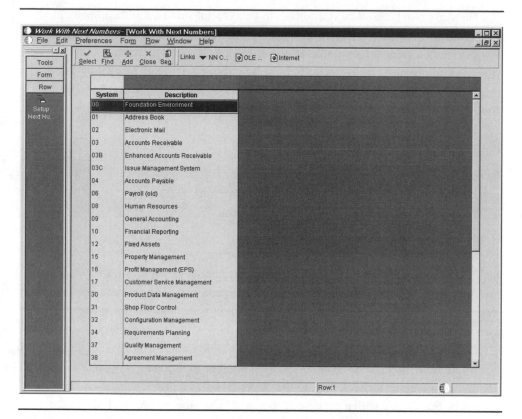

FIGURE 11-8.   The Work With Next Numbers application (P0002)

3. Enter the following values into the fields of the form:

Field	Value	Description
Use	NN Test 1	A meaningful title for the next number.
Next Number	1	The next-number value to be used when it is requested the next time by an application.
Check Digit Used	Disabled	To avoid number transposition, select the Check Digit Used check box for the next number.

4. Click the OK button when you have finished. To verify that the system saved the next numbers for system code 55, click the Find button on the Work With Next Numbers form. The system displays the next numbers you created.

5. Click the Close button when you have finished.

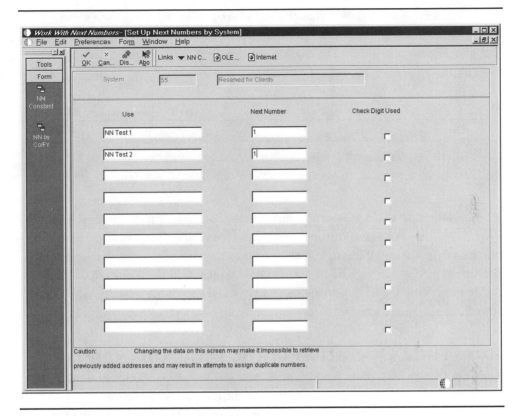

FIGURE 11-9.   The Set Up Next Numbers by System form of the Work With Next
Numbers application (P0002)

NOTE

*If you need to add a new next number to a system (or product) code, select the
code that needs the new next number from the grid in Figure 11-9. Then add
the new next number to an empty field on the form shown in Figure 11-9.*

Data Dictionary Items

The Data Dictionary manages the repository of data items for all environments,
applications, business views, business functions, and tables in OneWorld. The Data
Dictionary is dynamic because as changes are made to a data item, the changes are
automatically reflected in applications without having to recompile them.

A data item is a component that can be used by applications, business views, business functions, and tables in OneWorld, and it represents a unit of information. The unit of information could be anything from a temporary variable in an application to a column in a table.

NOTE

Just as a regular dictionary contains the definitions, spelling, and usage rules for words, the Data Dictionary in OneWorld is similarly a central repository that contains definitions, descriptions, and attributes of data items.

The definition of a data item controls how the data item is used throughout the system. The definitions can include a data item's name, alias, type, default values, number of decimals, UDC assignment, and next-number assignment. The data item definitions are used to validate and format the data that is entered into a field, assign the description to the field, provide text for help, and determine how the values are stored in a column of a table.

Run-Time Operation of the Data Dictionary

The Data Dictionary is global and dynamic, and it is actively working behind the scenes at all times. Any changes made to a data item in the Data Dictionary are reflected immediately across all OneWorld applications. The Data Dictionary updates clients with new or updated data items and validates the values assigned to a data item by the user.

The Data Dictionary is stored in two places on the corporate network: in the RDB specifications located in the Data Dictionary data source (DDB733), and locally on your client machine in Table Access Method (TAM) specifications.

The TAM specifications are updated for every client workstation when the client machine accepts a full or an update package (see Chapter 4). As applications execute, if the application finds that a data item that it needs isn't stored in TAM specifications, then it downloads the data item from the RDB specifications. This download procedure is called just-in-time installation (JITI), and it is discussed in Chapter 3.

The TAM specifications are located in the ddtext.*, dddict.*, glbltbl.* files in the spec directory of any valid OneWorld client or server. If the changes to Data Dictionary items do not occur dynamically, then you should delete the ddtext.*, dddict.*, and glbltbl.* TAM specs to force a JITI of all data items.

Data Item Specifications

The specifications for a data item identify it and describe how it is used in applications. The specifications for a data item are broken into three categories:

- **Data Item Definition** The definition of a data item determines how the values for the data item are stored in the database. Some examples of data item definitions are the name and alias.

- **Data Item Attributes** The attributes of a data item, such as its description, control type, and size, define how the data item is presented in applications.

- **Data Dictionary Triggers** The Data Dictionary triggers, such as formatting, next numbers, and UDCs, determine how the data item behaves in applications.

CAUTION

If you have to modify a data item, make sure that you only modify its attributes. Modifying the definition of a data item will affect how it is stored in the database, and will induce unpredictable behavior in your applications.

The starting point for viewing the specifications of a data item is the Work With Data Dictionary Items application (P92001), shown in Figure 11-10. The application is located on the Data Dictionary menu (GH951).

Data Item Definition

The data item definition establishes the data item name and alias that uniquely identify a data item in the Data Dictionary. The information for the definition of a data item is contained in the Item Specifications form of the Work With Data Dictionary Items application (P92001), shown in Figure 11-11. The Item Specifications form appears whenever you choose Select or Add from the Work With Data Items form.

Data Item Name

The data item name (the Data Item field in Figure 11-11), is a 40-character alphanumeric field that refers to a single data item. Special characters, such as spaces, the percent sign (%), ampersand (&), period (.), and plus sign (+), are not allowed to be used in the data item name. Usually the data item name is a combination of the product code and the description. For example, a system code of 56 and a data item

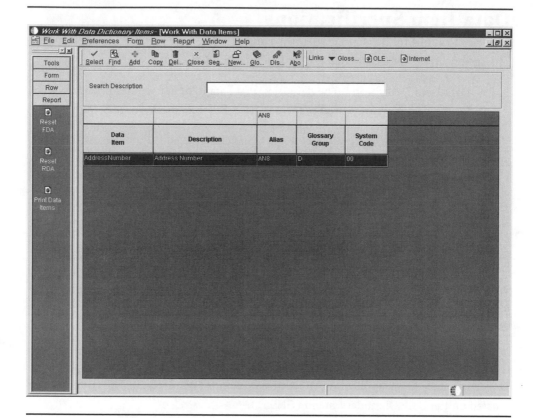

FIGURE 11-10. The Work With Data Items form of the Work With Data Dictionary
Items application (P92001)

with a description of customer name could have a data item name of
56CustomerName.

N O T E

*Once you create a data item with a specific data item name, it cannot be
changed at any time. Create another data item if you need to change its
data item name.*

The data item name forms the variable name that is used in C business functions
in OneWorld. Therefore, when you enter the name of the data item, ensure that it is

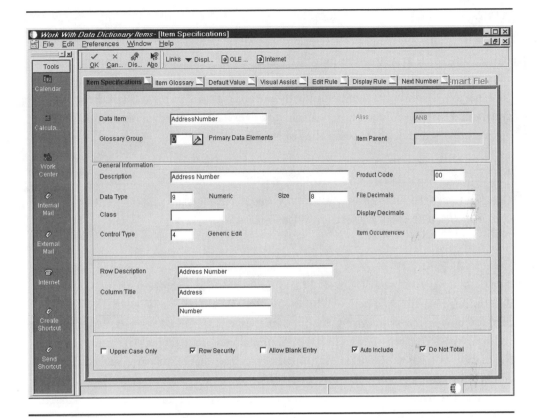

FIGURE 11-11. The Item Specifications form of the Work With Data Dictionary Items application (P92001)

meaningful enough that it makes sense when it is generated in C. An example of generating a data item to C is the math numeric data item, which is MATH01 and is displayed in a C program as mnMathNumeric.

CAUTION

Be sure to follow the naming convention of data items, because not doing so can have serious consequences when upgrading your OneWorld installation. The most current naming convention can be found in the Development Standards: Application Design manual that comes with the documentation CD for OneWorld.

Alias

A data item alias is an eight-character alphanumeric field that identifies a data item (the Alias field is grayed out in Figure 11-11). Just like the data item name, the alias cannot contain any special characters, such as spaces, the percent sign (%), ampersand (&), period (.), and plus sign (+). Usually the alias is the combination of the system code and a unique number. For example, the data item with a data item name of 56CustomerName might have an alias of 56010.

N O T E

Once you create the data item alias, you cannot change it at any time.
Create another data item if you need to change the alias.

Glossary Group

The glossary group uses UDC H98/DI and designates the type of data item, which determines how the data item will be used in OneWorld. Glossary group D is for primary data items, while group S is for data item arrays. D and S glossary groups are the only types that are allowed to have columns in database tables. An example of the S glossary group is the Address Line data item (ADD) that is the parent data item for Address Line data items ADD1 through ADD8.

Glossary groups E and K are for data items that are used for error messages and smart fields, respectively. Error messages are the pop-up messages you see in an interactive application when an error or warning occurs, and smart fields are used for cell calculations in financial reports.

Parent Data Item

The Item Parent field that is shown in Figure 11-11 defines the parent data item that is used as a template for defining many similar data items. Currently, the parent data item feature is not enabled for use in OneWorld through the Work With Data Dictionary Items application (P92001). An example of a data item that has a parent data item is the Address Category Codes, AC1 through AC10, which have the parent data item AC.

Data Item Attributes

The attributes of a data item define its behavior in different applications. The attributes define the row and column description, size, data type, among others. The attributes for a data item are entered on the Item Specifications form of the Work With Data Dictionary Items application (P92001), as shown in Figure 11-11. These available attributes for a data item are discussed next.

Description

The Description attribute is meant to provide a meaningful and qualitative title for a data item. The Description field accepts alphanumeric text, and it can be in upper- and lowercase.

TIP

As you create data items for your development projects, we encourage you to be consistent in the naming of your data items. This will increase your ability to search for data items in the Data Dictionary by using the Description.

Product Code

The Product Code attribute identifies which system or module a data item belongs to. For example, the AddressNumber data item, shown in Figure 11-11, belongs to product code 00, which is the Address Book module for OneWorld.

Data Type

The Data Type attribute classifies a data item by type, such as date, numeric, string, or character. Table 11-1 lists the valid data types that you can assign to a data item in OneWorld.

CAUTION

Do not change the data type of an existing data item. If you do, all of the applications, business views, reports, business functions, and data structures will have to be regenerated in order to use the new data type.

Data Type Code	Description	Purpose
1	Character	This data type is a single alphabetic character. The Event Point data item (EV01) is an example of this type of data item.
11	Date	This data type stores dates in the Julian date format. The Effective Date data item (EFT) is an example of this type of data item.
15	Integer	This data type is a number without decimals (an integer).
17	Character (BLOB)	This data type is used to store large data sets. The format in which the data set is stored is EBCDIC, which is typically used on the AS/400.
18	Binary (BLOB)	This data type is used to store large data sets. The format in which the data set is stored is machine code.
2	String	This data type is a static-sized array of characters. The Name data item (ALPH) is an example of this type of data item.
20	Variable string	This data type is a variable-sized array of characters.
7	Identifier (ID)	This data type holds integers used during the generation of C code, and it is the ID for a control on a form.
9	Numeric	This data type is used for long integers or floating point numbers. The Math Numeric data item (MATH01) is an example of this type of data item.

TABLE 11-1.   Valid Data Types for a Data Item

Size

The Size attribute determines to the field size of a data item. Numeric and currency data types usually have a field size of 15, whereas data items that represent Address Book numbers and business units usually have a field size of 8.

T I P

Some of the data types automatically enter the field size when you assign them to a data item. Except for character data types, you can modify the size of the fields without any problems.

File Decimals

For numeric and currency data types, the File Decimals value represents the number of digits to the right of the decimal point that are stored in a database table. This field is only used for AS/400 enterprise servers with DB2 databases.

Display Decimals

The Display Decimals attribute designates the number of digits to the right of the decimal point that are displayed in interactive and batch applications. For example, the U.S. dollar has a Display Decimal value of 2, while the Japanese yen has a value of 0. This attribute is needed because the decimal for a floating-point number is not stored in a table. When a numeric data type is extracted from a table, the system formats the numeric value based on its Display Decimals value.

Control Type

The Control Type attribute assigns the type of graphical control that will be the default for the data item. The types of graphical controls that are available for data items include push buttons, edit boxes, radio buttons, and check boxes. By assigning a graphical control to a data item, FDA automatically adds the correct graphical control for the data item that you add to a form. You can override the graphical control that you assign to a data item at the form level. Table 11-2 lists the graphical control types available in OneWorld forms.

Row Description

The Row Description attribute is the field description that appears on forms and reports. This description can be overridden on a form or a report. Use the abbreviations listed in Table 11-3 whenever you assign commonly used descriptions for data items.

Column Title

The Column Title attribute consists of two description lines. The first line is the primary descriptiong, used for all column headings for a data item in a form's grid or a report's column. The second line further describes the first line.

Control Type Code	Description
1	User-Defined Code (UDC) edit box
2	Check box
3	Radio button
4	Generic edit box
5	Push button

TABLE 11-2.   Valid Graphical Control Types for a Data Item

Advanced Application Development

Abbreviation	Full Description
U/M	Unit of measure
YTD	Year-to-date
MTD	Month-to-date
PYE	Period year end
QTY	Quantity
G/L	General ledger
A/P	Accounts payable
DEPR	Depreciation

TABLE 11-3.   Common Abbreviations for Data Item Descriptions

Class

The Class attribute is an information-only field that defines the general attributes and characteristics of a data item. This attribute is useful for identifying a special category of data items, such as a business unit or a Julian date. Table 11-4 lists the valid data item classes used in OneWorld.

Data Item Class Code	Description
COSTCTRSEC	Business unit
CURRENCY	Currency amount
DATEG	Gregorian date
DATEW	Julian date
DWAMT	Data warehouse amounts
DWQTY	Date warehouse quantity
HANDLE	Table handle
ONAT	Originator
QTYINV	Inventory quantities
TRACE	Units
VARLEN	Variable-length character field

TABLE 11-4.   Classes for Data Items

Item Occurrences

The Item Occurrences attribute for data items specifies the number of elements that are in an array, and these are only used for glossary groups of type S. Depending on the number of elements in the array, the array's data item names are restricted to certain lengths. For example, 3-byte name lengths are available for arrays with one to nine elements, 2-byte name lengths are used for arrays with 10 to 99 elements, and 1-byte name lengths are used for arrays with 100 to 999 elements.

Upper Case Only

The Upper Case Only attribute forces users to enter only uppercase characters into a field. You typically force uppercase characters in UDCs.

Allow Blank Entry

The Allow Blank Entry attribute permits a blank value to be entered in a graphical control that requires a value, including in an edit box whose UDC doesn't have a blank value in its valid values list.

Row Security

With row security, you limit the user's viewing and editing capabilities for rows in a table by assigning certain values that the user cannot see. This is done by activating the Row Security attribute and using the Security Manager to define which values the user cannot view or edit. To ensure that performance is not decreased by row security, the Row Security attribute can only be applied to data items that are a part of the primary key of a table.

NOTE

Enabling the Row Security check box in the Data Dictionary only makes the field available in the Security Manager. Security is not enabled for the data item until you set it up in the Security Manager application (P00950), which is discussed in Chapter 3.

Auto Include

The Auto Include attribute for data items ensures that the data item is included in any database fetch that contains it. This guarantees that accidentally forgetting to include the data item in the database fetch will never occur, and it is particularly useful for critical data items that are essential for database validation and security.

Do Not Total

The Do Not Total attribute ensures that no totaling of data occurs for this data item. You use this attribute to ensure that reports do not total the values related to a particular data item because it doesn't make sense. For example, totaling all Address Book numbers in a report results in wasted processing.

Data Dictionary Triggers

Data Dictionary triggers are an editing or display routine that you use for field-level data integrity. Triggers are attached to a data item and are automatically associated with an application that uses it. The primary advantage of Data Dictionary triggers is that they are reusable throughout all applications, which reduces development time and increases data integrity at the field level. The available Data Dictionary triggers are discussed next.

Glossary

The glossary provides a definition of the data item and is a useful mechanism for providing field-level, contextgsensitive help to users. You can view the glossary (definition) for a data item by pressing the F1 key when the cursor is in the field. Alternatively, you can right-click in the field and select the What's This? menu item from the pop-up menu.

The glossary information for a data item is entered into the Item Glossary form, as shown in Figure 11-12. You need to enter meaningful information in the glossary of every data item, because the system automatically uses it for field-level help. The Item Glossary form has all of the features and functionality of a typical text editor.

Default Value Trigger

A default value trigger automatically inserts a value into a control and helps increase the usability of a form. The default value is not used if a value is passed into the field through a processing option, business function, form interconnect, or data structure, or if a user types a value into the field. The default value is assigned to a control in a form if a control is exited or if a dialog box is initialized.

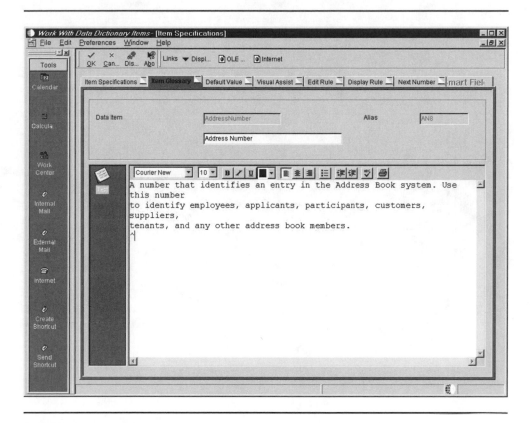

FIGURE 11-12.   The Item Glossary form of the Work With Data Dictionary Items
application (P92001)

Figure 11-13 shows the Default Value form for a data item. If you choose the Default
Value option, the system displays a field in which you can enter the default value.

Visual Assist Trigger

A visual assist trigger provides a link to a small application or form that is used to
provide assistance in entering data into the field. These triggers include Search and
Select forms that contain a valid list of values, a calendar in which you can choose the
date you want to enter into a field, or a calculator with which you can calculate a total
before entering it into a field, as shown in Figure 11-14.

Advanced Application Development

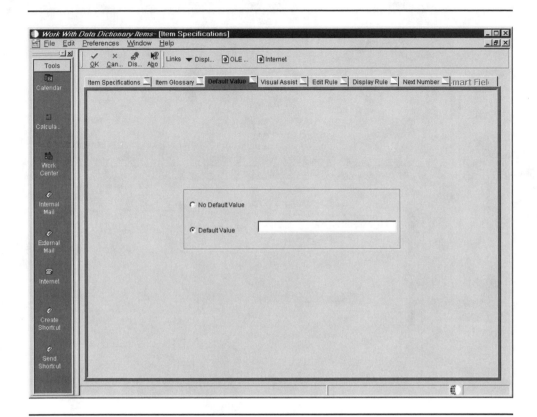

FIGURE 11-13. The Default Value form of the Work With Data Dictionary Items application (P92001)

The Search and Select form is invoked when a user clicks the Flashlight button located to the right of a field, and it provides a valid list of values that users can choose from. Users can also use the QBE line to search for a specific value.

NOTE

To display multiple values in a Search and Select form, insert the system command Suppress Default Visual Assist in the Call Visual Assist Before event. Then, use the form interconnect to call the Search and Select form that returns more than one value. An example of this approach is provided in Chapter 5.

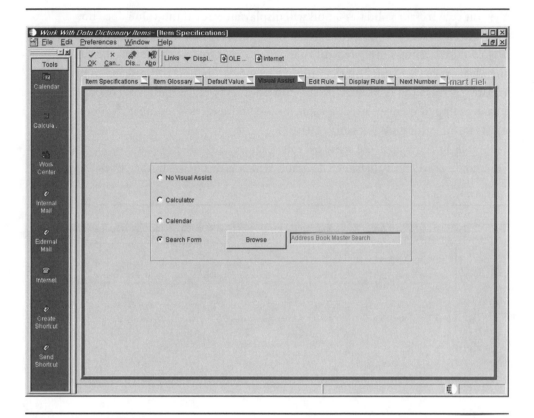

FIGURE 11-14. The Visual Assist form of the Work With Data Dictionary Items application (P92001)

The Calculator visual assist is invoked when a user clicks the Calculator button located to the right of a numeric field. The numeric field should only be assigned a Calculator visual assist if the value in the field can be edited.

The Calendar visual assist is invoked when a user clicks the Calendar button located to the right of a date field.

Edit Rule Trigger

You use edit rules to enforce data integrity in a field. Edit rules are based on either a business function or a rule. Any time a value is changed or entered into a data item,

Advanced Application Development

the edit rule trigger validates it and will display an error if the value does not pass the edit rule.

You use business function edit rules when you want to ensure that the value a data item has exists in a table. An example of a business function edit rule, as shown in Figure 11-15, is the Is Address Number in Address Book Column (B0100039). This business function ensures that a value for the Address Book Number data item (AN8) exists in the Address Book table (F0101).

Table 11-5 displays the standard rules that an edit rule can enforce. The most commonly used edit rule is the UDC rule, which is discussed in the "User-Defined

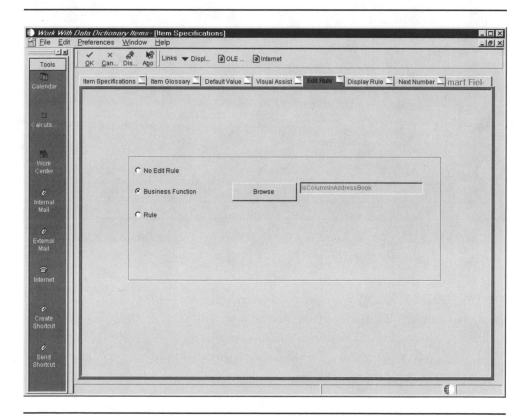

FIGURE 11-15.   The Edit Rule form of the Work With Data Dictionary Items application (P92001)

Edit Rule	Description
EQ	Equal to.
GE	Greater than or equal to.
GT	Greater than.
HNDL	This edit rule applies to table handles that are used to access a table more than once with a single database connection. Table handles are discussed in more detail later in this chapter.
LE	Less than or equal to.
LT	Less than.
NE	Not equal to.
NRANGE	Not between.
RANGE	Between.
UDC	User-Defined Code.
VALUE	In a list.
ZLNGTH	Allocated length.

TABLE 11-5. Standard Edit Rules

Codes" section earlier in this chapter. The UDC edit rule ensures that the value of a data item is one of the values contained in the UDC table.

For example, the UDC 01/01 governs the first category code for an Address Book entry. If the Address Book category code is set to a value that is not included in the UDC 01/01, then the edit rule highlights the field in red and displays an error message.

Display Rule Trigger

Display rule triggers determine how the values in a data item are presented on the screen. Any time a value is changed or entered into a data item, the display rule trigger changes the way it looks on the form, based on the rule. For example, if a numeric data item is defined to have two-digit precision, and a three-digit precision value is entered into it, then the trigger will automatically format the value entered to two-digit precision. Figure 11-16 shows the Display Rule form that you use to set the display rule for a data item.

You use business function display rules in situations where the other display rules cannot enforce the behavior required. For example, the Display Account Number

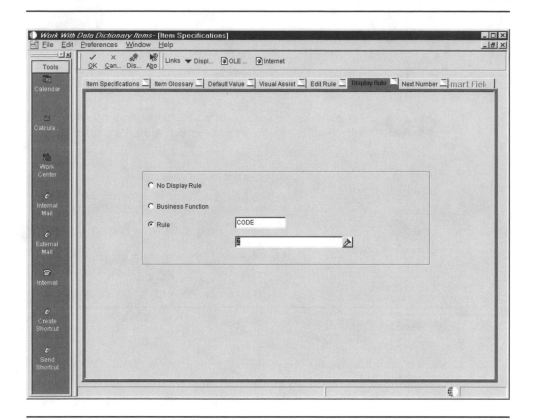

FIGURE 11-16. The Display Rule form of the Work With Data Dictionary Items application (P92001)

business function presents the account number on the form in a special format, which is Business Unit-Object Account-Subsidairy.

Table 11-6 displays the standard rules that a display rule can enforce. The most commonly used display rule is the CODE rule, which ensures that the value of a numeric data item is displayed with one of the formats listed in Table 11-7. For example, a currency data item will have the CODE K numeric format, while an integer will have a display rule of CODE Z for its numeric format.

UDC-Based Display Rule	Description
*RAB	The Business Unit data item (MCU) uses this rule to right-adjust the value and precede it with blanks.
*RABN	Numeric and alphanumeric data types use this rule to right-adjust the value and precede it with blanks.
*RAZ	Numeric and alphanumeric data types use this rule to right-adjust the value and precede it with zeroes. For example, a company data item would appear as 00001.
CODE	Numeric data items use this field to access special formats for numeric fields. The valid list of formats for numeric fields is located in UDC 98/EC.
MASK	String data items use this field to embed special characters within the data when it is displayed. For example, Social Security Numbers are embedded with dashes.

TABLE 11-6.   Standard Display Rules

Numeric Field Format	Special Purpose	Allow Zero Balance	Allow Commas	Symbol Denoting Negative Value
	Default value	NA	NA	NA
%	Trailing percent sign (%)	NA	NA	Minus sign
*	Leading asterisks	NA	Yes	Minus sign
1		Yes	Yes	No sign
2		No	Yes	No sign
3		Yes	No	No sign
4		No	No	No sign
A		Yes	Yes	CR
B		No	Yes	CR
C		Yes	No	CR
D		No	No	CR

TABLE 11-7.   Numeric Display Formats for Display Rules of Type CODE

Numeric Field Format	Special Purpose	Allow Zero Balance	Allow Commas	Symbol Denoting Negative Value
J		Yes	Yes	Minus sign
K		No	Yes	Minus sign
L		Yes	No	Minus sign
M		No	No	Minus sign
N		Yes	Yes	Float
O		No	Yes	Float
P		Yes	No	Float
Q		No	No	Float
R		Yes	Yes	<>
S		No	Yes	<>
T		Yes	No	<>
U		No	No	<>
X	Remove plus sign	NA	NA	NA
Y	Date field edit	NA	NA	NA
Z	Zero suppress	NA	NA	NA

TABLE 11-7.   Numeric Display Formats for Display Rules of Type CODE *(continued)*

Next Number Trigger

Next numbers, which are discussed in the "Next Numbers" section, earlier in this chapter, control the automatic numbering of values for data items that use them. Next numbering provides an automatic method of uniquely identifying a document or record in a table. Some data items that use next numbers are G/L account numbers, voucher numbers, and Address Book numbers.

NOTE

There are only ten next numbers available per system code. If you need more next numbers within a system code, you must build you own next-numbering mechanism.

When you create a record in OneWorld, such as a G/L account, the next-number trigger assigns a new number to the value in that data item. As shown in Figure 11-17, the next-number trigger is assigned a unique combination of the system code and an index for its data item. The system code and index must be unique, because only one data item in an environment is assigned to it. A further discussion on the purpose of indexes is provided in the "Tables" section, later in this chapter.

CAUTION

After you assign a next-number trigger to a data item, do not modify or reassign the next number. The values assigned before and after the modification are not guaranteed to be unique.

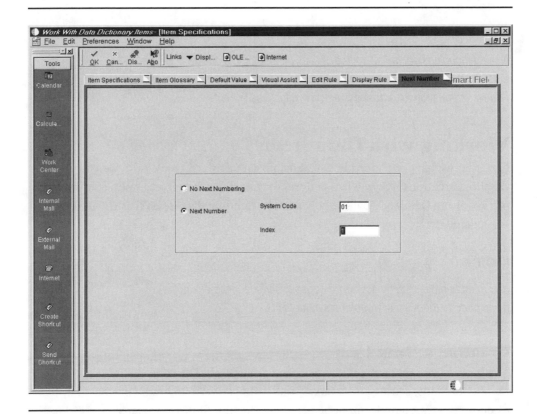

FIGURE 11-17. The Next Number form of the Work With Data Dictionary Items application (P92001)

Smart Field Trigger

Smart fields, which are discussed in more detail in Chapter 6, are data items with business functions that execute logic going beyond data validation and display. The advantage of using smart fields is that a user simply adds them as a column in a report, and the advanced logic that is assigned to the field is imbedded into the report. Smart fields are available only for columns in tabular sections of OneWorld reports.

An example of a smart field is the Account Balance data item (ASSETAB), which provides the balance for an account for a particular period and fiscal year (shown in Figure 11-18). The Smart Field Criteria form is used to assign the Business Function, the Named Mapping for the Business Function, and the event that will execute the Business Function for the smart field. In this case, the smart field relates to the Account Balance data item (ASSETAB).

DEFINITION

Named mappings define the source of each parameter in a business function's data structure. The advantage to named mappings is that they know where to retrieve information for a business function without user input.

Working with Data Items

Now that we have explained how you define data items in OneWorld, we will explain the three functions that you can perform on data items. These examples continue with the Supplier's Delivery Quality application by building data items that we need for our example.

NOTE

You need to have security access privileges to perform these examples if you perform them in an environment other than DEMOB73.

Creating a Data Item

The first example shows you how to create a data item. The steps include entering a number of fields, setting check boxes, and setting or verifying radio buttons. The example creates a simple, numeric-based data item. Follow these steps:

1. From OneWorld Explorer, type **DD** in the Fast Path edit box, and press the ENTER key. The Data Dictionary Design menu (GH951) appears in the right panel of OneWorld Explorer.

2. Execute Work With Data Dictionary Items (P92001) from the Data Dictionary Design menu (GH951).

3. Click the Add Button, and the Item Specifications form appears, as shown in Figure 11-11.

4. Enter the following information on the Item Specifications form, as shown in Figure 11-11.

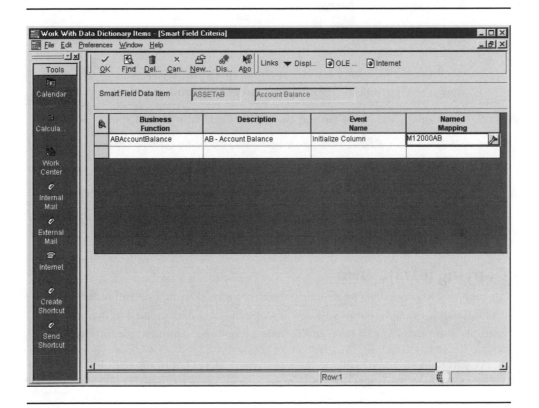

FIGURE 11-18. The Smart Field Criteria form of the Work With Data Dictionary Items application (P92001)

Field	Value
Data Item	55TestItem
Alias	55TSTITM
Glossary Group	D
Description	Test Item
System Code	55
Data Type	9
Size	15
Display Decimals	0
Control Type	4
Row Description	Test Item
Column Title 1	Test
Column Title 2	Item

5. Click the Item Glossary tab and enter the following text in the text editor shown in Figure 11-12: **This is a data item for testing purposes**.

6. Click the Visual Assist tab and choose the Calculator option shown earlier in Figure 11-14.

7. Click the OK button to save the data item to the Data Dictionary.

8. Click the Cancel button to return to the Work With Data Dictionary Items form.

9. To verify that the data item was added, type **55TSTITM** in the alias field, and click the Find button.

Copying a Data Item

An easy way to create data items quickly is to copy an existing one and rename it. The following example shows you how to copy the data item created in the previous example and rename it. To copy and rename a data item, complete the following steps:

1. On the Work With Data Items form, type **55TSTITM** in the QBE line of the Alias field, and click the Find button.

2. Highlight the data item, and click the Copy button.

3. Enter the following information on the Item Specifications form shown in Figure 11-11:

Field	Value
Data Item	55TestItem2
Alias	55TSTIT2
Description	Test Item 2
Row Description	Test Item 2
Column Title	Test Item 2

4. Click the Item Glossary tab and type the following text into the text editor shown in Figure 11-12: **This is another data item for testing purposes.**

5. Click the OK button to save the data item to the Data Dictionary.

6. Click the Cancel button to return to the Work With Data Dictionary Items form.

7. To verify that both data items exist, type **55TST*** in the alias field, and click the Find button on the toolbar.

Deleting Data Dictionary Items

We do not suggest that you delete J.D. Edwards data items, but you might have to delete some that *you* have created on occasion. The following steps show you how to delete data items from the Data Dictionary by deleting the data items created in the previous examples. To delete the data items you just created, follow these steps:

TIP

We suggest that you use the cross-reference application to search for the data item in all objects before you delete it, as discussed in Chapter 4. This will prevent any problems caused by objects that contain a data item that no longer exists.

1. On the Work With Data Items form, type **55TST*** in the Alias field, and click the Find button.

2. Highlight the first data item in the grid, and click the Delete button.

3. At the Confirm Delete dialog box, click the OK button to confirm that you want to delete the item. Repeat these steps for the other data item you created.

4. To verify that both data items have been deleted, type **55TST*** in the alias field, and click the Find button.

CAUTION

If you delete a data item that is attached to a table, business view, business function, or an application, it will cause the objects to fail. When you delete a data item, the system does not check to see if any objects are using that data item.

Creating Other Data Items

If you plan to perform any of the examples in this chapter, create the data items listed in Table 11-8. These data items are used to create a table, which is discussed in the next section, and they are all related to the Supplier's Delivery Quality application.

In this section, we discussed how data items are constructed and generated in OneWorld. However, there are general guidelines for creating specific types of data items, such as address book number, business units, and currency amounts. The

Alias	SLH001	SLH002	SLH003	SLH004	SLH005
Data Item	SLHNbrDaysFor NormalDelivery	SLHNbrDaysFor RushDelivery	SLHMatlQualityFor NormalDelivery	SLHMatlQualityFor RushDelivery	SLHLineNbr
Description	Nbr of Days for Normal Delivery	Nbr of Days for Rush Delivery	Material Quality for Normal Delivery	Material Quality for Rush Delivery	Line Number
Row Description	Number of Days	Number of Days	Quality	Quality	Line Number
Column Title (top)	Nbr of Days	Nbr of Days	Material Quality	Material Quality	Line
Column Title (bottom)	Normal Delivery	Rush Delivery	Normal Delivery	Rush Delivery	Nbr
System Code	SLH	SLH	SLH	SLH	SLH
Data Type	9	9	2	2	9
Size	15	15	4	4	4
Display Decimals	2	2	0	0	0
Control Type	4	4	1	1	4
Visual Assist	Calculator	Calculator	Select User-Defined Code	Select User-Defined Code	None
Edit Rule	None	None	UDC: SLH/MQ	UDC: SLH/MQ	None
Display Rule	None	None	None	None	CODE Z

TABLE 11-8. Data Items for the Table Example in This Chapter

following Developer's Corner, titled "Data Item Specification Settings for Common Data Types," discusses some common settings for basic data items.

Data Item Specification Settings for Common Data Types

It is good programming practice to have a predefined list of data items included in the design specifications for any OneWorld project. The list provides a template of commonly used data items that you will need. A small list of data item definitions is shown in Table 11-9. The benefit of the data items' specifications list is that every data item type is defined properly and consistently.

Data Item Attribute	Address Book Number	Monetary Amount	Business Unit	Material Quantity	Date
Data Type	9	9	2	9	11
Control Type	4	4	4	4	4
Data Size	8	15	12	15	6
Display Decimals	0	2	0	2	0
Visual Assist	Address Book Master Search Form (P0101S)	Calculator	Business Unit Master Search Form (P0006S)	Calculator	Calendar
Edit Rule	IsColumnInAddressBook (B0100039)		IsColumnInBusinessUnitTable (ISCOLBU)		
Display Rule	CODE Z	CODE K	*RAB		
Class		CURRENCY	COSTCTRSEC		

TABLE 11-9. Specifications for Commonly Used Data Items in OneWorld

Developer's Corner

You can employ several means to maintain lists of commonly used data items. The first is to store Data Dictionary definitions in a spreadsheet. Maintaining a spreadsheet ensures that you always have the definitions of commonly used data items on hand. However, this method requires that you manually enter the information every time you create a new data item.

Perhaps an easier and better way to store commonly used data item definitions without data-entry overhead is to maintain a master copy of each data item by product code. For example, suppose you maintain a list of the standard data items in product code 55. As you need new data items, you copy the data item from product code 55 and rename it to the specific data item that you need.

Tables

Virtually every application and system process in OneWorld uses one or more tables to store, retrieve, and manipulate information. In most cases, the tables are managed by a relational database management system (RDBMS). The RDBMS contains all of the features and functionality to support manipulation and administration of the tables. As discussed in Chapter 2, the most common databases that OneWorld uses are Oracle, Microsoft SQL Server, and IBM DB/2.

Given the importance of tables to the operation of applications and system processes in OneWorld, we feel it is necessary for you to understand how tables are designed, the structure of tables, the naming conventions of tables in OneWorld, and how to create tables in OneWorld.

How Tables Are Designed

The purpose of this section is to provide you with a quick overview of how tables are designed in OneWorld. We do not intend to spend a lot of time discussing analysis approaches for tables, since there are many books and white papers written on this topic. However, we do want to mention the design document that gives you the best results for constructing tables in OneWorld, and a simple example to reinforce the concept.

When designing a set of tables for your application it is important to derive the tables through several iterations of analysis and design. The analysis and design phase usually creates a document called the Entity Relationship Diagram (ERD). The ERD captures the essence of a business's operational model and requirements by depicting a model of entities and the relationships between them. A summary of the common elements that comprise an ERD document are displayed in Figure 11-19.

DEFINITION

*An **entity** in the ERD document is an object and its set of attributes, which become the tables and its columns, respectively. **Cardinality**, on the other hand, defines the relationship between two entities, and the quantity of entities that are required to support the relationship, such as one-to-many.*

In the ERD finished state, the diagram defines the overall database schema that is required to support business operations. Essentially, the ERD document contains the

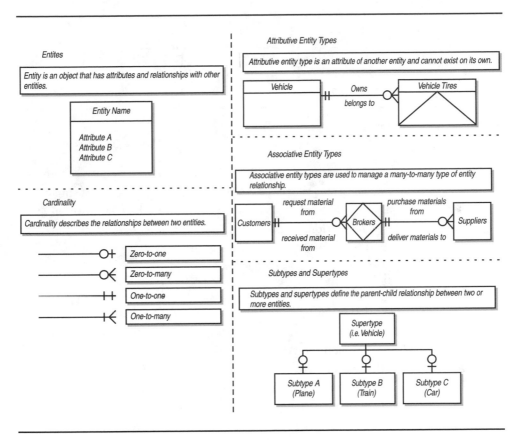

FIGURE 11-19. Summary of elements that comprise an Entity Relationship Diagram

Advanced Application Development

entities, their attributes, and their relationships with other entities. Typically, the entities in the ERD become the tables for your applications, and attributes for the entities become the columns in the tables. The relationship between two entities defines how many instances, such as one-to-many or many-to-many, of the entities are required to support the relationship.

For example, Figure 11-20 provides you with a simple ERD schematic of the sales order document. In Figure 11-20, the Sales Order Detail table has an attributive relationship with the Sales Order Header table, because detail items in a sales order cannot exist without the information in its header. The Sales Order Header table has a zero-to-many relationship with the Sales Order Detail table because there could be more than one item sold in a sales order.

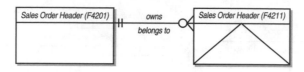

FIGURE 11-20.   Simple ERD schematic of a OneWorld sales order

Also, the ERD document names the relationships between the two entities to make it easier to understand. The name above the relationship defines the relationship of the left entity to the right. The name below the relationship defines the relationship of the right entity to the left. The relationship in Figure 11-20 is read as follows: the Sales Order Header owns zero-to-many Sales Order Detail items, and the Sales Order Detail item belongs to one-and-only-one Sales Order Header.

Structure of Tables

Tables store information about a specific entity or category of related data items, such as an address book, general ledger, or purchase order. They are physically implemented as two-dimensional entities that are derived from ERD schematics. A table is like a spreadsheet that contains information for applications and users to access and manipulate.

Tables are comprised of the following low-level components: rows, columns, and indexes.

Rows

A row in a table stores a unique set of information about an entity that applications access and manipulate as a single unit. For example, when the Address Book application (P01012) modifies the name of an employee, it updates the name in the row that represents the employee in the Address Book table (F0101).

TIP

You can think of a record in a table as a data structure that represents a specific entity. We can make this association because the Business View run-time data structure (BC) contains the current row available to an application after the system fetches it from the business view.

Columns

A column stores one piece of information for every record in a table, whether or not the record assigns a value to the column. A column has its own name and data type that is defined by a data item in the Data Dictionary. For example, the Social Security Number data item (SSN) is a column in the Address Book table (F0101) that is stored for every entity in the table.

It is a good idea to add the data items shown in Table 11-10 for all tables you create. These data items, which become columns in the table, provide an audit trail and a footprint of the last time a row was changed and by whom.

Indexes

An index of a table identifies a record or a set of records in the table. There can be many indexes attached to a table, but there must be one primary index (the primary key). The primary key consists of a data item or a group of data items that uniquely identify each record in the table. Without a primary key, the system and applications would not be able to access or manipulate records in a table.

Additional indexes are called secondary keys. You use secondary keys to arrange data in the table in ways that optimize search capabilities. Secondary keys can be unique or nonunique, depending on whether each record in the table must have a different key or whether duplicates are allowed.

For example, the Address Book table (F0101) has 13 secondary keys. The primary key is called Address Number, and it contains the Address Book Number data item (AN8) that is used to identify each record in the table. The Address Type 1 Description Compress secondary key contains the Search Type data item (AT1) and the Compressed Description data item (DC), which allow you to access and manipulate rows in the

Data Item	Description
USER	User ID
PID	Program ID
UPMJ	Date updated
JOBN	Workstation ID
UPMT	Time updated

TABLE 11-10.   Data Items for Table Audit Trail Purposes

table based on those two columns. The secondary key is useful in applications that allow you to search for Address Book entries that match a certain search type and compressed name.

DEFINITION

*A **compressed name** in OneWorld is the full name of an individual or business that has its spaces removed and all characters converted to uppercase.*

Another purpose of primary and secondary indexes is to maintain the relationship of tables defined in the ERD diagram. The tables store the columns that are defined in the keys of its related tables, and this allows tables to access records of their related tables.

The example shown in Figure 11-20 relates the Sales Order Header (F4201) and the Sales Order Detail (F4211) tables to support sales order contracts in the system. A single row in the Sales Order Header table (F4201) in Figure 11-20 is one sales contract for a particular customer, and all of the related records in the Sales Order Detail table (F4211) are the items contained in the order.

The relationship between the Sales Order Header (F4201) and Sales Order Detail (F4211) tables is implemented by the common columns contained in the primary keys of both tables. The primary key for the Sales Order Header table (F4201) contains the following columns: Document Order Number (DOCO), Document Order Type (DCTO), and Document Order Company (KCOO). The primary key for the Sales Order Detail table (F4211) contains the following columns: Document Order Number (DOCO), Document Order Type (DCTO), Document Order Company (KCOO), and Line Number (LNID).

The primary keys of the Sales Order Header (F4201) and the Sales Order Detail (F4211) tables contain the same three columns that uniquely identify a sales order so that a record in the Sales Order Header table (F4201) can relate to one or more records in the Sales Order Detail table (F4211). The Sales Order Detail table (F4211) contains one more column in its primary key to maintain the uniqueness of each record in both tables, and to identify all of the line numbers in the sales contract.

Naming Convention of Tables in OneWorld

The following guidelines are set forth by J.D. Edwards for naming tables and indexes in OneWorld. These guidelines can change from time to time, and therefore we recommend that you review the *OneWorld Application Design Standards Guide* from J.D. Edwards periodically.

Table-Naming Conventions

The object name for tables is *Fxxxxyyy*, where *F* identifies the object as a table, *xxxx* identifies the product code it belongs to, and *yyy* is the unique identifier for the table in the product code. You should use the description, which is 60 characters long, to qualitatively describe the purpose of the table.

Index-Naming Conventions

Index names can be 19 characters long. Use the data item description to name the index, and place a comma between each description. If the description is longer than 19 characters, put "+A" at the end of the index name to denote that the description name is longer than the index name. For example, the description for one of the indexes assigned to the Address Book table (F0101) is "Address Type 1, Desc Compresse."

Creating Tables in OneWorld

The following examples show you how to build, manipulate, and generate tables using the Table Design Aid (TDA) tool in OneWorld. The examples assume that you have already created the data items listed in Table 11-9. The table that you will create in this section is the Supplier's Delivery Quality table (FSLH002), which stores the condition of each item received from a supplier.

Creating a Table Object in the Object Librarian

To create a table OneWorld, you create it in the Object Librarian. The following steps show you how to create a table object:

1. From OneWorld Explorer, type **GH902** into the Fast Path edit box, and press the ENTER key. The Cross Application Development Tools menu appears.

2. Execute the Object Librarian application (P9860), and the Work With Object Librarian form appears, as shown in Figure 11-21.

3. In the Object Type field type **TBLE**, and click the Add button. The Add Object form, as shown in Figure 11-22, appears.

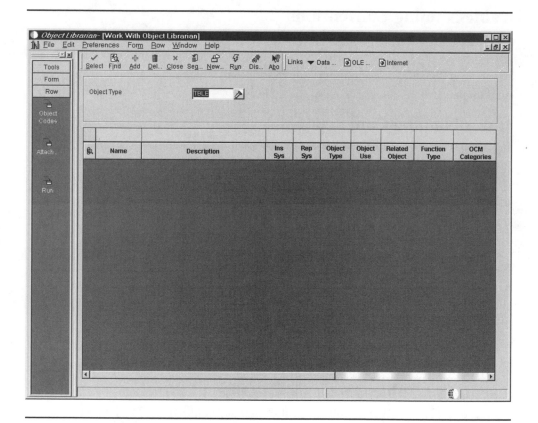

FIGURE 11-21. The Work With Object Librarian form of the Object Librarian application (P9860)

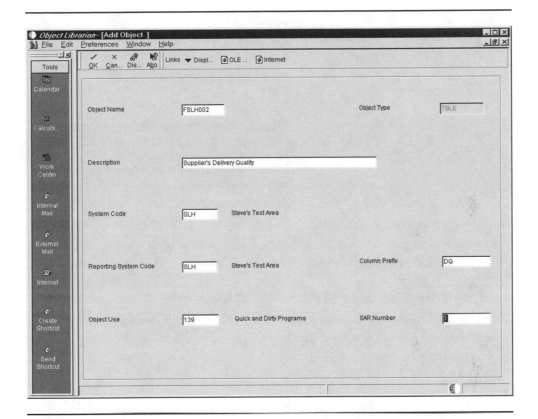

FIGURE 11-22. The Add Object form of the Object Librarian application (P9860)

4. On the Add Object form, fill in the fields with the following information to create the Object Librarian record for the Supplier's Delivery Quality table (FSLH002):

Field	Value	Description
Object Name	FSLH002	The unique identifier for the object in the system. It follows the naming convention mentioned in the preceding section.

Field	Value	Description
Description	Supplier's Delivery Quality	A meaningful name for the object.
System Code and Reporting System Code	SLH	The module that the table is assigned to.
Column Prefix	DQ	The table column prefix is appended to every data item alias when the table is generated in a particular RDBMS. For example, the Address Book Number (AN8) data item becomes DQAN8 in the FSLH002 table for the RDBMS that supports the table.
SAR Number	1	The value that assigns the object to a specific development project, modification, or fix.

5. When you have finished, click the OK button on the Add Object form. The Table Design Aid form appears, as shown in Figure 11-23.

Adding Items to a Table

After you have created the Object Librarian record for the table, you can create the table. You use the TDA tool to add data items to the table, and these data items become columns in the table.

To add data items to a table, complete the following steps:

1. To begin creating the table, click the Design button on the Table Design Aid form, as shown in Figure 11-23. The TDA form appears, as shown in Figure 11-24.

2. The TDA tool contains four child windows:

Child Window	Description
Properties window	This window displays the main properties for highlighted data items, indexes, and tables.
Data Dictionary Browser window	This window contains a QBE line for searching and selecting data items to be inserted into the table.
Table window	This window contains a list of all data items currently defined in the table.
Indices window	This window contains a list of all indexes the table has, and what data items make up each index.

3. To add a data item to the table, find the data item using the Data Dictionary Browser window.

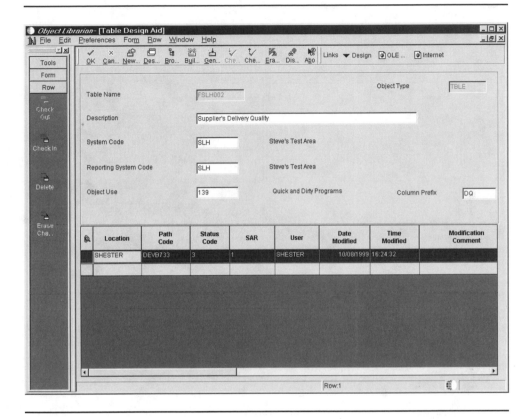

FIGURE 11-23. The Table Design Aid form of the Object Librarian application (P9860)

Advanced Application Development

NOTE

In order to view all windows in the TDA application, select the Window | Tile menu item. The application will tile all of the windows as shown later in Figure 11-25.

4. Drag and drop the data item into the table window, and the data item will now exist in the table you are currently designing. In Figure 11-24, the data item with the alias SLH005 is placed in the table window for the Supplier's Delivery Quality Columns.

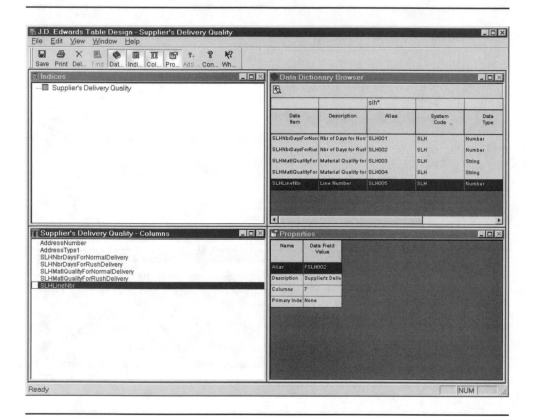

FIGURE 11-24. The Table Design Aid (TDA) development tool

5. If you need to delete a data item from the table, highlight the data item in the table window and click the Delete button on the TDA toolbar.

6. Click the Save button on the toolbar so that your changes will be saved.

Creating an Index

Now that you have added some columns to the table, you need to finish defining the table by adding a primary key index to the table. To create an index, complete the following steps:

1. Inside the Indices window of the TDA tool, choose Add New from the Index menu. Since this is the first index for this table, it will automatically become a primary key for the table.

2. Using the index-naming convention that is discussed in the preceding section, type the name of the index in the Indices window.

3. Now that the index exists, you can add data items to it. To add data items from the table to the index, select a data item from the table window, and drag it on top of the new key you just named in the Indices window.

4. To add another key, repeat steps 1 through 3. The next index you add will automatically become a secondary key, since the primary key already exists. Once you have finished building a new key, the indexes for the table should resemble those shown in Figure 11-25.

5. If the secondary key you just built needs to be unique, highlight the index, and choose Unique from the Index menu.

6. Click the Save button before you exit so that your changes will be saved.

7. Exit from the TDA tool. The system returns to the Table Design Aid form shown in Figure 11-23.

Generating a Table

Now that you have designed the table in the TDA application, you are ready for the system to create the table in a database. To create the table for a particular database data source, complete the following steps:

1. On the Table Design Aid form of the Object Librarian application, as shown earlier in Figure 11-24, click the Generate button. The Generate Table form appears, as shown in Figure 11-26.

2. In the Data Source field, select the database data source that you want the table to be generated from, as shown in Figure 11-26. If the data source requires a password to generate the table, then you must enter a password in the Password field.

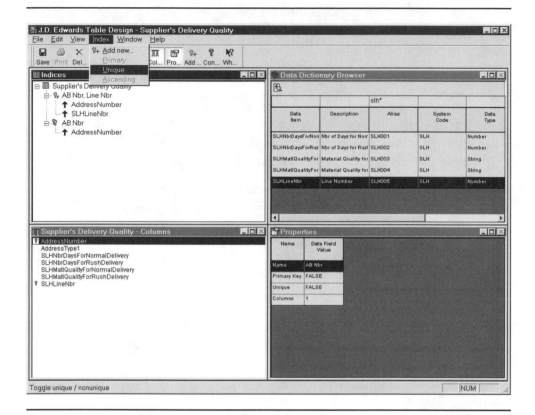

FIGURE 11-25. Creating a secondary key for a table with the TDA tool

NOTE

If you are generating the table locally, you will not have to provide a password. The local database for OneWorld is an Access database, and it does not support password protection.

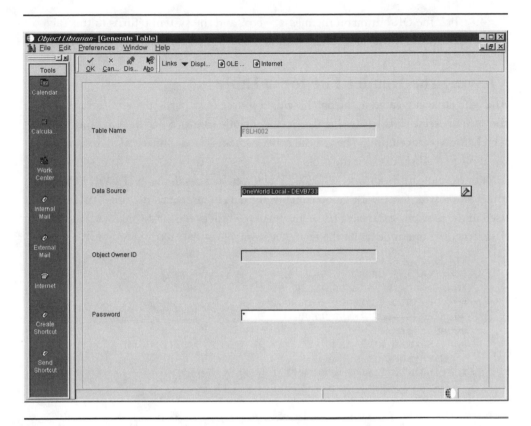

FIGURE 11-26. The Generate Table form of the Object Librarian application (P9860)

3. Click the OK button when you have finished, and the system will generate the table. When the table has been generated successfully, a message box appears to inform you.

4. Click the OK button on the message box, and the system returns to the Table Design Aid form, shown in Figure 11-23.

Viewing the Header File for a Table

After the table is created in the database data source for a particular environment, the system creates a C header file (.h) in the include directory for the environment in which you are developing. The C header file contains the definition of all data items in the table and all indexes for the table.

For example, the following FSLH002.h file, which exists in the \b7\DEVB733\include directory on your local workstation contains the data items, data structures, and indexes used in the previous examples. The contents of the header file for the table include the data structures and indexes for the table. The contents of FSLH002.h are shown here:

```
#ifndef __FSLH002__
#define __FSLH002__
#define DATA_VERSION_FSLH002   1
#define NID_FSLH002   "FSLH002"
#define STABLENAME_FSLH002   "FSLH002"
typedef struct {
#define NID_AN8   "AN8"
    MATH_NUMERIC   dqan8;
#define NID_SLH001   "SLH001"
    MATH_NUMERIC   dqslh001;
```

```
#define NID_SLH002  "SLH002"
    MATH_NUMERIC    dqslh002;
#define NID_SLH003  "SLH003"
    char            dqslh003[5];
#define NID_SLH004  "SLH004"
    char            dqslh004[5];
#define NID_SLH005  "SLH005"
    MATH_NUMERIC    dqslh005;
} FSLH002, FAR *LPFSLH002;

/* PRIMARY INDEX */
#define ID_FSLH002_AB_NBR__LINE_NBR  1L
typedef struct{
    MATH_NUMERIC    dqan8;
    MATH_NUMERIC    dqslh005;
} KEY1_FSLH002, FAR *LPKEY1_FSLH002;

#define ID_FSLH002_AB_NBR  2L
typedef struct {
    MATH_NUMERIC    dqan8;
} KEY2_FSLH002, FAR *LPKEY2_FSLH002;
#endif
```

In this section, we discussed how tables are constructed and generated in OneWorld. There are several issues, however, that affect how your tables are implemented in OneWorld; and they are discussed in the following Developer's Corner, titled "External Factors That Affect Table Design."

External Factors That Affect Table Design

Multiple databases can be integrated in OneWorld, but the functionality of the databases used will be limited to the capabilities of the least functional database.

For example, the Microsoft SQLServer has the lowest limits on the number and size of tables in a database, and therefore its limits become the limits for any database that operates in OneWorld. The database can only handle 2 billion tables per database. Each table can only handle 250 columns per table, and the maximum number of bytes per row is 1,962. If you exceed 1,962 bytes per row in a table, then the system produces an error message and the SQL statement fails.

When designing and implementing tables in OneWorld, there are a number of issues that you need to be aware of, relating to the following points:

- Applications and business functions

- Coexistence

- Microsoft Access database

- Microsoft SQLServer database

- IBM DB/2 database

- Oracle database

Issues Related to Applications and Business Functions

When applications and business functions need to access records from a table, it is more efficient for them to access only the records they need, instead of all the records in the table. The best way to limit the number of records the applications or business functions access is to build a secondary key that allows them to narrow the search down.

For example, an application needs to retrieve all records from the Address Book table (F0101) for employees that have the name John. The most efficient way to access the records is to search on the Address Type 1 Description Compress secondary key, which contains the Search Type data item (AT1) and the Compressed Description data item (DC).

For grids in forms that support them, it is crucial that the sort order of the grid match the sort order of the table. If the sort order does not match, then the system has to pause and sort the records to match the order defined in the grid. Therefore, you should create an index with the specific order you need for your applications.

For Find, Browse, Search, and Select forms in interactive applications, you can filter records in the grids of the forms by adding filter fields in the header portion of the form. However, the system will implicitly match the filter fields in the header to a secondary key in the table. If a match cannot be made, then the grid will not display any records. Therefore, for filtering records in the grid, you match the fields to a secondary key in the table.

Coexistence Issues

It is crucial that OneWorld and WorldSoftware tables match, because a mismatch will cause system and application errors. Any table that is modified in one system, such as WorldSoftware or OneWorld, the other definition for the table must be modified too. This includes the data item alias name and the column prefix used for the tables.

NOTE

The column prefix for tables in WorldSoftware have significance to the operation of its system, as opposed to OneWorld where they don't. This is due to the fact that the "Qx" series of column prefixes are reserved for client use only.

Microsoft Access Database Issues

Microsoft Access databases have the following limitations in OneWorld:

- Maximum number of indexes per table is 32.

- Maximum number of fields in an index is 10.

- Maximum number of fields in a record is 255.

- Maximum database size is 1GB.

Microsoft SQLServer Database Issues

Microsoft SQLServer databases have the following limitations in OneWorld:

- Maximum number of nonclustered (standard) indexes per table is 249.

- Maximum number of clustered indexes per table is 1.

- Maximum number of columns in a composite index is 16.

IBM DB/2 Database Issues

IBM DB/2 databases have the following limitations in OneWorld:

- Maximum number of identifiers for an index name is 10.

- Maximum size of an index is 1 TB.

- Maximum length of an index is 2,000 bytes.

- Maximum number of columns per index is 120.

- Maximum number of indexes per table is 4,000.

Oracle Database Issues

Oracle databases have the following limitations in OneWorld:

- Maximum length for an index is 254 bytes.

- Maximum number of columns per index is 16.

- Maximum index length is 900 bytes.

Business Views

All interactive and batch applications manipulate and access data from one or more tables by assigning business views to them. Business views provide access to data that is stored in a single column of a table or in many columns of several tables. The system uses business views to generate the appropriate structured query language (SQL) statements, which an application can then issue to a database.

DEFINITION

Structured Query Language (SQL) is an industry standard that uses statements to retrieve, insert, update, and delete data from one or many tables. The advantage of SQL statements is that they eliminate the need for applications to include file I/O routines to access the data stored in the tables, because the RDBMS manages that low-level file control.

Business views provide the link between the report or form you see on the computer screen and the data stored in a database, because they contain a list of data items and the tables to which they are assigned. As you assign business views to applications, the fields that are defined in the business view are automatically available for use in the applications.

Business views manage data at the application level by filtering out the columns in one or more tables that are used in the application. Using a business view to limit the number of columns retrieved ensures that only essential columns of data are transferred and the response time of the application is optimized.

Business views for two or more tables can also be used to enforce a relationship between the tables. For example, the Address Book table (F0101) and the Supplier Master table (F0401) are related through the Address Book Number data item (AN8), and frequently a business view join is used to extract information from both tables.

Relational Query Types

As mentioned earlier, business views that contain two or more joined tables enforce a relationship between the tables known as relational query. Relational queries define which rows are extracted from the tables that are assigned to a business view. There are three major types of relational queries for modern databases: join, union, and select distinct.

Joins

Joins identify the rows of information stored in tables that meet a specific search criteria. The search criteria contain the column restrictions of the tables, such as equals, greater than, or less than, that must be met in order for the row to qualify for a particular query. OneWorld supports three types of joins: simple, right, and left.

A simple join of two or more tables returns only the rows from the tables that explicitly match the criteria. The left-outer join of two tables returns rows from the tables that match the criteria, and all of the unmatched rows in the left table. The right-outer join returns rows from the tables that match the criteria, and all of the unmatched rows in the right table.

Unions

Unions include all of the rows for the tables assigned to the business view. This technique is not commonly used in applications, because a lot of the data that qualifies for a union of tables is redundant. Unions should be used only in applications that require virtually all of the data items in the business view.

Select Distinct

Select distinct is used for business views that contain tables with primary keys of more than one column, and it typically results in queries with redundant rows. The redundant data occurs when the search criteria don't restrict all columns in the primary key. The select distinct relational query ensures that all of the rows of data that meet the search criteria are unique.

Naming Convention of Business Views in OneWorld

The following guidelines are set forth by J.D. Edwards for naming business views in OneWorld. These guidelines can change from time to time, and therefore we recommend that you review the *OneWorld Application Design Standards Guide* from J.D. Edwards periodically.

The guidelines for the naming convention of business views is *Vsssstttt*, where *V* identifies that this is a business view, *ssss* is the view's product code, and *tttt* is a unique number or character sequence.

In this section, we discussed how business views are designed in OneWorld. There are several issues, however, that affect how your business views are implemented in OneWorld; and they are discussed in the following Developer's Corner, titled "Performance Considerations for Business Views."

Developer's Corner

Performance Considerations for Business Views

Properly designed business views can enhance the performance of your application. An application that uses a business view containing the same number of columns as there are fields in the application will ideally produce the best performance, because no unnecessary data is being transmitted over the network.

Each piece of information in a table is transmitted sequentially across the network. Thus, the amount of data that is transmitted across the network is determined by adding the binary lengths of each column and multiplying by the number of rows.

Therefore, to reduce the amount of data transmitted across the network you can limit either the number of records or columns transmitted across the network. This results in faster application response time..

For example, Table 11-11 compares the minimum delay time required for transmitting a single record over the network from the Address Book Master table (F0101), which has 77 columns. The comparison is made between two different business views: one that uses all columns in the table, and one that only uses nine columns from the table. As you can see, there is a substantial difference between the delay times, solely due to the fact that more data is being transmitted in one case than in the other.

Object	Number of Columns	Record Size (bits)	Minimum Delay Time on LAN (transmission rate = 10 Mbps)	Minimum Delay Time on WAN (transmission rate = 1.544 Mbps)	Minimum Delay Time on Dial Up (transmission rate = 56 Kbps)
Business vView for aAll cColumns in F0101	77	1027	0.0001 s	0.0065 ms	0.0185 s
Address Book Master Search business view (V0101C)	9	209	0.00002 s	0.00014 s	0.0035 s

TABLE 11-11. Comparison of Minimum Delay Time for Accessing One Record From Address Book Master table (F0101) With Two Different Business Views

The delay times may not be that noticeable for one record and one user in Table 11-11. However, the time delay becomes even longer when you consider that most applications access more than one table, and other message traffic on the network slows down the transmission rate.

Consider the following business view performance tips when you create applications:

- Take the time to determine what columns you really need for your applications. Trimmed-down business views help optimize applications and reduce unnecessary data transmission.

- Design business views for each application. This ensures that only the necessary data transmission will occur during application execution.

- Applications with grids generate the most data transmission in OneWorld. For grid-based applications, use business views that have at most the same number of data items as the grid has columns.

- Header and headerless detail forms have input-capable grids that require all of the items from the table to be displayed in the grid. Use as much filtering as possible on these forms to reduce the amount of data transmission.

- Search and Select forms are used only to identify data and select it. Use the minimum number of fields in a Search and Select form.

- For manipulating records in tables through Table I/O system calls, use a business view that minimizes the number of columns accessed by the call. Using direct table calls with Table I/O dramatically increases the transmission time required, because all columns are transmitted.

Creating Business Views

The following examples show you how to build, manipulate, and generate business views using the Business View Design Aid (BDA) tool. The examples assume that you have already created the table described earlier in this chapter. The business views that the BDA tool manipulates in these examples are the All Columns business view (VSLH002A) for the FSLH002 table and the join of F0101 and FSLH002 (VSLH002B).

Creating a Business View Object in the Object Librarian

Business view creation in OneWorld starts off by defining the Object Librarian record for the table. To create a business view object, complete the following steps:

1. Execute the Object Librarian application (P9860), and the Work With Object Librarian form appears, as shown in Figure 11-27.

2. In the Object Type field, type **BSVW**, and click the Add button. The Add Object form, shown in Figure 11-28, appears.

3. On the Add Object form, fill in the fields with the following information to create the Object Librarian record for the All Column View of FSLH002 (VSLH002A) business view.

Field	Value	Description
Object Name	VSLH002A	The unique identifler for the object in the system. It follows the naming convention mentioned in the preceding section.
Description	All Column View of FSLH002	A meaningful name for the object.
System Code and Reporting System Code	SLH	The module that the table is assigned to.
Column Prefix	DQ	The table column prefix is appended to every data item alias when the table is generated in a particular RDBMS.
SAR Number	1	The value that assigns the object to a specific development project, modification, or fix.

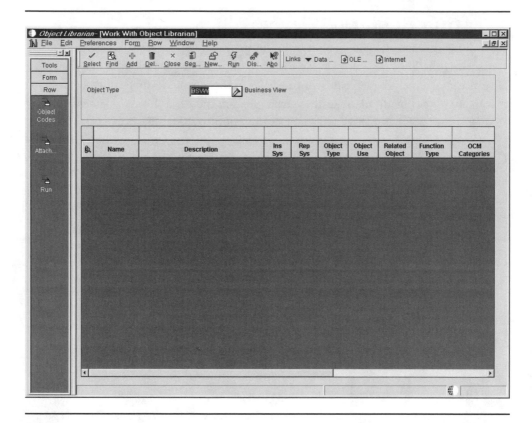

FIGURE 11-27.   The Work With Object Librarian form of the Object Librarian
application (P9860)

4. When you have finished, click the OK button. The Business View Design Aid
   form of the Object Librarian application appears, as shown in Figure 11-29. The
   object exists only on your workstation until you check the object into the
   environment in which you develop your applications.

5. After you finish defining the object for the All Column View of FSLH002
   (VSLH002A), repeat these steps for the other business view. The specifics on
   the next business view are as follows:

Field	Value	Description
Object Name	VSLH002B	The unique identifier for the object in the system. It follows the naming convention mentioned in the preceding section.

Field	Value	Description
Description	Join of F0101 and FSLH002	A meaningful name for the object.
System Code and Reporting System Code	SLH	The module that the table is assigned to.
Column Prefix	DQ	The table column prefix is appended to every data item alias when the table is generated in a particular RDBMS.
SAR Number	1	The value that assigns the object to a specific development project, modification, or fix.

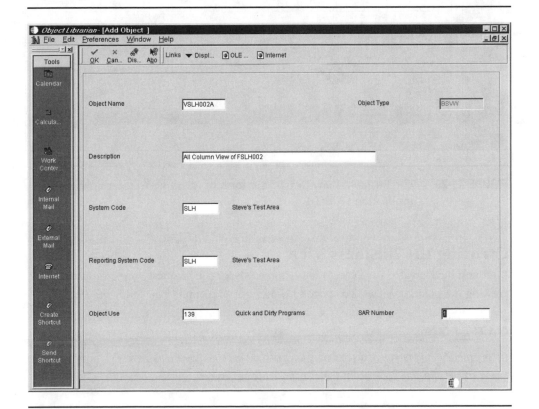

FIGURE 11-28.   The Add Object form of the Object Librarian application (P9860)

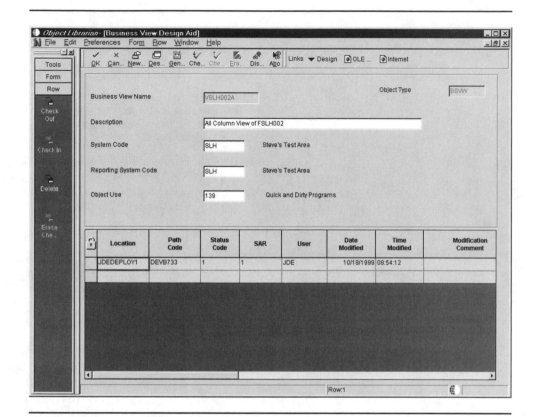

FIGURE 11-29.   The Business View Design Aid form of the Object Librarian
application (P9860)

Creating the Business View

After you have created the Object Librarian records for the business views, you can begin
creating the business views. To create a business view, complete the following steps:

CAUTION

*Do not modify the primary and secondary keys of the tables in a business view.
Doing so will affect all applications that use those tables.*

1. To begin designing the table, click the Design button on the Business View Design Aid form shown in Figure 11-29. The Business View Design window appears, as shown in Figure 11-30.

2. The Business View Design window contains three child windows:

Child Window	Description
Available Tables window	This window displays a QBE line that you use to find the tables that you want to insert into the business view.
Table Joins window	This window contains a list of all tables currently defined in the business view.

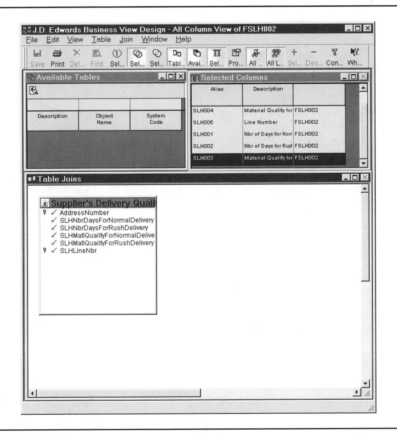

FIGURE 11-30.   The Business View Design window

Child Window	Description
Selected Columns window	This window contains a list of all columns that are currently selected for use in the business view and identifies the tables they belong to.

3. To add a table to the business view, find the table in the Available Tables window. You can find the table by using the QBE bar located in the window.

4. Drag and drop the table into the Table Joins window. In Figure 11-31, the Supplier's Delivery Quality table (FSLH002) is selected and placed in the Table Joins window.

5. To delete a table from the business view, highlight the table in the Table Joins window and click the Delete button.

6. To add a column from the Selected Columns window, double-click the column in the Table Joins window. The system adds a check mark to the left of the column to indicate that it has been selected. If you do not double-click columns in the Table Joins window, they will not be defined for use in the business view. For this example, all of the columns are selected.

7. Click the Save button before you exit so that your changes will be saved.

Creating a Table Join

The following steps show you how to create a table join using the BDA tool. If you have not looked at the previous example, please do so at this time because some of its material applies here. To create a table join with BDA, complete the following steps:

1. Open the Business View Design Aid form, shown in Figure 11-29, and click the Design button. The Business View Design window appears, as shown in Figure 11-31.

2. Choose the AddressNumber and NameAlpha columns from the Address Book table (F0101), and all of the columns in the Supplier's Delivery Quality table (FSLH002).

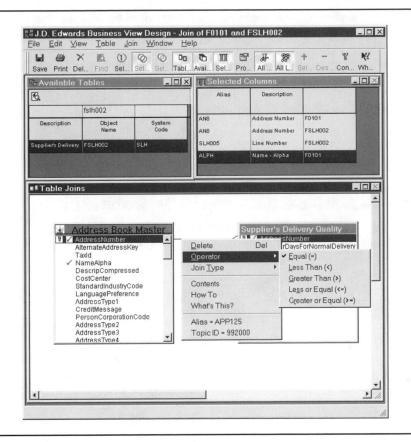

FIGURE 11-31. Placing the Supplier's Delivery Quality table in the Table Joins Window

3. To create a join between the two tables, highlight the AddressNumber column in the Address Book table (F0101), and drag it to the Supplier's Delivery Quality table (FSLH002). Drop the column on top of the AddressNumber column in the Supplier's Delivery Quality table (FSLH002). A one-to-many relationship sign appears between the two tables, as shown in Figure 11-31.

4. To define the relational query type for the join, right-click the relationship sign connecting the two tables. A pop-up menu appears, as shown in Figure 11-31.

5. Select the operator type and join type of the relationship. For this example, the join type is Simple, and the operator type is Equal.

6. Click the Save button on the toolbar before you exit so that your changes will be saved.

Generating a Business View

Generating a business view creates a header file (*.h). You do not have to generate business views for interactive and batch applications in OneWorld. However, you will need to generate the business view if you want to use the business view in a C-based business function. To generate a business view, complete the following steps:

1. Click the Generate button on the Business View Design Aid form, shown in Figure 11-29. When generation has finished, a message box appears stating that the business view was generated successfully.

2. To view the header file for the business view you just generated, go to the include directory for the environment. The header file for the VSLH002A business view is named BVSLH002A.h. Notice that the generation process added the letter B to the beginning of the object name for the business view.

3. The header file does not have any information about the tables where the data items originated, and therefore the use of the header file is minimal in most

C-based business functions. The contents of the header file for VSLH002A
are as follows:

```
#ifndef __VSLH002A__
#define __VSLH002A__
#define DATA_VERSION_VSLH002A  1
#define ID_BVSLH002A  "VSLH002A"
#define STABLENAME_BVSLH002A  "BVSLH002A"
typedef struct {
#define NID_AN8  "AN8"
      MATH_NUMERIC    dqan8;
#define NID_SLH001  "SLH001"
      MATH_NUMERIC    dqslh001;
#define NID_SLH002  "SLH002"
      MATH_NUMERIC    dqslh002;
#define NID_SLH003  "SLH003"
      char            dqslh003[5];
#define NID_SLH004  "SLH004"
      char            dqslh004[5];
#define NID_SLH005  "SLH005"
      MATH_NUMERIC    dqslh005;
} BVSLH002A, FAR *LPBVSLH002A;
#endif
```

Now that we have covered the basic objects that are required to build the Supplier's
Delivery Quality application, the following Developer's Corner, titled "The Missing
GUI Application Example," shows you how to finish constructing the application.

The Missing GUI Application Example

In this chapter, we showed you how to create the necessary OneWorld objects that comprise the Supplier's Delivery Quality application. However, we have not discussed the development of the application itself. The focus of this Developer's Corner is to show you the application and how it is built.

We realize that the detailed steps involved in building interactive applications have been covered in previous chapters, but we want to show you how quickly you can create an application and all of its corresponding objects. This exercise will show you the relative ease of the final steps in building the application.

The first step in creating the Supplier's Delivery Quality application is to create the application object in the Object Librarian (P9860). This is accomplished by executing the Object Librarian application (P9860) and clicking the Add button. Then, complete the fields on the Add Object form of the Object Librarian application, as shown in the Figure 11-32.

After you have finished filling in the fields on the Add Object form, click the OK button. The Application Design Aid form of the Object Librarian application appears, as shown in Figure 11-33.

The object currently resides on your local client workstation and will only be available for others after you check-in the object. To launch FDA to design the Supplier's Delivery Quality application, click the Design button.

We explained how to use FDA in previous chapters, so the steps on how to build this application are not covered. However, a discussion of the forms that were required and the supporting software code that was needed will be outlined in the following paragraphs.

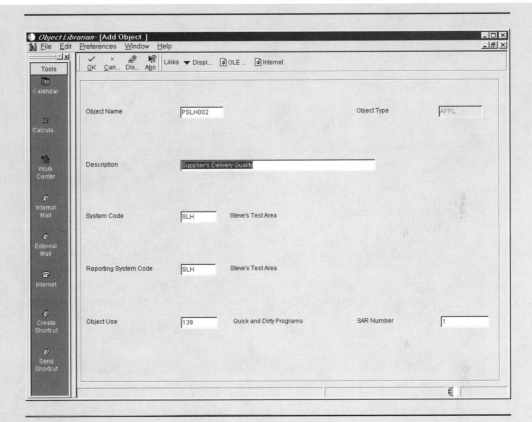

FIGURE 11-32. The Add Object form of the Object Librarian application (P9860)

The first form that was created was the Find/Browse form, shown in Figure 11-34. The form has only one filter field, which is the Address Number in the header. The filter field is used to show all of the shipments made by the supplier when the Find

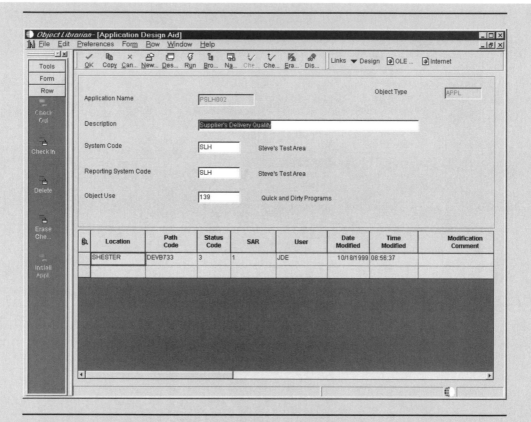

FIGURE 11-33. The Application Design Aid form of the Object Librarian application (P9860)

button is clicked. Each record in the grid represents one shipment and lists the quality of the receivables and number of days it took for normal or rush delivery. Add and Delete buttons were added to the form as well.

Developer's Corner

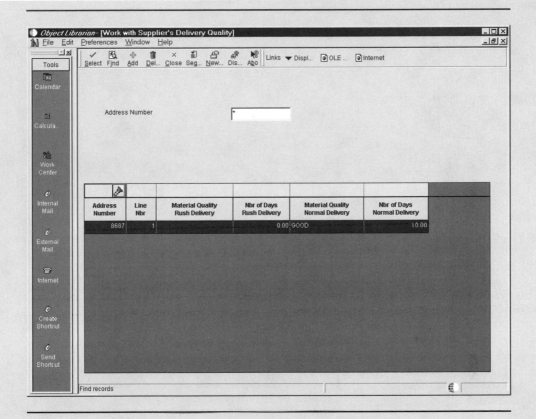

FIGURE 11-34. The Work With Supplier's Material Quality form for the new application

The only software code written for the Find/Browse form was the form interconnect statements for the Select and Add buttons. Both buttons launch the second form that was created for the application, which is the Supplier's Material Quality Revisions form shown in Figure 11-35.

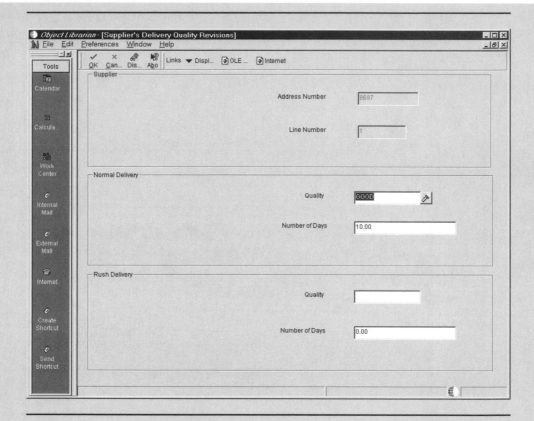

FIGURE 11-35. The Supplier's Material Quality Revisions form for the new application

This second form provides fields for adding or modifying the data for a particular record. The Quick Form technique was used to place the fields on the form, and then the fields were adjusted manually. No software code is written for this form.

Therefore, only two lines of code were needed for the Supplier's Delivery Quality application, and some minor tweaking was performed for cosmetic reasons. The entire time taken to build the application, starting from the UDCs, all the way to adding the application to the menu, was about an hour.

Menus

Applications must be attached to menus in OneWorld Explorer before users can access them. The primary purpose of menus is to logically arrange all of the applications in OneWorld Explorer, launch the application when selected, and provide security for certain menus.

Menus are the entry points to applications. The types of applications that menus can execute are: interactive and batch applications; WorldSoftware applications and reports; Windows applications; OneWorld-based Web applications; and other OneWorld menus.

Menus provide security features based on the user ID. This allows administrators and developers to maintain a single set of menus that are available for use, and then to restrict access for groups or individual users. For example, employees within a Human Resources department would be the only users to have access to the Human Resources Management menu, which may contain applications with confidential employee information.

The tables identified in Table 11-12 are used by the system to support menus.

Creating Menus in OneWorld

The following three examples show you how to build and manipulate menus that will launch OneWorld and non-OneWorld applications, by using the Menu Design tool. In particular, the examples show you how to attach the Supplier's Delivery Quality application to a menu in OneWorld Explorer.

Object Name	Description	Purpose
F0082	Menu Master	This table stores all of the definitions for menus.
F00821	Menu Selection	This table stores all of the menu-selection definitions.
F0083	Menu Text Override	This table provides the override text for menu-selection descriptions.
F0084	Menu Path	This table stores the icon definitions used for menu selections.

TABLE 11-12.   OneWorld Tables That Store Menus and Menu Selections

Advanced Application Development

Creating a Menu

The first step in creating menu items that launch applications in OneWorld Explorer is to define a menu on which you can place the menu items. Menus are used to group both applications and other menus, and when they are designed properly, they allow users to easily find the applications they need to perform their daily tasks. To create a menu, complete the following steps:

1. In OneWorld Explorer, type **GH9011** into the Fast Path box and press ENTER. The System Administration Tools menu (GH9011) appears.

2. Double-click the Menu Design application (P0082), and the Work With Menus form appears, as shown in Figure 11-36.

3. To add a new menu, click the Add button on the Work With Menus form, shown in Figure 11-36. The Menu Header Revisions form appears, as in Figure 11-37.

4. Enter the following information into the Menu Header Revisions form:

Field	Value	Description
Menu Identification	GSLH	The unique identifier for the menu in the system.
Menu Title	Special Programs	The description for the menu.
System Code	SLH	The module that the menu is assigned to.
Menu Classification	1	This field defined the type of menu that you are creating, and it is one of five values defined in the UDC (98/MN). This field has a value of 1 for OneWorld master menus; a value of 2 for company master menus; a value of 3 for personal menus; a value of 4 for Rumba menus; and a value of 5 for custom menus.
Level of Display		The Level of Display field contains a number identifying the logical level at which the menu is displayed. The values are Basic Operations (1), Intermediate Operations (2), Advanced Operations (3), Computer Operations (4), Programmers (5), and Senior Programmers (6).
Advanced Technical Operations		This field defines the menu selection that is used for the Advanced Technical Operations for a module.
Setup Menu		This field defines the menu selection that is used for the Setup Menu for a module.

5. Click the OK button when you have finished, and the system returns to the Work With Menus form. Type **GSLH** into the System Code field, and click the

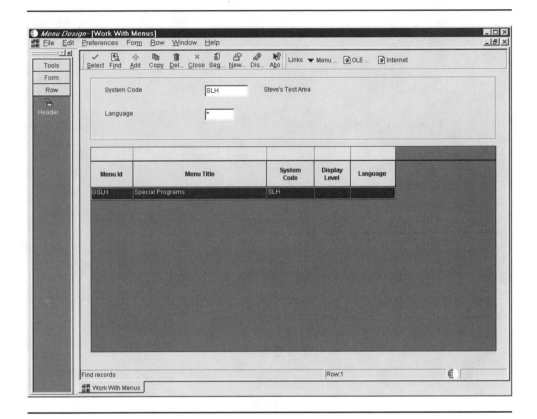

FIGURE 11-36.   The Work With Menus form of the Menu Design application (P0082)

Find button. If you created the menu properly, your menu will appear on the Work With Menus form, as shown in Figure 11-36.

6. To verify the proper operation of the new menu, type **GSLH** in the Fast Path box of OneWorld Explorer, and a menu should appear with no menu selections in it.

Creating a Menu Selection for a Windows Application

The following steps show you how to create a menu selection for a Windows application. After you create it, you will attach it to the menu you created in the previous example. Any Windows application can be launched from OneWorld

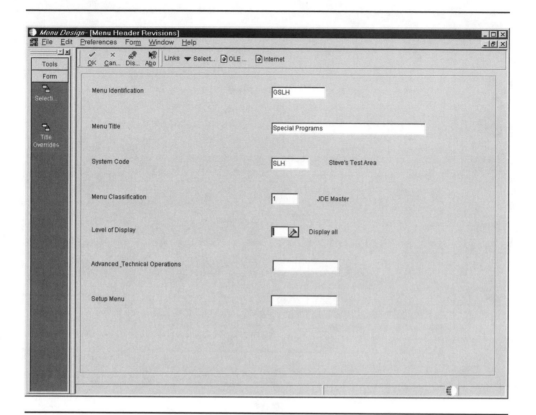

FIGURE 11-37. The Menu Header Revisions form of the Menu Design application (P0082)

Explorer, which can be extremely helpful to users who spend most of their day working inside OneWorld.

To create a menu selection for a Windows application, complete the following steps:

1. On OneWorld Explorer, type **GH9011** into the Fast Path box, and press ENTER. The System Administration Tools menu (GH9011) appears.

2. Double-click the Menu Design application (P0082), and the Work With Menus form appears, as shown in Figure 11-36.

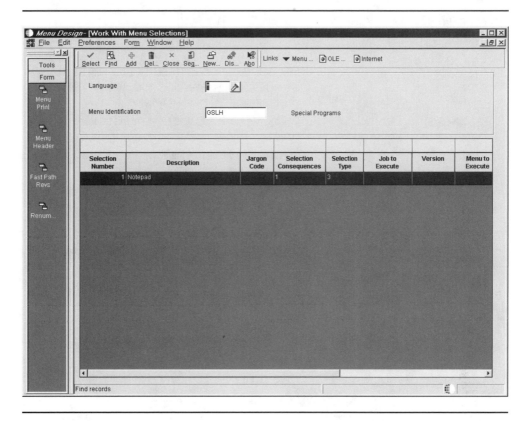

FIGURE 11-38.   The Work With Menu Selections form of the Menu Design application (P0082)

3. Type **GSLH** into the System Code field, and click the Find button. Highlight the Special Programs menu (GSLH), and click the Select button. The Work With Menu Selections form appears, as shown in Figure 11-38.

4. Click the Add button on the Work With Menu Selections form, and the Menu Selection Revisions form appears, as shown in Figure 11-39.

5. To create the definition of the menu selection, enter the following information into the Menu Selection Revisions form.

Field	Value	Description
Selection Number	1	The Selection Number field contains a unique number that you assign to identify the menu selection. By typing the combination of menu selection and menu (1GSLH) into the Fast Path box in OneWorld Explorer, you can launch the application without having to navigate through various menus.
Selection Description	Notepad	This is the title that is displayed for this menu selection on the menu.
Selection Consequences	1	This field notifies the user of the action that will happen when they select this menu selection.
Jargon Code		This field designates the product code that the text is assigned to.

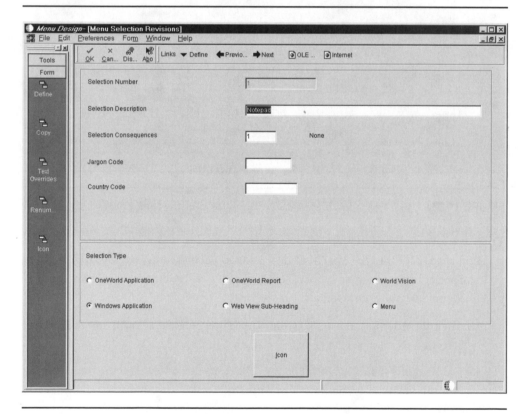

FIGURE 11-39.   The Menu Selection Revisions form of the Menu Design application (P0082)

Field	Value	Description
Country Code		This is used to define the country that the menu is assigned to.
Selection Type	Windows Application	This field defines the type of object that is launched by the menu: interactive and batch applications; WorldSoftware applications and reports; Windows applications; OneWorld-based Web applications; or other OneWorld mMenus.

6. Now that you have defined the menu selection, you need to assign the application to it. From the Form menu, choose Define. The Windows Application form appears, as shown in Figure 11-40.

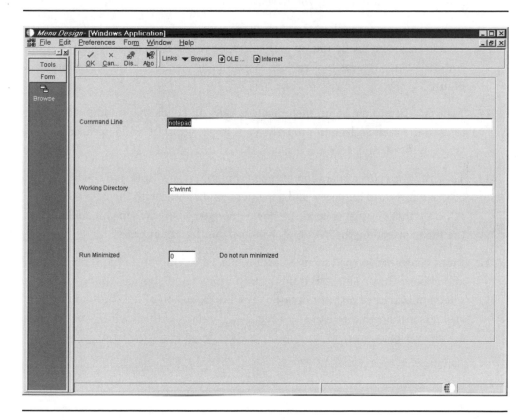

FIGURE 11-40. The Windows Application form of the Menu Design application (P0082)

7. To define which Windows application will execute when a user double-clicks the menu selection, enter the following information:

Field	Value	Description
Command Line	notepad	The name of the executable file.
Working Directory	C:\WINNT, (or your main Windows directory)	The directory where the executable file resides.
Run Minimized	0	This field specifies whether the system should start up the application as a minimized icon (1) or not (0).

8. Click the OK button when you have finished.

9. The system returns to the Menu Selection Revisions form, shown in Figure 11-39. To accept the definition of the new menu selection, click the OK button, and the system returns to the Work With Menu Selections form, shown in Figure 11-38.

10. Type **GSLH** into the Menu Identification field, and click the Find button. If you created the menu selection properly, your menu selection will appear in the Work With Menu Selections form, as shown in Figure 11-38.

11. To verify the proper operation of the new menu, type **GSLH** into the Fast Path box of OneWorld Explorer, and a menu should appear with the new menu selection that you just created, as shown in Figure 11-41. When you double-click the menu selection, the Windows Notepad application appears.

12. Right-click the Notepad menu selection located in OneWorld Explorer, and choose Create Shortcut from the pop-up menu. A shortcut to the menu selection is created on your desktop. The file extension of the shortcut is *.jde, and it is nothing more than a text file. The contents of the text file, notepad.jde, are shown as follows:

```
[OneWorld.Application]
Menu=GSLH
Selection=1
IsMenu=0
IconFile=D:\B7\DEVB733\res\ICONS\
IconIndex=0
```

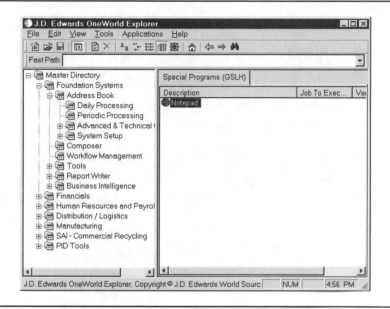

FIGURE 11-41. The Special Programs menu (GSLH) after adding a Windows application menu selection

As you can see from the code, the definition that you just created for the menu selection is included. The definition contains enough information to launch the application from your desktop. All you need to launch an application is the combination of menu selection and menu, which is 1GSLH in this example.

T I P

*You can execute any *.jde file at the MS-DOS command line to begin executing a OneWorld application. To execute the notepad.jde file at the command line, type the following: **Oexplore.exe notepad.jde**.*

Creating a Menu Selection for a OneWorld Application

The following steps show you how to create a menu selection for a OneWorld application. After you create it, you will attach it to the menu you created earlier. The application that this menu selection will launch is discussed in the Developer's

Corner titled "The Missing GUI Application Example," earlier in this chapter. To create the menu selection, complete the following steps:

1. On OneWorld Explorer, type **GH9011** into the Fast Path box, and press the ENTER key. The System Administration Tools menu (GH9011) appears.

2. Double-click the Menu Design application (P0082), and the Work With Menus form appears, as shown earlier in Figure 11-36.

3. Type **GSLH** into the Sytem Code field, and click the Find button.

4. Highlight the Special Programs menu (GSLH), and click the Select button. The Work With Menu Selections form appears, as shown in Figure 11-38.

5. Click the Add button on the Work With Menu Selections form, and the Menu Selection Revisions form appears, as shown in Figure 11-39.

6. Enter the following information into Menu Selection Revisions form:

Field	Value	Description
Selection Number	2	The Selection Number field contains a unique number that you assign to identify the menu selection. By typing the combination of menu selection and menu (2GSLH) into the Fast Path box in OneWorld Explorer you can launch the application without having to navigate through various menus.
Selection Description	Supplier's Delivery Quality	The title that is displayed for this menu selection on the menu.
Selection Consequences	1	This field notifies the user of the action that will happen when they select this menu selection.
Jargon Code		This field designates the product code that the text is assigned to.
Country Code		This is used to define the country that the menu is assigned to.
Selection Type	OneWorld Application	This field defines the type of object that is launched by the menu: interactive and batch applications; WorldSoftware applications and reports; Windows applications; OneWorld-based web applications; and other OneWorld menus.

7. Now that you have defined the menu selection, you need to assign the application to it. From the Form menu, choose Define, and the OneWorld Application form appears, as shown in Figure 11-42.

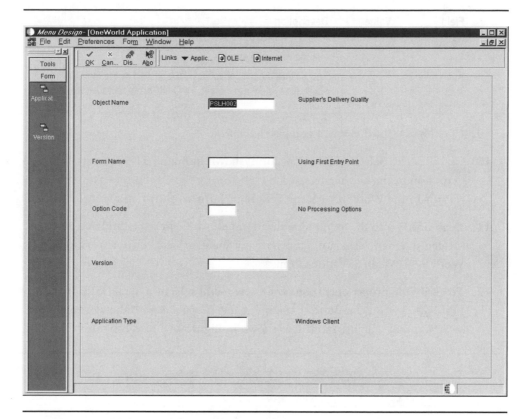

FIGURE 11-42. The OneWorld Application form of the Menu Design application (P0082)

8. To define which OneWorld application to execute when the menu selection is executed, enter the following information into the OneWorld Application form.

Field	Value	Description
Object Name	PSLH002	The object name of the application.
Form Name		The form name of the application, if you do not intend to execute the entry point form of the application.
Option Code	0	This field is used to prompt the user for additional information: processing options (0), blind execution (1), prompt for version (2), or prompt for values (3).

Field	Value	Description
Version		If the application has any versions attached to it, then enter the specific version to execute.
Application Type		This defines the type of application launched by the menu. If left blank, the system assumes it is a OneWorld application that is launched.

9. Click the OK button when you have finished.

10. On the Menu Selection Revisions form, shown in Figure 11-39, accept the definition of the new menu selection by clicking the OK button. The system returns to the Work With Menu Selections form, as shown in Figure 11-38.

11. Type **GSLH** into the Menu Identification field, and click the Find button. If you created the menu selection properly, your menu selection will appear in the Work With Menu Selections form.

12. To verify the proper operation of the new menu selection, type **GSLH** in the Fast Path box on OneWorld Explorer. A menu appears with the new menu selection that you just created, as shown in Figure 11-43. When you

FIGURE 11-43. The Special Programs menu (GSLH) after adding a OneWorld application menu selection

double-click the Supplier's Delivery Quality menu selection, the OneWorld application should appear.

Putting It All Together

The focus of this chapter is on how you construct the objects, such as tables, business views, and menus, that are used to support interactive and batch applications in OneWorld. These objects have a high degree of reusability, because the same object is usable for many interactive and batch applications.

Figure 11-1 provides you with a schematic diagram of the architecture for applications in OneWorld, which starts at OneWorld Explorer and drills down to the Data Dictionary. Application development, however, starts at the lowest level of the application architecture and works its way up to OneWorld Explorer. The Supplier's Delivery Quality application, which is the central example for this chapter, illustrates how the application development process progresses from start to finish: from UDCs, to next numbers, to tables, to business views, and finally to menus.

The rest of the chapters in this book build on the topics discussed in this chapter. Therefore, a thorough knowledge of this chapter's content is required.

CHAPTER 12

Processing Options

Processing options are a feature of OneWorld software that allow you to add subtle or large changes to your applications without changing the code. Processing options are used to pass default values, processing information, or display rules into an application or report. The processing option values can be configured by the user to meet specific business needs. For example, a user can change a processing option to control what is printed in a report.

A processing option is made up of a Data Dictionary item and a text description. A group of processing options is referred to as a *processing option template*, or sometimes simply as application processing options.

To help you understand how you can use processing options to increase the flexibility of your programs, the following topics are covered in this chapter:

- **Overview of Processing Options**   This overview explains the uses of processing options and describes the different categories of processing options.

- **Creating Processing Options**   To create a processing option template, you choose Data Dictionary items and add these items to a template.

- **Attaching Processing Options to Applications**   After you have created your processing option template, you need to attach the template to an application in order to allow the application to use the processing options.

- **Adding Logic to Use Processing Option Variables**   You need to add logic in order to use the processing options attached to an application. This logic is added to the application using Event Rules (ER).

- **Using Processing Options at Runtime**   After you've done all of the work, the processing options are ready to be configured and loaded with values. Processing options can be changed by using versions or by prompting for values when the application starts.

Overview of Processing Options

When users run an application or report, they often want to process certain information differently to suit their current needs. For example, they may want to alter data that prints on a report or change information that appears in an interactive application. The user could create multiple reports or applications to meet every business need, but this solution would be very time-consuming. The user could modify the code in the report each time to display different information, but this would be difficult for a typical user to do. To simplify the process of altering reports and applications to meet specific business needs, OneWorld provides processing options, which allow users to pass values into an application or report, so that they can change the way that information is displayed or processed based on their requirements.

The user can configure a set of processing options that is attached to an application or batch application. Inside the ER for an application, you can use these processing options to avoid needing to hard-code values or create different applications.

Uses of Processing Options

As a general rule, you should create processing options for anything that the user might want to configure within an interactive or batch application, including the appearance or processing of the application. Processing options apply to the entire application or report, not just a single form or section. You need to be sure your design takes this into consideration.

Processing options can be very beneficial to the user, but they can also become difficult to manage. If your application has too many processing options, it can become hard for the user to understand and set up. There needs to be a balance between the flexibility that your application or report provides and the functionality the user can understand.

N O T E

Not all interactive and batch applications use processing options. If your application is very simple, you may not need to use them.

The following are some common uses of processing options:

- **Provide default values**   You can add a processing option that will be used as a default value. The value that is placed inside a processing option usually will be assigned to a form field. For example, if an application has a default order type processing option, the application can assign this value to a form field, so users don't need to type this value in every time they create a new order.

Advanced Application Development

- **Limit what a user can do**   Default values can also be used to prevent users from changing certain values. For example, certain orders may have a status that describes the current stage of the order. You can design your application to only allow the user to modify orders that are less than the processing option status. To do this, the application can disable a grid line that has a status that is invalid (if the grid line status is less than the processing option), or the application can set an error if the user tries to modify an order with an invalid status.

- **Control what is displayed inside of an application or report**   Processing options can be created to hide certain information. For example, a user may want to configure a financial report to only display information over a certain calculated dollar value. During the processing of the report, if the calculated dollar value is less than the processing option value, the report will suppress the printing of that information. As another example, an application might display product and cost information, but in some cases you want to hide the cost information. To do this, you would use a processing option that could be configured to hide or show cost information. Then you could create two versions of the application with different processing option values.

- **Change how calculations are performed**   Processing options are useful for adapting calculations to specific needs. For example, one branch of your company might need to include overhead or transfer costs in a calculation, while another branch may not need to include those costs. To do this, you would need several processing options to allow the user to configure what to include in the calculation.

- **Determine acceptable criteria for a transaction**   Processing options also can be used to validate transactions. For example, you may not want your application to allow the inventory level to go below zero. By adding a processing option to validate this, you can allow the user to configure the application. If the transaction is invalid, the application should set an error.

Categories of Processing Options

You can use processing options for a wide variety of functions. Table 12-1 describes common categories of processing options.

Use	Description
Defaults	You can add processing options that will deliver default values.
Display	You can create processing options that allow the user to hide or show fields (or tabs) in an application. You can also enable or disable fields on a form based on values the user places in the processing options.
Versions	If your program calls other interactive or batch applications, you can add a processing option that allows users to choose which version of the interactive or batch application they want to use. For example, if batch application R550012 calls R550013, you can add a processing option for a version of R550013 to ensure that R550012 will call the correct version of R550013.
Interoperability	Some applications write information to interoperability tables. Each of these tables is a different transaction type. Instead of hard-coding this value, you can create a processing option that contains the transaction type. (See Chapter 14 for more information about interoperability.)
Process	This is a broad category that deals with how the application or batch application will process.
Edits	This is used to specify whether or not to perform editing on fields.
Currency	Any processing that deals with currency is placed in this category.
Print	This is used with batch applications to allow the user to configure how a report will print.

TABLE 12-1.   Generic Processing Option Categories

Advanced Application Development

Creating Processing Options

Creating a set of processing options is similar to creating any other object in OneWorld. Before you start to develop your processing options, you must first decide on what Data Dictionary items you want to use. After you have chosen the Data Dictionary items, you can create the processing option template.

As described in the previous section, processing options usually fall into groups (such as defaults, displays, and versions). You use tabs to organize your processing options into these groups. An example of a finished processing option template is shown here:

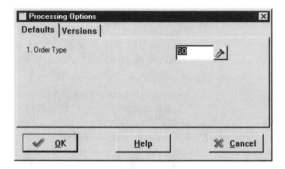

As you can see, the template contains several parts, including fields for user input, descriptions for each field, and the tabs for grouping the processing options.

This section describes how to create a process option template by selecting Data Dictionary items, creating the processing option template object in the Object Librarian, and designing the template.

Choosing Your Data Dictionary Items

Each field in a processing option template uses a Data Dictionary item. Any data items you add to a processing option template will include the same behavior that is set up in the Data Dictionary. For example, if you add an item that validates against a UDC table, it will perform the same function in the processing option template.

To decide which Data Dictionary items to use, you need to know how your processing options will be used. For example, if you want to create a default value for a sales order type (data item DCTO), you should include data item DCTO in your template. If you want to add a flag that will be used as an on/off switch for viewing information, you could either create a new data item (which we recommend) or use a generic item, such as EV01. The drawback to using generic items is that users might not easily understand what to enter in the field, because generic items do not contain a glossary or valid values.

NOTE

You cannot attach ERs to processing options. You will need to create new data items if you want to perform special validation against the item. For example, you may need to create a new data item that validates the information that a user enters in a field.

Creating the Processing Option Template in the Object Librarian

You perform two steps to create the template: you create the object in the Object Librarian, and then you design the template itself. When you create an object in Object Librarian, you need to give it a name. You can use any name for the template; however, the convention is to use the same name as your application or report, except start it with a *T* instead of a *P* or an *R*. For example, if your application is P550002, your processing option template is named T550002. Following this standard makes it easy to see which template goes with which application.

To create a new processing option template, follow these steps:

1. In the Object Librarian, create a new object of type DSTR. To do this, type **DSTR** in the Object Type field and click Add, as shown in Figure 12-1.

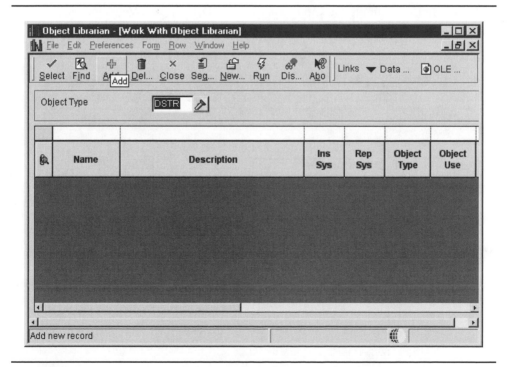

FIGURE 12-1. Adding a new object of type DSTR

2. Enter a name for your processing option template in the Object Name field.

3. Enter a description in the Description field. The description should be the same as the description of the application or report to which this template will be attached.

4. Enter the system code in both the Product Code and Product System Code fields. In this example, we used system code **55**.

5. Type **360** in the Object Use field. The value 360 is used for data structures.

6. Type **2** in the Structure Type field to specify that this is a processing option template. Figure 12-2 shows the completed Add Object form.

7. Click OK.

Designing a Processing Option Template

After you have created the template, you need to add the tabs and data items to the template. In this example, we will create two tabs: Defaults and Versions.

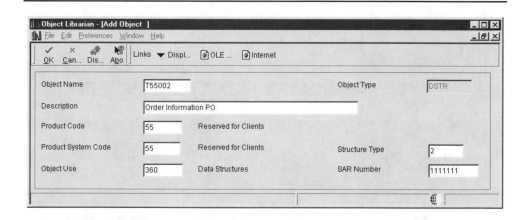

FIGURE 12-2.   The Add Object form for a processing option template

1. From the Object Librarian, click Design to start creating your template. Your form should look similar to Figure 12-3.

2. To begin, we will add the data item DCTO to the template. Type **DCTO** in the Alias field in the Data Dictionary Browser form and press ENTER.

3. Drag and drop the item from the grid on the right side of the screen to the form on the left side (or double-click the item). This will create a processing option field, as shown in Figure 12-4.

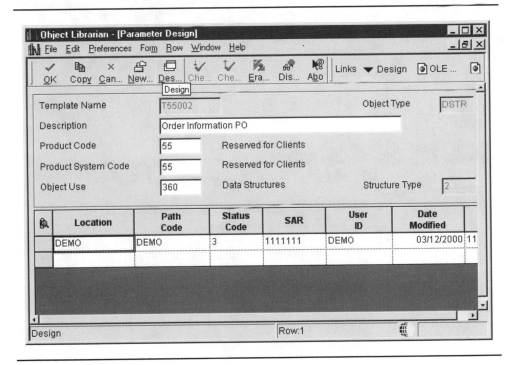

FIGURE 12-3. The processing option design form

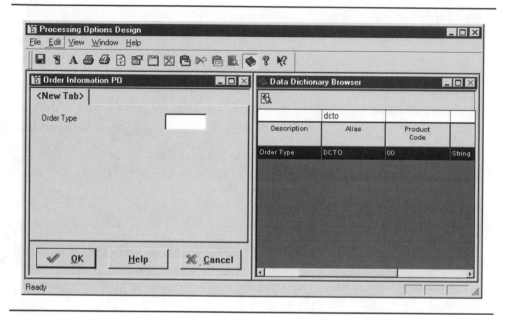

FIGURE 12-4.   The DCTO data item as a field on the processing option template

4. Right-click the data item on the template and select Properties from the menu to display the JDE.DataItem Properties form, as shown here:

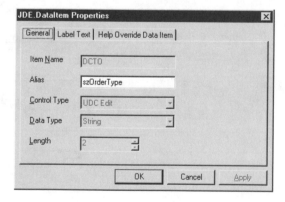

You can change the item name, label text, or override the Data Dictionary item. Make changes if necessary, and then click OK. The data item properties are explained in more detail in the next section.

5. Double-click the data item description in the option template to see an editing box in which you can change the description, as shown in Figure 12-5. The default description for the item is the Data Dictionary description. You can enter a more detailed description if necessary. To exit editing mode for the item, click another location on the form. Changing the description is explained in more detail in the next section.

If you want to add more fields to this tab, repeat steps 2 through 5.

T I P

You can add as many fields as you want, but you should try to keep the number of fields on a processing option tab on one page. This will allow the user to quickly review the options on each tab, without needing to scroll though all of the options on one tab.

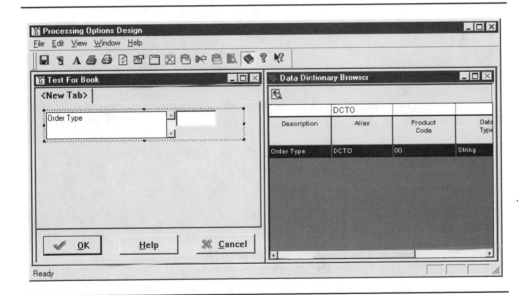

FIGURE 12-5. Changing the data item description

Advanced Application Development

6. To change the name of this tab, right-click the tab and select Current Tab Properties from the menu. You will see the Tab Properties form, as shown here:

Tab Properties	☒
Short Name	Defaults
Long Name	Defaults values
Tab Topic ID	3005500201 Override
Help File Name	
OK	Cancel

7. We will name this tab Defaults. Enter **Defaults** in the Short Name field and **Defaults values** in the Long Name field. Click OK.

T I P

For tab names, you should use one of the categories listed in Table 12-1, such as Defaults or Currency. If you give the tab another name, try to make it descriptive to help the user understand what this tab is used for. However, you also need to make sure that the title fits on the tab. A longer description helps the user understand what this tab is used for.

8. To add a new tab, choose New Tab from the Edit menu. Type **Versions** in the Short Name field and the Long Name field. Click OK.

9. Add the data item VER1 (Version) to the tab, as described in steps 2-5. In our example, this field will contain a version when the application calls Purchase Order Entry. The properties of this item are shown in Figure 12-6.

10. After you have finished adding your processing options, choose File | Save, and then choose File | Exit.

Changing Data Item Properties

As you saw in the previous example, the Properties form for a data item has three tabs that contain properties you can set for the data item. Through the General tab, you can change the name of the item; the other fields are defined in the Data Dictionary and can't be changed. Each of the data items in the processing option template is named. In some cases, you may want to change this name to something more descriptive. For

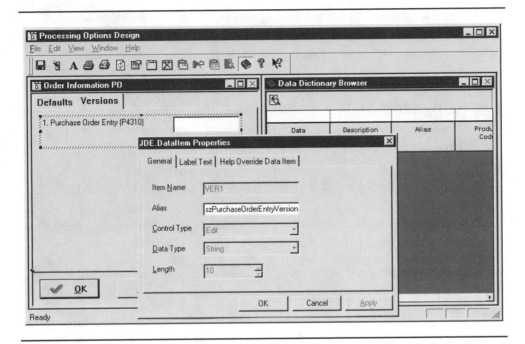

FIGURE 12-6.   The properties for the VER1 item

example, in more complex applications that contain many similar items, you will need to create a descriptive name in order to tell them apart in ER (in ER, you only see the field name).

The Label Text tab displays the description of the control. You can change the description here, as well as by double-clicking the data item on the form.

The Help Override Data Item tab, shown here, allows you to override the definition for this item to use a different Data Dictionary item:

To use another Data Dictionary item, simply type in the name of the Data Dictionary item you want to use. For example, the Data Dictionary item EV01 does not have any help text, so you might want to override this to use the help text for another data item.

Changing Data Item Descriptions

You may want to change the default description for the data item to provide a more informative description, such as to include valid values or information about the application it will affect. To change the description, simply double-click the text, and then type in a more detailed description. You have quite a bit of room to enter descriptive text.

Providing an adequate description is an important part of creating your processing options. Here are some examples of descriptions you might provide:

- If the processing option is a version of another application you will be calling, include the name of the application and the object name. For example, the description might read "Purchase Order (P4310)."

- If the field is used as an on/off switch, state what the valid values mean. For example, the description could be "To display the date, type 1; if blank, the date will not be displayed."

- If you want the processing options on each tab to be numbered, you can add a number to the description.

Adding a Comment to a Processing Option Template

You can add comments in your template to provide additional information about what the processing options will do. A comment is simply a control that contains only text.

To add a comment, follow these steps:

1. Select the tab you want to add the comment to by clicking it, and then select Edit | New Comment.

2. Place the comment on your form by clicking on the form (see Figure 12-7).

3. Double-click the comment to change the text, as shown in Figure 12-8. To exit editing mode for the comment, click another location on the form.

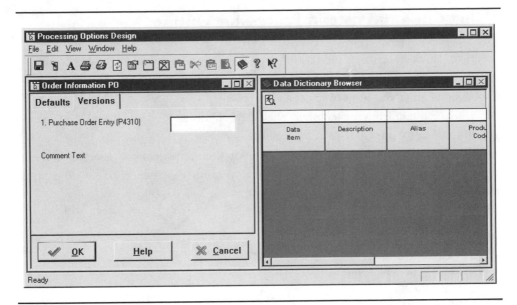

FIGURE 12-7.   The comment control placed on the form

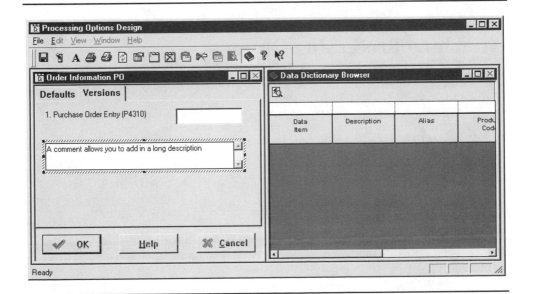

FIGURE 12-8.   The comment's edit control

Using Cut and Paste in Processing Options

You can cut and paste items to remove or move items in your processing option template. However, cutting and pasting processing option items is slightly different from cutting and pasting other types of items, because you have the extra step of choosing whether you want to select an item or a tab.

To cut an item from the template, click the field or the tab that you want to cut and select Edit | Cut. You will see a submenu with the options Item and Tab. If you select Tab, the entire tab will be removed. If you choose Item, the item you selected on the form will be cut. If you want to paste the item on another tab, you can select the tab and choose Edit | Paste.

Attaching Processing Options to Applications

After you've created your processing option template, your next step is to attach the template to an application, as described in this section. Then you need to add logic so that the processing options will be used in the application, as explained in the next section.

Attaching Processing Options to an Interactive Application

In this example, we are attaching the processing option template T55002 to the application P55002. To attach the processing options to the application, follow these steps:

1. From the Object Librarian, find and select the application that you want to attach the processing options to, and then click the Design button.

2. In Form Design Aid, choose Application | Select Processing Options.

3. In the Select Processing Option Template form, find and select the template you want to attach to the application. In our example, we select T55002, as shown next.

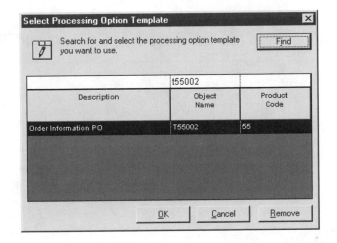

4. Click OK. The processing options are now attached to your application.

N O T E

Processing options apply to the entire application or report. They are not tied to a specific form or section.

Attaching Processing Options to a Batch Application

Attaching processing options to a report is similar to attaching processing options to an application. Processing options apply to the entire report, not just a particular section, so any processing options will be available to every section. (For more information about batch applications, see Chapter 6.)

In this example, we will attach the processing option template T55003 to batch application R55003. These processing options will be used by the application to control how the report is processed. To attach the processing options to the report, follow these steps:

1. From the Object Librarian, find and select the batch application to which you want to attach your processing options, and click the Design button, as shown in Figure 12-9.

2. In Report Design Aid, choose Report | Select Processing Options.

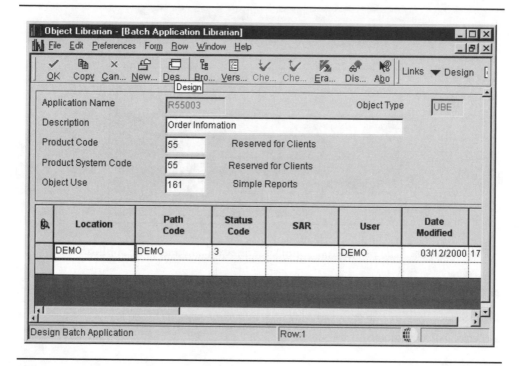

FIGURE 12-9.   The Batch Application Librarian form

3. In the Select Processing Option Template form, find and select the processing options you want to attach to the application. In this example, we select T55003.

4. Click OK. The processing options are now attached to your report.

Adding Logic to Use Processing Option Variables

When you attach a processing option template to an application or report, new variables are created. You need to provide the logic so that the application or report will use these variables to produce the effects you desire. You provide this logic through ER. (Using ER is discussed in detail in Chapter 7.)

The new variables are the fields that you added to the processing option template. These variables appear in the interactive or batch application list of available variables in ER. As mentioned earlier, the name that you gave the field is the name you see displayed in ER.

Processing options are normally used in Assignment and If statements. For example, if you were using processing options for a default value, in the Post Dialog Is Initialized event, you would have code similar to the code shown in Figure 12-10.

The T55002 processing option template includes a processing option field for the version of Purchase Order Entry. This field will be used in the row exit for Purchase

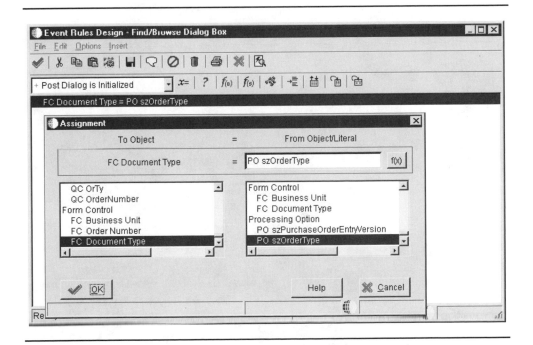

FIGURE 12-10.   The Assignment form in Event Rules Design

Advanced Application Development

Order Entry in the P55002 application. We will pass this processing option value to this form, as displayed in the upper-right corner of Figure 12-11.

These are only two examples of how to use processing option variables, but there are many more uses. For example, you can use processing options to keep a report from calling a custom section or to suppress record deletion in an application. To do this, create an If statement stating that if the processing option value is not valid, hide the control or don't call the custom section. Just remember that when you add a new processing option, you need to add logic to the interactive or batch application to make the processing option work.

Although processing options are designed to be used in applications, they can be used in business functions. For a description of how to do this, see the following Developer's Corner, titled "Attaching Processing Options to a Business Function."

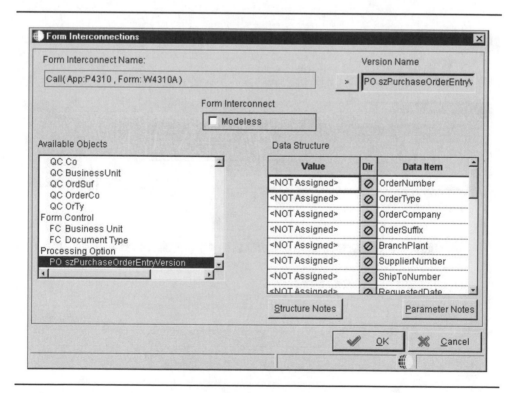

FIGURE 12-11. The code for using a processing option when calling another application

Attaching Processing Options to a Business Function

In this chapter, we have discussed how to create processing options for interactive or batch applications, but you are not limited to those two options. When you create MBFs, or even just large business functions, you may want to include the same type of processing options. For example, when you create a large business function, it might need default values or some processing options that the user can configure. (For more information about business functions, see Chapter 13.)

You cannot attach a processing option template directly to a business function. However, a business function can retrieve the processing options from any application or report in OneWorld. There are three things that you need to do in order for a business function to retrieve processing options from an application: create the processing option template, put the structure definition of the processing options in the business function, and then release the processing option values.

Creating the Processing Options for the Business Function

You create the processing options for a business function in the same way that you create them for any other type of application. If you retrieve the processing options from an existing application or report, the template should exist in the system and be attached to an application.

If you need to create a new processing option template, and this template will not be attached to any existing application or report, you will need to create a dummy application and attach the processing options to it. This dummy application will simply be made up of one form, and it does not need a business view since it will never be used. It should be named *XXXX* Processing Options, where *XXXX* is replaced by your function name, such as Customer Validation MBF Processing Options. Be sure to attach your processing options to this application.

Putting the Processing Option Structure Definition in the Business Function

Your next task is to get the structure definition of your processing options into your business function. The structure is often referred to as the *typedef*. In this example, we are retrieving the processing options from an application named P55002, and the processing option template is named T55002. To put the processing option structure definition in the business function, follow theses steps:

1. From the Object Librarian, select your processing option template. You will see the Parameter Design form.

2. In the Parameter Design form, choose Row | Typedef. At the bottom of the form, you will see the message "Your Typedef is on the clipboard."

3. Paste the typedef in your business function header file. The typedef will look something like the following code:

```
/*****************************************
 * TYPEDEF for Data Structure
            *       Template Name: Order Information PO
 *    Template ID:   T55002
 *    Generated:     Sun Mar 12 22:52:01 2000
 * DO NOT EDIT THE FOLLOWING TYPEDEF
 *    To make modifications, use the Everest Data Structure
 *    Tool to Generate a revised version, and paste from
 *    the clipboard.
 *
 *****************************************/
#ifndef DATASTRUCTURE_T55002
#define DATASTRUCTURE_T55002
typedef struct tagDST55002
{
  char              szOrderType[3];
  char              szPurchaseOrderEntryVersion[11];
} DST55002, *LPDST55002;
#define IDERRszOrderType_1                          1L
#define IDERRszPurchaseOrderEntryVersion_2          2L
#endif
```

Developer's Corner

Typedef in OneWorld is a generated data structure definition used in business functions.

4. After the typedef is in the header file, you need to add code to the business function. First, you need to declare a variable to get the values of the processing options. The following code shows how to declare a variable. In this code, the LPDST55001 is a pointer to your processing options.

```
LPDST55002      lpPOValues    =    (LPDST55002) NULL;
```

5. You need to call the API to retrieve the processing options and then use the API AllocatePOVersionData, as shown in the following code. In this code, the first parameter is hUser, which is described in more detail in Chapter 13. The second parameter is the application name to which the processing options are attached. The third parameter is the version name, which can be hard-coded or passed into the function. The last parameter is the size of the processing option structure.

```
lpPOValues = (LPDST55002) AllocatePOVersionData(hUser, "P55002",
                               lpDS->szInteractiveVersion,
                                    sizeof(DST55002));
```

6. After this API is called, the lpPOValues will be pointing to your processing options. You can then use the pointer lpPOValues to access the information. As in ER, the name of each processing option field is the name you gave it in Processing Option Design. The following code shows how to use the processing option szOrderType to load the variable szDefaultOrderType.

```
strcpy(szDefaultOrderType, lpPOValues->szOrderType);
```

Freeing Processing Option Values

After you have finished using the processing options, the last thing you need to do is free your processing option values to free memory. The following code shows how to free the memory associated with the processing option.

```
FreePODataStructure(lpPOValues);
```

Using Processing Options at Runtime

So far in this chapter, we have discussed how to create, attach, and code processing options inside applications and reports. In this section, we will discuss how to change processing options by using a version and by prompting for values.

Changing Processing Options for a Version

Versions, which were discussed in Chapter 10, allow the user to name a set of processing options and, in the case of batch applications, specify data selection and the sort sequence. When you create a version of an application, you can change the processing options.

Changing Processing Options for Interactive Applications

To change the processing options for a version of an application, follow these steps:

1. In OneWorld Explorer, type **IV** in the Fast Path box and press ENTER to access the Interactive Versions application.

2. Enter the name of the application that you want to attach the processing options to and click Find. In this example, we are attaching processing options to the Order Information application (P55002).

3. If you have not created a version for this application, you need to add one (for instructions on how to create a version, see Chapter 10). Highlight the row of the version whose processing options you want to change. In our example, we select the TMP0001 version.

4. Select Row | Processing Options, as shown in Figure 12-12. The system displays the Processing Option form.

5. Change or add values to the processing option fields, and then click OK.

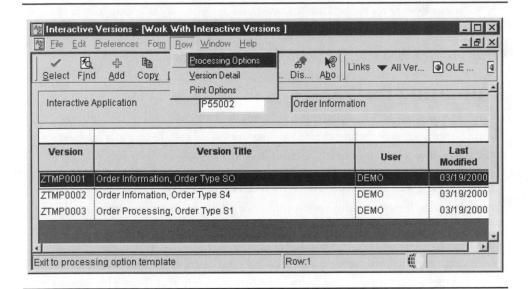

FIGURE 12-12.   Selecting the row of a version in the Interactive Versions form

Changing Processing Options for Batch Applications

To change the processing options for a version of a batch application, follow
these steps:

1. In OneWorld Explorer, type **BV** in the Fast Path box and press ENTER.
   The system displays the Batch Versions form.

2. Enter the name of the batch application whose processing options you want
   to change and click Find.

3. If you have not created a version for this report, you need to add one (for
   instructions on how to create a version, see Chapter 10). Highlight the version
   you want to change.

4. Select Row | Processing Options, as shown in Figure 12-13. You should see the processing option template.

5. Change or add values to the processing option fields and click OK.

Prompting for Values

Changing a version is the permanent way to set the values of processing options. Another approach is to change the processing option values as you enter an interactive application or as you start a batch application.

Prompting for Values in an Interactive Application

You can change the processing option values for an application on a menu before it is run. For example, you may need to configure an application to process certain orders or do a specific calculation, but don't change the version in the interactive versions screen. Instead, you can change the processing options from the OneWorld Explorer menu in OneWorld Explorer, right-click the Menu option, and choose Prompt for Values from the menu, as shown in Figure 12-14. This brings up the processing template. Change any values as desired, and then click OK.

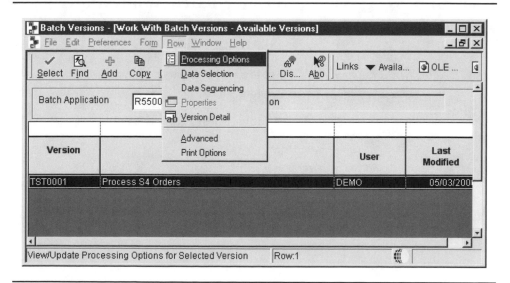

FIGURE 12-13. Selecting the row of a version in the Batch Versions form

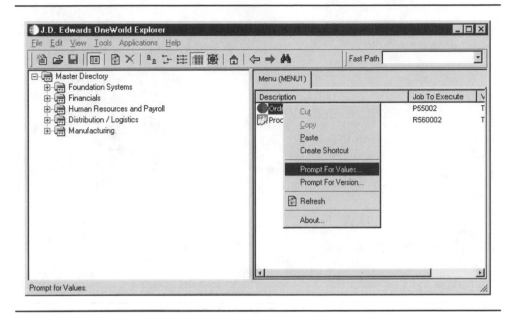

FIGURE 12-14. Selecting Prompt For Values for an Application in OneWorld Explorer

Prompting for Values in a Batch Application

You can create a version that prompts the user to change processing option values. To do this, follow these steps:

1. In OneWorld Explorer, type **BV** in the Fast Path box and press ENTER. The system displays the Batch Versions form.

2. Select the version you want to change and select Row | Version Detail.

3. Change the Prompting value to **2**, as shown in Figure 12-15. By changing the Prompting field to a 2, you allow the user to change the processing options every time a version is run.

4. Click OK.

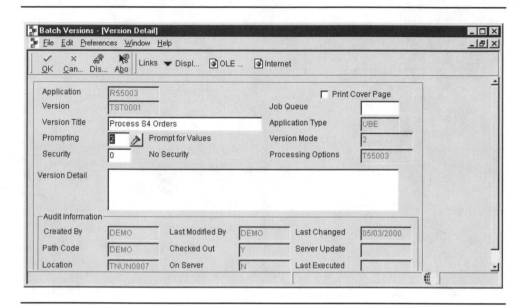

FIGURE 12-15. Changing the Prompting value for a version

Putting It All Together

In this chapter, we explained how to create and attach processing option templates to interactive and batch applications. We finished up the chapter by showing you how to change the processing option values.

You can use processing options to make your applications and reports more flexible and to reduce the need to hard-code values or create multiple applications or reports. To use processing options effectively, you need to understand how all of the parts work together. First, users enter values into the processing option fields. When the application runs, these values are passed into it. The application will use the values in ER to change the way that the application will run.

CHAPTER 13

Data Structures, Business Functions, and Table Event Rules

Data Structures

Business Functions

Business Function Design Tools

Table Event Rules (TER)

Putting It All Together

To increase the degree of maintainability and reusability of your OneWorld applications, you need to implement the logic in *business functions*. A business function is an executable function that can be used in any application in OneWorld. The advantages are that business functions allow you to reuse the same code in several applications; they provide a single point for maintaining code; and they can be mapped for execution on any computer on the network. As you build a store of business functions for your applications, you increase the likelihood that an existing business function with the required logic will fit a particular need in a particular application. Therefore, spending the time to build and maintain business functions will facilitate more efficient application development in the long run.

Deploying reusable business functions in your applications means those applications are easier to maintain. This link is made possible by having a central location for the code that executes the logic, and maintaining code in one location decreases the amount of time needed to modify and fix it.

A unique feature of OneWorld business functions is that they are easily mapped, using the Object Configuration Manager (OCM), to any client or server for execution. As shown in Chapter 1 in the Developer's Corner, "CNC's Impact on OneWorld Applications," you can increase the performance of your applications by mapping the business function to the server that has the database manipulated by that business function. You may not get the performance gain illustrated in Chapter 1, but you will improve the application's performance overall. The primary reason for the performance gain is the elimination of unnecessary data transmission and database requests across the network.

The topics in this chapter will give you a thorough understanding of how to create and modify business functions in OneWorld:

- **Data Structures**   Data structures pass information between a business function and the objects that invoke that business function. These objects provide an easy means of modifying the data passed between them, without drastically impacting them.

- **Business Functions**   Business functions are encapsulated functions that are written either in C or Named Event Rules (NER), and compiled into a DLL (dynamic link library). Business functions are intended to contain the business rules and logic required for various applications. For example, you typically use business functions when data manipulation in a set of tables is required, or when access to non-OneWorld applications is required.

- **Business Function Design Tools**   OneWorld provides a special set of design tools made specifically for use in business functions. The tools allow you to build business functions and maintain their documentation within the OneWorld environment.

- **Table Event Rules (TER)**   The TER language is used for building and defining table triggers that are assigned to a table. Table triggers help to maintain data integrity among tables as theses tables are modified by an application.

Data Structures

Data structures are a key component of any programming language. They pass information among objects and applications to assist with application execution. For example, when one UBE calls another UBE, or when a Find/Browse form calls a Fix/Inspect form, the two objects pass information that is jointly needed through the data structure. Let's take a look at how data structures are used in OneWorld.

An Infrastructure for Data Used by Objects

Λ data structure is essentially a group of data items in a single structure built specifically to pass information between two objects. The only types of objects in OneWorld that use data structures are forms, reports, and business functions. The information that the objects exchange are the calculated values that one object requires, or a Boolean flag that notifies an object of a special condition required during processing.

The system maximum for the number of data items in a data structure is 350. Creating a data structure of this size, however, will have a negative effect on the performance of the application using the data structure and will become a maintenance issue. We recommend that you not have more than 100 data items in a single data structure.

OneWorld uses two types of data structures: system-generated data structures and user-generated data structures.

System-Generated Data Structures

The system generates data structures for all interactive and batch applications when you create them through the Object Librarian. Maintained by the FDA or RDA development tools, these data structures allow information to be passed between one application and another application that calls it. You use system-generated data structures primarily for UBE or form-interconnect system calls.

DEFINITION

System-generated data structures *are used to communicate information from application to application and from the system to an application. These data structures are available once you create an application.*

Form Data Structures   Every form in the system has a *form data structure* that is available for use and modification by a developer. The form data structure receives and sends information to and from the calling object, such as another form or report. Form data structures contain data items that are

- From the processing option assigned to the form

- Required to be assigned when called by another form

- Passing information from one form to another to maintain the application flow

For example, when called from a Find/Browse form, a Search/Select form receives some values to populate in its QBE line.

Report Data Structures   Every batch application in the system has a *report data structure* that is available for use and modification by a developer. Like the form data structure, the report data structure receives and sends information from the calling object. For example, a batch application that updates delinquency notices in the A/R modules passes information to another batch application to print the report for the user to review.

NOTE

Initially, an empty report data structure is provided with a batch application, and you must manually define the data structure. This is unlike a form data structure, which is automatically populated with data items if it has a processing option assigned to it.

User-Generated Data Structures

The system requires data structures for media objects and business functions when you create them through the Object Librarian. You use the Data Structure Design tool to build and maintain the data structures. When you create a media object or business function, you must assign a data structure to it.

Media Object Data Structures   Media objects are supporting attachments that belong to a specific record in a table. Their purpose is to store related data about the record in the system. Such attachments include text files, images, and OLE connections to documents such as a spreadsheet. To enable media objects for an application, you must include a data structure that will pass information between the application and the Media Object table (F00165). Typically, the data items in the data structure are the same ones that make up the primary key of the record.

TIP

For the system to handle media objects properly, every media object attachment must have a unique identifier associated to one record in a table. To ensure that the system assigns a unique identifier, use the same data items making up the primary key for the record in the media object data structure.

Business Function Data Structures   Every business function, whether written in C or NER, requires a data structure. The business function data structure provides the parameters that allow communication between the function and its calling object, such as a form or report. The parameters are data items that are used for storing information sent to or from the business function.

Creating and Modifying Data Structures

This section contains examples of building and maintaining data structures in OneWorld. Included are the components of FDA and RDA that you use to modify form and report data structures, respectively. The Data Structure Design tool is covered in detail, and we also show you how you use it to modify media object and business function data structures. Also described here are the tools that generate the data structure definition in C for business functions covered.

N O T E

The system generates the C header and/or source code from the definition of the following objects: data structures, tables, C-based business functions, NER-based business functions, report application data structures, and interactive application data structures. The generated C code is provided so that you can use the objects in your C-based business functions.

Modifying a Form Data Structure

You use the form data structure to connect the variables within the form to the variables defined in the processing options, and to pass initial values for the form. The following steps show you how to modify the Work With Addresses form of the Address Book application (P01012):

1. Check out the Address Book application (P01012) from Object Librarian, and click the Design button to view the application in FDA.

2. From FDA, select the Work With Addresses form (W01012B).

3. From the Form menu, choose Data Structures. The form data structure appears in the Data Structure Design application, as shown in Figure 13-1.

4. To add a new data item to the form data structure, drag the data item from the Dictionary Items panel or Available Objects panel to the Structure Members grid. Use the QBE line to search for and select data items. The Available Objects panel contains a list of controls used by the form.

5. To remove a data item from the form data structure, highlight it in the Structure Members grid and click the Delete button.

Data Structure
Attachments button —

Data Structure Item
Attachments button

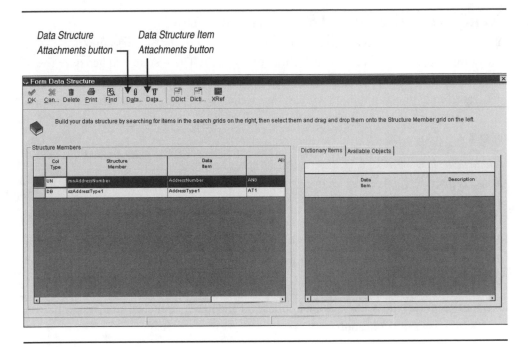

FIGURE 13-1. Using the Data Structure Design application to work with a form data structure

6. To rename a data item, double-click its name in the Structure Member column and edit it as desired. Use Hungarian notation rules when modifying the name, as discussed later in this chapter.

7. To add or modify design and business requirements information about the data structure, click the Data Structure Attachments button on the menu bar.

8. To add or modify design and business requirements information about the data item, select the data item and click the Data Structure Item Attachments button on the menu bar.

9. When you've finished modifying the form data structure, click the OK button. This stores your changes to the data structure; if you click the Cancel button, your changes aren't saved.

Advanced Application Development

Generating the Form Data Structure in C

You can call a form from a C-based business function, but the business function needs the definition of the data structure for the form it calls. The system will generate the C-based description of the form data structure when it is directed to. You use that generated code to communicate with an interactive application from a business function.

NOTE

A form data structure exists only when processing options are assigned to it. To modify or inspect a form data structure, a processing option must be assigned to the form.

The following steps show you how to generate the C-based description of the form data structure for the Work With Addresses form of the Address Book application (P01012):

1. Check out the Address Book application (P01012), and click the Design button to view the application in FDA.

2. From FDA, select the Work With Addresses form (W01012B).

3. From the Application menu, choose Application Properties to display the dialog box shown in Figure 13-2.

4. Click the Generate Form Data Structures button. After the system has generated the structure, a message box appears stating the location of the written file. The

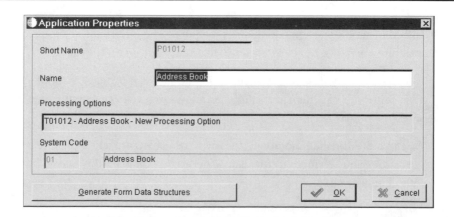

FIGURE 13-2. Application Properties dialog box

file is named after the object name of the interactive application, and is written to the source directory of the environment in which you are developing. For example, the full path of the file for this example is \B7\DEVB733\source\ P01012.txt.

5. Click OK to close the message box and then the Application Properties dialog box.

To see the definitions of the form data structure, edit the file in a text editor such as Notepad or Wordpad. For the Address Book application (P01012), several form data structures are generated for the application because each of its forms contains its own form data structure. Here is the code for the form data structure for the Work With Addresses form (W01012B):

```
/* Form Data Structure for : P01012 : W01012B */
typedef struct {
    MATH_NUMERIC    mnAddressNumber;
    char            szAddressType1[4];
} W01012B , *PW01012B;
```

NOTE

After the form data structures are generated, the code for the application is available for any C-based business function to use. Active messaging is a typical use for the C-based definition of the form data structure.

Modifying a Report Data Structure

The report data structure is used to communicate information to the structure's assigned batch application. You would pass data to the report data structure to initialize variables within the report, to define the records it must modify, or to connect the variables within the report to the variables defined in the processing options. Reports, forms, and business functions can call batch applications; therefore, the report data structure is available for use by objects such as reports and forms.

The following steps show you how to modify the Address Book Batch Load application (R01010Z):

1. Check out the Address Book Batch Load application (R01010Z) from the Object Librarian, and click the Design button to view the application in RDA.

2. From the Report menu, choose Report Data Structure to display the form shown in Figure 13-3.

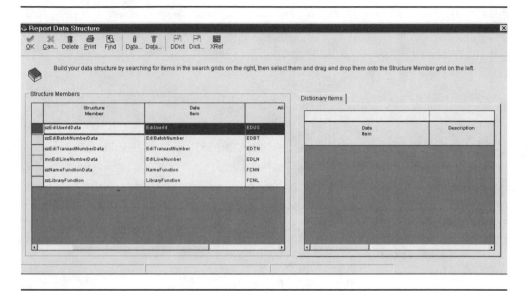

FIGURE 13-3. Report Data Structure form

3. To add a new data item to the report data structure, drag it from the Dictionary Items panel to the Structure Members grid. Use the QBE line to search for and select data items.

4. To remove a data item from the report data structure, highlight the item in the Structure Members grid and click the Delete button.

5. To rename a data item, double-click the name in the Structure Member column and edit it as desired. Use Hungarian notation rules when modifying the name, as discussed later in this chapter.

6. To add or modify design or business requirements information about the data structure, click the Data Structure Attachments button on the menu bar.

7. To add or modify design or business requirements information about the data item, select it and click the Data Structure Item Attachments button on the menu bar.

8. When you've finished modifying the report data structure, click OK. This stores changes you made to the data structure; if you click Cancel, your changes aren't saved.

Creating a Media Object Data Structure

Every media object requires a data structure. The data structure contains the data items that make up the primary key for the media object so that it can uniquely identify a record in a table. The following steps show you how to create the Media Object Data Structure Example data structure (D5600001), which is a clone of the Who's Who Generic Text media object data structure (GT0111):

1. From OneWorld Explorer, type **GH902** into the Fast Path box and press ENTER. The Cross Application Development Tools menu appears.

2. Execute the Object Librarian application (P9860); the Work With Object Librarian form appears (Figure 13-4).

3. Click the Add button on the menu bar to display the Add Object form (Figure 13-5).

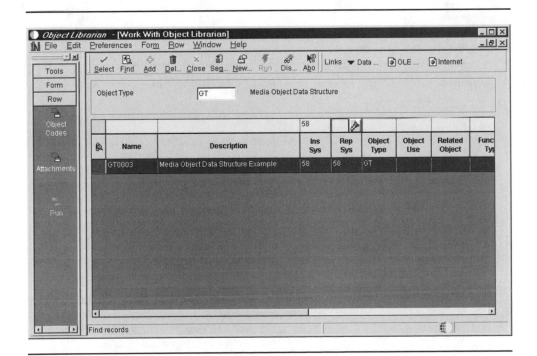

FIGURE 13-4.   Work With Object Librarian form of the Object Librarian application (P9860)

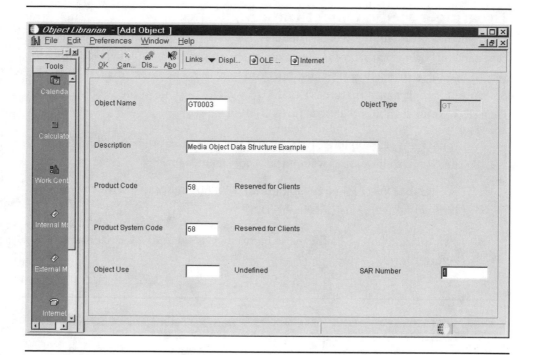

FIGURE 13-5.   Add Object form of the Object Librarian application (P9860)

4. Fill in the fields as follows:

Field	Entry	Notes
Object Name	GT0003	The naming convention for media object data structures is GT*xxxxyy,* where GT identifies the object as a media object data structure; *xxxx* identifies the system code; and *yy* is a unique two-digit number.
Description	Media Object Data Structure Example	A meaningful title for the object.
Product and Product System Codes	58	The product code that the object is assigned to.
SAR Number	1	The value that assigns the object to a specific development project, modification, or fix.

5. Click OK. The Parameter Design form of the Object Librarian application (P9860) appears, as shown in Figure 13-6.

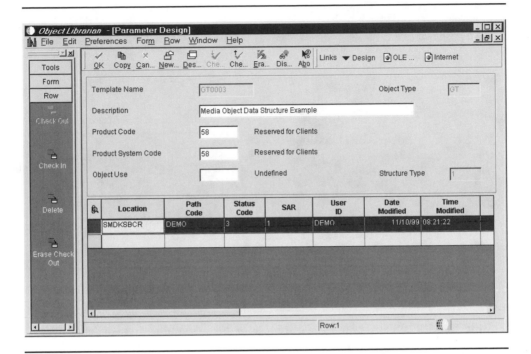

FIGURE 13-6.   Parameter Design form of the Object Librarian application (P9860)

6. To design the media object data structure, click the Design button. The Data Structure Design tool appears (Figure 13-7).

7. To add a new data item to the media object data structure, drag it from the Dictionary Items panel to the Structure Members grid. Use the QBE line to search for and select data items.

8. To remove a data item from the media object data structure, highlight it in the Structure Members grid and click the Delete button.

9. To rename a data item, double-click it in the Structure Member column and edit it as desired. Use Hungarian notation rules when modifying the name, as discussed later in this chapter.

10. To add or modify information about the data structure, click the Data Structure Attachments button on the menu bar.

Advanced Application Development

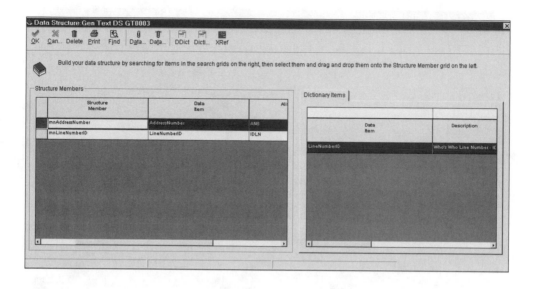

FIGURE 13-7. Data Structure Design application for working with media object data structure

11. To add or modify information about the data item, select the item and click the Data Structure Item Attachments button on the menu bar.

12. When you've finished modifying the media object data structure, click OK to save your changes.

Creating a Business Function Data Structure

Every business function requires a data structure to handle its input and output parameters. The parameters allow the business function to communicate information to the calling object (such as a batch or interactive application, or another business function) by allowing it to pass input and output values. The following steps show you how to create the Business Function Data Structure Example data structure (D5600001):

1. From OneWorld Explorer, type **GH902** into the Fast Path box and press ENTER. The Cross Application Development Tools menu appears.

2. Execute the Object Librarian application (P9860); the Work With Object Librarian form appears.

3. Click the Add button on the menu bar to display the Add Object form.

4. Fill in the fields as follows:

Field	Entry	Notes
Object Name	D5600001	The naming convention for business function data structures is D*xxyyyy*, where D identifies the object as a business function data structure, *xx* identifies the product code, and *yyyy* is a unique four-digit number.
Description	Business Function Data Structure Example	A meaningful title for the object.
Product and Product System Codes	56	The product code that the object is assigned to.
Structure Type	1	The value that defines the purpose of the data structure. A null value states that the object is not a data structure. A value of 1 defines the object as a function data structure, while a value of 2 defines the object as a processing option template.
SAR Number	1	The value that assigns the object to a specific development project, modification, or fix.

5. Click OK. The Parameter Design form of the Object Librarian application (P9860) appears.

6. To design the business function data structure, click the Design button. The Data Structure Design tool appears.

7. To add a new data item to the business function data structure, drag it from the Dictionary Items panel to the Structure Members grid. Use the QBE line to search for and select data items.

8. To remove a data item from the business function data structure, highlight it in the Structure Members grid and click the Delete button.

9. To rename a data item, double-click the name in the Structure Member column and edit it as desired. Use Hungarian notation rules when modifying the name, as explained later in this chapter.

10. To add or modify information about the data structure, click the Data Structure Attachments button on the menu bar.

11. To add or modify information about the data item, select the item and click the Data Structure Item Attachments button on the menu bar.

12. To require the use of the data item every time the data structure is used, click the button in the Req/Opt column. A check mark appears on the button to indicate that the data item is required. To remove the requirement from the data item, click the button again.

13. To require use of the data item for input or output every time the data structure is used, click the button in the I/O Type column. A directional arrow appears on the button to denote that parameter's use; each time you click the button, the directional arrow changes.

   - A right arrow indicates that the data item is only used for output.

   - A left arrow indicates input only.

   - A bidirectional arrow means the data item is used for both input and output.

   - A barred zero (Ø) indicates that the Input/Output direction for the data item is undefined.

14. When you've finished modifying the business function data structure, click OK to save your changes.

15. Click OK on the Parameters Design form to return to the Work with Object Librarian form.

Generating the Data Structure Definition in C

Every business function has a data structure assigned to it. For NER-based business functions, the system automatically provides the definition of the assigned data structure, but this is not the case for C-based business functions. For C-based business functions to access the data structure, you have to paste the definition into the business function's header file.

N O T E

The code defining the data structure in the header file of the business function must be changed when the data structure is modified. Always let the system generate the definition of the data structure. This ensures consistent, clean-running code.

The system generates the C-based description of the data structure, and then you insert it into the header file of the business function. The following steps show you how to generate the C-based definition of the business function:

1. From OneWorld Explorer, type **GH902** into the Fast Path box and press ENTER. The Cross Application Development Tools menu appears.

2. Execute the Object Librarian application (P9860); the Work With Object Librarian form appears.

3. On the Work With Object Librarian form, use the alias field of the QBE line to search for the Business Function Data Structure Example data structure (D5600001).

4. When you find the data structure, highlight it and click the Select button. The Parameter Design form of the Object Librarian application (P9860) appears, with the information about the Business Function Data Structure Example (D5600001).

5. From the Form menu, choose Typedef to generate the description in C. When the system has finished generating the C-based description of the data structure, the results are stored in the Clipboard.

6. To access the newly generated description, paste the C definition into the header file of the business function. Here's what gets pasted into the editor from the Clipboard:

```
/*****************************************
 * TYPEDEF for Data Structure
 *    Template Name: Business Function Data Structure Example
 *    Template ID:   D5600001
 * DO NOT EDIT THE FOLLOWING TYPEDEF
 *    To make modifications, use the Everest Data Structure
 *    Tool to Generate a revised version, and paste from
 *    the clipboard.
 ***************************************/
#ifndef DATASTRUCTURE_D5600001
#define DATASTRUCTURE_D5600001
typedef struct tagDSD5600001 {
  char              cOptionFlag;
  char              cResult;
```

```
    MATH_NUMERIC          mnValueOne;
} DSD5600001, *LPDSD5600001;
#define IDERRcOptionFlag_1          1L
#define IDERRcResult_2              2L
#define IDERRmnValueOne_3           3L
#endif
```

CAUTION

We recommend that you refrain from manually writing or changing the definition of the data structure in the header business function. Always let the system generate the code that defines the data structure.

Business Functions

There are two types of business functions in OneWorld: Named Event Rules (NER) and C based. NER business functions are written in the OneWorld Event Rules (ER) scripting language, which is the preferred method to write business functions for common table manipulation routines. C business functions are written in the C programming language and are used to enhance the performance of complex business logic or perform functions that are not available in ER scripting language.

This section discusses the components and structure of business functions, and how to create and modify them. It does not contain instruction for writing code in the ER and C languages.

Business Function Components

Business functions have several components that provide the required functionality and flexibility. When designed properly, the components form a unified architecture for the business functions and take the guesswork out of building them. Also, the components of OneWorld business functions are platform independent and can execute on multiple hardware platforms and operating systems.

Table 13-1 lists the components that make up C- and NER-based business functions, along with the applications used to create and build them. Every business function comprises specifications that uniquely identify the function, the data structure it uses to communicate with another object, the function's assigned parent DLL, and its .c and

BSFN Type	BSFN Component	Managing Applications
C, NER	BSFN specification	Object Librarian (P9860) Business Function Design (P9862)
C, NER	DSTR specification	Object Librarian (P9860) Business Function Design (P9862)
C, NER	Parent DLL	Object Librarian (P9860)
C	.c file	Generated by the Business Function Design form of the Object Librarian (P9860); modified with Visual C++ IDE
C	.h file	Generated by the Business Function Design form of the Object Librarian (P9860); modified with Visual C++ IDE
NER	Source code	Modified with NER Design Tool
NER	.c file	Generated by the Business Function Source Librarian form of the Object Librarian (P9860)
NER	.h File	Generated by the Business Function Source Librarian form of the Object Librarian (P9860)

TABLE 13-1. Components of C- and NER-Based Business Functions

.h files. NER-based business functions have one additional component: the NER source code that is used to generate the .c and .h files.

Figure 13-8 illustrates the Business Function Design form for the AAI Range Of Accounts business function (B0000115). It's an example of how the components for a business function work together. The C-based business function specifications are stored in the B000015 object. The AAI Range Of Accounts data structure (D0000115) is attached to this business function using the Parameters row exit.

The AAI Range Of Accounts business function (B0000115) contains four functions, as shown in Figure 13-8. The functions are contained within the same C file, named B0000115.c, and in the header file, named B0000115.h. In any environment, these files are stored in the source and include directories, respectively. For example, if the B0000115 business function were in the CRP environment, its files would be stored in the /b7/CRPB733/source and the /b7/CRPB733/include directories.

As shown in Figure 13-8, every OneWorld client and server accesses the runtime image of the AAI Range Of Accounts business function (B0000115), because it is compiled

Advanced Application Development

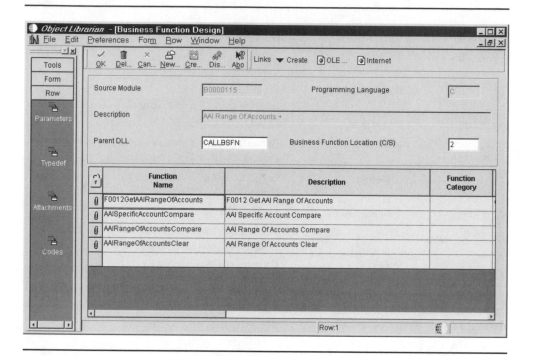

FIGURE 13-8. Business Function Design form for the Object Librarian application (P9860)

into the Callbsfn.dll file. The system cannot do JITI on business functions, because JITI can occur only on TAM spec objects such as interactive or batch applications. Therefore, every client and server for OneWorld contains the business function in one of its DLLs, and the OCM is used to map the function's execution location.

For example, before the AAIRangeOfAccountsClear function is called, the system refers to the OCM to determine which machine the B0000115 object is mapped to. The machine identified by the OCM mapping accomplishes execution of the business function by executing the AAIRangeOfAccountsClear function that is built into the machine's Callbsfn.dll file. All of the information between the calling application and the business function is communicated via the AAI Range Of Accounts data structure (D0000115).

The advantage of executing the B0000115 object on a server is that performance is improved if the object is located on a server that contains the tables that the object manipulates. A good example of this technique is shown in Chapter 1, in the Developer's Corner titled "CNC's Impact on OneWorld Applications."

Named Event Rules (NER) Business Functions

As mentioned, NER business functions are written using the OneWorld Event Rules (ER) scripting language. This scripting language provides all the commands, features, and functionality discussed in Chapter 7. Thus, you can leverage your knowledge of writing ER code used in interactive and batch applications, for building and modifying NER business functions as well.

In general, you should build NER business functions in the following circumstances:

- When you know you can write the code entirely in ER; for example, if your business function will contain only table I/O and system call statements

- When the business function can be reused in other applications; for example, if the logic in the business function is not specific to one application, such as validating a transaction before storing it in a table

T I P

If ER logic applies only to a particular application and is used in several events in the application, do not build an NER business function. Instead, attach ER logic to an event on a hidden control, such as on a Button Clicked event, and use a system function to execute the logic as needed.

- When the business function needs to be mapped by the OCM to decrease message traffic over the network; for example, if the logic in the business function generates a lot of database requests, and mapping the object on the server that contains the database will decrease message traffic because all database requests are maintained on one machine

The following examples will help you understand how NER business functions are built and modified.

Creating an NER Business Function

Start by creating the NER business function.

1. From OneWorld Explorer, type **OL** into the Fast Path box and press ENTER. The Work With Object Librarian form of the Object Librarian application (P9860) appears.

2. Type **BSFN** into the Object Type field and click the Add button. The Add Object form appears.

3. Fill in the fields as follows:

Field	Entry	Notes
Object Name	N550001	The object naming convention for NER business functions is N*xxxxyyyy,* where N identifies the object as a NER business function, *xxxx* is the product code, and *yyyy* is a unique identifier.
Description	NER Business Function Example	A meaningful title for the object.
Product and Product System Codes	55	The product code the object is assigned to.
Function Location	2	The Function Location item is actually a UDC (98/EB). The usual entry for this field is 2, which means that the business function can be executed on clients and servers. At times, however, the business function can execute on the client only, which needs an entry of 1; or on the server, which is 3.
Source Language	NER	The Source Language item is also a UDC (98/SL). The typical values in this field are **C** and **NER**; other valid languages that you can use include COBOL, FORTRAN, and PASCAL.
Object Use	139	The value for this field is defined in UDC (98/FU), and it is used to define the purpose of the object.
SAR Number	1	The value that assigns the object to a specific development project, modification, or fix.

4. Click OK. The Business Function Source Librarian form appears (Figure 13-9).

5. To assign the components to the business function, click the Design button. The Business Function Design form appears.

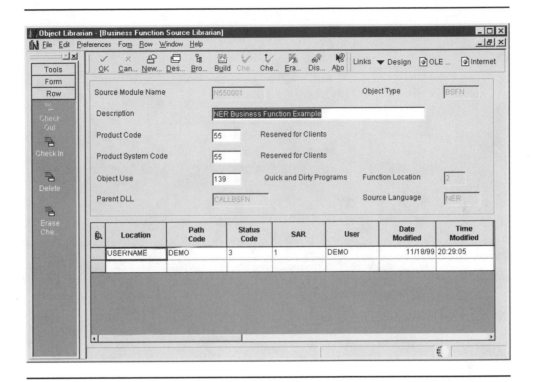

FIGURE 13-9.   Business Function Source Librarian form of the Object Librarian
application (P9860)

6. Fill in the fields as follows:

Field	Entry	Notes
Parent DLL	CALLBSFN	Parent DLL is explained in "Business Function Components," earlier in this chapter.
Function Name	NERBusiness FunctionExample	Always enter the business function name in the Function Name field without spaces.
Description	NER Business Function Example	The Description field contains additional information about the function.

7. To assign a data structure to the business function, highlight the row and
    choose Row | Parameters. The Select Business Function Parameters form
    appears, as shown in Figure 13-10. Use this form to search for and select
    the data structure you want to assign to the business function.

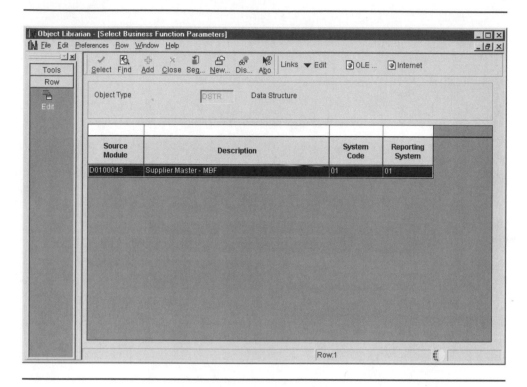

FIGURE 13-10. Select Business Function Parameters form of the Object Librarian application (P9860)

8. When you have selected the appropriate data structure, click OK. The NER business function is fully defined.

Modifying Event Rules for an NER Business Function

This example shows the details of an NER business function, using the Retrieve AAI Account For Journal Entry business function (N03B0144), as illustrated in Figure 13-11. This business function is assigned to the CALLBSFN Parent DLL. Its purpose is to return the account number in the standard ANI format that can be used for a journal entry.

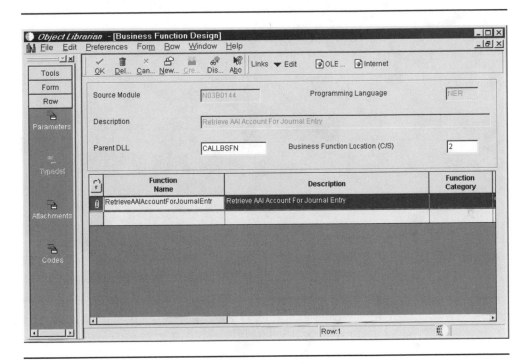

FIGURE 13-11. Business Function Design form for Retrieve AAI Account For Journal Entry business function (N03B0144)

NOTE

The ANI format for OneWorld is defined as BusinessUnit.Object.Subsidiary, *where* BusinessUnit *defines the organization unit affected by the transaction;* Object *is a description of the account; and* Subsidiary *is the expanded description of the account. For example, 1.1110.FNB refers to the Cash in Bank account for business unit 1, and the cash is maintained in the First National Bank (FNB).*

The data structure in this example is the Retrieve AAI Account For Journal Entry data structure (D03B0144), shown in Figure 13-12. Six data items are assigned to this data structure. The data items have an undefined input or output direction, and none

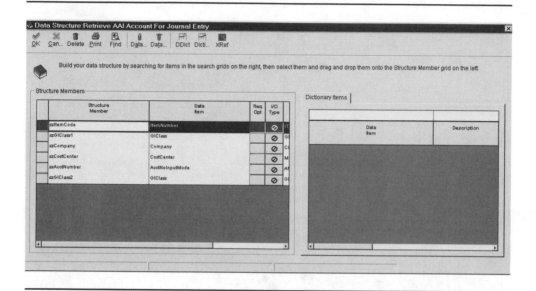

FIGURE 13-12. Data Structure design form for the Retrieve AAI Account For Journal
Entry data structure (D03B0144)

of them are required. Therefore, you can supply a portion of the information to the
business function through the data structure.

To examine the source code for the business function, select Form | Edit on the
Business Function Design form (see Figure 13-11). The Named Event Rules design
tool application appears.

As shown in Figure 13-13, the NER design tool is identical to the ER design tool,
so you use the same code-writing techniques. When you've finished modifying the
source code in the business function, click the Save & Exit button.

Building the NER Business Function

After you have built or modified a business function, you need to generate the .c and .h
files and build the function into the assigned DLL. The following steps show you how
to build the Retrieve AAI Account For Journal Entry business function (N03B0144):

1. From the Business Function Source Librarian form (Figure 13-14), click the Build button. The system generates the .c, .h, and Makefiles.

2. After the system generates the .c, .h, and Makefiles for the BusBuild application, the system builds the business function into the Callbsfn.dll file. The output of the build is shown in Figure 13-15.

3. To close the BusBuild form, choose File | Exit.

4. Click OK. The system returns to the Work With Object Librarian form.

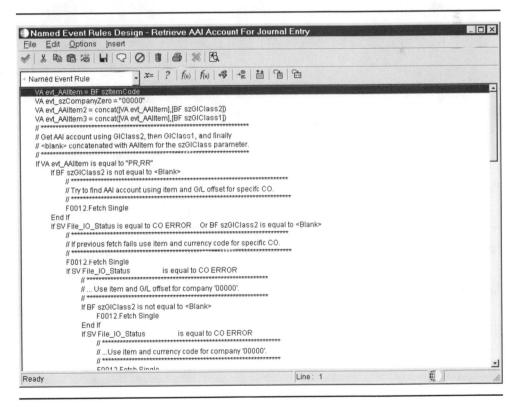

FIGURE 13-13. Named Event Rules Design form

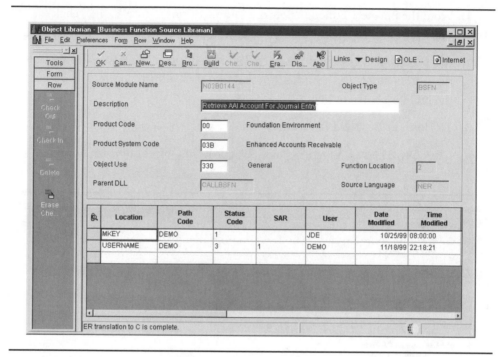

FIGURE 13-14. Business Function Source Librarian for the Retrieve AAI Account For Journal Entry business function (N03B0144)

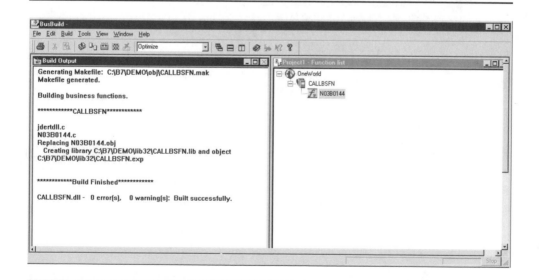

FIGURE 13-15. BusBuild form

C Business Functions

Writing C-based business functions requires that the developer have thorough knowledge of the C language. C business functions execute operations that go beyond the features and functionality of NER, and give the developer greater control of application code. Some of the C techniques ideally suited for C-based business functions are

- Manipulation of strings and arrays

- Execution of functions of low-level system APIs in OneWorld, such as JDEBASE and JDECACHE

- Communication to applications that are not native to OneWorld, such as a DLL that manipulates Access databases

In all cases, C-based business functions execute faster than their NER-based counterparts. The performance gain can be substantial, especially in mass database searches for data warehousing and data mining in OneWorld.

T I P

We strongly recommend that you initially build the business function in NER for proof-of-concept testing, if possible. Then, when the concept is solidified, write the business function in C. This will decrease the amount of time needed to build your business functions.

Structure of the Business Function Header File

Header files contain definitions of data types and variables used by the business function. Header files ensure that all definitions are located in a single file. OneWorld standardizes the header file even further by dividing it into sections to improve consistency and readability.

Here is a standard header file format:

```
/******************************************************************
*     Header File:  B550001.h
*     Description:  C Business Function Example Header File
*         History:
*            Date            Programmer   SAR# - Description
*            ----------      ----------
------------------------------------
*   Author 11/21/99    Unknown       1        - Created
```

```
* Copyright (c) J.D. Edwards World Source Company, 1996
* This unpublished material is proprietary to J.D. Edwards World Source
* Company.  All rights reserved.  The methods and techniques described
* herein are considered trade secrets and/or confidential.  Reproduction
* or distribution, in whole or in part, is forbidden except by express
* written permission of J.D. Edwards World Source Company.
**********************************************************************/
#ifndef __B550001_H
#define __B550001_H
/*********************************************************************
* Table Header Inclusions
**********************************************************************/
/*********************************************************************
* External Business Function Header Inclusions
**********************************************************************/
/*********************************************************************
* Global Definitions
**********************************************************************/
/*********************************************************************
* Structure Definitions
**********************************************************************/
/*********************************************************************
* DS Template Type Definitions
**********************************************************************/
/*********************************************************************
* Source Preprocessor Definitions
**********************************************************************/
#if defined (JDEBFRTN)
   #undef JDEBFRTN
#endif
#if defined (WIN32)
   #if defined (WIN32)
      #define JDEBFRTN(r) __declspec(dllexport) r
   #else
      #define JDEBFRTN(r) __declspec(dllimport) r
   #endif
#else
   #define JDEBFRTN(r) r
#endif
/*********************************************************************
```

```
* Business Function Prototypes
*********************************************************************/
JDEBFRTN (ID) JDEBFWINAPI CBusinessFunctionExample
         (LPBHVRCOM lpBhvrCom, LPVOID lpVoid, LPDSD4000481 lpDS);
/********************************************************************
* Internal Function Prototypes
*********************************************************************/
#endif    /* __B550001_H */
```

Header files include the following sections:

- **Table Header Inclusions**   Lists the header file for every table used in the business function.

- **External Business Function Inclusions**   Lists the header file for every business function called within the source file.

- **Global Definitions**   The global constants used in the business function.

- **Structure Definitions**   The data structures used within this business function only.

- **DS Template Type Definitions**   The data structures generated by the Business Function Design form of the Object Librarian application (P9860). You modify these data structures only through the Object Librarian.

- **Source Preprocessor Definitions**   Ensures that the business function is properly defined for compilation into its parent DLL through the use of the _declspec statement.

- **Business Function Prototypes**   The prototypes for every function defined in the business function through the Business Function Design form of the Object Librarian.

- **Internal Function Prototypes**   The prototypes for every internal function defined in the business function. The internal functions are defined here only, and are used only within the business function.

Structure of the Business Function Source File

Source files contain the actual C code. The definitions located in the header file are copied into the source file during the compilation process to ensure that the function will compile properly. Just like its header file counterpart, the OneWorld source file is sectioned off to improve consistency and readability.

Here is an example of a standard source file:

```
#include <jde.h>
#define b550001_c
/*********************************************************************
*     Source File:  b550001
*     Description:  C Business Function Example Source File
*         History:
*             Date        Programmer   SAR# - Description
*             ----------  ----------   ------------------------------------
*     Author 11/21/99   Unknown      1        - Created
* Copyright (c) J. D. Edwards World Source Company, 1996
* This unpublished material is proprietary to J. D. Edwards World Source
* Company. All rights reserved.  The methods and techniques described
herein are considered trade secrets and/or confidential.  Reproduction or
* distribution, in whole or in part, is forbidden except by express
* written permission of J. D. Edwards World Source Company.
*********************************************************************/
/*********************************************************************
* Notes:
*********************************************************************/
#include <b550001.h>
/*********************************************************************
*   Business Function:  CbusinessFunctionExample
*         Description:  C Business Function Example
*          Parameters:
*             LPBHVRCOM              lpBhvrCom     Business Function
                                                   Communications
*             LPVOID                 lpVoid        Void Parameter - DO NOT
                                                   USE!
```

```
*             LPDSD4000481          lpDS            Parameter Data Structure
                                                    Pointer
**********************************************************************/
JDEBFRTN (ID) JDEBFWINAPI CBusinessFunctionExample (LPBHVRCOM lpBhvrCom,
LPVOID lpVoid, LPDSD4000481 lpDS)  {
/***********************************************************************
*  Variable declarations
***********************************************************************/
/***********************************************************************
* Declare structures
***********************************************************************/
/***********************************************************************
* Declare pointers
***********************************************************************/
/***********************************************************************
* Check for NULL pointers
***********************************************************************/
    if ((lpBhvrCom == (LPBHVRCOM) NULL) ||
        (lpVoid   == (LPVOID)    NULL) ||
        (lpDS     == (LPDSD4000481) NULL))   {
      jdeErrorSet (lpBhvrCom, lpVoid, (ID) 0, "4363", (LPVOID) NULL);
      return ER_ERROR;
    }
/***********************************************************************
* Set pointers
***********************************************************************/
/***********************************************************************
* Main Processing
***********************************************************************/
/***********************************************************************
* Function Cleanup
***********************************************************************/
    return (ER_SUCCESS);
}
#endif
/***********************************************************************
```

```
*    Function:  Ixxxxxxx_a    // Replace "xxxxxxx" with source file number
*                             // and "a" with the function name
*      Notes:
*    Returns:
* Parameters:
*******************************************************************/
```

Source files include the following sections:

- **Notes**   Any relevant developer notes for the business function; they are copied into the business function documentation when it is generated.

- **Variable Declarations**   Defines all variables used in the business function. If the variable is a new data type, make sure it's defined in the business function's header file.

- **Declare Structures**   Declares all structures used in the business function. In this example, all data structures must be defined in either the header file or the Jde.h header file.

- **Declare Pointers**   Declares pointers to structures used in the business function.

- **Check for NULL Pointers**   Verifies that the lpbhvrcom, lpvoid, and lpdsxxxxyyyy pointers are not equal to NULL. The business function cannot execute properly if any of the values are equal to NULL.

N O T E

The lpbhvrcom pointer contains the environment handle from the calling object; the lpvoid pointer is used for error handling and security; and lpdsxxxxyyyy is the data structure assigned to the business function through the Business Function Design form.

- **Set Pointers**   Initializes the pointers declared in the Declare Pointers section to an address. The address is usually assigned to a value passed through the data structure pointer, which is denoted by lpdsxxxxyyyy.

- **Main Processing**   Performs all of the logic and operations required by the business function.

- **Function Cleanup**   Returns any memory allocated to the system that was requested by the business function, and returns the execute state of the function.

- **Function**   Defines internal functions used by the business function.

Creating a C Business Function

Sometimes you'll need to create a C business function for your projects. Situations requiring C business functions include the following: when an NER business function is too complex and hinders performance; when you need to integrate with a non-OneWorld application; or when the required functionality exists only in a system-level API, such as JDEBASE and JDECACHE.

To create a C business function, complete the following steps:

1. From OneWorld Explorer, type **OL** into the Fast Path box and press ENTER. The Work With Object Librarian form appears.

2. Type **BSFN** into the Object Type field, and click the Add button to display the Add Object form.

3. Fill in the fields as follows:

Field	Entry	Notes
Object Name	B550001	The object naming convention for C business functions is B*xxxxyyyy*, where B identifies the object as a C business function, *xxxx* is the system code, and *yyyy* is a unique identifier.
Description	C Business Function Example	A meaningful title for the object.
Product and Product System Codes	55	The product code the object is assigned to.
Object Use	139	The value for this field is defined in UDC (98/FU), and it is used to define the purpose of the object.
Function Location	2	The Function Location is actually a UDC (98/EB). The usual entry is a 2, which means the business function can be executed on clients and servers. At times, however, the business function should execute on the client only, which needs an entry of 1; or on the server, which is 3. Tip: Use client-only business functions when the function must access a Windows DLL. Use server-only business functions when you need to access special libraries on the server, such as a AS/400, HP 9000, or an RS6000.

Advanced Application Development

Field	Entry	Notes
Source Language	C	The Source Language is also a UDC (98/SL). The typical values are C and NER.
SAR Number	1	The value that assigns the object to a specific development project, modification, or fix.

4. Click OK, and the Business Function Source Librarian form appears. To create the other components of the C business function, click the Design button.

5. The Business Function Design form appears. Fill in the fields as follows:

Field	Entry	Notes
Parent DLL	CALLBSFN	The DLL that the business function is compiled into.
Function Name	CBusinessFunction Example	The name of the function that is assigned to the business function.
Description	C Business Function Example	The Description field contains additional information about the function.

6. To assign the data structure to the business function, highlight the row and select Row | Parameters. The Select Business Function Parameters form appears shown earlier in Figure 13-10. Use this form to search for and select the data structure you want to assign to the business function.

7. Click OK. The C business function is fully defined.

Modifying C Code for a Business Function

This example shows the details of the Convert String To Numeric business function (B4000770) shown in Figure 13-16. This function is assigned to the COPBASE parent DLL, and its purpose is to convert a string to a MATH_NUMERIC. The purpose of each parent DLL is discussed later in this section.

The data structure assigned to this business function is Convert String To Numeric (D4000481), shown in Figure 13-17. Three data items are assigned to the data structure. These data items have an undefined input/output direction, and none of them is required. You can provide whatever information you need.

To edit the source code for the Convert String To Numeric business function, choose Form | Edit on the Business Function Design form. This brings up the Microsoft Visual C++ application, which you use to edit the business function's .c and .h files. Following are guidelines for editing .c and .h files.

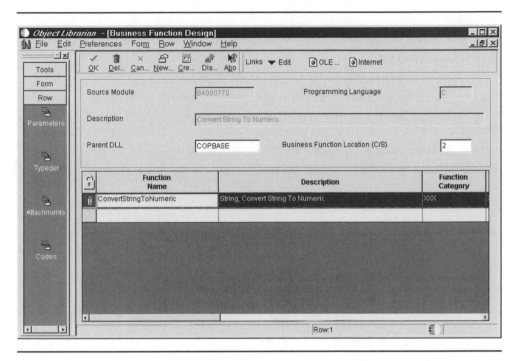

FIGURE 13-16. Business Function Design form for Convert String To Numeric business function (B4000770)

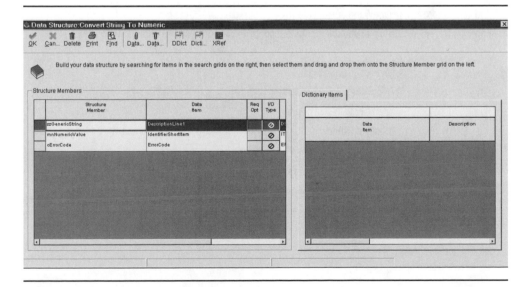

FIGURE 13-17. Data Structure design tool form for Convert String To Numeric data structure (D4000481)

Advanced Application Development

Hungarian Notation   Hungarian notation provides instant identification of variable types in C business functions. A two-letter prefix is appended to the name of every variable to denote its type. For example, a variable that is named Test and is a character will have a Hungarian notation variable name of cTest. Table 13-2 defines the Hungarian notation prefixes.

Data Structure   You can use any data structure in a C business function. All you have to do is include the typedef of the data structure in the DS Template Type Definition section of the function's .h file. The Convert String To Numeric data

Prefix	Description
b	Boolean
c	Character
sz	ASCII Null-terminated string
n	Short integer
l	Long integer
h	Handle
mn	MATH_NUMERIC
jd	OneWorld Julian date
lp	Pointer variable (long) that contains memory address of another variable
i	Integer
by	Byte or unsigned char
w	Word or unsigned integer
id	Identifier with size of unsigned long
u	Unsigned short
ds	OneWorld data structure
x, y	Coordinates with size of short
cx, cy	Distances with size of short

TABLE 13-2.   Hungarian Notation Standard for Variables

structure (D4000481) typedef description is shown here, and Figure 13-17 illustrates its definition in the Data Structure design tool application.

```
#ifndef DATASTRUCTURE_D4000481
#define DATASTRUCTURE_D4000481
typedef struct tagDSD4000481 {
  char                szGenericString[31];
  MATH_NUMERIC        mnNumericValue;
  char                cErrorCode;
} DSD4000481, FAR *LPDSD4000481;
#define     IDERRszGenericString_1    1L
#define     IDERRmnNumericValue       2L
#define     IDERRcErrorCode           3L
#endif
```

CAUTION

We recommend that you refrain from modifying the typedef for the data structure. If a change is made to the data structure, let the system regenerate it and paste the definition back into the header file.

NOTE

To insert the typedef for a data structure in a .h file, select Row | Typedef on the Business Function Design form. The definition is copied to the system Clipboard. You can then paste it directly into the header file.

Client-Side or Server-Side Code   Sometimes C code can only be compiled on the client or server. This usually occurs when the business function executes functions or APIs that only belong on the client or server—for example, when a business function accesses a function in a DLL that only exists in a Windows DLL file on a client machine. For the business function to properly compile on a client or server, special compiler directives are needed to ensure that no compilation problems occur.

For code specific to the client, the code is written between the following lines, which are special compiler directives for clients:

```
# ifdef JDENV_PC
#endif
```

Advanced Application Development

For code specific to the server, the code is inserted between the following lines, which are special compiler directives for servers:

```
#ifdef IAMASERVER
#endif
```

Building the C Business Function

After you've finished editing the C business function, you build it into the assigned DLL. We recommend that you use the Business Function Builder (BusBuild) utility, which is discussed later in this chapter, to compile and link your business functions into a DLL.

NOTE

The BusBuild utility has special settings and functionality that are unique to OneWorld and are not implemented in the standard version of Visual C/C++.

The following steps show you how to build the Convert String To Numeric business function (B4000770):

1. From the Business Function Source Librarian form, click the Build button. The system builds the business function into the Copbase.dll file. The build output is shown in Figure 13-18.

2. To close the BusBuild form, select File | Exit. The system returns to the Work With Object Librarian form.

3. Click OK.

Common OneWorld APIs

OneWorld contains an extensive set of APIs for use in C business functions. This section doesn't cover each API in detail, but rather lists the most common APIs and functions that you might need to use in your business functions.

MATH_NUMERIC API

The MATH_NUMERIC API contains all the logic required to manipulate numeric values in OneWorld. The API consists of a data structure and a set of C-based

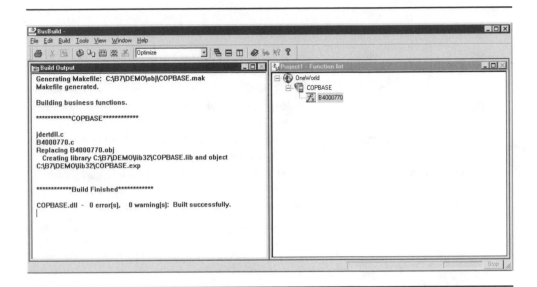

FIGURE 13-18.   Output from BusBuild after compiling the Convert String To Numeric
business function (B4000770)

functions to control the structure. The MATH_NUMERIC structure is defined in the
following C data structure, and Table 13-3 describes its elements:

```
struct tagMATH_NUMERIC {
        char String [MAXLEN_MATH_NUMERIC + 1];
        char Sign;
        char EditCode;
        short nDecimalPosition;
        short nLength;
        WORD wFlags;
        char szCurrency [4];
        short nCurrencyDecimals;
        short nPrecision;
};
typedef struct tagMATH_NUMERIC MATH_NUMERIC,
                FAR *LPMATH_NUMERIC;
```

NOTE

*As shown in the typedef statement, the MATH_NUMERIC data type is actually a
synonym for the tagMATH_NUMERIC data structure. The *LP_MATH_NUMERIC
is a pointer type that you can use in your business functions.*

Advanced Application Development

Element	Type	Description
String	char	A string that stores the digits of the number without formatting the characters. For example, 2,133.56 would be represented as a character string 213356.
Sign	char	Specifies whether the number is positive (Sign = zero) or negative (Sign = negative).
EditCode	char	Contains the edit that will be performed against the string value before it is displayed.
nDecimalPosition	short	Contains the number of digits that will appear on the right side of the decimal point.
nLength	short	Contains the total length of the number.
wFlags	WORD	Flag for the currency processing option. The option is N for Off, Y/Z for On, Y for multiplying the foreign amount by the exchange rate, or Z for dividing the foreign amount by the exchange rate.
szCurrency	char[4]	The currency code.
nCurrencyDecimals	short	The number of currency decimals.
NPrecision	short	Number of digits to the right of the decimal for currency.

TABLE 13-3. Elements for the MATH_NUMERIC Type

The following functions belong to the MATH_NUMERIC API that manipulates the MATH_NUMERIC data structure. These functions are the ones you're most likely to see in the MATH_NUMERIC API for your C business functions:

- **FormatMathNumeric** Converts the MATH_NUMERIC data type (MATH_NUMERIC FAR*) into a string (char FAR*).

```
void FormatMathNumeric (char FAR *.MATH_NUMERIC FAR *)
```

- **IncrementMathNumeric** Increments (nIncrement = 1) or decrements (nIncrement = −1) the MATH_NUMERIC value by 1.

```
void IncrementMathNumeric (LPMATH_NUMERIC lpIncremented,
                           int nIncrement)
```

- **IntToMathNumeric** Converts an integer to MATH_NUMERIC.

```
enum MathErrorCode IntToMathNumeric(int nNumberIn,
                                    LPMATH_NUMERIC lpmnMathOut)
```

- **LongToMathNumeric** Converts a long integer to MATH_NUMERIC.

```
enum MathErrorCode LongToMathNumeric(long lNumberIn,
                                     LPMATH_NUMERIC lpmnMathOut)
```

- **ParseNumericString** Converts a string to a MATH_NUMERIC. If the decimal point exists in the string, the function will process it properly.

```
enum MathErrorCode ParseNumericString
          ( LPMATH_NUMERIC lpmnMathOut, LPSTR lpszString);
```

- **ZeroMathNumeric** Sets the MATH_NUMERIC value to zero.

```
void ZeroMathNumeric (MATH_NUMERIC FAR *pZeroed);
```

JDEDATE API

The JDEDATE API contains all the logic required to manipulate dates in OneWorld. This API consists of a data structure and a set of C-based functions to control the structure. The JDEDATE structure is defined in the following C data structure, and Table 13-4 describes its elements:

```
struct tagJDEDATE {
      short nYear;
      short nMonth;
      short nDay;
};
typedef struct tagJDEDATE JDEDATE, FAR *LPJDEDATE;
```

N O T E

*As shown in the typedef statement, the JDEDATE data type is actually a synonym for the tag JDEDATE data structure. The * LPJDEDATE is a pointer type that you can use in your business functions.*

Element	Type	Description
Nyear	short	The four-digit numeric value that represents the year. All four digits are required for a year, such as 2005.
Nmonth	short	A numeric value that represents the month, such as January = 1, February = 2, and so on.
Nday	short	A numeric value that represents the day of the month. Values must be between 1 and 31.

TABLE 13-4.   Elements for the JDEDATE Type

All dates in OneWorld are stored in a database in a special Julian-date format defined by J.D. Edwards. This format is transparent to you because the JDEDATE API automatically handles its conversion. If you access the OneWorld database through the back end, however, you'll find that the dates are stored as long integers.

The format of the long integers representing J.D. Edwards Julian dates is *YYYJJJ* or *YYJJJ*. The *YYY* and *YY* are the number of years since 1900; *YY* is used for years less than 100, and *YYY* is used for years greater than 99. The *JJJ* identifies a particular date and month in a year by calculating the number of days since January 1 for that year. For example, 99365 represents December 31, 1999; 101022 represents January 22, 2001; and 0 represents December 31, 1899.

The following functions belong to the JDEDATE API that manipulates the JDEDATE data structure. These functions are the ones you'll use most often in the JDEDATE API for your C business functions:

- **FormatDATE**   Converts the jdeDate variable (lpjdDateIn) into a string (lpszDateStringOut):

```
Short FormatDate (char FAR *lpszDateStringOut,
JDEDATE FAR * lpjdDateIn,
char FAR * lpszFormatMask);
```

- **DeformatDate**   Converts the string variable (lpszDateString) into a jdeDate variable (lpjdDateOut):

```
Short DeformatDate (JDEDATE FAR * lpjdDateOut,
char FAR * lpszDateString,
char FAR * lpszFormatMask);
```

To convert variables from a jdeDate variable or from another variable type, the functions use a field called lpszFormatMask, which formats the date into a specific format. The mask values, shown in Table 13-5, can be combined to provide a unique date format. For example, the following line of code converts the date format from 02/14/2002 to the valid JDEDATE value, 102045, by using the mask string "OSASE":

```
JDEDATE jdNewDate;
char* szOldDate = "02/14/2002\n";
char* szDateMask = "OSASE";
nResult = DeformatDate (&jdNewDate, szOldDate, szDateMask);
```

Miscellaneous API

The Miscellaneous API contains a group of functions that are very useful for C-based business functions but have no common theme among them. No special logic is

Advanced Application Development

Mask	Description
D	A one- or two-digit value representing Day.
A	A two-digit value representing Day. Uses zero padding for one-digit numbers.
Y	A two-digit value representing Day. Uses space padding for one-digit numbers.
M	A one- or two-digit value representing Month.
O	A two-digit value representing Month. Uses zero padding for one-digit numbers.
N	A two-digit value representing Month. Uses space padding for one-digit numbers.
T	Month number, by language from UDC table.
B	Abbreviated name of Month from UDC table.
R	Two-digit Year number.
E	Four-digit Year number.
S	Date slash separator.
C	Date comma separator.

TABLE 13-5. Data Masks for jdeDate

performed; no particular data structure is manipulated by these functions. Following are the Miscellaneous API functions you'll use most often:

- **IsValidUDCValue**   Verifies that the UDC value is valid and exists in the UDC tables (F0004 and F0005); relevant parameters are defined in Table 13-6.

```
BOOL IsValidUDCValue(char FAR *szSystemCode,
                     char FAR *szUDCode,
                     char FAR *szValue);
```

- **JdeCallObject**   Initiates the execution of a business function. This is particularly useful when you need to execute a business function from another business function. Table 13-7 describes each parameter for the function.

```
ID jdeCallObject( char* szFunctionName,
                  LPFNBHVR lpFnBhvr,
                  LPBHVRCOM lpBhvrCom,
                  void* lpVoidInfo,
                  void* lpDS,
                  CALLMAP* lpErrorMap,
                  int nNumMap,
                  char* szLibName,
                  char* szExeLocation,
                  int nFlags);
```

- **StartFormDynamic**   Initiates the execution of a form from a business function. This technique is typically used in cases when user input must be verified before performing data manipulation that could seriously affect the behavior of OneWorld. Table 13-8 describes each parameter for the function.

```
int FAR_export StartFormDynamic (LPSTR lpszDLLName,
                                 WORD wFormOrdinal,
                                 HWND szValuehwnd,
                                 LPVOID lpFormDS );
```

Parameter	Description	Usage
szSystemCode	The system code that the UDC is assigned to, such as 02	Required
szUDCode	A UDC type for system code, such as MB	Required
szValue	The particular UDC value you need to validate, such as .01 for the UDC 02/MB	Required

TABLE 13-6.   Parameters in IsValidUDCValue Function

Parameter	Description	Usage
szFunctionName	The literal name of the function, placed within double quotes, such as "B550001"	Required
lpfnBhvr	Obsolete	Set to NULL
lpBhvrCom	Standard lpBhvrCom	Required
lpVoidInfo	Standard lpVoid	Required
lpDs	Pointer to the data structure of the called business function	Required
lpErrorMap	Pointer to the call address of the CALLMAP array	Optional (used for second level error messaging)
nNumMap	The #define variable describing the number of indices used in the CALLMAP array, such as IDERRszGenericString_1	Optional (used for second level error messaging)
szLibName	Reserved for future use	Required, but set equal to NULL
szExeLocation	Reserved for future use	Required, but set equal to NULL
nFlags	Error/warning suppress	Optional (usually set to zero)

TABLE 13-7.   Parameters in jdeCallObject Function

Advanced Application Development

Parameter	Description	Usage
lpszDLLName	Name of the interactive application, with .dll appended to the end; for instance, P01012.dll	Required
wFormOrdinal	Name of the form to display on the screen, such as W01012A	Required
szValuehwnd	Current window handle; accessed by passing the value lpBhvrCom->hDlg	Required
lpFormDS	Pointer to data structure to be passed to the form; generated by the system in FDA (see example in the earlier section, "Generating the Form Data Structure in C").	Required

TABLE 13-8.   Parameters in StartFormDynamic Function

Business Function Design Tools

To assist you with the creation or modification of business functions, OneWorld provides a special set of design tools, including the Business Function Parent Library, Business Function Builder, and Business Function Documentation. These utilities offer a full set of features and functionality necessary for the building, troubleshooting, and documentation of business functions.

Business Function Parent Library

As stated earlier in this chapter, every business function is assigned to one DLL. DLLs consolidate many business functions into a single file, gaining the following advantages over executable files that do not use DLLs:

- Savings in memory and hard disk space. DLLs provide a set of functions that are loaded by the application at runtime and allow many processes to access the same function in a DLL simultaneously. When DLLs are used, applications don't have to compile every function, thus reducing the file size of the application.

- Simplification of upgrades and modifications. You can compile just those DLLs that are affected by an upgrade or update. Modifications to a DLL do not affect applications because the library is loaded at runtime by the application.

- Support for multilanguage applications. As long as applications follow the same technique in calling a function from an application, programs written in other languages can use the same DLLs.

Table 13-9 lists all the DLLs included in a standard installation of OneWorld. Most of the DLLs correspond to major OneWorld packages, such as Financials and Human Resources. OneWorld also offers a standard DLL, CBUSPART, that J.D. Edwards business partners can use to isolate their functions from the standard system.

NOTE

Anyone can create their own custom DLLs in OneWorld without using the Cbuspart.dll file. Custom DLLs allows you to deliver made-to-order business functions to enhance OneWorld without conflicting with another DLL.

DLL Name	Assigned Category
CAEC	Architecture
CALLBSFN	Consolidated BSFN library
CBUSPART	Business Partner
CCONVERT	Conversion business functions
CCORE	Core business functions
CCRIN	Cross-industry application
CDBASE	Database tools
CDDICT	Data Dictionary tools
CDESIGN	Design business functions
CDIST	Distribution
CFIN	Financials
CHRM	Human Resources
CINSTALL	Installation tools
CINV	Inventory
CLOC	Localization
CLOG	Logistics
CMFG	Manufacturing
CMFG1	Manufacturing—Modified business functions
CMFGBASE	Base manufacturing functions
COBJLIB	Object Librarian tools
COBLIB	BusBuild business functions
COPBASE	Base distribution/logistics business functions
CRES	Resource scheduling
CRUNTIME	Runtime tools
CSALES	Sales ordering
CTOOL	Design tools
CTRAN	Transportation
CTRANS	Translations tools

TABLE 13-9.   Standard DLLs in OneWorld

Advanced Application Development

DLL Name	Assigned Category
CWARE	Warehouse
CWRKFLOW	Workflow tools
JDBTRG1	Table trigger library
JDBTRG2	Table trigger library
JDBTRG3	Table trigger library
JDBTRIG	Parent DLL for database triggers

TABLE 13-9. Standard DLLs in OneWorld (*continued*)

Creating a Custom DLL

If you're going to create several NER and C business functions, you need to make a custom DLL to contain the runtime image of your business functions. This will help prevent conflicts between the custom and standard DLLs. A major benefit of building custom DLLs is that the code is preserved during upgrades and re-installs of OneWorld. The following example shows you how to define a custom OneWorld DLL:

1. From OneWorld Explorer, type **OL** into the Fast Path box and press ENTER. The Work With Object Librarian form appears.

2. Type **BL** into the Object Type field. Click the Add button to display the Add Object form.

3. Fill in the fields as follows:

Field	Entry	Notes
Object Name	CALLCUST	The object-naming convention for DLLs is CALL*xxxx*, where CALL denotes the object as a DLL, and *xxxx* is the abbreviated and unique name of the DLL.
Description	Custom DLL Example	A meaningful name for the object.
Product and Product System Codes	55	The product code the object is assigned to.
Object Use	139	The value for this field is defined in UDC (98/FU), and it is used to define the purpose of the object.

Field	Entry	Notes
SAR Number	1	The value that assigns the object to a specific development project, modification, or fix.

4. The Business Function Parent Library form appears, as shown in Figure 13-19. As you add business functions to the parent DLL, they are displayed in the grid.

5. Click OK.

In most cases, OneWorld will use the DLLs that are defined in the Business Function Parent Library, but there is a technique available for accessing functions and resources from a non-OneWorld DLL. This technique is provided in the following Developer's Corner, titled "Business Functions That Execute Non-OneWorld DLLs."

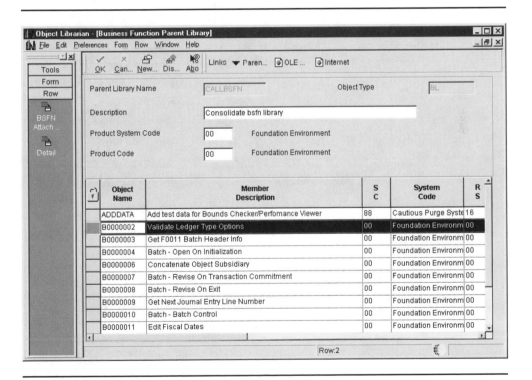

FIGURE 13-19.   Business Function Parent Library form of the Object Librarian application (P9860)

Advanced Application Development

Business Functions That Execute Non-OneWorld DLLs

There are many development projects in which you'll need to access applications or DLLs that do not belong to OneWorld. A good example is when you need to manipulate an Access database on a client machine by communicating to the set of DLLs that are available for Access. The example in this Developer's Corner illustrates how to write a business function that executes a non-OneWorld DLL. You'll be able to observe all the details required to execute a call from a business function to a function located in a non-OneWorld DLL.

To execute a non-OneWorld function from a business function, complete the following steps:

1. **Write and build the DLL.** In this first step, you build a Windows-based DLL that the business function will execute. You'll also see how to quickly build your own DLL for your projects. The following code represents the contents of the Dll_test.cpp file that compiled to a DLL. The function named fnDLL_Test is the external function that will be executed in later steps. As you can see, all the function does is return the value 47 to the calling business function.

NOTE

To quickly build the DLL in the Visual C++ IDE, create a new Win32 DLL. When the system asks you what kind of DLL to create, select the DLL that exports some symbols. The system will build most of the files necessary to compile and build a DLL.

```
#ifdef DLL_TEST_EXPORTS
#define DLL_TEST_API __declspec(dllexport)
#else
#define DLL_TEST_API __declspec(dllimport)
#endif
DLL_TEST_API int fnDLL_Test(void);
BOOL APIENTRY DllMain( HANDLE hModule,
                       DWORD  ul_reason_for_call,
                       LPVOID lpReserved ) {
```

```
    switch (ul_reason_for_call)      {
            case DLL_PROCESS_ATTACH:
            case DLL_THREAD_ATTACH:
            case DLL_THREAD_DETACH:
            case DLL_PROCESS_DETACH:
            break;
    }
    return TRUE;
}
DLL_TEST_API int fnDLL_Test(void) {
    return 47;
}
```

2. **Determine the location of the function in the DLL.** When a compiler builds the DLL, it modifies the DLL's name to indicate the function's location in memory. To determine this location, use the Dumpbin.exe application, which is usually located in the C:\Program Files\Microsoft Visual Studio\VC\Bin directory.

   The Dumpbin.exe application displays the modified name of the function when you type the following dumpbin statement at the command line. After the application is finished, it displays all the functions in the DLL. For this example, fnDLL_Test has been modified to ?fnDLL_Test@@YAHXZ, and it will be used later to reference the function in a OneWorld business function.

```
C:\dumpbin /EXPORTS Dll_test.dll
Microsoft (R) COFF Binary File Dumper Version 6.00.8168
Copyright (C) Microsoft Corp 1992-1998. All rights reserved.
Dump of file Dll_test.dll
File Type: DLL
  Section contains the following exports for Dll_test.dll
          0 characteristics
   383981D5 time date stamp Mon Nov 22 12:48:05 1999
       0.00 version
          1 ordinal base
          1 number of functions
          1 number of names
  ordinal hint RVA       name
          1    0 0000100A ?fnDLL_Test@@YAHXZ
  Summary
       4000 .data
       1000 .idata
       2000 .rdata
       2000 .reloc
      28000 .text
```

3. **Create a business function.** In Object Librarian (P9860), create a business function that will execute the function built in step 1. For this example, we use the C Business Function Example business function (B550001).

4. **Modify the header file of the business function.** The following code contains the sections of the header file (B550001.h) that are modified for this example. The Global Definitions section includes the standard Windows header file and defines a pointer type that is used for functions. The DS Template Section defines the data structure used for communicating with the calling object.

NOTE

If you execute a Windows-based DLL in your business function, you must wrap the code in a #ifdef compiler directive to ensure that only OneWorld client machines compile the lines of code.

```
/****************************************************************************
* Global Definitions
****************************************************************************/
#ifdef JDENV_PC
    #include <windows.h>
    typedef int (*PFNDLL_TEST) (void);
 #endif
/****************************************************************************
* Structure Definitions
****************************************************************************/
/****************************************************************************
* DS Template Type Definitions
****************************************************************************/
/***************************************
 * TYPEDEF for Data Structure
 *    Template Name: DSTR for BSFN B550001
 *    Template ID:   D550001
 *    Generated:     Mon Nov 22 05:58:25 1999
 * DO NOT EDIT THE FOLLOWING TYPEDEF
```

```
*    To make modifications, use the Everest Data Structure
*    Tool to Generate a revised version, and paste from
*    the clipboard.
****************************************/
#ifndef DATASTRUCTURE_D550001
#define DATASTRUCTURE_D550001
typedef struct tagDSD550001 {
  MATH_NUMERIC        mnResult;
} DSD550001, *LPDSD550001;
#define IDERRmnResult_1                 1L
#endif
```

5. **Modify the source file of the business function.** The following code contains the main section of the modified source file (B550001.c). These lines are wrapped around the #ifdef compiler directive so that the business function can compile on a server.

In order to access any DLL, you need to define two important pointers in the Declare Pointers section. The first pointer, hLibrary, provides access to a DLL after it is loaded into memory. The other pointer, lpfnDLL_Test, provides access to a function contained in the DLL you just loaded, and is used to execute the function stored in the DLL.

To access any functions or utilities built in a DLL, you must load the DLL into the memory space of your current application. Do this using the loadLibrary command; it returns a pointer to access the DLL, which is the C:\Dll_test.dll, and is stored in the hLibrary pointer.

CAUTION

It's important to unload the DLL from memory by using the FreeLibrary command. If you do not execute the FreeLibrary command, the memory will never be returned to the system and will cause a memory leak in your business function.

To determine the location of the function in memory, use the GetProcAddress command. The command searches for the function in the DLL and returns a pointer to the location of the function in memory. For this example, the *lpfnDLL_Test* pointer contains the location in memory where the function is, and executes it when you call it.

Note that you must use the modified name of the function, determined in step 2, so that the GetProcAddress command can find it.

```
JDEBFRTN (ID) JDEBFWINAPI CBusinessFunctionExample
                        (LPBHVRCOM lpBhvrCom,
                         LPVOID lpVoid,
                         LPDSD550001 lpDS)  {
    # ifdef JDENV_PC
/***********************************************************************
*  Variable declarations
***********************************************************************/
    int nResult = 0;
    int nMathReturn = MATH_SUCCESS;
/***********************************************************************
* Declare pointers
***********************************************************************/
    PFNDLL_TEST lpfnDLL_Test;
    HINSTANCE hLibrary;
/***********************************************************************
* Check for NULL pointers
***********************************************************************/
    if ((lpBhvrCom == (LPBHVRCOM) NULL) ||
        (lpVoid    == (LPVOID)    NULL) ||
        (lpDS      == (LPDSD550001)      NULL)) {
        jdeErrorSet (lpBhvrCom, lpVoid, (ID) 0, "4363", (LPVOID) NULL);
        return ER_ERROR;
    }
/***********************************************************************
* Set pointers
***********************************************************************/
    lpfnDLL_Test = (PFNDLL_TEST) NULL;
    hLibrary = (HINSTANCE) NULL;
/***********************************************************************
* Main Processing
***********************************************************************/
    hLibrary = LoadLibrary("C:\\Dll_test.dll");
    if(hLibrary) {
        lpfnDLL_Test = (PFNDLL_TEST) GetProcAddress
                                          (hLibrary,
                                           "?fnDLL_Test@@YAHXZ");
        if ( lpfnDLL_Test ) {
            nResult = lpfnDLL_Test ();
            nMathReturn = IntToMathNumeric
                                    (nResult, &lpDS->mnResult);
        }
        FreeLibrary (hLibrary);
    }
/***********************************************************************
* Function Cleanup
```

```
*************************************************************************/
    #endif
    return (ER_SUCCESS);
}
```

You have now written a business function to execute a function that is contained in a non-OneWorld DLL. This business function can be compiled to make it available for use by an application.

To show you that all of the code shown in this Developer's Corner works, we have built an interactive application to execute the business function. This application contains a button that, when clicked, executes the business function; and a field displays the value from the DLL_Test function that is contained in the foreign DLL. As shown in Figure 13-20, the proper value of 47, which is derived from the DLI_Test function, is displayed in the Result field.

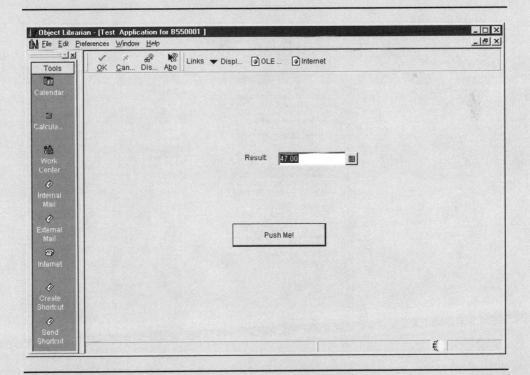

FIGURE 13-20.   Test application for B550001 application

Business Function Builder (BusBuild)

The Business Function Builder (BusBuild) development tool builds business functions into their assigned parent DLL. The tool compiles the source code that is found in C business functions, NER business functions, and Table Event Rules. After successful compilation of the business function, it is linked into its designated parent DLL.

Figure 13-21 illustrates the BusBuild development tool. The interface contains familiar elements: a menu bar, toolbar, three child windows, and a status bar at the bottom. Let's examine the elements of this interface and then look at BusBuild's output.

N O T E

BusBuild can execute without an active OneWorld session. This is very useful when you're only recompiling and building DLLs.

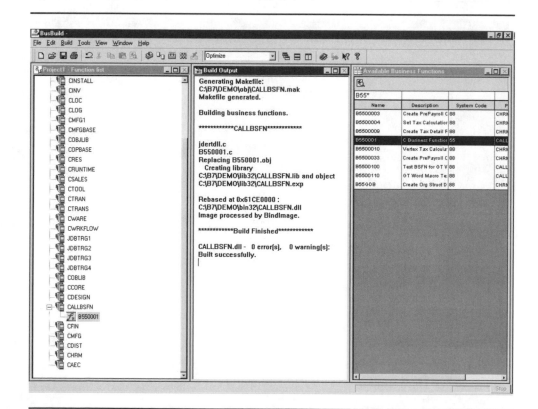

FIGURE 13-21. Business Function Builder application

BusBuild Child Windows

The three child windows of the Business Function Builder are as follows:

- **Available Business Functions** The Available Business Functions window contains a QBE line that allows you to search for one or more business functions to compile. To build a function, drag the business function from the grid of the Available Business Functions window into the Function List window.

- **Function List** The Function List window displays all the DLLs for OneWorld. Any functions listed in the window are available for building. To build the function, right-click to display the pop-menu shown here, and choose the Build menu item.

- **Build Output** The Build Output window displays the output of the build process. This allows you to view the progress of the build and to diagnose any problems identified by BusBuild. If the function is properly built, the output will display the message "Built successfully" (as in Figure 13-21).

Build Menu

The Build command on the menu bar provides the options shown here for building business functions:

- **Build** Generates a Makefile, compiles the business functions defined in the Makefile, and links the functions into their parent DLL. The purpose of the Makefile is to define all the libraries, compiler directives, and header files required to build a business function.

- **Compile** Generates a Makefile and compiles the selected business functions. Compiling a business function does not link the business function into its parent DLL file.

- **ANSI Check** Verifies that the business function is ANSI C compliant. Performing an ANSI Check on a business function guarantees that it can properly be built on any valid OneWorld client or server.

N O T E

We recommend that you regularly perform an ANSI Check on the business functions you develop. This prevents problems during packaging and deployment of your business functions to other clients and servers.

- **Link**   Generates a Makefile for a OneWorld DLL and links all the business functions that are assigned to it. The Link menu item does not compile any business functions.

- **Link All**   Generates a Makefile for all OneWorld DLLs and links all the business functions into them. The Link All menu item does not compile any business functions.

- **Rebuild Libraries**   Rebuilds the OneWorld DLL and static libraries from the .obj files of the business functions.

- **Build All**   Generates all business function Makefiles, compiles them, and links them into their parent DLL.

- **Stop Build**   Terminates processing of the build. Any partial processing of DLLs is not affected by stopping the build process; it only stops processing of DLLs that have been fully built before the Stop Build command is issued.

- **Suppress Output**   Limits the output that appears in the Build Output window.

- **Browse Info**   Generates browse information for the business function being compiled. This option increases time needed to compile the function; therefore, if time is a consideration, turn this option off.

- **Precompiled Header**   Expedites the time needed to compile a business function, by accessing an existing, precompiled header during the compilation process.

- **Debug Info**   Generates debugging information for the business function for use with the Visual C++ debugger. The debugging information is stored in Program Database Files (*.pdb), and the files are used by the debugger at runtime to store and process information about the program.

- **Full Bind**   Resolves the external runtime references for every OneWorld DLL.

Tools Menu

The Tools command on the menu bar provides the following advanced tools for building business functions:

- **Build**   Generates a Makefile, compiles the selected business functions, and links the functions into its parent DLL. The business function will only be built if its components are out-of-date.

- **Synchronize JDEBLC**   Reorganizes the business functions into new parent DLLs by updating the JDEBLC TAM spec with the F9860 table. You use this command when you change the parent DLL of a business function.

C A U T I O N

Do not execute Tools | Synchronize JDEBLC unless it is required, because the utility will permanently modify the JDEBLC spec based on the F9860 table. The Synchronize JDEBLC utility is used only after you have changed the parent DLL for one or more business functions and you are experiencing load library errors.

- **Dumpbin**   Initiates the execution of a utility that verifies whether a business function was properly built and linked into its parent DLL. The utility's run results are displayed in the Build Output window. Following is a partial listing of the Callbsfn.dll file:

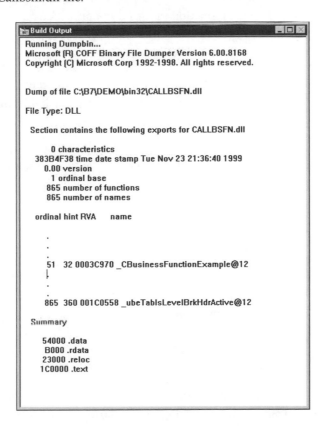

```
Build Output                                              _ □ ✕
Running Dumpbin...
Microsoft (R) COFF Binary File Dumper Version 6.00.8168
Copyright (C) Microsoft Corp 1992-1998. All rights reserved.


Dump of file C:\B7\DEMO\bin32\CALLBSFN.dll

File Type: DLL

  Section contains the following exports for CALLBSFN.dll

        0 characteristics
 383B4F38 time date stamp Tue Nov 23 21:36:40 1999
     0.00 version
        1 ordinal base
      865 number of functions
      865 number of names

 ordinal hint RVA      name

        .
        .
        .
       51   32 0003C970 _CBusinessFunctionExample@12
        .
        .
        .
      865  360 001C0558 _ubeTablsLevelBrkHdrActive@12

 Summary

     54000 .data
      B000 .rdata
     23000 .reloc
    1C0000 .text
```

- **PDB Scan** Searches for any PDB files (*.pdb) files that are used for debugging. This menu item is an important one because a business function cannot be linked into its parent DLLs until the function's *.pdb files are removed. The results of the PDB Scan are displayed in the Build Output window, as shown here:

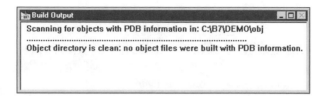

Understanding the Build Output

The build output contains several sections that display information about each step in the build process. The information in this section will help you determine whether the build process has finished successfully. If the process failed, the BusBuild tool lists the problems found. The information in the build output occurs in the same sequence as the build.

The build output sections include the following:

- **Makefile section** Provides information on the generation of the Makefile for each DLL that is built. If this step executes properly, the following statements are displayed in the Build Output window:

```
Generating Makefile:  C:\B7\DEMO\obj\Callbsfn.mak
Makefile generated.
```

- **Begin DLL section** Shows you the DLL currently being built. Here's an example of the section's output statements:

```
Building business functions.
************CALLBSFN***********
```

- **Compile section** Contains the results of the compilation process for each business function. If any errors or warnings occur during the process, the build output will display them and their corresponding messages. A successful compilation of the business function will display the following information:

```
B550001.c
Replacing B550001.obj
```

- **Link section** Contains the results of linking each business function into its parent DLL. If any errors or warnings occur during the process, the build output will display them and their corresponding messages. A successful link process of the business function will display the following information:

```
Creating library C:\B7\DEMO\lib32\Callbsfn.lib and object
C:\B7\DEMO\lib32\Callbsfn.exp
```

- **Rebase section**   Contains the results of performance tuning on the DLLs, which makes them load faster at runtime. As it performs rebasing of the DLL, the system tunes the DLL by changing its load address so that the system doesn't have to find it again when it's needed. A rebase process, which always occurs for every build, displays the following information:

```
Rebased at 0x61CE0000 : C:\B7\DEMO\bin32\Callbsfn.dll
Image processed by BindImage.
```

- **Summary section**   Displays the results of the build process for the tool. A successful build process displays the following message:

```
************Build Finished************
Callbsfn.dll - 0 error(s), 0 warning(s): Built successfully.
```

Business Function Documentation

Documentation is essential for understanding how to use a business function or a set of APIs. Maintaining a set of documentation for your business functions provides a definition of their purpose, and is an invaluable developer's tool for online help. The Business Function Documentation toolset helps you create documentation about a business function, generates it in a usable medium, and provides several means to view it.

The business function documentation is divided into the following sections:

- Purpose and logic for the business function

- Parameters and data structure used for the business function, and an explanation of each element in the data structure

- Related tables that the business function accesses and modifies

- Special handling instructions when accessing the business function

The following sections cover the process of managing the business function documentation for your projects.

Advanced Application Development

Creating or Modifying a Media Object Template for Documentation

You use *media object templates* to standardize the documentation for business functions and data structures. Your development team can use the template as a guide for what information is necessary to the object.

For business function documentation, the standard media object template from OneWorld contains the following sections:

- **Purpose**   An overview of the business function and its logical structure.

- **Setup Notes and Prerequisites**   Any special notes and functionality to assist in utilization of the business function.

- **Special Logic**   Information about any special logic required for the business function to operate properly.

- **Technical Specification**   Notes from the analysis and design phase of the business function project. We recommend that you include in this section information from the requirements document that applies to the business function.

For data structure documentation, the standard media object template from OneWorld contains the following sections:

- **Special Input Expected**   Information on the required input fields for the data structure.

- **Special Output Returned**   Information on the required output fields for the data structure.

- **Significant Data Values**   Information on the special values that have to be communicated to the business function.

To create or modify any media object template, follow these steps:

1. From OneWorld Explorer, type **GH9011** into the Fast Path box. The System Administration Tools menu (GH9011) appears.

2. Execute the Media Object Templates application (P98TMPL); the Work With Media Object Templates application (P98TMPL) appears, as shown in Figure 13-22.

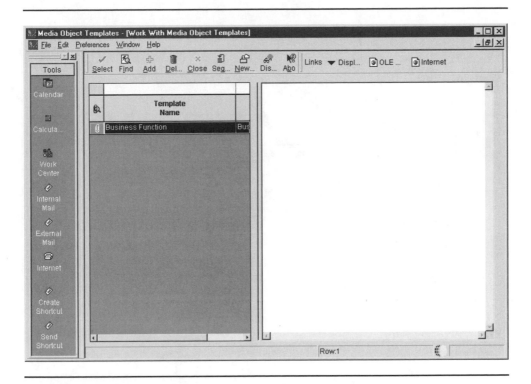

FIGURE 13-22. Work With Media Object Templates application (P98TMPL)

3. If you are modifying a media object template, click the Find button; the list of templates appears in the grid. Highlight the grid row of your choice and click the Select button. You can begin editing the template when the Media Object Template Revisions form appears (Figure 13-23).

4. If you are creating a new media object template, click the Add button in the Work with Media Object Templates application (Figure 13-22). When the Media Object Template Revisions form appears (Figure 13-23), enter a unique name into the Template Name field, and a description of the object in the Description field.

5. Define each section that the template will contain, as illustrated in Figure 13-23.

6. When you've finished, click OK. The template is stored in the system and available for use by other developers and users.

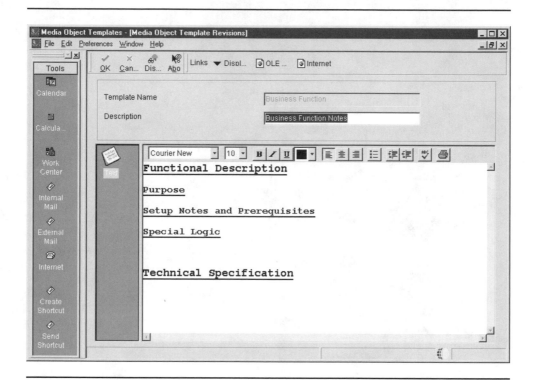

FIGURE 13-23. Media Object Template Revisions form of the Work With Media Object Templates application (P98TMPL)

Creating Business Function Documentation

You create business function documentation at several physical levels: for the business function, for its assigned data structure, and for each parameter that belongs to the data structure.

- The documentation for the business function provides a high-level overview and any special notes about the function itself.

- The data structure documentation allows you to write about the special logic needed to communicate to the business function.

- The parameter documentation provides special settings for using individual elements in the data structure.

Following are examples of creating these documents.

For Business Functions   To create documentation for business functions, complete
the following steps:

1. From the Business Function Design Form of the Object Librarian application
   (P9860), select the function you need to document and choose Row |
   Attachments. (An example of the Business Function Design form appeared
   earlier in Figure 13-16.) The Media Objects application appears, as shown in
   Figure 13-16.

2. To assign a media object template for documenting the business function,
   right-click the icon panel to the left of the Media Object application. From the
   pop-up menu, choose Templates.

3. On the Work With Media Object Template form, click the Find button to view
   a list of templates.

4. Highlight the grid row of your choice and click the Select button.

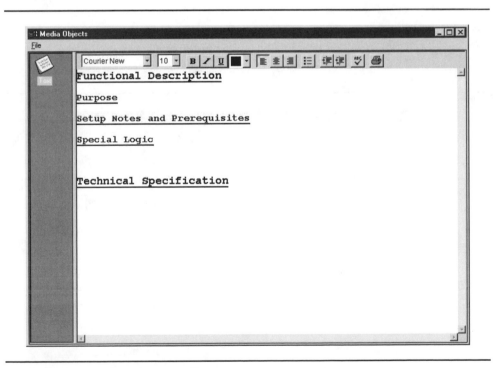

FIGURE 13-24.   Media Object application

5. The template is copied into the Media Objects application for the business function, as shown earlier in Figure 13-24, and you can begin documenting your business function.

N O T E

Another place to insert information about a business function is in the Notes section of the source file for a C business function. Any information written into the Notes section will appear in the business function documentation.

For Data Structures   To create documentation for data structures, complete the following steps:

1. From the Data Structure Design tool application (shown earlier in Figure 13-7), click the Data Structure Attachments button. The Data Structure Notes Revisions form of the Data Structure Notes application (P98DS) appears, as shown in Figure 13-25.

2. To assign a media object template for documenting the data structure, right-click in the icon panel to the left of the Media Object application. From the pop-up menu, choose Templates.

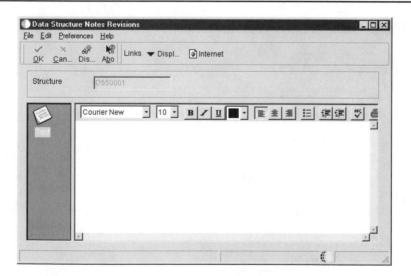

FIGURE 13-25.   Data Structure Notes Revisions form of the Data Structure Notes application (P98DS)

3. The template is copied into the Media Object application for the data structure, and you can begin documenting it.

For Data Structure Parameters To create documentation for data structure parameters, complete the following steps:

1. From the Data Structure Design tool application (shown earlier in Figure 13-7), click the Data Structure Item Attachments button. The Data Structure Item Notes Revisions form of the Data Structure Notes application (P98DS) appears, as shown in Figure 13-26.

2. Enter documentation about the data structure item.

3. To assign a media object template for documenting the data structure item, right-click in the icon panel to the left of the Media Object application. From the pop-up menu, choose Templates. The template is copied into the Media Object application for the data structure item, and you can begin documenting it.

Generating the Business Function Documentation

After you've finished creating or modifying the documentation for a business function, you can generate it. The system then compiles all of the documentation written about the business function and puts it into an easy-to-view medium. If any changes are

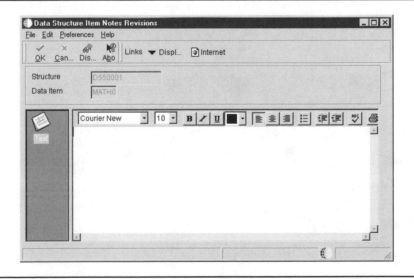

FIGURE 13-26. Data Structure Item Notes Revisions form of the Data Structure Notes application (P98DS)

Advanced Application Development

made after the system generates the documentation, you have to regenerate the documentation.

NOTE

The procedure for regenerating documentation is very time-consuming because it generates the documentation for all business functions. Try to generate the documentation only when you have finished writing it.

To generate the business function documentation, complete the following steps:

1. From OneWorld Explorer, type **GH902** into the Fast Path box. The Cross Application Development Tools menu appears.

2. Execute the Generate Business Function application (R98ABSFN). The Work With Batch Versions form of the Batch Version application (P98305) appears, as shown in Figure 13-27. It displays the Generate Business Function application and its versions in the form.

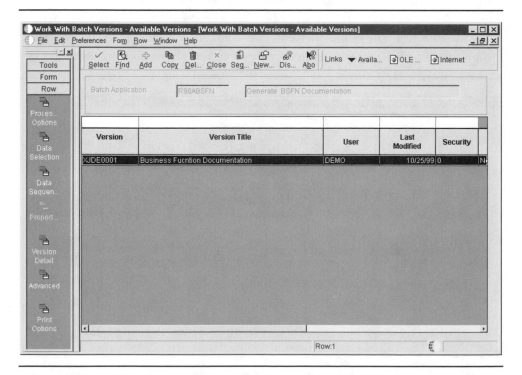

FIGURE 13-27. Work With Batch Versions form of the Batch Version application (P98305)

3. Highlight the Business Function Documentation version (XJDE0001), and click the Select button. The Version Prompting form appears.

4. Click the Submit button to execute the application.

5. On the Report Output Destination form, ensure that the On Screen check box is enabled.

6. Click OK to begin executing the batch application.

7. When the Generate Business Function Documentation application is finished, the report displays the business function documentation it generated, as shown in Figure 13-28, and stores the documentation locally on your machine.

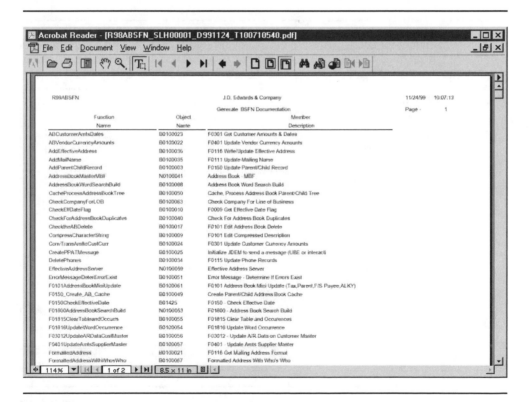

FIGURE 13-28. Generate Business Function Documentation (R98ABSFN) output report

Viewing the Business Function Documentation

After the system generates the documentation for a business function, it can be accessed through several different locations in OneWorld (where it is typically used the most). The documentation is accessible through the following applications:

- **Business Function Documentation Viewer**   You can find the Business Function Documentation Viewer application (P98ABSFN), shown in Figure 13-29, through the Cross Application Development Tools menu (GH902). This application displays the documentation in alphabetical order in an HTML format. To view it, click the links on the pages.

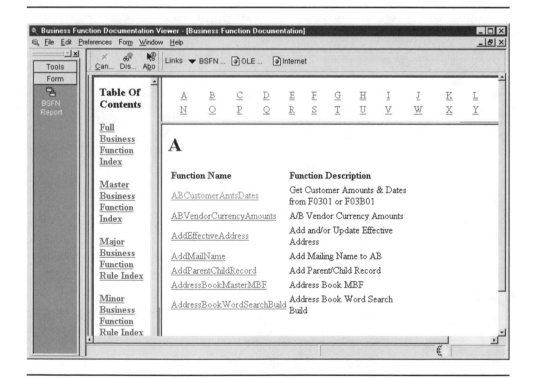

FIGURE 13-29.   Business Function Documentation Viewer application (P98ABSFN)

- **Business Function Search** When you click the Business Function button in the ER design tool, the Business Function Search form (Figure 13-30) appears. Here you can view the documentation through the use of attachments. You access the documentation by clicking the grid row button for the business function.

- **Business Functions, values to pass panel** After you select a business function from the Business Function Search form, the documentation for the business function, data structure, and data structure items all becomes available. They are displayed in the Value column of the Business Functions window shown in Figure 13-31. To access the business function documentation, click the Business Function Notes button. To access the data structure documentation, click the Structure Notes button, and click the Parameters Notes button to access the data structure item documentation.

Advanced Application Development

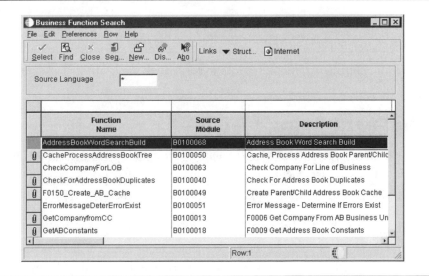

FIGURE 13-30.   Business Function Search form

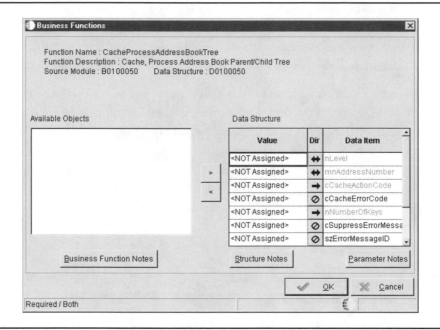

FIGURE 13-31. Business Function values to pass panel

Table Event Rules (TER)

All database tables in OneWorld have the ability to execute *table triggers*. Table triggers are functions that execute whenever a modification to the table occurs. The purpose of table triggers is to embed logic at the table level for enforcement of certain relationships between one or more tables, and to maintain data integrity.

For example, the Address Book module contains many tables that store information about your company's various clients. As you create, modify, and delete records from one or more of the tables in this module, the records in other related tables must be changed, as well, to maintain data integrity. Table triggers are used in the tables for the Address Book module to help maintain data integrity of related records in all tables for the module.

NOTE

Table triggers are only intended to maintain data integrity as well as relationships among tables in OneWorld. Therefore, the data must be valid and correct when the table trigger receives it.

Table triggers are written in the Table Event Rules (TER) language. TER is based on the ER code. The TER language is identical to the ER language; thus you can leverage your knowledge of ER for building TER code for table triggers. However, TER code contains a reduced set of system functions and interconnection commands, because the language is only intended to manipulate tables in OneWorld.

CAUTION

Do not write any data-validation logic in a table trigger. TER has no means to correct the logic or to notify the user of the error.

Probably the most difficult issue for working with table triggers concerns when and where to use them. This is because a business function or application can contain the same lines of code that are contained in a table trigger. Writing the logic in a business function or application, however, becomes burdensome when you always have to write and maintain the logic in every application that modifies the table.

Table triggers avoid duplicating the same logic in all applications that modify the table, because the logic is executed every time the table is modified. The primary advantage of table triggers is that, once you write the code into them, it doesn't have to be replicated throughout the applications. By implementing table logic for data integrity in table triggers, you make your applications more easily maintained.

TER Commands and Table Events

Figure 13-32 displays the available system commands for TER code. As you can see, compared to its ER code counerpart, TER has a dramatically scaled-down set of available commands. This is primarily because the scope of table triggers only includes OneWorld tables, resulting in TER code's inability to create a form or batch interconnect to an application.

TER code does contain all the commands for the Messaging and Workflow APIs. This lets you send messages to users, and control a workflow process from a table trigger.

NOTE

One interesting use of messaging and workflow in TER code is to monitor table changes for security purposes. System and security administrators can thus monitor changes made to tables, for the purpose of detecting fraudulent practices in the organization.

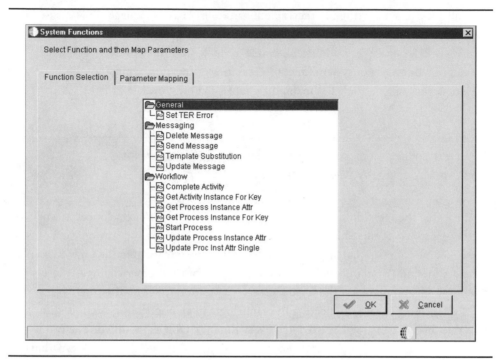

FIGURE 13-32. Available system commands for TER

TER code also uses one function in the General API, the Set TER Error. This command sets an error for the trigger by using an error message defined in the Error Messages application (P92002).

TER code also provides table I/O commands, shown in Figure 13-33. The table I/O commands in table triggers offer all the features and functionality of ER and NER code. For example, you can insert, fetch, select, open, and delete records in any table.

Every table trigger contains nine events that are used for before-and-after processing of the records in the table. You use these events to update all the dependent tables and validate that the record has been manipulated properly. Table 13-10 lists the table events available for table triggers.

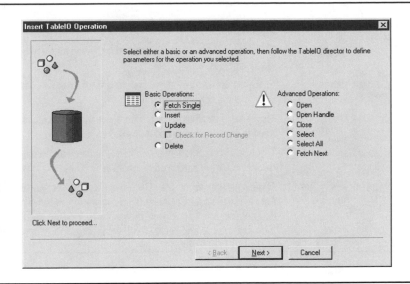

FIGURE 13-33.   Available table I/O commands for TER

Event	Description
Before Record Is Deleted	Executed before a record is deleted and is typically used for auditing purposes.
Before Record Is Fetched	Executed before a record is fetched and is used to validate any fields before they are fetched from the table.
Before Record Is Inserted	Executed before a record is inserted and is used to update records in other tables that are dependent on the current one.
Before Record Is Updated	This event is executed before a record is updated and is used to update records in other tables that are dependent on the current one. Tip: Issue all table manipulation commands to the dependent tables *before* the record is inserted or updated. That way, you can prevent data integrity problems if the commands fail, by stopping processing of the table trigger.

TABLE 13-10.   Available Events for Inserting TER into a Table

Event	Description
After Record Is Deleted	This event is executed after a record is deleted and is typically used for auditing purposes.
After Record Is Fetched	This event is executed after a record is fetched and is used to calculate fields that are columns of the buffer.
After Record Is Inserted	This event is executed after a record is inserted and is used to verify all records that were submitted to the table.
After Record Is Updated	This event is executed after a record is updated and is used to verify all records that were submitted to the table.
Currency Conversion Is On	This event replaces the After Record Is Fetched event and the Before Record Is Inserted event for currency processing, to convert the currency data coming out and going into the database. Use this event to retrieve the currency code and decimal for the currency amount data item.

TABLE 13-10.   Available Events for Inserting TER into a Table *(continued)*

Table Event Rule Examples

Creating and modifying TER for table triggers is a straightforward process. This is due, in part, to the limited number of events that can be used, and the few system commands that are available. The following two examples illustrate the process of creating and modifying table triggers.

Creating Table Triggers with TER

Since TER code is identical to ER code, writing TER for table triggers is less complex. The same Event Rule Design application is used for editing the code. Your knowledge of ER code helps you build powerful functionality into your table triggers.

The following steps show you how to write TER code for table triggers:

1. From OneWorld Explorer, type **OL** into the Fast Path edit box and press ENTER. The Object Librarian application (P9860) appears.

2. For this example, we are showing how to add table triggers to the F55TEST table. Highlight the table in the Work With Object Librarian form and

click the Select button. Next, you'll see the Table Design Aid form (Figure 13-34).

3. To begin editing the table trigger for the F55TEST table, click the Table ER form exit button on the left. The Event Rules Design Aid appears, as shown in Figure 13-35.

4. Edit the ER code for the table trigger as you normally would for a batch or interactive application. The ER commands available for table triggers are discussed in the preceding section, and in Chapter 7. When you've finished, select File | Save and Exit.

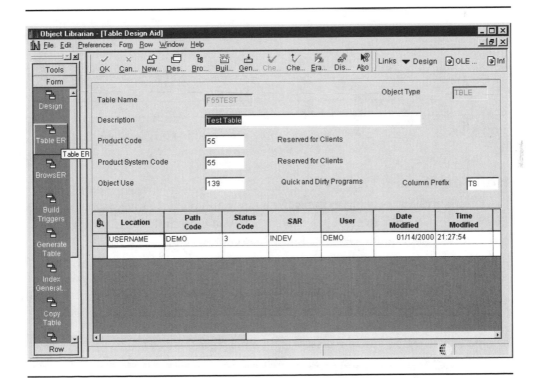

FIGURE 13-34. Table Design Aid form for the F55TEST table

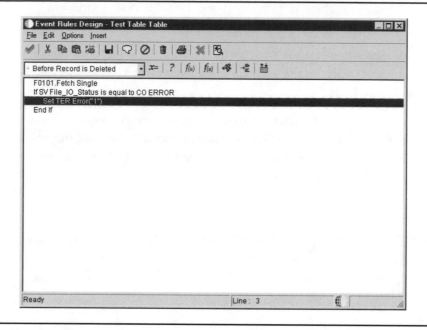

FIGURE 13-35.   Event Rules Design Aid application for the F55TEST table

Building Table Triggers

Continuing with the previous example, we'll now build the table trigger for a table. Every time you modify the TER in a table trigger, you must build the trigger. This is accomplished by compiling the TER into a OneWorld DLL file.

NOTE

Table triggers are built into a OneWorld DLL file and are executed when the system detects the table being modified from a native application. If you try to modify a OneWorld table from an application that is not native to OneWorld, the table trigger will not execute, because the system is not in control of the table during execution.

To write the TER code for table triggers, click the Build Triggers form exit row button in the Table Design Aid form (shown earlier in Figure 13-34). The system then converts the ER code to C. The source code file for this example is called F55test.c,

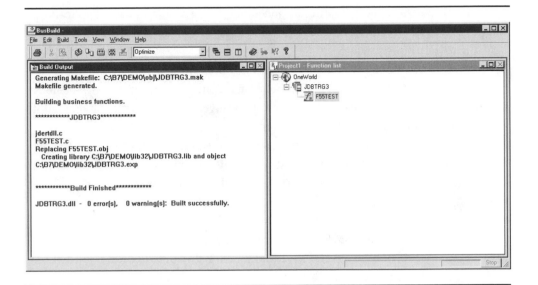

FIGURE 13-36. BusBuild application for the F55TEST table triggers

and the header file is called F55test.hxx. For other table triggers, you'll replace F55TEST with the object name of the table for which you're building triggers.

Next, the system creates the Makefile for the table trigger, and compiles it into one of the Jdbtrg$x$.dll files, where x is a value between 1 and 4. The BusBuild application is used to compile the table triggers, as shown in Figure 13-36. The F55TEST table triggers are successfully built into the Jdbtrg3.dll file.

When you've finished, you can close the BusBuild application and the Object Librarian application (P9860).

Putting It All Together

As you've seen in this chapter, you can create your own data structures and write customized business functions. By implementing your business requirements in business functions, you make them reusable throughout the system without having to duplicate the code. Also, they can be mapped to any machine on the network for execution by the OCM to increase the performance of applications.

Data structures support communication among objects such as batch applications, interactive applications, and business functions. This allows the objects to exchange data during runtime operation.

. Two types of business functions are available for use in OneWorld. You use NER business functions to perform data manipulation on one or more tables. NER business functions offer the ease of use of the ER scripting language, and you can rapidly build a business function using the ER Design tool.

When the logic for the NER becomes complex, it will impact the performance of the business function; or it may be that you require functionality not supported by the ER scripting language. That's when you need to build C-based business functions. C business functions are written in the C programming language and do require a developer experienced in C. Neverthless, C-based business functions give you advanced functionality, such string manipulation and calling a DLL, that is not native to OneWorld. An example of advanced functionality that you can implement in C-based business functions is illustrated in a Developer's Corner earlier in this chapter.

PART IV

Interfacing with OneWorld

CHAPTER 14

Interoperability

As corporations advance technologically, they depend more on technology to support their daily operations. Every day, technology enables companies and their employees to work better, faster, and more productively. The dependence on technology, however, makes corporations vulnerable and inefficient if the technology that supports them fails to work optimally and becomes outdated.

To keep up with advancing technology and to compete in the global market, many corporations have taken multiple vendor applications and built them to work together. The advantage of this approach is that your company can use the best features and functionality of each system to support daily operations.

The integration of Siebel with J.D. Edwards OneWorld is one example. Siebel has an enhanced set of sales force automation applications that improve the effectiveness of J.D. Edwards' sales and marketing departments, while J.D. Edwards OneWorld has superior financial and inventory applications to streamline Siebel's daily operations. This integration allows a company to use the best of both worlds without selecting one product over another.

To simplify the process of interfacing OneWorld with another system, J.D. Edwards has built an interoperability framework that lets OneWorld coordinate data flow and applications between it and another vendor's application. This framework allows OneWorld to be an open platform for other systems to interface with.

The following sections provide you with the information you need for your interoperability development project:

- **Overview of Interoperability**   Interoperability is more than building a few applications to facilitate the flow of data between different vendor's applications. It is an advanced approach to tackle the differences among applications in order to interface them. This section provides you with the core ideas to assist you during an interoperability development project.

- **Interoperability Processing Models**   OneWorld has a set of interoperability processing models that you use to implement the integration of OneWorld with external applications. These models are built directly into the system to avoid the problems of appending them after the fact.

Overview of Interoperability

Interoperability provides OneWorld with a well-defined framework that allows it to operate with an external system. The advantages of the framework are that it assists you in designing interfaces faster and implementing them with fewer defects, if built properly. This section explains how to use the interoperability framework effectively.

Interfacing Versus Integrating Two Systems

For development projects that are focused on operating OneWorld with an external system, the most difficult question to answer is, "How will the systems operate together?" When approaching this type of development project, the issues usually fall into one of two different categories: interfacing or integrating the systems.

Interfacing two systems together involves the flow of data between the systems. This technique usually consists of exchanging *flat files* between systems—that is, files consisting only of ASCII-defined characters. The advantage of this approach is that virtually no dependencies exist between the systems beyond the flat file. Therefore, interfacing systems together results in a minimal impact of each system on the other, and it is the fastest to implement. Some of the drawbacks of interfacing two systems together are the following: no real-time update of each system occurs, and little sharing of resources occurs besides the files sent between systems.

For example, OneWorld exports its data from one or more of its tables, usually by converting a table conversion application to a flat file. The external system then reads the data in the flat file at some point after the file is created and updates itself with the data.

On the other hand, integrating two systems involves coordinating data and applications between them. This technique usually consists of exchanging flat files or electronic documents and managing application execution in both systems for different processes.

The advantages of integrating two systems are that they behave as one system, and processing is usually performed in real time. However, one of the drawbacks of this approach is that it takes longer to implement. Also, dependencies are created between systems that make upgrading one of the systems difficult. For every upgrade, you have to verify that the interface has not been changed by the new release and modify it if it has.

N O T E

Presently, the interoperability framework is primarily based on interfacing OneWorld with an external system. In future releases, OneWorld will add more integration capabilities to the framework.

Interfacing with OneWorld

To reduce the dependency between systems, many third-party applications and industry standards already exist or are being developed to help you build and maintain the integration of the two systems. For example, IBM's MQ Series product is a message broker that allows two systems to communicate with each other. The product is delivered with a set of development tools for the creation of system integration, and it provides the technology to handle the flow of requests between the systems. The advantage of this approach is that the applications in both systems do not have to be modified.

Data Integrity

Because interoperability focuses on the flow of data and the coordination of application execution between OneWorld or another vendor's applications, the primary focus during a development project is the integrity of data flowing in and out of OneWorld.

DEFINITION

*OneWorld developers usually refer to the flow of data in and out of OneWorld as inbound and outbound data. **Inbound data** refers to data that OneWorld must enter into its application tables. **Outbound data** refers to data that OneWorld must extract from its application tables.*

Data integrity helps you maintain the validity of data flowing in and out of OneWorld. When properly implemented, data integrity prevents the corruption of data in both systems that can cause application failure and that can potentially cause system failures. You must perform two important tasks in any interoperability development to maintain the data integrity: data mapping and validation.

Data mapping defines each field required for both systems, and the table and column in which the data is stored in each system. Properly defining the data mapping between OneWorld and another system will help you identify which data has to be extracted or inserted from the tables and their columns in each system.

Data validation defines the valid values that each field in the interface can have. Properly defining the data validation between OneWorld and another system will help you maintain the integrity of each data item in the interface as data flows in and out of each system.

T I P

We recommend that you implement applications in both systems to validate data for an interoperability project. Even though this increases the workload required for the project, it dramatically reduces the problems associated with invalid data because all data is checked twice before it is processed into either system.

It is a good idea to thoroughly document the data mapping and data integrity rules that you build for the interface. When properly written, the interface documentation will capture the knowledge required to maintain the interface between OneWorld and other systems. This will cut your development time later when you modify the interface of the two systems for an upgrade.

Interoperability Framework

The interoperability framework includes a set of interoperability processing models that you use to define the objects and applications for a particular type of interface between OneWorld and another system. To determine which interoperability processing model you need to use for your interoperability development project, refer to the decision matrix in Figure 14-1.

For a OneWorld development project to interoperate with another system, you must determine the following: Is immediate processing or feedback required? Is individual processing of each transaction required?

Immediate processing or feedback is used in cases in which one system invokes the other system, and the invoking system has to know how the other system properly responded to its request. The synchronous model provides real-time interaction of OneWorld with external applications, and it forces the invoking system to wait on the other system. The primary benefit of this approach is that the invoking system knows when the other system has finished processing and whether the other system executed the request properly.

The system processes each transaction individually when it needs to be updated quickly, but the invoking system is not required to wait on the other system to finish processing. The asynchronous model allows you to update the system on a transaction-by-transaction basis within a short time after the request is generated.

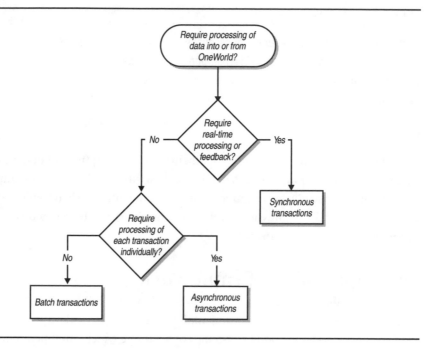

FIGURE 14-1.   A decision matrix for interoperability processing models

The advantage of this model is that it provides independent execution of OneWorld and an external application, because the systems do not have to pause and wait for each other to finish processing.

If you do not need real-time update and processing of individual transactions, you can use batch processing. The batch-processing model allows you to store transactions over time and submit them together for processing all at once. The advantage of this model is that processing can occur during off-hours, such as 2:00 A.M.

The interoperability framework can provide all of these models for integrating/ interfacing OneWorld with an external system because of the underlying system architecture, as shown in Figure 14-2. The top layer illustrates the actual applications that users execute to perform their daily tasks, whether they are OneWorld or external applications. The applications link to the OneWorld databases and business functions through the communication middleware, which is called JDENET (discussed in more detail in Chapter 15). JDENET provides the medium through which all clients and servers communicate to support the operation of application execution.

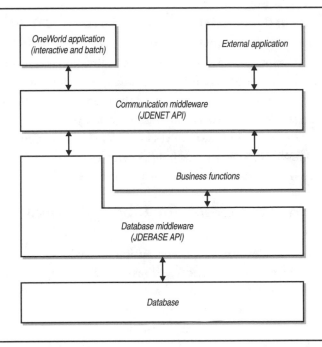

FIGURE 14-2.   OneWorld application architecture

Interoperability Processing Models

OneWorld has six different interoperability models: inbound synchronous, inbound asynchronous, inbound batch, outbound synchronous, outbound asynchronous, and outbound batch. Each one is based on a single data flow mode (inbound or outbound), and a processing mode (synchronous, asynchronous, or batch).

These models provide a set of structured approaches and techniques to transfer and retrieve information from OneWorld without risking its data and system integrity. Think of these models as a set of blueprints that provide you with the details about the interface that you must build between your applications and OneWorld.

The models give external applications the ability to operate with OneWorld without J.D. Edwards having to build an API for each one. This reduces the time you must spend designing the interface or integrating OneWorld with another system, because the framework for the OneWorld side of the design is already available. Also, the time you spend implementing is reduced on the OneWorld side, since most of the models already have their objects defined. Let's take a look at each model now.

Inbound Synchronous Processing Model

Inbound synchronous processing provides the framework for an external application to communicate directly with a OneWorld object in a bidirectional real-time mode. This model allows external applications to execute a function or application in OneWorld.

Figure 14-3 provides a schematic diagram of the inbound synchronous processing model. As you can see, there are two techniques in which you can provide data to a OneWorld table. The first technique involves establishing a valid OneWorld session to provide data to OneWorld. The other technique involves establishing an Open Database Connectivity (ODBC) connection to a database that OneWorld uses.

Using a OneWorld Session for Inbound Synchronous Processing

The first technique for an external application using inbound synchronous processing is to communicate through a valid OneWorld session. The external application is a valid OneWorld session, and it requires the same licensing and security restrictions as a regular OneWorld Explorer session. An example of an external application that uses this type of processing model is a data-warehousing application updated with information when data is changed in a OneWorld application table.

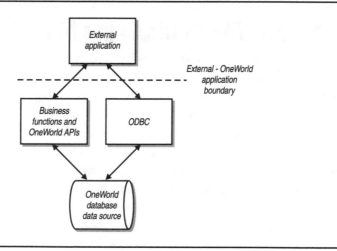

FIGURE 14-3.   A schematic diagram of inbound synchronous processing

N O T E

An example of using a OneWorld session for inbound synchronous processing is provided in Chapter 15, in the Developer's Corner titled "Using the JDEBASE API for Interoperability with OneWorld."

This processing model has a few advantages over the other models: after the execution of a call, the external application immediately determines if it executed successfully or not; and the external application has access to all OneWorld APIs and business functions. The disadvantage of this approach is that the portions of the external application that communicate with OneWorld must be written in C/C++, which creates a dependency when a developer or a new release of OneWorld modifies the function or application.

To enable an external application to provide inbound synchronous processing by using a valid OneWorld session, perform the following steps:

1. *Connect to OneWorld.* The external application has to create a valid connection to OneWorld, which it does by using the JDB_InitUser function. When the JDB_InitUser function executes, it displays the OneWorld sign-on screen to validate the user who is accessing OneWorld from an external application. The user executing the external application must pass sign-on security to acquire a OneWorld session.

N O T E

The JDB_InitUser function belongs to the JDEBASE API and is described in detail in Chapter 15.

2. *Call business functions or API functions.* Once you have a valid connection to OneWorld, any business function or API function is available for the external application to call. To execute a business function, execute the jdeCallObject function.

N O T E

The jdeCallObject function is described in detail in Chapter 13.

3. *Disconnect from OneWorld.* After your external application has made all the calls to OneWorld that it needs, the application must disconnect its session. To disconnect the session, execute the JDB_FreeUser function. This function will terminate any further communication with OneWorld and free the resources associated with the session.

N O T E

The JDB_FreeUser function belongs to the JDEBASE API, and is described in detail in Chapter 15.

Using an ODBC Connection for Inbound Synchronous Processing

The other technique for an external application using inbound synchronous processing is to communicate through an ODBC connection. The external application uses an ODBC connection to a OneWorld database. The external application must pass database security, but it avoids the licensing and security restrictions that the previous technique uses. An example of an external application that uses this type of processing model is a Visual Basic macro embedded in a Microsoft Office document that updates a table in OneWorld.

The advantage of this approach over the approach described in the preceding section is that users who know how to use an ODBC connection to insert data into a database table can use this technique. A disadvantage of this approach is that the external application has no access to the business functions and APIs that are available in OneWorld.

Perform the following steps to enable an external application to provide inbound synchronous processing by using an ODBC connection:

1. *Define an ODBC data source for the OneWorld database data source.* Define an ODBC data source that points to a valid OneWorld database data source. See Chapter 2 for further information on ODBC data sources.

2. *Create a connection to the database through the ODBC data source.* Connect to the database using the ODBC data source that you defined in the previous step. A login screen for the database will appear to require the user to pass login security for the database.

3. *Issue SQL commands to the ODBC data source.* If you have a valid connection to the database, then any SQL command can be issued to the ODBC data source to modify the database tables.

4. *Disconnect the ODBC data source connection to the database.* After your external application has issued all of the SQL commands to the ODBC data source connection, it must disconnect. This terminates communications to the ODBC data source and frees the resources associated with the connection.

Inbound Asynchronous Processing Model

The *inbound asynchronous processing model* allows external applications to execute transactions in OneWorld without waiting for the execution to finish. The transaction is inserted into an interoperability interface table, and OneWorld handles all of the validation and updating of the transaction into the system independent of the external application.

The advantage of this approach is that the external application need only contain logic to insert transactions into interoperability tables. Also, the external application does not have to maintain logic to validate and update the system with the transaction because all of that logic is maintained in OneWorld.

Figure 14-4 illustrates the inbound asynchronous processing model. To show you how OneWorld processes the transaction it received in its interoperability table, Figure 14-4 contains the object names that are required to import data into the Address Book module.

The following steps give you a better idea of the flow of inbound asynchronous processing, shown in Figure 14-4:

1. *Connect to OneWorld.* The external application has the same options to insert a transaction into the interoperability table (Z table). You can use the external

application to communicate to the Z table through a OneWorld user session or through the ODBC connection to the database that OneWorld uses.

2. *Add records to the interoperability or Z table.* Add records to the interoperability table for the process. For the Address Book example in Figure 14-4, you add the records to the Address Book Interoperability table (F0101Z2).

3. *Place the entry into the subsystem queue.* You must make an entry into the Subsystem Job Master table (F986113) so the system can process the transaction you just added in the previous step. When you add an entry into the table, make sure that you add the proper input batch application to process the transaction. To add an entry into the Subsystem Job Master table (F986113), execute the Add Transaction to Subsystem Queue business function (B0000176) by using the jdeCallObject function. For the address book example in Figure 14-4, make an entry into the Subsystem Job Master table (F986113) using the input batch application, Address Book Batch Upload application (R01010Z).

NOTE

The jdeCallObject function is described in detail in Chapter 13.

4. *Disconnect from OneWorld.* After your external application has made all of the calls to OneWorld that it needs, the application must disconnect its session, which is either a OneWorld or an ODBC session.

At this point, the input batch process executes. When the assigned time in the Subsystem Job Master table (F986113) occurs, the system executes the input batch process that you entered earlier. While the input batch process is executing, it usually requires a Master Business Function (MBF) to update the system with a record from the interoperability table. In most cases, the MBF requires a set of processing options, which are assigned to a dummy interactive application. For the Address Book example in Figure 14-4, the Address Book Batch Upload application (R01010Z) processes all of the records that the external application entered into the proper tables, sends a confirmation record to the user's Work Center Message Queue table (F01131), and prints out a report of what it did. The Address Book MBF (N0100041) updates the

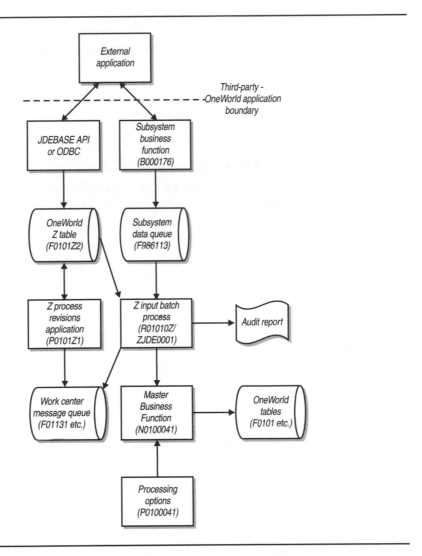

FIGURE 14-4. Schematic diagram of inbound asynchronous processing

system with one record at a time, and it uses the processing options assigned to the Address Book MBF PO application (P0100041) for certain settings.

NOTE

MBFs are explained in more detail later in this chapter, in the section "Master Business Functions."

The following sections describe the components that make up an inbound asynchronous process in more detail.

Interoperability Interface Tables (Z Tables)

The system uses interoperability interface tables to store information about transactions that occur between external applications and OneWorld. For example, the external application can be another ERP system, such as SAP or BAAN, or a third-party application used for special purposes, such as data warehousing and analysis. As the external application generates or requires information from OneWorld, it inserts or acquires information from interoperability interface tables.

NOTE

The client and server use the interoperability interface tables for communication between the store-and-forward mode for client/server operations. These tables store information generated by the client until the client is connected to the network and can communicate to the server.

The advantage of using the interoperability interface tables over the other models is that the application tables, such as the Journal Entry table (F0911), are isolated during insertion and extraction of data in the interoperability interface tables. Also, the external application does not have to contain all of the logic required to properly update a transaction in OneWorld.

The disadvantage of using the interoperability interface tables over direct table manipulation is that the records that are inserted by the external applications must contain valid values in each column. Therefore, the first step in your interoperability development project is determining the valid values for each column in the Z tables. This is a very tedious and heuristic approach that takes several iterations before it is finally ready for the production environment.

Table 14-1 lists the available interoperability interface transactions in OneWorld and the corresponding Z tables that they use. Table 14-1 also briefly describes the purpose of the transaction.

Interoperability Interface Transaction Types	Interoperability Interface Table(s)	Purpose of Transaction
Address Book	F0101Z2	Maintains information about companies and people with whom you do business
Customer Master	F03012Z1	Maintain information about customers and instructions the system uses to process their A/R accounts
Supplier Master	F0401Z1	Maintains information about suppliers and instructions the system uses to process their A/P accounts
Batch Invoice	F03B11Z1, F0911Z1, F0911Z1T	Maintains information about invoices charged to customers for services rendered
Batch Voucher	F0411Z1, F0911Z1	Maintains information about vouchers charged to your company for services rendered
Payment Order with Remittance	F0413Z1, F0414Z1	Issues payments for vouchers issued to your company
Journal Entry	F0911Z1, F0911Z1T	Creates transactions to accounts in your company's G/L
Fixed Asset Master	F1201Z1, F1217Z1	Maintains information about your company's equipment and assets
Account Balance	F0902Z1	Updates information about accounts assigned to the budget ledger of your company's G/L
Batch Cash Receipts	F03B13Z1	Issues cash receipts into automatic receipt processing
Payroll Time Entry	F06116Z1	Creates time cards in the payroll system
Purchase Order	F4301Z1, F4311Z1	Maintains information about purchase orders generated by your company
Outbound Purchase Receipts	F43121Z1	Outputs information about the purchase receipts in the system (intended to update an external system)
Receipt Routing	F43092Z1	Maintains information about the routing of an item on a purchase order after receipt of the item
Outbound Sales Order	F4201Z1, F4211Z1, F49211Z1	Outputs information about a sales order in the system (for updating an external system)
Outbound Shipment Confirmation	F4201Z1, F4211Z1, F49211Z1	Outputs information that verifies inventory has left the warehouse (for updating an external system)

TABLE 14-1. Interoperability Interface Tables in OneWorld

Interfacing with OneWorld

Interoperability Interface Transaction Types	Interoperability Interface Table(s)	Purpose of Transaction
Cycle Counts	F4141Z1	Maintains information about item numbers, descriptions, locations, and quantities for inventory records
Item Master	F4101Z1, F4101Z1A	Maintains information about the items your company stocks
Item Cost	F4105Z1	Maintains pricing information for items your company has in inventory
Warehouse Confirmations	F4611Z1	Maintains information about an existing suggestion
Work Order Header	F4801Z1	Outputs information about manufacturing work orders for the shop floor (intended to update an external system)
Work Order Parts List	F3111Z1	Outputs information about part requirements for maintenance tasks (for updating an external system)
Work Order Routing	F3112Z1	Outputs information about the work centers responsible for each maintenance task on a work order (for updating an external system)
Work Order Employee Time Entry	F31122Z1	Maintains information about the hours employees worked against a work order
Work Order Inventory Issues	F3111Z1	Maintains information that determines the actual quantities of parts used in a production process
Work Order Completions	F4801Z1	Maintains information about the completion of a production item into the inventory system
Super Backflush	F3112Z1	Creates backflush transactions against a work order at pay points defined in the routing
Bill of Material	F3002Z1	Maintains information about components used to assemble parent items
Routing Master	F3003Z1	Maintains information about the sequence of operations necessary to manufacture an item
Work Center Master	F30006Z1	Maintains information about work centers
Work Day Calendar	F0007Z1	Maintains information about days of the year that are work days

TABLE 14-1. Interoperability Interface Tables in OneWorld *(continued)*

Interoperability Interface Transaction Types	Interoperability Interface Table(s)	Purpose of Transaction
Planning Messages	F3411Z1	Maintains information about messages generated by Material Requirements Plan (MRP) and Master Production Schedule (MPS) systems
Detail Forecast	F3460Z1	Maintains information about the projected demand an inventory item will have based on its history
Kanban Transactions	F30161Z1	Maintains information about the consumption and production of work centers and what needs to be produced next

TABLE 14-1. Interoperability Interface Tables in OneWorld *(continued)*

Besides the data that accompanies every record in an interoperability interface table, additional fields are required for every record. The additional fields maintain information about the transaction and provide an audit trail for OneWorld. Table 14-2 lists the control columns, those that are required, and describes each one. Table 14-3 also lists the required user reference and audit trail columns and describes each one.

Data Item Alias	Data Item Name	Primary Key	Description
EDUS	User ID	Yes	The user ID of the OneWorld user who initiated the transaction
EDBT	Batch Number	Yes	The batch with which the transaction is associated
EDTN	Transaction Number	Yes	A unique number that identifies a transaction
EDLN	Line Number	Yes	A unique number that identifies a row belonging to a transaction
EDCT	Document Type	No	The OneWorld document type to which the transaction relates (always one of the values assigned to the UDC 00/DT)
TYTN	Transaction Type	No	The name of the transaction defined in the UDC 00/TT

TABLE 14-2. Control Columns for Interoperability Interface Tables

Data Item Alias	Data Item Name	Primary Key	Description
EDFT	Translation Format	No	A value that identifies a specific map used to process both inbound and outbound transactions
EDDT	Transmission Date	No	The date the transaction is transmitted
DRIN	Direction Indicator	No	A flag that identifies the record for either inbound (1) or outbound (2) processing
EDDL	Number of Detail Lines	No	The total number of rows to be processed
EDSP	Processed	No	A field that defines the final state of the transaction (equals Y when the transaction is completed successfully)
PNID	Trading Partner ID	No	The ID of the other party that is part of the transaction, such as a supplier, customer, or broker
TNAC	Action Code	No	The action to be taken on a row in a transaction—values are add (A), change (C), and delete (D)

TABLE 14-2.   Control Columns for Interoperability Interface Tables *(continued)*

Data Item Alias	Data Item Name	Description
URCD	User Reserved Code	A 2-character string data item available for the user
URDT	User Reserved Date	An 11-digit numeric data item available for the user and intended for dates
URAT	User Reserved Amount	A 15-digit numeric data item available for the user and intended for currency amounts
URAB	User Reserved Number	An 8-digit numeric data item available for the user
URRF	User Reserved Reference	A 15-character string data item available for the user
TORG	Transaction Originator	The user who initiated a request
USER	User ID	The user ID of a OneWorld user

TABLE 14-3.   User Reserved and Audit Trail Columns for Interoperability Interface Tables

Data Item Alias	Data Item Name	Description
PID	Program ID	The name of a OneWorld batch or interactive application that modifies the row
JOBN	Workstation ID	The name of the workstation that modified the row in a OneWorld table
UPMJ	Date Updated	The date the row was updated
TDAY	Time Updated	The time the row was updated

TABLE 14-3. User Reserved and Audit Trail Columns for Interoperability Interface Tables *(continued)*

Revisions Applications

Revisions applications are interactive applications in OneWorld that allow you to manage transactions located in the interoperability interface tables. These applications add, update, delete, and inspect transactions that are located in the Z tables. In addition, you can launch the execution of an input batch application to update the system with the transaction located in the Z table.

Table 14-4 lists all revisions applications in OneWorld and the particular interoperability interface transactions for which they are used.

Interoperability Interface Transaction Types	Revisions Application
Address Book	P0101Z1
Customer Master	P0101Z1
Supplier Master	P0401Z1
A/R Invoice	P03B11Z1
A/P Voucher	P0411Z1
Payment Order with Remittance	P0413Z1
Journal Entry	P0911Z1
Fixed Asset Master	P1201Z1
Account Balance	P0902Z1

TABLE 14-4. List of Revisions Applications in OneWorld

Interfacing with OneWorld

Interoperability Interface Transaction Types	Revisions Application
Payroll Time Entry	P05116Z1
Purchase Order	P4311Z1
Outbound Purchase Receipts	P43121Z1
Receipt Routing	P43092Z1
Outbound Sales Order	P4211Z1
Outbound Shipment Confirmation	P4211Z1
Cycle Counts	P4141Z1
Item Master	P4101Z1
Item Cost	P4105Z1
Warehouse Confirmations	P4611Z1
Work Order Header	P4801Z1
Work Order Parts List	P4801Z1
Work Order Routing	P4801Z1
Work Order Employee Time Entry	P31122Z1
Work Order Inventory Issues	P3111Z1
Work Order Completions	P4801Z1
Super Backflush	P3112Z1
Bill of Material	P3002Z1
Routing Master	P3003Z1
Work Center Master	P30006Z1
Work Day Calendar	P0007Z1
Planning Messages	P3411Z1
Detail Forecast	P3460Z1
Kanban Transactions	P30161Z1

TABLE 14-4. List of Revisions Applications in OneWorld (*continued*)

Add a Batch Using the Address Book Revisions Application

In the following example, we will add a new address book entry using the Address Book Revisions application (P0101Z1). These steps apply not only to this particular application, but to any other revisions applications listed previously in Table 14-4.

You use the Revisions application to manage all information stored in an interoperability interface table. For example, you can use it to inspect and modify existing batches that were added to the Z table, or you can use it to add a new batch to the Z table through the use of the Revisions application itself.

Follow these steps to use the Address Book Revisions application (P0101Z1):

1. From OneWorld Explorer, type **G0131** into the Fast Path box and press ENTER. The Address Book Advanced Technical Operations menu appears.

2. Double-click the Address Book Batch Revision application (P0101Z1), and the Address Book Batch Revision form appears, as shown in Figure 14-5.

3. To add a new customer, click the Add button, and the Batch Address Book Revision form appears, as shown in Figure 14-6.

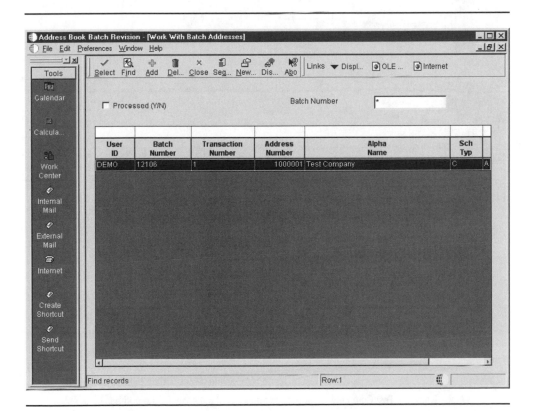

FIGURE 14-5. The Address Book Batch Revision form of the Address Book Batch Revision application (P0101Z1)

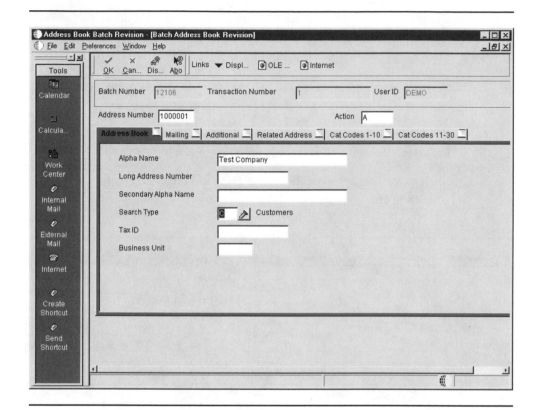

FIGURE 14-6. The Batch Address Book Revision form of the Address Book Batch Revision application (P0101Z1)

4. In the Batch Address Book Revision form, enter the following values into its fields:

Field	Value	Purpose
Address Number	1000001	A unique identifier for the address book entry. For this example, the value must not currently exist in the Address Book Master table (F0101), because we are adding a new entry.
Action	A	Defines the type of action to be taken for the address book entry, such as add (A), delete (D), or update (U).
Alpha Name	Test Company	Identifies the name of the entity for the address book entry.
Search Type	C	Identifies the type of address book entry you want to add, such as employee (E) or customer (C), and its value comes from the User Defined Code (01/ST).

5. Click the OK button when you have finished, and you will return to the Address Book Batch Revision form.

6. To ensure that the batch has been entered into the system, deselect the Processed (Y/N) check box, and click the Find button. By deselecting the Processed (Y/N) check box, you will examine all batches that have been entered into the system that have not been processed yet.

7. The address book entry you just entered should appear, as shown earlier in Figure 14-5.

8. To delete the batch from the system, highlight the batch you don't want and click the Delete button.

To have the system process the batch and create the address book entry, see "Update the System with the Address Book Input Batch Application," later in the chapter.

Input a Batch Application

You execute the *input batch application* after you add records to the Z table and after you have finished inspecting them using the Revisions application. The purpose of the input batch application is to update or create records that are stored in its corresponding Z table.

When the input batch application has finished executing, it generates a report that lists all of the records that it processed. The report provides information on the number of records it processed, the details on each record it processed, and any errors that occurred. If the input batch application encounters an error during processing, it sends an error message to the Employee Work Center (P012501).

Most input batch applications use two essential components: processing options and MBFs. The processing options assigned to the input batch application usually contain an option to run the application in final or proof mode. In final mode, all items that it processes are permanently updated in the system. However, proof mode allows you to execute the application without permanently affecting the system. The advantage of using proof mode is that you can run the application to determine if it will execute properly.

Most input batch applications use the MBF to process one record into the system. These MBFs, which are discussed in the section "Master Business Functions," have a processing option assigned to them. Therefore, the processing options for the input batch applications have an option that assigns which version of the MBF to execute.

Table 14-5 lists all input batch applications that are used for interoperability in OneWorld.

Interoperability Interface Transaction Types	Input Batch Application
Address Book	R01010Z – ZJDE0001
Customer Master	R01010Z – ZJDE0001
Supplier Master	R04010Z – ZJDE0001
A/R Invoice	R03B11Z1I – JDE0001
A/P Voucher	R04110Z – ZJDE0001
Journal Entry	R09110Z – ZJDE0002
Fixed Asset Master	R1201Z1I – XJDE0001
Account Balance	R14110M – XJDE0001, R14110 – XJDE0002
Batch Cash Receipts	R03B13Z1I – JDE0001
Payroll Time Entry	R05116Z1I – ZJDE0001
Purchase Order	R4311Z1I – XJDE0001
Receipt Routing	R43092Z1I – ZJDE0001
Cycle Counts	R4141Z1I – ZJDE0001
Item Master	R4101Z1I – ZJDE0001
Item Cost	R4105Z1I – XJDE0001
Warehouse Confirmations	R4611Z1I – ZJDE0001
Work Order Employee Time Entry	R31122Z1I – JDE0001
Work Order Inventory Issues	R31113Z1I – ZJDE0001
Work Order Completions	R31114Z1I – JDE0001
Super Backflush	R31123Z1I – ZJDE0001
Bill of Material	R3002Z1I – ZJDE0001
Routing Master	R3003Z1I – ZJDE0001
Work Center Master	R30006Z1I – ZJDE0001
Work Day Calendar	R0007Z1I – XJDE0001
Planning Messages	R3411Z1I – ZJDE0001
Detail Forecast	R3460Z1I – XJDE0001
Kanban Transactions	R30161Z1I – JDE0001

TABLE 14-5. List of Input Batch Applications in OneWorld

Update the System with the Address Book Input Batch Application

In a previous section, we created an address book entry and batch that were added to OneWorld's Address Book module. However, we only explained how to create a new address book entry. Now we'll explain how to update the system with the new address book entry that we created. You update the system by launching the corresponding input batch application for the particular Revisions application, as shown in the following steps:

1. From OneWorld Explorer, type G0131 into the Fast Path box and press ENTER. The Address Book Advanced Technical Operations menu appears.

2. Double-click the Address Book Batch Upload application (R0101Z1), and the Work With Batch Versions – Available Versions form appears.

3. To execute the Input Batch application, you need to execute the ZJDE0001 version. To do this, highlight the ZJDE0001 grid row and click the Select button. The Version Prompting form appears.

4. Click the Submit button on the Version Prompting form, and the processing options for the version appear.

5. Click the OK button on the Processing Options form, and the Report Output Destination form appears. On the Report Output Destination form, select the On Screen option, and click the OK button.

   The system launches the Address Book Batch Upload application (R0101Z1/ ZJDE0001). When the system has finished executing the application, the report appears, displaying all of the records processed during its execution, as shown in Figure 14-7.

6. To verify that the system properly processed the new address book entries, launch the Address Book Batch Revision application (P0101Z1). In the Work With Batch Addresses form, select the Processed (Y/N) check box and click the Find button. If the Address Book Batch Upload application (R0101Z1) properly processed the new entry, the new entry should appear in the grid, as shown in Figure 14-8.

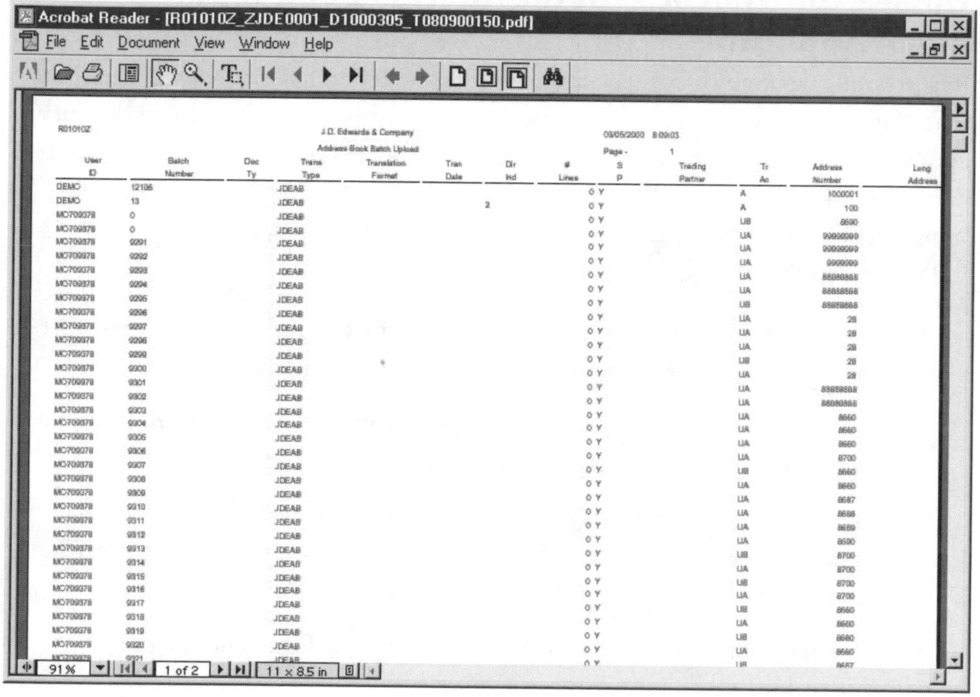

FIGURE 14-7. The Address Book Batch Upload application (R0101Z1/ZJDE0001) report

7. To verify that the new address book entry exists in the system, execute the Address Book Revisions application (P01012) and search for it. As shown in Figure 14-9, the address book entry created in a previous example now exists in the system.

Master Business Functions

MBFs are complex business functions that you can use to process business transactions, such as purchase orders. MBFs update the system properly when a business transaction

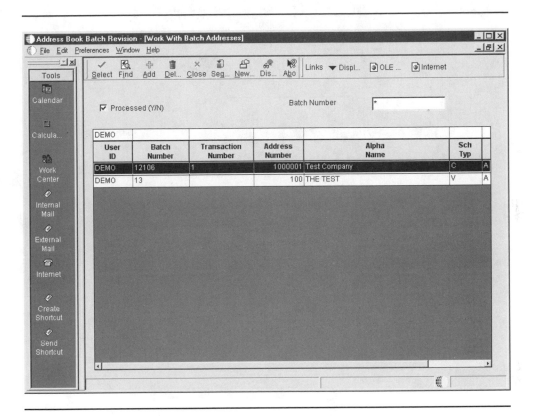

FIGURE 14-8. The Work With Batch Addresses form of the Address Book Batch Revision application (P0101Z1) for the new address book entry

is created, updated, voided, or deleted. To perform these tasks, MBFs usually have to call many different business functions.

Because MBFs perform complex processing, they usually have a processing option assigned to them. Since processing options cannot be directly assigned to business functions, you create a dummy interactive application and assign the processing options to it. For example, the Address Book MBF (N0100041) uses the Address Book MBF PO application (P0100041) to maintain its processing options.

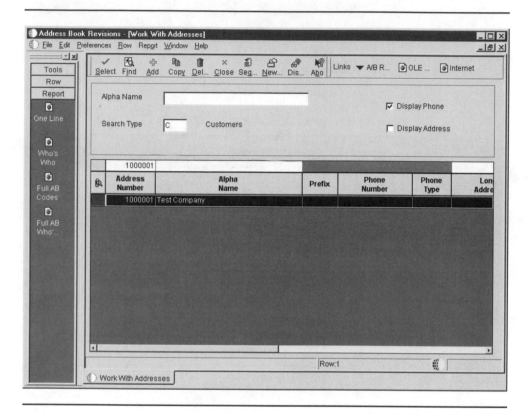

FIGURE 14-9. The Work With Addresses form of the Address Book Revisions
application (P01012) for the new address book entry

Table 14-6 lists all MBFs and the corresponding interactive application that each
one uses to manage its processing options.

Interoperability Interface Transaction Types	Master Business Function	Processing Option Application
Address Book	N0100041	P0100041
Customer Master	N0100042	P0100042
Supplier Master	N0100043	P0100043
A/R Invoice	B03B0011	P03B0011

TABLE 14-6. List of Master Business Functions and Their Corresponding
Processing Options

Interoperability Interface Transaction Types	Master Business Function	Processing Option Application
A/P Voucher	B0400047	P0400047
Payment Order with Remittance	B0400047	P0400047
Journal Entry	B0900049	P0900049
Fixed Asset Master	N1200010	P1201
Payroll Time Entry	B0500002	P050002A
Purchase Order	XT4311Z1	P4310
Outbound Purchase Receipts	XT4312Z1	
Receipt Routing	NXT43092	P43250
Cycle Counts	N4101050	
Item Master	XT4111Z1	P4113
Item Cost	XF4105	
Warehouse Confirmations	B4600440	P4617
Work Order Header	B3101420	
Work Order Parts List	B3101430	
Work Order Employee Time Entry	B3101040	P311221
Work Order Inventory Issues	B3100790	P31113
Work Order Completions	B3101480	
Super Backflush	B3101060	P31123
Bill of Material	N3002040	
Routing Master	N3001780	P3003
Work Center Master	N3001840	
Work Day Calendar	N000700	
Planning Messages	B3401360	P3411
Detail Forecast	N3401430	
Kanban Transactions	N3102010	P3157

TABLE 14-6.   List of Master Business Functions and Their Corresponding Processing Options (*continued*)

The Subsystem Business Function

You use the subsystem business function, which is actually called Add Inbound Transaction to Subsystem Queue business function (B0000176), to add an entry into the Subsystem Data Queue table (F986113). By placing an entry into the table, the system will execute the batch application defined in the entry. This is particularly

Interfacing with OneWorld

useful for the external applications that notify OneWorld when to execute the input batch application after it has inserted all records into a Z table.

The Add Inbound Transaction to Subsystem Queue business function (B0000176) uses the Add Inbound Transaction to Subsystem Queue data structure (D0000176A) to communicate information between the external application and itself. The parameters for the data structure are listed in Table 14-7. External applications use the jdeCallObject function in OneWorld to execute the Add Inbound Transaction to Subsystem Queue business function (B0000176).

NOTE

The jdeCallObject function is described in detail in Chapter 13.

Inbound Batch-Processing Model

Essentially, the *inbound batch-processing model* is a stripped down version of the inbound asynchronous processing model. The inbound batch-processing model allows external applications to insert a bulk amount of transactions into the Z tables. However, executing the input batch application to process the records in the Z tables is not the external application's concern in this model. A user executes the input batch application from a menu in a OneWorld Explorer session.

The advantage of this approach over the other models is that the external application only contains logic to insert transactions into interoperability tables. Also, the external

Parameter	Data Item Alias	Description
szUBEName	OBNM	Object Name
szVersion	VERS	Version History
szUserId	EDUS	EDI – User ID
szBatchNumber	EDBT	EDI – Batch Number
szTransactionNumber	EDTN	EDI – Transaction Number
szLineNumber	EDLN	EDI – Line Number
cSuppressErrorMessage	EV01	Error Message

TABLE 14-7. Parameters for the Add Inbound Transaction to Subsystem Queue Data Structure (D0000176A)

application requires no logic to launch insert records into the subsystem queue. The main disadvantage of this technique is that the input batch application must be manually executed after the external application has finished inserting its transactions into the interoperability tables.

Figure 14-10 provides a schematic diagram of the inbound batch-processing model. To show you how OneWorld processes the transaction it received in its interoperability table, Figure 14-10 contains the object names that are required to import data into the General Ledger module. Two approaches exist for implementing this model: inserting records directly into the Z table, and inserting records into the Z table by using the flat file conversion utility.

Add Records Directly into a Z Table

The first approach that you can take for the inbound batch-processing model, which is shown in Figure 14-10, is to use a stripped down version of the *inbound asynchronous processing model*. This approach requires the use of only the Z table and its corresponding input batch application. To use this approach, perform the following steps:

1. *Create a OneWorld or ODBC connection.* The external application has the same options to insert a transaction into the Z table. The external application communicates to the Z table through a OneWorld user session or an ODBC connection to the database that OneWorld uses.

2. *Add records to the interoperability or Z table.* Add records to the interoperability table for the process. For the example in Figure 14-10, the records are added to the General Ledger Interoperability table (F0911Z1).

N O T E

Figure 14-10 provides the schematic diagram of the components that make up the inbound asynchronous processing model. To assist you in your understanding of this model, each component in the figure provides the object name for processing Journal Entries using the inbound asynchronous processing model. The object names are given in parentheses after each component.

3. *Disconnect from OneWorld.* After your external application has made all of the calls to OneWorld it needs, the application must disconnect its session, which is either a OneWorld or ODBC session.

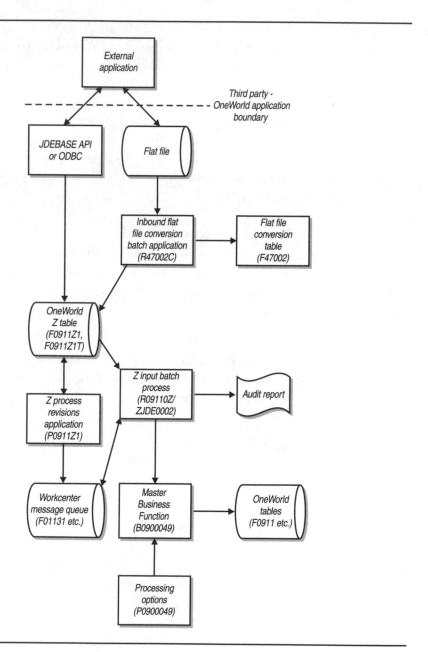

FIGURE 14-10.   Schematic diagram of inbound batch processing

4. *Examine records through the revisions application.* Use the corresponding Revisions application for the Z table to add, inspect, or modify records in the table. For the Journal Entries example in Figure 14-10, we used the Journal Entries Revision application (P0911Z1) to manage the General Ledger Interoperability table (F0911Z1).

5. *Execute the input batch process.* Now you can manually execute the input batch process. For the General Ledger example in Figure 14-10, the General Ledger Batch Upload application (R09110Z) processes all of the records that the external application entered into the proper tables, sends a confirmation record to the user's Work Center Message Queue table (F01131), and prints a report of what it did. The Journal Entries MBF business function (B0900049) updates the system, one record at a time, and uses the processing options assigned to the Journal Entry MBF PO application (P0900049) for certain settings.

Add Records Indirectly to a Z Table Through a Flat File

The other approach you can take using the inbound batch-processing model is to use the Inbound Flat File Conversion application (R47002C). This approach allows an external application to add records to a flat file that is not native to the OneWorld system without requiring any OneWorld or ODBC sessions. To use this approach, perform the following steps:

1. *Enter records into the flat file.* The external application enters records to be processed by OneWorld into the flat file. For the flat file conversion to work properly, the number of fields per record in the flat file must contain the same amount of columns in the destination table. Also, all of the fields in the flat file must correspond to the fields in the destination table in OneWorld. You define the fields in the flat file using the field delimiter assigned to the version for the particular Inbound Flat File Conversion application (R47002C).

2. *Execute the Inbound Flat File Conversion application (R47002C).* After the records are added to the flat file, a user signed on to OneWorld executes the Inbound Flat File Conversion application (R47002C). The application copies each record in the flat file to the corresponding Z table. When completed, the application automatically launches the input batch application to process the records in the Z table into the system. If any errors occur during the record copy process, the application stops processing.

The following sections outline the specific details on using the Inbound Flat File Conversion application (R47002C) for the inbound batch processing model.

Define a Transaction Type for Flat File Conversion

You must define a transaction type for every flat file conversion that the Inbound Flat File Conversion application processes (R47002C). The system uses the transaction type as an alias to uniquely identify a flat file conversion. You define transaction types in the UDC application (00/TT).

To define a transaction type for a flat file conversion, perform the following steps:

1. From OneWorld Explorer, type **UDC** into the Fast Path box and press ENTER. The Work With User Defined Codes form of the User Defined Codes application (P0004A) appears, as shown in Figure 14-11.

2. To create a new transaction type for your flat file conversion, click the Add button. The User Defined Codes form of the User Defined Codes application appears, as shown in Figure 14-12.

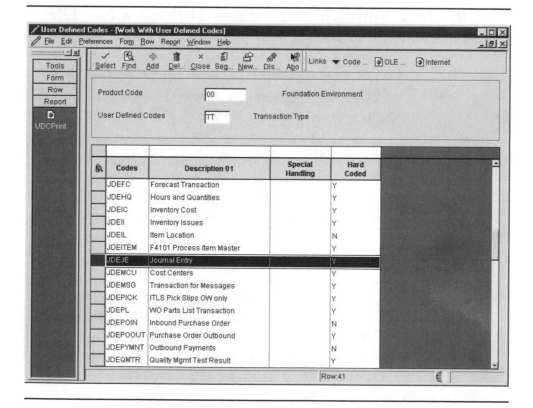

FIGURE 14-11.   The Work With User Defined Codes form of the User Defined Codes application (P0004A)

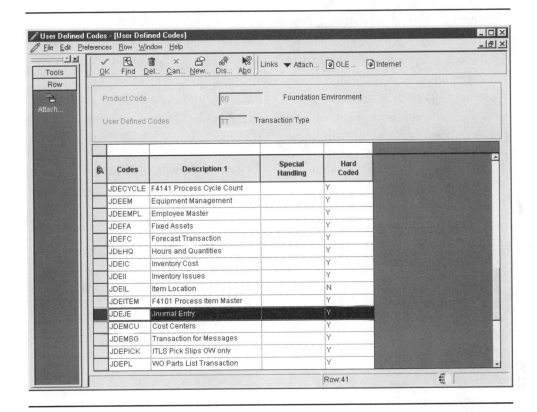

FIGURE 14-12. The User Defined Codes form of the User Defined Codes application (P0004A)

3. To define a transaction type for the Journal Entries transaction, go to the last row of the grid and complete the following fields:

Field	Value	Description
Codes	JDEJE	The short name of the transaction type. Comes preloaded with OneWorld.
Description 1	Journal Entry	A description of the transaction type.
Hard Coded	Y	The place where you define the UDC value as hard-coded. (See Chapter 11.)

4. Click the OK button.

5. Click the Close button to return to OneWorld Explorer.

Create a Version for Transaction Type

For the Inbound Flat File Conversion application (R47002C) to properly process your flat file, you have to provide information about the format of the contents in the flat file. You define the format by creating a new version of the Inbound Flat File Conversion application (R47002C) for the flat file.

To define a new version for the Inbound Flat File Conversion application (R47002C), perform the following steps:

1. From OneWorld Explorer, type BV into the Fast Path box and press ENTER. The Available Versions form of the Batch Versions application (P98305) appears, as shown in Figure 14-13.

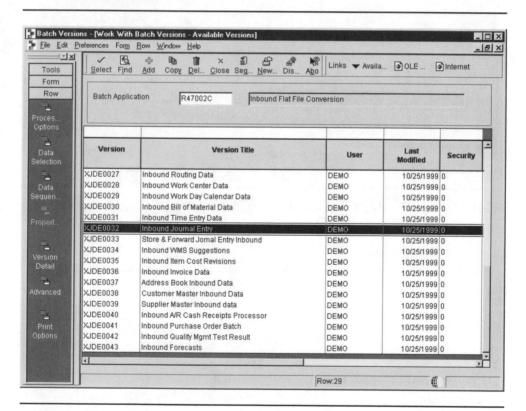

FIGURE 14-13. The Available Versions form of the Batch Versions application (P98305)

2. Type **R47002C** into the Batch Application field of the Available Versions form, and click the Find button. All of the versions for the Inbound Flat File Conversion application (R47002C) appear in the grid of the form.

3. To create a version, click the Add button and the Version Add form appears, as shown in Figure 14-14.

4. In the Version Add form, complete the following fields:

Field	Value	Description
Version	XJDE0032	This is a unique identifier for the new version, and this particular version comes preloaded with OneWorld.
Version Title	Inbound Journal Entry	The field provides a useful description for the version.

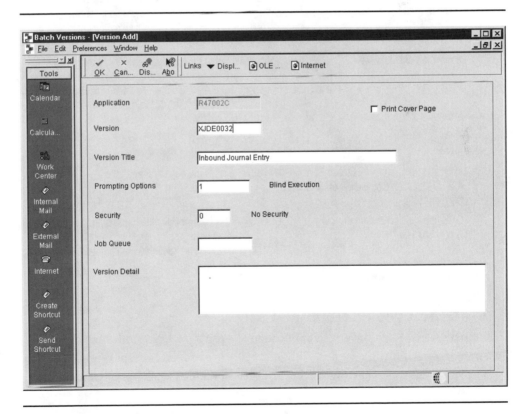

FIGURE 14-14. The Version Add form of the Batch Versions application (P98305)

5. Click the OK button to submit the new version to the system. You will return to the Available Versions form of the Batch Versions application (P98305).

6. Define the processing options for the new version you just made. From the Row menu on the Available Versions form, choose Processing Options, and the processing options for the version appear in the Transaction panel.

7. Enter the transaction type that you created in the previous section into the Enter The Transaction To Process field. In our example, we entered the value of **JDEJE**.

8. Select the Separators panel, and complete the following fields:

Field	Value	Description
Enter the Field Delimiter	,	The field delimiter defines the symbol that separates the fields in the flat file. We recommend that you use a comma; however, you can use any ASCII character that is not an alphanumeric value, such as a period, a semicolon, and so on.
Enter the Text Qualifier	"	The text qualifier defines the symbol that surrounds text for a field in the flat file, such as quotes or double quotes. The value in this field must not be equal to the value used as the field delimiter.

9. Select the Process panel, and complete the following fields:

Field	Value	Description
Enter the Inbound Processor to Run After Successful Completion of the Conversion	R09110Z	This is the object name of the input batch application.
Enter the Version of the Inbound Processor	ZJDE0005	This field provides the name of the version for the input batch application. If no value is provided, then version XJDE0001 will be used.

10. Click the OK button to save the values that you just entered.

Define the Cross-Reference Entry

The Inbound Flat File Conversion application (R47002C) requires information on the location of the flat file in which the inbound records exist and the OneWorld table that to receive the records. This information is stored in the Flat File Cross-Reference table (F47002).

The Flat File Cross-Reference table (F47002) stores the information required by the Inbound Flat File Conversion application (R47002C) by transaction type (UDC 00/TT). The information in this table is maintained with the Work With Flat File Cross-Reference application (P47002).

Follow these steps to properly define an entry in the Flat File Cross Reference table (F47002):

1. From OneWorld Explorer, type **P47002** into the Fast Path box and press ENTER. The Work With Flat File Cross-Reference application (P47002) appears, as shown in Figure 14-15.

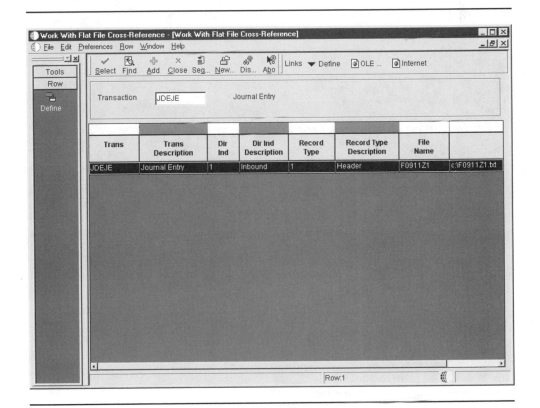

FIGURE 14-15. The Work With Flat File Cross-Reference form of the Work With Flat File Cross-Reference application (P47002)

2. Continuing with the Journal Entry transaction, type **JDEJE** into the Transaction field of the Work With Flat File Cross-Reference form. To enter new information about the transaction, click the Add button, and the Flat File Cross-Reference form appears, as shown in Figure 14-16.

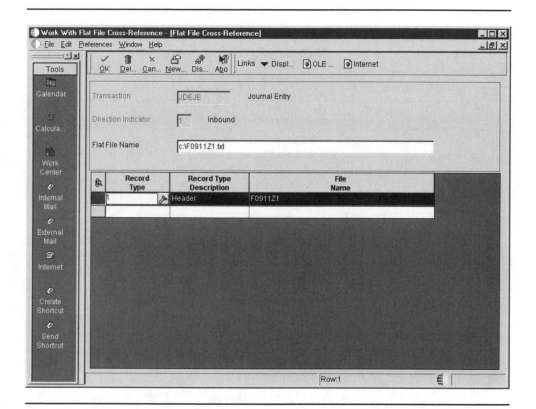

FIGURE 14-16. The Flat File Cross-Reference form of the Work With Flat File Cross-Reference application (P47002)

3. Enter the following information into the fields of the Flat File Cross-Reference form:

Field	Value	Description
Flat File Name	C:\F0911Z1.txt	This is where you enter the full directory path and filename that identifies the flat file you want to use.
Record Type	1	This is the UDC (00/RD) value that defines the record type for the flat file and OneWorld table. The UDC defines header, detail, and address record types.
File Name	F0911Z1	This is the OneWorld table that will receive the records from the flat file.

4. Click the OK button to save the information you just entered.

5. Click the Close button to return to OneWorld Explorer.

6. Now you can execute the Inbound Flat File Conversion application (R47002C) to import the records from the flat file into the Z table. When the application has finished, it will launch the particular input batch application for the transaction type. In this example, the application will launch the Journal Entries input batch application (R09110Z/ZJDE0005).

Until now, the discussion has focused on using OneWorld's Inbound Flat File Conversion application (R47002C) to import records into OneWorld. However, this is not the only option available for the inbound batch-processing model. The following Developer's Corner, titled "Importing Data into OneWorld Using Microsoft Access," shows you how to use Microsoft Access, instead of the Inbound Flat File Conversion application.

Interfacing with OneWorld

Importing Data into OneWorld Using Microsoft Access

In this Developer's Corner, you'll learn to quickly build an application using the inbound batch-processing model. The advantage of this technique is that it allows many users to enter records into OneWorld without using a OneWorld Explorer session. This technique is particularly useful for individuals who would use a OneWorld session to add entries only into something like the Address Book or Time Entry modules.

You build the application using Microsoft Access, and it uses an ODBC connection to implement the inbound batch-processing model. This application's only purpose is to insert records into the Address Book Interoperability Interface table (F0101Z2). As users enter records into the application, the system enters those records into the Address Book Interoperability Interface table (F0101Z2). This table is processed by the Address Book Inbound Process application (R01010Z/ZJDE0001) later. The following illustration shows you the Microsoft Access form that we created to enter new address book entries into the Address Book Interoperability Interface table (F0101Z2).

Developer's Corner

The following code is the only code required for this form, and it is attached to the Phone Number field, which is highlighted in the illustration. The code assigns values to the control columns of the Address Book Interoperability Interface table (F0101Z2). The control values are required so that the Address Book Inbound Process application (R01010Z/ZJDE0001) will properly execute when it is launched.

```
Private Sub SZPH1_BeforeUpdate(Cancel As Integer)
    SZEDUS = 'DEMO'
    SZEDBT = 15019
    SZEDLN = 1
    SZTYTN = 'JDEAB'
    SZDRIN = 1
    SZTNAC = A
End Sub
```

After the users have entered new address book entries, examine the records in the Address Book Revisions application (P0101Z1) to inspect and modify them. Once the entries are verified to be correct, launch the Address Book Inbound Process application (R01010Z/ZJDE0001) to submit the address book entries into the system.

Outbound Synchronous Processing Model

The *outbound synchronous processing model* is the counterpart to the inbound synchronous processing model. Like the inbound synchronous processing model, the outbound synchronous processing model allows an external application to communicate directly with OneWorld in real-time mode. The main difference between the two models, however, is that the outbound synchronous processing model is only used to retrieve data from OneWorld.

The advantage of this processing model over the other models is that it allows third-party applications to retrieve data for a OneWorld database data source. Therefore, applications such as Microsoft Excel and Seagate Crystal Reports can use this model to retrieve information from OneWorld for reporting purposes. The disadvantage of this approach is that you have to know where all of the data is stored in OneWorld to retrieve it, which is very cumbersome if you are not used to the object and data alias naming conventions for tables and their columns.

Figure 14-17 provides a schematic diagram of the outbound synchronous processing model. As you can see, the two means of retrieving data from OneWorld are available by using a OneWorld or ODBC connection. However, the outbound synchronous processing model includes one other technique to retrieve data from OneWorld. The new technique uses the Open Data Access (ODA) driver for OneWorld.

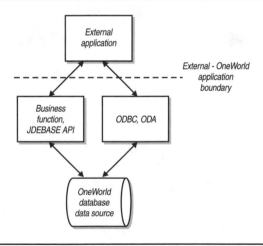

FIGURE 14-17. Schematic diagram of outbound synchronous processing

Perform the following steps to use the outbound synchronous processing model:

1. *Create a OneWorld or ODBC connection.* The external application has the same options to retrieve information from OneWorld tables. The external application can communicate with the tables through a OneWorld user session or an ODBC connection to the database that OneWorld uses.

2. *Retrieve records from a OneWorld table.* Retrieve records from the tables.

3. *Disconnect from OneWorld or the ODBC connection.* After your external application has retrieved all of the data from OneWorld it needs, the application must disconnect its session, which is either a OneWorld or an ODBC session.

Now let's examine how to use ODA for the outbound batch mode.

Overview of Open Data Access

ODA is a version 2.5 or higher ODBC driver that J.D. Edwards created for read-only purposes. ODA's main job is to be used for front-end query and reporting tools, such as Microsoft Query and Microsoft Access, to access any OneWorld table.

ODA sits between the calling application and OneWorld-configured ODBC drivers. This configuration provides the following features that no other ODBC drivers provide:

- *Long table and business view names.* ODA provides the long names of tables and business views in OneWorld instead of their object names. For example, you can view the name Address Book Master versus its object name F0101.

- *Long column names.* ODA provides the long names of columns in tables instead of their data item alias. For example, you can view the name AddressNumber rather than its data item alias ABAN8.

- *Julian date conversion.* ODA converts OneWorld Julian dates to a SQL-92 standard date.

- *Decimal shifting conversion.* ODA converts numeric columns that require decimal shifting as they are retrieved from a table. This allows your external application to retrieve a properly decimal-shifted numeric value from ODA, instead of the numeric value stored in the database tables.

- *Currency conversion.* ODA converts currency columns that require decimal shifting to their proper currency format as they are retrieved. This allows your external application to retrieve a properly formatted currency value from ODA, instead of the numeric value stored in the database tables.

- *Column and row security.* ODA allows you to select only columns and rows that you are allowed to view. If a row or column has security restrictions on it and you are not allowed to view it, then ODA will not retrieve any records.

- *User-defined code conversion.* ODA converts the internal code for a UDC to its associated description. This allows your external application to retrieve the first description of the UDC instead of its code.

Modifying an ODA Data Source

ODA is automatically registered as a part of the OneWorld installation process. At times, however, you may need to modify the data source to meet your needs. To modify an ODA data source, perform the following steps:

1. Click the Start button, and select Control Panel from the Settings menu.

2. Double-click the ODBC icon in the Control Panel. The ODBC Data Source Administrator application appears.

3. Select the System DSN dialog box, and in the System Data Sources list, you should see a driver called JD Edwards OneWorld ODA.

4. Double-click the JD Edwards OneWorld ODA driver, and the Configure Data Source dialog box appears, as shown in Figure 14-18.

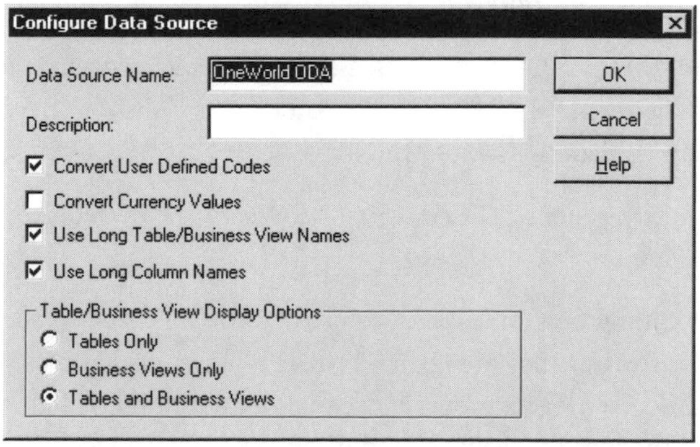

FIGURE 14-18. The Configure Data Source panel for an ODA driver

5. Modify the following fields to meet your needs:

Field	Description
Convert User Defined Codes	Enable this check box to have ODA convert all UDC alphanumeric values to descriptions.
Convert Currency Values	Enable this check box to have ODA convert all currency values to their proper format.
Use Long Table/Business View Names	Enable this check box to have ODA access the long names of tables and business views instead of their object names.
Use Long Column Names	Enable this check box to have ODA access the long names of the column in tables instead of their data item aliases.
Table/Business View Display Options	Enable one of the options in this group to allow your external applications to access data from either tables or business views, or from both.

6. Click the OK and Cancel buttons to save and return to the Control Panel.

Outbound Batch-Processing Model

The *outbound batch-processing model* is the counterpart to the inbound batch-processing model. Outbound batch processing allows OneWorld or the external application to execute separately. Like inbound batch processing, the external application only accesses an interoperability interface table, and very little communication with OneWorld is required. The main difference between the two processes, however, is that you use outbound batch processing only to retrieve data from OneWorld.

The main advantage of the outbound batch-processing model over the other models is that the application retrieves data from one or more of the Z tables. This approach isolates OneWorld application tables from external applications and helps you reduce the possibility of data corruption in the tables. The disadvantage of this approach is that OneWorld cannot maintain information about which external applications accessed the data from the Z tables.

Figure 14-19 provides a schematic diagram of the outbound batch-processing model.

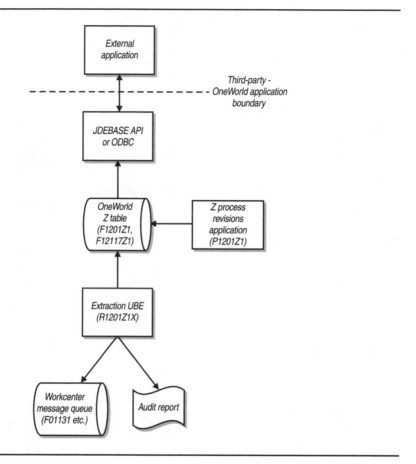

FIGURE 14-19. Schematic diagram of outbound batch processing

To use the outbound batch-processing model, follow these steps:

1. *Execute the outbound batch application.* The outbound batch application loads up the Z tables with data from the systems table for its module. In the upcoming example in Figure 14-20, the Fixed Asset Outbound batch application (R1201Z1X) loads up the Fixed Asset Interoperability Interface table (F1201Z1) with data from the Fixed Asset module.

2. *Create a OneWorld or ODBC connection.* The external application has the same options to retrieve information from a OneWorld table. The external application can communicate to the tables through a OneWorld user session or an ODBC connection to the database that OneWorld uses.

3. *Retrieve records from the Z table.* Now the system retrieves records from the Z tables. For the example in Figure 14-19, the external application retrieves the records from the Fixed Asset Interoperability Interface table (F1201Z1).

4. *Disconnect from OneWorld or from the ODBC connection.* After your external application has retrieved all of the data from OneWorld it needs, the application must disconnect its session, which is either a OneWorld or an ODBC session.

Outbound Batch Application

The *outbound batch application* is built similarly to the inbound batch application, except that it extracts records from a set of tables to one or more Z tables. The outbound batch application generates a report that lists all of the records that it has processed when it has finished executing. Also, the application provides information on the number of records it processed, the details on each record it processed, and any errors that occurred. If the outbound batch application encounters an error during processing, it sends an error message to the Employee Work Center (P012501).

Most outbound batch applications use two essential components: processing options and MBFs. The processing options assigned to the outbound batch application usually contain an option to run the application in final or proof mode. In final mode, all items that it processes are permanently updated in the system. However, proof mode allows you to execute the application without permanently affecting the system. The advantage of using proof mode is to run the application to determine if it will execute properly.

Most outbound batch applications use an MBF to process one record into the system. These MBFs, which are discussed in the next section, have a processing option assigned to them. Therefore, the processing options for the outbound batch applications have an option that assigns which version of the MBF to execute.

Table 14-8 lists all output batch applications that you can use for interoperability in OneWorld, their MBFs, and their processing options.

Interfacing with OneWorld

Interoperability Interface Transaction Types	Output Batch Application	Master Business Function	Processing Options
Address Book	R01010Z – ZJDE0002	N0100041	P0100041
Customer Master	R01010Z – ZJDE0002	N0100042	P0100042
Supplier Master	R04010Z – ZJDE0002	N0100043	P0100043
Fixed Asset Master	R1201Z1X – XJDE0001	N1200010	P1201
Work Order Header	R4101Z1O	B3101420	
Work Order Routing	R4801Z2X		

TABLE 14-8.   List of Output Batch Applications

Update the Z Tables with the Fixed Asset Master Outbound Batch Application

This section explains how to update the Z table with the outbound batch application. In this example, we will show you how to use the Outbound Asset Master/Equipment Tag Extraction application (R1201Z1X). Follow these steps to execute the Outbound Asset Master/Equipment Tag Extraction application (R1201Z1X):

1. From OneWorld Explorer, type **BV** into the Fast Path box and press ENTER. The Available Versions form of the Work With Batch Versions application appears, as shown in Figure 14-20.

2. Type **R1201Z1X** into the Batch Application field. The versions for the Outbound Asset Master/Equipment Tag Extraction application (R1201Z1X) appear in the grid of the form after you press ENTER or click the Find button.

3. We will be executing the XJDE0001 version of the Outbound Asset Master/Equipment Tag Extraction application (R1201Z1X). Therefore, highlight the XJDE0001 grid row, and then click the Select button.

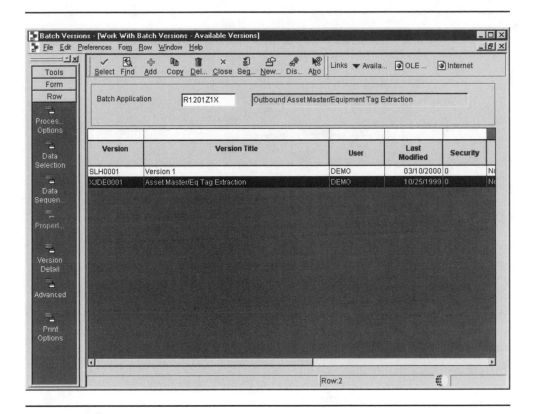

FIGURE 14-20.   The Available Versions form of the Work With Batch Versions
application (P98305)

4. The Version Prompting form appears. Click the Submit button to continue.

5. The Processing Options panel for the XJDE0001 version of the Outbound Asset
Master/Equipment Tag Extraction application (R1201Z1X) appears, as shown
in Figure 14-21.

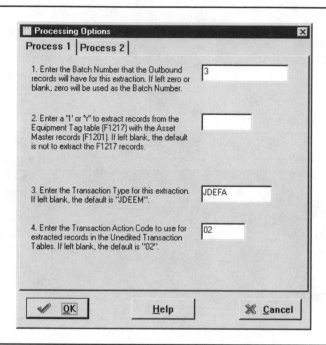

FIGURE 14-21. The Process 1 panel of the Processing Options form of the Outbound Asset Master/Equipment Tag Extraction application (R1201Z1X/XJDE0001)

6. The main purpose of the processing options is to populate the control columns in the Fixed Asset Interoperability Interface table (F1201Z1) with specific values that you assign. We mapped the following processing option values, as shown in Figure 14-21, to the control columns in the table:

Field	Value	Description
1	3	The value for the Batch Number column (EDBT) in the Z table.
2	*Leave blank*	While extracting data from the F1201 table, extract the corresponding records from the F1217 table. In this example, we want to extract only from the F1201 table.
3	JDEFA	The value for the Transaction Action column (TYTN) in the Z table.
4	02	The value for the Transaction Action Code column (TNAC) in the Z table.

7. Click the OK button on the Processing Options form, and the Report Output Destination form appears. Click the On Screen option, and then click the OK button.

8. Now the system launches the Address Book Batch Upload application (R0101Z1/ZJDE0001). The application provides a report displaying all of the records it processed.

9. To verify the extraction of data by the Address Book Batch Upload application (R0101Z1/ZJDE0001), type **G1233** into the Fast Path box and press ENTER. When the Asset Interoperability menu (G1233) appears, execute the Outbound Asset Master application (P1201Z1) to verify that your records exist in the Fixed Asset Interoperability Interface table (F1201Z1).

Outbound Asynchronous Processing Model

The *outbound asynchronous processing model* performs the same steps as the outbound batch-processing model to extract data to the Z tables. However, the outbound asynchronous processing model allows OneWorld to manage and monitor external applications that access data from its Z tables. The main advantage of this approach is that the system can provide an audit trail of records all the way to the external application.

The outbound asynchronous processing model requires a set of tables, applications, and business functions to manage the monitoring of external applications. The tables maintain a record of all external applications that have accessed OneWorld's Z table and show whether the applications finished retrieving data. The applications maintain the integrity of the tables that support the outbound asynchronous processing model. The external applications use the business functions to communicate when the applications have started or finished retrieving records from the Z tables.

However, the outbound asynchronous processing model is still in development, but it will be available soon for use in a future OneWorld release.

Putting It All Together

The primary advantage of interoperability is that it allows businesses to integrate multivendor applications to create new applications that will take a best-of-breed

Interfacing with OneWorld

approach. The primary benefit of a best-of-breed approach is that the features and functionality of multivendor applications are integrated into a single application.

Relative to the integration of OneWorld with other vendor's applications, OneWorld contains a whole host of integration architecture, or interoperability. Interoperability is not appended to OneWorld—it is built directly into the system. This allows OneWorld to have an open architecture that is easier for you to integrate with than its competitors.

For any development project that includes interoperability, you use one of the six interoperability processing models to integrate OneWorld with external applications. The models are based on the management of the data flow into and out of OneWorld and the synchronization of application execution to update the system with the new data. A summary of all the components, definitions, and objects required for each model is provided in Appendix D.

CHAPTER 15

Middleware APIs

JDENET

JDEBASE

Putting It All Together

O neWorld is a unique environment that allows you to execute applications across a variety of software and hardware platforms, and with more than one database from a mixture of vendors. This flexibility is testament to the powerful back-office infrastructure that supports OneWorld.

In order for disparate platforms to operate in harmony, OneWorld provides a set of middleware protocols and applications that allow all the platforms to communicate and interact. The middleware layer bridges the complexity of multiprotocol and multivendor differences, handling communications as well as data requests with consistency and accuracy. The common ground of the middleware allows the various protocols and platforms to exist cooperatively in the CNC architecture, and to operate seamlessly together.

The most important components of the middleware technology for OneWorld are the JDENET communication medium and the JDEBASE database environment.

- **JDENET**   JDENET is the medium that permits different platforms to communicate with one another. This middleware component allows all clients and servers to pass data and requests for action, as in data replication or execution of a batch application.

- **JDEBASE**   JDEBASE is a platform-independent environment for database manipulation and management. This middleware component provides a set of application programming interfaces (APIs) that remove many of the technical difficulties of integrating database systems. JDEBASE provides the functionality you need to develop applications in a multiprotocol and multivendor environment without having to contend with the details of integrating them.

JDENET

JDENET is a J.D. Edwards proprietary middleware package that is used for communication between servers, clients, and processes, and for monitoring of transaction processing. JDENET provides the client-to-server, server-to-server, and process-to-process communication that is required to support the system. The advantage is that any machine on a peer-to-peer network can function as a client or server at any time.

Communication among the machines on the JDENET-supported network occurs by exchanging messages. These messages contain requests for execution of sign-on security functions, business functions, launching of batch applications and reports, and data replication. Messaging between machines on the network can be either synchronous or asynchronous. Synchronous messaging, as in user validation, requires the sender of the message to wait until the request is fulfilled and the results are returned. Asynchronous messaging, as in execution of a batch application, allows the sender to continue processing while the other machine acts on the sender's message.

For example, OneWorld requires validation of all users who log in. The user provides a username and password, and the client to which they logged in issues a synchronous message that is sent to a security server, to validate the user. The security server validates the information provided by the user, and sends an acceptance or rejection response back to the client. If the user is accepted, then the client will proceed with execution of the client version of OneWorld. However, after three failed sign-ons, execution of OneWorld is halted and the sign-on screen is terminated.

JDENET Components

The JDENET middleware package consists of two components that support communication operations. Each component—the *network processes* and the *kernel processes*—performs a specific task, and together they provide the functionality required for distributed computing communication.

Network Processes

Network processes are applications that run continually and manage the point-to-point communication between computers on the TCP/IP network. (A TCP/IP network uses the TCP/IP protocol for communication.) The network process listens to the network for messages that refer to its machine or that send a message to another computer. The network processes are designed to operate just like *sockets* to provide dependable message delivery among network computers.

The concept of sockets is based on the idea of generalizing the operations of network I/O. Sockets can be viewed as files that are bound to the network instead of on your hard drive or floppy disk. Just as you create files on your hard drive, sockets create virtual files that point to a resource located on another computer on the network. Applications can read and write to the virtual file just as if it were a file on the hard drive.

Figure 15-1 shows how the network processes are implemented for OneWorld clients and servers. The client-side network processes are embedded in the Oexplore.exe application and only execute while a OneWorld Explorer session is active. The application manages the messages that are referred to it, and passes the messages to the JDENET subsystem.

There are two server-side network processes: JDESNET and JDENET_n. The JDESNET application constantly monitors the network for OneWorld messages. When it finds a message that refers to its server, JDESNET passes the message to a JDENET_n process, which performs further processing of the message. JDENET_n processes are responsible for routing messages to a database through the JDEBASE database middleware, or routing the message to 1 of 11 kernel processes (contained in JDENET_k) for logic processing.

DEFINITION

JDENET_n processes *manage the two-way routing of messages among clients and servers.*

As shown in Figure 15-1, there are several JDENET_n processes running on the server. Concurrent JDENET_n processes provide load balancing of message handling, which results in timely execution of requests.

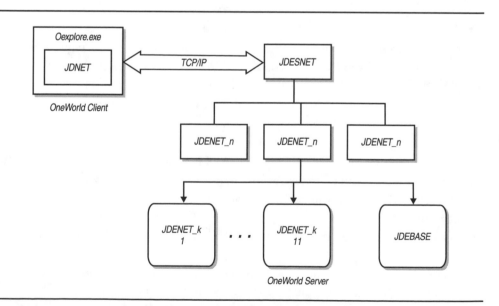

FIGURE 15-1.   JDENET communication middleware on the network

Kernel Processes

Kernel processes are a collection of specialized applications that support the OneWorld system. The kernel processes fill the roles of scheduling and dispatching of applications on the server. Scheduling enables OneWorld system administrators to launch the execution of an application at a predetermined time. Dispatching performs the necessary management of applications on the server, and cleans up when the application finishes execution.

A good example of kernel processes and when they are used is demonstrated in the scheduling of the A/R Credit/Cash Management Build application (R03B525). When you schedule the application to execute at night, the kernel process used for scheduling monitors the time on the computer throughout the day. As soon as the scheduler determines that it's time to execute the batch application, the scheduler notifies another kernel process, which launches or dispatches the batch application. After the batch application is finished, all of the kernels clean up the system resources and write entries into the job logs.

The kernel processes in OneWorld are implemented as JDENET_k jobs, and each process is responsible for supporting a specific task. You can view JDENET_k processes as virtual servers that are available to support OneWorld processing, as shown previously in Figure 15-1. The virtual servers are waiting to be notified to perform their jobs, and they are notified when the JDENET_n process sends a message to them.

Every message is labeled with an identifier that allows JDENET_n to route it to the proper JDENET_k kernel. Following is a list of message types and the kernels that process them:

Message Type	Processing Kernel
Type 1	OneWorld internal and testing processes
Type 2	OneWorld batch process (Universal Batch Engine, UBE) pass-through
Type 3	Data replication requests
Type 4	Security processes
Type 5	Transaction Manager and Lock Manager
Type 6	Remote Master Business Function (MBF)
Type 7	JDBNET Server to Server
Type 8	Package install
Type 9	Server Administration Workbench (SAW)
Type 10	Scheduler
Type 11	Package build

Interfacing with OneWorld

The JDENET_k processes are implemented in various forms, according to the hardware and software platform of the server on which they are installed (see Table 15-1). AS/400 platforms implement the processes as job queues, UNIX platforms implement them as shared library (SL or SO) files, and Windows NT platforms implement them as dynamic linked library (DLL) files.

JDENET Process Flow

Let's take a look at how the JDENET_n and JDENET_k processes work together, by examining the process flow between them step by step. In the following descriptions, the Jde.ini settings are displayed with the process flow to show you how the settings affect the system.

1. The JDESNET service accepts a request on its assigned port number. For example, these Jde.ini settings show that the service listens to port 6008:

   ```
   [JDENET]
   serviceNameListen=6008
   ```

2. The JDESNET service determines the maximum number of network processes and connections. It then uses the values to determine if the state of the system has exceeded the settings. If the system has not exceeded the settings, the JDESNET service creates another JDENET_n process and lets the new process handle the message. The following Jde.ini settings show a maximum value of 1 for network processes, and network connections at 50.

   ```
   [JDENET]
   netPgmName=jdenet_n.exe
   maxNetProcesses=1
   maxNetConnections=50
   ```

3. The assigned JDENET_n process receives the message and begins to process it. If the message is a logic request, the process determines the name of the appropriate JDENET_k process and then verifies the number of kernel processes that are active in the system. The following Jde.ini settings provide the kernel process name and the maximum number of active processes that can exist at one time:

   ```
   [JDENET]
   krnlPgmName=jdenet_k.exe
   maxKernelProcesses=1
   ```

JDENET_k Kernel Process	AS/400	UNIX	NT
Type 1: OneWorld internal and testing processes	JDENET	libjdenet.so (RS/6000 and Sun) libjdenet.sl (HP9000)	Jdenet.dll
Type 2: OneWorld batch process (UBE) pass-through	JDEKRNL	libjdeknet.so (Sun) libkjdekrnl.so (RS/6000) libjdeknet.sl (HP9000)	Jdekrnl.dll
Type 3: Data replication requests	JDEKRNL	libkjdekrnl.so (RS/6000) libjderepl.sl (HP9000) libjderepl.so (Sun)	Jdekrnl.dll
Type 4: Security processes	JDEKRNL	libjdeknet.so (Sun) libkjdekrnl.so (RS/6000) libjdeknet.sl (HP9000)	Jdekrnl.dll
Type 5: Transaction Manager and Lock Manager	JDEKRNL	libkjdekrnl.so (RS/6000) libtransmon.sl (HP9000) libtransmon.so (Sun)	Jdekrnl.dll
Type 6: Remote Master Business Function (MBF)	JDEKRNL	libjdeknet.so (Sun) libkjdekrnl.so (RS/6000) libjdeknet.sl (HP9000)	Jdekrnl.dll
Type 7: JDBNET Server to Server	JDEKRNL	libjdeknet.so (Sun) libkjdekrnl.so (RS/6000) libjdeknet.sl (HP9000)	Jdekrnl.dll
Type 8: Package install	JDEKRNL	libjdeknet.so (Sun) libkjdekrnl.so (RS/6000) libjdeknet.sl (HP9000)	Jdekrnl.dll
Type 9: Server Administration Workbench (SAW)	JDEKRNL	libjdesaw.sl (HP9000) libjdesaw.so (RS/6000, Sun)	Jdekrnl.dll
Type 10: Scheduler	JDEKRNL	libjdeschr.so (Sun) libkjdekrnl.so (RS/6000) libjdeschr.sl (HP9000)	Jdekrnl.dll
Type 11: Package build	JDEKRNL	libjdeknet.so (Sun) libkjdekrnl.so (RS/6000) libjdeknet.sl (HP9000)	Jdekrnl.dll

TABLE 15-1. JDENET_k Processes for Each Platform

4. The JDENET_k process examines the message to find the kernel type. This is determined by examining the message type number and comparing it to the range of message type numbers assigned to each kernel type. For example, if

Interfacing with OneWorld

the number assigned to a message is 562, the message is routed to the security kernel, which is kernel type 4. The following Jde.ini settings define the message range for kernel type 4, and any incoming message with the message type value between 551 and 580 is routed to it.

```
[JDENET_KERNEL_DEF4]
beginningMsgTypeRange=551
endingMsgTypeRange=580
```

5. Next, the JDENET_k process determines the maximum number of instances allowed for the particular kernel. If the number has not been exceeded, then the kernel is launched. In the following Jde.ini settings, the kernel type 4 is allowed only two instances at any time:

```
[JDENET_KERNEL_DEF4]
maxNumberOfProcesses=2
```

6. JDENET_k launches the kernel by examining the Jde.ini file to see where the library and function are located, and then executes the function. For the following settings in the Jde.ini file, JDENET_k loads the Jdekrnl.dll file for the Windows NT platform and executes the JDEK_DispatchSecurity function contained in that DLL file:

```
[JDENET_KERNEL_DEF4]
dispatchDLLName=jdekrnl.dll
dispatchDLLFunction=_JDEK_DispatchSecurity@28
```

JDEBASE

JDEBASE is the J.D. Edwards proprietary middleware package that is used for management of communication with databases that support OneWorld. This package supports database communication for all clients and servers in the system. The primary advantage offered by JDEBASE is that it provides a platform-independent API allowing any application in OneWorld to access a database regardless of the vendor.

Overview of the JDEBASE Architecture

OneWorld meets the technological challenge of integrating database management systems (DBMS) from multiple vendors to manage the system's information. Each DBMS implements its own Structured Query Language (SQL) to manipulate data in its tables. Until now, when you tried to build a set of applications for multiple databases, the application's complexity increased right along with the number of databases the application could use. Today, the JDEBASE architecture allows you to write one application for multiple databases.

JDEBASE provides a standard set of APIs that mask the differences between DBMSs used by OneWorld applications. Your applications in OneWorld can use the JDEBASE APIs to isolate the differences between the calls for a DB2, Oracle, or SQL Server database. This common programming ground ultimately reduces the overhead for maintaining a multiple-vendor database environment.

For an application to communicate to a DBMS, the functions in the JDEBASE APIs are used to translate the application's requests into SQL statements. The functions build the SQL statement for the particular vendor's DBMS by using its database data source definition, stored in the Object Configuration Manager (OCM). Then the function issues the statement to the DBMS and returns the result set to the application.

The following example illustrates how the JDEBASE APIs help your applications communicate with a database. The example steps through the processing of a request to access all records in the Address Book table (F0101). The steps are illustrated in Figure 15-2.

1. A call is made to a JDEBASE function by a batch application, interactive application, or business function. In Figure 15-2, the JDB_SelectAll function is executed. Its purpose is to retrieve all the records in the F0101 table.

2. JDEBASE checks for the location of the table on the network by querying the Object Configuration Master table (F986101). As you can see in Figure 15-2, the F0101 for the Production environment is located in the data source called OW2.

3. Using the name of the data source, JDEBASE checks for the details on the data source by querying the Data Source Master table (F98611). Figure 15-2 shows the OW2 data source located on the server named OneWorld (in this case, it's an Oracle database called JDEOW).

4. Now that JDEBASE knows the location of the database, and the OneWorld driver (Jdboci80.dll) to use for communicating with it, the driver translates the request to the vendor-specific SQL statement. In Figure 15-2, the SQL statement for the Oracle database is SELECT * FROM F0101;.

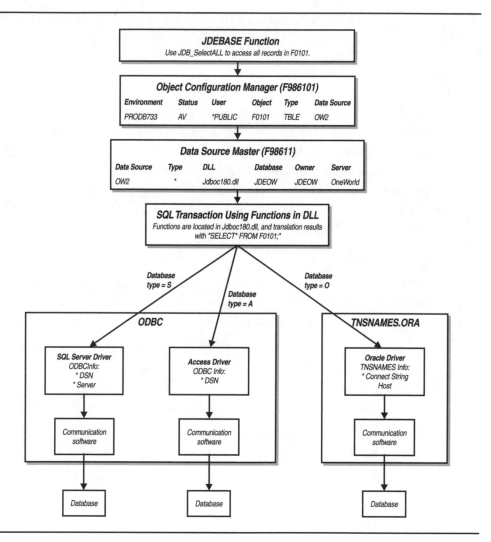

FIGURE 15-2. The process flow for a call to a JDEBASE function

5. The driver sends the SQL statement to the vendor's database driver, which manages all the connections and communication to the database. When the database has finished executing the SQL statement, the results are sent back to the calling application.

Commonly Used Functions of the JDEBASE API

There are many functions in the JDEBASE API—discussing each one is far beyond the scope of this book. In this section we'll list the most commonly used functions of the JDEBASE API, including an example of the function and a description of how you would typically use it in your applications.

Table 15-2 lists the parameters used in every function of the JDEBASE API. The parameters are used to communicate information to and from the business function, including user, database connection, environment, and execution state.

Some of the functions that are a part of the JDEBASE API write entries to the Jdedebug.log file. This log tells you how your application is communicating with the database. The following sections explain each function that writes an entry to the Jdedebug.log file and gives an example of the entry. The examples help you read the entries in the file properly, and also assist in troubleshooting your application.

N O T E

Keep in mind that all of the functions from the JDEBASE API that are presented here are usable only through C-based business functions. Therefore, you must know how to write applications in the C language in order to use any functions from the JDEBASE API.

Data Structure	Description
HENV	The environment information on the current connection to the database. This handle is usually passed into the business function through its data structure.
HUSER	The specific information for the current connection to the database. This handle must be initialized by the application in order to communicate with the database.
HREQUEST	The specific information for the current connection to a table. This handle is used for manipulation and communication with a table.
JDEDB_RESULT	Every function returns a value that describes the status of execution. If the function executed properly, the JDEDB_PASSED value is returned; otherwise, the JDEDB_FAILED value is returned.

TABLE 15-2. Data Structures Used by JDEBASE API Functions

Interfacing with OneWorld

Data Manipulation Functions

The Data Manipulation API provides the functions that manipulate records in a table. These functions perform the equivalent of SQL Select, Update, Delete, Insert, and Fetch commands. The API also provides the commit, rollback, and record locking functions that are needed for transaction processing. The most commonly used functions of the Data Manipulation API are JDB_InsertTable, JDB_SelectAll, JDB_SelectKeyed, and JDB_Fetch.

JDB_InsertTable   The JDB_InsertTable function adds a new row of data to a table. It is the equivalent of the SQL Insert command. Table 15-3 describes some of the parameters of JDB_InsertTable. Its syntax is as follows:

```
JDEDB_RESULT JDB_InsertTable( HREQUEST* hRequest, ID idTable,
                              ID idInstance, void* lpStruct );
```

The JDB_InsertTable function is one of the functions that writes an entry to the Jdedebug.log file. Here is a sample of the entry:

```
Entering JDB_InsertTable
INSERT INTO F0101 VALUES( 7777.000000,'jhsdkjaks',
                    'JHSDKJAKS','DEMO','EP01012',
                    1/1/2000,'USERNAME',104737.000000 );
```

JDB_SelectAll   JDB_SelectAll retrieves all records from a table for the requesting application. This function is available for sequencing to organize the records in ascending (the default) or descending order. The syntax for the JDB_SelectAll function follows:

JDB_InsertTable Parameters	Description
IdTable	ID for the table, which is located in the header file for the table.
IdInstance	ID for the table instance of a table join. If you are not using a table join, set the parameter to zero.
LpStruct	A data structure that contains the data to add to the table. The data structure is defined in the header file of the table.

TABLE 15-3.   Parameters for the JDB_InsertTable Function

```
JDEDB_RESULT JDB_SelectAll( HREQUEST hRequest );
```

The JDB_SelectAll function is one of the functions that writes an entry to the Jdedebug.log file, as shown here:

```
Entering JDB_Select
SELECT  *  FROM F0101 ORDER BY ABAN8 ASC;
```

JDB_SelectKeyed   JDB_SelectKeyed retrieves one or more records from a table based on the selection, sequencing, and index. This function is equivalent to a SQL Select command with a where clause. Table 15-4 defines the parameters of the JDB_SelectKeyed function. Here is the function's syntax:

```
JDEDB_RESULT JDB_SelectKeyed( HREQUEST* hRequest, ID idIndex,
                              void* lpKey, short nNumKeys );
```

Following is a sample of what the JDB_ SelectKeyed function writes to the Jdedebug.log file:

```
Entering JDB_SelectKeyed
SELECT  *  FROM F0005  WHERE  ( DRSY = '00' AND DRRT = 'FP' AND
                               DRKY = 'F0101' )  ORDER BY DRSY
                               ASC,DRRT ASC,DRKY ASC;
```

JDB_Fetch   JDB_Fetch returns one record from the result set of the JDB_SelectAll or JDBSelectKeyed functions. If more records exist in the result set, this function automatically advances the cursor to the next record in the set. Table 15-5 describes the parameters for the JDB_Fetch function. Its syntax is shown next.

JDB_SelectKeyed Parameters	Description
IdIndex	ID for the index to the table, which is located in the header file for the table.
LpKey	Pointer to the data structure for the index. The data structure is defined in the header for the table.
nNumKeys	Number of keys used to execute the Select statement.

TABLE 15-4.   Parameters for the JDB_SelectKeyed Function

Interfacing with OneWorld

```
JDEDB_RESULT JDB_Fetch( HREQUEST* hRequest, void* lpStruct,
                        int nNotUsed );
```

Following is a sample of what the JDB_Fetch function writes to the Jdedebug.log file:

```
Entering JDB_Fetch
```

Initialization Functions

The Initialization API provides functions that allow your business to acquire a connection to the database.

JDB_InitUser   JDB_InitUser initializes an application in OneWorld. The function returns an environment handle that groups a set of database requests together for the application. The parameters for JDB_InitUser are listed in Table 15-6. Here is the syntax for the function:

```
JDEDB_RESULT JDB_InitUser( HENV hEnv, HUSER* hUser,
                           char* szApp, JDEDB_COMMIT nCommitMode );
```

The JDB_InitUser function provides an entry into the Jdedebug.log file. Here is an example:

```
Entering JDB_InitUser with commit mode 0.
```

JDB_FreeUser   JDB_FreeUser releases the application from OneWorld. This function must be called every time JDB_InitUser is called. The function syntax is as follows:

```
JDEDB_RESULT JDB_FreeUser( HUSER hUser );
```

and here is the entry it makes into the Jdedebug.log:

```
Entering JDB_FreeUser
```

JDB_Fetch Parameters	Description
LpStruct	The pointer to the data structure to contain the result set.
NnotUsed	Currently, OneWorld is not using this parameter, and it is always zero.

TABLE 15-5.   Parameters for the JDB_Fetch Function

JDB_InitUser Parameters	Description
szApp	The pointer to the name of the active application.
nCommitMode	If transactions are committed automatically, set this to JDEDB_ COMMIT_AUTO. Otherwise, set to JDEDB_ COMMIT_MANUAL.

TABLE 15-6. Parameters for the JDB_InitUser Function

Request Settings Functions

The functions in the Request Settings API provide sorting and sequencing for the Data Manipulation API. These functions use a data structure called DBREF, which contains two strings: szDict and szTable. These strings identify which column (szDict) and table (szTable) will perform the sort or sequencing operation.

JDB_SetSequence   JDB_SetSequence defines the sort order of the result set that is returned when a JDB_Select or JDB_SelectAll is executed. If you use this function, it must be called before the JDB_Select or JDB_SelectAll commands. Table 15-7 defines the parameters for the JDB_SetSequence function. Its syntax is as follows:

```
JDEDB_RESULT JDB_ SetSequence( HREQUEST hRequest, LPSORT lpSort,
                               unsigned short nNumSort,
                               JDEDB_SET nMode );
```

JDB_SetSequence Parameters	Description
lpSort	A pointer to one or more Sort structures that define the sequence of the process.
nNumSort	The number of Sort data structures passed into the function.
nMode	If the sequence is to replace the existing definition, set this value to JDEDB_SET_REPLACE. Otherwise, set it to JDEDB_SET_APPEND.

TABLE 15-7. Parameters for the JDB_SetSequence Function

Interfacing with OneWorld

The lpSort parameter (see Table 15-7) contains a pointer to the Sort data structure. This data structure defines what column in the table is sequenced and how it is sequenced. The Sort data structure is defined as follows:

```
struct sequenceinfo {
     DBREF           Item;
     JDEDB_SORT      nSort;
};
```

Very important in the Sort data structure is the value for the nSort parameter. This parameter is of type JDEDB_SORT. It assumes one of two values:

- JDEDB_SORT_ASC, which sorts by the column in ascending order

- JDEDB_SORT_DESC, which sorts by the column in descending order

JDB_SetSelection   JDB_SetSelection defines what records are returned when a JDB_SelectAll is executed. This function is equivalent to the where clause of a SQL command. If JDB_SetSelection is used, it must be called before the JDB_Select command. Table 15-8 defines the parameters for this function. Its syntax is

```
JDEDB_RESULT JDB_ SetSelection( HREQUEST hRequest,
                                LPSELECT lpSelect,
                                unsigned short nNumSelect,
                                JDEDB_SET nMode );
```

Just like its JDB_SetSequence counterpart, the JDB_SetSelection function contains one parameter that is a pointer to the Select data structure. The data

JDB_SetSelection Parameters	Description
LpSelect	A pointer to one or more Select structures that define the selection of the process.
NnumSelect	This is the number of Select data structures passed into the function.
NMode	If the sequence is to replace the existing definition, set this value to JDEDB_SET_REPLACE. Otherwise, set it to JDEDB_SET_APPEND.

TABLE 15-8.   Parameters for the JDB_SetSelection Function

structure defines what rows in the table are to be selected. The Select data structure is defined as follows:

```
struct selectinfo {
     DBREF            Item1;
     DBREF            Item2;
     JDEDB_CMP        nCmp;
     JDEDB_ANDOR      nAndOr;
     void      *      lpValue;
     unsigned short   nValues;
};
```

If more than one Select data structure is applied to a table, the Select data structure provides two parameters to manage the relationship between the structures: nAndOr and nValues. The nValues parameter defines the number of Select data structures to be joined together, and the nAndOr parameter defines how the structure is joined with the other Select data structures. The join is defined by either the And (JDEDB_CMP_AND) operator or the Or (JDEDB_CMP_OR) operator.

The Select data structure contains two DBREF parameters in its definition. These two parameters are used to compare two columns and are the operands of the Select data structure. The nCmp parameter defines which operator is used to compare the two DBREF parameters. The nCmp parameter can have the following values:

JDEDB_CMP_LE	Less than or equal to
JDEDB_CMP_GE	Greater than or equal to
JDEDB_CMP_EQ	Equals
JDEDB_CMP_LT	Less than
JDEDB_CMP_GT	Greater than
JDEDB_CMP_NE	Not equal
JDEDB_CMP_IN	In
JDEDB_CMP_NI	Not in
JDEDB_CMP_BW	Between
JDEDB_CMP_NB	Not between
JDEDB_CMP_LK	Like

Table View Functions

The Table View API provides the functions that manage the tables in a database. The most commonly used functions in this API are JDB_OpenTable and JDB_CloseTable.

Interfacing with OneWorld

JDB_OpenTable   JDB_OpenTable opens a table and initializes it for processing. The table is initialized by returning a request handle that is associated with the table. The JDB_OpenTable function must be executed for a table before any operations are applied to it. Table 15-9 describes the parameters in JDB_OpenTable. Its syntax is

```
JDEDB_RESULT JDB_OpenTable( HUSER* hUser, ID idTable,
                            ID idIndex, LPID lpColSelect,
                            unsigned short nNumCols,
                            char* szOverrideDS,
                            HREQUEST* hRequest );
```

Here is the entry that the JDB_OpenTable function makes into the Jdedebug.log:

```
Entering JDB_OpenTable( Table = F0005 )
```

JDB_CloseTable   JDB_CloseTable releases the request handle obtained through the JDB_OpenTable function. This function must be called for every JDB_OpenTable that is called. Its syntax is as follows:

```
JDEDB_RESULT JDB_CloseTable( HREQUEST* hRequest );
```

Here is the entry made by JDB_ CloseTable into the Jdedebug.log:

```
Entering JDB_CloseTable( Table = F0005 )
```

JDB_OpenTable Parameters	Description
idTable	The ID for the table; located in the header file for the table.
idIndex	The ID for the index; located in the header file for the table.
lpColSelect	A pointer to an array of column IDs, which are located in the header file for the table. To access all of the columns in the table, set this value to NULL.
nNumCols	Number of columns required for this connection. To access all columns, set the value to zero.
szOverrideDS	To override the OCM mapping, set this string to the name of the data source. Otherwise, set the value to NULL.

TABLE 15-9.   Parameters for the JDB_OpenTable Function

Using the JDEBASE APIs

This section provides several examples of using the JDEBASE API. All of the examples are C-based business functions, and they increase in complexity from the simplest to the most complex. The examples are presented in this manner according to the technique we advocate for developing business functions that use functions from the JDEBASE API. The advantage to building the business functions in increasing order of complexity is that logic or syntax errors will be reduced.

N O T E

We strongly encourage you to examine the Jdedebug.log file as you develop C-based business functions with the JDEBASE API. This log file displays the status of JDEBASE API functions that write out to the file. It also shows you the SQL statement sent to the database to retrieve records from a table. You'll avoid many hours of grief if you pay attention to the Jdedebug.log file as you're developing business functions.

N O T E

To review the parameters and exact syntax of all functions from the JDEBASE APIs, examine the Help file attached to the Help menu in OneWorld Explorer. This will help you avoid the problems involved in writing code for an older release of OneWorld.

Retrieving All Records from a Table

A common technique for manipulating a table in OneWorld is to retrieve all of its records and search through them by using a business function. This example shows you how to open the Address Book table (F0101) and retrieve all of its records.

Entry to Jdedebug.log   If you have debugging enabled for your OneWorld session, you'll see the following SQL statement that is written by the business function to the Jdedebug.log file and sent to the database:

```
SELECT   *   FROM F0101
```

To retrieve all records from a table, perform the following steps:

Interfacing with OneWorld

1. Create the C-based business function, as explained in Chapter 13.

2. Open the business function for editing in the Visual C++ editor.

3. In the header file of the business function, insert the following lines of code into the Table Header Inclusions section:

```
#ifndef _F0101_H_
   #include <F0101.H>
#endif
```

4. Define the following variables in the Variable Declarations section:

```
JDEDB_RESULT    returnCode = JDEDB_PASSED;
NID             szTableF0101 = NID_F0101;
ID              idIndexF0101 = ID_F0101_ADDRESS;
HUSER           hUser = (HUSER) 0L;
HREQUEST        hRequestF0101 = (HREQUEST) 0L;
```

5. Define the following data structures in the Declare Structures section:

```
F0101           dsF0101Table = {0};
```

6. Define the following pointers in the Declare Pointers section:

```
LPF0101         lpDS0101 = (LPF0101) NULL;
LPKEY1_F0101    lpKey = (LPKEY1_F0101) NULL;
```

7. Assign the pointer to the proper data structure in the Set Pointers section:

```
lpDS0101 = &dsF0101Table;
```

8. In the Main Processing section, initialize a connection to the database and open the F0101 table:

```
returnCode = JDB_InitBhvr (lpBhvrCom, &hUser,
                (char*) NULL, JDEDB_COMMIT_AUTO);
if ( returnCode != JDEDB_PASSED ) {
   return (EXIT_FAILURE);
}
returnCode = JDB_OpenTable(hUser, szTableF0101,
                           idIndexF0101, NULL,
                           (unsigned short) 0, (char*) NULL,
                           hRequestF0101);
if ( returnCode != JDEDB_PASSED ) {
   return (EXIT_FAILURE);
}
```

9. In the Main Processing section, execute the JDB_SelectAll function to access all records in the F0101 table:

```
returnCode = JDB_SelectAll(hRequestF0101);
if ( returnCode != JDEDB_PASSED ) {
   return (EXIT_FAILURE);
}
```

10. In the Main Processing section, loop through the result set that is returned by the statements in step 9:

```
if(returnCode == JDEDB_PASSED)
   {
      returnCode = JDB_Fetch(hRequestF0101, lpDS0101, 0);
      while(returnCode == JDEDB_PASSED)
      {
         cout << "Answer: " << lpDS0101->abalph, << endl;
         returnCode = JDB_Fetch(hRequestF0101, lpDS0101,
                                          nNotUsed);
      }
   }
```

11. In the Function Clean Up section, release all handles that were opened by this business function, and exit:

```
returnCode = JDB_CloseTable (hRequestF0101);
if ( returnCode != JDEDB_PASSED ) {
   return (EXIT_FAILURE);
}
returnCode = JDB_FreeBhvr(hUser);
if ( returnCode != JDEDB_PASSED ) {
    return (EXIT_FAILURE);
}
return (EXIT_SUCCESS);
```

Retrieving All Records in Descending Order

Another common technique you might use when manipulating a table in a database is to sort the data in a specific order. This example shows you how to reverse the order of all records that are accessed by the JDB_SelectAll function. We'll use the example from the preceding section and add lines of code to perform a descending-order sequencing of the result set returned by the function.

Interfacing with OneWorld

Entry to Jdedebug.log   If you have debugging enabled for your OneWorld session, you'll see the following SQL statement written by the business function to the Jdedebug.log file and sent to the database:

```
SELECT  *  FROM F0101  ORDER BY ABAN8 DESC
```

To retrieve all records from a table in descending order, perform the following steps:

1. Create the C-based business function as shown in Chapter 13.

2. Open the business function for editing in the Visual C++ editor.

3. In the header file of the business function, insert the following lines of code into the Table Header Inclusions section:

```
#ifndef _F0101_H_
   #include <F0101.H>
#endif
```

4. Define the following variables in the Variable Declarations section:

```
JDEDB_RESULT    returnCode = JDEDB_PASSED;
NID             szTableF0101 = NID_F0101;
ID              idIndexF0101 = ID_F0101_ADDRESS;
HUSER           hUser = (HUSER) 0L;
HREQUEST        hRequestF0101 = (HREQUEST) 0L;
```

5. Define the following data structures in the Declare Structures section:

```
F0101           dsF0101Table = {0};
SORTSTRUCT      dsSortStruct = {0};
```

6. Define the following pointers in the Declare Pointers section:

```
LPF0101         lpDS0101 = (LPF0101) NULL;
LPKEY1_F0101    lpKey = (LPKEY1_F0101) NULL;
LPSORT          lpSort = (LPSORT) NULL;
```

7. Assign the pointer to the proper data structure in the Set Pointers section:

```
lpDS0101 = &dsF0101Table;
lpSort = &dsSortStruct;
```

8. In the Main Processing section, initialize a connection to the database and open the F0101 table:

```
returnCode = JDB_InitBhvr (lpBhvrCom, &hUser,
                (char*) NULL, JDEDB_COMMIT_AUTO);
if ( returnCode != JDEDB_PASSED ) {
   return (EXIT_FAILURE);
}
 returnCode = JDB_OpenTable(hUser, szTableF0101,
                          idIndexF0101, NULL,
                          (unsigned short) 0, (char*) NULL,
                          hRequestF0101);
if ( returnCode != JDEDB_PASSED ) {
   return (EXIT_FAILURE);
}
```

9. In the Main Processing section, execute the JDB_SetSequencing and JDB_SelectAll functions to access all records in descending order for the F0101 table:

```
jdeNIDcpy(lpSort->Item.szDict, NID_AN8);
jdeNIDcpy(lpSort->Item.szTable, NID_F0101);
lpSort->nSort = JDEDB_SORT_DESC;
returnCode = JDB_SetSequencing( hRequestF0101, lpSort,
                             1, JDEDB_SET_REPLACE);
if ( returnCode != JDEDB_PASSED ) {
   return (EXIT_FAILURE);
}
returnCode = JDB_SelectAll(hRequestF0101);
if ( returnCode != JDEDB_PASSED ) {
   return (EXIT_FAILURE);
}
```

10. In the Main Processing section, loop through the result set that is returned by the statements in step 9:

```
if(returnCode == JDEDB_PASSED)
   {
       returnCode = JDB_Fetch(hRequestF0101, lpDS0101, 0);
       while(returnCode == JDEDB_PASSED)
       {
          cout << "Answer: " << lpDS0101->abalph, << endl;
          returnCode = JDB_Fetch(hRequestF0101, lpDS0101,
                                         nNotUsed);
       }
   }
```

11. In the Function Clean Up section, release all handles that were opened by this business function, and exit:

```
returnCode = JDB_CloseTable (hRequestF0101);
if ( returnCode != JDEDB_PASSED ) {
   return (EXIT_FAILURE);
```

```
    }
    returnCode = JDB_FreeBhvr(hUser);
    if ( returnCode != JDEDB_PASSED ) {
        return (EXIT_FAILURE);
    }
    return (EXIT_SUCCESS);
```

Retrieving Selected Records in Descending Order

This example shows you how to access a small set of records from a database table. In particular, the business function retrieves all records that have equal values in columns AN8 and AN81. The records that meet the criteria are returned in descending order.

Entry to Jdedebug.log   If you have debugging enabled for your OneWorld session, you'll see the following SQL statement written by the business function to the Jdedebug.log file and sent to the database:

```
SELECT * FROM F0101 WHERE ( ABAN8 = ABAN81 ) ORDER BY ABAN8 DESC
```

To retrieve a set of records from a table in descending order, perform the following steps:

1. Create the C-based business function as shown in Chapter 13.

2. Open the business function for editing in the Visual C++ editor.

3. In the header file of the business function, insert the following lines of code into the Table Header Inclusions section:

   ```
   #ifndef _F0101_H_
       #include <F0101.H>
   #endif
   ```

4. Define the following variables in the Variable Declarations section:

   ```
   JDEDB_RESULT    returnCode = JDEDB_PASSED;
   NID             szTableF0101 = NID_F0101;
   ID              idIndexF0101 = ID_F0101_ADDRESS;
   HUSER           hUser = (HUSER) 0L;
   HREQUEST        hRequestF0101 = (HREQUEST) 0L;
   ```

5. Define the following data structures in the Declare Structures section:

   ```
   F0101           dsF0101Table = {0};
   SELECTSTRUCT    dsSelectStruct = {0};
   SORTSTRUCT      dsSortStruct = {0};
   ```

6. Define the following pointers in the Declare Pointers section:

```
LPF0101        lpDS0101 = (LPF0101) NULL;
LPKEY1_F0101   lpKey = (LPKEY1_F0101) NULL;
LPSELECT       lpSelect = (LPSELECT) NULL;
LPSORT         lpSort = (LPSORT) NULL;
```

7. Assign the pointer to the proper data structure in the Set Pointers section:

```
lpDS0101 = &dsF0101Table;
lpSelect = &dsSelectStruct;
lpSort = &dsSortStruct;
```

8. In the Main Processing section, initialize a connection to the database, and open the F0101 table:

```
returnCode = JDB_InitBhvr (lpBhvrCom, &hUser,
                (char*) NULL, JDEDB_COMMIT_AUTO);
if ( returnCode != JDEDB_PASSED ) {
   return (EXIT_FAILURE);
}
returnCode = JDB_OpenTable(hUser, szTableF0101,
                          idIndexF0101, NULL,
                          (unsigned short) 0, (char*) NULL,
                          hRequestF0101);
if ( returnCode != JDEDB_PASSED ) {
   return (EXIT_FAILURE);
}
```

9. In the Main Processing section, execute the JDB_SelectAll function to access all records in the F0101 table:

```
jdeNIDcpy(lpSort->Item.szDict, NID_AN8);
jdeNIDcpy(lpSort->Item.szTable, NID_F0101);
lpSort->nSort = JDEDB_SORT_DESC;
returnCode = JDB_SetSequencing( hRequestF0101, lpSort,
                               1, JDEDB_SET_REPLACE);
if ( returnCode != JDEDB_PASSED ) {
   return (EXIT_FAILURE);
}
jdeNIDcpy(lpSelect->Item1.szDict, NID_AN8);
jdeNIDcpy(lpSelect->Item1.szTable, NID_F0101);
jdeNIDcpy(lpSelect->Item2.szDict, NID_AN81);
jdeNIDcpy(lpSelect->Item2.szTable, NID_F0101);
lpSelect->nCmp = JDEDB_CMP_EQ;
returnCode = JDB_SetSelection(hRequestF0101, lpSelect,
                             1, JDEDB_SET_REPLACE);
if ( returnCode != JDEDB_PASSED ) {
   return (EXIT_FAILURE);
```

```
   }
   returnCode = JDB_SelectKeyed(hRequestF0101, 0, 0, 0);
   if ( returnCode != JDEDB_PASSED ) {
      return (EXIT_FAILURE);
   }
```

10. In the Main Processing section, loop through the result set that is returned by the statements in step 9:

```
if(returnCode == JDEDB_PASSED)
   {
      returnCode = JDB_Fetch(hRequestF0101, lpDS0101, 0);
      while(returnCode == JDEDB_PASSED)
      {
         cout << "Answer: " << lpDS0101->abalph, << endl;
      returnCode = JDB_Fetch(hRequestF0101, lpDS0101,
                                       nNotUsed);
      }
   }
```

11. In the Function Clean Up section, release all handles that were opened by this business function, and exit:

```
   returnCode = JDB_CloseTable (hRequestF0101);
   if ( returnCode != JDEDB_PASSED ) {
      return (EXIT_FAILURE);
   }
   returnCode = JDB_FreeBhvr(hUser);
   if ( returnCode != JDEDB_PASSED ) {
       return (EXIT_FAILURE);
   }
   return (EXIT_SUCCESS);
```

Another Technique for Retrieving Selected Records

This example, too, demonstrates accessing of a small set of records from a database table, but this one populates a data structure that is a parameter for the JDB_SelectKeyed function. The data structure is used to set the criteria to find records that are suppliers, and that have equal values in columns AN8 and AN81. Also, the records that meet the criteria are returned in ascending order.

Entry to Jdedebug.log   If you have debugging enabled for your OneWorld session, you'll see the following SQL statement written by the business function to the Jdedebug.log file and sent to the database:

```
SELECT * FROM F0101 WHERE ( ABAT1 = 'V' ) AND ( ABAN8 = ABAN81 )
        ORDER BY ABAT1 ASC, ABDC ASC
```

To retrieve selected records from a file, perform the following steps:

1. Create the C-based business function as shown in Chapter 13.

2. OPEN the business function for editing in the Visual C++ editor.

3. In the header file of the business function, insert the following lines of code into the Table Header Inclusions section:

   ```
   #ifndef _F0101_H_
       #include <F0101.H>
   #endif
   ```

4. Define the following variables in the Variable Declarations section:

   ```
   JDEDB_RESULT      returnCode = JDEDB_PASSED;
   NID               szTableF0101 = NID_F0101;
   ID                idIndexF0101 = ID_F0101_ADDRESS;
   ID                idIndexFiveF0101 =
                         ID_F0101_ADDRESS_TYPE_1__DESC_COMPRESSE;
   HUSER             hUser = (HUSER) 0L;
   HREQUEST          hRequestF0101 = (HREQUEST) 0L;
   ```

5. Define the following data structures in the Declare Structures section:

   ```
   F0101             dsF0101Table = {0};
   SELECTSTRUCT      dsSelectStruct = {0};
   SORTSTRUCT        dsSortStruct = {0};
   KEY5_F0101        dsKeyFiveStruct = {0};
   ```

6. Define the following pointers in the Declare Pointers section:

   ```
   LPF0101           lpDS0101 = (LPF0101) NULL;
   LPKEY1_F0101      lpKey = (LPKEY1_F0101) NULL;
   LPSELECT          lpSelect = (LPSELECT) NULL;
   ```

```
LPSORT          lpSort = (LPSORT) NULL;
LPKEY5_F0101    lpKeyFive = (LPKEY5_F0101) NULL;
```

7. Assign the pointer to the proper data structure in the Set Pointers section:

```
lpDS0101 = &dsF0101Table;
lpSelect = &dsSelectStruct;
lpSort = &dsSortStruct;
lpKeyFive = &dsKeyFiveStruct;
```

8. In the Main Processing section, initialize a connection to the database and open the F0101 table:

```
returnCode = JDB_InitBhvr (lpBhvrCom, &hUser,
                (char*) NULL, JDEDB_COMMIT_AUTO);
if ( returnCode != JDEDB_PASSED ) {
   return (EXIT_FAILURE);
}
returnCode = JDB_OpenTable(hUser, szTableF0101,
                        idIndexF0101, NULL,
                        (unsigned short) 0, (char*) NULL,
                        hRequestF0101);
if ( returnCode != JDEDB_PASSED ) {
   return (EXIT_FAILURE);
}
```

9. In the Main Processing section, execute the JDB_SetSequence, JDB_SetSelection, and JDB_SelectKeyed functions. These functions access all records in the F0101 table, in ascending order, and select those that are suppliers and with equal values in columns AN8 and AN81:

```
jdeNIDcpy(lpSort->Item.szDict, NID_AN8);
jdeNIDcpy(lpSort->Item.szTable, NID_F0101);
lpSort->nSort = JDEDB_SORT_ASC;
returnCode = JDB_SetSequencing( hRequestF0101, lpSort,
                            1, JDEDB_SET_REPLACE);
if ( returnCode != JDEDB_PASSED ) {
   return (EXIT_FAILURE);
}
jdeNIDcpy(lpSelect->Item1.szDict, NID_AN8);
jdeNIDcpy(lpSelect->Item1.szTable, NID_F0101);
jdeNIDcpy(lpSelect->Item2.szDict, NID_AN81);
jdeNIDcpy(lpSelect->Item2.szTable, NID_F0101);
```

```
lpSelect->nCmp = JDEDB_CMP_EQ;
returnCode = JDB_SetSelection(hRequestF0101, lpSelect,
                               1, JDEDB_SET_REPLACE);
if ( returnCode != JDEDB_PASSED ) {
   return (EXIT_FAILURE);
}
strcpy(lpKeyFive->abat1, "V");
returnCode = JDB_SelectKeyed(hRequestF0101,
                               idIndexFiveF0101, lpKeyFive, 1);
if ( returnCode != JDEDB_PASSED ) {
   return (EXIT_FAILURE);
}
```

10. In the Main Processing section, loop through the result set that is returned by the statements in step 9:

```
if(returnCode == JDEDB_PASSED)
   {
   returnCode = JDB_Fetch(hRequestF0101, lpDS0101, 0);
   while(returnCode == JDEDB_PASSED)
   {
       cout << "Answer: " << lpDS0101->abalph, << endl;
   returnCode = JDB_Fetch(hRequestF0101, lpDS0101,
                               nNotUsed);
   }
```

11. In the Function Clean Up section, release all handles that were opened by this business function, and exit:

```
returnCode = JDB_CloseTable (hRequestF0101);
if ( returnCode != JDEDB_PASSED ) {
   return (EXIT_FAILURE);
}
returnCode = JDB_FreeBhvr(hUser);
if ( returnCode != JDEDB_PASSED ) {
    return (EXIT_FAILURE);
}
return (EXIT_SUCCESS);
```

The previous examples showed you how to use the JDEBASE API to retrieve records from a database table. However, the examples provide only a hypothetical case for a particular JDEBASE API function. The following Developer's Corner, titled "Using the JDEBASE API for Interoperability with OneWorld," provides you with a real-world example of how to use the JDEBASE API to load an Interoperability Z table for importing data into OneWorld.

Using the JDEBASE API for Interoperability with OneWorld

This Developer's Corner continues the discussion of interoperability that was presented in Chapter 14. Here we discuss how to use the functions in the JDEBASE API for interoperability of OneWorld with a foreign system. This approach is different from the interoperability techniques shown in Chapter 14, because here we are constructing a OneWorld application that will import data. Previously, we focused on building an external application to import into OneWorld. The intent here, however, is to illustrate another viable technique that you can use for your projects developed specifically in the OneWorld environment.

By using the JDEBASE API for interoperability with OneWorld, you gain the following benefits:

- **Execution speed is improved.**   An interoperability application using the functions in the API executes much faster than other techniques, because you are using functions that are located in the low-level sections of the system. Use of these functions requires expertise in C programming, however.

- **The developed application is native to the system.**   The functions in the JDEBASE API are native to the system, and are controlled in the Security Manager, Object Configuration Master, and Data Source Master.

The following example is based on the Address Book Interoperability table (F0101Z2), which is used for importing and exporting data from the Address Book table (F0101) using the Address Book Z Process batch application (R0101Z1). We'll focus on the lines of code necessary to properly execute the functions in the JDEBASE API to insert a record into the F0101Z2 table. There are many sources from which you can import data into OneWorld, such as text files, spreadsheets, and database tables. For this reason, we'll show you how to insert data into the OneWorld database tables using JDEBASE.

This example also demonstrates how to access a next number for a data item. In the business function, you call X0010GetNextNumber. To use it correctly, you must know the particular "next number" and its product code. For this example, the next number for the Batch Number data item (EDBT) has a product code of 00, and the next number is 6.

To build the C-based business function that imports data into the Address Book Interoperability table (F0101Z2), perform the following steps:

1. Create the C-based business function using the Object Librarian (P9860).

2. Open the business function for editing in the Visual C++ editor.

3. In the header file of the business function, insert the following lines of code into the Table Header Inclusions section:

```
#ifndef _F0101Z2_H_
    #include <F0101Z2.H>
#endif
```

4. Define the following variables in the Variable Declarations section:

```
JDEDB_RESULT    returnCode = JDEDB_PASSED;
NID             szTableF0101Z2 = NID_F0101Z2;
ID              idIndexF0101Z2 =
                        ID_F0101Z2_USERID__BATCHNUMBER;
HUSER           hUser = (HUSER) 0L;
HREQUEST        hRequestF0101Z2 = (HREQUEST) 0L;
```

NOTE

The values, such as JDEDB_PASSED, that are referenced in the Variables Declaration section come from the header file of the F0101Z2 table. The header file, F0101Z2.h, is located in the include directory of the environment.

5. Define the following data structures in the Declare Structures section:

```
F0101Z2         dsF0101Z2Table = {0};
DSD0000065      dsX0010GetNextNumber = {0};
```

NOTE

The F0101Z2 data structure is defined in the header file of the F0101Z2 table. The header file, F0101Z2.h, is located in the include directory of the environment.

6. Define the following pointers in the Declare Pointers section:

```
LPF0101Z2       lpDS0101Z2 = (LPF0101Z2) NULL;
```

NOTE

*The LPF0101Z2 pointer is defined in the header file of the F0101Z2 table. The
header file, F0101Z2.h, is located in the include directory of the environment.*

7. Assign the pointer to the proper data structure in the Set Pointers section:

```
lpDS0101Z2 = &dsF0101Z2Table;
```

8. In the Main Processing section, assign values to elements for the F0101Z2 data
structure. In particular, get the next number for the EDBT data item by using
the X0010GetNextNumber function. Also, the following lines of code contain
the elements that must have data assigned to them in order for the F0101Z2
table's Z process to handle the entry correctly.

```
lpDS0101Z2->szdrin = '2';
strcpy(lpDS0101Z2->szedus, "DEMO");
strcpy(lpDS0101Z2->sztnac, "A");
strcpy(lpDS0101Z2->szat1, "V");
strcpy(lpDS0101Z2->sztytn, "JDEAB");
strcpy(lpDS0101Z2->szalph, "THE TEST");
ParseNumericString( &lpDS0101Z2->szan8, "100");
ParseNumericString( &lpDS0101Z2->szedln, "1");
strncpy(dsX0010GetNextNumber.szSystemCode,
        (const char *)("00"),
        sizeof(dsX0010GetNextNumber.szSystemCode));
ParseNumericString(
        &dsX0010GetNextNumber.mnNextNumberingIndexNo, "6");
returnCode = jdeCallObject("X0010GetNextNumber", NULL,
                            lpBhvrCom, (void *)lpVoid,
                            &dsX0010GetNextNumber,
               (CALLMAP *)NULL, (int)0,
                            (char *)NULL, (char *)NULL,
                            (int)0);
FormatMathNumeric( lpDS0101Z2->szedbt,
               dsX0010GetNextNumber.mnNextNumber001);
```

9. In the Main Processing section, initialize a connection to the database and open
the F0101Z2 table:

```
returnCode = JDB_InitBhvr (lpBhvrCom, &hUser,
                (char*) NULL, JDEDB_COMMIT_AUTO);
if ( returnCode != JDEDB_PASSED ) {
   return (EXIT_FAILURE);
}
returnCode = JDB_OpenTable(hUser, szTableF0101Z2,
                           idIndexF0101Z2, NULL,
                           (unsigned short) 0, (char*) NULL,
                           &hRequestF0101Z2);
if ( returnCode != JDEDB_PASSED ) {
   return (EXIT_FAILURE);
}
```

10. In the Main Processing section, execute the JDB_InsertTable to add a new entry in the F0101Z2 table:

```
returnCode = JDB_InsertTable (hRequestF0101Z2,
                             szTableF0101Z2, 0,
                             lpDS0101Z2);
if ( returnCode != JDEDB_PASSED ) {
   return (EXIT_FAILURE);
}
```

11. In the Function Clean Up section, release all handles that were opened by this business function, and exit:

```
returnCode = JDB_CloseTable (hRequestF0101);
if ( returnCode != JDEDB_PASSED ) {
   return (EXIT_FAILURE);
}
returnCode = JDB_FreeBhvr(hUser);
if ( returnCode != JDEDB_PASSED ) {
    return (EXIT_FAILURE);
}
return (EXIT_SUCCESS);
```

At this point, you can compile your business function and use it in an application to import data into the F0101Z2 table. We suggest that you examine the records through the Address Book Revisions application (P0101Z1). When you are ready, execute the Address Book Z Process batch application (R0101Z2) to import data from the F0101Z2 table into the application tables in the Address Book module. The report provided by the batch application after you execute it will tell you what records were properly processed into the system.

Putting It All Together

In this chapter, you've observed that OneWorld's power and flexibility spring in large part from its middleware components: JDENET and JDEBASE. Each of these components provides the features and functionality required to isolate and bridge the differences between various computers on a network operating in a OneWorld environment. Even, for example, a Windows 98 client and a UNIX-based server can efficiently communicate, because their hardware and software differences are ameliorated through the JDENET and JDEBASE components.

The JDENET component provides the medium for communication between all clients and servers. This message-based architecture allows two or more computers to issue requests to each other and to communicate the completion status of the requests.

The JDEBASE component provides a unified mechanism for accessing data from more than one type of database, such as Oracle, SQL Server, or DB2. JDEBASE provides a set of APIs with powerful functions that help you manage connections to a database and manipulate its data.

If you are wondering how you can use the JDEBASE APIs for your applications, the next chapter will provide some answers. In Chapter 16, we build on the topics discussed here and expand the JDEBASE API into transaction-based processing.

CHAPTER 16

Transaction Processing

For mission-critical business applications, it is essential to maintain the integrity of the data at all times. Achieving this goal is more difficult than ever, considering the time frame for business transactions in modern applications. A few years ago, business transactions were performed manually by clerks, and transaction time frames were measured in days and weeks. Now business transactions are digitally transmitted between systems in a matter of seconds.

To maintain the integrity of the data in databases, developers use transaction processing in their business applications. Transaction processing involves a set of SQL statements that work together to process the parts of a business transaction as a single unit. OneWorld implements transaction processing through a set of business functions that include all of the logic required to start transactions, issue SQL statements, and terminate transactions.

To assist you in using transaction processing, the following topics are provided in this chapter:

- **Overview of Transaction Processing**   The overview explains how to implement transaction processing and the benefits it offers. The information in this section is not specific to OneWorld; you can apply it to any system that supports transaction processing.

- **Transaction Master Business Functions**   Transaction Master Business Functions (MBFs) are the objects that support transaction processing in OneWorld. All transaction MBFs adhere to a standard that allows maximum flexibility and reusability in any application.

- **Implementing Transaction Processing in Your Applications**   After you have built your transaction MBF, you need to implement it. This section explains the standard techniques for connecting the transaction MBFs to OneWorld interactive applications, batch applications, and business functions.

Overview of Transaction Processing

Transaction processing is implemented in an application by defining a set of SQL statements that comprise a single logical operation that manipulates the database. The purpose of grouping the statements together is to issue the SQL statements in a single step to maintain the integrity of the database. You can think of a transaction as a wrapper for several lines of SQL that define a more sophisticated SQL statement.

DEFINITION

Transaction processing *is a manipulation technique for databases, and its primary purpose is to maintain the integrity of data in one or more databases.*

As the application executes, it creates SQL statements for the transaction. The SQL statements are issued to the transaction server, which, in turn, verifies each SQL statement for the transaction. Upon successful verification of the SQL statements, the transaction server issues the statements to the database to modify its data. Because the manipulation of the database occurs only when there are no errors in any of the SQL statements that compose the transaction, the integrity of the database is maintained at all times.

As an example of how transaction processing maintains data integrity, Figure 16-1 illustrates what happens when two computers—one that uses transaction processing and one that does not—each submits a single sales-order document to the database during execution of the Sales Order application (P4210).

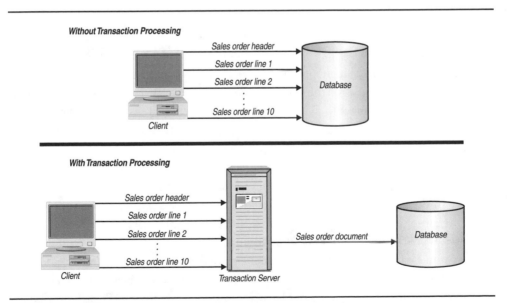

FIGURE 16-1. Two clients submitting a sales-order document to the database

Interfacing with OneWorld

In the example, the computer that does not use transaction processing submits the sales header and each of its ten detail items separately to the database. The problem with this approach is that the integrity of the database is violated during the transmission of the each sales-order header and detail item. If the client or database suddenly stopped operating during the transmission, the information related to the sales order would be invalid and incomplete, because only part of the entire document had been issued to the database.

The client that uses transaction processing issues the sales-order header and detail items to a transaction server that validates and temporarily maintains all of the data for the entire document. When the transaction server is notified that the transaction is complete, it issues the sales-order document to the database in one step. If the transaction server can't submit the document to the database, or the data in the document is invalid, the server notifies the client of the problem and prevents any modification of the database. Therefore, the integrity of the database is maintained at all times. The transaction server is discussed in the upcoming Developer's Corner, titled "Where's the Transaction Server?"

The only drawback of transaction processing is that it degrades the performance of your system, because extra processing is required to verify the SQL statements before they are issued to the database.

Characteristics of Transaction Processing

The SQL statements in a single transaction are dependent on each other, and they all must execute successfully for the transaction to execute properly. The dependencies of the SQL statements come into play when one of two scenarios occur in an application. The first scenario is when the application modifies more than one table at a time, and the records that are created in the tables must exist to guarantee the integrity of the database. The other scenario is when more than one form in an interactive application, or a section in a batch application, modifies the same table. If one of the forms or sections in the application did not execute, there would be a data-integrity problem.

For example, the A/P Standard Voucher Entry application (P0411), which uses transaction processing, manipulates the Accounts Payable Ledger table (F0411) and the Account Ledger table (F0911). As vouchers are created, modified, and deleted, the use of transaction processing ensures that entries exist in both tables to support the vouchers. Any voucher that does not have a record in either the F0411 or F0911 table is invalid and will generate an error the next time it is processed by an application. The data is guaranteed to exist in both tables when transaction processing is properly used, because the transaction is not successful until both SQL statements that affect the tables have successfully executed. Otherwise, the transaction will not be issued to the database to permanently change it.

Transaction processing includes four criteria—atomicity, consistency, isolation, and durability (ACID)—that assist the database in maintaining the integrity of its data:

- **Atomicity** Atomicity is a grouping of operations that act as a complete unit. This requires that all of the SQL statements for a particular transaction must execute successfully, or no changes are made to the database. For example, in order for the voucher-entry transaction to properly affect the data in the database, all of the SQL statements in the transaction must execute properly.

- **Consistency** Consistency requires a group of operations to maintain the integrity of the system. This requires that modifications to the database transform it from a valid state to another valid state. Therefore, the database at any point in time is always in a valid state, and this property assists the system in ensuring that no invalid records exist in any table at any time. In the voucher-entry transaction example, transaction processing ensures that a voucher entry generates a record in the F0411 and F0911 tables to ensure that the database tables are not in an invalid state.

- **Isolation** Isolation is a group of operations that have no dependencies with any other operations in the system. Therefore, it requires that concurrent applications that are executed by different users do not conflict with each other. This ensures that simultaneous updates of transactions never conflict with each other. For example, two clerks who submit a voucher to the system will not interfere with each other as the vouchers are processed. Therefore, the data each clerk submits does not change the other's data in the F0411 and F0911 tables.

- **Durability** Durability is a group of operations that persist, even if the system crashes. This requires that when all of the SQL statements are successfully executed by the database for a transaction, the changes that are made by the transaction are permanent. Any previous information that existed before the transaction is not present in the records of the tables, which prevents any data corruption caused by glitches in the system.

Each criterion provides a specific set of features and functionality that ensure that the records in one table never reference one or more nonexistent records in another table.

Where's the Transaction Server?

You are probably wondering about the transaction server that validates and temporarily maintains the data for the transaction. We only mentioned the transaction server briefly, because it is more of a system administration setting than an application developer requirement.

DEFINITION

*A **transaction server** is an enterprise server used as a manager for all transactions processes. The server has the Transaction Manager process used to manage all database transactions.*

The transaction server for OneWorld is actually the JDENET kernel process that is constantly executing on the enterprise server (JDENET is discussed in Chapter 15). The transaction server is defined in the JDE.INI file for all enterprise servers, and it is shown in following table. Typically, the settings in the following table are preloaded with OneWorld and do not require any modifications.

Section	Key	Value	Description
JDENET_KERNEL_DEF5	dispatchDLL-Name	Jdekrnl.dll	The name of the library (*.dll or *.so) that contains the kernel for the Transaction Manager.
	dispatchDLL-Function	_TM_Dispatch-Transaction-Message@28	The name of the function in the dispatchDLL-Name library that is executed for the particular kernel
	maxNumberOf-Processes	1	The maximum number of kernel processes that can be running at one time for this dedicated server process
	beginningMsg-TypeRange	601	The starting message type ID for this dedicated server process
	endingMsg-TypeRange	650	The ending message type ID for this dedicated server process
	newProcess-Threshold-Requests	0	The total number of outstanding requests each dedicated server process can have before starting a new dedicated server process

To enable transaction processing for every client and server that operates in the OneWorld environment, you must manually change a few settings in the JDE.INI file.

The settings are used to define the transaction server for OneWorld and to identify the service that it provides.

Server JDE.INI File Modifications

To define the enterprise server that is the transaction server in the JDE.INI file for every server, enter the information from the following table into the appropriate section of the server's JDE.INI file.

Section	Key	Value	Description
LOCK MANAGER	Server	oneworld server	Identifies the name of the server acting as the Lock Manager.
	Available-Service	TS	Indicates the type of service that the enterprise server provides. The service that is currently being provided is time stamping (TS) only.
	Requested-Service	TS	Indicates the type of service that the workstation requests from the enterprise server. The service that is currently being provided by servers is time stamping (TS) only.

Client JDE.INI File Modifications

Every OneWorld client requires its JDE.INI file to be manually modified to enable it to perform transaction processing. This allows the client to direct all transaction processing requests to the proper enterprise server that is the transaction server. To enable transaction processing for a client, enter the information from the following table into the appropriate section of the client's JDE.INI file.

Section	Key	Value	Description
LOCK MANAGER	Server	oneworldserver	Identifies the name of the server acting as the Lock Manager.
	Requested-Service	TS	Indicates the type of service that the workstation issues to the enterprise server. The service that is currently being provided by servers is time stamping (TS) only.

Transaction-Processing Boundaries

As stated earlier, transactions are constructed by wrapping several SQL statements into a single statement to manipulate the database tables. The data in each SQL statement has one or more dependencies on the data in the other SQL statements, and this means that all of the data must exist in the database in order to guarantee its integrity. The set of data and the tables in which they reside defines its *boundary*.

DEFINITION

A ***transaction-processing boundary*** *defines the tables and data that are manipulated for a transaction. Defining the boundaries of a transaction assists you in designing a transaction, and what it manipulates.*

In the voucher-entry example described in the previous section, transaction processing manipulated the Accounts Payable Ledger (F0411) and the Account Ledger (F0911) tables. The transaction includes both tables, because some of the data that is in the F0411 table requires entries in the F0911 table to support it, and this creates dependencies in the data for the tables. Therefore, the transaction boundary for the voucher-entry transaction is the data that resides in the F0411 and F0911 tables.

Transaction-processing boundaries are important because they define the starting and ending points for a transaction. The starting point notifies the database that the SQL statements that follow are a part of a transaction, and the database executes the statements without changing the tables to ensure their proper execution. The ending point of the transaction notifies the database of the end of the transaction, and it will update the tables if the SQL statements executed properly.

Commit and Rollback Mechanisms

In order for databases to manage transaction processing, they use the commit and rollback mechanisms. These mechanisms ensure that either the entire transaction is completed or none of the transaction is completed.

Commit

The commit mechanism for transaction processing manages the way the database is manipulated by the SQL statements after they successfully execute. There are three types of commits for a database:

- **Automatic commit**   An automatic commit (or auto-commit) records a change to the database immediately after each SQL statement is executed, which is the technique employed when transaction processing is not used. It is important to note that automatic commits immediately modify the records, regardless of whether or not the previous SQL statements have successfully executed, so they will leave the database susceptible to integrity problems.

- **Manual commit**   A manual commit tells the database to modify the tables based on the SQL statements. The manual commit is issued after the SQL statements have executed properly, and there are no more statements to be issued for the transaction. The manual commit also notifies the database that the transaction is completed and terminates processing after the changes to the tables have been made.

- **Two-phase commit**   A two-phase commit manages transactions that encompass more than one data source. The two-phase commit usually occurs when the transaction needs to access and manipulate data that exists in more than one database or server. The two-phase commit verifies that the SQL statements that are issued to each database successfully execute before notifying each database to manipulate its tables based on the statements that were issued to it.

Rollback

Rollbacks are the opposite of commits for databases, because they manipulate the database after an unsuccessful end to a transaction. A rollback notifies the database to reject the modifications that the SQL statements made during the transaction. Therefore, the modifications that exist in the transaction boundary are deleted.

For example, when a user clicks the Cancel button on a form, the logic behind the event issues a command to perform a rollback of the transaction. Another example is when a catastrophic failure, such as a network crash, occurs during a transaction. This failure causes an automatic rollback of the transaction, because the data is incomplete and will jeopardize the integrity of the database.

Transaction Master Business Functions

OneWorld implements transaction processing through a set of business functions referred to as transaction Master Business Functions (MBFs). Transaction MBFs include all of the logic required to start transactions, issue SQL statements, and terminate transactions.

You can develop transaction MBFs for any application or business function in OneWorld. They provide a standard interface for issuing transactions from any module. For example, an entry that originates from an inventory transfer uses the same transaction MBF to update the General Ledger module as a voucher entry in the Accounts Payable module.

This section describes how to assign processing option templates to transaction MBFs, the standard functions in transaction MBFs, and the naming conventions for transaction MBFs.

Processing Option Templates for Transaction Master Business Functions

To reduce the number of input parameters required by a transaction MBF, you should assign a processing option template to it. This template allows you to set parameters that are required each time the transaction MBF is called. Use the following guidelines when creating a processing option template for a transaction MBF:

- The processing option template must use the following object naming convention: T*xxxxyyyy*, where *xxxxyyyy* is the same system code unique identifier combination as the object name for the transaction MBF. For example, the Journal Entry MBF (B0900049) includes a processing option template with the name Journal Entry MBF Processing Options (T0900049).

- You must include a dummy interactive application to support the processing option template, because you can apply a version only to a processing option that is assigned to an application. The naming convention for the dummy interactive application is P*xxxxyyyy*, where *xxxxyyyy* is the same product code unique identifier combination as the object name for the transaction MBF. For example, the Journal Entry MBF (B0900049) includes a dummy interactive application with the name Journal Entry MBF Processing Options (P0900049).

TIP

To access the values assigned to a processing option, you must acquire the values in the Begin Document function of the transaction MBF. Then use the AllocatePOVersionData function for a C-based business function to retrieve the values assigned by the version for the processing option.

- To create several versions of the processing options for the transaction MBF, set up each version through the Interactive Versions application (P983051).

N O T E

To use a specific version of a transaction MBF, pass the version name into the version parameter of the Begin Document function of the transaction MBF. This will ensure that the parameters set for that version are used for the transaction.

Standard Functions Contained in Transaction Master Business Functions

Each transaction MBF contains several functions that provide the features and functionality required for proper operation of a transaction. The functions are available for use by both batch and interactive applications.

Three standard elements are used by the functions in the transaction MBF: job number, cache file, and document. The job number uniquely identifies an instance of a transaction. The job number is assigned by the *00/04* next number, where 00 is the system code and 04 is the next number value. The job number is passed between the functions in transaction MBFs to ensure that the functions perform their operations on the correct transaction.

You use the job number in conjunction with the cache files to identify the records that apply to a particular transaction. Cache files are used by transaction MBFs to store information that is generated during the transaction but has not been permanently stored in the database. This keeps the data that is processed by the transaction separate from the data in the database and ensures database integrity during processing of the transaction.

The cache files are structured in a header-detail document format. The format assigns two cache files (header and detail) for each transaction MBF. The header and detail cache files are organized in the same manner as the corresponding Header-Detail form that users interact with for entering records. For example, the Journal Entry header (F09UI002) and detail (F09UI003) cache files are organized as the Header-Detail form for the Standard Journal Entry application (P0911).

The cache file naming convention is FxxUIyyy, where xx is the product code, yyy is a unique identifier for the table, and UI identifies the table as a cache file. The header and detail cache files are usually numbered consecutively, such as F09UI002 and F09UI003 for the Journal Entry files.

To ensure that the functions manipulate the cache files properly and to correctly define the transaction boundary, the functions in the transaction MBF treat the cache files as documents. The Begin Document function creates the header cache file and starts the transaction boundary for the transaction. As the process continues, various functions manipulate the data in specific sections of the document, such as the header or detail section. For example, detail lines in the document are manipulated by the Edit Line function, and the document header is manipulated by the Begin Document function.

The end of the transaction boundary is defined by two functions: Cancel Document and End Document. The Cancel Document function ends the transaction by providing the rollback SQL command to the database, and the End Document function ends the transaction by providing the commit SQL command to the database.

The Begin Document, Edit Line, Cancel Document, and End Document functions are always present in any transaction MBF. The following sections describe the transaction MBF functions in more detail.

Begin Document Function

The Begin Document function (BeginDoc), which follows the naming convention FXXXXBeginDoc, is the first function executed in a transaction process. The primary purpose of the function is to initialize transaction processing with the database that begins the transaction boundary. The BeginDoc function also provides default values and settings for the document and edits the data in the header portion of the document.

The BeginDoc function performs the following steps:

1. It creates the cache file that is used during the transaction for storage of data until it is submitted to the database.

2. It retrieves the values from the processing option template for the transaction MBF, if the version data item (VERS) contains a value. It then saves the values

in the cache file. Use the AllocatePOVersionData function to retrieve the values from the processing options.

3. It uses the business function X0010GetNextNumber if the job number data item (JOBS) that uniquely identifies the transaction is not assigned. The next number that is used for assigning the job number for transactions is system code 00 with index number 04.

4. Subsequent calls to the BeginDoc function during the transaction will update the fields to the header data of the document.

Table 16-1 lists all of the data items that are required in the BeginDoc data structure. The data structure contains a set of header fields that are used to pass values to the header portion of the document. Also, work fields are used in the data structure to communicate information among the functions that are a part of the transaction, as well as to store the values that are assigned by the processing option version for the transaction MBF in the header document.

Use the following guidelines when calling the BeginDoc function:

- The BeginDoc function must be called first to initialize the transaction.

- You can call the BeginDoc function more than once to edit the values in the document header of the transaction. To call the function again in an interactive application, add a hidden button on the form to encapsulate the ER code that calls the function.

- The BeginDoc function must be called again if it terminates with an error, and it ensures that all errors have been cleared for the transaction.

Edit Line Function

The Edit Line function (EditLine), which follows the naming convention F*XXXXX*EditLine, is used to maintain the detail records for the document that is submitted during the transaction. This function validates the input that the user provides, performs any calculations that are required for the document, and retrieves any default information for the document. The EditLine function is executed each time new detail records are added to the document.

Name	Data Item Alias	I/O	Description
Job number	JOBS	I/O	The job number is the unique identifier for the transaction. If you do not provide a value, the function will assign one.
Document action	ACTN	I	The document action is the action to perform on the entire document: A or 1 = Add C or 2 = Change D = Delete
Process edits	EV01	I	Partial editing of the document header does not apply to this function: 0 = No edits Any other = Full edits
Error conditions	EV01	O	The error conditions identify any errors: Space = No errors 1 = Warning 2 = Error
Version	VERS	I	The version identifies the version that is used when acquiring the values assigned in the processing options for the transaction MBF.
Header fields		I/O	The header fields list and assign the fields that are required by the header portion of the document for the transaction.
Work fields		I	These fields are used to list and assign any work fields that are required to support the other functions of the transaction.

TABLE 16-1.　Data Structure Elements in the BeginDoc Function

The EditLine function performs the following steps:

1. As each column is validated, the EditLine function validates columns in the record that are dependent on each other. This ensures that no conflicts exist for the information in the record of the document.

2. EditLine creates a detail cache file for the storage of detail records, if the detail cache file does not exist.

3. If the record does not exist in the detail cache file, EditLine writes the record to the detail cache file before the EditLine function. Otherwise, it updates the record in the detail cache file.

The Process Edit flag for EditLine determines what type of editing is performed, and it can only be used for interactive applications. For example, use EditLine to create the detail record and perform high-level defaulting in the Grid Record Is Fetched event, and perform the rest of the editing during the Row Is Exited and Changed events.

Table 16-2 lists all of the data items that are required in the EditLine data structure. The data structure contains a set of detail fields that are used to pass values to the detail record of the document. Also, work fields are used in the data structure to communicate information among the functions that are a part of the transaction.

Name	Data Item Alias	I/O	Description
Job number	JOBS	I	This field is used to pass the value that was assigned from the BeginDoc function.
Line number	LNID	I/O	This field contains the line number for the detail record. It must be a unique value.
Line action	ACTN	I	The line action is the action to perform for the detail record: A or 1 = Add C or 2 = Change D or 3 = Delete
Process edits	EV01	I	Process edits is used for partial editing of the document for interactive applications: 0 = No edits 1 = Full edits 2 = Partial edits
Error conditions	ERRC	O	The error conditions identify any errors: Space = No errors 1 = Warning 2 = Error
Update or write to work file	EV01	I	A value of 1 notifies the function to write or update records to the work file.
Record written to work file	EV01	I/O	A value of 1 notifies that the function wrote records to the work file. A value of Space notifies that no records were written to the work file. Space = No record was written to the work file 1 = Record was written to the work file

TABLE 16-2. Data Structure Elements in the EditLine Function

Name	Data Item Alias	I/O	Description
Detail fields		I/O	The detail fields list and assign all of the fields that are required by the detail portion of the document for the transaction.
Work fields		I	These fields are used to list and assign any work fields that are required to support the other functions of the transaction.

TABLE 16-2.   Data Structure Elements in the EditLine Function (*continued*)

Edit Document Function

The Edit Document function (EditDoc), which follows the naming convention F*XXXX*EditDoc, is used to perform the final validation of the document created during the transaction before it is submitted to the database. User inputs are not required, since the header and detail cache files contain all of the information for the transaction. The primary purpose of the EditDoc function is to validate any data dependencies that exist between the fields in the detail records and the header portion of the document.

The EditDoc function performs the following steps:

1. It verifies that certain values that are used in the document total correctly. For example, it verifies fields that provide information on totaling, balancing, and percentages.

2. It finishes processing fields in the header or detail portions of the document that can't be processed until the information for the entire document has been submitted.

Table 16-3 lists the data items that are required in the EditDoc data structure. The data structure only needs the specific transaction number (JOBS) to process the document, and the data item (EV01) for the execution status of the EndDoc function.

Clear Cache Function

The Clear Cache function (ClearCache), which follows the naming convention F*XXXX*ClearCache, is used to remove the header and detail records for the document that

Name	Alias	I/O	Description
Job number	JOBS	I	The job number is used to pass the value that was assigned from the BeginDoc function.
Error conditions	EV01	O	The error conditions identify any errors: Space = No errors 1 = Warning 2 = Error

TABLE 16-3.   Data Structure Elements in the EditDoc Function

is stored in cache. This function is particularly useful when the transaction is canceled during processing, or when the document for the transaction has been stored in the database. Table 16-4 lists the parameters that are used in the ClearCache function.

Cancel Document Function

The Cancel Doc function (CancelDoc), which follows the naming convention F*XXXXX*CancelDoc, is used when the transaction is canceled during processing. The ClearCache function deletes all of the header and detail records that were created during transaction processing. The function also performs a database rollback to restore the database to its original state before the transaction. The only user input

Name	Alias	I/O	Description
Job number	JOBS	I	The job number is used to pass the value that was assigned from the BeginDoc function.
Clear header	EV01	I	A value of 1 notifies the function to clear the header cache.
Clear detail	EV01	I	A value of 1 notifies the function to clear the detail cache.
Line number	LNID	I	The line number for the detail cache notifies the function where to start deleting the detail cache. If this parameter is left blank, the function starts at line number 1.

TABLE 16-4.   Data Structure Elements in the ClearCache Function

that is required to cancel the transaction is the job number (JOBS) that uniquely identifies the transaction, as shown in Table 16-5.

End Document Function

The End Document function (EndDoc), which follows the naming convention F*XXXX*EndDoc, is used when the transaction is permanently written to the database. This function performs a database commit to write all entries to the database and cleans up the records in the cache files used during processing using the ClearCache function. At this point, all of the data in the document has been validated for the transaction, and it maintains the integrity of the database after the records have been written to the database.

The EndDoc function performs the following steps:

1. It assigns the next number for the document. This value is not the same as the job number (JOBS) for the transaction, because it applies only to uniquely identified transactions and specific documents in the system.

2. It reads the header and detail records in the cache files.

3. It performs a SQL INSERT for creating records, an UPDATE for modifying existing records, and a DELETE for removing records from the database tables.

Table 16-6 lists the data items that are required in the EndDoc data structure. The data structure requires the specific transaction number (JOBS) to submit the document to the database, and it provides the error status of the EndDoc function after it executes.

Name	Alias	I/O	Description
Job number	JOBS	I	The job number is used to pass the value that was assigned from the BeginDoc function.

TABLE 16-5. Data Structure Elements in the CancelDoc Function

Name	Alias	I/O	Description
Job number	JOBS	I	The job number is used to pass the value that was assigned from the BeginDoc function.
Computer ID	CTID	I	The value that is assigned from the GetAuditInfo business function (B9800100).
Error conditions	EV01	O	The error conditions identify any errors: Space = No errors 1 = Warning 2 = Error
Program ID	PID	I	A hard-coded value that represents the object name of the application.

TABLE 16-6.   Data Structure Elements in the EndDoc Function

Naming Conventions for Transaction Master Business Functions

All transaction MBFs adhere to the following naming conventions:

- The name of the transaction MBF object follows the same naming convention as business functions, which is B*xxxxyyyy*, where *xxxx* is the system code, and *yyyy* is the unique identifier for the object.

- The data structures for the transaction MBF follow the naming convention of D*xxxxyyyy*A, D*xxxxyyyy*B, D*xxxxyyyy*C, and D*xxxyyyy*D, where *xxxx* is the system code, and *yyyy* is the unique identifier for the object. The last letter of the object name refers to the particular function in the transaction MBF. For example, A is for BeginDoc, B is for EditLine, C is for EditDoc, and D is for EndDoc.

- The individual business functions in the transaction MBF are in the format *filename function-name*, such as F0411BeginDoc and F0911EndDoc.

- Use code 192 in the Functional Use field of the Object Librarian to designate the function as a transaction MBF.

Interfacing with OneWorld

Implementing Transaction Processing in Your Applications

Transaction processing is not enabled when you create applications. You need to enable the application for transaction processing and define transaction boundaries each time you create a transaction.

This section explains how to enable transaction processing in interactive applications, in batch applications, and in business functions. You will also learn how to extend the transaction boundary for the application to the objects that it calls during execution.

Implementing Transaction Processing in Interactive Applications

Enabling a form in an interactive application for transaction processing is easy. However, defining the transaction boundary across the events of a form can be difficult, because you need to consider all of the actions that users might take when executing an interactive application.

Enabling Transaction Processing for a Form

You enable transaction processing for a form through the Form Properties dialog box, as shown in Figure 16-2. To open this dialog box, select Form Properties from the Form menu. Select the Transaction check box at the bottom of the dialog box to enable transaction processing.

Implementing Transaction Processing in a Form

Enhancing a form to manage and execute transaction processing is straightforward when you select the proper events to execute the business functions in an application. Figure 16-3 is provided as a guideline to assist you in implementing transaction processing for forms in interactive applications.

Figure 16-3 defines the typical transaction boundary that is used for forms, and it also shows the events where each function of a transaction MBF needs to be executed. The transaction boundary starts at the BeginDoc function and is located in the Set Focus On Grid event. The function belongs in this event because users typically enter the grid of a form after they have completed entering data in the header of the document.

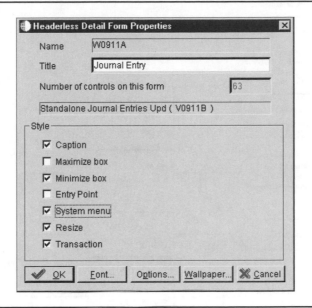

FIGURE 16-2. The Form Properties dialog box with Transaction selected to enable transaction processing

TIP

Transaction MBFs perform all of the table I/O for the transaction. Therefore, insert the ER code "Suppress Add" for the Add Grid Record To DB – Before event, the ER code "Suppress Update" for the Update Grid Record To DB – Before event, and the ER code "Suppress Delete" for the Delete Grid Record To DB – Before event.

The EditLine function executes once the user has completed entering data into a row of the grid. You place this function in the Row Exited And Changed – Async event to ensure that its execution does not prevent users from entering more data into the grid. As the user continues to enter data into the next row of the grid, the system initiates a background process that executes the EditLine function.

The EditDoc function executes in the OK Button Clicked event. When the EditDoc function finishes execution, the document that is issued to the database cannot contain any errors, which means that this is your last chance to validate the document. The

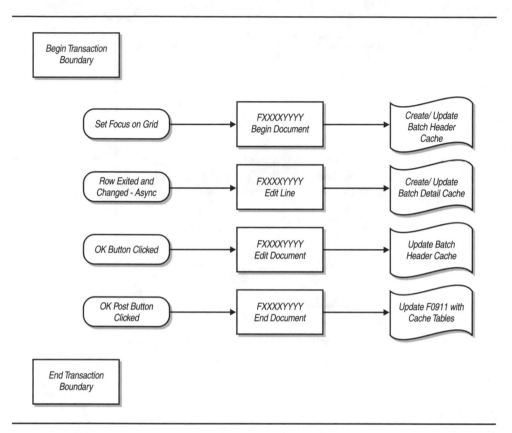

FIGURE 16-3.   Transaction processing flow for a form

document cannot contain any errors because the OK Button Clicked event is the last event in which you can stop processing in the form and prompt the user to fix the document.

If the OK Button Clicked event does not stop processing in the form, the OK Post Button Clicked event will execute. This event will execute the EndDoc function, which will commit the document to the tables defined for the transaction and end the transaction boundary for the form.

N O T E

You should add the ClearCache function to the Cancel Button Clicked event to ensure that stranded records in the cache do not overtake the available hard disk space.

Implementing Transaction Processing in Batch Applications

You enable and implement transaction processing for batch applications in much the same way as you do for interactive applications. However, unlike interactive applications, batch applications do not involve user interaction, so it's easier to implement transaction processing in them.

Enabling Transaction Processing for a Batch Application

You enable transaction processing for a batch application through the Advanced tab of the report's Properties dialog box, as shown in Figure 16-4. To open this dialog box, select Report Properties from the Report menu. Select the Enabled check box in the Transaction Processing group box to enable transaction processing for the batch application.

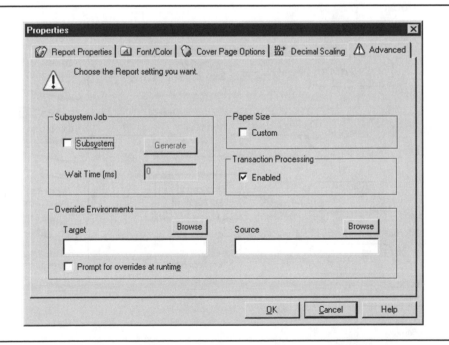

FIGURE 16-4. The Properties dialog box with Enabled selected to enable transaction processing

Implementing Transaction Processing in a Batch Application

Although you don't need to worry about user interaction during batch application execution, the number of events in which you can execute transaction-processing functions can be daunting. Figure 16-5 is provided as a guideline to assist you in implementing transaction processing in batch applications.

Figure 16-5 defines the typical transaction boundary that is used for batch applications, and it also shows the events where each function of a transaction MBF needs to be executed. The transaction boundary starts at the BeginDoc function, as it does in an interactive application, and is located in the Do Section event for the group or columnar section that is the Level One section of the report. The Level One section

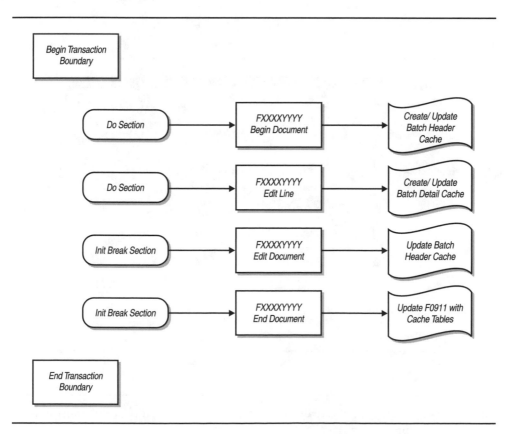

FIGURE 16-5.   Transaction processing flow for a batch application

creates a document to be processed by the transaction for each value passed into the Data Selection structure of the report. For example, users typically post a single batch at a time to the system to update the General Ledger, Accounts Payable, and Accounts Receivable ledgers, and the Data Selection structure only passes one batch number to post it.

You attach the EditLine function to the Do Section event; however, it must execute after the BeginDoc function finishes executing. The EditLine function retrieves and processes the detail items that are assigned to the document that was created by the BeginDoc function. Typically, a batch that contains one or more vouchers will post the vouchers to the ledgers of the financial modules using the EditLine function.

The EditDoc and EndDoc functions execute, respectively, in the Init Break Section event for the batch application. The EditDoc function validates the document. If the document is valid, the EndDoc function will execute and commit the document to the database; otherwise, the ClearCache function will be called.

Extending the Transaction Boundary

Most OneWorld applications, whether batch or interactive, make several calls to other objects in the system through the use of interconnects. In most cases, the interconnect calls manipulate data that is a part of the transaction boundary. Therefore, it becomes paramount to extend the transaction boundary to include interconnects that are called by an application. You can use business function interconnects, table I/O interconnects, form interconnects, and batch application interconnects to extend the boundary of a transaction.

Business Function Interconnects

You can include any business function in the system in the transaction boundary. Business function interconnects are typically used for interacting with the database in auto-commit mode. For example, you might call the Get Next Number business function (X0010) in an application to execute that function for one of the application's fields.

You include the business function in the transaction boundary of the application through the Business Functions dialog box when you are defining the business function interconnect, as shown in Figure 16-6.

NOTE

For more information on the Business Functions dialog box, see Chapter 13.

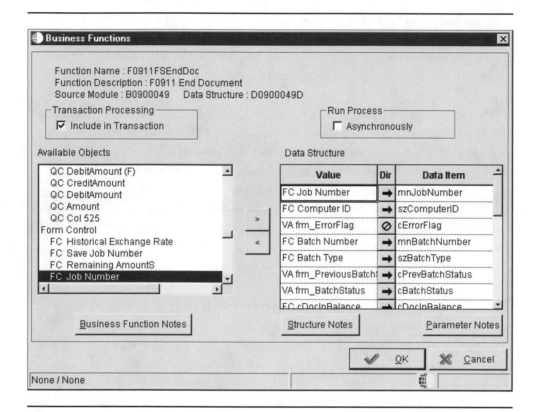

FIGURE 16-6. The Business Functions dialog box with the Include in Transaction check box selected

When you select the Include in Transaction check box in this dialog box, the calling business function will inherit the database commitment mode of the application. The records that are created or updated in the business function will not be committed until the calling application explicitly executes the SQL commit command.

Table I/O Interconnects

A table I/O interconnect is only available for inclusion in an application's transaction boundary when you enable the Open Table operation for it. You include the table I/O interconnect in the transaction boundary of the application through the Data Source dialog box when you are defining the table I/O interconnect, as shown in Figure 16-7.

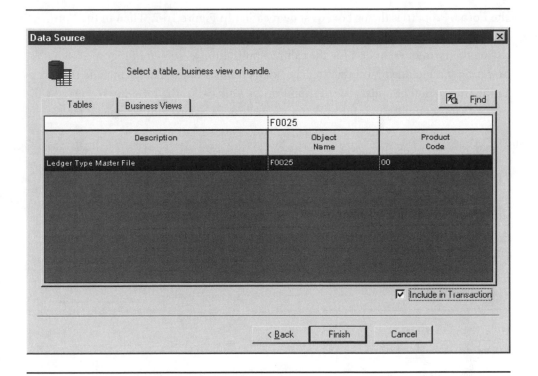

FIGURE 16-7. The Tables tab of the Data Source dialog box I/O Interconnect dialog box with the Include in Transaction check box selected

NOTE

For more information on the Data Source dialog box, see Chapter 7.

When you select the Include in Transaction check box in this dialog box, the system will include the table I/O interconnect in the transaction. Otherwise, the table I/O interconnect will use the auto-commit mode for updating or inserting a record into a database table.

Form Interconnects

You can also include a form interconnect in an application transaction boundary. To include the form interconnect in the transaction, select the Transaction check box in the Forms Properties dialog box, as shown earlier in Figure 16-2. Then in the Form Interconnections dialog box, select the Include in Transaction check box when you define the form interconnect for the calling application, as shown in Figure 16-8. Selecting the Include in Transaction check box notifies the system to include the form in the transaction boundary for the application. Otherwise, the form interconnect will use the auto-commit mode for updating or inserting a record into a database table.

NOTE

For more information on the Form Interconnections dialog box, see Chapter 5.

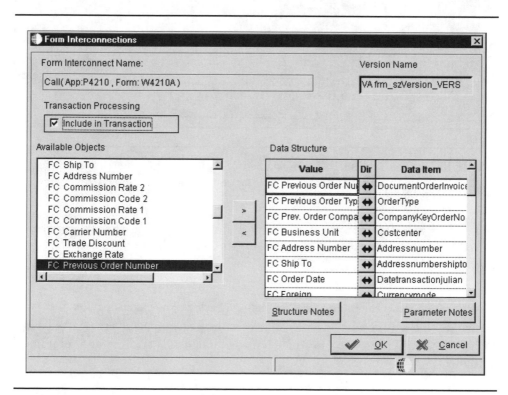

FIGURE 16-8.   The Form Interconnections dialog box with the Include in Transaction check box selected

Batch Application Interconnects

To include a batch application interconnect in an application transaction boundary, select the Enabled check box on the Advanced tab of the report's Properties dialog box, as shown earlier in Figure 16-4. Then in the UBE Interconnections dialog box, select the Include in Transaction check box when you define the batch application interconnect for the calling application, as shown in Figure 16-9. Selecting the Include in Transaction check box notifies the system to include the batch application interconnect in the transaction. Otherwise, the batch application interconnect will use the auto-commit mode for updating or inserting a record into a database table.

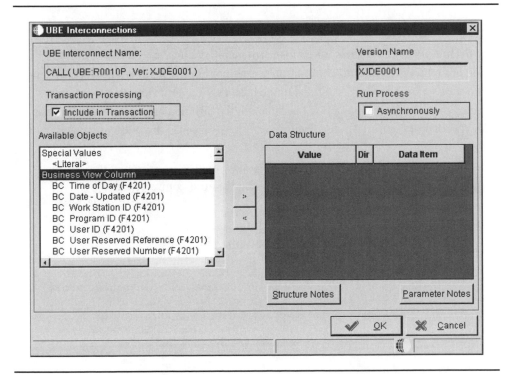

FIGURE 16-9. The UBE Interconnections dialog box with the Include in Transaction check box selected

NOTE

For more information on the UBE Interconnections dialog box, see Chapter 7.

Implementing Transaction Processing in Business Functions

Currently, C-based business functions are the only type of business functions that allow transaction processing. Therefore, developing these business functions requires a thorough knowledge of C-based business functions and transaction processing.

There are two database modes involved in transaction processing for business functions: auto-commit and manual commit.

Auto-Commit

The default mode for business functions when manipulating the database is the auto-commit mode. The auto-commit mode does not implement transaction processing, so no transaction boundary is defined in the business function. However, if you have selected the Include in Transaction check box in the Business Functions dialog box, as shown earlier in Figure 16-6, the database calls in the business function are included in the transaction.

The following lines of code illustrate the statements that are generated by a business function to update the database using the auto-commit mode:

```
. . .
JDBReturn = JDB_InitBhvr (lpBhvrCom, &hUser, (char*)NULL,
                          JDEDB_COMMIT_AUTO);
. . .
JDBReturn = JDB_OpenTable (hUser, NID_Fxxxx, ID_Fxxxx_yyyy, NULL,
                           (ushort)0, (char*)NULL, &hRequestFxxxx);
. . .
JDBReturn = JDB_UpdateTable (hRequestFxxxx, NID_Fxxxx, (ID)NULL,
                             ID_Fxxxx_yyyy, (void*)&dsFxxxxKey,
                             nNumKeys, (void*)&dsColFxxxxx);
```

```
. . .
JDBReturn = JDB_CloseTable (hRequestFxxxx);
. . .
JDBReturn = JDB_FreeBhvr (hRequestFxxxx);
. . .
```

Notice that one of the parameters in the JDB_InitBhvr function explicitly defines the communication with the database to be the auto-commit mode. This is the defined mode until the connection with the database is closed with the JDB_FreeBhvr function. The statements between the JDB_InitBhvr and JDB_FreeBhvr functions update a generic table in the database, and the updates to the tables are automatically committed to the database.

Manual Commit

The manual commit mode for business functions allows you to define when all of the records for your transaction are committed to the database tables. You can use the manual commit feature whether or not the calling application uses transaction processing.

For calling applications that do not use transaction processing, the business function will still use manual commits to the database; however, it will only affect records that are defined in the business function. You would commonly use this technique for master file tables in OneWorld that must enforce database integrity with critical tables that it references in order for the system to properly operate. Some examples of master files are the Address Book Master table (F0101), Business Unit Master table (F0006), and the Data Item Master table (F9200). A further discussion on master files is provided in the upcoming Developer's Corner, titled "Using Master Files in Your Development Projects."

N O T E

When you create a master file in OneWorld, you identify it by the Object Use code 210 in the Object Librarian.

If you have selected the Include in Transaction check box in the Business Functions dialog box, the business function is included in the transaction boundary. The database calls issued by a business function that use manual commits becomes a micro-transaction. If the micro-transaction fails, the overall transaction fails, and none of the tables in the database are modified.

DEFINITION

Micro-transaction boundaries are transaction boundaries that are defined within a larger transaction boundary. Micro-transaction boundaries are useful in cases in which the data within them is not defined until the processing of the transaction occurs, and the data must exist in order for the overall transaction to successfully execute.

Micro-transaction boundaries exist because the calling application transaction boundary does not affect the transaction boundary defined in the business function. Micro-transaction boundaries are used in situations in which transactions contain data dependencies. This prevents the transaction from being committed to the database, because some of the data in the transaction must exist before the records are committed to the database. You can avoid this situation by defining the micro-transaction boundary within the transaction, and commit the data that has dependencies on it to the database before the rest of the transaction is committed.

The following lines of code illustrate the statements that are generated by a business function to update the database using the manual commit mode:

```
. . .
JDBReturn = JDB_InitBhvr (lpBhvrCom, &hUser, (char*)NULL,
                          JDEDB_COMMIT_MANUAL);
. . .
JDBReturn = JDB_OpenTable (hUser, NID_Fxxxx, ID_Fxxxx_yyyy, NULL,
                           (ushort)0, (char*)NULL, &hRequestFxxxx);
. . .
JDBReturn = JDB_UpdateTable (hRequestFxxxx, NID_Fxxxx, (ID)NULL,
                             ID_Fxxxx_yyyy, (void*)&dsFxxxxKey,
                             nNumKeys, (void*)&dsColFxxxxx);
if (JDBReturn == JDEDB_PASSED) {
    JDB_CommitUser (&hUser);
} else (
    JDB_RollbackUser (&hUser);
}
. . .
JDBReturn = JDB_CloseTable (hRequestFxxxx);
. . .
JDBReturn = JDB_FreeBhvr (hRequestFxxxx);
. . .
```

Notice that one of the parameters in the JDB_InitBhvr function explicitly defines the communication with the database to be the manual commit mode. This is the defined mode until the connection with the database is closed with the JDB_FreeBhvr function. The statements between the JDB_InitBhvr and JDB_FreeBhvr functions issue their SQL statements to modify the database tables, and all of them must successfully execute before the commit statement, JDB_CommitUser, is issued to the database. After the commit statement is issued, all of the modifications are permanently made to the tables in the database.

Interfacing with OneWorld

Using Master Files in Your Development Projects

As you read through the previous section on business functions and transaction processing, a lot of questions probably entered your mind. In particular, you are probably wondering what master files are and why transaction processing is essential to managing them.

Master files are critical for the proper operation of OneWorld because they define the basic components of data that is used throughout all transactions. For example, master files store critical information about business units, companies, address book information, security settings, machine definitions, inventory items, vehicles used for transportation, and much more.

If the integrity of the master file is violated at any time, the transactions will refer to data in the master files that does not exist, and this will cause many operations and applications to fail. For example, if an application tries to update a sales order that requires information that does not exist in the Address Book (F0101), Business Unit (F0006), and Inventory Item (F4101) master files, the application will not execute properly because there is no data to manipulate in the tables.

To maintain the integrity of the master files, you use business functions with transaction processing built into them. These business functions validate SQL commands that manipulate the data in the tables, which, in turn, maintain the validity of the data in the table. They also maintain the validity of data that references records in other essential tables.

The two main problems that can occur if you don't take care of your master files are intermittent problems in your applications and a lack of data integrity in databases that are distributed across the network.

Reducing Intermittent Application Problems

As your support staff members maintain and troubleshoot new applications, they will find that a lack of data integrity in the master files can wreak havoc on your applications. This problem becomes increasingly obvious when you find yourself needing to constantly manipulate the data in the tables to fix the applications your development project creates. The reason for the data-integrity problem is that virtually all development projects end up with a set of tables that hinge on a few critical tables.

DEFINITION

*In OneWorld, **master tables** are core system tables that must have the integrity of their data maintained at all times. Data integrity is required by master tables, because without it, the system-level and module-level applications either propagate data-integrity problems throughout the system or cause applications to fail.*

The critical tables in your development project become the master files for your applications and modules. Therefore, the only way to fix the data-integrity problem is to create business functions with transaction processing for the master tables.

Rather than creating the business functions in the first phase of your development project, we suggest that you implement transaction processing in the second or third phase. During the first phase, you should be concentrating on developing the base functionality of the first version of your product. Also, it is very difficult to define transaction boundaries for tables that are still in the definition and initial development stage. Unfortunately, this means that you will have data-integrity problems when the first phase of the development project is rolled out to the production environment.

During the second or third phase of your development project, the layout of the master files will be stabilized. Then you can add the business functions for transaction processing, without worrying about needing to redesign them every time a change to the master file occurs.

TIP

After you create the business functions that contain transaction processing for your critical tables, you need to attach them to an event that will be executed every time the tables are accessed. The best events in which these business functions should be executed are in the table events that manipulate the records before they are added, updated, or deleted from the table.

Maintaining Data Integrity in Distributed Databases

In typical relational database systems, enforcing data and referential integrity of two tables in the same database is relatively easy, because the functionality is built into the system. However, maintaining data and referential integrity between tables that are located on different servers and databases is more difficult. You may not be able to find a development or management tool for maintaining database integrity between tables that reside in different databases, and if such a tool exists, you may find that it requires quite a bit of manual administration.

All of the functions in the JDEBASE APIs use the OCM to manage the location of the tables on the network, so tables that are scattered across multiple databases become easier to maintain. The OCM mappings store information on the location of the tables, and the JDEBASE functions use this information to issue the SQL commands to the proper tables.

The only way you can properly enforce data and referential integrity in a CNC environment that has two tables located in different databases is to use C-based business functions that implement transaction processing. Transaction processing will ensure that the tables are only updated by the SQL statements that successfully execute, since the JDEBASE functions use the OCM. Regardless of the end result of executing the SQL commands, transaction processing in the business function will issue the proper commit or rollback command to update the tables.

Putting It All Together

Transaction processing is a useful tool that can provide a lot of power and flexibility to maintain the data integrity of your databases. Like most powerful development tools, transaction processing is complex. In most cases, only experienced application developers will be able to implement transaction processing in their applications.

The Accounts Payable Standard Voucher Entry application (P0411) is a good example of the most common usage of transaction processing in an application. Transaction processing is used to ensure that records in the Account Payable Ledger table (F0411) and the Account Ledger table (F0911) are created, modified, and deleted in a manner that ensures integrity of the data. Transaction processing provides this guarantee because the transaction is not successful until both SQL statements that affect the tables have executed successfully.

This chapter explained how transaction processing works and how to implement transaction processing in your applications. As you read in this chapter, transaction processing for an interactive application occurs around the actions of users as they are clicking buttons on the form. Transaction processing for a batch application occurs as the application retrieves and manipulates tables in the database. You also learned how to use the JDEBASE API in your C-based business functions to build business functions that use transaction processing internally.

However, you may be left wondering how to build a transaction MBF for your development projects. The problem with showing you how to build transaction MBFs is that we haven't covered how to manipulate cache tables, which is the subject of Chapter 17. Cache tables are used in transaction MBFs to temporarily store data during processing of the transaction and until the data for the transaction is issued to the database.

Interfacing with OneWorld

CHAPTER 17

JDE Cache

Cache Definition and Creation

Cache Manipulation APIs

Example of a Cache Business Function

Putting It All Together

When developing code in OneWorld, you'll often want to save information, such as records in a file, into a temporary location. Creating and maintaining hundreds of variables is a very difficult proposition. You might create a work table inside the database to store the information, but this table would be a permanent table even if it is empty. And fetching the widely disbursed records from this database would be a slow and cumbersome process. OneWorld provides a better solution: you can create a temporary data store using JDE Cache functions. A JDE Cache is a piece of memory that is analogous to a table in RAM. The cache can contain many records and will have an associated index or indices to aid in fetching and updating.

You can use JDE Cache in Master Business Functions (MBFs) as well as I/O-intensive functions. For example, suppose a function will hit a database table hundreds or thousands of times, and the function will typically access the same information. You can create a cache to store the information that the system will access. Loading the cache one time from the database and fetch from the cache each time a record is needed is a much faster process than repeatedly fetching the same record from the database. You can also use cache to save and manipulate a large number of records before you update them to the database. Records saved in cache can be manipulated much faster than fetching and updating from the database (see Figure 17-1).

When should you use JDE Cache? Before you decide, it's important to understand what you can and can't do with it. Currently, you can create a cache only inside a business function written in C. You can also create a business function that will manipulate a cache that can be called by other functions, applications, and batch applications, but you cannot access the cache like a table using table I/O functions.

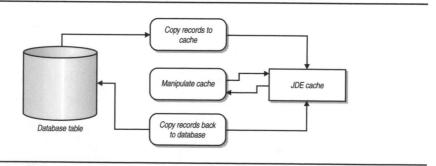

FIGURE 17-1.   Manipulating records in cache

Cache is saved inside RAM; so if a computer goes down, all the cached information is lost. Thus, you'll need to be careful about the size of the cache. There's no strict rule about the size of a cache, but you're limited by the amount of RAM on the computer. If a cache takes up all available RAM or even a large portion of it, you must consider the significant impact on operating system performance for your application and any other application running on the same machine. As a general rule, when your temporary data store is small (under 3MB), cache is a very good alternative if your application will be complete within a few minutes. A cache larger than 3MB is still beneficial, depending on how much RAM is on the system. If the cache grows to over 10MB, however, you need to measure the importance of your cache. Is it worth taking up the majority of the available RAM to do this process? Will this process run using this RAM for an extended amount of time? These questions will help determine what size cache is acceptable. If you determine that the temporary data store will be too large for the machine on which it will run, a work table may be a better choice.

What are the performance issues of running JDE Cache? Cached records are not stored in shared memory; so if a function using cache is running on the server, for example, different processors cannot access the same cache because the memory is not visible to all those processors. Since cache uses pointers and is stored in RAM, there is potential for serious memory leaks if you're not careful.

Machine name and user ID uniquely identify a cache. For example, if a business function is running on the server and two people from two different client machines are accessing the same server function, two different caches will be created. Problems with cache can occur when a threaded business function destroys the cache in one thread while another thread is trying to access it. Problems can also arise when two users are using the same sign-on through a Windows Terminal Server. We will discuss some tips and techniques for avoiding these potential conflicts in the upcoming section "Cache Name."

This chapter discusses the following topics:

- **Cache Definition and Creation** We will start with a discussion of how to define a cache naming standard, as well as the APIs that are involved in creating it.

- **Cache Manipulation APIs** This section discusses how to add, update, and delete records from a cache.

- **Example of a Cache Business Function** We will end by showing an example C business function that will create and manipulate a cache.

Cache Definition and Creation

This section explains the steps for creating a cache: naming it, creating a structure, defining one or more indices, and initializing the cache.

Cache Name

You must first name the cache and determine if you want to include a job number inside the cache name. A cache name usually includes the name of the business function, such as B5600002Cache. When creating multiple caches inside the same function, you can append a letter after the function name, as in B5600002ACache, and B5600002BCache. The cache name is used when you initialize your cache.

Adding a Job Number

If you are calling the same function multiple times, or from different processes or threads, consider adding a job number to your cache. This is like creating a batch of cache records that are used by one process. In the introduction to this chapter, we mentioned that a cache is uniquely identified by machine and user. By adding a job number, you add a third key that will make the cache unique. For example, if the cache will be used for creating an order, the cache will save all the records needed to complete this order. Therefore, the first time an order is created, the job number will be 1; the second time the order is created, the job number will be 2; and so on. Your cache name would be something like B5600002_10, where 10 is the job number (see Figure 17-2).

Adding a job number ensures that the two different processes (jobs) will have two completely different caches instead of sharing the same cache. Job numbers also preserve the unique identity of the cache records and the cache itself when there is

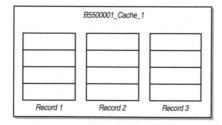
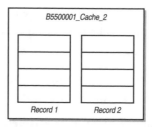

FIGURE 17-2. Job number attached to a cache name

threading or access by multiple users. Although it's not absolutely required that you add a job number, following this practice will help avoid problems with multiple threads or multiple users with the same sign-on.

A cache name cannot exceed 50 characters and cannot contain any reserved characters such as / or &. The following section of code shows how to append the job number:

```
/* this converts a math numeric to a string */
FormatMathNumeric(szJobNumber, &lpDS->mnJobNumber);
sprintf(szCacheName,"%s%s","B5600002_",(const char *)szJobNumber);
```

The next section of code shows how to use the function JDB_GetInternalNext-Number to get a job number. This function starts at 1 every time the computer restarts, and increments by one every time the function is called. Using this function is faster than using other next number functions.

```
nJobNumber = JDB_GetInternalNextNumber();
if (nJobNumber)
{
    LongToMathNumeric(nJobNumber, pmnNewJobNumber);
}
```

Alternate Cache Naming Methods

There are various techniques for coding caches, and not all programmers follow the guidelines described in this chapter. For example, some programmers will put a job number inside the cache record itself, as well as inside all cache indexes, as shown in Figure 17-3. By doing this, they have created one large cache instead of multiple caches. Rather than terminating the cache, they delete all records inside it that match their job number.

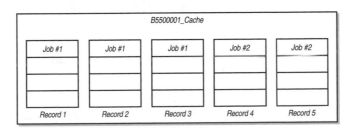

	B5500001_Cache			
Job #1	Job #1	Job #1	Job #2	Job #2
Record 1	Record 2	Record 3	Record 4	Record 5

FIGURE 17-3.   Job number inside the cache records

Cache Structure

The cache structure itself is easy to define: it is a structure inside your code and can contain any elements you wish it to have. Of more important consideration is the size of the structure. A structure that contains unused elements wastes space with every record you save.

For this example, we will define a cache structure inside the header file of a business function. This structure has seven members.

```
typedef struct tagDS5600002Cache
{
  MATH_NUMERIC        mnIdentifierShortItem;
  char                szCostCenter[13];
  char                szLocation[21];
  char                szLot[31];
  MATH_NUMERIC        mnQtyOnHandPrimaryUn;
  MATH_NUMERIC        mnQuantitySoftCommitted;
  MATH_NUMERIC        mnQtyHardCommitted;
} DS5600002Cache,  *LPDS5600002Cache;
```

The cache structure is named DS5600002Cache. As mentioned earlier, when you have multiple cache structures inside the same function, you place a letter after the function number, as in DS5600002A_Cache. In some code you'll notice that an additional structure has been created for the cache key. This is unnecessary; you can use the same structure for both the key and the cache. In fact, using a separate key structure can cause problems if the offsets of the key fields are different inside the key structure versus the cache structure. Offsets are discussed in the next section.

Index Definition

A cache, like a database table, includes indices to allow for fast access. A cache needs to have at least one index, and the first index should be your primary index that is unique across all the records in the cache. The code will be slightly different for a cache with one index and a cache with multiple indexes. To define an index, you'll use a structure called JDECMINDEXSTRUCT, which includes the members listed in Table 17-1.

To define each field inside an index, you use the data structure JDECMKEYSEGMENT. This structure is loaded with several pieces of information, including the location of each index member, as well as the member's size and type. This information is used when the cache APIs fetch, update, and delete records. Table 17-2 describes the parts of the structure JDECMKEYSEGMENT.

Interfacing with OneWorld

Data Structure Member	Description
nKeyID	The number of the key. Use it only when creating multiple indexes.
nNumSegments	The number of fields inside the index. For example, if your key is Item and Branch, then nNumSegments will be 2 because there are two items in the key.
CacheKey	An array of structures of type JDECMKEYSEGMENT, used to define each field inside your index

TABLE 17-1.   Members of the Structure JDECMINDEXSTRUCT

Figure 17-4 displays an example of a cache record. The cache record may comprise many fields, but the most important are the key fields needed by the cache APIs. Although several of the key fields are located in different areas inside the cache, you can still use them as key fields. In this example, one member of the cache is the first element (Item Number) in the cache, so the offset is 0. Another field (Branch) is located inside the cache, and its offset (or distance from the start of the structure) is 256.

Data Structure Member	Description
nOffset	The location, in bytes, from the top of the cache structure. To find this, use the function offsetof.
nSize	An integer that contains the size of the key field, in bytes. To find the field size, use the sizeof function.
idDataType	The data type member must be one of the following constants: EVDT_CHAR, EVDT_SZCHAR, EVDT_STRING EVDT_SHORT, EVDT_USHORT, EVDT_LONG EVDT_ULONG, EVDT_ID, EVDT_MATH_NUMERIC EVDT_MATHNUM, EVDT_JDEDATE, EVDT_BYTE EVDT_BOOL, EVDT_INT, EVDT_HANDLE EVDT_LONGVARCHAR, EVDT_LONGVARBINARY EVDT_BINARY, EVDT_VARSTRING, EVDT_TEXT EVDT_NID, EVDT_UINT, EVDT_TIMESTAMP EVDT_PROMO, EVDT_CATEGORY EVDT_PERMISSION, EVDT_VARCHAR The four constants used most often are EVDT_STRING for a string, EVDT_MATH_NUMERIC for a number, EVDT_JDEDATE for a date, and EVDT_CHAR for a character.

TABLE 17-2.   Members of the Structure JDECMKEYSEGMENT

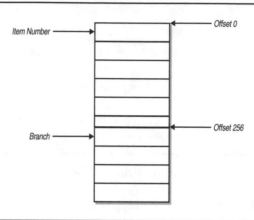

FIGURE 17-4.   A cache structure with key fields

T I P

Indices are automatically set up in ascending order; there is no way to set up a cache index in descending order. For example, if you want all quantities in order largest to smallest, you can't create an index that would sort the cache this way. To set up an index in descending order, you can add an additional parameter to your cache and use it for sorting instead. To do this, you'd make the additional field the quantity field, but change the sign of this quantity so it will be in reverse order. You can then use this additional parameter inside a key, and its order would be the opposite of your original quantity.

The two data structures described in Tables 17-1 and 17-2 are used in the following code to define a cache with two indexes. The first key, or index, contains four fields; the second key has only 2 fields. In this code, two indexes are created for our cache.

- The first index contains the members mnIdentifierShortItem, szCostCenter, szLocation, and szLot. The order of these members determines the sort order. The first member is sorted first; the second is sorted second, and so on.

- The second index contains szLocation and szLot. If you use this key, your records will be sorted by these two fields.

```
/*******************************************************************
*  Variable declarations
*******************************************************************/
   JDECM_RESULT        idJCMReturn        = JDECM_PASSED;
char              szCacheName[50]    = {0};
char              szJobNumber[32]    = {0};
/*******************************************************************
* Declare structures
 *******************************************************************/
   DS5600002Cache          dsCache;
   JDECMINDEXSTRUCT        dsKey[2];
/*************************************************************
* Main Processing
*************************************************************/
   /*  Setup and Initialize CACHE-keys    */
   dsKey[0].nKeyID                 = 1;
   dsKey[0].nNumSegments           = 4;
   dsKey[0].CacheKey[0].nOffset    = offsetof (DS5600002Cache,
                                     mnIdentifierShortItem);
   dsKey[0].CacheKey[0].nSize=sizeof(dsCache.mnIdentifierShortItem);
   dsKey[0].CacheKey[0].idDataType = EVDT_MATH_NUMERIC;
   dsKey[0].CacheKey[1].nOffset    = offsetof (DS5600002Cache,
                                     szCostCenter);
   dsKey[0].CacheKey[1].nSize      = sizeof (dsCache.szCostCenter);
   dsKey[0].CacheKey[1].idDataType = EVDT_STRING;
   dsKey[0].CacheKey[2].nOffset    = offsetof (DS5600002Cache,
                                          szLocation);
   dsKey[0].CacheKey[2].nSize      = sizeof (dsCache.szLocation);
   dsKey[0].CacheKey[2].idDataType = EVDT_STRING;
   dsKey[0].CacheKey[3].nOffset    = offsetof (DS5600002Cache,
                                          szLot);
   dsKey[0].CacheKey[3].nSize      = sizeof (dsCache.szLot);
   dsKey[0].CacheKey[3].idDataType = EVDT_STRING;

   dsKey[1].nKeyID                 = 2;
   dsKey[1].nNumSegments           = 2;
   dsKey[1].CacheKey[0].nOffset    = offsetof (DS5600002Cache,
                                          szLocation);
   dsKey[1].CacheKey[0].nSize      = sizeof (dsCache.szLocation);
   dsKey[1].CacheKey[0].idDataType = EVDT_STRING;
   dsKey[1].CacheKey[1].nOffset    = offsetof (DS5600002Cache,szLot);
   dsKey[1].CacheKey[1].nSize      = sizeof (dsCache.szLot);
   dsKey[1].CacheKey[1].idDataType = EVDT_STRING;
```

Cache Initialization

The final step in creating a cache is to call an API to initialize the cache. If you use only one index, you call jdeCacheInit. If you use multiple indices, you call jdeCacheInitMultipleIndex. These functions must be called to create a cache with the name you specified.

The initialization function also generates a cache handle, which is used in the cache APIs. Do not confuse a *cache handle* with a *cache cursor*. A cache cursor resembles a structure that points to records inside a cache; a cache handle on the other hand, is a pointer to the entire cache. This difference is illustrated in Figure 17-5.

Table 17-3 describes the parameters contained inside jdeCacheInit and jdeCacheInitMultipleIndex.

In the following section of code, the API jdeCacheInitMultipleIndex initializes a cache. The first parameter is hUser, created during a call to InitBhvr. The pCacheHandle is actually a pointer to a pointer that receives the cache handle, which is used by other cache APIs. The third parameter is a string that contains the cache name. The fourth

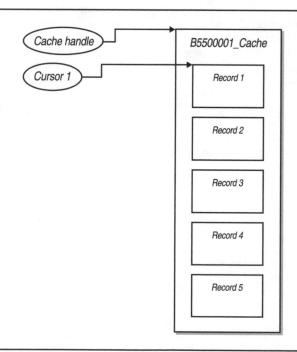

FIGURE 17-5. Cache handle vs. cache cursor

Parameter	Single or Multiple Index API	Description
HUSER	Both	The user handle that must be passed into the function. Use the JDB_InitBhvr function to generate a user handle.
HCACHE	Both	The cache handle created by the API.
szCache	Both	The name of the cache; for example, B5500001Cache. If you attached a job number, the name would be B5500001_Cache1.
lpIndex	Both	A pointer to the key structure you created. It uses the structure JDECMINDEXSTRUCT and defines the index or indices used in this cache.
nNumIndices	Multiple index only	The number of indexes.

TABLE 17-3.   Parameters in jdeCacheInit and jdeCacheInitMultipleIndex

parameter is dsKey, which contains the definition of the cache indexes. The last parameter is a 2 because there are two keys defined in the dsKey.

```
idJCMReturn = jdeCacheInitMultipleIndex (hUser, pCacheHandle,
                                         szCacheName, dsKey, 2);
if (idJCMReturn != JDECM_PASSED)
{
    /*  Failed to Initialize CACHE  */
    strcpy (lpDS->szErrorMessageID, "032E");
}
```

To create a cache handle, pCacheHandle, the function jdeCacheInitMultipleIndex uses the user handle hUser, the cache name szCacheName, the index structure dsKey, and the parameter 2, (which states the number of indexes). You can call the cache initialization functions multiple times without damaging the cache itself. This allows two different business functions to access the same cache (because both functions need to call CacheInit. Similarly, the same business function can call the initializing API multiple times to get a cache handle when needed. In other words, if the initializing API is called and the cache does not exist, the API creates the cache. Conversely, if the cache already exists, the API simply passes a pointer to the cache and does not re-create the cache.

These two APIs (jdeCacheInit and jdeCacheInitMultipleIndex), like all the other cache APIs, may return a JDECM_PASSED or JDECM_FAILED message. We recommend that you test the return by comparing against JDECM_PASSED. If you want to test for success, test

```
idJCMReturn == JDECM_PASSED
```

To test for failure, test

```
idJCMReturn!= JDECM_PASSED
```

Cache Manipulation APIs

Now that you've learned how to define and initialize a cache, this section shows you how to manipulate a cache. A cache contains records that you insert, fetch, update, or delete. As mentioned earlier, the cache is not a database, so it doesn't have the same functions as a database—for example, a cache has no "selection" operation. In this section, we discuss the programming you do to accomplish functions such as selection, adding and deleting records, and so on.

Cache Cursors

All cache manipulation APIs (other than Add) require a cache cursor—a structure that keeps track of which record is currently being used inside the cache. Every cursor needs to be opened before it's used and closed after it's used, and this is accomplished with the APIs that open, close, and reset the cache cursor.

During processing, you may need to have multiple cursors inside the cache at the same time. Figure 17-6 illustrates a situation in which you may need to fetch two records from the cache using two different keys.

The APIs that deal with cursors are as follows:

- jdeCacheCursorOpen

- jdeCacheCursorReset

- jdeCacheCursorClose

- jdeCacheSetIndex

NOTE

No more than 100 cursors can be used inside your cache, so make sure to close the cursors after you're finished using them.

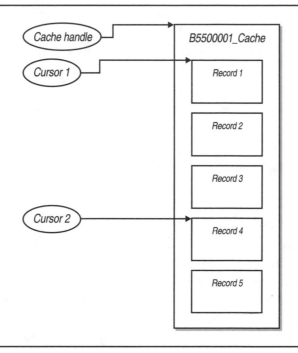

FIGURE 17-6.   Multiple cursors inside one cache

The following code creates the cache cursor hCursor by using the cache handle pCacheHandle:

```
idJCMReturn = jdeCacheOpenCursor ((HCACHE)pCacheHandle, &hCursor);
```

If you're using multiple indexes inside your cache, you need to set the cursor to a specific index. In the following section of code, the variable hCursor is set to an index.

```
idJCMReturn = jdeCacheSetIndex(pCacheHandle,
                          hCursor,
                          lpDS->nIndexNumber);
```

In this example, the index number is passed into the function, but it can also be hard-coded to a value if the logic requires it. Here, the lpDS->nIndexNumber could be either a 1 or a 2. Because we have two keys, we're using a variable, but you could just as well hard-code this to a 1 or a 2. If there's only one index in the cache, this API will not be called.

When you need to use the same cursor again, you have the option of resetting the cursor before using it. This method is used in many of the manipulation APIs.

As stated, a cursor should always be closed after you have finished using it. This frees any memory associated with the cursor. Here's how to close a cursor:

```
if(hCursor != NULL)
{
    jdeCacheCloseCursor ((HCACHE)pCacheHandle, hCursor);
}
```

Adding Cache Records

To add cache records, you use the jdeCacheAdd API. You must have a cache handle in order to do an Add, but you don't need to have a cache cursor. In fact, if you try to open a cursor on an empty cache, it will fail.

Before you call the API to do the insert, make sure you load your cache structure. Simply copy information into the cache structure that you will be inserting into the cache, as shown in the following code. This is simply copying information from the business function data structure to the cache data structure.

```
strcpy(lpdsCache->szCostCenter          ,lpDS->szCostCenter);
strcpy(lpdsCache->szLocation            ,lpDS->szLocation);
strcpy(lpdsCache->szLot                 ,lpDS->szLot);
MathCopy(&lpdsCache->mnQtyOnHandPrimaryUn,
         &lpDS->mnQtyOnHandPrimaryUn);
```

Next, we'll add a record to the cache. Calling a cache initialization function, as discussed earlier, retrieves the first parameter, pCacheHandle. The second parameter, pdsCache, is a pointer to a structure that is loaded with a new cache record. The last parameter is the size of the cache record. You should always use the sizeof function to reserve the size of the cache record.

```
idJCMReturn = jdeCacheAdd ((HCACHE)pCacheHandle,
                           (void *)pdsCache,
                           (long)sizeof(DS5600002Cache));
```

Fetching a Single Cache Record

There are a number of APIs that fetch from a cache; but for our purposes here, you're only concerned with two of them: jdeCacheFetchPosition and jdeCacheFetch. You use these functions to do one of two things: fetch to a position inside the cache, or advance the cursor and then fetch a record. Various other APIs will do these tasks, such as jdeCacheCursorFetchForUpdate, but they include the same functionality as jdeCacheFetchPosition and jdeCacheFetch. For additional information about JDE Cache APIs, see the OneWorld online help.

The basic difference between jdeCacheFetchPosition and jdeCacheFetch is how they position the cache cursor. The jdeCacheFetchPosition function fetches the first record matching the key passed in and does not advance the cursor, as shown here:

```
idJCMReturn = jdeCacheFetchPosition ((HCACHE)pCacheHandle,hCursor,
                                     (void *)pdsCacheKey,
                                     (short int)lpDS->nNumberOfKeys,
                                     (void *)pdsCache,
                                      sizeof (DS5600002Cache));
```

The pdsCacheKey is a pointer to a cache structure that is used in the comparison of key values. The parameter pdsCache is a pointer to a structure that receives the record fetched. The order of records is determined by the index that is used. For example, if you have a multiple-index cache, the index order will be that used in the jdeCacheSetIndex API.

The function jdeCacheFetch retrieves a cache record, too, but the API first advances the cursor to the next record in the cache before retrieving a record. This API does not have parameters for a key; it just fetches the next record in the cache. If this is the first time the cursor has been used, it fetches the first record in the cache. This is illustrated in Figure 17-7. Here is the code:

```
idJCMReturn = jdeCacheFetch ((HCACHE)pCacheHandle,hCursor,
                             (void *)pdsCache,
                             (void *)NULL);
```

Updating Cache Records

Before records can be updated into a cache, you must have a cache handle and a cursor, and then you must position the cursor on the correct cache record. To position

Interfacing with OneWorld

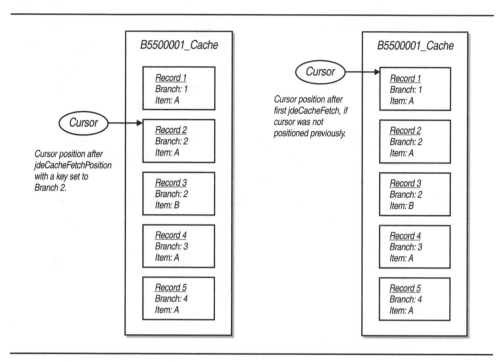

FIGURE 17-7.   Using jdeCacheFetch

the cursor, use the jdeCacheFetchPosition API. This API does two things: first, it ensures that the record exists; and second, it positions the cursor. The following code uses the fetch and update APIs to update a cache record.

```
/* Fetch a record and positions the cursor */
    idJCMReturn = jdeCacheFetchPosition((HCACHE)pCacheHandle,
                                    hCursor ,
                                    (void *) pdsCacheKey,
                                    (short int)lpDS->nNumberOfKeys,
                                    (void *) pdsCache,
                                     sizeof (DS5600002Cache));
/* If successful update the record */
    if(idJCMReturn == JDECM_PASSED)
    {
        I5600002_CopyToStruct (lpDS, pdsCache);
        /* Update the cache record */
        idJCMReturn = jdeCacheUpdate((HCACHE)pCacheHandle,hCursor,
                            (void *) pdsCache,
                             sizeof (DS5600002Cache));
```

The internal function I5600002_CopyToStruct (which is displayed in its entirety at the end of this chapter) simply loads the cache structure with what is in the business function data structure.

Deleting Cache Records

Two different APIs can be used to delete records from a cache. The first is jdeCacheDelete. This function simply deletes the record that the cache cursor is currently on. To use it, do a fetch position (jdeCacheFetchPosition), as discussed earlier, and then call the API as shown here:

```
idJCMReturn =jdeCacheDelete((HCACHE)idCacheHandle, hCursor);
```

The second function you can use for deleting records is jdeCacheDeleteAll, which deletes all records that match key fields that are passed in. This function has a parameter that designates how many elements of the key to look at. For the index that was defined in the "Index Definition" section earlier, that index is the first one with four fields in the key: mnIdentifierShortItem, szCostCenter, szLocation, and szLot. If you are using this index and you pass in a 2, then you'd use the first two fields of the key: mnIdentifierShortItem and szCostCenter. You must go in order of the key—in other words, you cannot pass in a 2 and then load mnIdentifierShortItem and szLocation, because of the order of the key. If you pass a 2, it means the first two fields of the key. In this example, the first field is mnIdentifierShortItem and the second is szCostCenter.

The following code shows how to call the DeleteAll function. If the number of keys is 0, all records will be deleted in the cache.

```
idJCMReturn = jdeCacheDeleteAll((HCACHE)pCacheHandle, hCursor,
                           pdsCacheKey,
                           (ushort)lpDS->nNumberOfKeys);
```

CAUTION

Avoid having two cursors pointing to the same cache record if you are going to delete or update using one of the cursors.

Fetching Multiple Cache Records

As mentioned in the introduction to this chapter, a cache is not a database and there is no "Select" statement per se. To fetch all the records that match a key inside your cache, you must program for it. Since the cache is ordered by the index you are using, all the records that match the passed-in key are grouped together. The API jdeCacheFetchPosition fetches the first record inside the cache that matches the key passed in. On the other hand, the API jdeCacheFetch fetches the next record inside the cache and does not look at the key.

Figure 17-8 shows how the cache functions go through the cache to find all the records in which Branch equals 2. First, we do a jdeCacheFetchPosition using Branch 2 in the key. This fetches the first record with Branch 2 and positions the cursor. Then a jdeCacheFetch fetches the next record. We can continue to do this; but because jdeCacheFetch does not compare against the key values, the third fetch retrieves a record in Branch B.

To avoid getting unwanted records, after fetching the record, we need to do the comparison of the key fields explicitly. This is demonstrated in the following code.

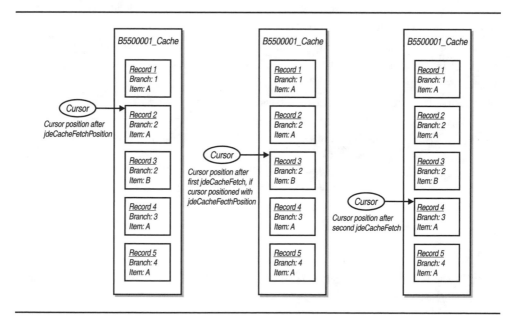

FIGURE 17-8. Fetching multiple records from a cache

Adding the code to do the comparison is currently the only way to ensure that a record fetched by jdeCacheFetch matches the key we want.

```
idJCMReturn = jdeCacheFetch ((HCACHE)pCacheHandle,hCursor,
                             (void *)lpdsCache,
                             (void *)NULL);
  if (idJCMReturn == JDECM_PASSED)
  {
     switch (lpDS->nIndexNumber)
     {
        case 1:
           switch (lpDS->nNumberOfKeys)
           {
              case  4:
                 if (jdestrcmp (lpdsCache->szLot,
                                lpDS->szLot) != 0)
                 {
                    bMatchKey = FALSE;
                 }
              case  3:
                 if (jdestrcmp (lpdsCache->szLocation,
                                lpDS->szLocation) != 0)
                 {
                    bMatchKey = FALSE;
                 }
              case  2:
                 if (jdestrcmp (lpdsCache->szCostCenter,
                                lpDS->szCostCenter) != 0)
                 {
                    bMatchKey = FALSE;
                 }
              case  1:
                 if (MathCompare(&lpdsCache->mnIdentifierShortItem,
                                 &lpDS->mnIdentifierShortItem)!= 0)
                 {
                    bMatchKey = FALSE;
                 }
              default:
                 break;
           }
           break;
        case 2:
           switch (lpDS->nNumberOfKeys)
           {
              case  2:
                 if (jdestrcmp (lpdsCache->szLot,
                                lpDS->szLot) != 0)
                 {
```

```
            bMatchKey = FALSE;
        }
    case 1:
        if (jdestrcmp (lpdsCache->szLocation,
                        lpDS->szLocation) != 0)
        {
            bMatchKey = FALSE;
        }
    default:
        break;
    }
    break;
default:
    break;
}
```

Clearing and Terminating Cache

After you finish using cache, always clear the records or terminate the cache. If you included your job number inside cache records as part of the cache structure, then you can delete all the records that match your job number. If you included your job number inside the cache name and you've finished with the cache, you can terminate the cache as shown in the following code example:

```
jdeCacheTerminateAll (hUser, (HCACHE)pCacheHandle);
```

There are two APIs that terminate cache: jdeCacheTerminate and jdeCacheTerminateAll. Before memory is freed and the entire cache destroyed, there must be as many jdeCacheTerminate calls as there are jdeCacheInit calls. If you call jdeCacheTerminateAll, it frees the cache regardless of how often jdeCacheInit was called. We recommend, if you're going to terminate cache, that you call jdeCacheTerminateAll to ensure that the entire cache is eliminated. This API frees all memory associated with a cache and closes any cursors that are open on the cache as well.

So far in this chapter you have seen how to use the different cache APIs. For a discussion of how cache is used in Master Business Functions, see the following Developer's Corner, titled "Cache and Transaction Master Business Functions."

Cache and Transaction Master Business Functions

As mentioned in the introduction of this chapter, cache is often used in Master Business Functions (MBFs). It's used in these functions because it can provide a convenient place to save the information until the user is ready to commit the data to the database. Transaction MBFs are made up of several functions: Begin Doc, Edit Line, Edit Doc, End Doc, and Cancel Doc (fully explained in Chapter 16). As shown in Figure 17-9, these functions work together to add or modify information in the cache and will eventually be used to update the database. Each of these functions uses cache in a slightly different way.

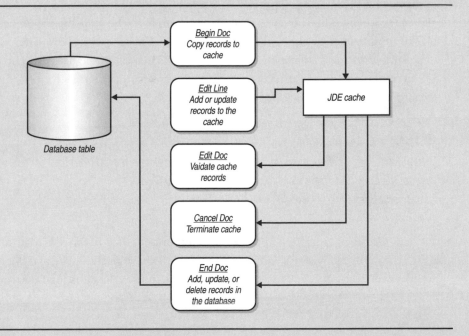

FIGURE 17-9.   Master Business Functions and cache

Begin Doc is responsible for initializing the cache and, in some cases, multiple caches. If a transaction has header and detail information, it's easiest to have a header and detail cache. That way the data will be logically and physically separated. When there is a header cache, Begin Doc inserts a record there; typically, there's only one record in the header cache. If the MBF is editing an existing transaction, such as an order, there may be several existing detail lines. Begin Doc loads this order information from the database into the cache. To do this, you'll use the following functions: jdeCacheInit, jdeCacheAdd, and database APIs discussed in Chapters 15 and 16. The jdeCacheInit gets a cache handle, and the jdeCacheAdd function adds the existing records to the cache.

Edit Line is called in one of three modes: add, update, or delete. The purpose of Edit Line is to validate a single detail line and save the record. The record isn't changed in the database but rather in the cache. To do this, the function uses jdeCacheInit, jdeCacheAdd, jdeCacheOpenCursor, jdeCacheFetchPosition, and jdeCacheUpdate. When Edit Line is called, it needs a cache handle, which it gets using jdeCacheInit. If Edit Line is called in add mode, it inserts a record to cache by using jdeCacheAdd. If called in update or delete mode, Edit Line uses jdeCacheOpenCursor to get a cursor. The cursor is used in the fetch and update APIs. Then Edit Line uses this cursor during a call to jdeCacheFetchPosition to fetch the cache record. After it's fetched, the cache record is modified and updated.

N O T E

When Edit Line is called in delete mode, this does not delete a record from the cache; it simply flags the record to be deleted. The actual delete from the database doesn't take place until End Doc.

Edit Doc is not included in all MBFs, but if present, it is used to validate an entire transaction. In many cases, Edit Doc simply loops through the cache and does any validations necessary. To loop through the cache, it uses the APIs jdeCacheInit, jdeCacheOpenCursor, and jdeCacheFetch. The jdeCacheInit and jdeCacheOpenCursor functions are used to get a handle and a cursor. The jdeCacheFetch is used to loop through all the records in the cache.

Cancel Doc is used if the user cancels a transaction. This function simply calls jdeCacheInit to open a cache handle and then calls one of two APIs, depending on how the cache is organized. If the cache includes a job number in the cache name, Cancel Doc calls jdeCacheTerminateAll to destroy the cache and clean up memory. If the job number is not in the cache name, then Cancel Doc deletes all records from the cache that it created using jdeCacheDeleteAll.

End Doc is called when the user decides to process the transaction. End Doc's processing involves looping through the cache and then updating the database for each record necessary. To do this, the function calls jdeCacheInit, and jdeCacheOpenCursor is used to get a handle and a cursor. The jdeCacheFetch is called multiple times in a loop to process all records in the cache. As each record is fetched from the cache, End Doc updates the database. After all records are processed, it either terminates the cache or deletes all records from the cache (similar to Cancel Doc).

By using a Master Business Function and the correct cache APIs, you'll be able to safely process a transaction and modify the database only after all the validation is complete.

Example of a Cache Business Function

Often, when using cache, you'll want to set up a business function to insert, add, update, and delete from the cache. Then you can call this function from ER or from another function. The cache processing function has several modes, allowing you to do each of the following operations:

- Add

- Update

- Fetch Single

- Fetch Multiple

- Delete

- Terminate Cache

The rest of this chapter contains the code for such a cache-processing operation. This example, called "Cache Item Location," employs all of the concepts we've discussed in this chapter. Let's first walk through the code and see how to design a cache business function. When you create a function similar to this one, you can access and use this cache from any business function, or any object that allows Event Rules. This example also passes pointers back to the calling application. For an explanation of these APIs, see the Developer's Corner, titled "Passing Pointers Inside OneWorld," at the end of this chapter.

The code will perform a number of tasks. Letters within the code correspond to the following explanation:

A. This function also calls initBhvr to get a user handle. If any value is incorrect, the function sets an error.

B. This function validates that the user is passing in valid information. It checks the modes and the number of keys. The *number of keys* validate that the user has not sent in a number of keys greater than the number defined for the index. The *mode* is a number that the user passes in to identify the function desired, as follows:

Mode 1 = Add
Mode 2 = Update
Mode 3 = Fetch Single
Mode 4 = Fetch Next
Mode 5 = Delete
Mode 6 = Terminate

C. This function initializes the cache. As mentioned earlier, the cache can be initialized without affecting the contents of the cache.

D. After initialization, this function loads a structure that contains the key.

E. Loads the key fields.

F. Adds a record to the cache.

G. Changes a cache record.

H. Fetches one record from the cache or fetches the first record in a series of records.

I. Fetches the next record from a cache.

J. Deletes records from the cache.

K. Terminates the cache.

```
/****************************************************************
*     Source File:   b5600002
*     Description:   Cache Item Location Source File
*          Date          Programmer    SAR# - Description
*          ----------    ----------    -------------------------------
*     Author 02/05/2000  C.Enyeart     1          - Created
****************************************************************/
#include <b5600002.h>
/****************************************************************
*   Business Function:   CacheItemLocationQuantity
*         Description:   Cache Item Location Quantity
*         Parameters:
*     LPBHVRCOM       lpBhvrCom      Business Function Communications
*         LPVOID      lpVoid         Void Parameter - DO NOT USE!
*     LPDSD5600002    lpDS           Parameter Data Structure
```

```
*******************************************************************/
JDEBFRTN (ID) JDEBFWINAPI CacheItemLocationQuantity (LPBHVRCOM lpBhvrCom, LPVOID
lpVoid, LPDSD5600002 lpDS)
{
  /****************************************************************
   *  Variable declarations
   ****************************************************************/
  HUSER            hUser              = (HUSER)NULL;
  HCACHE           pCacheHandle       = (HCACHE)NULL;
  /****************************************************************
   * Declare structures
   ****************************************************************/
  DS5600002Cache          dsCacheKey;
  DS5600002Cache          dsCache;
  DSDE0022                dsDE0022;
  /****************************************************************
   * Declare pointers
   ****************************************************************/
  HJDECURSOR      hCursor  = NULL;
  /****************************************************************
   * Check for NULL pointers  and INVALID input keys
   ****************************************************************/
  if ((lpBhvrCom == (LPBHVRCOM) NULL) ||
      (lpVoid    == (LPVOID)    NULL) ||
      (lpDS      == (LPDSD5600002) NULL))
  {
     strcpy (lpDS->szErrorMessageID, "078S");
     if (lpDS->cSuppressErrorMessage != '1')
     {
        jdeErrorSet (lpBhvrCom, lpVoid, (ID) 0,
                   "078S", (LPVOID) NULL);
     }
     return (ER_ERROR);
  }
  else
  {
     /* A */
     JDB_InitBhvr (lpBhvrCom, &hUser,
                 (char *) NULL,JDEDB_COMMIT_AUTO);
  }
  if (lpDS->nIndexNumber < 1 )
  {
     lpDS->nIndexNumber = 1;
  }
  /*  B This if statement will validate that the
   *    input is correct before proceeding  */
  if  ((lpDS->cCacheActionCode  < '1')   ||
       (lpDS->cCacheActionCode  > '6')   ||
       (lpDS->nIndexNumber  >  2 )   ||
```

```
             (lpDS->nNumberOfKeys <  0 )  ||
           ((lpDS->nIndexNumber     == 1 )  &&
            (lpDS->nNumberOfKeys      >  4 )) ||
           ((lpDS->nIndexNumber     == 2 )  &&
            (lpDS->nNumberOfKeys      >  2 )))
   {
      strcpy (lpDS->szErrorMessageID, "032E");
      if (lpDS->cSuppressErrorMessage != '1')
      {
         memset((void *)(&dsDE0022), (int)('\0'), sizeof(dsDE0022));
         strncpy(dsDE0022.szDescription, (const char *) ("B5600002"),
                 sizeof(dsDE0022.szDescription));
         jdeSetGBRErrorSubText(lpBhvrCom, lpVoid, (ID) 0, "078L",
                               &dsDE0022);
      }
      return (ER_ERROR);
   }
/*****************************************************************
 * Main Processing
 ****************************************************************/
strcpy (lpDS->szErrorMessageID, " ");
/* C */
/* If Job Number is 0 get job number */
if(MathZeroTest(&lpDS->mnJobNumber)==0)
{
    /*  All the internal functions would have prototypes in
     *  the header file */
    I_B5600002_GetJobNumber(&lpDS->mnJobNumber);
}
/* D - Always get a handle to the cache */
I5600002_CreateInitCache (lpDS, hUser, &pCachcHandle);
/*  E Load the key structure with information from the
    business function data structure */
I5600002_CopyToKey (lpDS,&dsCacheKey);
switch (lpDS->cCacheActionCode)
{
    case '1':/* F  - Add record CACHE Table,
              *        always uses primary index*/
        I5600002_AddProcessing (lpBhvrCom, lpVoid,lpDS,hUser,
                                pCacheHandle,&dsCacheKey,&dsCache);
        break;
    case '2' : /* G - Change record CACHE Table  */
        I5600002_UpdateProcessing (lpBhvrCom, lpVoid,
                                   lpDS,hUser,
                                   pCacheHandle,
                                   &dsCacheKey,&dsCache);
        break;
    case '3': /*H - Get single, matching record from CACHE Table*/
        I5600002_FetchProcessing ( lpBhvrCom, lpVoid,lpDS,hUser,
                                   pCacheHandle,
                                   &dsCacheKey,&dsCache);
```

```
            break;
      case '4':  /* I - Get NEXT element in Cursor
                  *      CACHE (keyed or keyless) */
          I5600002_FetchNextProcessing ( lpBhvrCom, lpVoid,
                                          lpDS,hUser,
                                          pCacheHandle,
                                          &dsCacheKey,&dsCache);
            break;

      case '5':  /*J - Delete record(s) in CACHE Table*/
          I5600002_DeleteProcessing ( lpBhvrCom, lpVoid,lpDS,hUser,
                                      pCacheHandle,&dsCacheKey);
            break;

      case '6':    /* K - Terminate CACHE */
          jdeCacheTerminateAll (hUser, (HCACHE)pCacheHandle);
          hCursor = NULL;
          break;
      default:
          strcpy (lpDS->szErrorMessageID, "032E");
          if (lpDS->cSuppressErrorMessage != '1')
          {
              jdeErrorSet (lpBhvrCom, lpVoid, (ID) 0,
                          "032E", (LPVOID) NULL);
          }
          break;
  }
  /****************************************************************
   * Function Clean Up
   ****************************************************************/
  JDB_FreeBhvr (hUser);
  if (!IsStringBlank(lpDS->szErrorMessageID))
  {
      if (lpDS->cSuppressErrorMessage != '1')
      {
          memset((void *)(&dsDE0022), (int)('\0'), sizeof(dsDE0022));
          strncpy(dsDE0022.szDescription, (const char *) ("B5600002"),
                  sizeof(dsDE0022.szDescription));
          jdeSetGBRErrorSubText(lpBhvrCom, lpVoid, (ID) 0, "078L",
                                &dsDE0022);
      }
      return (ER_ERROR);
  }
  else
  {
      return (ER_SUCCESS);
  }
}
/****************************************************************
 *   Function: I5600002_CreateInitCache
 ****************************************************************/
```

```
void I5600002_CreateInitCache (LPDSD5600002 lpDS,
                               HUSER hUser,
                               HCACHE *pCacheHandle)
{
    /****************************************************************
     *  Variable declarations
     ****************************************************************/
    JDECM_RESULT        idJCMReturn        = JDECM_PASSED;
    char                szCacheName[50]    = {0};
    char                szJobNumber[32]    = {0};
    /****************************************************************
     * Declare structures
     ****************************************************************/
    DS5600002Cache          dsCache;
    /* if you have more keys you will need to
     * increase the size of this array
     */
    JDECMINDEXSTRUCT        dsKey[2];
    /****************************************************************
     * Main Processing
     ****************************************************************/
    /*  Setup and Initialize CACHE-keys */
    dsKey[0].nKeyID                  = 1;
    dsKey[0].nNumSegments            = 4;
    dsKey[0].CacheKey[0].nOffset     =offsetof(DS5600002Cache,
                                                 mnIdentifierShortItem);
    dsKey[0].CacheKey[0].nSize=sizeof(dsCache.mnIdentifierShortItem);
    dsKey[0].CacheKey[0].idDataType = EVDT_MATH_NUMERIC;
    dsKey[0].CacheKey[1].nOffset    = offsetof (DS5600002Cache,
                                                 szCostCenter);
    dsKey[0].CacheKey[1].nSize      = sizeof (dsCache.szCostCenter);
    dsKey[0].CacheKey[1].idDataType = EVDT_STRING;
    dsKey[0].CacheKey[2].nOffset    = offsetof (DS5600002Cache,
                                                 szLocation);
    dsKey[0].CacheKey[2].nSize      = sizeof (dsCache.szLocation);
    dsKey[0].CacheKey[2].idDataType = EVDT_STRING;
    dsKey[0].CacheKey[3].nOffset    = offsetof (DS5600002Cache, szLot);
    dsKey[0].CacheKey[3].nSize      = sizeof (dsCache.szLot);
    dsKey[0].CacheKey[3].idDataType = EVDT_STRING;
    dsKey[1].nKeyID                 = 2;
    dsKey[1].nNumSegments           = 2;
    dsKey[1].CacheKey[0].nOffset    = offsetof (DS5600002Cache,
                                                 szLocation);
    dsKey[1].CacheKey[0].nSize      = sizeof (dsCache.szLocation);
    dsKey[1].CacheKey[0].idDataType = EVDT_STRING;
    dsKey[1].CacheKey[1].nOffset    = offsetof (DS5600002Cache,szLot);
    dsKey[1].CacheKey[1].nSize      = sizeof (dsCache.szLot);
    dsKey[1].CacheKey[1].idDataType = EVDT_STRING;
    FormatMathNumeric(szJobNumber, &lpDS->mnJobNumber);
    sprintf(szCacheName,"%s%s","B5600002_",(const char *)szJobNumber);
    idJCMReturn = jdeCacheInitMultipleIndex (hUser, pCacheHandle,
                            szCacheName, dsKey, 2);
```

Interfacing with OneWorld

```
   if (idJCMReturn != JDECM_PASSED)
   {
      /*  Failed to Initialize CACHE */
      strcpy (lpDS->szErrorMessageID, "032E");
   }
   return;
}
/******************************************************************
 *    Function: I5600002_CopyToLPDS
 ******************************************************************/
void I5600002_CopyToLPDS (LPDSD5600002 lpDS, LPDS5600002Cache lpdsCache)
{
/* This function will copy values from the
 * cache struct to the BF struct */
   MathCopy(&lpDS->mnIdentifierShortItem,
            &lpdsCache->mnIdentifierShortItem);
   strcpy(lpDS->szCostCenter,
          lpdsCache->szCostCenter);
   strcpy(lpDS->szLocation,
          lpdsCache->szLocation);
   strcpy(lpDS->szLot                          ,lpdsCache->szLot);
   MathCopy(&lpDS->mnQtyOnHandPrimaryUn,
            &lpdsCache->mnQtyOnHandPrimaryUn);
   MathCopy(&lpDS->mnQuantitySoftCommitted,
            &lpdsCache->mnQuantitySoftCommitted);
   MathCopy(&lpDS->mnQtyHardCommitted,
            &lpdsCache->mnQtyHardCommitted);   }
/******************************************************************
 *    Function: I5600002_CopyToStruct
 ******************************************************************/
void I5600002_CopyToStruct (LPDSD5600002 lpDS, LPDS5600002Cache lpdsCache)
{
/* This function will copy values from
 * the BF struct to the cache struct */
   MathCopy(&lpdsCache->mnIdentifierShortItem,
            &lpDS->mnIdentifierShortItem);
   strcpy(lpdsCache->szCostCenter,
          lpDS->szCostCenter);
   strcpy(lpdsCache->szLocation,
          lpDS->szLocation);
   strcpy(lpdsCache->szLot,lpDS->szLot);
   MathCopy(&lpdsCache->mnQtyOnHandPrimaryUn,
            &lpDS->mnQtyOnHandPrimaryUn);
   MathCopy(&lpdsCache->mnQuantitySoftCommitted,
            &lpDS->mnQuantitySoftCommitted);
   MathCopy(&lpdsCache->mnQtyHardCommitted,
            &lpDS->mnQtyHardCommitted);
}
```

```
/*****************************************************************
 *    Function: I5600002_CopyToKey
 *****************************************************************/
void I5600002_CopyToKey (LPDSD5600002        lpDS,
                         LPDS5600002Cache    lpdsCacheKey)
{
  /* Copy all the members of any index
   * into the lpdsCacheKey struct
   */
  MathCopy(&lpdsCacheKey->mnIdentifierShortItem,
           &lpDS->mnIdentifierShortItem);
   strcpy(lpdsCacheKey->szCostCenter,
          lpDS->szCostCenter);
   strcpy(lpdsCacheKey->szLocation            ,lpDS->szLocation);
   strcpy(lpdsCacheKey->szLot                 ,lpDS->szLot);
}
/*****************************************************************
 *    Function: I5600002_ReadNext
 *****************************************************************/
void I5600002_GetNext        (LPDSD5600002        lpDS,
                              LPDS5600002Cache    lpdsCache,
                              HCACHE              pCacheHandle,
                              HJDECURSOR          hCursor)

{
   /*************************************************************
    *  Variable declarations
    *************************************************************/
   BOOL          bMatchKey          = TRUE;
   JDECM_RESULT  idJCMReturn        = JDECM_PASSED;
   /*************************************************************
    * Main Processing
    *************************************************************/
/* Fetch the next record and compare it to the keys */
   idJCMReturn = jdeCacheFetch ((HCACHE)pCacheHandle,hCursor,
                                (void *)lpdsCache,
                                (void *)NULL);

   if (idJCMReturn == JDECM_PASSED)
   {
      switch (lpDS->nIndexNumber)
      {
         case 1:
            switch (lpDS->nNumberOfKeys)
            {
               case  4:
                  if (jdestrcmp (lpdsCache->szLot,
                                 lpDS->szLot) != 0)
                  {
                     bMatchKey = FALSE;
                  }
               case  3:
                  if (jdestrcmp (lpdsCache->szLocation,
```

```
                                  lpDS->szLocation) != 0)
                    {
                  .     bMatchKey = FALSE;
                    }
                case  2:
                    if (jdestrcmp (lpdsCache->szCostCenter,
                                lpDS->szCostCenter) != 0)
                    {
                        bMatchKey = FALSE;
                    }
                case  1:
                    if (MathCompare(&lpdsCache->mnIdentifierShortItem,
                                &lpDS->mnIdentifierShortItem)!= 0)
                    {
                        bMatchKey = FALSE;
                    }
                default:
                    break;
            }
            break;
        case 2:
            switch (lpDS->nNumberOfKeys)
            {
                case  2:
                    if (jdestrcmp (lpdsCache->szLot,
                                lpDS->szLot) != 0)
                    {
                        bMatchKey = FALSE;
                    }
                case  1:
                    if (jdestrcmp (lpdsCache->szLocation,
                                lpDS->szLocation) != 0)
                    {
                        bMatchKey = FALSE;
                    }
                default:
                    break;
            }
            break;
        default:
            break;
    }
    if (bMatchKey != TRUE)
    {
        idJCMReturn = JDEDB_FAILED;
    }
}
if (idJCMReturn == JDECM_PASSED)
{
```

```
        I5600002_CopyToLPDS (lpDS, lpdsCache);
    }
    else
    {
        lpDS->cLastRecord = '1';
        strcpy (lpDS->szErrorMessageID, "032E");
    }
}
/*******************************************************************
 *   Function: I5600002_AddProcessing
 *******************************************************************/
void I5600002_AddProcessing ( LPBHVRCOM          lpBhvrCom,
                              LPVOID             lpVoid,
                              LPDSD5600002       lpDS,
                              HUSER              hUser,
                              HCACHE             pCacheHandle,
                              LPDS5600002Cache   pdsCacheKey,
                              LPDS5600002Cache   pdsCache)
{
    /*******************************************************************
     *   Variable declarations
     *******************************************************************/
    HJDECURSOR       hCursor             = NULL;
    JDECM_RESULT     idJCMReturn         = JDECM_PASSED;
    int              nPrimaryIndex       = 1;
    int              nKeysInPrimary      = 4;
    /*******************************************************************
     * Main Processing
     *******************************************************************/
    idJCMReturn = jdeCacheOpenCursor((HCACHE)pCacheHandle,&hCursor);

    /* If a cursor can be opened, then search for a matching entry.
     *Only add new record if no matching entry exists. */
    if (idJCMReturn == JDECM_PASSED)
    {
      idJCMReturn = jdeCacheSetIndex(pCacheHandle, hCursor,
                                     nPrimaryIndex);
      idJCMReturn = jdeCacheFetchPosition ((HCACHE)pCacheHandle,
                                           hCursor,
                                           (void *)pdsCacheKey,
                                           (short int)nKeysInPrimary,
                                           (void *)pdsCache,
                                           sizeof (DS5600002Cache));
      if (idJCMReturn == JDECM_PASSED)
      {
         strcpy (lpDS->szErrorMessageID, "0780");
         if (lpDS->cSuppressErrorMessage != '1')
         {
```

```
            jdeErrorSet (lpBhvrCom, lpVoid, (ID) 0,
                        "0780", (LPVOID) NULL);
        }
    }
  }
  /* Either the fetch or the cursor open failed.
   * If the fetch failed, no matching record exists
   * so add the new record.
   */
  /* If the cursor open failed then the cache didn't already
   * exist, so add the new record. */
  if (idJCMReturn != JDECM_PASSED)
  {
     I5600002_CopyToStruct (lpDS, pdsCache);
     idJCMReturn = jdeCacheAdd ((HCACHE)pCacheHandle,
                               (void *)pdsCache,
                               (long)sizeof(DS5600002Cache));
     if (idJCMReturn != JDECM_PASSED)
     {
        strcpy (lpDS->szErrorMessageID, "0780");
        if (lpDS->cSuppressErrorMessage != '1')
        {
           jdeErrorSet (lpBhvrCom, lpVoid, (ID) 0,
                       "0780", (LPVOID) NULL);
        }
     }
  }
  /*  Close Cursor */
  if(hCursor != NULL)
  {
     jdeCacheCloseCursor ((HCACHE)pCacheHandle, hCursor);
  }
}
/********************************************************************
 *   Function: I5600002_UpdateProcessing
 ********************************************************************/
void I5600002_UpdateProcessing ( LPBHVRCOM        lpBhvrCom,
                                 LPVOID           lpVoid,
                                 LPDSD5600002     lpDS,
                                 HUSER            hUser,
                                 HCACHE           pCacheHandle,
                                 LPDS5600002Cache pdsCacheKey,
                                 LPDS5600002Cache pdsCache)
{
  /********************************************************************
   *  Variable declarations
   ********************************************************************/
  HJDECURSOR    hCursor           = NULL;
  JDECM_RESULT  idJCMReturn       = JDECM_PASSED;
```

```
/***************************************************************
 * Main Processing
 ***************************************************************/
idJCMReturn = jdeCacheOpenCursor ((HCACHE)pCacheHandle,
                                  &hCursor);
/* If a cursor can be opened to the cache, only change a
 * record if it can be found. */
if (idJCMReturn == JDECM_PASSED)
{
   idJCMReturn = jdeCacheSetIndex(pCacheHandle, hCursor,
                                  lpDS->nIndexNumber);
   idJCMReturn = jdeCacheFetchPosition((HCACHE)pCacheHandle,
                                  hCursor ,
                                  (void *) pdsCacheKey,
                                  (short int)lpDS->nNumberOfKeys,
                                  (void *) pdsCache,
                                  sizeof (DS5600002Cache));
   if(idJCMReturn == JDECM_PASSED)
   {
       I5600002_CopyToStruct (lpDS, pdsCache);
       idJCMReturn = jdeCacheUpdate((HCACHE)pCacheHandle,hCursor,
                                  (void *) pdsCache,
                                  sizeof (DS5600002Cache));
       if (idJCMReturn != JDECM_PASSED)
       {
           strcpy (lpDS->szErrorMessageID, "078P");
           if (lpDS->cSuppressErrorMessage != '1')
           {
               jdeErrorSet (lpBhvrCom, lpVoid, (ID) 0,
                            "078P", (LPVOID)
                            NULL);
           }
       }
   }
}
/* Either the cursor open failed or
 * there was no matching record in the
 * cache.  Either way, set the error. */
if (idJCMReturn != JDECM_PASSED)
{
   strcpy (lpDS->szErrorMessageID, "078N");
   if (lpDS->cSuppressErrorMessage != '1')
   {
       jdeErrorSet (lpBhvrCom, lpVoid, (ID) 0,
                    "078N", (LPVOID) NULL);
   }
}
/*  Close Cursor */
if(hCursor != NULL)
```

```
      {
         jdeCacheCloseCursor ((HCACHE)pCacheHandle, hCursor);
      }
}
/******************************************************************
 *    Function: I5600002_DeleteProcessing
 ******************************************************************/
void I5600002_DeleteProcessing ( LPBHVRCOM          lpBhvrCom,
                                 LPVOID             lpVoid,
                                 LPDSD5600002       lpDS,
                                 HUSER              hUser,
                                 HCACHE             pCacheHandle,
                                 LPDS5600002Cache pdsCacheKey)
{
   /******************************************************************
    *  Variable declarations
    ******************************************************************/
   HJDECURSOR      hCursor                 = NULL;
   JDECM_RESULT    idJCMReturn             = JDECM_PASSED;

   /******************************************************************
    * Main Processing
    ******************************************************************/
   idJCMReturn = jdeCacheOpenCursor ((HCACHE)pCacheHandle, &hCursor);
   if (idJCMReturn == JDECM_PASSED)
   {
      idJCMReturn = jdeCacheSetIndex(pCacheHandle, hCursor,
                                  lpDS->nIndexNumber);
      idJCMReturn = jdeCacheDeleteAll((HCACHE)pCacheHandle, hCursor,
                                     pdsCacheKey,
                                     (ushort)lpDS->nNumberOfKeys);
   }
   if (idJCMReturn != JDECM_PASSED)
   {
      strcpy (lpDS->szErrorMessageID, "078Q");
      if (lpDS->cSuppressErrorMessage != '1')
      {
         jdeErrorSet (lpBhvrCom, lpVoid, (ID) 0,
                    "078Q", (LPVOID) NULL);
      }
   }
   /*  Close Cursor */
   if(hCursor != NULL)
   {
      jdeCacheCloseCursor ((HCACHE)pCacheHandle, hCursor);
   }
}
/******************************************************************
 *    Function: I5600002_FetchProcessing
 ******************************************************************/
void I5600002_FetchProcessing (  LPBHVRCOM          lpBhvrCom,
```

```
                        LPVOID          lpVoid,
                        LPDSD5600002    lpDS,
                        HUSER           hUser,
                        HCACHE          pCacheHandle,
                        LPDS5600002Cache pdsCacheKey,
                        LPDS5600002Cache pdsCache)
{
   /****************************************************************
    *  Variable declarations
    ****************************************************************/
   HJDECURSOR     hCursor            = NULL;
   JDECM_RESULT   idJCMReturn        = JDECM_PASSED;
   /****************************************************************
    * Main Processing
    ****************************************************************/
   idJCMReturn = jdeCacheOpenCursor ((HCACHE)pCacheHandle, &hCursor);
   if (idJCMReturn == JDECM_PASSED)
   {
      idJCMReturn = jdeCacheSetIndex(pCacheHandle, hCursor,
                                     lpDS->nIndexNumber);
      idJCMReturn = jdeCacheFetchPosition ((HCACHE)pCacheHandle,
                                     hCursor,
                                     (void *)pdsCacheKey,
                                     (short int)lpDS->nNumberOfKeys,
                                     (void *)pdsCache,
                                     sizeof (DS5600002Cache));

      if(idJCMReturn == JDECM_PASSED)
      {
         I5600002_CopyToLPDS (lpDS, pdsCache);
      }
   }
   /* Either the cursor open failed or there was no matching
    * record in the cache.  Either way, set the error.
    */
   if (idJCMReturn != JDECM_PASSED)
   {
      strcpy (lpDS->szErrorMessageID, "078N");
      if (lpDS->cSuppressErrorMessage != '1')
      {
         jdeErrorSet (lpBhvrCom, lpVoid, (ID) 0,
                      "078N", (LPVOID) NULL);
      }
   }
   /*  Close Cursor */
   if(hCursor != NULL)
   {
     jdeCacheCloseCursor ((HCACHE)pCacheHandle, hCursor);
   }
}
```

Interfacing with OneWorld

```
/******************************************************************
 *   Function: I5600002_ FetchNextProcessing
 ******************************************************************/
void I5600002_FetchNextProcessing ( LPBHVRCOM        lpBhvrCom,
                                     LPVOID           lpVoid,
                                     LPDSD5600002     lpDS,
                                     HUSER            hUser,
                                     HCACHE           pCacheHandle,
                                     LPDS5600002Cache pdsCacheKey,
                                     LPDS5600002Cache pdsCache)
{
   /******************************************************************
    *  Variable declarations
    ******************************************************************/
   HJDECURSOR      hCursor             = NULL;
   JDECM_RESULT    idJCMReturn         = JDECM_PASSED;
   /******************************************************************
    * Main Processing
    ******************************************************************/
   lpDS->cLastRecord = '0';
   /* If the cursor was not passed in then this is the
    * first fetch of the get next. */
   if (lpDS->idCursor != 0)
   {
      hCursor  =  jdeRetrieveDataPtr(hUser, lpDS->idCursor);
   }
   else
   {
       idJCMReturn = jdeCacheOpenCursor ((HCACHE)pCacheHandle,
                                          &hCursor);
       if (idJCMReturn == JDECM_PASSED)
       {
          idJCMReturn = jdeCacheSetIndex(pCacheHandle, hCursor,
                                        lpDS->nIndexNumber);
       }
       else
       {
          strcpy (lpDS->szErrorMessageID, "032M");
          if (lpDS->cSuppressErrorMessage != '1')
          {
             jdeErrorSet (lpBhvrCom, lpVoid, (ID) 0, "032M",
                      (LPVOID) NULL);
          }
       }
   }
   if(lpDS->idCursor == 0)
   {
     idJCMReturn = jdeCacheFetchPosition ((HCACHE)pCacheHandle,
                                     hCursor,
                                     (void *)pdsCacheKey,
                                     (short int) lpDS->nNumberOfKeys,
```

```
                                    (void *)pdsCache,
                                    sizeof (DS5600002Cache));
      if (idJCMReturn == JDECM_PASSED)
      {
         lpDS->idCursor  = jdeStoreDataPtr(hUser, hCursor);
         I5600002_CopyToLPDS (lpDS, pdsCache);
      }
      else
      {
         lpDS->cLastRecord = '1';
         strcpy (lpDS->szErrorMessageID, "078N");

         if (lpDS->cSuppressErrorMessage != '1')
         {
            jdeErrorSet (lpBhvrCom, lpVoid, (ID) 0,
                        "078N", (LPVOID) NULL);
         }
      }
   }
   else
   {
     I5600002_GetNext (lpDS, pdsCache, pCacheHandle, hCursor);
   }
   if(lpDS->cLastRecord == '1')
   {
     if(hCursor != NULL)
     {
        jdeCacheCloseCursor ((HCACHE)pCacheHandle, hCursor);
     }
     if(lpDS->idCursor)
     {
        jdeRemoveDataPtr(hUser, lpDS->idCursor);
        lpDS->idCursor  = 0;
     }
   }
}
/*******************************************************************
*   Function:  I_B5600002_GetJobNumber
********************************************************************/
static void I_B5600002_GetJobNumber(LPMATH_NUMERIC   pmnNewJobNumber)
{
   unsigned long      nJobNumber     = {0};
   /* Retrieve Next Number */
   nJobNumber = JDB_GetInternalNextNumber();
   if (nJobNumber)
   {
      LongToMathNumeric(nJobNumber, pmnNewJobNumber);
   }
   return;
}
```

Passing Pointers Inside OneWorld

Inside a cache business function, or inside functions that are fetching multiple records many times, it becomes necessary to pass a pointer outside the business function and then pass it back in. Two examples of this are a loop through a table in which you need to save the hRequest, and a loop through cache in which you want to save your cache cursor.

You may be tempted to pass the pointer back through the function data structure. That might work, but it won't always and is potentially very dangerous. Your OneWorld installation might span different machines, and thus you run the risk of truncating your pointer. For example, you might pass a pointer from an AS/400, on which the pointer size is larger than on a PC, which would change the value of the pointer. Using the pointer could then cause a memory violation. Fortunately, OneWorld provides a way around this.

Three APIs used inside a business function enable you to pass a pointer without worrying if it will be truncated: jdeStoreDataPtr, jdeRetrieveDataPtr and jdeRemoveDataPtr. Note that you still cannot use a pointer on another machine, but you *can* pass it back and forth. In other words, if you pass a pointer from machine 1 to machine 2, you cannot use the pointer on machine 2. But if you pass the pointer from machine 1 to machine 2 and back to machine 1, these three functions will ensure that your value remains the same.

Using these three functions is a simple process: The basic idea is to create a place in which to save and retrieve data pointers. Instead of passing the pointer itself, you get a number that corresponds to a small table and saves the value of the pointer. For example, if your cache pointer has a value of 0x5678954, you can call the function jdeStoreDataPtr, which returns a value of 1 to 100. You can only save 100 data pointers.

Here's how it looks:

```
lpDS->idCursor = jdeStoreDataPtr(hUser, hCursor);
```

In this line of code, the hCursor value is saved in the list, and the lpDS->idCursor receives a number from 1 to 100. For example, let's say the number is 5. A value of 5 can be passed back and forth between machines.

If the value is passed back in, you can use the function jdeRetrieveDataPtr to retrieve the value of the pointer:

```
hCursor = jdeRetrieveDataPtr(hUser, lpDS->idCursor);
```

In this statement, the function takes the value inside the idCursor, such as 5; looks it up in the table; and returns the value of the pointer, such as 0x5678954.

As mentioned, you have a maximum of 100 saves per user, so you want to make sure you remove your saved pointer when you have finished. In this example, you'd use the following code to remove the data pointer.

```
jdeRemoveDataPtr(hUser, lpDS->idCursor);
```

NOTE

The store and remove functions do nothing to the memory. The functions do not allocate or free memory; they simply save the value of the pointer.

Putting It All Together

Cache is a very significant tool that helps you save information into memory. It allows you to speed up processing or defer table I/O until all validations and manipulations are complete. To use JDE Cache, you'll employ a number of APIs, and it's important to understand how the APIs use cursors. OneWorld includes APIs that will add, update, fetch, and delete records from cache.

PART V

Appendixes

APPENDIX A

OneWorld Developer Quick Tips

OneWorld Modules (UDC = 98/SY)

Frequently Used Fast Path Commands
(UDC = 00/FP)

Frequently Used Menus

Data Dictionary Item Types (UDC = H98/DT)

Data Dictionary Edit Codes (UDC = 98/EC)

Object Naming Conventions

Frequently Used Business Functions

Audit Information Fields

Frequently Used Business Views and
Their Tables

Commonly Used OneWorld Acronyms

OneWorld Modules (UDC = 98/SY)

Number	Module
00	Foundation Systems
01	Address Book
02	Electronic Mail
03	Accounts Receivable
03B	OneWorld Accounts Receivable
04	Accounts Payable
05	Base Human Resource Management and Time Accounting
05A	OneWorld Human Resource Management and Time Accounting
07	Payroll
08	Human Resources
09	General Accounting
10	Financial Reporting
11	Multi-Currency
12	Fixed Assets
13	Equipment and Plant Management
14	Modeling, Planning, and Budgeting
15	Property Management
30	Product Data Management
31	Shop Floor Control
32	Configuration Management
34	Requirements Planning
35	Enterprise Facility Planning
36	Forecasting
37	Quality Management
38	Agreement Management
39	Advanced Stock Valuation
41	Inventory Management
42	Sales Order Processing
43	Purchase Order Processing

Number	Module
44	Contract Management
45	Advanced Pricing
46	Warehouse Management
47	Electronic Data Interchange
48	Work Order Processing
49	ECS Load and Delivery Management
51	Job Cost Accounting
52	Job Cost Billing
53	Change Management
55–59	Reserved for Clients
60–69	Reserved for J.D. Edwards Custom
71	Client/Server Applications
72	WorldVision
74	EMEA Localization
75	ASEAN Localization
76	Latin America Localization
77	Canadian Payroll
80	Business Intelligence
81	DREAM Writer
82	World Writer
83	Management Reporting
98	Technical Tools
H90	OneWorld Tools
H91	Design Tools
H92	Graphical User Interactive Engine and Object Librarian
H93	Database and Communications
H94	Universal Batch Engine
H95	Technical Resources and Applications
H96	Deployment
H97	Benchmarking and Performance
H98	Internet
H99	Product Version Control

Appendixes

Frequently Used Fast Path Commands (UDC = 00/FP)

Command	Description
1K	Address Book constants
3K	Accounts Receivable constants
4K	Accounts Payable constants
9K	General Accounting constants
AAI	Automatic Accounting Instructions
BV	Batch Versions
DD	Data Dictionary
DEBUG	Debug
EM	Employee Queue Manager
IV	Interactive Versions
MENUS	Menus
NN	Next numbers
OCM	Object Configuration Manager
OL	Object Librarian
OPM	Path Code Master
PATH	Environments
PKG	Packages
PM	Promotion Manager
PO	Processing Options
RDA	Report Design Aid application
SARS	SAR system
UDC	User-Defined Codes
USERS	User Profile revisions
UTB	Universal Table Browser
XREF	Cross-Reference facility

Frequently Used Menus

Menu Object Name	Description
GH901	Application Development Tools
GH9011	System Administration Tools
GH908	Packaging & Deployment Tools
GH9081	Object Management (Promotion Manager)
GH961	System Installation Tools
GH910	Internet Tools
GH909	Application Documentation Tools
GH902	Cross-Application Development Tools
GH907	Analysis & Modeling Tools
GH903	Interactive Development Tools
GH904	Batch Development Tools
GH902222	Data-Modeling Programs

Data Dictionary Item Types (UDC = H98/DT)

Code	Description
1	Character
2	String
7	Identifier (ID)
9	Numeric
11	Date
15	Integer
17	Character (BLOB)
18	Binary (BLOB)
20	Variable string

Appendixes

Data Dictionary Edit Codes (UDC = 98/EC)

Code	Commas (Y/N)	Zero Balance (Y/N)	Negative Amount Notations
A	Yes	Yes	CR
B	Yes	No	CR
C	No	Yes	CR
D	No	No	CR
J	Yes	Yes	Trailing minus sign
K	Yes	No	Trailing minus sign
L	No	Yes	Trailing minus sign
M	No	No	Trailing minus sign
N	Yes	Yes	Preceding minus sign
O	Yes	No	Preceding minus sign
P	No	Yes	Preceding minus sign
Q	No	No	Preceding minus sign
R	Yes	Yes	< >
S	Yes	No	< >
T	No	Yes	< >
U	No	No	< >
1	Yes	Yes	*No notation*
2	Yes	No	*No notation*
3	No	Yes	*No notation*
4	No	No	*No notation*

Object Naming Conventions

Naming Convention	Object Type
Z*xxxdddd*	Data Dictionary
F*xxxxyyy*	Tables
19 characters	Indices
V*ffffffff*{A}	Business views
P*xxxxyyy*	Applications
ppp_hhzzzzzz_ddalias	Event Rule variables
N*xxxxyyyy*	NER-based business functions

Naming Convention	Object Type
B*xxxyyyy*	C-based business functions
D*xxxyyyy*{A}	Data structures
GT*xxxyy*	Media object data structures
T*xxxyyyy*	Processing option data structures
R*xxxyyyy*	Reports

dddd = Data Item Name
ffffffff = Characters of the primary table
hh = Hungarian notation for data type
ppp = Auto-assigned scope prefix, such as a form or event
xxxx = System code
yyy or *yyyy* = Next number
zzzzzz = Programmer-supplied name

Frequently Used Business Functions

Business Function Object Name	Description
B0000027	Calculate currency conversion
B0000033	Get exchange rate
B0000045	Convert math numeric to string
B0000049	Convert character to math numeric
B0000128	Get company currency code
B0000560	Convert integer to math numeric
B0000580	Convert string to math numeric
B0800013	Convert string to JDEDate
B0900102	Write to Jdedebug.log
B1100007	Get decimal trigger by company and currency code
B7400150	Convert CR and LR to hexadecimal
B8000030	Convert math numeric to integer
B9800009	Convert local time to UTC
B9800009	Convert UTC to local time
B9800100	Get audit information
B9800210	Convert JDEDate to Julian date
B9800210	Convert Julian date to JDEDate
B9800460	Convert JDEDate to string
B9800460	Convert character to string

Appendixes

Business Function Object Name	Description
BDDVAL	Data Dictionary validation
BD3N070	Convert string to math numeric
MD_DEBUG	M and D debug
X0010	Get next number

Audit Information Fields

Data Item Name	Description
USER	User ID
UPMJ	Date updated
UPMT	Time last updated
JOBN	Workstation ID
PID	Program ID

Frequently Used Business Views and Their Tables

Module	Business View Title	Business View Object Name	Tables Defined in the Business View
Address Book	Address Book	V0101E	F0101
Financial	A/R Detail Reports	V03B11P	F0101, F03B11
	A/R Account Status Summary	V03B15A	F03B15
	A/R Collection Manager	V03B15B	F0101, F03B15
	A/P Detail Reports	V0411G	F0101, F0411
	Account Balances	V0902JC	F0902
	Account Ledger	V0911F	F0911
	Business Units and Accounts	V1011	F0006, F0901
	Fixed Assets	V1201H	F1201, F1202
	Cost Analyzer Balances	V1602A	F1602
Human Resources	Employee Master	V060116Z	F060116
Distribution	Sales Order Detail	V4211L	F4211

Module	Business View Title	Business View Object Name	Tables Defined in the Business View
	Sales Order Header and Detail	V4211M	F4201, F4211
	Shipment Header/Routing Step	V4215A	F4215, F4941
	Purchase Order Header	V4301G	F4301
	Purchase Order Detail	V4311R	F4311
	Purchase Order Receiver	V43121E	F43121
Inventory	Item Master, Branch, Location	V4101D	F4101, F4102, F41021
	Item Location, Lot Join	V41021Y	F4108, F41021
	Item Cost, Item Master Join	V4105B	F4101, F4105
	Inventory Journal	V4111D	F4111
	Item Master, Branch	V4101F	F4101, F4102
Manufacturing	Equipment Master/PM Schedule	V1201E	F1201, F1207
	Equipment Master/Work Orders	V1201JE	F1201, F4801
	Work Center Master Report	V30006C	F30006
	Bill of Material Report	V3002P	F3002
	Routing Master Report	V3003I	F3003
	Work Order Variances	V3102C	F3102, F3102T
	Work Order Master	V4801AJ	F4801
	Manufacturing Work Order Header	V4801C	F4801
Transportation	Shipment Header/Routing Step	V4215A	F4215, F4941
	Load Header/Load Legs	V4960C	F4960, F4961
	Freight Audit History	V4981A	F4981
Warehouse	Location Driver Processing	V4600A	F4600
	Item Profiles	V46010	F46010
	Item Unit Measure Definition	V46011A	F46011
	Location Detail Information	V4602A	F4602
	Warehouse Suggestions	V4611A	F4611
Management Reporting	Financial Reporting	V8300001	F0006, F0901, F0902
	Financial Reporting for 52-Period Accounting	V8300002	F0006, F0901, F0902B
	Cost Management System Reporting	V8300003	F0006, F0901, F1602
	Date Effective Financial Report	V8300004	F0901, F0902, F0006S

Commonly Used OneWorld Acronyms

Acronym	Description
APPL	Application
BDA	Business View Design Aid
BF or BSFN	Business function
BSVW	Business view
CRP	Conference Room Pilot
DD	Data Dictionary
DLL	Dynamic link library
DS or DSTR	Data structure
ER	Event Rule
FDA	Forms Design Aid
NER	Named Event Rules
OCM	Object Configuration Manager
OL	Object Library
PODA	Processing Option Design Aid
PROCOPTS	Processing options
QBE	Query By Example
RDA	Report Design Aid
SAR	Software Action Request
SPECS	Specifications
TAM	Table Access Method
TBLE	Table
TC	Table Conversion
TDA	Table Design Aid
TER	Table Event Rules
UBE	Universal Batch Engine (reports)
WF	Workflow

APPENDIX B

Summary of Interactive Application Properties

Form Properties

Events by Control

Form Properties

	Available Forms						
	Find/ Browse	Search/ Select	Fix/ Inspect	Header Detail	Headerless Detail	Parent/ Child	Confirmation Message
Form Properties							
Add			✓	✓	✓	✓	
Change			✓	✓	✓		
Inquire	✓	✓	✓	✓	✓	✓	
Delete	✓		✓	✓	✓	✓	
Entry Point	✓	✓		✓	✓	✓	✓
Processing Options	✓	✓	✓	✓	✓	✓	✓
Query-by-example (QBE)	✓	✓		✓	✓	✓	
Transaction Processing			✓	✓	✓		
Business View	✓	✓	✓	✓	✓	✓	
Toolbar Functionality							
Select	✓	✓				✓	
Find	✓	✓		✓	✓	✓	
Close	✓	✓				✓	
Copy	✓					✓	
Delete	✓			✓	✓	✓	
Ok			✓	✓	✓		✓
Cancel			✓	✓	✓		✓
Add	✓					✓	
Event Rule Logic							
Form	✓	✓	✓	✓	✓	✓	✓
Grid	✓	✓		✓	✓	✓	
Controls	✓	✓	✓	✓	✓	✓	✓
Menu/Toolbar	✓	✓	✓	✓	✓	✓	
Form Interconnect Data Structure	✓	✓	✓	✓	✓	✓	
Modal	✓	✓	✓	✓	✓	✓	✓
Modeless			✓	✓	✓		
Form Interconnect	✓	✓	✓	✓	✓	✓	✓
Runtime Data Structures							
Business View (BC)	✓	✓	✓	✓	✓	✓	
Constant (CO)	✓	✓	✓	✓	✓	✓	

Available Forms

	Find/ Browse	Search/ Select	Fix/ Inspect	Header Detail	Headerless Detail	Parent/ Child	Confirmation Message
Form Control (FC)	✓	✓	✓	✓	✓	✓	✓
Form Interconnect (FI)	✓	✓	✓	✓	✓	✓	✓
Grid Column (GC)	✓	✓		✓	✓	✓	
Grid Buffer (GB)	✓	✓		✓	✓	✓	
Hyper Control (HC)	✓	✓	✓	✓	✓	✓	
Processing Option (PO)	✓	✓	✓	✓	✓	✓	✓
Query-by-Example Column (QC)	✓	✓		✓	✓	✓	
System Literal (SL)	✓	✓	✓	✓	✓	✓	
System Variables (SV)	✓	✓	✓	✓	✓	✓	
Tab Page (TP)	✓	✓	✓	✓	✓	✓	

Events by Control

Available Forms

Control	Events	Find/ Browse	Search/ Select	Fix/ Inspect	Header Detail	Headerless Detail	Parent/ Child	Confirmation Message
Forms	Dialog Is Initialized	1	1	1	1	1	1	1
	Post Dialog Is Initialized	2	2	3	3	3	2	
	Clear Screen Before Add			2	2	2		
	Clear Screen After Add			✓	✓	✓		
	Grid Record Is Fetched	3	3		4	4	3	
	Write Grid Line Before	4	4		5	5	4	
	Write Grid Line After	5	5		6	6	5	
	Last Grid Record Has Been Read	6	6		7	7	6	
	Add Record to DB Before			✓	✓			
	Add Record to DB After			✓	✓			

		Available Forms						
		Find/ Browse	Search/ Select	Fix/ Inspect	Header Detail	Headerless Detail	Parent/ Child	Confirmation Message
	Update Record to DB Before			✓	✓	✓		
	Update Record to DB After			✓	✓	✓		
	Delete DB Record Verify Before				✓	✓		
	Delete DB Record Verify After				✓	✓		
	Delete Record from DB Before	✓		✓	✓	✓	✓	
	Delete Record from DB After	✓		✓	✓	✓	✓	
	End Dialog	7	7	4	8	8	7	
	Call Is Alerting	✓		✓	✓	✓	✓	
Edit	Control Is Entered	1	1	1	1	1	1	
	Control Exited/ Changed-Asynchronous	4	4	4	4	4	4	
	Control Is Exited	2	2	2	2	2	2	
	Control Exited/ Changed-Inline	3	3	3	3	3	3	
	Visual Assist Button Clicked	✓	✓	✓	✓	✓	✓	
	Post Visual Assist Clicked	✓	✓	✓	✓	✓	✓	
Check Box	Selection Changed	✓	✓	✓	✓	✓	✓	
Radio Button	Selection Changed	✓	✓	✓	✓	✓	✓	
Push Button	Button Clicked	✓	✓	✓	✓	✓	✓	✓
	Post Button Clicked	✓	✓	✓	✓	✓	✓	✓
Bitmap	Button Clicked	✓	✓	✓	✓	✓	✓	✓
Tab Control	Tab Page Is Selected	✓	✓	✓	✓	✓	✓	✓
	Tab Page Is Initialized	✓	✓	✓	✓	✓	✓	✓
Tree Control	Get Custom Tree Node	✓	✓	✓	✓	✓	✓	✓
	Tree Node Is Deleted	✓	✓	✓	✓	✓	✓	✓

		Available Forms						
		Find/ Browse	Search/ Select	Fix/ Inspect	Header Detail	Headerless Detail	Parent/ Child	Confirmation Message
	Double-Click on Leaf Node	✓	✓	✓	✓	✓	✓	✓
	Tree Node Is Collapsing	✓	✓	✓	✓	✓	✓	✓
	Tree Node Is Expanding	✓	✓	✓	✓	✓	✓	✓
	Tree Node Is Selected	✓	✓	✓	✓	✓	✓	✓
Grid, Parent/Child	Double-Click on Row Header	✓	✓		✓	✓	✓	
	Set Focus on Grid	✓	✓		✓	✓		
	Kill Focus on Grid	✓	✓		✓	✓		
	Add Grid Record to DB Before				✓	✓		
	Add Grid Record to DB After				✓	✓		
	All Grid Records Added to DB				✓	✓		
	Add Last Entry Row to Grid				✓	✓		
	Update Grid Record to DB Before				✓	✓		
	Update Grid Record to DB After				✓	✓		
	All Grid Records Updated to DB				✓	✓		
	Delete Grid Record/ Verify Before	✓			✓	✓	✓	
	Delete Grid Record/ Verify After	✓			✓	✓	✓	
	Delete Grid Record from DB Before	✓			✓	✓	✓	
	Delete Grid Record from DB After	✓			✓	✓	✓	
	All grid Records Deleted from DB	✓			✓	✓	✓	
	Column Is Exited							
	Column Is Exited and Changed-Asynchronous							

Appendixes

		Find/ Browse	Search/ Select	Fix/ Inspect	Header Detail	Headerless Detail	Parent/ Child	Confirmation Message
					Available Forms			
	Column Is Exited and Changed-Inline							
	Row Is Exited and Changed-Inline				✓	✓		
	Row Is Exited	✓	✓		✓	✓		
	Row Is Exited and Changed-Asynchronous				✓	✓		
	SetFocusOnControl						✓	
	Tree Node Level Changed						✓	
	Tree Node Selection Changed						✓	
	Tree Drag Over Node						✓	
	Tree-Cancel Drag and Drop						✓	
	Tree-Begin Drag and Drop Operation						✓	
	Tree-End Drag and Drop Operation						✓	
	Tree Node Is Expanding						✓	
	Tree Node Is Collapsing						✓	
	Row Is Entered	✓	✓		✓	✓		
	Get Custom Grid Row	✓	✓		✓	✓		
	Get Custom Tree Node						✓	
	Tree Node Is Deleted						✓	
	Kill Focus on Control						✓	
Hyperitem (Select)	Button Clicked	✓	✓				✓	
	Post Button Clicked	✓	✓				✓	
Hyperitem (OK)	Button Clicked			✓	✓	✓		✓
	Post Button Clicked			✓	✓	✓		✓

		Available Forms						
		Find/ Browse	Search/ Select	Fix/ Inspect	Header Detail	Headerless Detail	Parent/ Child	Confirmation Message
Hyperitem (Find)	Button Clicked	✓	✓		✓	✓	✓	
	Post Button Clicked	✓	✓		✓	✓	✓	
Hyperitem (Cancel)	Button Clicked			✓	✓	✓		✓
	Post Button Clicked			✓	✓	✓		✓
Hyperitem (Close)	Button Clicked	✓	✓				✓	
	Post Button Clicked	✓	✓				✓	
Hyperitem (User Defined)	Button Clicked	✓	✓	✓	✓	✓	✓	
	Post Button Clicked	✓	✓	✓	✓	✓	✓	
Hyperitem (Add)	Button Clicked	✓	✓				✓	
	Post Button Clicked	✓	✓				✓	
Hyperitem (Delete)	Button Clicked	✓	✓		✓	✓	✓	
	Post Button Clicked	✓	✓		✓	✓	✓	
Hyperitem (Copy)	Button Clicked	✓	✓		✓	✓	✓	
	Post Button Clicked	✓	✓		✓	✓	✓	

Appendixes

APPENDIX C

Summary of Batch Application Properties

Summary of Properties for Level-One Sections

Summary of Properties for Level-Two Sections

Summary of Events for Level-One Sections

Summary of Events for Level-Two Sections

Smart Fields

Summary of Properties for Level-One Sections

Level-one sections are independent sections in batch applications. At least one level-one section must exist in a batch application in order for it to execute.

Components Available for Use by Sections	Group	Columnar	Tabular
Processing Options	✓	✓	✓
Report Interconnect Data Structure	✓	✓	✓
Assigned a Business View	✓	✓	✓
Data Selection	✓	✓	✓
Data Sequencing	✓	✓	✓
Subsection Join	✓	✓	✓
Smart Fields			✓
Transaction Processing	✓	✓	✓
Available Interconnects			
Report	✓	✓	✓
Table I/O	✓	✓	✓
Business Function	✓	✓	✓
Section Features and Functionality			
Free Form Layout	✓		
Column Style Layout		✓	✓
Used as a Conditional Section	✓	✓	
Used as a Subsection Join Section	✓	✓	
Used as a Level Break Header	✓		
Used as a Level Break Footer	✓	✓	
Able to Format Headers and Footers	✓	✓	
Implicit Totaling on Level Break			✓
Auto-Generation of Grand Totals			✓
Data Selection at the Column Level			✓
Auto-Population of Descriptions			✓
Drill Down Capability			✓

Components Available for Use by Sections	Group	Columnar	Tabular
Runtime Data Structures			
Business View (BC)	✓	✓	✓
Constant (CO)	✓	✓	✓
Processing Option (PO)	✓	✓	✓
Report Constant (RC)	✓	✓	✓
Report Interconnect (RI)	✓	✓	✓
Report Section (RS)	✓	✓	✓
Report Variable (RV)	✓	✓	✓
System Literal (SL)	✓	✓	✓
System Variables (SV)	✓	✓	✓

Summary of Properties for Level-Two Sections

Level-two sections are dependent sections in batch applications. At least one Level-one section must exist in a batch application in order for a level-two section to be used in the application.

Components Available for Use by Sections	Report Header	Page Header	Page Footer	Report Footer	Level-Break Header	Level-Break Footer
Processing Options	✓	✓	✓	✓	✓	✓
Report Interconnect Data Structure	✓	✓	✓	✓	✓	✓
Transaction Processing	✓	✓	✓	✓	✓	✓
Interconnects						
Report Interconnect	✓	✓	✓	✓	✓	✓
Table I/O	✓	✓	✓	✓	✓	✓
Business Function	✓	✓	✓	✓	✓	✓
Runtime Data Structures						
Business View (BC)					✓	✓
Constant (CO)	✓	✓	✓	✓	✓	✓
Processing Option (PO)	✓	✓	✓	✓	✓	✓
Report Constant (RC)	✓	✓	✓	✓	✓	✓
Report Interconnect (RI)	✓	✓	✓	✓	✓	✓
Report Section (RS)	✓	✓	✓	✓	✓	✓

Appendixes

Components Available for Use by Sections	Report Header	Page Header	Page Footer	Report Footer	Level-Break Header	Level-Break Footer
Report Variable (RV)	✓	✓	✓	✓	✓	✓
System Literal (SL)	✓	✓	✓	✓	✓	✓
System Variables (SV)	✓	✓	✓	✓	✓	✓

Summary of Events for Level-One Sections

The following table provides you with all of the events available for use in level-one sections and their supporting components. The numeric values in the columns represent the execution flow of the events for the section by the Universal Batch Engine.

Object	Events	Level-One Sections		
		Group	Columnar	Tabular
Common	Refresh Section	✓	✓	
	Initialize Section	1	1	1
	Advance Section	2	2	2
	Do Section	4	4	5
	Suspend Section	✓	✓	✓
	End Section	6	6	7
	Clear Space	✓	✓	✓
	Initialize Break Section	✓	✓	✓
	End Break Section	✓	✓	✓
	Initialize Level Break rFooter Section			✓
	End Level Break Footer Section			✓
	Initialize Level Break Header Section			✓
	End Level Break Header Section			✓
	After Last Object Printed	5	5	6
	Before Level Break	3	3	✓
	Do Tabular Break			4
	Do Balance Auditor			✓
Constant	Initialize Constant	✓	✓	✓
	End Constant	✓	✓	✓

Object	Events	Level-One Sections		
		Group	**Columnar**	**Tabular**
	Suspend Constant	✓	✓	✓
	Skip Constant	✓	✓	✓
	Do Constant	✓	✓	✓
	Do Column Heading	✓	✓	✓
Variable	Initialize Variable	✓	✓	✓
	End Variable	✓	✓	✓
	Suspend Variable	✓	✓	✓
	Skip Variable	✓	✓	✓
	Do Variable	✓	✓	✓
	Column Inclusion			3
	Initialize Column	✓	✓	✓
	End Column	✓	✓	✓

Summary of Events for Level-Two Sections

The following table provides you with all of the events available for use in level-two sections and their supporting components. The numeric values in the columns represent the execution flow of the events for the section by the Universal Batch Engine.

Object	Events	Level-Two Sections					
		Report Header	**Page Header**	**Page Footer**	**Report Footer**	**Level-Break Header**	**Level-Break Footer**
Common	Refresh Section					✓	✓
	Initialize Section					1	1
	Advance Section					4	4
	Do Section	2	2	2	2	2	2
	Suspend Section					✓	✓
	End Section						
	Clear Space					✓	✓
	Initialize Break Section					✓	✓
	End Break Section					✓	✓
	Initialize Level Break Footer Section						

Object	Events	Level-Two Sections					
		Report Header	Page Header	Page Footer	Report Footer	Level-Break Header	Level-Break Footer
	End Level Break Footer Section						5
	Initialize Level Break Header Section						
	End Level Break Header Section					5	
	After Last Object Printed	3	3	3	3	3	3
	Before Level Break						
	Do Tabular Break						
	Do Balance Auditor						
Header	Initialize Report Header	1					
	Initialize Page Header		1				
	End Page Header		4				
	End Report Header	4					
Footer	Initialize Report Footer				1		
	Initialize Page Footer			1			
	End Report Footer				4		
Constant	Initialize Constant	✓	✓	✓	✓	✓	✓
	End Constant	✓	✓	✓	✓	✓	✓
	Suspend Constant	✓	✓	✓	✓	✓	✓
	Skip Constant	✓	✓	✓	✓	✓	✓
	Do Constant	✓	✓	✓	✓	✓	✓
	Do Column Heading						
Variable	Initialize Variable	✓	✓	✓	✓	✓	✓
	End Variable	✓	✓	✓	✓	✓	✓
	Suspend Variable	✓	✓	✓	✓	✓	✓

		Level-Two Sections					
Object	Events	Report Header	Page Header	Page Footer	Report Footer	Level-Break Header	Level-Break Footer
	Skip Variable	✓	✓	✓	✓	✓	✓
	Do Variable	✓	✓	✓	✓	✓	✓
	Column Inclusion						
	Initialize Column						
	End Column						

Smart Fields

Module	Description	Data Item
Financial	52 Period Reporting Account Balance	WKRPTAB
	52 Period Reporting Period Activity	WKRPTPA
	Account Balance	FINRPTAB
	Approved Budget	FINRPTBA
	Create Journal Entry	FINRPTJE
	Current Semester	FINRPTSC
	Final Budget	FINRPTBO
	First Quarter	FINRPTQ1
	Fourth Quarter	FINRPTQ4
	Inception to Date Through Current Period	FINRPTIC
	Inception to Date Year End	FINRPTIY
	Period Activity	FINRPTPA
	Prior Semester to Date	FINRPTPS
	Prior Year End Balance Forward	FINRPTPB
	Prior Year End Net Postings	FINRPTPY
	Prior Year's Account Balance	FINRPTPC
	Prior Year's YTD to Current Period	FINRPTPR
	Requested Budget	FINRPTBR
	Second Quarter	FINRPTQ2
	Third Quarter	FINRPTQ3

Appendixes

Module	Description	Data Item
	Year to Date Through Current Period	FINRPTYC
	Year to Date Through Year End	FINRPTYY
Enterprise-Wide	Cost Analyzer Account Balance	CMSRPTAB
Profitability	Cost Analyzer Period Activity	CMSRPTPA
	Net Balance Account Balance	CMSNBAB
	Net Balance Period Activity	CMSNBPA
Fixed Assets	Account Balance	ASSETAB
	Annual Depreciation	ASSETAN
	Asset Additions Current Year	ASSETAD
	Computation Method – ITD or Rem	ASSETCM
	Create Fixed Asset Journal Entry	ASSETJE
	Date – Depreciation Started	ASSETDD
	Depreciation Information	ASSETDI
	Depreciation Method	ASSETDM
	Disposal Cost	ASSETDC
	First Quarter	ASSETQ1
	Fourth Quarter	ASSETQ4
	Inception to Date Through Current Period	ASSETIC
	Inception to Date Year End	ASSETIY
	Life Months	ASSETLM
	Method Percent	ASSETMP
	Period Activity	ASSETPA
	Prior Year End Balance Forward	ASSETPB
	Prior Year End Net Postings	ASSETPY
	Prior Year's Account Balance	ASSETPC
	Prior Year's Year to Date to Current Period	ASSETPR
	Retirement Amount	ASSETRT
	Salvage Value	ASSETSV
	Schedule No/Method 9	ASSETSN
	Second Quarter	ASSETQ2

Module	Description	Data Item
	Third Quarter	ASSETQ3
	Transfer In Amount	ASSETTI
	Transfer Out Amount	ASSETTO
	Year to Date Through Current Period	ASSETYC
	Year to Date Through Year End	ASSETYY
Work Order	Invoice Summary Alpha	SF4822A
	Work Order Master Alpha	WRKORDA
	Work Order Master Numeric	WRKORDN

Appendixes

APPENDIX D

Summary of Interoperability Processing Modes

Summary of Interoperability Model Properties

Model Properties	Inbound Synchronous	Inbound Asynchronous	Inbound Batch	Outbound Synchronous	Outbound Asynchronous	Outbound Batch
Master Business Function (MBF)		✓	✓		✓	✓
Transaction name (UDC 00/TT)		✓	✓		✓	✓
Interface or Z tables		✓	✓		✓	✓
Revision application		✓	✓		✓	✓
Inbound processor		✓	✓			
Flat-file version for inbound processor		✓	✓			
Flat-file cross-reference table (F47002)		✓	✓		✓	
Log changes logic for MBF					✓	
Retrieval API				✓		
Purge processor		✓	✓		✓	✓

Summary of Interoperability Transactions

Transaction	Table	Inbound Batch Subsystem Process	Inbound Batch Process	Outbound Batch Process	Revision Application	Purge Batch Process	Master Business Function	Processing Option for MBF
Address Book	F0101Z2		R01010Z–ZJDE0001	R01010Z–ZJDE0002	P0101Z1	R0101Z1P	N0100041	P0100041
Customer master	F03012Z1		R01010Z–ZJDE0001	R01010Z–ZJDE0002	P0101Z1	R0101Z1P	N0100042	P0100042
Supplier master	F0401Z1		R04010Z–ZJDE0001	R04010Z–ZJDE0002	P0401Z1	R0101Z1P	N0100043	P0100043
A/R invoice	F03B11Z1I, F0911Z1, F0911Z1T	R03B11Z1I	R03B11Z1I–ZJDE0001		P03B11Z1	R03B11Z1P	B03B0011	P03B0011
A/P voucher	F0411Z1, F0911Z1	R04110Z–ZJDE0002	R04110Z–ZJDE0001		P0411Z1	R0411Z1P	B0400047	P0400047

Transaction	Table	Inbound Batch Subsystem Process	Inbound Batch Process	Outbound Batch Process	Revision Application	Purge Batch Process	Master Business Function	Processing Option for MBF
Payment order with remittance	F0413Z1, F0414Z1				P0413Z1	R0413Z1	B0400047	P0400047
Journal entry	F0911Z1, F0911Z1T	R09110Z–ZJDE0005	R09110Z–ZJDE0002		P0911Z1	R0911Z1P	B0900049	P0900049
Fixed asset master	F1201Z1, F1217Z1	R1201Z1I–XJDE0002	R1201Z1I–XJDE0001	R1201Z1X–XJDE0001	P120 1Z1	R1201Z1P	N1200010	P1201
Account balance	F0902Z1		R14110M–XJDE0001, R14110–XJDE0002		P0902Z1	R0902ZP		
Batch cash receipts	F03B13Z1		R03B13Z1I–ZJDE0001 (R03B50)					
Payroll time entry	F06116Z1	R05116Z1I	R05116Z1I–ZJDE0001		P05116Z1	R05116Z1P	B0500002	P050002A
Purchase order	F4301Z1, F4311Z1	R4311Z1I–XJDE0002	R4311Z1I–XJDE0001		P4311Z1	R4301Z1P	XT4311Z1	P4310
Outbound purchase receipts	F43121Z1				P43121Z1	R43121Z1P	XT4312Z1	
Receipt routing	F43092Z1	R43092Z1I–XJDE0002	R43092Z1I–ZJDE0001		P43092Z1	R43092Z1P	NXT43092	P43250
Outbound sales order	F4201Z1, F4211Z1, F49211Z1				P4211Z1	R4211Z1P		
Outbound shipment confirmation	F4201Z1, F4211Z1, F49211Z1				P4211Z1	R4211Z1P		
Cycle counts	F4141Z1	R4141Z1I	R4141Z1I–ZJDE0001		P4141Z1	R4141Z1P	N4101050	
Item master	F4101Z1, F4101Z1A	R4101Z1I	R4101Z1I–ZJDE0001		P4101Z1		XT4111Z1	P4113
Item cost	F4105Z1		R4105Z1I–XJDE0001		P4105Z1	R4105Z1P	XF4105	
Warehouse confirmations	F4611Z1	R4611Z1I	R4611Z1I–ZJDE0001		P4611Z1	R4611Z1P	B4600440	P4617
Work order header	F4801Z1			R4101Z1O	P4801Z1	R4801Z1P	B3101420	
Work order parts list	F3111Z1				P4801Z1	R3111Z1P	B3101430	
Work order routing	F3112Z1			R4801Z2X (R4801Z1O)	P4801Z1	R3112Z1P		
Work order employee time entry	F31122Z1	R31122Z1I–XJDE0002	R31122Z1I–XJDE0001		P31122Z1	R31122Z1	B3101040	P311221

Transaction	Table	Inbound Batch Subsystem Process	Inbound Batch Process	Outbound Batch Process	Revision Application	Purge Batch Process	Master Business Function	Processing Option for MBF
Work order inventory issues	F3111Z1	R31113Z1I–ZJDE0002	R31113Z1I–ZJDE0001		P3111Z1	R3111Z1P	B3100790	P31113
Work order completions	F4801Z1	R31114Z1I–XJDE0002	R31114Z1I–XJDE0001		P4801Z1	R4801Z1P	B3101480	
Super backflush	F3112Z1	R31123Z1I	R31123Z1I–ZJDE0001		P3112Z1	R3112Z1P	B3101060	P31123
Bill of material	F3002Z1	R3002Z1I–ZJDE0002	R3002Z1I–ZJDE0001		P3002Z1	R3002Z1P	N3002040	
Routing master	F3003Z1	R3003Z1I–ZJDE0002	R3003Z1I–ZJDE0001		P3003Z1	R3003Z1P	N3001780	P3003
Work Center master	F30006Z1	R30006Z1I–ZJDE0002	R30006Z1I–ZJDE0001		P30006Z1	R30006Z1P	N3001840	
Workday calendar	F0007Z1	R0007Z1I–XJDE0002	R0007Z1I–XJDE0001		P0007Z1	R0007Z1P	N000700	
Planning messages	F3411Z1	R3411Z1I–ZJDE0002	R3411Z1I–ZJDE0001		P3411Z1	R3411Z1P	B3401360	P3411
Detail forecast	F3460Z1	R3460Z1I–XJDE0002	R3460Z1I–XJDE0001		P3460Z1	R3460Z1P	N3401430	
Kanban transactions	F30161Z1	R30161Z1I–XJDE0002	R30161Z1I–XJDE0001		P30161Z1	R30161Z1P	N3102010	P3157

APPENDIX E

Summary of System Functions

Group	System Function	Application Design Tool				
		FDA	RDA	NER	TER	TC
Control	Clear control error	✓				
	Disable control	✓				
	Disable tab page	✓				
	Enable control	✓				
	Enable tab page	✓				
	Go to URL	✓				
	Hide control	✓				
	Hide tab page	✓				
	Set control error	✓				
	Set control text	✓				
	Set current tab page	✓				
	Set tab page text	✓				
	Set Data Dictionary item	✓				
	Set Data Dictionary overrides	✓				
	Set edit control color	✓				
	Set edit control font	✓				
	Set status bar text	✓				
	Show control	✓				
	Was value entered	✓				
Grid	Clear grid buffer	✓				
	Clear grid cell error	✓				
	Clear QBE column	✓				
	Clear selection	✓				
	Clear sequencing	✓				
	Copy grid row to grid buffer	✓				
	Delete grid row	✓				
	Disable grid	✓				
	Enable grid	✓				
	Get grid row	✓				
	Get max grid rows	✓				
	Get selected grid row count	✓				
	Get selected grid row number	✓				

Group	System Function	Application Design Tool				
		FDA	RDA	NER	TER	TC
	Hide column	✓				
	Hide grid row	✓				
	Insert grid buffer row	✓				
	Insert grid row	✓				
	Set Data Dictionary item	✓				
	Set Data Dictionary overrides	✓				
	Set grid cell error	✓				
	Set grid color	✓				
	Set grid column heading	✓				
	Set grid font	✓				
	Set grid row bitmap	✓				
	Set lower limit	✓				
	Set QBE column compare style	✓				
	Set selection	✓				
	Set sequencing	✓				
	Show grid column	✓				
	Show grid row	✓				
	Suppress gridline	✓				
	Update grid buffer row	✓				
	Was grid cell value entered	✓				
Parent Child	Clear grid buffer	✓				
	Clear gridline	✓				
	Contract tree node	✓				
	Copy grid row to grid buffer	✓				
	Delete all tree nodes	✓				
	Delete grid row	✓				
	Expand tree node	✓				
	Get grid row	✓				
	Get max grid rows	✓				
	Get node level	✓				
	Get selected grid row count	✓				
	Get selected grid row number	✓				

Appendixes

Group	System Function	Application Design Tool				
		FDA	RDA	NER	TER	TC
	Get tree node handle	✓				
	Hide grid column	✓				
	Insert grid buffer row	✓				
	Set Data Dictionary item	✓				
	Set Data Dictionary overrides	✓				
	Set drag cursor	✓				
	Set grid color	✓				
	Set grid column heading	✓				
	Set grid font	✓				
	Set grid row bitmap	✓				
	Set tree bitmap	✓				
	Set tree node font	✓				
	Set tree node handle	✓				
	Show grid column	✓				
	Suppress fetch on node expand	✓				
	Suppress gridline	✓				
	Update grid buffer row	✓				
	Write custom gridline	✓				
Tree	Contract tree node	✓				
	Delete grid row	✓				
	Expand tree node	✓				
	Get node information	✓				
	Get node level	✓				
	Get tree node handle	✓				
	Insert tree node	✓				
	Set bitmap scheme	✓				
	Set node bitmap	✓				
	Set node information	✓				
	Set pre-expand mode	✓				
	Set tree node handle	✓				
General	Cancel user transaction	✓				
	Continue custom data fetch	✓				

Group	System Function	Application Design Tool				
		FDA	RDA	NER	TER	TC
	Copy currency information	✓	✓			
	Press button	✓				
	Run executable	✓				
	Set control focus	✓				
	Set form title	✓				
	Stop processing	✓				
	Suppress add	✓				
	Suppress default visual assist form	✓				
	Suppress delete	✓				
	Suppress update	✓				
	Was form record fetched?	✓				
	Check data selection/sequence		✓			
	Clear user selection		✓			
	Clear user sequence		✓			
	Initialize local printer name		✓			
	Log message		✓			
	Set language preference		✓			
	Set report display scale		✓			
	Set selection append flag		✓			
	Set sequence append flag		✓			
	Set error		✓	✓	✓	
	Set user selection		✓			
	Set user sequence		✓			
	Stop batch processing		✓			
	Stop event processing		✓			
	Use data selection and sequencing from a section		✓			
	Delete current input row					✓
	Stop conversion processing					✓
	Stop event processing					✓
	Table copy insert row					✓
	Update current input row					✓
	User input row					✓

Group	System Function	Application Design Tool				
		FDA	RDA	NER	TER	TC
Messaging	Delete message	✓	✓	✓	✓	
	Forward message	✓	✓	✓	✓	
	Send message	✓	✓	✓	✓	
	Template substitution	✓	✓	✓	✓	
	Update message	✓	✓	✓		
Workflow	Complete activity	✓	✓	✓		
	Get activity instance for key	✓	✓	✓		
	Get process instance attribute	✓	✓	✓		
	Get process instance for key	✓	✓	✓		
	Start composer process	✓	✓	✓		
	Start process	✓	✓	✓		
	Update process instance attribute	✓	✓	✓		
	Update process instance attribute single	✓	✓	✓		
Workflow Administration	Change activity action	✓				
	Change activity status	✓				
	Copy activity definition	✓				
	Delete process GUI file	✓				
	Display process GUI	✓				
	Higher level override	✓				
	Process activity definition	✓				
	Resume process	✓				
	Suspend process	✓				
	Terminate process	✓				
	Validate workflow process	✓				
	Workflow activity commitment	✓				
Telephony	Answer call	✓				
	Conference call	✓				
	Drop call	✓				
	Extend call	✓				
	Get agent state	✓				
	Get call data	✓				
	Get call handle	✓				

Group	System Function	FDA	RDA	NER	TER	TC
		Application Design Tool				
	Get call handle count	✓				
	Get call party number	✓				
	Hold call	✓				
	Log agent in	✓				
	Log agent out	✓				
	Make call	✓				
	Park call	✓				
	Redirect call	✓				
	Reject call	✓				
	Retrieve call	✓				
	Set agent state	✓				
	Transfer call	✓				
Media Object Functions	Activate item	✓				
	Hide the viewer icon panel	✓				
	Lock the viewer splitter bar	✓				
	Set form text indicator	✓				
	Set grid text indicator	✓				
	Start the web browser	✓				
Combo Box Functions	Select item	✓				
	Get description	✓				
Text Control Functions	Add segment	✓				
	Get last clicked segment	✓				
	Get segment information	✓				
	Remove segment	✓				
	Update segment	✓				
Object	Hide object		✓			
	Set object display scale		✓			
	Show object		✓			
Section	Do custom section		✓			
	Do running total		✓			
	Hide section		✓			
	Initialize running total		✓			

Appendixes

Group	System Function	Application Design Tool				
		FDA	RDA	NER	TER	TC
	Set section display scale		✓			
	Show section		✓			
	Stop section processing		✓			
	Suppress section write		✓			
	Zero running total		✓			
Media objects	Media object structures	✓	✓			
Transaction processing	Begin transaction		✓			
	Commit transaction		✓			
	Roll back transaction		✓			
Copy table	Copy table data source					✓
	Copy table environment					✓

APPENDIX F

Client-Side Settings for the Jde.ini File

Section	Key	Value	Purpose
DB System Settings	Version	43	The version number of the Jde.ini file that matches with the current version of OneWorld.
	BD	POOH	For OneWorld stand-alone mode only, enables or disables the sign-on screen.
	Default User	JDE	The user account name for the OneWorld databases.
	Default Env	CRP733	The default environment for the workstation.
	Default PathCode	PRDB733	The default path code for the sign-on screen.
	Base Datasource	Access 32	The database data source that contains the sign-on information.
	Object Owner		The owner of the system database tables.
	Server	*Server name*	The server on which the database resides.
	Database	Access 32	The name of the database in which the system tables reside.
	Load Library	Jdbodbc.dll	The JDE database driver used to access the database. There are two values: Jdboci80.dll, for Oracle databases; and Jdbodbc.dll, for all others.
	Decimal Shift	N	A flag that indicates whether decimal shifting is used for numeric data. The values are N for no (the default) and Y for yes.
	Julian Dates	N	A flag that indicates whether dates are stored in Julian or database-specific format. The values are N for no (the default) and Y for yes.
	Use Owner	N	A flag that indicates whether the table names are to be qualified by the owner. The values are N for no (the default) and Y for yes.
	Secured	N	A flag that indicates whether the database is secured and requires a user and password login. The values are N for no (the default) and Y for yes.

Section	Key	Value	Purpose
	Type	A	A flag that indicates the type of database. The values are O (Oracle), A (MS Access), S (SQL Server), and I (DB2).
	LibraryList		This string is used for the AS/400 only; it contains the library name for the system tables.
Debug	TAMMultiUserOn	0	For internal use only.
	Output	None	Determines when data is written to the Jdedebug.log file. The valid values are None, for no output; File, for output; Excfile, for output written to another file stated in the DebugFile key; and Both, for information written to the Jde.log and Jdedebug.log.
	ServerLog	0	Determines when data is written to the Jdedebug.log file for the server. The valid values are 0, for disabling output; and 1, for enabling output to the Jde.log and Jdedebug.log files.
	LEVEL	BSFN, Events	Controls what information is written to the Jdedebug.log file. The valid values are Events, for tracing when events are entered and exited; BSFN, for tracing when business functions are entered and exited when they return; and SF_x, for tracing when systems are executed. The valid values for the x variable are one of the families of system functions: SF_GRID; SF_PARENT_CHILD; SF_GENERAL; SF_MESSAGING; SF_WORKFLOW; SF_WORKFLOW_ADMIN; SF_MEDIA_OBJ; and SF_CONTROL.
	DebugFile	c:\Jdedebug.log	The location and name of the Jdedebug.log file.
	JobFile	c:\Jde.log	The location and name of the Jde.log file.
Everest	ShowAlias	1	Enables (1) or disables (0) the ability to right-click a field in a form of an interactive application and displays its Data Dictionary alias.
Install	DefaultSystem	System	The name of the subdirectory under the \B7 directory that contains the OneWorld foundation code and tools.

Appendixes

Section	Key	Value	Purpose
	ClientPath	OneWorld Client Install	The name of the directory on the deployment server that contains the workstation installation program for clients.
	PackagePath	Package	The name of the subdirectory under any path code on the deployment server that contains the packages built for that path code.
	DataPath	Data	The name of the subdirectory under any path code on the deployment server that contains the Access database delivered for all packages for that path code.
	HOSTS	Hosts	The name of the directory on the deployment server that contains all the host files.
	HP9000	HP9000	The name of the subdirectory under the HOSTS directory on the deployment server that contains HP9000 files.
	RS6000	RS6000	The name of the subdirectory under the Hosts directory on the deployment server that contains RS/6000 files.
	AS400	AS400	The name of the subdirectory under the Hosts directory on the deployment server that contains AS400 files.
	SUN	Sun	The name of the subdirectory under the Hosts directory on the deployment server that contains AS400 files.
	LocalCodeSet	WE_ISO88591	Used to determine the language used for the client.
Interactive Runtime	DefaultMailServer	C:\Program Files\Microsoft Exchange\ Exchange32.exe	The default mail application launched when the user clicks the e-mail form exit button.
	DefaultBrowser	Default.htm	The default web page to load when a web browser is invoked from a OneWorld application.
	PwdBackground	Onemenu.bmp	The bitmap file used for the default background for the sign-on screen.
	BITMAP_StatusBar	Stbr1.bmp	The bitmap displayed in the status bar of OneWorld forms.

Section	Key	Value	Purpose
	OBJECTQUEUE		The path to store OLE objects that are created from OW grids.
	FONT_FaceName	Arial	Defines the font name for the forms and controls; it excludes grid and parent/child controls.
	FONT_Height	−12	Specifies the height of the FONT_FaceName value.
	COLOR_Weight	400	Specifies the weight of the FONT_FaceName value.
	COLOR_Grid-Background	255,255,128	These values define the background color of the grid in RGB (Red, Green, Blue) format.
	COLOR_Grid-Foreground	0,0,0	These values define foreground color of the grid in RGB (Red, Green, Blue) format.
	COLOR_Grid-Desktop	64,128,128	These values define the desktop color of the grid in RGB (Red, Green, Blue) format.
	COLOR_UseCache	0,0,0	These values define the grid lines color of the grid in RGB (Red, Green, Blue) format.
	CACHE_UseCache	1	Instructs forms to use caching.
	CACHE_Maximum-Nodes	50	Indicates the maximum number of nodes to store in the cache file for forms.
	GRID_Grid-IntegralRows	1	Determines if rows should be cut off (0) or not (1) at the bottom of the visible portion of the grid.
	GRID_FONT_Face-Name	Arial	Defines the font for text in grids and parent/child controls.
	GRID_FONT_Height	−12	Specifies the height of the FONT_FaceName value.
	GRID_FONT_Weight	400	Specifies the weight of the FONT_FaceName value.
	EXCEPTION_Enabled	True	Indicates whether structured exception handling is enabled.
	Initial_Language_Code		Used to determine the language used for the controls.
	TextLimit	80	Defines the average character width when displaying text for controls in the FDA.

Appendixes

Section	Key	Value	Purpose
	TAMMenus	Show	Enables the Universal Table Browser to view local and remote RDB and TAM specs.
	PWndLocation	11,132,827,738, 327681	The first four values define the location of the OneWorld Explorer on the client's screen. The fifth value controls whether the exit bar and type-ahead feature is enabled. The valid values for the fifth value are as follows: 1114113, for disabling the exit bar and type-ahead features; 65537, for disabling the exit bar and enabling type-ahead features; 1376257, for enabling the exit bar and disabling type-ahead features; and 327681, for enabling the exit bar and type-ahead features.
JDE_CG	STDLIBDIR	$(COMP)\VD98\Lib	The path to the Lib directory used by the MSVC compiler.
	TARGET	Release	Used by the code generator and global build program to determine the type of build; its valid values are Debug and Release. The settings are normally Release, unless you need to compile applications with debug information.
	INCLUDES	$(COMP)\VD98\ Include; $(SYSTEM)\Include; $(SYSTEM)\CG; $(APP)\Include; $(SYSTEM)\Includev	The directories in which the header files are located for use by the Microsoft Visual C compiler.
	LIBS	$(COMP)\VC98\Lib; $(SYSTEM)\Lib32; $(SYSTEM)\Lib32; $(APP)\Lib32; $(SYSTEM)\Libv32	The directories where libraries are located for the Microsoft Visual C compiler and OneWorld.
	MAKEDIR	$(COMP)\VC98\Bin; $(COMP)\Common\ MSDev98\Bin	The directories in which the Makefiles are built by the Microsoft Visual C compiler.
	USER	Shester	The user ID of the user who performed the workstation installation.

Section	Key	Value	Purpose
JDEMAIL	mailProfile	Default profile	The name of the profile used by the OneWorld Work Center to access external mail systems.
	mailServer	mail.mycompany. com	The domain name of the SMTP server from which to send server mail messages.
JDENET	netPgmName	Jdenet_n.exe	The name of the JDENET_N executable.
	krnlPgmName	Jdenet_k.exe	The name of the JDENET_K executable.
	serviceNameListen	6008	The network I/O port from which JDENET receives messages.
	serviceNameConnect	6008	The network I/O port to which JDENET transmits messages.
	maxNetProcesses	1	Determines the maximum number of JDENET_N processes that can be running at any time.
	maxNetConnections	50	Determines the total number of connections that all JDENET_N processes can handle.
	maxKernelProcesses	11	Determines the maximum number of JDENET_K processes that can be running at any time.
	maxKernelRanges	9	Determines the total number of JDENET_K processes loaded into memory at any time.
	singleTimeout	30	The total number of seconds to wait before a connection request expires.
	singleProcess	1	Determines whether only one OneWorld process is allowed on the computer; valid values are 1 for workstations, and 0 for servers.
	gdmRetryInterval	0	Enables the guaranteed delivery of messages. If the value is set to 0, the messages will only be retried at startup; otherwise, they will be retried according to the number of seconds specified by the setting.
	newProcess-Threshold Connects	0	The number of active connections a JDENET_N process can handle before starting a new JDENET_N process.
	kernelDelay	0	The number of seconds a JDENET_K process will sleep when started.

Appendixes

Section	Key	Value	Purpose
	netBroadcast-Address	10.255.255.255	The address used to broadcast datagram control messages.
JDENET_KERNEL_DEF1	dispatchDLLName	Jdenet.dll	Identifies the name of the library (*.dll or *.so) that contains the kernel for internal server testing.
	dispatchDLLFunction	_JDENET_Dispatch-Message@28	The name of the function in the dispatchDLLName library executed for the particular kernel.
	maxNumberOf-Processes	2	The maximum number of kernel processes that can be running at one time for this dedicated server process.
	beginningMsgType-Range	0	The starting message type ID for this dedicated server process.
	endingMsgType-Range	255	The ending message type ID for this dedicated server process.
	newProcess-ThresholdRequests	2	The total number of outstanding requests each dedicated server process can have before starting a new dedicated server process.
JDENET_KERNEL_DEF2	dispatchDLLName	Jdekrnl.dll	Identifies the name of the library (*.dll or *.so) that contains the kernel for executing UBE requests.
	dispatchDLLFunction	_JDEK_Dispatch UBEMessage@28	The name of the function in the dispatchDLLName library executed for the particular kernel.
	maxNumberOf-Processes	1	The maximum number of kernel processes that can be running at one time for this dedicated server process.
	beginningMsgType-Range	256	The starting message type ID for this dedicated server process.
	endingMsgType-Range	511	The ending message type ID for this dedicated server process.
	newProcess ThresholdRequests	0	The total number of outstanding requests each dedicated server process can have before starting a new dedicated server process.
JDENET_KERNEL_DEF3	dispatchDLLName	Jdekrnl.dll	Identifies the name of the library (*.dll or *.so) that contains the kernel for data replication.

Section	Key	Value	Purpose
	dispatchDLLFunction	_DispatchRep-Message@28	The name of the function in the dispatchDLLName library executed for the particular kernel.
	maxNumberOf-Processes	1	The maximum number of kernel processes that can be running at one time for this dedicated server process.
	beginningMsgType-Range	512	The starting message type ID for this dedicated server process.
	endingMsgType-Range	550	The ending message type ID for this dedicated server process.
	newProcess-ThresholdRequests	0	The total number of outstanding requests each dedicated server process can have before starting a new dedicated server process.
JDENET_KERNEL_DEF4	dispatchDLLName	Jdekrnl.dll	Identifies the name of the library (*.dll or *.so) that contains the kernel for security server requests.
	dispatchDLLFunction	_JDEK_Dispatch-Security@28	The name of the function in the dispatchDLLName library executed for the particular kernel.
	maxNumberOf-Processes	1	The maximum number of kernel processes that can be running at one time for this dedicated server process.
	beginningMsgType-Range	551	The starting message type ID for this dedicated server process.
	endingMsgType-Range	600	The ending message type ID for this dedicated server process.
	newProcess-ThresholdRequests	0	The total number of outstanding requests each dedicated server process can have before starting a new dedicated server process.
JDENET_KERNEL_DEF5	dispatchDLLName	Jdekrnl.dll	Identifies the name of the library (*.dll or *.so) that contains the kernel for the transaction manager.
	dispatchDLLFunction	_TM_Dispatch-Transaction-Message@28	The name of the function in the dispatchDLLName library executed for the particular kernel.
	maxNumberOf-Processes	1	The maximum number of kernel processes that can be running at one time for this dedicated server process.

Appendixes

Section	Key	Value	Purpose
	beginningMsgType-Range	601	The starting message type ID for this dedicated server process.
	endingMsgType-Range	650	The ending message type ID for this dedicated server process.
	newProcess-ThresholdRequests	0	The total number of outstanding requests each dedicated server process can have before starting a new dedicated server process.
JDENET_KERNEL_DEF6	dispatchDLLName	Jdenet.dll	This identifies the name of the library (*.dll or *.so) that contains the kernel for remote BSFN execution.
	dispatchDLLFunction	_JDEK_DispatchCall-ObjectMessage@28	The name of the function in the dispatchDLLName library executed for the particular kernel.
	maxNumberOf-Processes	1	The maximum number of kernel processes that can be running at one time for this dedicated server process.
	beginningMsgType-Range	901	The starting message type ID for this dedicated server process.
	Endingmsgtyperange	1156	The ending message type ID for this dedicated server process.
	newProcess-ThresholdRequests	0	The total number of outstanding requests each dedicated server process can have before starting a new dedicated server process.
JDENET_KERNEL_DEF7	dispatchDLLName	Jdekrnl.dll	This identifies the name of the library (*.dll or *.so) that contains the kernel for JDBNET server-to-server communication.
	dispatchDLLFunction	_JDEK_Dispatch-JDBNET-Message@28	The name of the function in the dispatchDLLName library that is executed for the particular kernel.
	maxNumberOf-Processes	1	The maximum number of kernel processes that can be running at one time for this dedicated server process.
	beginningMsgType-Range	1201	The starting message type ID for this dedicated server process.
	endingMsgType-Range	1456	The ending message type ID for this dedicated server process.

Section	Key	Value	Purpose
	newProcess-ThresholdRequests	0	The total number of outstanding requests each dedicated server process can have before starting a new dedicated server process.
JDENET_KERNEL_DEF8	dispatchDLLName	Jdekrnl.dll	Identifies the name of the library (*.dll or *.so) that contains the kernel for package installation requests.
	dispatchDLLFunction	_TM_DispatchTransactionMessage@28	The name of the function in the dispatchDLLName library executed for the particular kernel.
	maxNumberOfProcesses	1	The maximum number of kernel processes that can be running at one time for this dedicated server process.
	beginningMsgType-Range	1501	The starting message type ID for this dedicated server process.
	endingMsgType-Range	1756	The ending message type ID for this dedicated server process.
	newProcess-ThresholdRequests	0	The total number of outstanding requests each dedicated server process can have before starting a new dedicated server process.
JDENET_KERNEL_DEF9	dispatchDLLName	Jdesaw.dll	Identifies the name of the library (*.dll or *.so) that contains the kernel for the system administration workbench application.
	dispatchDLLFunction	_JDEK_DispatchSAWMessage@28	The name of the function in the dispatchDLLName library executed for the particular kernel.
	maxNumberOfProcesses	1	The maximum number of kernel processes that can be running at one time for this dedicated server process.
	beginningMsgType-Range	2001	The starting message type ID for this dedicated server process.
	endingMsgType-Range	2256	The ending message type ID for this dedicated server process.
	newProcess-ThresholdRequests	0	The total number of outstanding requests each dedicated server process can have before starting a new dedicated server process.

Appendixes

Section	Key	Value	Purpose
JDENET_ KERNEL_DEF10	dispatchDLLName	Jdekrnl.dll	Identifies the name of the library (*.dll or *.so) that contains the kernel for the Scheduler application.
	dispatchDLLFunction	_JDEK_Dispatch-Scheduler@28	The name of the function in the dispatchDLLName library executed for the particular kernel.
	maxNumberOf-Processes	1	The maximum number of kernel processes that can be running at one time for this dedicated server process.
	beginningMsgType-Range	2501	The starting message type ID for this dedicated server process.
	endingMsgType-Range	2756	The ending message type ID for this dedicated server process.
	newProcess-ThresholdRequests	0	The total number of outstanding requests each dedicated server process can have before starting a new dedicated server process.
JDENET_ KERNEL_DEF11	dispatchDLLName	Jdekrnl.dll	Identifies the name of the library (*.dll or *.so) that contains the kernel for package builds.
	dispatchDLLFunction	_JDEK_Dispatch PkgBuild-Message@28	The name of the function in the dispatchDLLName library that is executed for the particular kernel.
	maxNumberOf-Processes	1	The maximum number of kernel processes that can be running at one time for this dedicated server process.
	beginningMsgType-Range	3001	The starting message type ID for this dedicated server process.
	endingMsgType-Range	3256	The ending message type ID for this dedicated server process.
	newProcess-ThresholdRequests	0	The total number of outstanding requests each dedicated server process can have before starting a new dedicated server process.
Lock Manager	Server	*Server name*	Identifies the name of the server acting as the lock manager.

Section	Key	Value	Purpose
	RequestedService	None	Indicates the type of service the workstation requests from the Lock Manager. The service that is currently being provided by servers is time stamping (TS) only.
Network Queue Settings	UBEQueue	Qbatch	The batch name the client submits for report application execution and package installations to the server.
	UBEPriority	5	The priority set when the UBE is submitted to the UBEQueue. The valid values are 1 to 5, where 1 is the highest priority and 5 is the lowest.
	PrintImmediate	True	The UBEQueue stores files that are submitted to it (False) or submits the files for printing to a print queue (True).
	SaveOutput	False	States whether the user wants to save the log files generated by the UBE (True) or not (False).
	InstallSpecs	Y	States whether the user wants to install specifications when submitting UBEs (Y) or not (N).
	JDENETTimeout	60	The time-out value for clients to attempt to connect to the server.
Object Librarian	OLTLogMode	Yes	Specifies whether the Object Librarian Transaction log (Olt.log) is generated. There are three valid values: Yes, No, and Append. The Yes value generates a new file for each transaction, while Append writes the information to the end of the Olt.log file.
	OLTLogContents	General	Specifies whether detail information about specification records will be generated in the Olt.log file. The valid values are General, for no detail information written to the file, and Detail, for writing detail information to the file.
Replication	DefaultEnvironment	*Environment name*	The default environment in which the publisher resides.
	RepTrace	0 (default) or 1	Enables replication logging (1) or disables replication logging (0).

Section	Key	Value	Purpose
	ForcedSync		A system-controlled value that determines whether replication was performed on the client at the startup of a OneWorld session.
Security	SecurityServer	*Server name*	Identifies the name of the server acting as the security server.
	DataSource	ORACLE PVC	The database data source name for the security tables.
	DefaultEnvironment	*Environment name*	The valid environment in which the F98OWSEC table is located.
	UnifiedLogon	0 (default), or 1	Specifies whether the unified logon feature is on (1) or the standard logon is on (1).
	UnifiedLogonServer	*Server name*	Identifies the name of the server acting as the unified logon server.
	ShowUnifiedLogon	0 or 1 (default)	Determines whether the OneWorld environment selection form appears when the unified logon feature is used.
SVR	SourcePath	Source	On a client, the subdirectory under the path code in which the business function source files are stored.
	ObjectPath	Obj	On a client, the subdirectory under the path code in which the business function object files are stored.
	HeaderPath	Include	On a client, the subdirectory under the path code and system directory in which the business function and system header files are stored.
	HeaderVPath	Includedev	On a client, the subdirectory under the system directory in which the foundation code header files are stored.
	BinPath	Bin32	On a client, the subdirectory under the path code and system directory in which the replicated set of business functions, applications, and DLLs are stored.
	LibPath	Lib32	On a client, the subdirectory under the path code and system directory in which the business function and system library files are stored.

Section	Key	Value	Purpose
	LibVPath	Libv32	On a client, the subdirectory under the path code and system directory in which third-party libraries are stored.
	MakePath	Make	On a client, the subdirectory under the path code used to store the Makefiles for business functions.
	WorkPath	Work	On a client, the subdirectory under the path code used to store the replicated set of application temp files created during a build.
	CodeGeneratorPath	CG	On a client, the subdirectory under the system directory used to store the interactive application form templates.
	ResourcePath	Res	On a client, the subdirectory under the path code used to store the replicated set of bitmaps.
	IconPath	Res\Icons	On a client, the subdirectory under the path code used to store the replicated set of icons.
	HelpPath	Helps	On a client, the path that stores the client-accessible set of replicated help files.
	TreeBmpPath	Res\Treebmps	On a client, the subdirectory under the path code used to store the tree bitmap files.
	ModelPath	Models	On a client, the subdirectory under the path code used to store the model files for OneWorld models.
	LocalePath	Locale	On a client, the base directory for the National Language Support (NLS) conversion tables.
	IconVPath	Locale\Iconv	On a client, the directory for the National Language Support (NLS) conversion map.
	ProgIDOWTAPI		The name of the third-party telephony product.
	Host Port		These values define the host and port number for the third-party telephony product.

Appendixes

Section	Key	Value	Purpose
	UBEDebugLevel	0	Sets the level of debugging information that is provided when UBE debug logging is on (1–6) or off (0). The descriptions for the debugging levels when it is enabled are as follows: information messages (1); section level messages (2); object level messages (3); Event Rules messages (4); SQL statements (5); UBE function messages (6); and display all messages (9).
TAPI	UBESaveLogFile	0	Determines whether UBE debug log files will be saved (1) or not (0).
TAPI – *driver*	UBEShowPDFLink	0	Enables a rectangle to be displayed (1) or prevents a rectangle from being displayed (2) around a link in a PDF file.
UBE	UBEFont_PointSize	80	Defines the font size used for a font that is not the default language preference for the system.

Glossary

AAI   *See* automatic accounting instruction.

action message   A OneWorld message containing a shortcut to a OneWorld interactive application that is sent to a user's mailbox. Action messages are normally sent by workflow processes, but they can also originate from a third-party e-mail system.

alphabetic characters   All of the characters on a standard computer keyboard, excluding the numbers zero through nine. These include all letters of the alphabet, and special characters such as *, @, #, $, ^, and /. This group contains all alphabetic characters: ZDE*Q$Q; this group does not: A123.

alphanumeric character   The complete set of characters on a standard computer keyboard. These include all letters of the alphabet, special characters, and numerals. This is a group of alphanumeric characters: Z222,UE1.

alternate language   A language other than English that is assigned to a user.

American Standard Code for Information Interchange (ASCII)   The single-byte character set that defines the standard encoding format to represent alphanumeric characters for personal computers. ASCII is based on the English alphabet.

API   *See* application programming interface.

APPL   *See* interactive application.

applet   A small application that is built using the Java programming language. Applets are used for web-based applications and can be used to deliver data over the network from a web server to a client.

application   Applications are executable files that users launch on a computer to perform one or more tasks, such as updating the General Ledger. In OneWorld, users launch the execution of an application that is attached to a menu in OneWorld Explorer. There are two types of applications in OneWorld: interactive and batch.

application programming interface (API)   A library of software functions that is executed by an application to access features and functionality provided by another application.

application server   A server on a LAN that contains a set of applications available for use by clients on the LAN.

architecture   The underlying design of a hardware or software platform. The architecture defines how data and applications are stored and manipulated by one or more systems.

ASCII   *See* American Standard Code for Information Interchange.

asynchronous   A processing mode that describes the operation of two applications after one application begins the execution of the other one. In asynchronous mode, the invoking application can continue execution after starting the other application, whether or not the other application has finished executing. *See also* synchronous.

audit trail   Information that is stamped onto every record in a table that uses that record. The audit trail information consists of the user who accessed the records, and the program, workstation, date, and time that the records were accessed. The purpose of this information is to provide a history of the record.

automatic accounting instruction (AAI)   An alphanumeric code that refers to an account in the chart of accounts. The primary purpose of AAIs is to define an application's generation of automatic journal entries from a module such as A/P, A/R, Inventory, and so on. Each module that interfaces with the General Accounting system contains its own set of AAIs.

B2B   *See* business-to-business.

B2C   *See* business-to-customer.

B2E   *See* business-to-employee.

backbone   A series of high-capacity network communication lines for a company or a country.

bandwidth   The amount of information that a network can carry at any point in time.

batch application   A task or group of tasks you submit for processing to the Universal Batch Engine (UBE). Batch applications require no user input during execution, and upon completion normally output a PDF file, hard-copy output, or a comma-separated value (CSV) text file.

batch-of-one   A transaction mode between clients and servers in which the clients automatically enter data into the Z tables of the server. That data is then processed into the application tables when the Z process for the tables is executed.

batch server   A OneWorld application server that processes batch applications for clients on the network.

batch type   The batch type data item (ICUT) defines the system from which a particular transaction for a batch application originated. The list of valid values for batch type is assigned in the UDC 98/IT. For example, the batch type O represents all transactions from the Procurement module.

BDA   *See* Business View Design Aid.

binary large object (BLOB)   A database field that has no maximum size limit and stores its data in a binary format. BLOBs are used to store images, applets, and object specifications.

bitmap   A two-dimensional image composed of pixels.

bits per second (bps)   Measurement for the data transmission rate over a communication medium such as a modem or a network.

BLOB   *See* binary large object.

Boolean logic   Instructs the system to compare the values contained in two variables or parameters, using the following operators: Equal To (EQ); Less Than (LT); Less Than or Equal To (LE); Greater Than (GT); Greater Than or Equal To (GE); Not Equal To (NE); Not Less Than (NL); Not Greater Than (NG).

browser   A client application that translates HTML files received from a web server, and issues HTTP requests for information from a web server.

BSFN   *See* business function.

BSVW   *See* business view.

bug   A programming error that causes a program or computer system to perform erratically, produce incorrect results, or crash. The term "bug" was coined when a real insect was discovered to have fouled up one of the circuits of the first electronic digital computer, the ENIAC. *See also* glitch.

business function   An encapsulated set of functions that is reusable by one or more applications. Business functions can be combined with other business functions, forms, Event Rules, and other components to make up an application. Business functions can be created with the Event Rules language or with third-generation languages such as C.

business-to-business   A portal for a company's suppliers to do business electronically. All supplier-based transactions, such as the sending of quotes to your company, are performed in real-time and immediately affect your inventories, procurement, and financial modules.

business-to-customer   A portal for a company's customers to do business electronically. All customer-based transactions, such as submitting purchase orders to your company, are performed in real time and immediately affect your inventories, sales orders, and financial modules.

business-to-employee   A portal for a company's employees to do business electronically. All employee-based transactions, such as submitting a résumé to Human Resources for a job posting, are performed in real time and immediately affect your human resources and payroll modules.

business view   Business views are used by interactive and batch applications to access data from database tables. A business view is a means for selecting specific columns from one or more tables whose data will be used in an application, but the business view does not select specific rows and does not contain any physical data.

Business View Design Aid (BDA)   A OneWorld GUI-based development tool for creating, modifying, and copying business views.

cache   Caches are temporary tables that store information during the execution of an application. Cache tables increase the performance of an application because the read and write delay times are much shorter than for data stored in a database. Cache tables are also used for transaction processing, to store information for the process during the lifetime of its execution. *See* JDE Cache.

category codes   A data field used to categorize or classify data for reporting purposes. For example, a category code that classifies business units by sales region might be named Sales Region and have possible values of E (East), W (West), N (North), and S (South).

central objects   The master version of all objects in OneWorld. Central objects reside on enterprise and deployment servers and consist of two parts: the central objects data source and the central C components. The central object's data source contains RDB specs, OneWorld master specifications that are stored in a relational database. The central C components are the master copies that contain business function source, header, object, library, and DLL files, and are usually stored in directories on the deployment server.

chart of accounts   The definitions of accounts available in the General Ledger. The chart of accounts defines the types and gives descriptions for each account. Also, it assigns the account numbers and posting edit codes for each account.

check in   The process of copying an object stored on a local machine to central objects. This includes translating the object's TAM specification stored on the local machine, into RDB specs for storage in the central objects data source. After the check-in process is finished, the system removes the object's corresponding checkout entry in the Object Librarian application (P9860).

check-in location   The path code locations for the storage of objects in OneWorld; for example, DEVB733.

checkout   The process of copying an object stored in central objects to a local machine. This includes translating the object's RDB specification that is stored in the central objects database data source, into TAM specifications for your machine. After the checkout process is finished, the system enters a checkout entry for the object in the Object Librarian application (P9860).

classes   Classes are the design-time definitions of objects based on OOT. The class definition can only be modified during development time of the class. A class contains the definition of the attributes and methods that make up the class, which provide the class's features and functionality. Because instances of classes are created during application execution, classes are called objects.

client   The client computer on the network typically generates requests to one or more users, and, in most cases, the clients are the computers with which users interact. For OneWorld, all clients are computers that provide a OneWorld Explorer session for users.

client/server   A relationship between processes running on separate machines that use the services of a computer that shares resources such as files, printers, and databases. The server process is a provider of application and database services, and it waits for requests from clients to provide this support. The client generates requests to servers to access the shared services and resources.

cluster   A group of two or more servers that are identically configured to operate as one server. The cluster's primary role is to provide continued processing when one server fails or is too busy to process another request.

CNC   *See* Configurable Network Computing.

coexistence   A J.D. Edwards special configuration that provides a shared data interface between OneWorld and WorldSoftware products. This configuration is only available for AS/400-based enterprise servers.

comma-separated value (CSV)   A text file that stores information as alphanumeric characters, in a free-form format. In OneWorld, CSV files are an alternate output medium for batch applications.

commit   A database process that defines when a set of SQL statements that modify one or more tables are permanently written to the tables. The modifications are treated as a single unit, and this helps to maintain the integrity of the database. *See* rollback.

Conference Room Pilot (CRP)   CRP is a OneWorld environment that is used for staging the Production environment. This environment is used to test the configuration of OneWorld before it is made available to all users in a company.

Configurable Network Computing (CNC)   An application architecture that allows interactive and batch applications to execute across a TCP/IP network of multiple-server platforms and SQL databases. The applications consist of reusable business functions and associated data that can be configured across the network dynamically. The overall objective for CNC is to support a computing platform that enables businesses to independently change organizational structures, business processes, and technologies.

control   Any point of data entry that allows the user to interact with an interactive application. Check boxes, pull-down lists, hyperbuttons, entry fields, and grids are all examples of controls.

CRP   *See* Conference Room Pilot.

CSV   *See* comma-separated value.

data   Any information that is stored in a database or cache tables, or that is generated during the execution of an application.

Data Dictionary (DD)   A set of database tables that manage all definitions of data-item specifications, and definitions that are used as controls, fields, and columns in OneWorld. You manage the DD through a OneWorld GUI-based development tool called the Data Dictionary application (P9200). It allows you to dynamically change the definition or specification of a data item, and the changes take effect immediately.

data replication   The process of synchronizing data that is maintained across multiple databases. There must be a single source that contains the master copy of the data (publisher); other databases (subscribers) are duplicates of the data. This technique ensures that the latest copy of data can be applied to a primary place and then replicated when appropriate.

data source   One of the building blocks for OneWorld; the data source identifies the database that is available for use by the system, or an enterprise server that is available for processing business functions and batch applications.

data structure (DSTR)   A group of data items that pass information among objects. For example, data structures can pass information between two forms, between forms and business functions, or between reports and business functions.

database   A collection of information stored in one or more tables, which enables indexing and cross-referencing of information in those tables.

database driver   An application that allows other applications to store and retrieve data from a database.

database management system (DBMS)   A software system that manages databases and their tables by providing centralized control over them. DBMS fosters a more productive environment for maintenance, administration, and integrity of the databases.

database server   A server that stores and manages a database.

DCE   *See* distributed computing environment.

DD   *See* Data Dictionary.

Deployment environment (DEP)   A OneWorld environment that only exists on the deployment server. The primary purpose of the Deployment environment (DEP) is to install and upgrade OneWorld on a network.

deployment server   A OneWorld server that installs OneWorld onto the network and builds packages for all OneWorld clients and servers on the network. The deployment server also maintains license security, as well as the source files, include files, and DLLs for the central objects.

Development environment   A OneWorld environment that is used for constructing and modifying objects. The primary purpose of the Development environment (DEV) is to provide a single environment in which application developers can freely build applications in OneWorld without interfering with the CRP and Production environments.

direct connect   A transaction mode between clients and servers, in which the clients communicate directly with the server. All transactions and database manipulations occur immediately.

distributed computing environment (DCE)   A set of integrated software services that allow software running on multiple computers to perform seamlessly and transparently to the end users. DCE provides security, directory services, time services, remote procedure calls, and file services across computers running on a network.

DLL   *See* dynamic link library.

Do not translate (DNT)   A type of database data source for AS/400 platforms; it prevents the AS/400 from translating fields passed back and forth through an ODBC data source. This is due to the fact that translation of the fields will corrupt them, if they are BLOB fields.

double-byte character set   An encoding scheme in which each character is represented by two bytes. This technique is used for languages that employ characters that are not alphabetic and cannot fit in a single byte, such as Japanese, Korean, and Chinese. *See* single-byte character set.

DSTR   *See* data structure.

duplicated database   A database that contains a copy of operational data from a master database. The duplicated database offers improved performance for application execution, because the availability of the duplicated database is much higher than for the master database.

dynamic link library (DLL)   A set of program modules designed to be invoked from executable files when the executable files are run, without having to be linked to the executable files. DLLs typically contain commonly used functions. Since DLLs are shared resources, many applications can simultaneously use the same functions.

dynamic partitioning   The ability for client/server-based applications to dynamically distribute logic or data across the network. In dynamic partitioning, any change to the network location of logic and data occurs immediately, without recompiling any applications on either the server or a client.

Electronic Data Interchange (EDI)   A paperless exchange of business transactions between two computers, primarily focused on the transmission business documents of purchase orders, invoices, vouchers, and so on. The two standards for EDI transactions are ANSI X12, for U.S.-based companies, and EDIFACT, defined by the United Nations.

embedded Event Rules   Event Rules (ER) are code embedded into a specific table (TBLE), interactive application (APPL), or batch application (UBE). Examples of events include form-to-form calls and business function calls.

Employee Work Center   A central location in OneWorld for sending and receiving messages. Each OneWorld user has a Work Center mailbox that contains workflow messages and other messages from external mail servers. *See* Work Center mailbox.

encapsulation   Confining access to and manipulation of data from an object to the procedures that contribute to the definition of that object.

enterprise server   The main server for OneWorld that shares all database information and applications for OneWorld clients on the network.

environment   A OneWorld environment is a collection of applications and databases for use by clients and servers on the network. The primary purpose of the environment is to provide an isolated set of OneWorld applications for development, installation, testing, or production use. There are four typical environments (Pristine, Development, Conference Room Pilot, and Production) and two special environments (Deployment and Test) that are loaded along with OneWorld.

ER   *See* Event Rules.

event   For applications that are based on the event-driven model, an event is a pause in the processing of the runtime engine that processes the application. The runtime engine pauses to execute a block of code that a developer wrote for that event. An interactive application generates an event when a user tabs out of an edit control, or clicks a push button, or clicks a row exit button. A batch application generates an event by processing certain components in the report, including initializing a section, retrieving data from the database, or exporting the value for a field to the output medium.

event-driven model   An architecture that defines a particular type of application and is typically used for GUI-based applications. This type of architecture divides an application into two major components: the runtime engine and the user application. The user application generates events as the users interact with the application, and the events issue messages to a runtime engine that processes the messages and any code written for the events.

Event Rules (ER)   Event Rules (ER) is the scripting language developed by J.D. Edwards for OneWorld's applications. ER code is written into the following OneWorld objects: interactive applications, batch applications, business functions, table events, and table conversions. Applications based on ER code are stored in TAM specifications on each OneWorld client and server. The primary advantage of an arrangement of ER-based applications is that if a client does not have the application it needs to execute, the client can perform a just-in-time installation (JITI) to download the objects for the application, without performing a full or update package installation for the client.

Extensible Markup Language (XML)   A document formatting language that is used to transfer data between two different systems. XML defines how the data is formatted within a document, and the meaning of the formatting codes that determine the uses of the data. Therefore, any system can examine an XML document to extract the data easily, because the data and its meaning are contained within the same document.

extranet   A private and smaller version of the Internet that is normally confined to a company's suppliers and business partners. The extranet uses the functionality of the Internet but replaces management of it for the company.

facility   Within a business, a facility is a separate entity for which you want to track costs. For example, a facility might be a warehouse location, job, project, work center, or branch/plant. Also called a business unit.

fat client   A client machine that operates in a two-tier architecture, and is required to perform most of the application execution. For OneWorld, a fat client is a machine that can directly interact with the enterprise server.

FDA   *See* Form Design Aid.

file   A document that stores information, in ASCII or binary format, that is managed by the operating system of a computer.

find/browse form   In an interactive application, a type of form that allows users to search, view, delete, and select multiple records in a grid. The find/browse form usually serves as the entry point for OneWorld applications.

firewall   A device on the network that physically separates the private and public portions of a network from each other. Firewalls are primarily used to keep unauthorized outsiders from gaining access to the private network, which is usually a company's LAN or WAN.

fix/inspect   In an interactive application, a form that allows users to view, add, or modify a single record at a time. The fix/inspect form does not contain a grid.

form   A main component for an interactive application, and the main graphical interface by which a user interacts with applications. Forms contain edit boxes, grids, buttons, parent/child controls, and drop-down boxes. Seven types of forms are available for interactive applications: find/browse, fix/inspect, search/select, header detail, headerless detail, parent/child, and message box.

Form Design Aid (FDA)   The OneWorld GUI-based development tool for building interactive applications.

form interconnection   Allows one form to access and pass data to another form; form interconnection is generated by the event code in an event.

glitch   A computer hardware defect that induces errors into software applications. *See also* bug.

graphical user interface (GUI)   An application interface that is graphically based rather than character based. GUI-based applications employ pictures and other graphical images to give people visual clues on how to operate the computer. Any application that executes in the Microsoft Windows environment is a GUI.

grid   In an interactive application, a control stores data in rows and columns.

GUI   *See* graphical user interface.

GUI runtime engine   The GUI runtime engine is the background application that monitors and manages the execution of interactive applications. When a user clicks a control in an interactive application, that application generates an event that is issued to the GUI runtime engine, which causes the runtime engine to execute code written for the event.

header detail   For interactive applications, a type of form that allows users to add, modify, or delete records from two different business views. One business view is for the fields in the header, and the other business view is for the fields in the grid. The header detail form is useful in cases in which the data in the header and grid of the form have a parent/child or a one-to-many relationship.

headerless detail   For interactive applications, a type of form that allows users to add, modify, or delete records from a single business view. The business view is for the fields in the header and the grid of the form. The headerless detail form is useful when the data in the business view uses a nonunique secondary key for a table that points to a group of records in the table.

host   In the centralized computer model, the host is a large time-sharing computer system that terminals communicate with and rely on for processing.

Hypertext Markup Language (HTML)   A document formatting language that defines the structure of a document rather than its physical layout. HTML provides platform-independent documents that any web browser can view, and it contains graphics, applets, and other links to HTML documents.

index   An index groups and orders records in a table by assigning one or more columns to the records. A *primary* index uniquely identifies each record in a table; a *secondary* index groups one or more records in a table. The advantage of maintaining primary and secondary indices is that together they provide efficient access to data in the rows of a table.

inheritance   The ability of a class to receive all or parts of the data and procedure definitions from a parent class. Inheritance enhances development through the reuse of classes and their related code.

integration   A link between two or more computer systems that allows these systems to share features and functionality.

interactive application (APPL)   A GUI-based application comprising one or more forms that provide you with the functionality to manipulate the system or database. During execution of the interactive application, the user is in direct communication with the system.

interface   A link between two or more computer systems that allows these systems to share data.

Internet   An international system of linked computer networks that facilitates data communication services. The Internet is a way of connecting existing computer networks, and thus greatly extending the reach of each participating system. The Internet is composed of thousands of wide area networks (WANs) and local area networks (LANs), which use TCP/IP to provide worldwide communications to homes, schools, businesses, and governments.

Internet Protocol (IP)   A connectionless communications protocol that provides a datagram service. *Datagrams* are created by dividing data into multiple packets for transmission over a network. These packets are then forwarded by routers, based on the packet's address and the routing table information.

Internet Protocol address (IP address)   The standard way of identifying computers connected to a network; IP addresses work much the same as telephone numbers on a telephone network.

interoperability   The integration or interface of discrete computer systems, networks, operating systems, and applications so that they operate together.

interoperability interface process   *See* Z process.

interoperability interface table   *See* Z table.

intranet   A private and smaller version of the Internet that is normally confined to a company or organization. The intranet uses the functionality of the Internet. Management of the intranet is maintained by the company.

IP   *See* Internet Protocol.

JAS   *See* Java Application Server.

Java   The software programming language developed by Sun Microsystems that is specifically designed for writing programs and can be executed by any computer that has a Java runtime engine installed on it. Java is ideal for creating applets and applications for the Internet, intranets and any other complex, distributed network.

Java Application Server (JAS)   A OneWorld server that provides web-based applications to clients using a web browser. JAS can provide Java/HTML or HTML-only applications to a client.

Java Database Connectivity (JDBC)   The standard method for a Java application to access databases, by means of a JDBC driver database.

JDBC   *See* Java Database Connectivity.

JDE Cache   An API that allows applications to temporarily store data from a table in computer's memory (RAM). Using JDE Cache increases the performance of an application because all execution is kept locally in RAM. It is used in situations in which work files or temporary files are required by applications. The JDE Cache API can be used on any platform that supports OneWorld.

JDEBASE   The J.D. Edwards proprietary database middleware package comprising a set of platform-independent APIs for multidatabase access. JDEBASE provides client-to-server and server-to-server database access. These APIs are used by interactive and batch engines to dynamically generate platform-specific SQL, depending on the data source request. The APIs are also available for C-based business functions.

Jdedebug.log   A J.D. Edwards file containing diagnostic information from the execution of the GUI and UBE runtime engines for a client or server. This file has several levels of detail for the execution flow of a runtime engine. Typically, the Jdedebug.log file resides on every machine running OneWorld, and it always exists in the root directory of the primary drive.

Jde.ini   A J.D. Edwards file that provides the runtime settings for OneWorld initialization. Specific versions of the file must reside on every machine running OneWorld.

Jde.log   A J.D. Edwards file containing diagnostic information from OneWorld Explorer. The file contains status and error messages occurring between the startup and shutdown operations of OneWorld Explorer. Typically, the Jde.log file resides on every machine running OneWorld, and it always exists in the root directory of the primary drive.

JDENET   The J.D. Edwards proprietary communications middleware package for OneWorld. JDENET provides client-to-server and server-to-server communications for all OneWorld-supported platforms. It is a peer-to-peer, message-based, socket-based, multiprocess communications middleware solution.

JITI   *See* just-in-time installation.

job queue   A queue residing on an enterprise server, for temporary storage of batch applications waiting for processing by the server.

just-in-time installation (JITI)   OneWorld's method of dynamically replicating objects from RDB specifications to a client's TAM specifications during execution of the application on the client.

key   *See* index.

LAN   *See* local area network.

leading zeros   A series of zeros in front of the value in an alphanumeric field. Leading zeros appear when the value in the field is shorter than the field length. For example, if you enter 3245 in an alphanumeric field that should contain eight characters, the value appears as 00003245 in the system.

level of detail   Levels within the General Ledger chart of accounts that summarize a set of similar accounts. This reporting arrangement is useful when the balances are more important than the detail that derives them. The level of detail ranges from one to nine, where one provides the least amount of detail. For example, if you are reporting at the fifth level of detail, the detail is presented from level one down to the fifth level, and all other detail below the fifth level is summarized into a single value.

local area network (LAN)   A network that covers a small geographical area, such as a building. The only purpose of a LAN is to provide a common communication medium for the computers on the LAN. LANs do not have any telecommunication equipment for communication outside of the LAN.

login   *See* sign-on.

mailbox   An application that stores and manages your e-mail messages. *See* Work Center mailbox.

MAPI   *See* Messaging Application Programming Interface.

master table   A database table that manages data essential to the system's operation and configuration. Such information includes business units, suppliers, employees, accounts, and other system settings.

media objects   Any file that relates to a record in table to provide further information about the record. Media objects include text files, images, and OLE pointers to documents on the network.

menu   A panel in an application that provides a list of available applications to execute, or other menus.

Messaging Application Programming Interface (MAPI)   A messaging architecture that defines how messages are managed in the system and routed to their destinations and users.

middleware   A software architecture design that defines the execution of distributed applications between clients and servers. Middleware includes client-to-server and server-to-server communication and database manipulation. For OneWorld, JDEBASE and JDENET are middleware applications that allow OneWorld to execute over a network.

modal   A modal form restricts a user's interaction with other forms and requires certain action within the current form in order to proceed to another.

modeless   A modeless form allows the form's user to interact with other forms.

multitier architecture   A client/server architecture that allows multiple levels of processing. A tier defines the number of computers that support a system. For example, in OneWorld, a two-tier architecture comprises a fat client and an enterprise server; a three-tier architecture comprises a Java server, enterprise server, and a thin client.

Named Event Rules (NER)   Business functions written using the Event Rules (ER) language.

National Language Support (NLS)   The system-level mechanisms that enable OneWorld to configure itself for other countries besides the U.S. Through the NLS mechanisms, the system and user-application layers modify themselves for a particular country.

network computing   A type of computing that contains a set of applications that execute across a network rather than within a single computer. The applications and resources used in network computing are distributed throughout a network, as opposed to residing on one or more stand-alone computers.

next numbers (NN)   A feature used to control the automatic numbering of certain fields, such as General Ledger accounts, vouchers, and addresses.

NLS   *See* national language support.

NN   *See* next numbers.

numeric character   Any field that uses only the digits 0 through 9 and the decimal point to represent data.

object   For OneWorld, an object is a reusable entity based on software specifications created by the development toolset. Some examples of objects are tables, business functions, data structures, and applications. For OOT-based objects, an object is the runtime instance of a class.

Object Configuration Manager (OCM)   OneWorld's "object request broker." The OCM directs the request for an object to a particular computer on the network. The OCM is used when a business function, table I/O, interactive application, or batch application makes a request for an object.

Object Librarian (OL)   A repository of all versions, applications, and business functions in the OneWorld environment. It provides checkout and check-in capabilities for developers, and it controls the creation, modification, and use of OneWorld objects. The Object Librarian supports multiple environments (such as Production and Development) and allows objects to be easily moved from one environment to another.

object linking   When an object is linked to another document, a reference is created including the file the object is stored in and the application that created it. When the object is modified, either from the compound document or directly through the file in which it is saved, the change is reflected in that application as well as anywhere the object has been linked.

Object Linking and Embedding (OLE)   A way to integrate objects from diverse applications into a single document. The main document contains references to the objects that are linked or embedded into the document. Object linking allows an object to be modified by either the main document or the application that created the object. Object embedding allows only the main document to modify the object.

object-based technology (OBT)   An object containing a data structure that represents the attributes of the object, and a set of functions that are used to manipulate the data structure. Objects based on OBT only follow the encapsulation principle of OOT objects.

object-oriented technology (OOT)   An object contains a set of attributes, which are the fields of the object; and a set of methods, which are the functions used to manipulate the object. Objects based on OOT also have the following properties: class, polymorphism, encapsulation, and inheritance.

OBT   *See* object-based technology.

OCM   *See* Object Configuration Manager.

ODBC   *See* Open Database Connectivity.

OL   *See* Object Librarian.

OLE   *See* Object Linking and Embedding.

OLE DB   An open specification from Microsoft that is designed to access data from any database over a network. OLE DB is different from ODBC, which is used to access data from relational databases, because OLE DB is designed to access data from any source, including a relational database, mainframe ISAM/VSAM files, e-mail, text, graphics, and more.

OneWorld   A comprehensive suite of business applications that includes its own set of application development tools. OneWorld is built on the Configurable Network Computing technology that extends client/server functionality to new levels of configurability, adaptability, and stability.

OOT   *See* object-oriented technology.

Open Database Connectivity (ODBC)   An industry standard interface created by Microsoft that allows applications to access data from a variety of relational database systems. Applications are thus independent of any relational database systems from which they access data. The ODBC interface is composed of an API, several methods of database connectivity, and a standard set of data types for all databases.

Open Systems Interconnection (OSI) model   The OSI model was developed by the International Standards Organization (ISO) in the early 1980s to define the protocols and standards for interconnection of computers and network equipment.

order company   The order company data item (KCOO) identifies the company assigned to the document for a transaction. This enables retrieval of a document for a particular company in an organization. Order company is used in conjunction with the order number and order type data items to uniquely identify a document in the system.

order number   The order number data item (DOCO) defines the number that identifies a document for the transaction. This data item is used for vouchers, invoices, journal entries, and so on. It is used in conjunction with the order company and order type data items to uniquely identify a document in the system.

order type   The order type data item (DCTO) identifies the type of document for a transaction. Order type is used for vouchers, invoices, journal entries, and so on. The list of values for this data item are defined in UDC 00/DT. Some examples of order types are automatic entry (AE) and journal entry (JE). Order type is used in conjunction with the order number and order type data items to uniquely identify a document in the system.

OSI   *See* Open Systems Interconnection model.

package   A set of OneWorld objects that install or update OneWorld software for clients and servers. A package is a point-in-time snapshot of the central objects on the deployment server.

parameter   A set of alphanumeric and numeric fields that you provide for or retrieve from an object that you are invoking, such as a business function or an application. Parameters are typically used with commands to provide additional information for invoking special options of the commands.

parent/child form   A type of form for interactive applications that presents parent/child relationships within it. The left portion of the form presents a tree view that displays the hierarchical relationship of parents, and the right portion of the form displays the children of a specific parent.

partitioning   A technique for distributing data and applications onto machines across a network. There are two types of partitioning: static and dynamic.

password   A confidential text string that you type into the sign-on screen of OneWorld to gain access privileges to the system.

path code   A pointer to a specific set of objects located in a computer's directory. The path code provides the location of central and replicated objects.

Planner environment   *See* Deployment environment.

platform independence   A benefit of open systems and configurable network computing that allows applications to execute on any machine across the network.

PODA   *See* Processing Option Design Aid.

polymorphism   A principle of object-oriented technology that allows an object to behave differently based on the type of object that invoked it.

port   A network-based input/output connection for computers using TCP/IP through which applications receive and send messages. For example, the World Wide Web operates on either port 80 or 8080; OneWorld usually operates on port 6008.

portability   The ability of a system or application to execute on various operating systems and hardware platforms.

portal   A web site that offers a broad array of resources and services to a particular group (such as suppliers, customers, and employees) for the purpose of extending the business operations to the individuals of that group.

primary key   A column or combination of columns that uniquely identifies each row in a table.

Pristine environment   A OneWorld environment (PRT) used to test and maintain unaltered objects. This provides the means to compare pristine objects with modified objects in other environments.

processing option   A feature available in some OneWorld applications that allows you to supply parameters to change the application's features and functionality.

Processing Option Design Aid (PODA)   The OneWorld GUI-based development tool for building processing options.

product code   *See* system code.

Production environment   A OneWorld environment (PRD) that is the live environment. The Production environment maintains all objects and data that support the day-to-day operations of a company.

protocol   A technical standard that is managed, and developed by a governing body, such as the IEEE, for activities such as the communication between computers over a network.

proxy server   A network device that translates addresses from one network to another.

published table   A table that maintains the central copy of records for an organization. The published table is used to replicate its data to other machines, called subscribers. The Data Replication Publisher Table (F98DRPUB) identifies all the published tables and their associated publishers in the enterprise.

publisher   The server that is responsible for the published table.

pull replication   One of the OneWorld methods for replicating data to individual subscriber workstations. The only time pull subscribers are notified of changes, updates, and deletions is when they request such information.

push replication   One of the OneWorld methods for replicating data to individual subscriber workstations. The publisher notifies all subscribers that changes, updates, and deletions have occurred for a publisher table. This approach allows the publisher to immediately update its subscriber tables when the publisher tables are modified.

QBE   *See* Query By Example.

query   A question that is issued to a database or a search engine to find data within a particular file, web site, record, or set of records in a database.

Query By Example   The topmost grid line on a OneWorld form, in which you can enter data to narrow the search for information from the database.

queue   An object or application that temporarily stores messages, applications, or printouts that are generated by clients for a server. The queue manages requests for resources when a server is too busy to service the request. When the server becomes available, it retrieves the next request from the queue.

RDA   *See* Report Design Aid.

RDB   Relational database. *See* RDB specs, central objects.

RDB specs   Another name for central object specifications. RDB (relational database) specs are the master specifications for all OneWorld objects.

record   A collection of related fields of data that together represent a single unit of information, such as a sales order header, address book entry, or journal entry. A record is a row of data that is stored in a database table.

referential integrity   In tables that have relationships with other tables, records have to be added, modified, and deleted as a single unit to maintain the relationship. If a record is missing from a table, it violates the integrity of the records in other tables that are dependent on that table. For example, referential integrity is maintained as long as the detail items for a sales order (F4211) have a corresponding record for its header table (F4211).

regenerable application   The ability of an application to generate itself from a master specification. For OneWorld, this is performed by copying the RDB specs to TAM specs during a package build or JITI.

replicated object   A runtime copy, stored in TAM specifications, of the central objects that reside on each client and server for a OneWorld environment. The path code indicates the directory in which these objects are located.

report application   *See* batch application.

Report Design Aid   The OneWorld GUI-based development tool for building batch applications.

rollback   A database process that defines the acceptable circumstances for rejecting a set of SQL statements that modify one or more tables. The primary purpose of a rollback is to return the database to its previous state, before it was modified by a set of SQL statements. *See* commit.

runtime engine   A runtime engine is a background process that monitors, manages, and processes applications. The background process translates the scripting language of the application to machine code, initializes the application in the computer system, and processes any requests that are sent to it from the application. In OneWorld, there are two types of runtime engines: GUI and UBE.

runtime object   *See* replicated objects.

SAR   *See* software action request.

scalability   The ability of a system to grow in size relative to the size and resource requirements set forth by the company.

script   A software language for applications that are executed by a runtime engine. Scripts need not be compiled into machine code in order to be executed, a requirement that restricts the portability of an application. Via scripts, the application can be executed on any computer that has the runtime engine installed. The only drawback to script-based applications is that performance is inferior to that of machine code–based applications, because the runtime engine has to compile the script to machine code before it can be executed.

search/select   In interactive applications, a type of form used to search for a value and return it to the calling field.

secondary key   A column or combination of columns that identify one or more rows in a table. A secondary key groups records by columns in a table to simplify access to the records.

server   A computer on the network that provides essential services and shared resources to clients. In most cases, it is not possible for one server to support all requests for clients on the network. Some examples of servers are web servers, enterprise servers, mail servers, archive servers, and database servers.

sign-on   A form that prompts you to enter your user account name and password to gain access to OneWorld Explorer.

single-byte character set   An encoding scheme in which each alphanumeric character is represented by one byte. English is a common language that is represented by a single-byte character set, and it is defined in the ASCII standard. *See* double-byte character set.

socket   A communications end point that provides applications to send or receive packets of data across a network. Sockets were developed at the University of California at Berkeley, and, therefore, another name for sockets is Berkeley sockets.

software action request   A request sent to J.D. Edwards for a software modification.

source code   A text file that contains a set of computer instructions written in a software language that an application is compiled from.

special character   A symbol used to represent data. Some examples are *, &, #, and /.

specifications   A complete description of a OneWorld object. There are two types of specifications in OneWorld: RDB and TAM.

SQL   Pronounced "sequel." *See* Structured Query Language.

static partitioning   The ability for client/server-based applications to statically distribute logic or data of an application across the network. Any change to the network location of logic and data only occurs by compiling all applications for servers and clients on the network.

static text   Short, descriptive text that appears next to a control variable or field in a form.

store and forward   A transaction mode between clients and servers in which the clients enter data into its Z tables. When the client has a connection to the server, the data is then moved from the client's to the server's Z table. The data is then processed into the application tables when the Z process for the tables is executed.

Structured Query Language (SQL)   A fourth-generation language used as an industry standard for accessing and modifying data from a relational database system.

subscriber   The server that is responsible for maintaining the duplicate copy of data for published tables stored on it.

subscriber table   A table (F98DRSUB) maintained on the publisher server that identifies al of the subscriber machines for each published table.

subsystem job   Batch applications that continually run independently of OneWorld applications.

synchronous   A processing mode that describes how two applications execute after one application begins the execution of the other one. In this mode, the invoking application cannot continue execution after starting the execution of the other application, until the other application has finished execution or not. *See* asynchronous.

system code   A numerical representation of a module in OneWorld. For example, 01 is the system code for Address Book. System codes 55 through 59 are reserved for customer development.

system function   A program function provided by OneWorld that is available to applications and reports for processing system-level tasks.

T-1   A leased-line connection capable of carrying data at 1,544,000 bits per second.

T-3   A leased-line connection capable of carrying data at 44,736,000 bits per second.

table   A two-dimensional entity made up of rows and columns. All physical data in a database are stored in tables. A row in a table contains a record of related information, while a column in a table contains a field of information for the records.

Table Access Method (TAM)   The J.D. Edwards proprietary format for the storage and management of the runtime definition of OneWorld objects. *See also* regenerable object, replicated object.

table conversion   Table conversions can import, export, delete, and translate records in tables. The Table Conversion tool is a special batch application that manipulates data in one or more tables.

Table Design Aid (TDA)   A OneWorld GUI-based development tool for creating, modifying, copying, and printing database tables.

Table Event Rules   Any time an action occurs against a table, such as before update or delete, the table generates an event. If the event contains any Event Rules code, the system executes the lines of code inside the event. The execution of this code is called a database trigger. Table Event Rules allow you to embed logic at the table level for maintaining data integrity between one or more tables.

TAM   *See* Table Access Method.

TAM specifications   The runtime descriptions of an application used by the OneWorld runtime engines to execute an application. *See* Table Access Method.

TBLE   *See* table.

TC   *See* table conversion.

TCP   *See* Transmission Control Protocol.

TCP/IP   *See* Transmission Control Protocol/Internet Protocol.

TDA   *See* Table Design Aid.

TER   *See* Table Event Rules.

Test environment   A OneWorld environment (TST) that uses the data from the Conference Room Pilot environment, and applications from the Development environment. This provides the means to test development objects for accuracy with the configuration and business data for the particular installation.

thin client   A computer with which a user interacts, that is part of a three-tier architecture system. The thin client's only task is the control of a GUI application. For OneWorld, a thin client is a machine that can interact with the enterprise server through a Java server in Java/HTML mode.

Transmission Control Protocol (TCP)   A networking protocol that controls transmission of packets of data over a network and the Internet. Some of TCP's tasks are to verify that packets are not lost, to arrange data from multiple packets in the correct order, and to request that missing or damaged packets be resent.

Transmission Control Protocol/Internet Protocol (TCP/IP)   An integrated set of protocols that are used together to enable Telnet, FTP, e-mail, and other services among computers. The purpose of the TCP/IP protocols is to establish a connection between two computers for reliable delivery of messages and data. The communication takes place through one or more ports.

UBE   *See* Universal Batch Engine.

UDC   *See* user-defined code.

uniform resource locator (URL)   A string that supplies the Internet address of resources on the Internet, such as a web page.

Universal Batch Engine   The Universal Batch Engine is the runtime engine that monitors and manages the execution of batch applications. As a batch application processes a control, it generates an event that is issued to the UBE and causes it to execute code written for the event.

UNIX   The UNIX operating system was invented by Dennis Ritchie in 1969 at AT&T Bell Laboratories and made available to researchers and students in 1973. It was used to develop the Internet's communication software protocols.

URL   *See* uniform resource locator.

user-defined code (UDC)   A set of codes within OneWorld software that users can define, associate with code descriptions, and assign valid values. Some examples of UDCs are unit-of-measure codes, state names, and employee type codes.

username   The name you use to sign on to OneWorld.

visual assist   Forms that are invoked from a control to assist the user in determining which data belong in the control.

WAN   *See* wide area network.

web browser   *See* browser.

web page   A single HTML file that is displayed by a web browser.

web server   Any workstation that contains a web server and provides web pages for web browsers to access.

WF   *See* workflow.

wide area network (WAN)   A computer network that connects two or more LANs together in a common network. In most circumstances, there is a substantial physical distance between the LANs, such as across a state or country.

Work Center mailbox This is a central location for sending and receiving all OneWorld messages regardless of the originating application or user. Each user has a mailbox that contains workflow and other messages, including active messages.

workflow (WF) The automation of a business process, in whole or part, through which documents, information, and tasks are passed from one participant to another for action, according to a set of procedural rules.

World Wide Web (WWW) A group of worldwide web servers that your web browser can access.

XML *See* Extensible Markup Language.

Z files or tables An interoperability interface table in OneWorld; used for storing data for inbound or outbound transactions on either the client or server. Z files allow isolation of the application tables from inadvertent corruption by the flow of inbound or outbound data, while importing or exporting data into OneWorld.

Z process An interoperability interface batch application in OneWorld; used for importing or exporting data from the Z tables into OneWorld's application tables.

zero client A computer a user interacts with that is part of a three-tier architecture system. The zero client only displays information and captures input from users; it has all of its execution performed on a server. There are two types of zero clients in OneWorld: the HTML mode of the OneWorld Java Server and the Windows Terminal Server.

Index

T